COUNCIL OF LITERARY MAGAZINES AND PRESSES

# THE LITERARY PRESS AND MAGAZINE DIRECTORY 2006/2007

D0315485

COUNCIL OF LITERARY MAGAZINES AND PRESSES

# THE LITERARY PRESS AND MAGAZINE DIRECTORY 2005/2006

 Soft Skull Press, Brooklyn NY

Published by Soft Skull Press
55 Washington St.
Suite 804
Brooklyn NY 11201
www.softskull.com

Distributed by Publishers Group West
1-800-788-3123  www.pgw.com

Cover and interior design: Nick Stone Design

Printed in Canada

# Table of Interviews

# Foreword
## by Rick Moody

This is a foreword that means to incite!

Do you think things are bad out there in the big, bad world of commercial publishing? Me too! It *is* bad out there in the big, bad publishing world! Think that the kinds of work that you hold dear are in short supply out there in the commercial publishing world? Me too! Whatever kind of work it is that you favor, whether it's creative non-fiction, or experimental short-fiction, any kind of poetry, even the gentle realistic fiction that would seem to be immune to trend-mongering in the globalized publishing marketplace, it's doing *badly* out there in the big box retailers. Unless you are surpassingly beautiful or you know someone in high places, you are going to have a rough time getting the message out, and you are going to endure manifold rejections, much waiting, much doubting, many reversals, etc. This is the state of things!

There is one place, however, where this headlong rush toward cookie-cutter formula is in disrepute, and that's in the world of independent publishing. No matter how stupid things get in the culture as a whole, and they are dispiriting, there still seem to be many intrepid magazine publishers and small book publishers who are getting into the business on their own, for the simple reason that they *love good writing*. There's absolutely no practical reason why these people should be undertaking these businesses, because it's likely they will never get rich doing it, and their kids will have no enormous inheritance, and yet they are doing it anyhow. For love. I can think, without even working at it, of eight or ten very good American literary magazines that are less than ten years old, despite the fact that these have probably been the ten worst years for publishing serious literature since I began reading and paying attention. The same is true of our many independent book publishers, of course, of whom I can say with total conviction that they are now publishing some of the finest literature written in this country.

What do you require in order to get in touch with these intrepid, heroic souls? What do you, dear reader, require to *supply* these heroic souls, whose only wish is to have good work to publish, whether in magazine or book form? You need only the one thing, and that thing is information. You need only the means to locate the editors in question and to ascertain which is the best venue for the particular sort of work that you do, or the kind of work you represent, whether it be language poetry, poetry in translation, cyberpunk, experimental fiction, or memoirs. Whatever is the manner of your work, there's a place for you out there, and the one book you need to find these unusual businesses, whether for work or pleasure, is the volume you have in your hands now. (By the way, I think I got my first copy of this directory sometime in the late eighties, and I kept that copy for about five years, it was so handy, and I have used its various annual incarnations, ever since.)

Information is liberation! Information is a energy in potential! Maybe there's something at the center of American culture that these days *hates* the news that literature brings. That's what I think on the rough days. And yet, as the CLMP has been proving for a long time now, proving beyond even the proverbial shadow of doubt, there is another way of looking at the world, one that cherishes what literary writers do. Here is that world view! In your hands!

This book gives you the information you need, dear reader and/or writer. There are two things you can do with this information. You can a) begin sending out your stories, or poems, to such places as you have never heard of before, new magazines—*Golden Handcuffs Review,* e.g., or *Swink,* or *Circumference,* or *Unpleasant Event Schedule,* or *Land Grant Review,* just to pick a few magazines with beguiling names—or you can send competed manuscripts to the independent presses that may well publish your *book,* and then, when you have done that, you can think about b) *starting* one of these presses yourself. This foreword means to incite! This book means to incite! Take back your means of production, maker and consumer of American literature! It belongs to you!

# Directory Note

All publishers in this Directory are listed in alphabetical order (additional indices appear in the back). The Directory includes print magazines, online publishers, and small presses in the United States, Canada, and England. Publishers who fit into more than one of these categories may have multiple listings—be sure to check under "Publisher Type." For writers, here are a few tips to keep in mind:

- Support independent publishing by buying literary magazines and books.

- Read a publication and learn about its editorial viewpoint and specific areas of interest before sending work.

- Follow all the submission guidelines provided by each publisher.

- Always include a self-addressed stamped envelope with enough postage for return of your work and/or a reply. Make clear to the editors whether or not your manuscript should be returned.

- Check your manuscript carefully for spelling and grammatical errors; if possible, have someone else proofread the work as well.

- Include a brief cover letter about who you are, and mention if you've read the publication.

- Include contact information on every page (including phone number and e-mail address) unless otherwise stated in the publisher's guidelines. Never send the only copy of your work.

- Check policies on simultaneous submissions and whether submissions via e-mail or fax are acceptable.

- Keep a log of where you have submitted. Be sure to notify any publishers if a simultaneously submitted work sent to them has subsequently been accepted for publication.

We hope you are well served by this edition of The Literary Press and Magazine Directory. For more information about the Council of Literary Magazines and Presses, visit http://www.clmp.org.

## & Journal for the Arts

**Type:** magazine
**CLMP member:** yes
**Address:** 18908 Briargate Ln., Apt 2D
Parker, CO 80134
**Publishes:** essays
**Reading Period:** Year-round
**Reporting Time:** 1 to 2 months
**Author Payment:** none
**Non Profit:** yes
**Backfile Available:** yes

## 13th Moon

**Type:** magazine
**CLMP member:** no
**Primary Editor/Contact Person:** Judith Johnson
**Address:** Department Of English, HU 378
SUNY Albany
Albany, NY 12222
**Web Site Address:**
http://www.albany.edu/13thMoon/index.html
**Publishes:** fiction, poetry, art, and translation
**Editorial Focus:** 13th Moon's wide array of contributors creates a dynamic journal that constantly evolves to meet the needs of literature.
**Representative Authors:** Ursula Le Guin, Carolee Schneeman, and Ethal Schwabacher
**Submissions Policy:** We welcome submissions from all women as well as men who write about women or translate women's writings.
**Simultaneous Subs:** no
**Reading Period:** 9/1 to 5/31
**Reporting Time:** 5 to 6 months
**Author Payment:** none
**Founded:** 1973
**Non Profit:** yes
**Paid Staff:** 0
**Unpaid Staff:** 4
**Distributors:** EBSCO, Swets Blackwell
**ISSN Number/ISBN Number:** ISSN 0094-3320
**Total Circulation:** 1,200

## 2River

**Type:** online
**CLMP member:** yes
**Primary Editor/Contact Person:** Richard Long
**Address:** 7474 Drexel Dr.
University City, MO 63130
**Web Site Address:** http://www.2River.org
**Publishes:** poetry and art
**Editorial Focus:** 2River publishes The 2River View and the 2River Chapbook Series, and podcasts poems from Muddy Bank.
**Representative Authors:** Wendy Taylor Carlisle, Robert Creeley, and Ann Politte
**Submissions Policy:** Submit no more than four poems, along with a brief bio. Paste poems and bio into e-mail or use Word or RTF attachments.
**Simultaneous Subs:** no
**Reading Period:** Year-round
**Reporting Time:** 1 to 3 months
**Author Payment:** copies
**Founded:** 1996
**Non Profit:** yes
**Paid Staff:** no
**Unpaid Staff:** yes
**ISSN Number/ISBN Number:** 15636-2280/1536-2086
**Average Page Views per Month:** 2,500
**Average Unique Visitors per Month:** 1,800
**Frequency per Year:** 4
**Publish Print Anthology:** no
**Average Percentage of Pages per Category:** Poetry 95%, Art 5%
**Ads:** no

## 32 Poems

**Type:** magazine
**CLMP member:** yes
**Primary Editor/Contact Person:** Deborah Ager
**Address:** P.O. Box 5824
Hyattsville, MD 20782
**Web Site Address:** http://www.32poems.com
**Publishes:** poetry
**Editorial Focus:** 32 Poems is a semiannual. Each issue contains only 32 poems so that readers may give intimate, unhurried attention to each.
**Representative Authors:** Medbh McGuckian, B.H. Fairchild, and Brigit Pegeen Kelly
**Submissions Policy:** Please visit http://www.32poems.com/submit.html for latest guidelines.
**Simultaneous Subs:** no
**Reading Period:** 9/1 to 5/31
**Reporting Time:** 2 to 4 months
**Author Payment:** copies
**Contests:** See Web Site for Contest Guidelines.
**Founded:** 2003
**Non Profit:** yes

**Paid Staff:** 0
**Unpaid Staff:** 3
**Distributors:** available exclusively via subscription
**ISSN Number/ISBN Number:** ISSN pending
**Total Circulation:** 300
**Paid Circulation:** 200
**Subscription Rate:** Individual $12/Institution $12
**Single Copy Price:** $6
**Current Volume/Issue:** 1/2
**Frequency per Year:** 2
**Backfile Available:** yes
**Unsolicited Ms. Received:** yes
**% of Unsolicited Ms. Published per Year:** 50%
**Format:** stapled
**Size:** H 5" W 7"
**Ads:** yes
See Web Site for Details.

# 3rd bed

**Type:** magazine
**CLMP member:** yes
**Primary Editor/Contact Person:** Vincent Standley
**Address:** 68 Third St.
Lincoln, RI 02906
**Web Site Address:** http://3rdbed.com
**Publishes:** essays, fiction, nonfiction, poetry, art, and translation
**Editorial Focus:** Absurdist prose, poetry, and art.
**Representative Authors:** Brian Evenson, Diane Williams, and Lisa Jarnot
**Submissions Policy:** Paper submissions: Cover letter and SASE. Electronic submissions: Please refer to our webpage.
**Simultaneous Subs:** yes
**Reading Period:** Year-round
**Reporting Time:** 2 to 4 months
**Author Payment:** copies and subscription
**Founded:** 1998
**Non Profit:** yes
**Paid Staff:** 0
**Unpaid Staff:** 7
**Distributors:** Ingram, SPD
**ISSN Number/ISBN Number:** ISSN 1523-6773
**Total Circulation:** 1,500
**Paid Circulation:** 150
**Subscription Rate:** Individual $18/Institution $20
**Single Copy Price:** $10
**Current Volume/Issue:** Issue 9
**Frequency per Year:** 2
**Backfile Available:** yes

**Unsolicited Ms. Received:** yes
**% of Unsolicited Ms. Published per Year:** 5%
**Format:** perfect
**Size:** H 8.5" W 6"
**Average Pages:** 200
**Ads:** no

# 580 Split

**Type:** magazine
**CLMP member:** yes
**Primary Editor/Contact Person:** Michell Simotas
**Address:** P.O. Box 9982
Mills College
Oakland, CA 94613-0982
**Web Site Address:** http://www.mills.edu/580Split/
**Publishes:** fiction, poetry, and art
**Editorial Focus:** Innovative prose, poetry, and art
**Representative Authors:** Victo LaValle, Lisa Jarnot, and Cecile Pineda
**Submissions Policy:** see website
**Simultaneous Subs:** no
**Reading Period:** 7/1 to 11/1
**Reporting Time:** 3 to 6 months
**Author Payment:** copies
**Founded:** 1998
**Non Profit:** yes
**Paid Staff:** 0
**Unpaid Staff:** 12
**Distributors:** Ingram
**ISSN Number/ISBN Number:** ISSN 1523-4762
**Total Circulation:** 650
**Average Print Run:** 750
**Subscription Rate:** Individual $14/2 yrs./Institution $12/2 yrs.
**Single Copy Price:** $7.50
**Current Volume/Issue:** Issue 8
**Frequency per Year:** 1
**Backfile Available:** yes
**Unsolicited Ms. Received:** yes
**% of Unsolicited Ms. Published per Year:** 5%
**Format:** perfect
**Size:** H 8.5" W 5.5"
**Average Pages:** 110
**Ads:** yes
**Ad Rates:** $25 1/4 page, $50 1/2 page, $100 full page
See Web Site for Details.

# 6x6

**Type:** magazine
**CLMP member:** yes
**Primary Editor/Contact Person:** Matvei Yankelevich
**Address:** 106 Ferris St.
2nd Floor
Brooklyn, NY 11231
**Web Site Address:**
http://www.uglyducklingpresse.org
**Publishes:** poetry
**Editorial Focus:** 6x6 publishes six poets with six pages each in every issue. Our tastes change and so do our editors. We also do translations.
**Representative Authors:** Frank Lima, Jacqueline Waters, and Steve Dalachinsky
**Submissions Policy:** Send by mail. Enough for six pages. Interested in work designed specifically for the format. Must read mag. before sending.
**Simultaneous Subs:** yes
**Reading Period:** 5/1 to 9/1
**Reporting Time:** 1 to 3 months
**Author Payment:** copies and subscription
**Founded:** 2000
**Non Profit:** yes
**Paid Staff:** 0
**Unpaid Staff:** 3
**Distributors:** Ugly Duckling Presse
**ISSN Number/ISBN Number:** ISSN 1533-9459
**Total Circulation:** 600
**Paid Circulation:** 30
**Subscription Rate:** Individual $10/Institution $20
**Single Copy Price:** $3
**Current Volume/Issue:** Issue 8
**Frequency per Year:** 3
**Backfile Available:** no
**Unsolicited Ms. Received:** yes
**% of Unsolicited Ms. Published per Year:** 25%
**Format:** Industrial Rubber Band Binding
**Size:** H 7" W 7"
**Average Pages:** 52
**Ads:** no

# 88: A Journal of Contemporary American Poetry

**Type:** magazine
**CLMP member:** yes
**Primary Editor/Contact Person:** Ian Randall Wilson
**Address:** P.O. Box 2872
Venice, CA 90294
**Web Site Address:** http://www.hollyridgepress.com
**Publishes:** essays, poetry, and reviews
**Representative Authors:** Thomas Lux, Dean Young, and Jesse Lee Kercheval
**Submissions Policy:** Unsolicited subs 3/1-5/31. Unsolicited subs outside window returned unread.
**Simultaneous Subs:** no
**Reading Period:** Year-round
**Reporting Time:** 3 to 6 months
**Author Payment:** none
**Founded:** 2001
**Non Profit:** no
**Paid Staff:** 0
**Unpaid Staff:** 3
**Wholesalers:** Ingram, Baker & Taylor
**Total Circulation:** 500
**Average Print Run:** POD
**Single Copy Price:** $13.95
**Current Volume/Issue:** Issue 5
**Frequency per Year:** 1
**Backfile Available:** yes
**Unsolicited Ms. Received:** yes
**% of Unsolicited Ms. Published per Year:** 5%
**Format:** perfect
**Size:** H 9" W 6"
**Average Pages:** 180
**Ads:** yes
**Ad Rates:** Full Page: $300, 1/2 Page: $175, 1/4 Page: $100

# A Gathering of the Tribes

**Type:** magazine
**CLMP member:** yes
**Primary Editor/Contact Person:** Steve Cannon
**Address:** P.O. Box 20693
Tompkins Square Station
New York, NY 10009
**Web Site Address:** http://www.tribes.org/
**Publishes:** essays, fiction, poetry, and art
**Simultaneous Subs:** yes
**Reading Period:** Year-round
**Reporting Time:** 1 to 2 months
**Author Payment:** none
**Founded:** 1991
**Non Profit:** yes
**Paid Staff:** 1
**Unpaid Staff:** 10
**Total Circulation:** 2,000
**Paid Circulation:** 150
**Subscription Rate:** Individual $12.50/Institution $30
**Single Copy Price:** $12.50

**Current Volume/Issue:** Issue 13
**Frequency per Year:** 2
**Backfile Available:** yes
**Unsolicited Ms. Received:** yes
**Format:** perfect

## Abraxas Press

**Type:** press
**CLMP member:** no
**Primary Editor/Contact Person:** Ingrid Swanberg
**Address:** P.O. Box 260113
Madison, WI 53726-0113
**Web Site Address:**
http://www.geocities.com/Paris/4614
**Publishes:** essays, poetry, reviews, art, and translation
**Editorial Focus:** Abraxas Magazine is interested in lyrical and experimental poetry, translations of poetry, and essays on contemporary poetry.
**Representative Authors:** d.a.levy, prospero saiz, and Andrea Moorhead
**Submissions Policy:** No unsolicited manuscripts except as announced when projects arise.
**Simultaneous Subs:** no
**Reading Period:** none
**Author Payment:** copies
**Founded:** 1968
**Non Profit:** yes
**Paid Staff:** 0
**Unpaid Staff:** 5
**Distributors:** none currently
**Wholesalers:** none currently
**ISSN Number/ISBN Number:** 0361-1663/0-932868
**Number of Books Published per Year:** 0
**Titles in Print:** 9
**Average Percentage Printed:** Paperback 60%, Chapbook 40%

## The Absinthe Literary Review

**Type:** online
**CLMP member:** yes
**Primary Editor/Contact Person:** Charles Allen Wyman
**Address:** P.O. Box 328
Spring Green, WI 53588
**Web Site Address:** http://www.absinthe-literary-review.com
**Publishes:** essays, fiction, poetry, reviews, and art
**Editorial Focus:** ALR publishes work of high literary caliber dealing with excess, sex, death, disease, philosophy, experiment, and language.
**Recent Awards Received:** Voted most important online journal by LOCKSS program. Lit Rep panel judges from Stanford, IU, Harvard, FSU, UW, UM, Penn ++
**Representative Authors:** Norman Lock, Virgil Suarez, and Davis Schneiderman
**Submissions Policy:** See detailed guidelines at http://www.absinthe-literary-review.com/submit.htm. Failure to do so generally results in sub dismissal.
**Simultaneous Subs:** yes
**Reading Period:** Year-round
**Reporting Time:** 1 to 5 months
**Author Payment:** cash
**Founded:** 1998
**Non Profit:** yes
**Paid Staff:** 1
**Unpaid Staff:** 6
**Distributors:** Online only (print version expected 2006 or 2007)
**Wholesalers:** Online only
**ISSN Number/ISBN Number:** ISSN pending
**Average Page Views per Month:** 1,000,000
**Average Unique Visitors per Month:** 250-300K
**Frequency per Year:** 4
**Publish Print Anthology:** no
**Average Percentage of Pages per Category:** Fiction 24%, Poetry 24%, Reviews 24%, Essays 4%, Art 24%
**Ads:** no

## Absinthe: New European Writing

**Type:** magazine
**CLMP member:** yes
**Primary Editor/Contact Person:** Dwayne D. Hayes
**Address:** Absinthe Arts 21
P.O. Box 11445
Detroit, MI 48211-1445
**Web Site Address:** http://www.absinthenew.com
**Publishes:** essays, fiction, nonfiction, poetry, reviews, art, and translation
**Editorial Focus:** Poetry and prose by contemporary European writers.
**Representative Authors:** Christa Wolf, Herberto Helder, and Ulrike Draesner
**Submissions Policy:** See web site
**Simultaneous Subs:** yes
**Reading Period:** Year-round
**Reporting Time:** 1 to 2 months
**Author Payment:** copies and subscription

**Founded:** 2003
**Non Profit:** yes
**Paid Staff:** 0
**Unpaid Staff:** 6
**Distributors:** DeBoer
**ISSN Number/ISBN Number:** ISSN 1543-8449
**Total Circulation:** 500
**Paid Circulation:** 100
**Average Print Run:** 1,000
**Subscription Rate:** Individual $12/Institution $25
**Single Copy Price:** $7
**Current Volume/Issue:** Issue 4
**Frequency per Year:** 2
**Backfile Available:** yes
**Unsolicited Ms. Received:** yes
**Format:** perfect
**Size:** H 9" W 6"
**Average Pages:** 104
**Ads:** yes

## Accent Miami

**Type:** magazine
**CLMP member:** no
**Primary Editor/Contact Person:** Augusto Maxwell
**Address:** 736 13th St. #111
Miami Beach, FL 33139
**Web Site Address:** http://www.accentmiami.org
**Publishes:** essays, fiction, nonfiction, poetry, reviews, art, and translation
**Editorial Focus:** Focus on Miami, Florida and publishes on a quarterly basis works from area writers or matters of interest to Miami readers.
**Representative Authors:** Rick Jervis, Bob Williamson, and Cecilia Fernandez
**Submissions Policy:** Three double-spaced copies accompanied by a cover page with your name, address, phone number, e-mail address and a brief bio.
**Simultaneous Subs:** yes
**Reading Period:** Year-round
**Reporting Time:** 2 to 3 months
**Author Payment:** copies and subscription
**Founded:** 2001
**Non Profit:** yes
**Paid Staff:** 0
**Unpaid Staff:** 10
**Total Circulation:** 1,200
**Paid Circulation:** 200
**Subscription Rate:** Individual $20/Institution $20
**Single Copy Price:** $5.95

**Current Volume/Issue:** Issue 4
**Frequency per Year:** 4
**Backfile Available:** yes
**Unsolicited Ms. Received:** yes
**% of Unsolicited Ms. Published per Year:** 50%
**Format:** stapled
**Size:** H 10" W 6.5"
**Average Pages:** 44
**Ads:** yes
**Ad Rates:** Full page $1,200
See Web Site for Details.

## The Adirondack Review

**Type:** online
**CLMP member:** no
**Primary Editor/Contact Person:** Colleen Marie Ryor
**Address:** P.O. Box 46
Watertown, NY 13601
**Web Site Address:** http://www.adirondackreview.com
**Publishes:** essays, fiction, nonfiction, poetry, reviews, and art
**Representative Authors:** Lee Upton, D.C. Berry, and Ilya Kaminsky
**Submissions Policy:** See website for guidelines.
**Simultaneous Subs:** yes
**Reading Period:** Year-round
**Reporting Time:** 1 to 12 weeks
**Author Payment:** none
**Contests:** The St. Lawrence Book Award for a first collection: $1,000 and publication. The 46er Prize for Short Fiction: $500.
See Web Site for Contest Guidelines.
**Founded:** 2000
**Non Profit:** yes
**Paid Staff:** 0
**Unpaid Staff:** 9
**ISSN Number/ISBN Number:** ISSN 1533-2063
**Average Page Views per Month:** 18,000
**Average Unique Visitors per Month:** 5,000
**Frequency per Year:** 4
**Publish Print Anthology:** no
**Average Percentage of Pages per Category:** Fiction 25%, Nonfiction 10%, Poetry 45%, Reviews 10%, Essays 2%, Art 3%, Translation 5%
**Ad Rates:** $40/classified ad with graphic (three months), discounts
See Web Site for Details.

# African American Review

**Type:** magazine
**CLMP member:** yes
**Primary Editor/Contact Person:** Joycelyn Moody/Aileen Keenan
**Address:** 3800 Lindell Blvd.
Humanities 317, 3800 Lindell Blvd.
St. Louis, MO 63108
**Web Site Address:** http://aar.slu.edu
**Publishes:** essays, fiction, poetry, and reviews
**Editorial Focus:** African American Review promotes a lively exchange among writers and scholars in the arts, humanities, and social sciences who hold diverse perspectives on African American literature and culture. AAR publishes essays on African American literature, theatre, film, art, and culture generally; interviews; poetry; fiction; and book reviews.
**Representative Authors:** Farah Jasmine Griffin, Kalamu ya Salaam, and Sandra Shannon
**Submissions Policy:** http://aar.slu.edu/submsinf.html
**Simultaneous Subs:** no
**Reading Period:** Year-round
**Reporting Time:** 6 to 7 months
**Author Payment:** cash and copies
**Founded:** 1967
**Non Profit:** yes
**Paid Staff:** 2
**Unpaid Staff:** 0
**ISSN Number/ISBN Number:** ISSN 1062-4783
**Paid Circulation:** 1,800
**Average Print Run:** 2,400
**Subscription Rate:** Individual $40/Institution $80
**Single Copy Price:** $12
**Current Volume/Issue:** 38/1-4
**Frequency per Year:** 4
**Backfile Available:** yes
**Unsolicited Ms. Received:** yes
**% of Unsolicited Ms. Published per Year:** 15%
**Format:** perfect
**Size:** H 10" W 7"
**Average Pages:** 176
**Ads:** yes
**Ad Rates:** $120 1/2 page, $200 full page
See Web Site for Details.

# African Heritage Press

**Type:** press
**CLMP member:** yes
**Primary Editor/Contact Person:** Basil Njoku
**Address:** P.O. Box 1433
New Rochelle, NY 10802
**Web Site Address:**
http://www.africanheritagepress.com
**Publishes:** essays, fiction, nonfiction, and poetry
**Editorial Focus:** we are committed to publishing original poetry, prose fiction and drama that uniquely inform, reveal and project the rich socio-cultural experiences and worlds of the diverse peoples of African descent, beyond borders.
**Recent Awards Received:** ANA Best Poetry Prize, 2003 BBC Drama Documentary, Radio Drama.
**Representative Authors:** Tess Onwueme, Tanure Ojaide, and Ernest Emenyonu
**Submissions Policy:** Include a hard copy printed on one side only and double-spaced. Pages should be numbered, and manuscripts bound or securely clipped without rubber bands, staples, paper clips, or loose pages. An author's bio must include address, phone number, and e-mail. Include a one-page description of the subject and purpose of the book, and a disk or CD copy developed in Microsoft Word.
**Simultaneous Subs:** yes
**Reading Period:** Year-round
**Reporting Time:** 1 to 2 months
**Author Payment:** royalties and copies
**Founded:** 2000
**Non Profit:** yes
**Paid Staff:** 4
**Unpaid Staff:** 3
**Distributors:** http://www.africanbookscollective.com
**Wholesalers:** African books collective/Michigan State University
**Number of Books Published per Year:** 5
**Titles in Print:** 8
**Average Percentage Printed:** Paperback 100%
**Average Price:** $14.95

# African Voices Communications

**Type:** magazine
**CLMP member:** yes
**Primary Editor/Contact Person:** Carolyn A. Butts
**Address:** 270 West 96th St.
New York, NY 10025
**Web Site Address:** http://www.africanvoices.com/
**Publishes:** essays, fiction, nonfiction, poetry, reviews, art, and translation
**Editorial Focus:** African Voices publishes compelling short stories, poetry and art by people of color.
**Representative Authors:** Willie Perdomo, Nalo Hopkinson, and Ngugi wa Thiong'o

**Submissions Policy:** Please submit no more than 3 poems at a time. Fiction stories between 300 to 2,500 words are considered for publication.
**Simultaneous Subs:** yes
**Reading Period:** Year-round
**Reporting Time:** 1 to 3 months
**Author Payment:** copies
**Contests:** Periodic fiction and poetry contests are announced.
**Founded:** 1992
**Non Profit:** yes
**Unpaid Staff:** 7
**Distributors:** Ingram and Ubiquity
**ISSN Number/ISBN Number:** ISSN 1530-0668
**Total Circulation:** 20,000
**Paid Circulation:** 95%
**Subscription Rate:** Individual $12/Institution $12
**Single Copy Price:** $4
**Current Volume/Issue:** 10/17
**Frequency per Year:** 4
**Backfile Available:** yes
**Unsolicited Ms. Received:** yes
**% of Unsolicited Ms. Published per Year:** 80%
**Format:** saddle stitched
**Size:** H 11" W 8.5"
**Average Pages:** 44
**Ads:** yes
**Ad Rates:** Full page $1,200
See Web Site for Details.

# AGNI

**Type:** magazine
**CLMP member:** yes
**Primary Editor/Contact Person:** Sven Birkerts, Editor
**Address:** Boston University
236 Bay State Road
Boston, MA 02215
**Web Site Address:** http://www.agnimagazine.org
**Publishes:** essays, fiction, nonfiction, poetry, art, and translation
**Editorial Focus:** Following Ezra Pound's dictum that "artists are the antennae of the race," we publish the best, most provocative "signals."
**Recent Awards Received:** Two Pushcart Prizes for 2006. A story published at AGNI Online was named one of the Top Ten Online Stories of 2004.
**Representative Authors:** Seamus Heaney, David Foster Wallace, and Alden Jones
**Submissions Policy:** Mail one story, essay, or 1-5 poems per submission, with SASE, addressed to

Fiction, Poetry, or Nonfiction Editor. No e-mail.
**Simultaneous Subs:** yes
**Reading Period:** 9/1 to 5/31
**Reporting Time:** 2 to 4 months
**Author Payment:** cash, copies, and subscription
**Founded:** 1972
**Non Profit:** yes
**Paid Staff:** 6
**Unpaid Staff:** 3-4
**Distributors:** Ingram, DeBoer
**ISSN Number/ISBN Number:** ISSN 0191-3352
**Total Circulation:** 3,000
**Paid Circulation:** 1,100
**Average Print Run:** 3,500
**Subscription Rate:** Individual $17/Institution $20
**Single Copy Price:** $10
**Current Volume/Issue:** Issue 62
**Frequency per Year:** 2
**Backfile Available:** yes
**Unsolicited Ms. Received:** yes
**% of Unsolicited Ms. Published per Year:** 1%
**Format:** perfect
**Size:** H 8.5" W 5-3/8"
**Average Pages:** 240
**Ads:** yes
**Ad Rates:** $500 full page; $350 half, sold with Harvard Review
See Web Site for Details.

# Ahsahta Press

**Type:** press
**CLMP member:** yes
**Primary Editor/Contact Person:** Janet Holmes
**Address:** Boise State University
1910 University Dr.
Boise, ID 83725-1525
**Web Site Address:** http://ahsahtapress.boisestate.edu
**Publishes:** poetry
**Editorial Focus:** We publish full-length collections and seek out work that surprises and innovates. Annual Sawtooth Prize honors new poetry.
**Representative Authors:** Noah Eli Gordon, Sandra Miller, and Liz Waldner
**Submissions Policy:** 48-80 pages. Cover letter with bio info, description of manuscript, list of publications (if applicable). SASE.
**Simultaneous Subs:** yes
**Reading Period:** 3/1 to 5/30
**Reporting Time:** 1 to 2 months
**Author Payment:** royalties and copies

**Contests:** See Web Site for Contest Guidelines.
**Founded:** 1974
**Non Profit:** yes
**Paid Staff:** 0
**Unpaid Staff:** 7
**Distributors:** SPD
**Wholesalers:** Baker & Taylor
**ISSN Number/ISBN Number:** ISBN 0-916272-
**Number of Books Published per Year:** 3-5
**Titles in Print:** 71
**Average Print Run:** 1,000
**Average Percentage Printed:** Paperback 100%
**Average Price:** $16

# Akashic Books

**Type:** press
**CLMP member:** yes
**Primary Editor/Contact Person:** Johnny Temple
**Address:** P.O. Box 1456
New York, NY 10009
**Web Site Address:** http://www.akashicbooks.com
**Publishes:** fiction and nonfiction
**Editorial Focus:** Brooklyn-based independent company dedicated to publishing urban literary fiction and political nonfiction.
**Recent Awards Received:** Edgar, Miriam Bass, Anthony
**Representative Authors:** Arthur Nersesian, Kaylie Jones, and T. Cooper
**Submissions Policy:** Currently not accepting new submissions, but okay to e-mail or mail inquiry and short synopsis.
**Simultaneous Subs:** yes
**Reading Period:** Year-round
**Reporting Time:** 1 to 8 months
**Author Payment:** royalties
**Founded:** 1997
**Non Profit:** no
**Paid Staff:** 3
**Unpaid Staff:** 2
**Distributors:** Consortium
**Wholesalers:** Ingram, Koen, Baker & Taylor, SPD, Turnaround-UK
**ISSN Number/ISBN Number:** 1-888451/0-9719206
**Number of Books Published per Year:** 24
**Titles in Print:** 90
**Average Print Run:** 5,000
**Average Percentage Printed:** Hardcover 20%, Paperback 80%
**Average Price:** $14.95

# Alaska Quarterly Review

**Type:** magazine
**CLMP member:** yes
**Primary Editor/Contact Person:** Ronald Spatz
**Address:** University of Alaska Anchorage
3211 Providence Dr.
Anchorage, AK 99508
**Web Site Address:** http://aqr.uaa.alaska.edu
**Publishes:** essays, fiction, nonfiction, poetry, and translation
**Editorial Focus:** publishing fiction, short plays, poetry and literary nonfiction in traditional and experimental styles.
**Representative Authors:** Jane Hirshfield, Douglas Light, and Howard Norman
**Submissions Policy:** Alaska Quarterly Review is a literary journal devoted to literary art, publishing fiction, short plays, poetry and literary nonfiction in traditional and experimental styles. The editors encourage new and emerging writers, while continuing to publish award-winning and established writers.
**Simultaneous Subs:** yes
**Reading Period:** 8/15 to 5/15
**Reporting Time:** 1 to 6 months
**Author Payment:** cash, copies, and subscription
**Founded:** 1981
**Non Profit:** yes
**Paid Staff:** 1
**Unpaid Staff:** 6
**Distributors:** Ingram, DeBoer
**ISSN Number/ISBN Number:** ISSN 0737-268X
**Total Circulation:** 3,500
**Paid Circulation:** 160
**Average Print Run:** 4,000
**Subscription Rate:** Individual $10/Institution $10
**Single Copy Price:** $6.95
**Current Volume/Issue:** V22/3 and 4
**Frequency per Year:** 2
**Backfile Available:** yes
**Unsolicited Ms. Received:** yes
**% of Unsolicited Ms. Published per Year:** 1/2%
**Format:** perfect
**Size:** H 9" W 6"
**Average Pages:** 250
**Ads:** no

# Alice James Books

**Type:** press
**CLMP member:** yes
**Primary Editor/Contact Person:** April Ossmann
**Address:** 238 Main St.
Farmington, ME 04938
**Web Site Address:** http://www.alicejamesbooks.org
**Publishes:** poetry
**Editorial Focus:** Publishes poetry by established and beginning poets, both national and regional; emphasizes involving poets in publishing process.
**Representative Authors:** B.H. Fairchild, Matthea Harvey, and Cole Swensen
**Submissions Policy:** The cooperative board selects manuscripts through annual regional and national competitions. See website for guidelines.
**Simultaneous Subs:** yes
**Reading Period:** 7/1 to 12/1
**Reporting Time:** 3 to 4 months
**Author Payment:** cash
**Contests:** See Web Site for Contest Guidelines.
**Founded:** 1973
**Non Profit:** yes
**Paid Staff:** 4
**Unpaid Staff:** 5
**Distributors:** Consortium, SPD
**Wholesalers:** Ingram, Baker & Taylor
**ISSN Number/ISBN Number:** ISBN 0-914086; 1-882295
**Number of Books Published per Year:** 6
**Titles in Print:** 120
**Average Percentage Printed:** Paperback 100%
**Average Price:** $14.95

# All Info-About Poetry

**Type:** online
**CLMP member:** no
**Primary Editor/Contact Person:** Paula Bardell
**Address:** Pussy Willow
2 Singrett Hill
Llay, Wr LL12 0NS
**Web Site Address:** http://poetry.allinfo-about.com
**Publishes:** essays, nonfiction, poetry, reviews, and translation
**Editorial Focus:** We are pleased to accept well-crafted poetry and verse; book, film and performance reviews; essays and articles concerning poets and poetry; and any other appropriate contribution.
**Representative Authors:** Ruth Daigon, Liam Wilkinson, and Karen Alkalay-Gut

**Submissions Policy:** Submit your work to the e-mail address: mailto:poets@allinfo-about.com with "submission AIAP" in the subject heading. Please do not send attachments.
**Simultaneous Subs:** yes
**Reading Period:** Year-round
**Reporting Time:** 4 to 8 weeks
**Author Payment:** none
**Contests:** See Web Site for Contest Guidelines.
**Founded:** 2001
**Non Profit:** yes
**Paid Staff:** 0
**Unpaid Staff:** 1
**ISSN Number/ISBN Number:** ISSN 1740-4428
**Average Page Views per Month:** 10,000
**Average Unique Visitors per Month:** 8,000
**Publish Print Anthology:** no
**Average Percentage of Pages per Category:** Nonfiction 10%, Poetry 50%, Reviews 20%, Essays 20%
**Ad Rates:** See Web Site for Details.

# Alligator Juniper

**Type:** magazine
**CLMP member:** yes
**Primary Editor/Contact Person:** Miles Waggener
**Address:** 220 Grove Ave.
220 Grove Ave.
Prescott, AZ 86301
**Web Site Address:** http://www.prescott.edu/highlights/alligator_juniper
**Publishes:** fiction, nonfiction, and poetry
**Editorial Focus:** Literary fiction, poetry, nonfiction, and black and white photography.
**Recent Awards Received:** AWP Director's Prize for Content in 2001 and 2004.
**Representative Authors:** Wendy Bishop, Kurt Brown, and Fatima Lim-Wilson
**Submissions Policy:** The majority of our material comes from contest submissions. Please read our guidelines before entering.
**Simultaneous Subs:** yes
**Reading Period:** 5/1 to 10/1
**Reporting Time:** 3 to 5 months
**Author Payment:** copies
**Contests:** See Web Site for Contest Guidelines.
**Founded:** 1994
**Non Profit:** yes
**Paid Staff:** 3
**Unpaid Staff:** 24

**Distributors:** Ingram
**ISSN Number/ISBN Number:** ISSN 1547-187X
**Total Circulation:** 1,200
**Paid Circulation:** 150
**Average Print Run:** 2,000
**Subscription Rate:** Individual $12/2 years/Institution $12/2 years
**Single Copy Price:** $7.50
**Current Volume/Issue:** 10/2005
**Frequency per Year:** 1
**Backfile Available:** yes
**Unsolicited Ms. Received:** yes
**% of Unsolicited Ms. Published per Year:** 90%
**Format:** perfect
**Size:** H 9" W 6"
**Average Pages:** 180
**Ads:** no

# American Book Review

**Type:** magazine
**CLMP member:** yes
**Primary Editor/Contact Person:** Rebecca Kaiser
**Address:** ISU Campus Box 4241
Normal, IL 61790-4241
**Web Site Address:** http://www.litline.org/abr
**Publishes:** essays and reviews
**Editorial Focus:** Reviews of literary books.
**Submissions Policy:** contact for guidelines
**Simultaneous Subs:** yes
**Reading Period:** Year-round
**Reporting Time:** 2 to 8 weeks
**Author Payment:** cash, copies, and subscription
**Founded:** 1977
**Non Profit:** yes
**Paid Staff:** 3
**Unpaid Staff:** 16
**Distributors:** Ingram, Interstate
**ISSN Number/ISBN Number:** ISSN 0149-9408
**Total Circulation:** 5,000
**Paid Circulation:** 2,000
**Subscription Rate:** Individual $24/Institution $30
**Single Copy Price:** $4
**Current Volume/Issue:** 25/1
**Frequency per Year:** 6
**Backfile Available:** yes
**Unsolicited Ms. Received:** yes
**% of Unsolicited Ms. Published per Year:** 15%
**Format:** tabloid
**Size:** H 17" W 11"
**Average Pages:** 32

**Ads:** yes
**Ad Rates:** full page $1,050, half page $750, 2 half-columns $300

# American Letters & Commentary

**Type:** magazine
**CLMP member:** yes
**Primary Editor/Contact Person:** David Vance, Catherine Kasper
**Address:** P.O. Box 830365
San Antonio, TX 78283
**Web Site Address:** http://www.amletters.org
**Publishes:** essays, fiction, nonfiction, poetry, reviews, art, and translation
**Editorial Focus:** Challenging, innovative work in all genres
**Representative Authors:** Ann Lauterbach, Charles Bernstein, and Marjorie Perloff
**Submissions Policy:** Only unpublished work, simultaneous submissions accepted if notified
**Simultaneous Subs:** yes
**Reading Period:** 10/1 to 3/1
**Reporting Time:** 1 to 4 months
**Author Payment:** copies
**Founded:** 1987
**Non Profit:** yes
**Paid Staff:** 0
**Unpaid Staff:** 4
**Distributors:** Ingram, DeBoer, SPD, Ubiquity
**ISSN Number/ISBN Number:** ISSN 1049-7153
**Total Circulation:** 1,500
**Paid Circulation:** 200
**Average Print Run:** 1,600
**Subscription Rate:** Individual $8/Institution $8
**Single Copy Price:** $8
**Current Volume/Issue:** 15/15
**Frequency per Year:** 1
**Backfile Available:** yes
**Unsolicited Ms. Received:** yes
**% of Unsolicited Ms. Published per Year:** 95%
**Format:** perfect
**Size:** H 7" W 8"
**Average Pages:** 200
**Ads:** yes
**Ad Rates:** $35 half page, $50 whole page
See Web Site for Details.

## American Literary Review

**Type:** magazine
**CLMP member:** no
**Primary Editor/Contact Person:** John Tait, Editor
**Address:** P.O. Box 311307
University of North Texas
Denton, TX 76203-1307
**Web Site Address:** http://www.engl.unt.edu/alr
**Publishes:** essays, fiction, nonfiction, poetry, reviews, and art
**Editorial Focus:** Well-crafted stories that reveal the complexities of characters. Poetry that uses fresh language and formal artistry.
**Representative Authors:** Mark Jacobs, David Citino, and Mark Irwin
**Submissions Policy:** We accept previously unpublished short stories, poems, essays, and reviews. Submit no more than one story or five poems.
**Simultaneous Subs:** yes
**Reading Period:** 9/1 to 5/1
**Reporting Time:** 8 to 12 weeks
**Author Payment:** copies
**Contests:** Each year we run a contest with a $1,000 prize. The contest is for fiction in the even years and poetry in the odd years.
See Web Site for Contest Guidelines.
**Founded:** 1990
**Non Profit:** yes
**Paid Staff:** yes
**Unpaid Staff:** yes
**ISSN Number/ISBN Number:** 1051-5062/PS24437-3/31
**Total Circulation:** 500
**Paid Circulation:** 350
**Subscription Rate:** Individual $10/Institution $25
**Single Copy Price:** $6
**Current Volume/Issue:** 14/2
**Frequency per Year:** 2
**Backfile Available:** yes
**Unsolicited Ms. Received:** yes
**% of Unsolicited Ms. Published per Year:** 2%
**Format:** perfect
**Size:** H 9" W 6"
**Average Pages:** 130
**Ads:** no

## The American Poetry Review

**Type:** magazine
**CLMP member:** yes
**Primary Editor/Contact Person:** David Bonanno
**Address:** 117 S. 17th St. #910
Philadelphia, PA 19103
**Web Site Address:** http://www.aprweb.org
**Publishes:** essays, fiction, nonfiction, poetry, reviews, and translation
**Editorial Focus:** Broad range of poetry, translations, criticism, reviews, interviews, and columns.
**Representative Authors:** Louise Gluck, Dana Levin, and W.S. Merwin
**Submissions Policy:** Send 1-5 poems with SASE
**Simultaneous Subs:** no
**Reading Period:** Year-round
**Reporting Time:** 8 to 12 weeks
**Author Payment:** cash, copies, and subscription
**Contests:** See Web Site for Contest Guidelines.
**Founded:** 1972
**Non Profit:** yes
**Paid Staff:** 6
**Unpaid Staff:** 4
**Distributors:** Ingram, DeBoer, Ubiquity, Media Solutions, Armadillo
**ISSN Number/ISBN Number:** ISSN 0360-3709
**Total Circulation:** 16,000
**Paid Circulation:** 11,000
**Average Print Run:** 17,500
**Subscription Rate:** Individual $19/Institution $19
**Single Copy Price:** $3.95
**Current Volume/Issue:** 35/200
**Frequency per Year:** 6
**Backfile Available:** yes
**Unsolicited Ms. Received:** yes
**% of Unsolicited Ms. Published per Year:** .6%
**Format:** tabloid
**Size:** H 13" W 9 1/2"
**Average Pages:** 52
**Ads:** yes
**Ad Rates:** See Web Site for Details.

## American Short Fiction

**Type:** magazine
**CLMP member:** yes
**Address:** P.O. Box 301209
Austin, TX 78703
**Web Site Address:** http://www.badgerdog.org
**Publishes:** fiction
**Reading Period:** Year-round
**Reporting Time:** 1 to 2 months
**Author Payment:** none
**Non Profit:** no
**Backfile Available:** yes

# anderbo.com

**Type:** online
**CLMP member:** yes
**Primary Editor/Contact Person:** Rick Rofihe
**Address:** 341 Lafayette St. #974
New York, NY 10012
**Web Site Address:** http://www.anderbo.com
**Publishes:** fiction, nonfiction, and poetry
**Editorial Focus:** Look at our first online issue.
**Representative Authors:** Martha Wilson, Jeff
Clinkenbeard, and Wayne Conti
**Submissions Policy:** Fiction up to 3,500 words.
"Fact" up to 750 words. Poems, submit up to 6.
Photographs, submit photocopies, snail mail only.
**Simultaneous Subs:** yes
**Reading Period:** Year-round
**Reporting Time:** 0 to 4 weeks
**Author Payment:** none
**Founded:** 2005
**Non Profit:** no
**Paid Staff:** 0
**Unpaid Staff:** 6
**Average Page Views per Month:** unknown
**Average Unique Visitors per Month:** unknown
**Frequency per Year:** 3
**Publish Print Anthology:** yes
Price: $10
**Average Percentage of Pages per Category:** Fiction
60%, Nonfiction 20%, Poetry 20%
**Ads:** yes
**Ad Rates:** Sliding scale.

# Anhinga Press

**Type:** press
**CLMP member:** yes
**Primary Editor/Contact Person:** Rick Campbell
**Address:** P.O. Box
Tallahassee, FL 32302
**Web Site Address:** http://www.anhinga.org
**Publishes:** poetry
**Editorial Focus:** We are looking for good poetry; it's
that simple.
**Representative Authors:** Naomi Shihab Nye, Robert
Dana, and Frank X. Gaspar
**Submissions Policy:** Send submissions to our post
office address; we don't accept electronic submis-
sions.
**Simultaneous Subs:** yes
**Reading Period:** Year-round

**Reporting Time:** 6 to 10 weeks
**Author Payment:** royalties, cash, and copies
**Contests:** Anhinga Prize for Poetry. For 1st or 2nd
books. Reading period 2/15-5/1. Fee: $20.
See Web Site for Contest Guidelines.
**Founded:** 1973
**Non Profit:** yes
**Paid Staff:** 2
**Unpaid Staff:** 6
**Distributors:** SPD
**ISSN Number/ISBN Number:** ISBN 0938078
**Number of Books Published per Year:** 4
**Titles in Print:** 35
**Average Percentage Printed:** Hardcover 5%,
Paperback 95%
**Backfile Available:** yes

# Another Chicago Magazine/Left Field Press

**Type:** magazine
**CLMP member:** no
**Address:** 3709 N. Kenmore
Chicago, IL 60613-2905
**Web Site Address:**
http://www.anotherchicagomag.com
**Publishes:** essays, fiction, poetry, reviews, art, and
translation
**Reading Period:** Year-round
**Reporting Time:** 1 to 2 months
**Author Payment:** none
**Founded:** 1977
**Non Profit:** no
**Frequency per Year:** Biannual
Price: $8

# Antioch Review

**Type:** magazine
**CLMP member:** yes
**Primary Editor/Contact Person:** Robert Fogarty
**Address:** P.O. Box 148
Yellow Springs, OH 45387
**Web Site Address:** http://www.review.antioch.edu
**Publishes:** essays, fiction, nonfiction, poetry, and
translation
**Editorial Focus:** A quarterly of critical and creative
thought printing fiction, poetry and essays. We print
the best words in the best order.
**Representative Authors:** Bruce Fleming, Peter
LaSalle, and Edith Pearlman

**Submissions Policy:** Send only one story at a time. Do not mix poetry and prose. Rarely do we publish anything over 8,000 words.
**Simultaneous Subs:** no
**Reading Period:** 9/1 to 6/1
**Reporting Time:** 4 to 6 months
**Author Payment:** cash and copies
**Founded:** 1941
**Non Profit:** yes
**Paid Staff:** 1.5
**Unpaid Staff:** 1
**Distributors:** Ingram, Media Solutions, Ubiquity, Central Bks.—UK
**ISSN Number/ISBN Number:** ISSN 0003-5769
**Total Circulation:** 2,850
**Paid Circulation:** 1,000
**Average Print Run:** 3,000
**Subscription Rate:** Individual $40/Institution $76
**Single Copy Price:** $9.50
**Current Volume/Issue:** 64/1
**Frequency per Year:** 4
**Backfile Available:** yes
**Unsolicited Ms. Received:** yes
**% of Unsolicited Ms. Published per Year:** 1%
**Format:** perfect
**Size:** H 9" W 6"
**Average Pages:** 200
**Ads:** yes
**Ad Rates:** $250 full page, $150 1/2 page, $100 1/4 page
See Web Site for Details.

## Anvil Press

**Type:** press
**CLMP member:** no
**Primary Editor/Contact Person:** Brian Kaufman
**Address:** 6 West 17th Ave.(Rear)
Vancouver, BC V5T2C2
**Web Site Address:** http://www.anvilpress.com
**Publishes:** fiction, nonfiction, and poetry
**Editorial Focus:** Anvil Press publishes contemporary and exciting work by Canadian writers. We look for work that is fresh, edgy and unique.
**Representative Authors:** Lincoln Clarkes, Jim Christy, and Mark Anthony Jarman
**Submissions Policy:** Only Canadian authors. No genre fiction, self-help, cookbooks, etc. Enclose SASE for reply or sufficient postage for return of ms.
**Simultaneous Subs:** yes
**Reading Period:** Year-round

**Reporting Time:** 4 to 6 months
**Author Payment:** royalties and cash
**Contests:** See Web Site for Contest Guidelines.
**Founded:** 1988
**Non Profit:** no
**Paid Staff:** 3
**Unpaid Staff:** 0
**Distributors:** University of Toronto Press
**Number of Books Published per Year:** 10
**Titles in Print:** 53
**Average Percentage Printed:** Paperback 100%

## Apalachee Review

**Type:** magazine
**CLMP member:** yes
**Primary Editor/Contact Person:** Laura Newton
**Address:** P.O. Box 10469
Tallahassee, FL 32302
**Web Site Address:** http://www.apalacheereview.org
**Publishes:** essays, fiction, poetry, reviews, art, and translation
**Editorial Focus:** The best writing we can get our hands on.
**Representative Authors:** Rita Mae Reese, Marilyn Abildskov, and Marlin Barton
**Simultaneous Subs:** yes
**Reading Period:** Year-round
**Reporting Time:** 3 to 6 months
**Author Payment:** copies
**Contests:** no
**Founded:** 1978
**Non Profit:** yes
**Paid Staff:** 0
**Unpaid Staff:** 9
**Distributors:** DeBoer
**ISSN Number/ISBN Number:** ISSN 0890-6408
**Total Circulation:** 500
**Paid Circulation:** 200
**Average Print Run:** 750
**Subscription Rate:** Individual $15/Institution $20
**Single Copy Price:** $8
**Current Volume/Issue:** Issue 54
**Frequency per Year:** 2
**Backfile Available:** yes
**Unsolicited Ms. Received:** yes
**% of Unsolicited Ms. Published per Year:** 10%
**Format:** perfect
**Size:** H 8 1/2" W 5 1/2"
**Average Pages:** 100
**Ads:** o

## Apogee Press

**Type:** press
**CLMP member:** yes
**Primary Editor/Contact Person:** Editor
**Address:** P.O. Box 8177
Berkeley, CA 94707-8177
**Web Site Address:** http://www.apogeepress.com
**Publishes:** poetry
**Editorial Focus:** innovative poetry
**Simultaneous Subs:** yes
**Reading Period:** Year-round
**Reporting Time:** 2 to 4 months
**Author Payment:** royalties and copies
**Founded:** 1998
**Non Profit:** yes
**Paid Staff:** 0
**Unpaid Staff:** 0
**Distributors:** SPD
**Number of Books Published per Year:** 3-4
**Titles in Print:** 18
**Average Print Run:** 1,000
**Average Percentage Printed:** Paperback 100%
**Average Price:** $14.95

## Archipelago Books

**Type:** press
**CLMP member:** yes
**Primary Editor/Contact Person:** Jill Schoolman
**Address:** 25 Jay St., #203
Brooklyn, NY 11201
**Web Site Address:** http://www.archipelagobooks.org
**Publishes:** fiction, poetry, art, and translation
**Editorial Focus:** Archipelago Books focuses on bringing classic and contemporary works of literature to an American audience.
**Representative Authors:** Witold Gombrowicz, Ahmed Hamdi Tanpinar, and Elias Khoury
**Submissions Policy:** We are not accepting submissions at this time.
**Simultaneous Subs:** no
**Reading Period:** Year-round
**Reporting Time:** 1 to 2 months
**Author Payment:** royalties, cash, and copies
**Founded:** 2003
**Non Profit:** yes
**Paid Staff:** 2
**Unpaid Staff:** 2
**Distributors:** Consortium
**ISSN Number/ISBN Number:** ISBN 0-9728692, 0-9749680

**Number of Books Published per Year:** 8
**Titles in Print:** 20
**Average Print Run:** 2,500
**Average Percentage Printed:** Hardcover 50%, Paperback 50%
**Average Price:** $14/$24

## Archipelago

**Type:** online
**CLMP member:** no
**Primary Editor/Contact Person:** Katherine McNamara, Editor
**Address:** Box 2485
Charlottesville, VA 22902-2485
**Web Site Address:** http://www.archipelago.org
**Publishes:** essays, fiction, nonfiction, poetry, reviews, art, translation, and audio
**Editorial Focus:** Intelligent writing for educated readers formed by more than one culture, knowing the world is larger than the US.
**Submissions Policy:** Query required first for electronic submission. Paper with SASE.
**Simultaneous Subs:** no
**Reading Period:** Year-round
**Reporting Time:** 1 to 6 months
**Author Payment:** none
**Founded:** 1997
**Non Profit:** yes
**Paid Staff:** 1
**Unpaid Staff:** yes
**Average Page Views per Month:** 44,000
**Average Unique Visitors per Month:** 12,000
**Frequency per Year:** 4
**Average Percentage of Pages per Category:** Audio 100%

## Arctos Press

**Type:** press
**CLMP member:** yes
**Primary Editor/Contact Person:** C.B. Follett
**Address:** P.O. Box 401
Sausalito, CA 94966
**Web Site Address:** http://members.aol.com/Runes
**Publishes:** poetry
**Editorial Focus:** From our contest and regular submissions, we select the best 100 poems on our annual theme.
**Representative Authors:** David St. John, Jane Hirshfield, and Li-Young Lee

**Submissions Policy:** Up to 5 poems on theme-'06 is "hearth" (literal/metaphorical). SASE required.
**Simultaneous Subs:** yes
**Reading Period:** 4/5 to 5/31
**Reporting Time:** 2 to 4 months
**Author Payment:** copies
**Contests:** See Web Site for Contest Guidelines.
**Founded:** 1996
**Non Profit:** yes
**Paid Staff:** 0
**Unpaid Staff:** 4
**Distributors:** SPD
**Wholesalers:** Baker & Taylor
**ISSN Number/ISBN Number:** ISBN 0-9725384-
**Number of Books Published per Year:** 1-3
**Titles in Print:** 15
**Average Print Run:** 1,200
**Average Percentage Printed:** Paperback 100%
**Average Price:** $12

# Argonne House Press

**Type:** press
**CLMP member:** no
**Primary Editor/Contact Person:** R.D. Baker
**Address:** 1620 Argonne Place NW
Washington, DC 20009
**Web Site Address:** http://www.wordwrights.com
**Publishes:** essays, fiction, nonfiction, and poetry
**Editorial Focus:** We publish books by authors previously published in Wordwrights Magazine.
**Representative Authors:** Judith Podell, Grace Cavalieri, and Richard Peabody
**Submissions Policy:** We publish books by authors previously published in Wordwrights Magazine.
**Simultaneous Subs:** yes
**Reading Period:** Year-round
**Reporting Time:** 3 to 6 months
**Author Payment:** royalties
**Founded:** 1993
**Non Profit:** no
**Paid Staff:** 0
**Unpaid Staff:** 25
**Distributors:** Argonne House Press
**Wholesalers:** Argonne House Press
**Number of Books Published per Year:** 12
**Titles in Print:** 48
**Average Percentage Printed:** Paperback 10%, Chapbook 90%

# Arkansas Review: A Journal of Delta Studies

**Type:** magazine
**CLMP member:** yes
**Primary Editor/Contact Person:** Tom Williams
**Address:** P.O. Box 1890
Arkansas State University
State University, AR 72467
**Web Site Address:** http://www.clt.astate.edu/arkreview
**Publishes:** essays, fiction, nonfiction, poetry, reviews, and art
**Editorial Focus:** Material that evokes or responds to the Mississippi River Delta region.
**Representative Authors:** Sterling Plump, Pia Erhardt, and George Singleton
**Submissions Policy:** All submissions must address the journal's regional focus.
**Simultaneous Subs:** yes
**Reading Period:** Year-round
**Reporting Time:** 1 to 4 months
**Author Payment:** copies
**Founded:** 1996
**Non Profit:** yes
**Paid Staff:** 5
**Unpaid Staff:** 0
**ISSN Number/ISBN Number:** ISSN 0022-8745
**Total Circulation:** 500
**Paid Circulation:** 250
**Average Print Run:** 550
**Subscription Rate:** Individual $20/Institution $20
**Single Copy Price:** $7.50
**Current Volume/Issue:** 34/3
**Frequency per Year:** 3
**Backfile Available:** yes
**Unsolicited Ms. Received:** yes
**% of Unsolicited Ms. Published per Year:** 50%
**Format:** stapled
**Size:** H 11" W 8 1/2"
**Average Pages:** 88
**Ads:** no

# Arsenal Pulp Press

**Type:** press
**CLMP member:** yes
**Primary Editor/Contact Person:** Blaine Kyllo
**Address:** 103, 1014 Homer St.
Vancouver, BC V6B 2W9
**Web Site Address:** http://www.arsenalpulp.com
**Publishes:** fiction, nonfiction, and art

**Editorial Focus:** Arsenal Pulp Press books subvert genres and speak with authority from the fringes of society.
**Representative Authors:** Hiromi Goto, Ivan Coyote, and Nalo Hopkinson
**Submissions Policy:** Query with sample and SASE (IRCs from outside Canada). Non-Canadians only in anthologies.
**Simultaneous Subs:** yes
**Reading Period:** Year-round
**Reporting Time:** 3 to 4 months
**Author Payment:** royalties and copies
**Founded:** 1971
**Non Profit:** no
**Paid Staff:** 4
**Unpaid Staff:** 0
**Distributors:** US: Consortium, Canada: Jaguar, UK: Turnaround, Austrailia: Wakefield
**Wholesalers:** Ingram, Baker/Taylor, Koen, Bookazine et. al.
**ISSN Number/ISBN Number:** ISBN 0-888978; 1-55152
**Number of Books Published per Year:** 20
**Titles in Print:** 165
**Average Percentage Printed:** Paperback 100%

# Arte Público Press

**Type:** press
**CLMP member:** yes
**Primary Editor/Contact Person:** Nicolas Kanellos
**Address:** University of Houston
452 Cullen Performance
Houston, TX 77204-2004
**Web Site Address:** http://www.artepublicopress.com
**Publishes:** fiction, nonfiction, poetry, and translation
**Editorial Focus:** To broaden America's vision of itself by increasing awareness and appreciation of Hispanic Culture.
**Representative Authors:** Pat Mora, Victor Villaseʾor, and Diane Gonzales Betrand
**Submissions Policy:** available on our website
**Simultaneous Subs:** no
**Reading Period:** Year-round
**Reporting Time:** 3 to 6 months
**Author Payment:** royalties, cash, and copies
**Founded:** 1979
**Non Profit:** yes
**Paid Staff:** 30
**Unpaid Staff:** 2
**Distributors:** APP works with all the major book dis-tributors
**Wholesalers:** APP works with all the major book wholesalers
**ISSN Number/ISBN Number:** ISBN 0-934770 and 1-55885
**Number of Books Published per Year:** 30
**Titles in Print:** 500
**Average Print Run:** 3,000
**Average Percentage Printed:** Hardcover 25%, Paperback 75%
**Average Price:** $10

# Artful Dodge

**Type:** magazine
**CLMP member:** yes
**Primary Editor/Contact Person:** Daniel Bourne
**Address:** Department of English
The College of Wooster
Wooster, OH 44691
**Web Site Address:** http://www.wooster.edu/artful-dodge
**Publishes:** essays, fiction, nonfiction, poetry, reviews, art, and translation
**Editorial Focus:** Along with the best new American work we can find, we're also open to literature in translation from all over the world.
**Representative Authors:** Dan Chaon, Tess Gallagher, and Charles Simic
**Submissions Policy:** SASE; no previously published work; no more than 6 poems or 30 pages of prose, though long poems are encouraged.
**Simultaneous Subs:** yes
**Reading Period:** Year-round
**Reporting Time:** 3 to 12 months
**Author Payment:** cash and copies
**Founded:** 1979
**Non Profit:** yes
**Paid Staff:** 1
**Unpaid Staff:** 6
**Distributors:** DeBoer, Ubiquity
**ISSN Number/ISBN Number:** ISSN 0196-091X
**Total Circulation:** 900
**Paid Circulation:** 100
**Average Print Run:** 1,000
**Subscription Rate:** Individual $7/Institution $10
**Single Copy Price:** $7
**Current Volume/Issue:** Issue 44/5
**Frequency per Year:** 1
**Backfile Available:** yes
**Unsolicited Ms. Received:** yes

**% of Unsolicited Ms. Published per Year:** 2%
**Format:** perfect
**Size:** H 9" W 6"
**Average Pages:** 170
**Ads:** yes
**Ad Rates:** See Web Site for Details.

## Arts & Letters

**Type:** magazine
**CLMP member:** no
**Primary Editor/Contact Person:** Martin Lammon
**Address:** Campus Box 89
Georgia College & State University
Milledgeville, GA 31061
**Web Site Address:** http://al.gcsu.edu
**Publishes:** essays, fiction, nonfiction, poetry, reviews, art, and translation
**Editorial Focus:** The best contemporary literature available.
**Representative Authors:** Margaret Gibson, Dinty W. Moore, and Daniel Wallace
**Submissions Policy:** Poetry, fiction, creative nonfiction. Query first for other kinds of work. No electronic submissions. Include SASE.
**Simultaneous Subs:** yes
**Reading Period:** 9/1 to 4/1
**Reporting Time:** 3 to 6 weeks
**Author Payment:** cash, copies, and subscription
**Contests:** Annual Arts & Letters prizes in fiction, poetry, and drama. $1,000 prize to each winner, publication, and visit to campus.
See Web Site for Contest Guidelines.
**Founded:** 1999
**Non Profit:** yes
**Paid Staff:** 18
**Unpaid Staff:** 0
**ISSN Number/ISBN Number:** ISSN 1523-4592
**Total Circulation:** 1,200
**Paid Circulation:** 900
**Subscription Rate:** Individual $15/Institution $15
**Single Copy Price:** $8
**Current Volume/Issue:** Issue 10
**Frequency per Year:** 2
**Backfile Available:** yes
**Unsolicited Ms. Received:** yes
**% of Unsolicited Ms. Published per Year:** .5%
**Format:** perfect
**Size:** H 10" W 7"
**Average Pages:** 184
**Ads:** yes

**Ad Rates:** $50 for 6" x 9" full-page ad; contact al@gcsu.edu

## ArtsEditor

**Type:** online
**CLMP member:** no
**Primary Editor/Contact Person:** S. Edward Burns
**Address:** Postal Box 636
Concord, MA 01742
**Web Site Address:** http://www.ArtsEditor.com
**Publishes:** essays, nonfiction, poetry, reviews, and art
**Editorial Focus:** ArtsEditor develops and publishes articles in the areas of visual, performing, literary, film, and musical arts.
**Representative Authors:** Jeremy Perkins, Scott Ruescher, and Paul Jump
**Submissions Policy:** Send via the postal mail, a letter of introduction including a current resume, two writing samples, and three references.
**Simultaneous Subs:** yes
**Reading Period:** Year-round
**Reporting Time:** 2 to 3 weeks
**Author Payment:** none and cash
**Founded:** 1999
**Non Profit:** no
**Paid Staff:** 1
**Unpaid Staff:** 7
**Average Page Views per Month:** 18,000
**Average Unique Visitors per Month:** 4,000
**Frequency per Year:** 18
**Publish Print Anthology:** no
**Average Percentage of Pages per Category:**
Nonfiction 20%, Poetry 10%, Reviews 45%, Essays 15%, Art 10%
**Ad Rates:** $45, $70, and $475
See Web Site for Details.

## Ascent

**Type:** magazine
**CLMP member:** yes
**Primary Editor/Contact Person:** W. Scott Olsen
**Address:** Dept. of English/Concordia College
901 8th St. S.
Moorhead, MN 56562
**Web Site Address:** http://www.cord.edu/dept/english/ascent/
**Publishes:** essays, fiction, nonfiction, and poetry
**Editorial Focus:** We are open to all styles and lengths.
**Representative Authors:** Peter Chilson, Edith

## Profile: Johnny Temple,
## Publisher, Akashic Books

**1) How did you arrive at your current position?**
I founded the company.

**2) What is the staff structure like at your press/magazine?**
We have a staff of 7—2 full-time (myself and Johanna Ingalls, our Managing Editor), 3 part-time, and 2 interns.

**3) How do you keep your press/magazine running?**
Selling enough books to keep the company afloat.

**4) What do or don't you hope to see in a cover letter?**
I don't want to read sarcasm or over-confidence in a cover letter. I want to read something that perks my interest. One example would be Caribbean themes and settings.

**5) What do you look for in a submission?**
Something that gives me goose bumps.

**6) How are submissions processed at your press/magazine?**
I have a crew of editors and readers who help me evaluate submissions. Ultimately, it comes down to a gut feeling about a book.

**7) Do you have a favorite unsolicited submission discovery or story?**
Well, once it took me about 6 months to track down an author—Yongsoo Park—after falling in love with his unsolicited manuscript. Now we've published his first two books. I wanted to write my own book called "Searching for Yongsoo Park."

**8) Do you have any advice for first-time submitters?**
Have patience, and listen to the feedback that others give you. Be prepared to rewrite, rewrite, rewrite.

Pearlman, and Kate Coles
**Simultaneous Subs:** yes
**Reading Period:** Year-round
**Reporting Time:** 1 to 4 months
**Author Payment:** none, copies, and subscription
**Founded:** 1975
**Non Profit:** yes
**Paid Staff:** 0
**Unpaid Staff:** 1
**ISSN Number/ISBN Number:** ISSN 0098-9363
**Total Circulation:** 750
**Paid Circulation:** 700
**Subscription Rate:** Individual $12/Institution $12
**Single Copy Price:** $5
**Current Volume/Issue:** 28/3
**Frequency per Year:** 3
**Backfile Available:** yes
**Unsolicited Ms. Received:** yes
**Format:** perfect
**Size:** H 9" W 6"
**Average Pages:** 115
**Ads:** no

# The Asian American Writers' Workshop

**Type:** press
**CLMP member:** no
**Primary Editor/Contact Person:** Noel Shaw
**Address:** 16 West 32nd St. #10A
New York, NY 10001
**Web Site Address:** http://www.aaww.org
**Publishes:** essays, fiction, nonfiction, poetry, reviews, art, and translation
**Editorial Focus:** We publish literature that focuses on underrepresented Asian American ethnic groups and topics absent from the mainstream.
**Representative Authors:** Ishle Yi Park, Ed Lin, and Eric Gamalinda
**Submissions Policy:** For submissions guidelines please go to http://www.aaww.org/publications/sub-missions.html
**Simultaneous Subs:** yes
**Reading Period:** Year-round
**Reporting Time:** 3 to 4 months
**Author Payment:** copies and subscription
**Contests:** See Web Site for Contest Guidelines.
**Founded:** 1991
**Non Profit:** yes
**Paid Staff:** 6
**Unpaid Staff:** 0

**Distributors:** Temple University Press
**Number of Books Published per Year:** 1
**Titles in Print:** 9
**Average Percentage Printed:** Hardcover 10%, Paperback 90%

# Asphodel Press

**Type:** press
**CLMP member:** no
**Address:** Master of Arts in Writing Program, Rowan University
Glassboro, NJ 8028
**Web Site Address:** http://www2.rowan.edu/open/communic/asphodel/
**Publishes:** essays, fiction, nonfiction, poetry, and art
**Reading Period:** Year-round
**Reporting Time:** 1 to 2 months
**Author Payment:** none
**Founded:** 1990
**Non Profit:** no
**Average Percentage Printed:** Hardcover 100%

# At Length

**Type:** magazine
**CLMP member:** yes
**Address:** P.O. Box 594
New York, NY 10185
**Web Site Address:** http://www.atlengthmag.com
**Publishes:** fiction and poetry
**Reading Period:** Year-round
**Reporting Time:** 1 to 2 months
**Author Payment:** none
**Founded:** 2003
**Non Profit:** yes
**Backfile Available:** yes

# Atlanta Review

**Type:** magazine
**CLMP member:** no
**Primary Editor/Contact Person:** Dan Veach
**Address:** Poetry Atlanta
P.O. Box 8248
Atlanta, GA 31106
**Web Site Address:** http://www.atlantareview.com/
**Publishes:** fiction and poetry
**Editorial Focus:** Quality poetry of genuine human appeal.
**Representative Authors:** Seamus Heaney, Derek

Walcott, and Maxine Kumin
**Submissions Policy:** Up to five poems. SASE for reply.
**Simultaneous Subs:** yes
**Reading Period:** Year-round
**Reporting Time:** 2 to 3 weeks
**Author Payment:** copies
**Contests:** Poetry 2004 International Poetry Competition
See Web Site for Contest Guidelines.
**Founded:** 1994
**Non Profit:** yes
**Paid Staff:** 0
**Unpaid Staff:** 4
**Distributors:** Ingram, Media Solutions, EBSCO, Blackwell
**ISSN Number/ISBN Number:** ISSN 1073-9696
**Total Circulation:** 2,000
**Paid Circulation:** 1,000
**Subscription Rate:** Individual $10/Institution $12
**Single Copy Price:** $6
**Current Volume/Issue:** 10/1
**Frequency per Year:** 2
**Backfile Available:** yes
**Unsolicited Ms. Received:** yes
**% of Unsolicited Ms. Published per Year:** 1%
**Format:** perfect
**Size:** H 9" W 6"
**Average Pages:** 128
**Ads:** yes
**Ad Rates:** 500/250/125

## Atomic Quill Press

**Type:** press
**CLMP member:** yes
**Primary Editor/Contact Person:** Timothy Dugdale
**Address:** P.O. Box 39859
Detroit, MI 48240
**Web Site Address:** http://press.atomicquill.com
**Publishes:** essays, fiction, nonfiction, and audio
**Editorial Focus:** We are interested in compelling fiction and nonfiction. We have an academic imprint and a spirituality imprint as well.
**Representative Authors:** Isaiah McKinnon, Lincoln Swain, and Bruce Henricksen
**Submissions Policy:** Previously published authors only. Please send a proposal and two sample chapters. No electronic submissions, please.
**Simultaneous Subs:** yes
**Reading Period:** Year-round

**Reporting Time:** 1 to 2 months
**Author Payment:** royalties and copies
**Founded:** 2004
**Non Profit:** no
**Paid Staff:** 1
**Unpaid Staff:** 0
**Distributors:** Ingram via Pathway Book Service
**ISSN Number/ISBN Number:** ISBN 09760535
**Number of Books Published per Year:** 4
**Titles in Print:** 4
**Average Print Run:** 1,000
**Average Percentage Printed:** Paperback 100%
**Average Price:** $14.95

## Aufgabe

**Type:** magazine
**CLMP member:** yes
**Primary Editor/Contact Person:** E. Tracy Grinnell
**Address:** Litmus Press
P.O. Box 25526
Brooklyn, NY 11202-5526
**Web Site Address:** http://www.litmuspress.org
**Publishes:** essays, fiction, poetry, reviews, art, and translation
**Editorial Focus:** Emerging and established American writers working in the experimental tradition and writing/poetry in translation.
**Representative Authors:** Rosmarie Waldrop, Xue Di, and Jen Hofer
**Submissions Policy:** Submission via regular mail should be accompanied by cover letter and current contact information.
**Simultaneous Subs:** yes
**Reading Period:** 12/1 to 1/1
**Reporting Time:** 4 to 6 weeks
**Author Payment:** copies
**Founded:** 2000
**Non Profit:** yes
**Paid Staff:** 1
**Unpaid Staff:** 1-4
**Distributors:** SPD
**ISSN Number/ISBN Number:** ISSN 1532-5539
**Total Circulation:** 400
**Paid Circulation:** 25
**Average Print Run:** 500
**Subscription Rate:** Individual $20/Institution $30
**Single Copy Price:** $12
**Current Volume/Issue:** Issue 5
**Frequency per Year:** 1
**Backfile Available:** yes

**Unsolicited Ms. Received:** yes
**% of Unsolicited Ms. Published per Year:** 60%
**Format:** perfect
**Size:** H 9" W 6"
**Average Pages:** 250
**Ads:** no

# Ausable Press

**Type:** press
**CLMP member:** yes
**Primary Editor/Contact Person:** Chase Twichell
**Address:** 1026 Hurricane Rd.
Keene, NY 12942
**Web Site Address:** http://www.ausablepress.org
**Publishes:** poetry
**Editorial Focus:** full-length collections of poetry
**Recent Awards Received:** Kate Tufts Discovery
Award Finalist, National Book Critics Circle Award
**Representative Authors:** Laura Kasischke, Eric
Pankey, and James Richardson
**Submissions Policy:** We accept unsolicited submissions during the month of June. Please see guidelines for details.
**Simultaneous Subs:** yes
**Reading Period:** 6/1 to 6/30
**Reporting Time:** 2 to 4 months
**Author Payment:** royalties, cash, and copies
**Founded:** 1999
**Non Profit:** yes
**Paid Staff:** 3
**Unpaid Staff:** 1
**Distributors:** Consortium; SPD
**Wholesalers:** Amazon.com
**ISSN Number/ISBN Number:** ISBN 1-931337
**Number of Books Published per Year:** 4
**Titles in Print:** 20
**Average Print Run:** 1,500
**Average Percentage Printed:** Paperback 100%
**Average Price:** $14

# Autumn House Press

**Type:** press
**CLMP member:** yes
**Primary Editor/Contact Person:** Michael Simms
**Address:** 87 1/2 Westwood St.
Pittsburgh, PA 15211
**Web Site Address:** http://autumnhouse.org
**Publishes:** poetry and audio
**Recent Awards Received:** Maurice English Poetry

Award (selected by Naomi Shihab Nye), Brockman-Campbell Award (Selected by Colette Inez)
**Representative Authors:** Ed Ochester, Gerald Stern, and Sue Ellen Thompson
**Submissions Policy:** We ask that all submissions come through our annual contest. Please see our website for guidelines
**Simultaneous Subs:** yes
**Reading Period:** Year-round
**Reporting Time:** 1 to 4 months
**Author Payment:** royalties, cash, and copies
**Contests:** See Web Site for Contest Guidelines.
**Founded:** 1998
**Non Profit:** yes
**Paid Staff:** 0
**Unpaid Staff:** 6
**Wholesalers:** Baker & Taylor, Book House, Coates, etc.
**Number of Books Published per Year:** 4-5
**Titles in Print:** 20
**Average Print Run:** 1,500
**Average Percentage Printed:** Hardcover 25%, Paperback 75%
**Average Price:** $14-$30

# Avenue B

**Type:** press
**CLMP member:** no
**Primary Editor/Contact Person:** Stephen Ratcliffe
**Address:** P.O. Box 714
Bolinas, CA 94924
**Web Site Address:** http://durationpress.com
**Publishes:** poetry
**Editorial Focus:** contemporary poetry in "experimental/innovative" forms
**Representative Authors:** Clark Coolidge, Jackson
Mac Low, and Ron Padgett
**Submissions Policy:** no unsolicited manuscripts
**Simultaneous Subs:** no
**Reading Period:** Year-round
**Reporting Time:** 2 to 3 months
**Author Payment:** copies
**Contests:** no
**Founded:** 1986
**Non Profit:** yes
**Distributors:** SPD
**ISSN Number/ISBN Number:** none/0-939691-xx-x
**Number of Books Published per Year:** 0-1
**Titles in Print:** 14
**Average Percentage Printed:** Paperback 100%

## Backwards City Review

**Type:** magazine
**CLMP member:** yes
**Primary Editor/Contact Person:** Gerry Canavan
**Address:** P.O. Box 41317
Greensboro, NC 27404-1317
**Web Site Address:** http://www.backwardscity.net
**Publishes:** fiction, nonfiction, poetry, and art
**Editorial Focus:** Prose, poetry, and comics. We favor literary and experimental work.
**Recent Awards Received:** One of Library Journal's top ten new journals of 2004.
**Representative Authors:** Kurt Vonnegut, Chris Bachelder, and Kenneth Koch
**Submissions Policy:** See website for full guidelines and contest details.
**Simultaneous Subs:** yes
**Reading Period:** Year-round
**Reporting Time:** 1 to 2 months
**Author Payment:** copies
**Contests:** We have an annual literary contest and a chapbook contest with deadlines in March. Check the website for details.
See Web Site for Contest Guidelines.
**Founded:** 2004
**Non Profit:** yes
**Paid Staff:** 0
**Unpaid Staff:** 5
**Total Circulation:** 550
**Paid Circulation:** 300
**Average Print Run:** 750
**Subscription Rate:** Individual $12/Institution $20
**Single Copy Price:** $7
**Current Volume/Issue:** Issue 3
**Frequency per Year:** 2
**Backfile Available:** yes
**Unsolicited Ms. Received:** yes
**% of Unsolicited Ms. Published per Year:** 50%
**Format:** perfect
**Size:** H 9" W 6"
**Average Pages:** 128
**Ads:** yes
**Ad Rates:** E-mail ads@backwardscity.net for rates. Open to ad swaps.

## The Backwaters Press

**Type:** press
**CLMP member:** yes
**Primary Editor/Contact Person:** Greg Kosmicki
**Address:** 3502 N. 52nd St.
Omaha, NE 68104-3506
**Web Site Address:**
http://www.thebackwaterspress.homestead.com
**Publishes:** poetry
**Editorial Focus:** Regional-Great Plains-Nebraska-Women-National-Poets who win the prize.
**Representative Authors:** Aaron Anstett, Michelle Gillett, and Steve Langan
**Submissions Policy:** No longer running contests. Open to all submissions. Please see website for guidelines or e-mail for guidelines.
**Simultaneous Subs:** yes
**Reading Period:** Year-round
**Reporting Time:** 4 to 6 weeks
**Author Payment:** copies
**Contests:** None.
**Founded:** 1997
**Non Profit:** no
**Paid Staff:** 0
**Unpaid Staff:** 2-6
**Distributors:** Amazon.com, LightningSource
**Wholesalers:** LightningSource
**Number of Books Published per Year:** 4
**Titles in Print:** 15
**Average Print Run:** 300
**Average Percentage Printed:** Paperback 100%
**Average Price:** $14-$16

## Ballyhoo Stories

**Type:** magazine
**CLMP member:** yes
**Primary Editor/Contact Person:** Joshua Mandelbaum
**Address:** 18 Willoughby Ave., #3
Brooklyn, NY 11205
**Web Site Address:** http://www.ballyhoostories.com
**Publishes:** essays, fiction, and nonfiction
**Submissions Policy:** Visit http://www.ballyhoostories.com
**Simultaneous Subs:** yes
**Reading Period:** Year-round
**Reporting Time:** 2 to 3 months
**Author Payment:** copies
**Founded:** 2005
**Non Profit:** no
**Paid Staff:** 0
**Unpaid Staff:** 3
**Distributors:** Ingram
**ISSN Number/ISBN Number:** ISSN 1554-6950
**Total Circulation:** 400
**Paid Circulation:** 16
**Average Print Run:** 1,000

**Subscription Rate:** Individual $16/Institution $16
**Single Copy Price:** $8
**Current Volume/Issue:** 1/2
**Frequency per Year:** 2
**Backfile Available:** yes
**Unsolicited Ms. Received:** yes
**% of Unsolicited Ms. Published per Year:** 100%
**Format:** perfect
**Average Pages:** 88
**Ads:** yes
**Ad Rates:** exchange

# The Baltimore Review

**Type:** magazine
**CLMP member:** yes
**Primary Editor/Contact Person:** Barbara Diehl/Lalita Noronha
**Address:** P.O. Box 410
Riderwood, MD 21286
**Web Site Address:** http://www.baltimorewriters.org
**Publishes:** fiction and poetry
**Editorial Focus:** Literary fiction and poetry
**Submissions Policy:** Traditional and experimental prose and poetry. No themes, or previously published work.
**Simultaneous Subs:** yes
**Reading Period:** Year-round
**Reporting Time:** 2 to 4 months
**Author Payment:** copies
**Contests:** See Web Site for Contest Guidelines.
**Founded:** 1980
**Non Profit:** yes
**Paid Staff:** no
**Unpaid Staff:** 10
**Distributors:** Ingram
**ISSN Number/ISBN Number:** ISSN 1092-5716
**Total Circulation:** 600
**Paid Circulation:** 100
**Subscription Rate:** Individual $14.75/Institution $14.75
**Single Copy Price:** $7.95
**Current Volume/Issue:** VII/2
**Frequency per Year:** 2
**Backfile Available:** yes
**Unsolicited Ms. Received:** yes
**% of Unsolicited Ms. Published per Year:** 95%
**Format:** perfect
**Size:** H 9" W 6"
**Average Pages:** 128
**Ads:** no

# Bamboo Ridge

**Type:** magazine
**CLMP member:** yes
**Primary Editor/Contact Person:** Eric Chock
**Address:** P.O. Box 61781
Honolulu, HI 96839-1781
**Web Site Address:** http://www.bambooridge.com
**Publishes:** essays, fiction, poetry, art, and audio
**Editorial Focus:** Literature by, for, and about the people of Hawaii.
**Recent Awards Received:** Pushcart Prize, O. Henry
**Representative Authors:** Juliet S. Kono, Lee Cataluna, and Ian MacMillan
**Submissions Policy:** 10 pages poetry, 20 pages prose, double-spaced. SASE required.
**Simultaneous Subs:** no
**Reading Period:** Year-round
**Reporting Time:** up to 12 months
**Author Payment:** cash, copies, and subscription
**Contests:** Submissions selected for publication are automatically entered in the Bamboo Ridge Writing Contest. Cash awards.
**Founded:** 1978
**Non Profit:** yes
**Paid Staff:** 4
**Unpaid Staff:** yes
**Distributors:** Booklines Hawaii, SPD
**Wholesalers:** Booklines Hawaii, SPD
**ISSN Number/ISBN Number:** 0733-0308/0-910043-xx-x
**Total Circulation:** 1,500
**Paid Circulation:** 500
**Average Print Run:** 2,000
**Subscription Rate:** Individual $25/2 issue/Institution $35/2-issue
**Single Copy Price:** $15
**Current Volume/Issue:** Issue #84
**Frequency per Year:** Biannual
**Backfile Available:** yes
**Unsolicited Ms. Received:** yes
**Format:** perfect
**Size:** H 9" W 6"
**Average Pages:** 300
**Ads:** yes
**Ad Rates:** $150 full page, $100 half page

## Barrelhouse Journal

**Type:** magazine
**CLMP member:** yes
**Address:** 3701 5th St. S., #308
Arlington, VA 22204
**Web Site Address:** http://www.barrelhousemag.com
**Publishes:** essays, fiction, and poetry
**Reading Period:** Year-round
**Reporting Time:** 1 to 2 months
**Author Payment:** none
**Founded:** 2004
**Non Profit:** yes
**Backfile Available:** yes

## Barrow Street

**Type:** magazine
**CLMP member:** yes
**Primary Editor/Contact Person:** Lois Hirshkowitz
**Address:** P.O. Box 1831
New York, NY 10156-1831
**Web Site Address:** http://barrowstreet.org
**Publishes:** essays, poetry, and reviews
**Editorial Focus:** To publish a literary journal dedicated to giving new and established authors a forum and to publish their highest quality work
**Representative Authors:** Donald Revell, Lyn Hejinian, and Ira Sadoff
**Submissions Policy:** Submit up to five of your best, unpublished poems. Include a SASE and a short bio, please. We accept reviews/essays as well.
**Simultaneous Subs:** yes
**Reading Period:** Year-round
**Reporting Time:** 1 to 3 months
**Author Payment:** copies
**Contests:** Barrow Street Annual Book Prize, deadline on or about July 1, for an unpublished manuscript of 48-70 pages of poetry.
See Web Site for Contest Guidelines.
**Founded:** 1998
**Non Profit:** yes
**Paid Staff:** 1
**Unpaid Staff:** 30
**Distributors:** Ingram, Armadillo, DeBoer
**ISSN Number/ISBN Number:** 0-9728302/1522-2160
**Total Circulation:** 2,000
**Paid Circulation:** 350
**Subscription Rate:** Individual $15/Institution $8
**Single Copy Price:** $8
**Current Volume/Issue:** 5/1
**Frequency per Year:** 2

**Backfile Available:** no
**Unsolicited Ms. Received:** yes
**% of Unsolicited Ms. Published per Year:** 10%
**Format:** perfect
**Size:** H 9" W 6"
**Average Pages:** 110
**Ads:** no

## Barrytown/Station Hill Press

**Type:** press
**CLMP member:** no
**Primary Editor/Contact Person:** George Quasha or Jenny Fox
**Address:** 120 Station Hill Road
Barrytown, NY 12507
**Web Site Address:** http://www.stationhill.org
**Publishes:** essays, fiction, nonfiction, poetry, art, translation, and video
**Editorial Focus:** The focus is open and variable; unique or innovative contribution to language, poetics, art, thinking; bodywork; maybe other.
**Representative Authors:** Maurice Blanchot, Deane Juhan, and Rosmarie Waldrop
**Submissions Policy:** Letter of inquiry must precede submission. E-mail preferred: publishers@stationhill.org.
**Simultaneous Subs:** yes
**Reading Period:** Year-round
**Reporting Time:** 1 to 6 months
**Author Payment:** royalties and copies
**Founded:** 1977
**Non Profit:** yes
**Paid Staff:** 2
**Unpaid Staff:** 2
**Distributors:** Midpoint
**Wholesalers:** Ingram, Baker & Taylor, SPD, etc.
**ISSN Number/ISBN Number:** ISBN 1-58177-/0-88268-
**Number of Books Published per Year:** 6+/-
**Titles in Print:** 300+/-
**Average Print Run:** 1,000
**Average Percentage Printed:** Paperback 100%
**Average Price:** $19.95

## Bathtub Gin

**Type:** magazine
**CLMP member:** no
**Primary Editor/Contact Person:** Christopher Harter
**Address:** P.O. Box 178
Erie, PA 16512

**Web Site Address:** http://www.bluemarble.net/~charter/btgin.htm
**Publishes:** essays, fiction, nonfiction, poetry, reviews, art, and translation
**Editorial Focus:** Publishes work not found in overly academic or post-Beat journals. Strong emphasis on imagery.
**Representative Authors:** Mark Terrill, Kell Robertson, and Mike James
**Submissions Policy:** 4-5 poems. Prose not over 3,000 words. Eclectic in the styles and works accepted.
**Simultaneous Subs:** yes
**Reading Period:** 6/1 to 9/15
**Reporting Time:** 4 to 6 weeks
**Author Payment:** copies
**Founded:** 1997
**Non Profit:** yes
**Paid Staff:** 0
**Unpaid Staff:** 1
**Distributors:** Via website and catalogs
**Wholesalers:** Baker & Taylor
**ISSN Number/ISBN Number:** ISSN 1094-7965
**Total Circulation:** 300
**Paid Circulation:** 60
**Average Print Run:** 400
**Subscription Rate:** Individual $8/Institution $8
**Single Copy Price:** $5
**Current Volume/Issue:** Issue 17
**Frequency per Year:** 2
**Backfile Available:** yes
**Unsolicited Ms. Received:** yes
**% of Unsolicited Ms. Published per Year:** 1%
**Format:** stapled
**Size:** H 8.5" W 5.5"
**Average Pages:** 52
**Ads:** yes
**Ad Rates:** See Web Site for Details.

# Bayou

**Type:** magazine
**CLMP member:** yes
**Primary Editor/Contact Person:** Joanna Leake, Editor
**Address:** University of New Orleans
Dept. of English/Lakefront
New Orleans, LA 70148
**Web Site Address:**
http://www.uno.edu/%7Ecww/bayou.htm
**Publishes:** essays, fiction, nonfiction, poetry, reviews, and translation
**Editorial Focus:** Partner UWF reads for Spring 11/7-2/15: Univ. of West Florida/Laurie O' Brien, ed./11000 Univ Pkwy/Pensacola, FL 32514
**Submissions Policy:** 3-5 poems. Fiction and essays of reasonable length (one submission/writer) SASE for reply. We continue Panhandler's 25-year tradition.
**Simultaneous Subs:** yes
**Reading Period:** 9/1 to 11/7
**Reporting Time:** 1 to 8 months
**Author Payment:** copies
**Founded:** 2000
**Non Profit:** yes
**Paid Staff:** 0
**Unpaid Staff:** varies
**Distributors:** We do this ourselves.
**Wholesalers:** We do this ourselves.
**ISSN Number/ISBN Number:** None yet/None yet
**Total Circulation:** 500
**Paid Circulation:** varies
**Subscription Rate:** Individual $10/Institution $10
**Single Copy Price:** $5
**Current Volume/Issue:** Issue #41
**Frequency per Year:** 2
**Backfile Available:** yes
**Unsolicited Ms. Received:** yes
**Format:** perfect
**Size:** H 9" W 6"
**Average Pages:** 128

# Beach Holme Publishing

**Type:** press
**CLMP member:** no
**Primary Editor/Contact Person:** Michael Carroll
**Address:** 1010-409 Granville St.
Vancouver, BC V6C 1T2
**Web Site Address:** http://www.beachholme.bc.ca
**Publishes:** fiction, nonfiction, and poetry
**Editorial Focus:** Adult literary fiction, nonfiction, and poetry. Also publishes historical young adult fiction and juvenile books.
**Representative Authors:** Eric Walters, Marilyn Bowering, and David Watmough
**Submissions Policy:** Please submit with a SASE, first three chapters, synopsis, and author bio.
**Simultaneous Subs:** yes
**Reading Period:** Year-round
**Reporting Time:** 4 to 6 months
**Author Payment:** royalties
**Contests:** none

See Web Site for Contest Guidelines.
**Founded:** 1971
**Non Profit:** no
**Paid Staff:** 2
**Unpaid Staff:** 0
**Distributors:** LitDistCo
**Wholesalers:** LitDistCo
**ISSN Number/ISBN Number:** ISBN 088878
**Number of Books Published per Year:** 13
**Titles in Print:** 91
**Average Percentage Printed:** Paperback 100%

## Beacon Press

**Type:** press
**CLMP member:** no
**Primary Editor/Contact Person:** Hilary Jaccqmin
**Address:** 25 Beacon St.
Boston, MA 02108
**Web Site Address:** http://www.beacon.org
**Publishes:** essays and nonfiction
**Editorial Focus:** Beacon Press, the non-profit publisher owned by the Unitarian Universalist Association, publishes scholarly works for the general reader.
**Submissions Policy:** If you would like Beacon Press to consider publishing your work, please submit a letter of inquiry, proposal, and current CV.
**Simultaneous Subs:** yes
**Reading Period:** Year-round
**Reporting Time:** 8 to 12 weeks
**Author Payment:** royalties and copies
**Founded:** 1854
**Non Profit:** yes
**Paid Staff:** 26
**Unpaid Staff:** 5
**Distributors:** Houghton Mifflin Co.
**Number of Books Published per Year:** 65
**Titles in Print:** 500
**Average Print Run:** Varies
**Average Percentage Printed:** Hardcover 60%, Paperback 40%
**Average Price:** Varies

## The Bear Deluxe Magazine

**Type:** magazine
**CLMP member:** no
**Primary Editor/Contact Person:** Tom Webb
**Address:** P.O. Box 10342
Portland, OR 97296
**Web Site Address:** http://www.orlo.org

**Publishes:** essays, fiction, nonfiction, poetry, reviews, and art
**Editorial Focus:** We take a pretty open-minded, creative look at environmental/landscape issues and how those often overlap with culture.
**Recent Awards Received:** Print Magazine Literary Arts, Inc. Portland Monthly Regional Arts and Culture Council
**Representative Authors:** Gina Ochsner, David James Duncan, and Amy Roe
**Submissions Policy:** See guides at http://www.orlo.org. 4,000 word max for fiction and essay. 50 line max on poetry. Best to query on nonfiction.
**Simultaneous Subs:** yes
**Reading Period:** Year-round
**Reporting Time:** 2 to 6 months
**Author Payment:** cash and subscription
**Founded:** 1993
**Non Profit:** yes
**Paid Staff:** .5
**Unpaid Staff:** 8
**Distributors:** in house
**ISSN Number/ISBN Number:** ISSN 1074-2700
**Total Circulation:** 44,000
**Paid Circulation:** 500
**Average Print Run:** 20,000
**Subscription Rate:** Individual $16/Institution $16
**Single Copy Price:** $3
**Current Volume/Issue:** Issue 22
**Frequency per Year:** 4
**Backfile Available:** yes
**Unsolicited Ms. Received:** yes
**% of Unsolicited Ms. Published per Year:** 10%
**Format:** magazine format, saddle stitched
**Size:** H 11" W 9"
**Average Pages:** 48
**Ads:** yes
**Ad Rates:** $800 full-page, black and white, color available
See Web Site for Details.

## Bear Star Press

**Type:** press
**CLMP member:** yes
**Primary Editor/Contact Person:** Beth Spencer
**Address:** 185 Hollow Oak Dr.
Cohasset, CA 95973
**Web Site Address:** http://www.bearstarpress.com
**Publishes:** poetry

**Editorial Focus:** We publish the best poetry we can attract from US writers living west of the central time zone.
**Representative Authors:** Lynne Knight, Rick Bursky, and Joshua McKinney
**Submissions Policy:** Send 50-65 pages of poems, not counting sec seps, front matter, etc. Any theme, subject. New writers especially welcome!
**Simultaneous Subs:** yes
**Reading Period:** 9/1 to 11/30
**Reporting Time:** 1 to 4 months
**Author Payment:** copies
**Contests:** See Web Site for Contest Guidelines.
**Founded:** 1996
**Non Profit:** no
**Paid Staff:** 0
**Unpaid Staff:** 3
**Distributors:** SPD
**ISSN Number/ISBN Number:** ISBN 0-9179607...
**Number of Books Published per Year:** 2
**Titles in Print:** 17
**Average Print Run:** 750
**Average Percentage Printed:** Paperback 80%, Chapbook 20%
**Average Price:** $12-$14

## Beginnings Publishing

**Type:** magazine
**CLMP member:** no
**Primary Editor/Contact Person:** Jenine Boisits, Editor/Publisher
**Address:** P.O. Box 92
Shirley, NY 11967
**Web Site Address:** http://www.scbeginnings.com
**Publishes:** fiction and poetry
**Editorial Focus:** We cater strictly to the novice writer. We believe in giving the new writer a chance to be heard.
**Representative Authors:** Ben Ogle, Beverly Jo Dittmer, and Johnathon Madden
**Submissions Policy:** Only one submission at a time, please. Cover letters are appreciated but not required.
**Simultaneous Subs:** yes
**Reading Period:** Year-round
**Reporting Time:** 6 to 12 weeks
**Author Payment:** copies
**Contests:** Four contests per year with substantial cash prizes for fiction and poetry.
See Web Site for Contest Guidelines.
**Founded:** 1999

**Non Profit:** yes
**Paid Staff:** 5
**Unpaid Staff:** 10
**Distributors:** Ingram
**Total Circulation:** 2,000
**Paid Circulation:** 400
**Subscription Rate:** $14
**Single Copy Price:** $5.50
**Current Volume/Issue:** Fall
**Frequency per Year:** 3
**Backfile Available:** yes
**Unsolicited Ms. Received:** yes
**% of Unsolicited Ms. Published per Year:** 100%
**Format:** perfect
**Size:** H 8" W 11"
**Average Pages:** 48
**Ads:** yes
**Ad Rates:** $200 full page, $50 business card
See Web Site for Details.

## Belladonna*

**Type:** press
**CLMP member:** yes
**Primary Editor/Contact Person:** Erica Kaufman/Rachel Levitsky
**Address:** 458 Lincoln Place #4B
Ste. 4B
Brooklyn, NY 11238
**Web Site Address:**
http://www.durationpress.com/belladonna
**Publishes:** fiction, nonfiction, poetry, and translation
**Editorial Focus:** Belladonna is a reading series and small press that promotes the work of women writers of diverse backgrounds and cultures.
**Representative Authors:** Alice Notley, Lydia Davis, and Mei-mei Berssenbrugge
**Simultaneous Subs:** yes
**Reading Period:** Year-round
**Reporting Time:** 2 to 3 months
**Author Payment:** cash and copies
**Founded:** 1999
**Non Profit:** yes
**Paid Staff:** 0
**Unpaid Staff:** 3
**Number of Books Published per Year:** 15
**Titles in Print:** 35
**Average Percentage Printed:** Chapbook 95%, Other 5%
**Backfile Available:** yes

## The Bellevue Literary Review

**Type:** magazine
**CLMP member:** yes
**Primary Editor/Contact Person:** Danielle Ofri
**Address:** NYU School of Medicine, Dept. of Medicine
550 First Ave.-OBV-612
New York, NY 10016
**Web Site Address:** http://www.BLReview.org
**Publishes:** essays, fiction, nonfiction, and poetry
**Editorial Focus:** The BLR examines the human condition through the prism of health, healing, illness, disease, the mind and body.
**Recent Awards Received:** Grants from NYSCA, NY Council for the Humanities, CLMP, private foundations.
**Representative Authors:** Abraham Verghese, Sheila Kohler, and Rafael Campo
**Submissions Policy:** 3 poems, prose up to 5,000 words. Submit online at http://www.BLReview.org
**Simultaneous Subs:** yes
**Reading Period:** Year-round
**Reporting Time:** 2 to 5 months
**Author Payment:** copies and subscription
**Contests:** Annual contest for superlative writing related to health, healing, illness, disease, mind and body. See Web Site for Contest Guidelines.
**Founded:** 2000
**Non Profit:** yes
**Paid Staff:** 1
**Unpaid Staff:** 6
**Distributors:** Ingram, DeBoer
**ISSN Number/ISBN Number:** 1537-5048/with each issue
**Total Circulation:** 4,000
**Paid Circulation:** 1,500
**Average Print Run:** 4,000
**Subscription Rate:** Individual $12/Institution $18
**Single Copy Price:** $7
**Current Volume/Issue:** 5/2
**Frequency per Year:** 2
**Backfile Available:** yes
**Unsolicited Ms. Received:** yes
**% of Unsolicited Ms. Published per Year:** 3%
**Format:** perfect
**Size:** H 9" W 6"
**Average Pages:** 160-200
**Ads:** yes
**Ad Rates:** exchange ads and paid ads
See Web Site for Details.

## Bellingham Review

**Type:** magazine
**CLMP member:** yes
**Primary Editor/Contact Person:** Brenda Miller, Editor-in-Chief
**Address:** Mail Stop 9053
Western Washington U.
Bellingham, WA 98225
**Web Site Address:** http://www.wwu.edu/~bhreview/
**Publishes:** essays, fiction, nonfiction, and poetry
**Submissions Policy:** Prose under 9,000 words, 3-5 poems. Must be previously unpublished in North America. We do not accept e-submissions.
**Simultaneous Subs:** yes
**Reading Period:** 10/1 to 2/1
**Reporting Time:** 1 to 6 months
**Author Payment:** none
**Contests:** See Web Site for Contest Guidelines.
**Founded:** 1977
**Non Profit:** no
**Paid Staff:** 2
**Unpaid Staff:** 1-6
**ISSN Number/ISBN Number:** ISSN 0734-2934
**Total Circulation:** 2,000
**Paid Circulation:** 1,480
**Average Print Run:** 2,000
**Subscription Rate:** Individual $14/Institution $28
**Single Copy Price:** $7
**Current Volume/Issue:** 28/56
**Frequency per Year:** 2
**Backfile Available:** yes
**Unsolicited Ms. Received:** yes
**Format:** perfect

## Beloit Poetry Journal

**Type:** magazine
**CLMP member:** yes
**Primary Editor/Contact Person:** John Rosenwald and Lee Sharkey
**Address:** P.O. Box 151
Farmington, ME 04938
**Web Site Address:** http://www.bpj.org
**Publishes:** poetry and reviews
**Editorial Focus:** We publish poets without regard to their reputation. Our tastes are eclectic, but we're looking for quickened language.
**Recent Awards Received:** Karl Elder's "Everything I Wanted to Know" republished in Best American Poetry 2005.
**Representative Authors:** Susan Tichy, Karl Elder, and

Albert Goldbarth

**Submissions Policy:** Five pages or so of poetry, unless it's a long poem. No cover letter required.
**Simultaneous Subs:** no
**Reading Period:** Year-round
**Reporting Time:** 1 to 14 weeks
**Author Payment:** copies
**Contests:** No contests, but we award annual $3,000 Chad Walsh Prize to the strongest poem we've published.
**Founded:** 1950
**Non Profit:** yes
**Paid Staff:** 0
**Unpaid Staff:** 7
**Distributors:** DeBoer, Ubiquity, Media Solutions
**Wholesalers:** Subscription services: EBSCO, Swets, Harrassowitz
**ISSN Number/ISBN Number:** ISSN 0005-8661
**Total Circulation:** 1,100
**Paid Circulation:** 573
**Average Print Run:** 1,300
**Subscription Rate:** Individual $18/Institution $23
**Single Copy Price:** $5
**Current Volume/Issue:** 56/1
**Frequency per Year:** 4
**Backfile Available:** yes
**Unsolicited Ms. Received:** yes
**% of Unsolicited Ms. Published per Year:** 0.5%
**Format:** stapled
**Size:** H 9" W 6"
**Average Pages:** 48
**Ads:** no

## The Berkeley Fiction Review

**Type:** magazine
**CLMP member:** yes
**Primary Editor/Contact Person:** Juliana Yee
**Address:** 10 B Eshleman Hall
University of California
Berkeley, CA 94720
**Web Site Address:** http://www.ocf.berkeley.edu/~bfr/
**Publishes:** fiction
**Editorial Focus:** Short (less than 10,000 words) fiction, particularly experimental work
**Submissions Policy:** No e-mail submissions accepted.
**Simultaneous Subs:** yes
**Reading Period:** Year-round
**Reporting Time:** 12 to 18 months
**Author Payment:** copies

**Contests:** Sudden Fiction Contest (1,000 words or less)
See Web Site for Contest Guidelines.
**Founded:** 1983
**Non Profit:** yes
**Paid Staff:** no
**Unpaid Staff:** 30
**Distributors:** Ubiquity Publishing
**ISSN Number/ISBN Number:** ISSN 1087-7053
**Total Circulation:** 300
**Paid Circulation:** none
**Average Print Run:** 300
**Subscription Rate:** Individual $8.50/Institution $8.50
**Single Copy Price:** $8.50
**Current Volume/Issue:** Issue 25
**Frequency per Year:** 1
**Backfile Available:** yes
**Unsolicited Ms. Received:** yes
**% of Unsolicited Ms. Published per Year:** 2%
**Format:** perfect
**Ads:** yes
**Ad Rates:** e-mail if interested

## Best of Branches

**Type:** magazine
**CLMP member:** no
**Primary Editor/Contact Person:** Toni Bennett
**Address:** P.O. Box 85394
Seattle, WA 98145-1394
**Web Site Address:**
http://www.branchesquarterly.com
**Publishes:** essays, fiction, nonfiction, poetry, reviews, art, and translation
**Editorial Focus:** Seeking an eclectic mix of quality poetry, short prose, photography (JPGs), drawing, short fiction, and essays.
**Representative Authors:** John Amen, Nathan Leslie, and A.E. Stallings
**Submissions Policy:** Submissions can be e-mailed to: submit@branchesquarterly.com with cover letter, bio, and work in body of e-mail or mailed
**Simultaneous Subs:** yes
**Reading Period:** Year-round
**Reporting Time:** 3 to 6 months
**Author Payment:** copies
**Contests:** See Web Site for Contest Guidelines.
**Founded:** 2001
**Non Profit:** no
**Paid Staff:** 0
**Unpaid Staff:** 1

**ISSN Number/ISBN Number:** ISSN 1536-2051
**Total Circulation:** 100
**Paid Circulation:** 25
**Subscription Rate:** Individual $8/Institution $8
**Single Copy Price:** $8
**Current Volume/Issue:** 1/1
**Frequency per Year:** 1
**Backfile Available:** yes
**Unsolicited Ms. Received:** yes
**% of Unsolicited Ms. Published per Year:** 95%
**Format:** perfect
**Size:** H 8.5" W 5.5"
**Average Pages:** 64
**Ads:** no
**Ad Rates:** See Web Site for Details.

# The Best of Carve Magazine

**Type:** magazine
**CLMP member:** yes
**Primary Editor/Contact Person:** Melvin Sterne
**Address:** P.O. Box 1573
Tallahassee, FL 32302
**Web Site Address:** http://www.carvezine.com
**Publishes:** fiction
**Editorial Focus:** The Best of Carve Magazine is a print anthology of the best stories published online in Carve. US and world literary fiction.
**Representative Authors:** Lynn Stegner, Kate Braverman, and Clarinda Harriss
**Submissions Policy:** Electronic OK, mail-ins OK. 8,500 words. No reprints. Guidelines on our website http://www.carvezine.com.
**Simultaneous Subs:** yes
**Reading Period:** Year-round
**Reporting Time:** 1 to 3 months
**Author Payment:** copies
**Founded:** 2000
**Non Profit:** no
**Paid Staff:** 0
**Unpaid Staff:** 6
**ISSN Number/ISBN Number:** ISBN 0-9707221-2-5 (2002)
**Total Circulation:** 500
**Average Print Run:** 500
**Subscription Rate:** Individual $15/Institution $15
**Single Copy Price:** $14.99
**Current Volume/Issue:** 5/1
**Frequency per Year:** 1
**Backfile Available:** yes
**Unsolicited Ms. Received:** yes

**% of Unsolicited Ms. Published per Year:** 100%
**Format:** perfect
**Size:** H 9" W 6"
**Average Pages:** 220
**Ads:** no

# Big Bridge

**Type:** online
**CLMP member:** no
**Primary Editor/Contact Person:** Michael Rothenberg
**Address:** 16083 Fern Way
Guerneville, CA 95446
**Web Site Address:** http://www.bigbridge.org
**Publishes:** essays, fiction, nonfiction, poetry, reviews, art, translation, and audio
**Editorial Focus:** Language, sonnets, haiku, spoken word, experimental, workshop agit-smut poetry. We want art of whimsy, passion, and urgency.
**Representative Authors:** Philip Whalen, Joanne Kyger, and David Meltzer
**Submissions Policy:** We only accept online submission to walterblue@bigbridge.org. Paste work into body of e-mail and include word doc attachment.
**Simultaneous Subs:** yes
**Reading Period:** Year-round
**Reporting Time:** 1 to 2 weeks
**Author Payment:** none
**Founded:** 1997
**Non Profit:** no
**Paid Staff:** 0
**Unpaid Staff:** 2
**Distributors:** online
**ISSN Number/ISBN Number:** ISSN: 1529-7136
**Average Page Views per Month:** 40,000
**Average Unique Visitors per Month:** 800
**Publish Print Anthology:** no
**Average Percentage of Pages per Category:** Fiction 15%, Nonfiction 5%, Poetry 40%, Reviews 3%, Essays 5%, Art 30%, Translation 1%, Audio 1%
**Ads:** no

# Bilingual Review Press

**Type:** press
**CLMP member:** no
**Primary Editor/Contact Person:** Karen Van Hooft
**Address:** Hispanic Research Center
Arizona State University, Box 875303
Tempe, AZ 85287-5303
**Web Site Address:** http://www.asu.edu/brp

**Publishes:** fiction, nonfiction, poetry, art, and translation

**Editorial Focus:** Literary works, criticism, and art books by or about US Hispanics. English, Spanish, and bilingual editions.

**Representative Authors:** Ana Castillo, Lourdes Vazquez, and Stella Pope Duarte

**Submissions Policy:** See website for details.

**Simultaneous Subs:** no

**Reading Period:** Year-round

**Reporting Time:** 1 to 2 months

**Author Payment:** royalties and copies

**Founded:** 1973

**Non Profit:** yes

**Paid Staff:** 6

**Unpaid Staff:** 0

**Distributors:** Ingram, Baker & Taylor, SPD

**Number of Books Published per Year:** 8

**Titles in Print:** 150

**Average Print Run:** 5,000

**Average Percentage Printed:** Hardcover 5%, Paperback 95%

**Average Price:** $16

# Bilingual Review

**Type:** magazine

**CLMP member:** no

**Primary Editor/Contact Person:** Karen Van Hooft

**Address:** Hispanic Research Center
Arizona State University, Box 872702
Tempe, AZ 85287-2702

**Web Site Address:** http://www.asu.edu/brp

**Publishes:** essays, fiction, poetry, and translation

**Editorial Focus:** Bilingual Review focuses on bilingualism, bilingual education and ethnic scholarship, and features Hispanic creative writing.

**Submissions Policy:** See our website.

**Simultaneous Subs:** no

**Reading Period:** Year-round

**Reporting Time:** 1 to 2 months

**Author Payment:** copies

**Founded:** 1973

**Non Profit:** yes

**Paid Staff:** 6

**Unpaid Staff:** 0

**Distributors:** Distributed directly by publisher.

**ISSN Number/ISBN Number:** ISSN 0094-5366

**Total Circulation:** 1,000

**Paid Circulation:** 500

**Subscription Rate:** Individual $25/Institution $25

**Single Copy Price:** $12-28

**Current Volume/Issue:** 26/1

**Frequency per Year:** 3

**Backfile Available:** yes

**Unsolicited Ms. Received:** yes

**Format:** perfect

**Size:** H 7" W 10"

**Average Pages:** 90

**Ads:** yes

# The Bitter Oleander

**Type:** magazine

**CLMP member:** yes

**Primary Editor/Contact Person:** Paul B. Roth

**Address:** 4983 Tall Oaks Dr.
Fayetteville, NY 13066-9776

**Web Site Address:** http://www.bitteroleander.com

**Publishes:** essays, fiction, poetry, and translation

**Editorial Focus:** TBO publishes poetry and fiction in pursuit of the imagination unfolding specific aspects of the concrete particular.

**Recent Awards Received:** Best of American Poetry 1999

**Representative Authors:** Duane Locke, Christine Boyka Kluge, and Ray Gonzalez

**Submissions Policy:** e-mail submissions allowed only from outside the US All others use SASE and consult our website.

**Simultaneous Subs:** yes

**Reading Period:** 8/6 to 1/30

**Reporting Time:** 1 to 2 months

**Author Payment:** copies

**Contests:** The Frances Locke Memorial Poetry Award See Web Site for Contest Guidelines.

**Founded:** 1974

**Non Profit:** no

**Paid Staff:** 1

**Unpaid Staff:** 2

**Distributors:** Ingram, SPD

**ISSN Number/ISBN Number:** ISSN 1087-8483

**Total Circulation:** 1,500

**Paid Circulation:** 200

**Average Print Run:** 2,000

**Subscription Rate:** Individual $15/Institution $12

**Single Copy Price:** $8

**Current Volume/Issue:** 11/2

**Frequency per Year:** 2

**Backfile Available:** yes

**Unsolicited Ms. Received:** yes

**% of Unsolicited Ms. Published per Year:** .1%

# Profile: Marc Fitten, Editor, Chattahoochie Review

### 1) How did you arrive at your current position?

Grit, tooth, nail, and a cadre of truncheon wielding fairy godmothers. That's the short version. Nobody believes the longer one:

I moved to Hungary a year after high school, when I was nineteen, to write a novel. I lived in the middle of the Hungarian Steppes. Four years into it, I was broke and eating from a bushel of old apples. I had a second-hand fur coat and was friendly with every bum in town. Winters were brutal. I thought I was living the dream. I thought I was living just like my heroes at the time had lived before—Dostoevsky and Miller. Only, I ended up hospitalized, seriously infected after an emergency trip to a quack dentist. The infection was spreading down my throat. The doctors said it would eat my heart. I couldn't speak. I couldn't breathe. I should have been scared, but I was more upset because I'd been trying for brain fever—a curious, nineteenth-century Russian malady that enough people don't suffer from anymore. The doctors lanced my throat to get me breathing. They hooked me up to an antibiotic drip. They didn't use anesthetics. I was twenty-three. Confined to a bed, I started thinking that maybe I wasn't making good choices. I figured that if I wanted to be a writer, besides reading and writing as much as I was able, I should try to find a rewarding job in publishing to learn a little about how it really works. Ah, the slippery mind of a convalescent. I left Hungary in '98 and returned to the States. I figured I'd have a snowball's chance in hell trying to compete for a job in NYC with all those talented kids at schools like NYU and Columbia . . .not to mention Barnard, the rest of the northeast, and frankly, the entire country. I figured the front door would be rightly shut to me and that if I wanted in I'd have to get in through a back door or pantry window. So, I went to Atlanta and walked into the offices of *The Chattahoochee Review* right off of the street. They were shocked. Surprisingly, nobody in my generation had thought of it. Too busy chasing the MFA. I've been there ever since. My entire professional life has been at *The Chattahoochee Review*. I made myself indispensable. Worked like hell. Changed the way we did everything and put myself in the middle of it. Jimmy Olsen on crank. People quit, died, and retired. I moved up the masthead. Nobody noticed until I became editor. I have no first-hand experience with a traditional MFA program. They sound like fun. I read their stuff all the time. If I could find a school that would accept me, I might even go.

### 2) What is the staff structure like at your press/magazine?

There are presently only two full-time positions. I'm one. The managing editor is the other. She's a real doll. 76

years old. She's partied with Bob Hope, Jimmy Carter, Ben Heppner, and Ru Paul. A grande dame. She handles the bookkeeping and enjoys line editing. I also edit and do everything besides. After I was well ensconced, I began a more formal internship program. Résumé's, interviews, deadlines, the works. We have between two and four interns per semester. None of them have had an MFA. A couple of MBAs, a comp & rhetoric guy, some undergrads, but no MFAs. I've actually had people tell me that it wouldn't be worth it to an MFA student to intern at an established literary review. That they wouldn't do it. I can't understand that. It seems more valuable an experience to me than tutoring in a writing lab or teaching English Comp. If you're an MFA student who wants an internship and you live in the south, give us a call.

### 3) How do you keep your press/magazine running?

On the one hand you have things like the NEA's Reading at Risk report and magazine editors talking about dwindling subscriptions. Somehow, these things portend the end of literature and a dismal future. On the other hand you have folks at RH who are flat out making money, not to mention B&N and Borders who are posting strong retail sales. New York is Book Country goes kaput, *The Atlantic Monthly* stops publishing fiction, and everybody throws a fit like it's the end of the literary world. Agents say that they can't sell short story collections, so don't bother. Fiction is in big trouble. Poetry? Ha! Not unless your Billy Collins.

However, Decatur Book Festival in Atlanta announces that they're starting a major national book festival. Little Brown & RH are already sending authors. The AJC—a newspaper who's own subscription rates fall in double digits, ponies up $100,000 in advertising. Corporations and colleges start donating cash. Miami's book fair is a monster. Then, back at *The Atlantic*, the numbers are out, and big surprise, that fiction issue they published actually made a profit. Michael Curtis spoke for us at an event in Atlanta and said something like that issue sold more newsstand copies than any other issue in that magazine's history. It goes on . . .one minute CLMP is worried about bankruptcy, the next, they are getting help from some kind of Venture fund. The AWP conference can't stop growing. They're doing so well, they double their sponsorship levels. Writing programs are bursting at the seams. This is not a dying industry.

My problem as a publisher is simply this: The talented reader holding this book is wondering where to submit, even better, maybe he's wondering where to subscribe. Well, I want him to do both. I want him to submit and subscribe to *The Chattahoochee Review*. So does *Tin House*. So does *McSweeneys*. So do *Fence*, *Open City*, *The Georgia Review*, *A Public Space*, and on and on. So do *Harpers*, *Playboy*, and *Time*. How do I do get him to consider *The Chattahoochee Review* over the others?

How can I compete?

The issues for publishers aren't the issues of art and literature. That is, there is no dearth of quality content. The issue for all of us is recognizing that we are an industry and that the rules of capitalism apply. We're cannibalizing each other and we don't even know it. My prediction: things will stay the same until the market corrects itself. As a small publisher it will become more important to find a niche and capitalize on that. Rain Taxi is the perfect example of this.

The problem that a lot of small publishers have is accepting the fact that they are in a business and will eventually have to contend with the bottom line, if they want to continue publishing. If they don't care and they just want to do something fun for a few years, then that's different. To create something that lasts, to impact culture, well, that requires a plan and as much of an interest in the How To as in the What to Publish.

### 4) What do or don't you hope to see in a cover letter?

I don't need your photograph. I don't need a listing of pubs. I don't need a synopsis. Four sentences should cover it. Get to the point. Something like: I read and like The Chattahoochee Review. I'm submitting a short story or poem(s), X. I'm a student or I sell flowers for a living. Thanks for your time.

### 5) What do you look for in a submission?

Something confident. I can sense a person's confidence right away. The writing punches from the first sentence. The author knows what he's doing. That's what I want to see. I'll read that. After that, all the normal rules apply: story arc, characters, etc. I guess it's something about the tone. I don't mean cocky. I mean confidently written. Polished. Like glass. It's just something you see when you read a lot of manuscripts.

### 6) How are submissions processed at your press/magazine?

The mailman comes. He has tea and chips. He chats up the interns. They laugh and take the mail from him. They open it, log it, and put it in a box. It stays there until someone reads it and comments. A second person reads and comments. The managing editor reads and comments. If all those people comment positively, I read and comment. Typical over the transom kind of thing. I spend a lot of time in the world as well. I like to think I have good instincts and a good eye. I have no problem asking perfect strangers to email me something. I've been wrong, but I've been right more times than wrong.

### 7) Do you have a favorite unsolicited submission discovery or story?

Volume 23 Double Issue2/3

"A Family of Breast Feeders" by Starkey Flythe, Jr. It came in over the transom when I was assistant editor. The story was hilarious. Starkey is a great comic writer, an even greater guy. He needs more recognition, I think. I didn't know him at the time, but we've become friends since. The story was later picked up by Shannon Ravenel at Algonquin for the New Stories from the South anthology.

### 8) Do you have any advice for first-time submitters?

Get over yourself. Get over your anxieties. Read as much as you can. Read more than you can. Know the journal you're submitting to. Get an internship. Inevitably, the Law of Averages will work in your favor. You'll be published. Being published is the only way to get that posting at a college you never heard of somewhere in rural America. Who knows? You might even end up teaching poetry in the south.

**Format:** perfect
**Size:** H 9" W 6"
**Average Pages:** 128
**Ads:** yes
**Ad Rates:** whole: $200 half: $125
See Web Site for Details.

## The Bitter Oleander Press

**Type:** press
**CLMP member:** yes
**Primary Editor/Contact Person:** Paul B. Roth
**Address:** 4983 Tall Oaks Dr.
Fayetteville, NY 13066-9776
**Web Site Address:** http://www.bitteroleander.com
**Publishes:** poetry
**Editorial Focus:** Aside from our journal, our books represent the total imaginative work of a single poet.
**Representative Authors:** Anthony Seidman, Benjamin P/ret, and Christine Boyka Kluge
**Submissions Policy:** Ask with a SASE or via e-mail whether we are looking for manuscripts.
**Simultaneous Subs:** yes
**Reading Period:** Year-round
**Reporting Time:** 1 to 2 months
**Author Payment:** copies
**Founded:** 1974
**Non Profit:** no
**Paid Staff:** 1
**Unpaid Staff:** 2
**Distributors:** Ingram and SPD
**ISSN Number/ISBN Number:** ISBN 0-9664358
**Number of Books Published per Year:** 2
**Titles in Print:** 10
**Average Percentage Printed:** Paperback 100%

## BkMk Press

**Type:** press
**CLMP member:** yes
**Primary Editor/Contact Person:** Ben Furnish, Managing Editor
**Address:** University of Missouri-Kansas City
5101 Rockhill Road
Kansas City, MO 64110
**Web Site Address:** http://www.umkc.edu/bkmk
**Publishes:** essays, fiction, and poetry
**Editorial Focus:** Contemporary writers
**Representative Authors:** Marilyn Kallet, John Knoepfle, and Billy Lombardo
**Submissions Policy:** Poetry, short fiction, creative

nonfiction
**Simultaneous Subs:** yes
**Reading Period:** 1/1 to 6/30
**Reporting Time:** 6 to 8 months
**Author Payment:** royalties
**Contests:** See Web Site for Contest Guidelines.
**Founded:** 1971
**Non Profit:** yes
**Paid Staff:** 2
**Unpaid Staff:** 4
**Distributors:** SPD
**Wholesalers:** Baker & Taylor
**ISSN Number/ISBN Number:** ISBN 0-933532, 1-886157
**Number of Books Published per Year:** 5
**Titles in Print:** 90
**Average Print Run:** 800
**Average Percentage Printed:** Paperback 100%
**Average Price:** $13.95

## Black Clock

**Type:** magazine
**CLMP member:** no
**Primary Editor/Contact Person:** Steve Erickson/Dwayne Moser
**Address:** CalArts
24700 McBean Parkway
Valencia, CA 91355
**Web Site Address:** http://www.blackclock.org
**Publishes:** essays, fiction, nonfiction, and poetry
**Editorial Focus:** Featuring works by some of the most prominent writers of our time, talented regional authors, and selected CalArts students.
**Representative Authors:** David Foster Wallace, Joanna Scott, and Jonathan Lethem
**Submissions Policy:** At this point we are not accepting unsolicited submissions.
**Author Payment:** cash
**Founded:** 2004
**Non Profit:** yes
**Paid Staff:** 3
**Unpaid Staff:** 3
**Wholesalers:** BigTop Newsstand Services
**ISSN Number/ISBN Number:** ISSN 7447058384
**Total Circulation:** 2,500
**Paid Circulation:** 120
**Subscription Rate:** Individual $20/Institution $20
**Single Copy Price:** $12
**Current Volume/Issue:** Issue 1
**Frequency per Year:** 2

**Backfile Available:** no
**Unsolicited Ms. Received:** no
**Format:** Smythe Sewn, very nice
**Size:** H 12" W 9"
**Average Pages:** 160
**Ads:** yes
**Ad Rates:** See Web Site for Details.

# Black Issues Book Review

**Type:** magazine
**CLMP member:** yes
**Primary Editor/Contact Person:** Angela P. Dodson
**Address:** Empire State Building
350 Fifth Ave., Ste. 1522
New York, NY 10118-0165
**Web Site Address:** http://www.bibookreview.com
**Publishes:** reviews
**Simultaneous Subs:** no
**Reading Period:** Year-round
**Reporting Time:** 1 to 2 months
**Author Payment:** none
**Founded:** 1999
**Non Profit:** no
**Paid Staff:** 14
**Unpaid Staff:** 3
**ISSN Number/ISBN Number:** ISSN 1522-0524
**Paid Circulation:** 18,000
**Average Print Run:** 75,000
**Subscription Rate:** Individual $14.95/Institution $14.95
**Single Copy Price:** $4.95
**Current Volume/Issue:** S/O/5
**Frequency per Year:** 6
**Backfile Available:** yes
**Unsolicited Ms. Received:** no
**Format:** stapled
**Size:** H 11" W 8"
**Average Pages:** 64
**Ads:** yes

# Black Lawrence Press

**Type:** press
**CLMP member:** no
**Primary Editor/Contact Person:** Colleen Ryor
**Address:** P.O. Box 46
Watertown, NY 13601
**Web Site Address:**
http://www.blacklawrencepress.com
**Publishes:** fiction, nonfiction, poetry, and translation

**Editorial Focus:** Contemporary fiction, poetry, politics, culture, and some translation (German and French only).
**Representative Authors:** D.C. Berry, Frank Matagrano, and James Owens
**Submissions Policy:** See websites for guidelines or write to us.
**Simultaneous Subs:** yes
**Reading Period:** Year-round
**Reporting Time:** 1 to 4 months
**Author Payment:** royalties and copies
**Contests:** The St. Lawrence Book Award for a first collection: $1,000 prize and publication. The 46er Prize for Short Fiction: $500
See Web Site for Contest Guidelines.
**Founded:** 2003
**Non Profit:** yes
**Paid Staff:** 1
**Unpaid Staff:** 1
**Number of Books Published per Year:** 2-4
**Average Percentage Printed:** Paperback 100%

# Black Square Editions/Hammer Books

**Type:** press
**CLMP member:** no
**Primary Editor/Contact Person:** John Yau
**Address:** 1200 Broadway (3C)
New York, NY 10001
**Web Site Address:** http://blacksquareeditions.com
**Publishes:** essays, fiction, nonfiction, poetry, art, and translation
**Editorial Focus:** Innovative poetry and fiction, essays about postwar and contemporary art, translations of the above.
**Representative Authors:** Gary Lutz, Jacques Dupin, and Albert Mobilio
**Submissions Policy:** queries preferred.
**Simultaneous Subs:** yes
**Reading Period:** Year-round
**Reporting Time:** 4 to 6 months
**Author Payment:** copies
**Contests:** no
**Founded:** 1999
**Non Profit:** yes
**Paid Staff:** 0
**Unpaid Staff:** 3
**Distributors:** SPD and PGW
**ISSN Number/ISBN Number:** ISBN 0-9744065, 0-9712485

**Number of Books Published per Year:** 2-5
**Titles in Print:** 17
**Average Percentage Printed:** Paperback 75%,
Chapbook 20%, Other 5%
**Backfile Available:** yes

# Black Warrior Review

**Type:** magazine
**CLMP member:** yes
**Primary Editor/Contact Person:** Aaron Welborn,
Editor
**Address:** Box 862936
Tuscaloosa, AL 35486-0027
**Web Site Address:** http://webdelsol.com/bwr
**Publishes:** essays, fiction, nonfiction, poetry, and art
**Editorial Focus:** The freshest work out there, by new
and established writers.
**Representative Authors:** Tomaz Salamun, Judy
Budnitz, and Larissa Szporluk
**Submissions Policy:** Send 5-7 poems. Fiction up to
7,500 words; short-shorts welcome. Address to
appropriate genre editor. No e-mail submissions.
**Simultaneous Subs:** yes
**Reading Period:** Year-round
**Reporting Time:** 1 to 5 months
**Author Payment:** cash and subscription
**Founded:** 1974
**Non Profit:** yes
**Paid Staff:** 4
**Unpaid Staff:** 30
**Distributors:** Ingram
**Wholesalers:** Ingram
**ISSN Number/ISBN Number:** ISSN 0193-6301
**Total Circulation:** 1,500
**Paid Circulation:** 500
**Subscription Rate:** Individual $14/Institution $20
**Single Copy Price:** $8
**Current Volume/Issue:** 31/1
**Frequency per Year:** 2
**Backfile Available:** yes
**Unsolicited Ms. Received:** yes
**% of Unsolicited Ms. Published per Year:** 1%
**Format:** perfect
**Size:** H 9" W 6"
**Average Pages:** 168
**Ads:** yes
**Ad Rates:** See Web Site for Details.

# Blackbird

**Type:** online
**CLMP member:** no
**Primary Editor/Contact Person:** Anna Journey,
Associate Editor
**Address:** P.O. Box 843082
Richmond, VA 23284-3082
**Web Site Address:** http://www.blackbird.vcu.edu
**Publishes:** essays, fiction, nonfiction, poetry, reviews,
art, translation, and audio
**Representative Authors:** Hal Crowther, Norman
Dubie, and Lily Tuck
**Submissions Policy:** We accept submissions in fic-
tion and poetry only. All other material is solicited.
**Simultaneous Subs:** yes
**Reading Period:** 9/15 to 4/15
**Reporting Time:** 3 to 5 months
**Author Payment:** cash
**Founded:** 2001
**Non Profit:** yes
**Paid Staff:** 1
**Unpaid Staff:** 8
**ISSN Number/ISBN Number:** ISSN 1540-3068
**Average Page Views per Month:** 200,000
**Average Unique Visitors per Month:** 20,000
**Frequency per Year:** 2
**Publish Print Anthology:** no
**Average Percentage of Pages per Category:** Fiction
25%, Nonfiction 5%, Poetry 25%, Reviews 5%, Essays
5%, Art 15%, Translation 5%, Audio 15%
**Ads:** no

# Blithe House Quarterly

**Type:** online
**CLMP member:** yes
**Primary Editor/Contact Person:** Aldo Alvarez
**Address:** 5100 N. Winchester #3
Chicago, IL 60640
**Web Site Address:** http://www.blithe.com
**Publishes:** fiction and translation
**Editorial Focus:** BHQ features a diversity of new short
stories by emerging and established gay, lesbian,
bisexual, and transgendered authors.
**Submissions Policy:** Stories should be between
1,500 and 7,500 words in length. We ask for First
Serial Rights—all rights return to the author on publi-
cation. We do not consider previously published mate-
rial. We only accept submissions via e-mail. For more
details, submission guidelines are available on site.
**Simultaneous Subs:** yes

**Reading Period:** 9/1 to 12/1
**Reporting Time:** 2 to 4 months
**Author Payment:** none
**Founded:** 1997
**Non Profit:** yes
**Paid Staff:** 0
**Unpaid Staff:** 6
**Average Page Views per Month:** 50,000
**Average Unique Visitors per Month:** 8,000
**Frequency per Year:** 4
**Average Percentage of Pages per Category:** Fiction 98%, Translation 2%
**Ads:** no

## Blood and Thunder

**Type:** magazine
**CLMP member:** yes
**Address:** 941 Stanton L Young Blvd.
BSEB Room 100
Oklahoma City, OK 73190
**Web Site Address:** http://www.bloodandthunder.org
**Publishes:** essays, fiction, nonfiction, poetry, and art
**Reading Period:** Year-round
**Reporting Time:** 1 to 2 months
**Author Payment:** none
**Founded:** 2000
**Non Profit:** no
**Backfile Available:** yes

## The Blood Moon Productions

**Type:** press
**CLMP member:** no
**Primary Editor/Contact Person:** Danforth Prince
**Address:** 75 Saint Marks Place
Staten Island, NY 10301
**Web Site Address:**
http://www.BloodMoonProductions.com
**Publishes:** fiction and nonfiction
**Editorial Focus:** Controversial but carefully researched Hollywood biographies. Potboiling novels for sexually sophisticated adults.
**Representative Authors:** Darwin Porter and Danforth Prince
**Submissions Policy:** Author's contact info, a plot synopsis, 2-3 sample chapters.
**Simultaneous Subs:** yes
**Reading Period:** Year-round
**Reporting Time:** 1 to 3 months
**Author Payment:** royalties and cash

**Founded:** 1997
**Non Profit:** no
**Paid Staff:** 4
**Unpaid Staff:** 2
**Distributors:** Bookazine, Ingram, Baker & Taylor, Turnaround
**ISSN Number/ISBN Number:** ISBN 09668030 and 9748118
**Number of Books Published per Year:** 3
**Titles in Print:** 8
**Average Percentage Printed:** Hardcover 20%, Paperback 80%

## Bloom: Queer Fiction, Art, Poetry and More

**Type:** magazine
**CLMP member:** yes
**Primary Editor/Contact Person:** Charles Flowers
**Address:** 210 W.19th St. Apt. 2B
Old Chelsea Station
New York, NY 10011
**Web Site Address:** http://www.bloommagazine.org
**Publishes:** essays, fiction, nonfiction, poetry, art, and translation
**Editorial Focus:** Authors must identify as queer, but Bloom does not discriminate against the imagination.
**Representative Authors:** Adrienne Rich, Andrew Holleran, and Carl Phillips
**Submissions Policy:** SASE required. Prose: up to 25 pages. Poems: up to 10 pages. Art: slides or disk.
**Simultaneous Subs:** yes
**Reading Period:** Year-round
**Reporting Time:** 2 to 3 months
**Author Payment:** copies and subscription
**Founded:** 2003
**Non Profit:** yes
**Paid Staff:** 0
**Unpaid Staff:** 4
**Distributors:** Bookazine
**ISSN Number/ISBN Number:** ISSN 1550-3291
**Total Circulation:** 1,500
**Paid Circulation:** 300
**Subscription Rate:** Individual $16/Institution $40
**Single Copy Price:** $10
**Current Volume/Issue:** 1/2
**Frequency per Year:** 2
**Backfile Available:** yes
**Unsolicited Ms. Received:** yes
**% of Unsolicited Ms. Published per Year:** 20%
**Format:** perfect

**Size:** H 8" W 5"
**Average Pages:** 200
**Ads:** yes
**Ad Rates:** $100 1/2 page, $175 full page, $250 bookmark flap

## Blue Collar Review

**Type:** magazine
**CLMP member:** no
**Primary Editor/Contact Person:** Al Markowitz
**Address:** P.O. Box 11417
Norfolk, VA 23517
**Web Site Address:** http://Partisanpress.org
**Publishes:** essays, poetry, and reviews
**Editorial Focus:** Our mission is the preservation, expansion, and promotion of the literature of our working class, primarily poetry, which might not find a place in profit-driven publishing channels.
**Representative Authors:** Marge Piercy, Robert Edwards, and Jim Daniels
**Submissions Policy:** Submissions should have name and address on each page. SASE for response. Prose limit 2,500 words. Send no more than 4 poems
**Simultaneous Subs:** no
**Reading Period:** Year-round
**Reporting Time:** 4 to 8 weeks
**Author Payment:** copies
**Contests:** See Web Site for Contest Guidelines.
**Founded:** 1997
**Non Profit:** yes
**Paid Staff:** 0
**Unpaid Staff:** 4
**ISSN Number/ISBN Number:** ISSN 1535-136X
**Total Circulation:** 520
**Paid Circulation:** 350
**Subscription Rate:** Individual $15/Institution $15
**Single Copy Price:** $5
**Current Volume/Issue:** 6/4
**Frequency per Year:** 4
**Backfile Available:** yes
**Unsolicited Ms. Received:** yes
**% of Unsolicited Ms. Published per Year:** 5%
**Format:** stapled
**Size:** H 8.5" W 5.5"
**Average Pages:** 60
**Ads:** yes
**Ad Rates:** $40 half page $70 full page

## Blue Mesa Review

**Type:** magazine
**CLMP member:** no
**Primary Editor/Contact Person:** Julie Shigekuni
**Address:** Dept. of English, Humanities Bldg.
University of New Mexico
Albuquerque, NM 87131-1106
**Web Site Address:** http://www.unm.edu/~bluemesa/
**Publishes:** essays, fiction, nonfiction, poetry, and reviews
**Submissions Policy:** Four poems or six pages of poetry, or one story fewer than 7,500 words, or one work of creative nonfiction
**Simultaneous Subs:** yes
**Reading Period:** 7/1 to 10/1
**Reporting Time:** 3 to 6 months
**Author Payment:** copies
**Founded:** 1989
**Non Profit:** yes
**Paid Staff:** 5
**Unpaid Staff:** 15
**Distributors:** University of New Mexico Press
**ISSN Number/ISBN Number:** ISBN 1-885290-15-2
**Total Circulation:** 1,000
**Paid Circulation:** 100
**Subscription Rate:** Individual $12/Institution $12
**Single Copy Price:** $12
**Current Volume/Issue:** Issue 16
**Frequency per Year:** 1
**Backfile Available:** yes
**Unsolicited Ms. Received:** yes
**% of Unsolicited Ms. Published per Year:** 90%
**Format:** perfect
**Size:** H 9" W 6"
**Average Pages:** 250
**Ads:** yes

# The Blue Moon Review

**Type:** online
**CLMP member:** no
**Primary Editor/Contact Person:** Doug Lawson,
Executive Editor
**Address:** 14313 Winter Ridge Ln.
Midlothian, VA 23113
**Web Site Address:** http://thebluemoon.com
**Publishes:** fiction
**Editorial Focus:** Narrative fiction up to 4,500 words.
**Submissions Policy:** We only accept submissions via
e-mail. Please review website for all guidelines, cur-
rent needs, and submission addresses.
**Simultaneous Subs:** no
**Reading Period:** Year-round
**Reporting Time:** 1 to 4 months
**Author Payment:** none
**Founded:** 1994
**Non Profit:** yes
**Paid Staff:** 0
**Unpaid Staff:** 1
**ISSN Number/ISBN Number:** ISSN 1079-042x
**Average Page Views per Month:** 34,000
**Average Unique Visitors per Month:** 17,500
**Frequency per Year:** 12
**Publish Print Anthology:** no
**Average Percentage of Pages per Category:** Fiction
100%
**Ads:** no

# Blueline

**Type:** magazine
**CLMP member:** yes
**Primary Editor/Contact Person:** Rick Henry
**Address:** 122 Morey Hall, Dept. of English
125 Morey Hall
Potsdam, NY 13676
**Web Site Address:**
http://www.potsdam.edu/ENGL/Blueline/default
**Publishes:** essays, fiction, nonfiction, poetry, reviews,
and art
**Editorial Focus:** Literary work relating to the
Adirondacks and regions similar in geography and
spirit, or on the shaping influence of nature.
**Representative Authors:** M.J. Iuppa, Susan J.
Newell, and Elizabeth Biller Chapman
**Submissions Policy:** Submissions must not have
been previously published. Simultaneous submissions
as long as they are announced as such.
**Simultaneous Subs:** yes

**Reading Period:** 9/1 to 11/30
**Reporting Time:** 2 to 3 months
**Author Payment:** copies
**Founded:** 1979
**Non Profit:** yes
**Paid Staff:** 0
**Unpaid Staff:** 6
**Distributors:** EBSCO
**Total Circulation:** 400
**Paid Circulation:** 250
**Average Print Run:** 400
**Subscription Rate:** Individual $10/Institution $10
**Single Copy Price:** $10
**Current Volume/Issue:** Issue XXVI
**Frequency per Year:** 1
**Backfile Available:** yes
**Unsolicited Ms. Received:** yes
**% of Unsolicited Ms. Published per Year:** 100%
**Format:** perfect
**Size:** H 9" W 6"
**Average Pages:** 200
**Ads:** no

# BOA Editions, Ltd.

**Type:** press
**CLMP member:** yes
**Primary Editor/Contact Person:** Thom Ward
**Address:** 260 East Ave.
Rochester, NY 14604-2608
**Web Site Address:** http://www.boaeditions.org
**Publishes:** poetry and translation
**Editorial Focus:** Contemporary American poetry and
poetry in translation and prose on poetry and poetics.
**Recent Awards Received:** National Book Award for
Poetry
**Representative Authors:** Lucille Clifton, Li-Young Lee,
and Louis Simpson
**Submissions Policy:** Look at our submissions policies
on our website
**Simultaneous Subs:** yes
**Reading Period:** Year-round
**Reporting Time:** 3 to 4 months
**Author Payment:** royalties and copies
**Contests:** See Web Site for Contest Guidelines.
**Founded:** 1976
**Non Profit:** yes
**Paid Staff:** 3
**Unpaid Staff:** 1
**Distributors:** Consortium
**ISSN Number/ISBN Number:** ISBN 1-929918

**Number of Books Published per Year:** 10
**Titles in Print:** 150
**Average Print Run:** 1,500
**Average Percentage Printed:** Hardcover 30%,
Paperback 70%
**Average Price:** $14.95

## Bogg

**Type:** magazine
**CLMP member:** yes
**Primary Editor/Contact Person:** John Elsberg
**Address:** 422 N. Cleveland St.
Arlington, VA 22201
**Publishes:** essays, fiction, poetry, reviews, and art
**Editorial Focus:** A journal of contemporary writing,
combining innovative US work with a leavening of
British and Commonwealth writing.
**Representative Authors:** Ann Menebroker, Richard
Peabody, and Kathy Ernst
**Submissions Policy:** Poems can be single-spaced;
double-spaced copy for fiction, interviews, reviews.
Stamped return envelope required.
**Simultaneous Subs:** no
**Reading Period:** Year-round
**Reporting Time:** 1 to 2 weeks
**Author Payment:** copies
**Founded:** 1968
**Non Profit:** no
**Paid Staff:** 0
**Unpaid Staff:** 3
**ISSN Number/ISBN Number:** ISSN 0882-648X
**Total Circulation:** 750
**Paid Circulation:** 350
**Average Print Run:** 750
**Subscription Rate:** Individual $15/Institution $20
**Single Copy Price:** $6
**Current Volume/Issue:** Issue 73
**Frequency per Year:** 2
**Backfile Available:** yes
**Unsolicited Ms. Received:** yes
**% of Unsolicited Ms. Published per Year:** 1%
**Format:** stapled
**Size:** H 9" W 6"
**Average Pages:** 56
**Ads:** no

## BOMB Magazine

**Type:** magazine
**CLMP member:** yes
**Primary Editor/Contact Person:** Nell McClister
**Address:** 594 Broadway, Ste. 905
80 Hanson Place #703
New York, NY 11217
**Web Site Address:** http://www.bombsite.com/
**Publishes:** essays, fiction, nonfiction, poetry, reviews,
art, and translation
**Editorial Focus:** Peer-to-Peer interviews with artists,
writers, musicians, architects, playwrights, filmmak-
ers, and actors.
**Representative Authors:** Eric Bogosian, Peter Carey,
and Laurie Anderson
**Simultaneous Subs:** yes
**Reading Period:** Year-round
**Reporting Time:** 4 to 6 months
**Author Payment:** subscription
**Founded:** 1981
**Non Profit:** yes
**Paid Staff:** 6
**Unpaid Staff:** 3
**Distributors:** BigTop Newsstands, a division of the IPA
**ISSN Number/ISBN Number:** ISSN 0743-3204
**Total Circulation:** >55,000
**Subscription Rate:** Individual $18/Institution $24
**Single Copy Price:** $4.95
**Current Volume/Issue:** Issue 85
**Frequency per Year:** 4
**Backfile Available:** yes
**Unsolicited Ms. Received:** yes
**Format:** perfect
**Size:** H 10.75" W 8.25"
**Average Pages:** 112
**Ads:** yes
**Ad Rates:** See Web Site for Details.

## Book/Mark Small Press Quarterly Review

**Type:** magazine
**CLMP member:** yes
**Primary Editor/Contact Person:** Mindy Kronenberg
**Address:** P.O. Box 516
Miller Place, NY 11764
**Web Site Address:** http://www.writersnetwork.com
**Publishes:** essays and reviews
**Editorial Focus:** To bring attention to the variety of
books by small press publishers. We are eclectic and
include the arts and popular culture.

**Representative Authors:** Richard Kostelanetz, Thomas Fink, and Laura Stamps
**Submissions Policy:** We accept freelance submissions and prefer reviews that are empathetic to the genre or subject of the book, citing excerpts.
**Simultaneous Subs:** yes
**Reading Period:** Year-round
**Reporting Time:** 2 to 5 weeks
**Author Payment:** copies and subscription
**Founded:** 1994
**Non Profit:** yes
**Paid Staff:** 0
**Unpaid Staff:** 15
**Distributors:** Suffolk Cooperative Library System
**ISSN Number/ISBN Number:** ISSN 1081-3209
**Total Circulation:** 850
**Paid Circulation:** 125
**Average Print Run:** 1,000
**Subscription Rate:** Individual $12/Institution $15
**Single Copy Price:** $3
**Current Volume/Issue:** 11/3
**Frequency per Year:** 4
**Backfile Available:** yes
**Unsolicited Ms. Received:** yes
**% of Unsolicited Ms. Published per Year:** 50%
**Format:** stapled
**Size:** H 11" W 8 1/2"
**Average Pages:** 12
**Ads:** yes
**Ad Rates:** $75/quarter page, $135/column

# Border Crossings

**Type:** magazine
**CLMP member:** no
**Primary Editor/Contact Person:** Meeka Walsh, Editor
**Address:** 500-70 Arthur St.
Winnipeg, MB R3B 1G7
**Web Site Address:**
http://www.bordercrossingsmag.com
**Publishes:** essays, fiction, nonfiction, poetry, reviews, and art
**Editorial Focus:** Exploring the boundaries of culture with intelligence and savvy, the magazine covers all areas of contemporary art.
**Representative Authors:** Meeka Walsh, Robert Enright, and Martha Langford
**Submissions Policy:** Border Crossings prefers that contributors clear any submissions with the Editor prior to submission.
**Simultaneous Subs:** yes

**Reading Period:** Year-round
**Reporting Time:** 1 to 6 months
**Author Payment:** cash
**Founded:** 1982
**Non Profit:** yes
**Paid Staff:** 4
**Unpaid Staff:** 0
**Distributors:** DeBoer, Ubiquity, Small Changes, Armadillo
**ISSN Number/ISBN Number:** ISSN 0831-2559
**Total Circulation:** 5,000
**Paid Circulation:** 2,500
**Subscription Rate:** Individual $32/Institution $40
**Single Copy Price:** $9.95
**Current Volume/Issue:** 23/3
**Frequency per Year:** 4
**Backfile Available:** yes
**Unsolicited Ms. Received:** yes
**% of Unsolicited Ms. Published per Year:** 10%
**Format:** perfect
**Size:** H 11" W 8.5"
**Average Pages:** 120
**Ads:** yes
**Ad Rates:** See Web Site for Details.

# Born Magazine

**Type:** online
**CLMP member:** no
**Primary Editor/Contact Person:** Anmarie Trimble
**Address:** P.O. Box 1313
Portland, OR 97215
**Web Site Address:** http://www.bornmagazine.org
**Publishes:** essays, fiction, nonfiction, poetry, art, translation, and audio
**Editorial Focus:** Experimental collaborations between writers and interactive artists.
**Representative Authors:** Michele Glazer, Major Jackson, and Joyelle McSweeney
**Submissions Policy:** 3-5 poems or 1-2 short prose works (e-mailed MS Word documents preferred). Accepts both new and previously published works.
**Simultaneous Subs:** no
**Reading Period:** Year-round
**Reporting Time:** 3 to 5 months
**Author Payment:** none
**Founded:** 1997
**Non Profit:** yes
**Paid Staff:** 0
**Unpaid Staff:** 11
**Average Page Views per Month:** 300,000

**Average Unique Visitors per Month:** 35,000
**Frequency per Year:** 4
**Publish Print Anthology:** no
**Average Percentage of Pages per Category:** Fiction 8%, Poetry 40%, Essays 1%, Art 50%, Translation 1%
**Ads:** no

# Boston Review

**Type:** magazine
**CLMP member:** yes
**Primary Editor/Contact Person:** Joshua J. Friedman
**Address:** E53-407 MIT
30 Wadsworth St.
Cambridge, MA 02139
**Web Site Address:** http://bostonreview.net
**Publishes:** essays, fiction, nonfiction, poetry, and reviews
**Editorial Focus:** Public policy, progressive politics and political science, culture, art, poetry, writing, film, mind/brain, book reviews
**Representative Authors:** Susie Linfield, James K. Galbraith, and Bin Ramke
**Simultaneous Subs:** yes
**Reading Period:** Year-round
**Reporting Time:** 1 to 2 months
**Author Payment:** none and cash
**Contests:** Annual poetry and short story contests. Winners of each receive publication in Boston Review plus $1,000 prize.
**Founded:** 1975
**Non Profit:** yes
**Paid Staff:** yes
**Unpaid Staff:** 4
**Distributors:** BigTop
**Total Circulation:** 10,000
**Paid Circulation:** 7,000
**Average Print Run:** 10,000
**Subscription Rate:** Individual $20/Institution $40
**Single Copy Price:** $5
**Current Volume/Issue:** 30/5
**Frequency per Year:** 6
**Backfile Available:** yes
**Unsolicited Ms. Received:** yes
**% of Unsolicited Ms. Published per Year:** .01%
**Format:** tabloid
**Average Pages:** 64
**Ads:** yes
**Ad Rates:** See Web Site for Details.

# Bottom Dog Press

**Type:** press
**CLMP member:** yes
**Primary Editor/Contact Person:** Larry Smith
**Address:** P.O. Box 425
Huron, OH 44839
**Web Site Address:** http://members.aol.com/lsmith-dog/bottomdog
**Publishes:** essays, fiction, nonfiction, and poetry
**Editorial Focus:** Midwest-Working Class-Buddhist-Performance Poets
**Representative Authors:** Jim Ray Daniels, Ray McNiece, and Richard Hague
**Simultaneous Subs:** yes
**Reading Period:** Year-round
**Reporting Time:** 1 to 3 months
**Author Payment:** royalties and copies
**Founded:** 1985
**Non Profit:** yes
**Paid Staff:** 1
**Unpaid Staff:** 1
**Distributors:** SPD, Baker & Taylor, direct from publisher
**ISSN Number/ISBN Number:** ISBN 0-933087-
**Number of Books Published per Year:** 5
**Titles in Print:** 91
**Average Print Run:** 1,000
**Average Percentage Printed:** Hardcover 10%, Paperback 85%, Other 5%
**Average Price:** $12.95

# Branches Quarterly

**Type:** online
**CLMP member:** no
**Primary Editor/Contact Person:** Toni Bennett
**Address:** P.O. Box 85394
Seattle, WA 98145-1394
**Web Site Address:**
http://www.branchesquarterly.com
**Publishes:** essays, fiction, nonfiction, poetry, reviews, art, and translation
**Editorial Focus:** Seeking an eclectic mix of quality poetry, short prose, photography (JPGs), drawing, short fiction, and essays.
**Representative Authors:** John Amen, Nathan Leslie, and Corrine De Winter
**Submissions Policy:** Submissions can be e-mailed to: submit@branchesquarterly.com with cover letter, bio, and work in body of e-mail or mailed.
**Simultaneous Subs:** yes

**Reading Period:** Year-round
**Reporting Time:** 3 to 6 months
**Author Payment:** none
**Contests:** See Web Site for Contest Guidelines.
**Founded:** 2001
**Non Profit:** no
**Paid Staff:** 0
**Unpaid Staff:** 1
**ISSN Number/ISBN Number:** ISSN 1536-2043
**Average Page Views per Month:** 400-500
**Average Unique Visitors per Month:** 250
**Frequency per Year:** 4
**Publish Print Anthology:** yes
**Price:** $8
**Average Percentage of Pages per Category:** Fiction 10%, Nonfiction 5%, Poetry 40%, Essays 3%, Art 40%, Translation 2%
**Ads:** no

# The Briar Cliff Review

**Type:** magazine
**CLMP member:** yes
**Primary Editor/Contact Person:** Tricia Currans-Sheehan
**Address:** Briar Cliff University
3303 Rebecca St.
Sioux City, IA 51104-0100
**Web Site Address:** http://briarcliff.edu/bcreview
**Publishes:** essays, fiction, nonfiction, poetry, reviews, and art
**Editorial Focus:** The Briar Cliff Review is an eclectic literary/cultural magazine focusing on, but not limited to, Siouxland writers/subjects
**Representative Authors:** Josip Novakovich, Lee Ann Roripaugh, and Brian Bedard
**Submissions Policy:** Unpublished work. No e-mail submissions. Send cover letter with SASE.
**Simultaneous Subs:** yes
**Reading Period:** 8/1 to 11/1
**Reporting Time:** 3 to 5 months
**Author Payment:** copies
**Contests:** See Web Site for Contest Guidelines.
**Founded:** 1989
**Non Profit:** yes
**Paid Staff:** 0
**Unpaid Staff:** 7-12
**Distributors:** Tricia Currans-Sheehan and Briar Cliff Bookstore
**ISSN Number/ISBN Number:** 1550-0926/0
**Total Circulation:** 750

**Paid Circulation:** 100
**Average Print Run:** 750
**Subscription Rate:** Individual $12/Institution $12
**Single Copy Price:** $12
**Current Volume/Issue:** Issue 18
**Frequency per Year:** 1
**Backfile Available:** yes
**Unsolicited Ms. Received:** yes
**% of Unsolicited Ms. Published per Year:** 10%
**Format:** perfect
**Size:** H 11" W 81/2"
**Average Pages:** 80
**Ads:** no

# Brick, A Literary Journal

**Type:** magazine
**CLMP member:** no
**Primary Editor/Contact Person:** Michael Redhill
**Address:** Box 537, Stn. Q
Toronto, ON M4T 2M5
**Web Site Address:** http://www.brickmag.com
**Publishes:** essays, fiction, nonfiction, poetry, reviews, art, and translation
**Editorial Focus:** We are interested in literary nonfiction essays. We do not accept unsolicited fiction or poetry.
**Simultaneous Subs:** yes
**Reading Period:** Year-round
**Reporting Time:** 1 to 9 months
**Author Payment:** cash and copies
**Founded:** 1977
**Non Profit:** yes
**Paid Staff:** 3
**Unpaid Staff:** 5+
**Distributors:** CMPA, Ubiquity, Pan Macmillan (Australia), DeBoer
**ISSN Number/ISBN Number:** ISSN 0382-8565
**Total Circulation:** 4,500
**Paid Circulation:** 1,000
**Average Print Run:** 5,000
**Subscription Rate:** Individual $38 CAD/$41 US/Institution varies
**Single Copy Price:** $12
**Current Volume/Issue:** Issue 76
**Frequency per Year:** 2
**Backfile Available:** yes
**Unsolicited Ms. Received:** yes
**Format:** perfect
**Average Pages:** 150
**Ads:** yes
**Ad Rates:** See Web Site for Details.

# Bright Hill Press

**Type:** press
**CLMP member:** yes
**Primary Editor/Contact Person:** Bertha Rogers
**Address:** P.O. Box 193
94 Church St.
Treadwell, NY 13846-0193
**Web Site Address:** http://www.brighthillpress.org
**Publishes:** essays, fiction, nonfiction, poetry, and art
**Editorial Focus:** Finely crafted poetry by accomplished poets; no memoiristic poems or poetry that sounds more like prose.
**Recent Awards Received:** Best Book of Poetry Published by a North Carolina poet, 2004 (Possum by Shelby Stephenson)
**Representative Authors:** Shelby Stephenson, Victoria Hallerman, and Bruce Bennett
**Submissions Policy:** Query letter only, with 10-poem sample. Reading January-March only.
**Simultaneous Subs:** yes
**Reading Period:** 1/3 to 1/31
**Reporting Time:** 4 to 12 months
**Author Payment:** cash and copies
**Contests:** See Web Site for Contest Guidelines.
**Founded:** 1992
**Non Profit:** yes
**Paid Staff:** 2-4
**Unpaid Staff:** 2
**Distributors:** North Country Books, SPD
**Wholesalers:** Baker & Taylor
**ISSN Number/ISBN Number:** ISBN 1-892471
**Number of Books Published per Year:** 7-10
**Titles in Print:** 35
**Average Print Run:** 1,000
**Average Percentage Printed:** Paperback 50%, Chapbook 50%
**Average Price:** $10

# Brilliant Corners

**Type:** magazine
**CLMP member:** no
**Primary Editor/Contact Person:** Sascha Feinstein
**Address:** Lycoming College
Williamsport, PA 17701
**Web Site Address:**
http://www.lycoming.edu/BrilliantCorners
**Publishes:** essays, fiction, nonfiction, poetry, reviews, and art
**Editorial Focus:** Exclusively publishes jazz-related literature.

**Representative Authors:** Yusef Komunyakaa, Jayne Cortez, and Philip Levine
**Submissions Policy:** Nothing electronic. SASE a must. Bio pref. but not essential.
**Simultaneous Subs:** no
**Reading Period:** 9/15 to 5/1
**Reporting Time:** 1 to 3 months
**Author Payment:** copies
**Founded:** 1996
**Non Profit:** yes
**Paid Staff:** 1
**Unpaid Staff:** 3
**Distributors:** Ingram
**ISSN Number/ISBN Number:** ISSN 1091-1197
**Total Circulation:** 600
**Paid Circulation:** 150
**Average Print Run:** 900
**Subscription Rate:** Individual $12/Institution $12
**Single Copy Price:** $7
**Current Volume/Issue:** IX/2
**Frequency per Year:** 2
**Backfile Available:** yes
**Unsolicited Ms. Received:** yes
**% of Unsolicited Ms. Published per Year:** 95%
**Format:** perfect
**Size:** H 9" W 6"
**Average Pages:** 90
**Ads:** yes
**Ad Rates:** $125 per page

# Brindle & Glass Publishing

**Type:** press
**CLMP member:** no
**Primary Editor/Contact Person:** Lee Shedden
**Address:** 132 Hallbrook Dr SW
Calgary, AB T2V 3H6
**Web Site Address:** http://www.brindleandglass.com
**Publishes:** fiction and nonfiction
**Editorial Focus:** Fiction, creative nonfiction, and drama by leading and emerging Canadian writers.
**Representative Authors:** Fred Stenson, T.J. Dawe, and Grant MacEwan
**Submissions Policy:** Prospective authors should query via e-mail before submitting. We only publish Canadian citizens or landed immigrants.
**Simultaneous Subs:** yes
**Reading Period:** Year-round
**Reporting Time:** 2 to 6 months
**Author Payment:** royalties
**Founded:** 2000

**Non Profit:** no
**Paid Staff:** 0
**Unpaid Staff:** 2
**Distributors:** Sandhill Book Marketing, Kelowna, BC
**ISSN Number/ISBN Number:** ISBN 0-9732481
**Number of Books Published per Year:** 7
**Titles in Print:** 18
**Average Percentage Printed:** Hardcover 10%, Paperback 90%

# Bristol Banner Books

**Type:** press
**CLMP member:** no
**Primary Editor/Contact Person:** Melody Myers
**Address:** 14041 C.R. 8
Middlebury, IN 46540
**Publishes:** fiction, nonfiction, and poetry
**Simultaneous Subs:** yes
**Reading Period:** Year-round
**Reporting Time:** 1 to 12 months
**Author Payment:** none
**Founded:** 1877
**Non Profit:** no
**Paid Staff:** 0
**Unpaid Staff:** 0
**ISSN Number/ISBN Number:** ISSN 1-879183
**Number of Books Published per Year:** 4
**Titles in Print:** 20
**Average Print Run:** 5
**Average Percentage Printed:** Paperback 100%
**Average Price:** $24.95

# Broken Pencil

**Type:** magazine
**CLMP member:** yes
**Address:** P.O. Box 203
Station P
Toronto, Ontario M5S2S7, Canada
**Web Site Address:** http://www.brokenpencil.com
**Publishes:** essays, fiction, nonfiction, and reviews
**Reading Period:** Year-round
**Reporting Time:** 1 to 2 months
**Author Payment:** none
**Founded:** 1995
**Non Profit:** yes
**Backfile Available:** yes

# Brook Street Press

**Type:** press
**CLMP member:** no
**Primary Editor/Contact Person:** James Pannell
**Address:** P.O. Box 20284
St. Simons Island, GA 31522
**Web Site Address:** http://www.brookstreetpress.com
**Publishes:** fiction and nonfiction
**Editorial Focus:** We publish literary fiction and creative nonfiction. We look for quality works (new/reissue) that deal with moral dilemmas.
**Representative Authors:** Frederick Buechner, Thomas McMahon, and Robert A.G. Monks
**Submissions Policy:** See web site for detailed submission guidelines.
**Simultaneous Subs:** yes
**Reading Period:** Year-round
**Reporting Time:** 3 to 6 months
**Author Payment:** royalties and copies
**Founded:** 2002
**Non Profit:** no
**Paid Staff:** 4
**Unpaid Staff:** 0
**Distributors:** Midpoint Trade Books
**Wholesalers:** Baker & Taylor, Ingram
**ISSN Number/ISBN Number:** ISBN 0-9724295
**Number of Books Published per Year:** 10
**Titles in Print:** 7
**Average Print Run:** 2,000
**Average Percentage Printed:** Hardcover 20%, Paperback 80%
**Average Price:** $14

# Bullfight Media

**Type:** magazine
**CLMP member:** yes
**Address:** P.O. Box 362
Walnut Creek, CA 94597-4512
**Web Site Address:** http://www.bullfightreview.com
**Publishes:** essays, fiction, nonfiction, and poetry
**Reading Period:** Year-round
**Reporting Time:** 1 to 2 months
**Author Payment:** none
**Non Profit:** yes
**Backfile Available:** yes

## Bureau of Public Secrets

**Type:** press
**CLMP member:** no
**Primary Editor/Contact Person:** Ken Knabb
**Address:** P.O. Box 1044
Berkeley, CA 94701
**Web Site Address:** http://www.bopsecrets.org
**Publishes:** essays, nonfiction, reviews, and translation
**Editorial Focus:** Radical political and cultural critique. Texts by Guy Debord, Situationist International, Kenneth Rexroth
**Representative Authors:** Guy Debord, Kenneth Rexroth, and Raoul Vaneigem
**Simultaneous Subs:** no
**Reading Period:** Year-round
**Reporting Time:** 1 to 2 weeks
**Author Payment:** none
**Founded:** 1973
**Non Profit:** yes
**Paid Staff:** 0
**Unpaid Staff:** 1
**Distributors:** AK Distribution, Small Press Dist., Koen Dist.
**ISSN Number/ISBN Number:** ISSN 0-939682
**Number of Books Published per Year:** 1
**Titles in Print:** 3
**Average Percentage Printed:** Paperback 100%

## Burning Bush Publications

**Type:** online
**CLMP member:** no
**Primary Editor/Contact Person:** Amanda Majestie
**Address:** P.O. Box 9636
Oakland, CA 94613
**Web Site Address:** http://www.bbbooks.com
**Publishes:** essays, fiction, nonfiction, and poetry
**Editorial Focus:** Social and economic justice, love, romance, beauty.
**Representative Authors:** Lyn Lifshin, Abby Bogomolny, and Abdul Jabbar
**Submissions Policy:** Send paper copy to US mail address. No e-mail submissions.
**Simultaneous Subs:** yes
**Reading Period:** 4/1 to 8/1
**Reporting Time:** 2 to 5 months
**Author Payment:** none
**Contests:** People Before Profits Poetry Prize. See http://www.bbbooks.com/contest.html
See Web Site for Contest Guidelines.
**Founded:** 1996

**Non Profit:** yes
**Paid Staff:** 0
**Unpaid Staff:** 2
**ISSN Number/ISBN Number:** ISSN 0965066592
**Average Page Views per Month:** 160,000
**Average Unique Visitors per Month:** 100,000
**Frequency per Year:** 1
**Average Percentage of Pages per Category:** Fiction 10%, Nonfiction 10%, Poetry 70%, Essays 10%
**Ad Rates:** See Web Site for Details.

## Cabinet

**Type:** magazine
**CLMP member:** yes
**Primary Editor/Contact Person:** Sina Najafi
**Address:** 181 Wyckoff St.
Brooklyn, NY 11217
**Web Site Address:** http://www.cabinetmagazine.org/
**Publishes:** essays
**Editorial Focus:** nonfiction essays and art projects
**Representative Authors:** Tom Vanderbilt, Margaret Wertheim, and Slavoj Zizek
**Submissions Policy:** we will only accept full manuscripts for consideration.
**Simultaneous Subs:** yes
**Reading Period:** Year-round
**Reporting Time:** 1 to 2 months
**Author Payment:** none
**Founded:** 2000
**Non Profit:** yes
**Paid Staff:** 2
**Unpaid Staff:** 7
**Distributors:** DAP, Ingram, IPD, Central Books, etc.
**ISSN Number/ISBN Number:** ISSN 1531-1430
**Total Circulation:** 10,000
**Paid Circulation:** 2,800
**Average Print Run:** 11,000
**Subscription Rate:** Individual $28/Institution $34
**Single Copy Price:** $10
**Current Volume/Issue:** Issue 19
**Frequency per Year:** 4
**Backfile Available:** yes
**Unsolicited Ms. Received:** yes
**% of Unsolicited Ms. Published per Year:** 5%
**Format:** perfect
**Size:** H 10" W 8"
**Average Pages:** 112
**Ads:** yes
**Ad Rates:** See Web Site for Details.

# The Cafe Irreal

**Type:** online
**CLMP member:** yes
**Primary Editor/Contact Person:** G.S. Evans
**Web Site Address:** http://www.cafeirreal.com
**Publishes:** essays, fiction, and translation
**Editorial Focus:** We present a kind of fantastic fiction infrequently published in English, resembling the work of Kafka, Borges, or Barthelme.
**Recent Awards Received:** One of the top five "online markets" according to the June 2003 issue of Writer's Digest magazine.
**Representative Authors:** Ana Mar,a Shua, Charles Simic, and Norman Lock
**Submissions Policy:** We accept unsolicited fiction up to 2,000 words in length. There is no minimum length. We accept only electronic submissions.
**Simultaneous Subs:** no
**Reading Period:** Year-round
**Reporting Time:** 1 to 2 months
**Author Payment:** cash
**Founded:** 1998
**Non Profit:** yes
**Paid Staff:** 0
**Unpaid Staff:** 2
**Average Page Views per Month:** 20,000
**Average Unique Visitors per Month:** 10,000
**Frequency per Year:** 4
**Average Percentage of Pages per Category:** Fiction 75%, Essays 5%, Art 5%, Translation 15%
**Ads:** no

# Cairn

**Type:** magazine
**CLMP member:** no
**Primary Editor/Contact Person:** Tom Heffernan/Lindsay Hess
**Address:** 1700 Dogwood Mile
Laurinburg, NC 28352
**Web Site Address:** http://www.sapc.edu/sapress
**Publishes:** fiction, nonfiction, and poetry
**Editorial Focus:** We look for excellent literary prose and poetry. Our name means marking the way. New writers are our mission.
**Representative Authors:** Robert Creeley, Dana Levin, and Ilya Kaminsky
**Submissions Policy:** SASE, manuscripts not returned, electronic submissions okay, up to 20 pages of fiction/nonfiction, 10 pages of poetry
**Simultaneous Subs:** yes
**Reading Period:** 9/1 to 12/15

**Reporting Time:** 8 to 12 weeks
**Author Payment:** copies and subscription
**Contests:** See Web Site for Contest Guidelines.
**Founded:** 1969
**Non Profit:** yes
**Paid Staff:** 3
**Unpaid Staff:** 4
**Total Circulation:** 500
**Paid Circulation:** 100
**Average Print Run:** 1,000
**Subscription Rate:** Individual $6/Institution $6
**Single Copy Price:** $8
**Current Volume/Issue:** Issue 37
**Frequency per Year:** 1
**Backfile Available:** yes
**Unsolicited Ms. Received:** yes
**% of Unsolicited Ms. Published per Year:** 5%
**Format:** perfect
**Size:** H 8.5" W 5.5"
**Average Pages:** 150
**Ads:** no

# Calaca Press

**Type:** press
**CLMP member:** no
**Primary Editor/Contact Person:** Brent E. Beltran
**Address:** P.O. Box 2309
National City, CA 91951
**Web Site Address:** http://calacapress.com
**Publishes:** fiction
**Editorial Focus:** Calaca Press is dedicated to publishing and producing works by progressive Chicano and Latino voices.
**Representative Authors:** Raul R. Salinas, Alurista, and Tatiana de la Tierra
**Submissions Policy:** Calaca only accepts submissions when we make a call. No unsolicited manuscripts.
**Simultaneous Subs:** yes
**Reading Period:** 11/11 to 2/2
**Reporting Time:** 1 to 12 months
**Author Payment:** copies
**Founded:** 1997
**Non Profit:** no
**Paid Staff:** 0
**Unpaid Staff:** 2
**Distributors:** SPD and Baker & Taylor
**Number of Books Published per Year:** 2.333
**Titles in Print:** 15
**Average Percentage Printed:** Paperback 50%, Chapbook 25%, Other 25%

# Callaloo

**Type:** magazine
**CLMP member:** yes
**Primary Editor/Contact Person:** Charles H. Rowell
**Address:** Department of English
Texas A&M University 4227 TAMU
College Station, TX 77843-4227
**Publishes:** essays, fiction, nonfiction, poetry, reviews, art, and translation
**Editorial Focus:** A forum for new and established creative writers, literary and cultural critics, and visual artists in the African Diaspora.
**Representative Authors:** Rita Dove, Percival Everett, and Yusef Komunyakaa
**Submissions Policy:** All manuscripts should be submitted in triplicate, with name/address on one page and SASE. Documented articles in MLA format.
**Simultaneous Subs:** no
**Reading Period:** Year-round
**Reporting Time:** 3 to 6 months
**Author Payment:** copies
**Founded:** 1976
**Non Profit:** yes
**Paid Staff:** 3
**Unpaid Staff:** 6
**Distributors:** Johns Hopkins Press
**ISSN Number/ISBN Number:** ISSN 0161-2492
**Total Circulation:** 1,110
**Paid Circulation:** 1,003
**Subscription Rate:** Individual $39/Institution $107
**Single Copy Price:** $15
**Current Volume/Issue:** 26/4
**Frequency per Year:** 4
**Backfile Available:** yes
**Unsolicited Ms. Received:** yes
**% of Unsolicited Ms. Published per Year:** 100%
**Format:** perfect

# Calyx, A Journal of Art and Lit by Women

**Type:** magazine
**CLMP member:** yes
**Primary Editor/Contact Person:** Margarita Donnelly, Director
**Address:** P.O. Box B
216 SW Madison Ave. E#7
Corvallis, OR 97339
**Web Site Address:** http://www.calyxpress.com
**Publishes:** essays, fiction, nonfiction, poetry, reviews, art, and translation
**Editorial Focus:** Publish fine art and literature by women in an elegant format.
**Representative Authors:** Marianne Villanueva, Susan Elbe, and Ingrid Wendt
**Submissions Policy:** Submit up to 6 poems, prose 5,000 words, reviews 500-1,000 words, art 6 slides or black and white photos-all with bio and SASE.
**Simultaneous Subs:** yes
**Reading Period:** 10/1 to 12/31
**Reporting Time:** 6 to 8 months
**Author Payment:** copies and subscription
**Contests:** Lois Cranston Memorial Poetry Prize, 3 poems, March 1-May 31, $15 submission fee per entry.
See Web Site for Contest Guidelines.
**Founded:** 1976
**Non Profit:** yes
**Paid Staff:** 4
**Unpaid Staff:** 75
**Distributors:** Ingram, Periodicals, Armadillo, Small Changes
**ISSN Number/ISBN Number:** ISSN 0147-1627
**Total Circulation:** 2,500
**Paid Circulation:** 900
**Average Print Run:** 3,000
**Subscription Rate:** Individual $21/Institution $27
**Single Copy Price:** $9.50
**Current Volume/Issue:** 22/3
**Frequency per Year:** 2
**Backfile Available:** yes
**Unsolicited Ms. Received:** yes
**% of Unsolicited Ms. Published per Year:** 100%
**Format:** perfect
**Size:** H 8" W 6"
**Average Pages:** 128
**Ads:** yes
**Ad Rates:** $550/full page, $285/half page, $150/quarter page

# Canadian Literature

**Type:** magazine
**CLMP member:** no
**Primary Editor/Contact Person:** Laurie Ricou
**Address:** Buchanan E158
1866 Main Mall
Vancouver, BC V6T 1Z1
**Web Site Address:** http://www.canlit.ca
**Publishes:** essays, nonfiction, poetry, reviews, and translation
**Editorial Focus:** Canadian Literature welcomes sub-

missions of articles, interviews, and brief commentaries on writers and writing in Canada,
**Representative Authors:** George Elliott Clarke, Anne Carson, and W.H. New
**Submissions Policy:** Articles should follow current MLA bibliographic format. Maximum word length for articles is 6,500 words.
**Simultaneous Subs:** no
**Reading Period:** Year-round
**Reporting Time:** 2 to 3 months
**Author Payment:** none
**Founded:** 1959
**Non Profit:** yes
**Paid Staff:** 2
**Unpaid Staff:** 5
**ISSN Number/ISBN Number:** ISSN 0008-4360
**Total Circulation:** 1,200
**Paid Circulation:** 1,000
**Subscription Rate:** Individual $69 US/Institution $89 US
**Single Copy Price:** $19
**Current Volume/Issue:** Issue 181
**Frequency per Year:** 4
**Backfile Available:** yes
**Unsolicited Ms. Received:** yes
**% of Unsolicited Ms. Published per Year:** 10%
**Format:** perfect
**Size:** H 9" W 6"
**Average Pages:** 208
**Ads:** yes
**Ad Rates:** $400 US
See Web Site for Details.

## Canadian Poetry: Studies, Documents, Reviews

**Type:** magazine
**CLMP member:** no
**Primary Editor/Contact Person:** D.M.R. Bentley
**Address:** Department of English
University of Western Ontario
London, ON N6A 3K7
**Web Site Address:** http://www.canadianpoetry.ca
**Publishes:** essays and reviews
**Editorial Focus:** Canadian Poetry publishes scholarly article, documents and reviews on poetry from all periods and regions in Canada.
**Representative Authors:** Frank Davey, W.H. New, and Tracy Ware
**Submissions Policy:** Submissions should follow the MLA style, and be submitted in duplicate and with an accompanying stamped, addressed envelope.
**Simultaneous Subs:** yes
**Reading Period:** Year-round
**Reporting Time:** 3 to 6 weeks
**Author Payment:** none and copies
**Founded:** 1977
**Non Profit:** yes
**Paid Staff:** 0
**Unpaid Staff:** 2
**Distributors:** Canada Post, IUTS
**ISSN Number/ISBN Number:** ISSN 0704 5646
**Total Circulation:** 400
**Paid Circulation:** 400
**Average Print Run:** 400
**Subscription Rate:** Individual $15/Institution $18
**Single Copy Price:** $7.50
**Current Volume/Issue:** Issue 55
**Frequency per Year:** 2
**Backfile Available:** yes
**Unsolicited Ms. Received:** yes
**% of Unsolicited Ms. Published per Year:** 40%
**Format:** perfect
**Size:** H 9" W 6"
**Average Pages:** 130
**Ads:** yes
**Ad Rates:** Exchange
See Web Site for Details.

## The Canary

**Type:** magazine
**CLMP member:** yes
**Primary Editor/Contact Person:** Joshua Edwards
**Address:** 512 Clear Lake Road
Kemah, TX 77565
**Web Site Address:** http://www.thecanary.org
**Publishes:** poetry
**Editorial Focus:** The Canary publishes poems that, like the eponymous bird, venture into the labyrinthine mineshafts of mind and culture.
**Recent Awards Received:** Best American Poetry
**Representative Authors:** D.A. Powell, Rae Armantrout, and Fanny Howe
**Submissions Policy:** August 1-December 1. E-mail (as Word or RTF) up to six poems w/ a brief cover letter to: submissions@thecanary.org
**Simultaneous Subs:** yes
**Reading Period:** 8/1 to 12/1
**Reporting Time:** 2 to 4 months
**Author Payment:** copies
**Contests:** See Web Site for Contest Guidelines.

**Founded:** 2002
**Non Profit:** no
**Paid Staff:** 0
**Unpaid Staff:** 3
**Distributors:** DeBoer, Ingram
**ISSN Number/ISBN Number:** ISSN 1543-0030
**Total Circulation:** 700
**Paid Circulation:** 100
**Average Print Run:** 1,100
**Subscription Rate:** Individual $30/Institution $30
**Single Copy Price:** $10
**Current Volume/Issue:** Issue 5
**Frequency per Year:** 1
**Backfile Available:** yes
**Unsolicited Ms. Received:** yes
**% of Unsolicited Ms. Published per Year:** 2%
**Format:** perfect
**Size:** H 8" W 7"
**Average Pages:** 120
**Ads:** no

## The Caribbean Writer

**Type:** magazine
**CLMP member:** yes
**Primary Editor/Contact Person:** Mr. Marvin E. Williams
**Address:** University of the Virgin Islands
RR 1, Box 10,000
Kingshill, St. Croix, VI 00850
**Web Site Address:**
http://www.TheCaribbeanWriter.com
**Publishes:** essays, fiction, nonfiction, poetry, reviews, art, and translation
**Editorial Focus:** International literary anthology with Caribbean focus. Work should reflect Caribbean heritage, experience or perspective.
**Recent Awards Received:** Pushcart Prize (2000)
**Representative Authors:** Mervyn Morris, Geoffrey Philp, and Frank Birbalsingh
**Submissions Policy:** Put name, address, and title of work on separate sheet. Title only on work. Include brief bio. Type (double-space) all work.
**Simultaneous Subs:** yes
**Reading Period:** 8/1 to 1/30
**Reporting Time:** 2 to 3 months
**Author Payment:** copies
**Contests:** Prizes awarded for best poetry, short fiction, first-time publication, Caribbean author and Virgin Islands author.
See Web Site for Contest Guidelines.

**Founded:** 1987
**Non Profit:** yes
**Paid Staff:** 2
**Unpaid Staff:** 0
**Distributors:** Ubiquity (US), Novelty Trading (Jam), Lexicon (Trinidad)
**ISSN Number/ISBN Number:** ISBN 0-9769273-0-6
**Total Circulation:** 1,000
**Paid Circulation:** 175
**Average Print Run:** 1,200
**Subscription Rate:** Individual $25/Institution $40
**Single Copy Price:** $15
**Current Volume/Issue:** Volume 19
**Frequency per Year:** 1
**Backfile Available:** yes
**Unsolicited Ms. Received:** yes
**% of Unsolicited Ms. Published per Year:** 80%
**Format:** perfect
**Size:** H 9" W 6"
**Average Pages:** 304
**Ads:** yes
**Ad Rates:** Full page $250, 1/2 page $150, 1/4 page $100
See Web Site for Details.

## The Carolina Quarterly

**Type:** magazine
**CLMP member:** no
**Primary Editor/Contact Person:** Tessa Joseph
**Address:** CB 3520, Greenlaw Hall
UNC-Chapel Hill
Chapel Hill, NC 27599
**Web Site Address:** http://www.unc.edu/depts/cqonline
**Publishes:** essays, fiction, nonfiction, poetry, reviews, and art
**Representative Authors:** Elizabeth Spencer, Ha Jin, and Richard Wilbur
**Submissions Policy:** No e-mail submissions. One clean copy addressed to appropriate genre editor, containing contact information.
**Simultaneous Subs:** no
**Reading Period:** 8/3 to 4/4
**Reporting Time:** 4 to 6 months
**Author Payment:** copies
**Founded:** 1948
**Non Profit:** yes
**Paid Staff:** 0
**Unpaid Staff:** 50
**Distributors:** Ingram, EBSCO, Swets Blackwell

**Total Circulation:** 600
**Paid Circulation:** 400
**Subscription Rate:** Individual $18/Institution $21
**Single Copy Price:** $6
**Current Volume/Issue:** 56/55.3
**Frequency per Year:** 3
**Backfile Available:** yes
**Unsolicited Ms. Received:** yes
**Format:** perfect
**Average Pages:** 100
**Ads:** yes

# Carousel

**Type:** magazine
**CLMP member:** yes
**Primary Editor/Contact Person:** Mark Laliberte,
Managing Editor
**Address:** UC274
University of Guelph
Guelph, ON N1G 2W1
**Web Site Address:** http://www.carouselmagazine.ca
**Publishes:** fiction, poetry, and art
**Editorial Focus:** We are a hybrid literary and arts
mag: from cover to cover, we act as a venue for those
interested in "exploring the page."
**Recent Awards Received:** Honorable Mention for
"Best Art Direction for an Entire Issue, 2004" by The
National Magazine Awards Foundation (Canada)
**Submissions Policy:** Please visit website for our most
current submission guidelines. E-mail submissions are
accepted.
**Simultaneous Subs:** yes
**Reading Period:** Year-round
**Reporting Time:** 1 to 2 months
**Author Payment:** cash, copies, and subscription
**Contests:** Occasional contests and special projects
**Founded:** 1983
**Non Profit:** yes
**Paid Staff:** 0
**Unpaid Staff:** 1
**Distributors:** Magazines Canada, Ubiquity, DeBoer
**ISSN Number/ISBN Number:** ISSN 0835-7994
**Total Circulation:** 1,000
**Paid Circulation:** 300
**Average Print Run:** 1,200
**Subscription Rate:** Individual $25/2 years/Institution
$34/2 years
**Single Copy Price:** $10
**Current Volume/Issue:** Issue 18
**Frequency per Year:** 2

**Backfile Available:** yes
**Unsolicited Ms. Received:** yes
**Format:** perfect
**Size:** H 9.5" W 7.5"
**Average Pages:** 76
**Ads:** yes
**Ad Rates:** See Web Site for Details.

# Carve Magazine

**Type:** online
**CLMP member:** yes
**Primary Editor/Contact Person:** Melvin Sterne
**Address:** P.O. Box 1573
Tallahassee, FL 95617
**Web Site Address:** http://www.carvezine.com
**Publishes:** fiction
**Editorial Focus:** We publish short stories only, literary
fiction. Open to new authors but only strong, polished
writing.
**Representative Authors:** Sallie Bingham, Lynn
Stegner, and Kate Braverman
**Submissions Policy:** Electronic submission preferred,
mail-ins OK provided author can furnish electronic
copy on request. Guidelines per website.
**Simultaneous Subs:** yes
**Reading Period:** Year-round
**Reporting Time:** 1 to 3 months
**Author Payment:** none
**Contests:** See Web Site for Contest Guidelines.
**Founded:** 2000
**Non Profit:** no
**Paid Staff:** 0
**Unpaid Staff:** 9
**ISSN Number/ISBN Number:** ISSN 1529-272X
**Backfile Available:** no
**Average Page Views per Month:** 17,143
**Average Unique Visitors per Month:** 9,505
**Frequency per Year:** 6
**Publish Print Anthology:** yes
Price: $10
**Average Percentage of Pages per Category:** Fiction
100%
**Ads:** no

## CavanKerry Press, Ltd.

**Type:** press
**CLMP member:** yes
**Primary Editor/Contact Person:** Joan Cusack Handler
**Address:** 6 Horizon Rd #2901
Fort Lee, NJ 07024
**Web Site Address:** http://www.cavankerrypress.org
**Publishes:** poetry
**Representative Authors:** Mary Ruefle, Robert Cording, and Howard Levy
**Simultaneous Subs:** yes
**Reading Period:** 5/06 to 7/06
**Reporting Time:** 6 to 12 months
**Author Payment:** cash and copies
**Founded:** 1999
**Non Profit:** yes
**Paid Staff:** 5
**Unpaid Staff:** 3
**Distributors:** SPD
**Number of Books Published per Year:** 3
**Titles in Print:** 19
**Average Percentage Printed:** Paperback 100%
**Backfile Available:** yes

## The Center for Literary Publishing

**Type:** press
**CLMP member:** yes
**Primary Editor/Contact Person:** Stephanie G'Schwind
**Address:** Department of English
Colorado State University
Fort Collins, CO 80523
**Web Site Address:**
http://coloradoreview.colostate.edu
**Publishes:** essays, fiction, nonfiction, poetry, reviews, and translation
**Editorial Focus:** Publisher of Colorado Review, the Colorado Prize for Poetry, and the Series in Contemporary Fiction.
**Representative Authors:** Rusty Morrison, Dean Young, and G.C. Waldrep
**Submissions Policy:** See guidelines for Colorado Prize for Poetry on our website. Not currently accepting submissions to Series in Cont. Fiction.
**Simultaneous Subs:** yes
**Reading Period:** 9/1 to 5/1
**Reporting Time:** 1 to 3 months
**Author Payment:** royalties, cash, and copies
**Contests:** Colorado Prize for Poetry and the Nelligan

Prize for Short Fiction.
See Web Site for Contest Guidelines.
**Founded:** 1992
**Non Profit:** yes
**Paid Staff:** 1
**Unpaid Staff:** 20
**Distributors:** Ingram, Kent News, UP of Colorado, U of Oklahoma P
**ISSN Number/ISBN Number:** 1046-3348/0-885635
**Number of Books Published per Year:** 1
**Titles in Print:** 12
**Average Print Run:** 750
**Average Percentage Printed:** Paperback 100%
**Average Price:** $14.95

## Century Press

**Type:** press
**CLMP member:** no
**Primary Editor/Contact Person:** Robert W. Olmsted
**Address:** PO BOX 298
Thomaston, ME 04861
**Web Site Address:** http://www.americanletters.org
**Publishes:** fiction, nonfiction, and poetry
**Editorial Focus:** Anything!
**Representative Authors:** Diane Lau Cordrey, Steven Janasik, and Nora Hamilton
**Submissions Policy:** Send personal marketing plan first. No electronic submissions or queries.
**Simultaneous Subs:** yes
**Reading Period:** Year-round
**Reporting Time:** 1 to 2 weeks
**Author Payment:** royalties
**Founded:** 1999
**Non Profit:** yes
**Paid Staff:** 1
**Unpaid Staff:** 1
**Distributors:** Baker & Taylor, Ingram, Barnes & Noble, amazon.com
**ISSN Number/ISBN Number:** ISBN 0-89754-xxx-x
**Number of Books Published per Year:** 2
**Titles in Print:** 6
**Average Percentage Printed:** Hardcover 5%, Paperback 95%

## Chain Magazine/'A 'A Arts

**Type:** magazine
**CLMP member:** yes
**Address:** Dept. of English, Mills College
5000 MacArthur Blvd.

Oakland, CA 94613
**Web Site Address:** http://www.temple.edu/chain
**Publishes:** essays, fiction, nonfiction, poetry, and art
**Reading Period:** Year-round
**Reporting Time:** 1 to 2 months
**Author Payment:** none
**Founded:** 1993
**Non Profit:** no
**Backfile Available:** yes

## Chapman Magazine

**Type:** magazine
**CLMP member:** no
**Primary Editor/Contact Person:** Joy Hendry
**Address:** 4 Broughton Place
Edinburgh, UK EH1 3RX
**Web Site Address:** http://www.chapman-pub.co.uk
**Publishes:** essays, fiction, nonfiction, and poetry
**Editorial Focus:** The best in Scottish and international poetry, short stories and critical essays. Scottish in location, international in outlook.
**Representative Authors:** Alasdair Reid, Louise Welsh, and Sorley MacLean
**Submissions Policy:** Covering letter w/ enough IRCs to cover reply. No IRCs means a reply is not likely. Guidelines on request.
**Simultaneous Subs:** yes
**Reading Period:** Year-round
**Reporting Time:** 4 to 8 weeks
**Author Payment:** cash, copies, and subscription
**Founded:** 1970
**Non Profit:** yes
**Paid Staff:** 2
**Unpaid Staff:** 4
**ISSN Number/ISBN Number:** 0308-2695/1-903700
**Total Circulation:** 2,000
**Paid Circulation:** 1,000
**Average Print Run:** 2,000
**Subscription Rate:** Individual $48/Institution $58
**Single Copy Price:** $12.50
**Current Volume/Issue:** Issue 107
**Frequency per Year:** 3
**Backfile Available:** yes
**Unsolicited Ms. Received:** yes
**% of Unsolicited Ms. Published per Year:** 0.5%
**Format:** perfect
**Size:** H 8.5" W 6"
**Average Pages:** 144
**Ads:** yes
**Ad Rates:** ad sheet on request (e-mail)

## Chatoyant

**Type:** press
**CLMP member:** yes
**Primary Editor/Contact Person:** Suki Wessling
**Address:** P.O. Box 832
Aptos, CA 95001
**Web Site Address:** http://chatoyant.com
**Publishes:** poetry
**Editorial Focus:** Well-crafted poetry.
**Representative Authors:** Penny Cagan, Virginia Chase Sutton, and William Minor
**Submissions Policy:** No unsolicited submissions. All unsolicited mail and e-mail will not receive a reply.
**Simultaneous Subs:** no
**Reading Period:** Year-round
**Reporting Time:** 3 to 6 months
**Author Payment:** royalties
**Founded:** 1997
**Non Profit:** no
**Paid Staff:** 1
**Unpaid Staff:** 1
**Wholesalers:** Baker & Taylor
**ISSN Number/ISBN Number:** ISBN 0-9661452
**Number of Books Published per Year:** 1
**Titles in Print:** 4
**Average Percentage Printed:** Paperback 90%, Chapbook 10%
**Backfile Available:** yes

## The Chattahoochee Review

**Type:** magazine
**CLMP member:** yes
**Primary Editor/Contact Person:** Marc Fitten
**Address:** 2101 Womack Road
Dunwoody, GA 30338-4497
**Web Site Address:** http://www.chattahoochee-review.org
**Publishes:** essays, fiction, nonfiction, poetry, reviews, art, and translation
**Editorial Focus:** Literary quality in a variety of genres and subject matter. See website for details,
**Representative Authors:** George Singleton, Ignacio Padilla, and William Gay
**Submissions Policy:** See website for details
**Simultaneous Subs:** yes
**Reading Period:** Year-round
**Reporting Time:** 2 to 3 months
**Author Payment:** cash and copies
**Contests:** See Web Site for Contest Guidelines.
**Founded:** 1980

**Non Profit:** yes
**Paid Staff:** 3
**Unpaid Staff:** 10
**ISSN Number/ISBN Number:** ISSN 0741-9155
**Total Circulation:** 1,250
**Paid Circulation:** 800
**Average Print Run:** 1,250
**Subscription Rate:** Individual $20/Institution $20
**Single Copy Price:** $6
**Current Volume/Issue:** 26/1
**Frequency per Year:** 4
**Backfile Available:** yes
**Unsolicited Ms. Received:** yes
**% of Unsolicited Ms. Published per Year:** 1%
**Format:** perfect
**Size:** H 6" W 9"
**Average Pages:** 120
**Ads:** yes
**Ad Rates:** $200 for full page

## Chelsea Editions

**Type:** press
**CLMP member:** no
**Primary Editor/Contact Person:** Alfredo de Palchi
**Address:** P.O. Box 773 Cooper Station
New York, NY 10276-0773
**Publishes:** poetry and translation
**Editorial Focus:** Translations of modern Italian poetry into English. Bilingual edition
**Representative Authors:** Milo De Angelis, Giorgio Caproni, and Camillo Sbarbaro
**Submissions Policy:** Send 10-12 translations plus bio
**Simultaneous Subs:** yes
**Reading Period:** 9/1 to 5/31
**Reporting Time:** 2 to 4 months
**Author Payment:** cash
**Founded:** 2002
**Non Profit:** yes
**Paid Staff:** 0
**Unpaid Staff:** 1
**ISSN Number/ISBN Number:** 0009-2185/0-9725271
**Number of Books Published per Year:** 2
**Titles in Print:** 2
**Average Percentage Printed:** Paperback 100%

## Chelsea

**Type:** magazine
**CLMP member:** yes
**Primary Editor/Contact Person:** Alfredo de Palchi
**Address:** P.O. Box 773 Cooper Station

New York, NY 10276-0773
**Web Site Address:** http://www.chelseamag.org
**Publishes:** essays, fiction, nonfiction, poetry, reviews, and translation
**Editorial Focus:** Original and eclectic
**Recent Awards Received:** Pushcart Prize 2005 for Fiction
**Submissions Policy:** 3-6 poems, 25-30 pp double-spaced prose. Query for book reviews.
**Simultaneous Subs:** no
**Reading Period:** 9/1 to 6/30
**Reporting Time:** 2 to 4 months
**Author Payment:** copies
**Contests:** Annual deadlines: Short Fiction: June 15. Poetry: December 15. Send SASE or check our web-site for complete guidelines
See Web Site for Contest Guidelines.
**Founded:** 1958
**Non Profit:** yes
**Paid Staff:** 0
**Unpaid Staff:** 6
**Distributors:** DeBoer, Ingram, Ubiquity
**Wholesalers:** EBSCO, Swets, Blackwell, Huber & Lang
**ISSN Number/ISBN Number:** ISSN 0009-2185
**Total Circulation:** 2,200
**Paid Circulation:** 700
**Average Print Run:** 2,200
**Subscription Rate:** Individual $13/Institution $18
**Single Copy Price:** $8
**Current Volume/Issue:** Issue 79
**Frequency per Year:** 2
**Backfile Available:** yes
**Unsolicited Ms. Received:** yes
**% of Unsolicited Ms. Published per Year:** 2%
**Format:** perfect
**Size:** H 9" W 6"
**Average Pages:** 200
**Ads:** yes
**Ad Rates:** $125 full page, $75 1/2 page

## Chicago Review

**Type:** magazine
**CLMP member:** yes
**Primary Editor/Contact Person:** Eirik Steinhoff
**Address:** 5801 S. Kenwood Ave.
Chicago, IL 60637
**Web Site Address:** humanities.uchicago.edu/review
**Publishes:** essays, fiction, nonfiction, poetry, reviews, art, and translation
**Submissions Policy:** read the magazine before sub-

mitting.
**Simultaneous Subs:** yes
**Reading Period:** 9/30 to 5/31
**Reporting Time:** 3 to 6 months
**Author Payment:** copies
**Founded:** 1946
**Non Profit:** yes
**Paid Staff:** 3
**Unpaid Staff:** 15
**Total Circulation:** 2,000`
**Paid Circulation:** 900
**Subscription Rate:** Individual $18/Institution $42
**Single Copy Price:** $6
**Current Volume/Issue:** 49/2
**Frequency per Year:** 3
**Backfile Available:** yes
**Unsolicited Ms. Received:** yes
**Format:** perfect

# Chicory Blue Press

**Type:** press
**CLMP member:** yes
**Primary Editor/Contact Person:** Sondra Zeidenstein
**Address:** 795 East St. N.
Goshen, CT 06756
**Web Site Address:** http://www.chicorybluepress.com
**Publishes:** poetry
**Editorial Focus:** focuses on strong voices of women poets over 65
**Representative Authors:** Honor Moore, Betty Buchsbaum, and Nellie Wong
**Submissions Policy:** send ten poems and brief cover letter
**Simultaneous Subs:** yes
**Reading Period:** Year-round
**Reporting Time:** 3 to 4 months
**Author Payment:** none, royalties, and copies
**Founded:** 1986
**Non Profit:** no
**Paid Staff:** no
**Unpaid Staff:** no
**Distributors:** SPD
**Number of Books Published per Year:** 1-2
**Titles in Print:** 12
**Average Print Run:** 750
**Average Percentage Printed:** Paperback 100%
**Average Price:** $16

# Cimarron Review

**Type:** magazine
**CLMP member:** yes
**Primary Editor/Contact Person:** E.P. Walkiewicz
**Address:** 205 Morrill
Oklahoma State University
Stillwater, OK 74078-0135
**Web Site Address:** http://cimarronreview.okstate.edu
**Publishes:** essays, fiction, nonfiction, poetry, reviews, art, and translation
**Editorial Focus:** Gritty realism with healthy doses of irony, humor (when possible), drama, intelligence and humanity.
**Recent Awards Received:** N/A
**Representative Authors:** Rick Moody, Kim Addonizio, and Gary Fincke
**Submissions Policy:** Send 3-6 poems, 1 short story or 1 nonfiction piece with an SASE. E-mail submissions accepted from foreign countries only.
**Simultaneous Subs:** yes
**Reading Period:** Year-round
**Reporting Time:** 2 to 6 months
**Author Payment:** copies
**Contests:** none
**Founded:** 1967
**Non Profit:** yes
**Paid Staff:** 3
**Unpaid Staff:** 17
**Distributors:** Ingram, Kent News
**ISSN Number/ISBN Number:** 0009-6849
**Total Circulation:** 600
**Paid Circulation:** 260
**Average Print Run:** 600
**Subscription Rate:** Individual $24/Institution $24
**Single Copy Price:** $7
**Current Volume/Issue:** 152
**Frequency per Year:** 4
**Backfile Available:** yes
**Unsolicited Ms. Received:** yes
**% of Unsolicited Ms. Published per Year:** 3%
**Format:** perfect
**Size:** H 9" W 6"
**Average Pages:** 112
**Ads:** yes
**Ad Rates:** Contact us via e-mail: cimarronreview@yahoo.com

## The Cincinnati Review

**Type:** magazine
**CLMP member:** yes
**Primary Editor/Contact Person:** Nicola Mason, Managing Editor
**Address:** University of Cincinnati
P.O. Box 210069
Cincinnati, OH 45221-0069
**Web Site Address:** http://cincinnatireview.com
**Publishes:** essays, fiction, nonfiction, poetry, reviews, art, and translation
**Editorial Focus:** We publish poetry and prose of any stripe provided there is great care given to craft.
**Recent Awards Received:** Poems and fiction appeared in Best American Poetry and New Stories from the South
**Representative Authors:** Antonya Nelson, Rosanna Warren, and George Singleton
**Submissions Policy:** Submit up to ten pages of poetry or up to forty pages of fiction. SASE required for response. No e-mail or fax submissions.
**Simultaneous Subs:** yes
**Reading Period:** 9/1 to 5/31
**Reporting Time:** 1 to 2 months
**Author Payment:** cash, copies, and subscription
**Founded:** 2003
**Non Profit:** yes
**Paid Staff:** 5
**Unpaid Staff:** 8
**ISSN Number/ISBN Number:** ISSN 1546-9034
**Total Circulation:** 500
**Paid Circulation:** 500
**Average Print Run:** 1,000
**Subscription Rate:** Individual $15/Institution $30
**Single Copy Price:** $9
**Current Volume/Issue:** 2/2
**Frequency per Year:** 2
**Backfile Available:** yes
**Unsolicited Ms. Received:** yes
**% of Unsolicited Ms. Published per Year:** 25%
**Format:** perfect
**Size:** H 9" W 6"
**Average Pages:** 225
**Ads:** yes
**Ad Rates:** upon request
See Web Site for Details.

## Cinco Puntos Press

**Type:** press
**CLMP member:** no
**Primary Editor/Contact Person:** Lee or Bobby Byrd
**Address:** 701 Texas Ave.
El Paso, TX 79901
**Web Site Address:** http://www.cincopuntos.com
**Publishes:** fiction and nonfiction
**Editorial Focus:** Literatures of Southwest, the Border region, and Latin America. Known for bilingual children's books with political edge.
**Recent Awards Received:** Lannan Foundation 2005 Cultural Freedom Foundation
**Representative Authors:** Benjamin Alire Saenz, Luis Alberto Urrea, and Joe Hayes
**Submissions Policy:** Contact Lee Byrd before submitting. We do not accept unsolicited manuscripts. Please study our list before sending blindly.
**Simultaneous Subs:** yes
**Reading Period:** Year-round
**Reporting Time:** 2 to 3 months
**Author Payment:** royalties
**Contests:** See Web Site for Contest Guidelines.
**Founded:** 1985
**Non Profit:** no
**Paid Staff:** 7
**Unpaid Staff:** 0
**Distributors:** Consortium
**Wholesalers:** All
**ISSN Number/ISBN Number:** ISBN 0-938317
**Number of Books Published per Year:** 6-8
**Titles in Print:** 70
**Average Print Run:** 7,000
**Average Percentage Printed:** Hardcover 40%, Paperback 60%
**Average Price:** $15.95

## Circumference

**Type:** magazine
**CLMP member:** yes
**Primary Editor/Contact Person:** J. Kronovet, S. Heim
**Address:** P.O. Box 27
New York, NY 10159
**Web Site Address:**
http://www.circumferencemag.com
**Publishes:** poetry and translation
**Editorial Focus:** Circumference publishes new translations of poetry. We print original poems side-by-side with translations.
**Submissions Policy:** Mail 5-10 translations. Include originals.
**Simultaneous Subs:** yes
**Reading Period:** Year-round

**Reporting Time:** 1 to 5 months
**Author Payment:** copies and subscription
**Founded:** 2002
**Non Profit:** yes
**Paid Staff:** 0
**Unpaid Staff:** 3
**Distributors:** Ingram, DeBoer, Ubiquity
**Total Circulation:** 1,800
**Paid Circulation:** 400
**Average Print Run:** 2,000
**Subscription Rate:** Individual $15/Institution $40
**Single Copy Price:** $10
**Current Volume/Issue:** 2/2
**Frequency per Year:** 2
**Backfile Available:** yes
**Unsolicited Ms. Received:** yes
**Format:** perfect
**Ads:** yes

## City Lights Books

**Type:** press
**CLMP member:** no
**Primary Editor/Contact Person:** Editorial Staff/City
Lights Books
**Address:** 261 Columbus Ave.
San Francisco, CA 94133
**Web Site Address:** http://www.citylights.com
**Publishes:** fiction, nonfiction, and poetry
**Editorial Focus:** Literary fiction, translations, poetry
and books on radical politics, social and cultural histo-
ry, and current events.
**Representative Authors:** Julio CortΩzar, Rebecca
Brown, and Michael Parenti
**Submissions Policy:** Please see our website for sub-
mission guidelines.
**Simultaneous Subs:** no
**Reading Period:** Year-round
**Reporting Time:** 2 to 6 months
**Author Payment:** royalties
**Founded:** 1955
**Non Profit:** no
**Paid Staff:** 4
**Unpaid Staff:** 2
**Distributors:** Consortium Books
**Wholesalers:** Ingram, Baker & Taylor, and all majors
**ISSN Number/ISBN Number:** ISBN 0-87286
**Number of Books Published per Year:** 12
**Titles in Print:** 200
**Average Percentage Printed:** Paperback 100%

## Cleveland State University Poetry Center

**Type:** press
**CLMP member:** no
**Primary Editor/Contact Person:** Dr. Ted Lardner
**Address:** 2121 Euclid Ave.
Cleveland, OH 44115-2214
**Web Site Address:** http://www.csuohio.edu/poet-
rycenter
**Publishes:** poetry
**Representative Authors:** Tim Seibles and Jared
Carter
**Submissions Policy:** Only through annual contests.
2004 contests have been suspended.
**Simultaneous Subs:** yes
**Reading Period:** 11/1 to 6/15
**Reporting Time:** 7 to 8 months
**Author Payment:** cash and copies
**Contests:** Have offered first book and "open" compe-
titions. Contests have been suspended for 2004. See
website.
See Web Site for Contest Guidelines.
**Founded:** 1971
**Non Profit:** yes
**Paid Staff:** 1
**Unpaid Staff:** 1
**Distributors:** Spring Church, Ingram
**Wholesalers:** Baker & Taylor, Coutts, Midwest Library
Service
**ISSN Number/ISBN Number:** ISBN 1-880834-
**Number of Books Published per Year:** 4
**Titles in Print:** 120
**Average Percentage Printed:** Hardcover 15%,
Paperback 65%, Chapbook 20%

## Coach House Books

**Type:** press
**CLMP member:** yes
**Primary Editor/Contact Person:** Alana Wilcox
**Address:** 401 Huron St. (rear)
Toronto, ON M5S 2G5
**Web Site Address:** http://www.chbooks.com
**Publishes:** fiction and poetry
**Editorial Focus:** Innovative/experimental fiction and
poetry by Canadian authors
**Representative Authors:** Christian Bˉk, Nicole
Brossard, and Steve McCaffery
**Submissions Policy:** Query letter, CV and sample-
from Canadian authors only
**Simultaneous Subs:** yes

**Reading Period:** Year-round
**Reporting Time:** 2 to 6 months
**Author Payment:** royalties, cash, and copies
**Founded:** 2001
**Non Profit:** no
**Paid Staff:** 3
**Unpaid Staff:** 0
**Distributors:** LitDistCo (Canada), SPD
**Wholesalers:** Ingram, Baker & Taylor
**ISSN Number/ISBN Number:** ISBN 1 55245
**Number of Books Published per Year:** 16
**Titles in Print:** 120
**Average Percentage Printed:** Paperback 100%
**Backfile Available:** yes

# Codhill Press

**Type:** press
**CLMP member:** yes
**Primary Editor/Contact Person:** David Appelbaum
**Address:** 1 Arden Ln.
New Paltz, NY 12561
**Web Site Address:** http://codhill.com
**Publishes:** nonfiction and poetry
**Editorial Focus:** The union of philosophy, poetry, and spirit.
**Representative Authors:** Frederick Franck, Laura Simms, and Christopher Bamford
**Submissions Policy:** query first
**Simultaneous Subs:** no
**Reading Period:** 5/1 to 8/15
**Reporting Time:** 1 to 12 weeks
**Author Payment:** none
**Founded:** 2000
**Non Profit:** no
**Paid Staff:** 0
**Unpaid Staff:** 1
**Distributors:** Steinerbooks
**ISSN Number/ISBN Number:** ISBN 1930337
**Number of Books Published per Year:** 5
**Titles in Print:** 21
**Average Print Run:** 1,000
**Average Percentage Printed:** Paperback 80%, Chapbook 20%
**Average Price:** $14

# Coelacanth Magazine

**Type:** online
**CLMP member:** no
**Primary Editor/Contact Person:** William Delman

**Address:** 35 Gardner St. #10
Allston, MA 02134
**Web Site Address:**
http://www.coelacanthmagazine.com
**Publishes:** essays, fiction, poetry, and art
**Editorial Focus:** To explore the role of classic forms and themes in modernity.
**Representative Authors:** Eleanor Lerman, Janet Buck, and Nick Wolven
**Submissions Policy:** Rolling Deadline. Please include brief bio and cover letter. Electronic submissions preferred.
**Simultaneous Subs:** yes
**Reading Period:** Year-round
**Reporting Time:** 1 to 2 months
**Author Payment:** none
**Founded:** 2001
**Non Profit:** yes
**Paid Staff:** 0
**Unpaid Staff:** 2
**Average Page Views per Month:** 1,550
**Average Unique Visitors per Month:** 657
**Frequency per Year:** 4
**Publish Print Anthology:** no
**Average Percentage of Pages per Category:** Fiction 35%, Poetry 55%, Art 10%
**Ads:** no

# Coffee House Press

**Type:** press
**CLMP member:** yes
**Primary Editor/Contact Person:** Allan Kornblum/Chris Fischbach
**Address:** 27 N. Fourth St, Ste. 400
Minneapolis, MN 55401
**Web Site Address:** http://www.coffeehousepress.org
**Publishes:** essays, fiction, and poetry
**Editorial Focus:** New York School poets, Minnesota Writers, African American and Asian American poetry and fiction, characterized by excellence
**Representative Authors:** Anne Waldman, Karen Tei Yamashita, and Quincy Troupe
**Simultaneous Subs:** no
**Reading Period:** Year-round
**Reporting Time:** 1 to 2 months
**Author Payment:** royalties
**Founded:** 1984
**Non Profit:** yes
**Paid Staff:** 6
**Unpaid Staff:** 3

**Distributors:** Consortium/SPD
**Wholesalers:** Ingram, Baker & Taylor, other major wholesalers
**ISSN Number/ISBN Number:** ISBN 1-56689
**Number of Books Published per Year:** 13
**Titles in Print:** 225
**Average Percentage Printed:** Hardcover 10%, Paperback 90%
**Backfile Available:** yes

## Cold Mountain Review

**Type:** magazine
**CLMP member:** yes
**Address:** Dept. of English, ASU
Boone, NC 28608
**Web Site Address:** http://www.coldmountain.app-state.edu
**Publishes:** poetry and reviews
**Reading Period:** Year-round
**Reporting Time:** 1 to 2 months
**Author Payment:** none
**Founded:** 1972
**Non Profit:** no
**Backfile Available:** yes

## College Literature

**Type:** magazine
**CLMP member:** yes
**Primary Editor/Contact Person:** Kostas Myrsiades
**Address:** 210 E. Rosedale Ave.
West Chester University
West Chester, PA 19383
**Web Site Address:** http://www.collegeliterature.org
**Publishes:** essays and reviews
**Editorial Focus:** College Literature features a wide variety of approaches to textual analysis and the teaching of literary texts.
**Representative Authors:** Henry Giroux, Mustapha Marrouchi, and Jeffrey Williams
**Submissions Policy:** 8,000-10,000 words on textual analysis, literary theory, and pedagogy for today's college English classroom.
**Simultaneous Subs:** yes
**Reading Period:** Year-round
**Reporting Time:** 1 to 4 months
**Author Payment:** none
**Founded:** 1974
**Non Profit:** yes
**Paid Staff:** 2

**Unpaid Staff:** 0
**ISSN Number/ISBN Number:** ISSN 0093-3139
**Total Circulation:** 800
**Paid Circulation:** 600
**Average Print Run:** 900
**Subscription Rate:** Individual $40/Institution $100
**Single Copy Price:** $10
**Current Volume/Issue:** 32/4
**Frequency per Year:** 4
**Backfile Available:** yes
**Unsolicited Ms. Received:** yes
**% of Unsolicited Ms. Published per Year:** 75%
**Format:** perfect
**Size:** H 9" W 6"
**Average Pages:** 220
**Ads:** yes
**Ad Rates:** $175 full page; discount for successive issues
See Web Site for Details.

## Colorado Review

**Type:** magazine
**CLMP member:** yes
**Primary Editor/Contact Person:** Stephanie G'Schwind
**Address:** Dept. of English
Colorado State University
Fort Collins, CO 80523
**Web Site Address:**
http://coloradoreview.colostate.edu
**Publishes:** essays, fiction, nonfiction, poetry, and translation
**Representative Authors:** Paul Mandelbaum, Ann Hood, and Fanny Howe
**Submissions Policy:** Please submit no more than one story or essay, and no more than five poems at a time.
**Simultaneous Subs:** yes
**Reading Period:** 9/1 to 5/1
**Reporting Time:** 2 to 3 months
**Author Payment:** cash and copies
**Contests:** See Web Site for Contest Guidelines.
**Founded:** 1956
**Non Profit:** yes
**Paid Staff:** 1
**Unpaid Staff:** 20
**Distributors:** Ingram, Kent
**ISSN Number/ISBN Number:** ISSN 1046-3348
**Total Circulation:** 1,100
**Paid Circulation:** 800

# Profile: Alana Wilcox
## Senior Editor, Coach House Books

**1) How did you arrive at your current position?**

Through serendipity. As an undergrad student I edited literary journals that were printed on Coach House's presses. Then, years later, after grad school and working for ages in a bookstore, I was doing freelance editing, and Stan Bevington, the owner, suggested I come in one day a week to help with sales. As these things tend to go, that quickly turned into seven days a week and, before I knew it, I was the editor. I've been here six and a half years now.

**2) What is the staff structure like at your press/magazine?**

We have an owner/publisher. I'm the editor, so I take care of all acquisitions and editing, and I oversee the running of the company. We also have a publicist, a managing editor and a web editor.

**3) How do you keep your press/magazine running?**

I'm sure every publisher would say the same thing: money. It's tough to compete with the giant media conglomerates—with their endless resources, it's easier for them to attract media attention and to lure good authors.

**4) What do you hope to see in a cover letter?**

I like to see "Coach House" in the cover letter. It's important to me to know that the writer has done some research and wants not simply to be published but to be published by Coach House. I automatically pay more attention to those letters that mention some of the books we've published, especially if the writer explains why he/she likes them.

I am wary of letters that have "bestseller" in them. It is unrealistic to think that a first book by an unknown writer published by a small press would ever be a bestseller; of course we'd love to have a bestseller (we have had one!), but if the writer goes into it with such unreasonable expectations, it can only go badly.

**5) What do you look for in a submission?**

Excellent writing, appropriate to our list. Writing that is innovative, dextrous, spellbinding, unique, superlative.

**6) How are submissions processed at your press/magazine?**

Every couple of months I go through the whole pile and send back all the ones that are wildly inappropriate—cookbooks, fantasy novels, collections of limericks. I read as much as I can of the more appropriate ones, gradually whittling the pile until I have just a few to choose from. Those final decisions are the hardest, and they often take me a long time.

**7) Do you have a favorite unsolicited submission discovery or story?**

One unsolicited writer once sent me five novels at once. One of them was a mystery novel about an unpublished writer killing off editors who had rejected him. "You see that man in the dark alley?" it began. "Yes, it's you he's after. He's going to kill you." Not recommended as a submission strategy.

Another time, a writer sent a query letter about a novel he'd written called "All My Friends Are Superheroes." I told him to send it. He did, but neglected to enclose any contact information. I finally tracked him down and called. He'd been saying for years that he'd pack it in if he hadn't been published by 35. It was the day after his 35th birthday. When I said I wanted to publish the book, he laughed. "Uh, yeah, sure," he said. "That's a mean joke." It took about five minutes to persuade him that I was really from Coach House and wanted to publish the book. It's gone on to be one of our best-selling books.

**8) Do you have any advice for first-time submitters?**

Do a lot of research. Think about the books that you read—what press are they from? That's probably where you should submit. Write a cover letter that's not obnoxiously sycophantic but that does demonstrate familiarity with the publisher's list, and explain why you would fit on the list. Keep it relatively concise, and make sure your spelling and grammar are correct—I once received a letter by a "writter." Enclose a writing sample, a literary CV and, of course, an SASE. And be patient. I work seven days a week but am still a few months behind on submissions. And do let us know if you're submitting elsewhere—nothing irritates a publisher more than spending hours reading a manuscript only to find it's been accepted elsewhere.

**Average Print Run:** 1,400
**Subscription Rate:** Individual $24/Institution $34
**Single Copy Price:** $9.50
**Current Volume/Issue:** 32/3
**Frequency per Year:** 3
**Backfile Available:** yes
**Unsolicited Ms. Received:** yes
**% of Unsolicited Ms. Published per Year:** 40%
**Format:** perfect
**Size:** H 6" W 9"
**Average Pages:** 224
**Ads:** yes
**Ad Rates:** whole page $150, half page $75
See Web Site for Details.

## Columbia: A Journal of Literature & Art

**Type:** magazine
**CLMP member:** yes
**Primary Editor/Contact Person:** Lytton Smith
**Address:** 415 Dodge Hall, Columbia University
2960 Broadway
New York, NY 10027
**Web Site Address:**
http://www.columbia.edu/cu/arts/journal
**Publishes:** essays, fiction, nonfiction, poetry, art, and translation
**Representative Authors:** Gary Lutz, Yusef Komunyakaa, and Phillip Lopate
**Submissions Policy:** see website
**Simultaneous Subs:** yes
**Reading Period:** Year-round
**Reporting Time:** 8 to 12 weeks
**Author Payment:** copies
**Contests:** See Web Site for Contest Guidelines.
**Founded:** 1977
**Non Profit:** yes
**Paid Staff:** 0
**Unpaid Staff:** 30
**Distributors:** Ingram, Ubiquity, DeBoer
**Wholesalers:** EBSCO
**ISSN Number/ISBN Number:** ISBN 7-4470867-6-4
**Total Circulation:** 2,000
**Paid Circulation:** 100
**Subscription Rate:** Individual $15/Institution $15
**Single Copy Price:** $10
**Current Volume/Issue:** Issue 39
**Frequency per Year:** 2
**Backfile Available:** yes
**Unsolicited Ms. Received:** yes

**% of Unsolicited Ms. Published per Year:** 30%
**Format:** perfect
**Size:** H 9" W 6"
**Average Pages:** 180
**Ads:** yes
**Ad Rates:** see web
See Web Site for Details.

## COMBAT

**Type:** online
**CLMP member:** no
**Primary Editor/Contact Person:** Ed Staff
**Address:** P.O. Box 3
Circleville, WV 26804-0003
**Web Site Address:** http://www.combat.ws/
**Publishes:** essays, fiction, nonfiction, poetry, art, and translation
**Editorial Focus:** non-partisan analysis and depiction of war and its aftermath
**Submissions Policy:** electronic submissions only
**Simultaneous Subs:** yes
**Reading Period:** Year-round
**Reporting Time:** 2 to 4 weeks
**Author Payment:** none
**Founded:** 2002
**Non Profit:** yes
**Paid Staff:** 0
**Unpaid Staff:** 5
**ISSN Number/ISBN Number:** ISSN 1542-1546
**Average Page Views per Month:** x
**Average Unique Visitors per Month:** x
**Frequency per Year:** 4
**Publish Print Anthology:** no
**Average Percentage of Pages per Category:** Fiction 25%, Nonfiction 25%, Poetry 25%, Essays 25%
**Ads:** no
**Ad Rates:** x

## The Common Review

**Type:** magazine
**CLMP member:** no
**Primary Editor/Contact Person:** J.A. Smith
**Address:** 35 E. Wacker Dr.
Ste. 2300
Chicago, IL 60601
**Web Site Address:** http://www.thecommonreview.org
**Publishes:** essays, poetry, reviews, and art
**Editorial Focus:** We publish intelligent, but not only academic writing including book reviews, literary trav-

el pieces, and author profiles.
**Representative Authors:** Phillip Lopate, Regina Barreca, and Michael Berube
**Submissions Policy:** Unsolicited manuscripts should be preceded by a query. All others via e-mail or disk in MS Word/RTF with works/quotes cited.
**Simultaneous Subs:** yes
**Reading Period:** Year-round
**Reporting Time:** 1 to 2 months
**Author Payment:** cash
**Founded:** 2001
**Non Profit:** yes
**Paid Staff:** 3
**Unpaid Staff:** 2
**Distributors:** Ingram, DeBoer
**ISSN Number/ISBN Number:** ISSN 1535-4784
**Total Circulation:** 10,000
**Paid Circulation:** 1,100
**Average Print Run:** 10,000
**Subscription Rate:** Individual $17.95/Institution $17.95
**Single Copy Price:** $4.95
**Current Volume/Issue:** 4/3
**Frequency per Year:** 4
**Backfile Available:** yes
**Unsolicited Ms. Received:** yes
**% of Unsolicited Ms. Published per Year:** 10%
**Format:** perfect
**Size:** H 10" W 8"
**Average Pages:** 64
**Ads:** yes
**Ad Rates:** Negotiable/swap-ads

## Conduit

**Type:** magazine
**CLMP member:** yes
**Primary Editor/Contact Person:** William Waltz
**Address:** 510 8th Ave. N.E.
Minneapolis, MN 55413
**Web Site Address:** http://www.conduit.org
**Publishes:** essays, fiction, nonfiction, poetry, art, and translation
**Representative Authors:** James Tate, Dean Young, and Sarah Manguso
**Submissions Policy:** Send 3-5 poems or 1-3 prose pieces (3,500 word maximum) with SASE. No electronic submissions.
**Simultaneous Subs:** no
**Reading Period:** Year-round
**Reporting Time:** 1 to 9 months

**Author Payment:** copies and subscription
**Founded:** 1992
**Non Profit:** yes
**Paid Staff:** 0
**Unpaid Staff:** 4
**Distributors:** DeBoer, Don Olson Distribution
**ISSN Number/ISBN Number:** ISSN 1073-6182
**Total Circulation:** 900
**Paid Circulation:** 400
**Average Print Run:** 1,000
**Subscription Rate:** Individual $15/Institution $25
**Single Copy Price:** $8
**Current Volume/Issue:** Issue 15
**Frequency per Year:** 2
**Backfile Available:** yes
**Unsolicited Ms. Received:** yes
**% of Unsolicited Ms. Published per Year:** 5%
**Format:** perfect
**Size:** H 11" W 5"
**Average Pages:** 80
**Ads:** no

## Confrontation Magazine

**Type:** press
**CLMP member:** yes
**Primary Editor/Contact Person:** Martin Tucker
**Address:** English department, C.W. Post of L.IU.
same
Brookville, NY 11548
**Web Site Address:** http://www.liu.edu
**Publishes:** essays, fiction, nonfiction, poetry, reviews, art, and translation
**Editorial Focus:** literary Journal open to all forms and style; merit of style is criterion.
**Representative Authors:** David Ray, Nadine Gordimer, and Cynthia Ozick
**Submissions Policy:** open to poetry and stories. Essays for special topic supplement usually assigned; memoirs a regular feature.
**Simultaneous Subs:** yes
**Reading Period:** Se/Ma to pt/31
**Reporting Time:** 6 to 8 weeks
**Author Payment:** cash and copies
**Founded:** 1968
**Non Profit:** yes
**Paid Staff:** 2
**Unpaid Staff:** 8
**Distributors:** Ubiquity, DeBoer
**Wholesalers:** Baker & Taylor
**ISSN Number/ISBN Number:** 0010-5716/many

**Number of Books Published per Year:** 2
**Titles in Print:** 19
**Average Percentage Printed:** Hardcover 20%,
Paperback 70%, Chapbook 10%

## Confrontation

**Type:** magazine
**CLMP member:** yes
**Primary Editor/Contact Person:** Martin Tucker
**Address:** CW Post of Long Island University
720 Northern Blvd/English Department
Brookville, NY 11548-1300
**Publishes:** essays, fiction, nonfiction, poetry, reviews,
art, and translation
**Editorial Focus:** open to all forms and styles; quality
is our main concern. We are an eclectic mix.
**Representative Authors:** Cynthia Ozick, David Ray,
and Ihab Hassan
**Submissions Policy:** We do not consider mss. during
June, July, August. Stories in print version only, poetry
may be in e-mail submission. SASE
**Simultaneous Subs:** yes
**Reading Period:** Year-round
**Reporting Time:** 1 to 2 months
**Author Payment:** cash and copies
**Founded:** 1968
**Non Profit:** yes
**Paid Staff:** 2
**Unpaid Staff:** 6
**Distributors:** DeBoer, Ubiquity
**ISSN Number/ISBN Number:** ISSN 0010 5716
**Total Circulation:** 2,000
**Paid Circulation:** 500
**Average Print Run:** 2,000
**Subscription Rate:** Individual $10/Institution $10
**Single Copy Price:** $10
**Current Volume/Issue:** Issue 90
**Frequency per Year:** 2
**Backfile Available:** yes
**Unsolicited Ms. Received:** yes
**% of Unsolicited Ms. Published per Year:** 80%
**Format:** perfect
**Size:** H 9" W 6"
**Average Pages:** 300
**Ads:** yes
**Ad Rates:** varies

## Conjunctions

**Type:** magazine
**CLMP member:** yes
**Primary Editor/Contact Person:** Bradford Morrow
**Address:** Bard College
Annandale-on-Hudson, NY 12504
**Web Site Address:** http://www.conjunctions.com
**Publishes:** essays, fiction, nonfiction, poetry, art, and
translation
**Editorial Focus:** Features previously unpublished
innovative contemporary fiction, poetry, drama, art,
essays, interviews, and translations.
**Representative Authors:** William H. Gass, Joyce
Carol Oates, and Rick Moody
**Submissions Policy:** Accepts previously unpublished
submissions only. No electronic submissions will be
considered. Please include an SASE.
**Simultaneous Subs:** no
**Reading Period:** Year-round
**Reporting Time:** 1 to 2 months
**Author Payment:** none, cash, and copies
**Founded:** 1981
**Non Profit:** no
**Paid Staff:** Six
**Unpaid Staff:** 0
**Distributors:** Distributed Art Publishers
**ISSN Number/ISBN Number:** ISSN 0278-2324
**Total Circulation:** 4,000
**Paid Circulation:** 1,000
**Average Print Run:** 5,000
**Subscription Rate:** Individual $18/Institution $25
**Single Copy Price:** $15
**Current Volume/Issue:** 45/45
**Frequency per Year:** 2
**Backfile Available:** yes
**Unsolicited Ms. Received:** yes
**% of Unsolicited Ms. Published per Year:** 33%
**Format:** perfect
**Size:** H 9" W 5"
**Average Pages:** 400
**Ads:** yes
**Ad Rates:** $350 per full page

## Connecticut Review

**Type:** magazine
**CLMP member:** yes
**Address:** 39 Woodland St.
Hartford, CT 06790
**Web Site Address:**
http://www.connecitcutreview.com

**Publishes:** essays, fiction, nonfiction, poetry, reviews, and translation
**Reading Period:** Year-round
**Reporting Time:** 1 to 2 months
**Author Payment:** none
**Founded:** 1967
**Non Profit:** no
**Backfile Available:** yes

# Contemporary Poetry Review

**Type:** online
**CLMP member:** yes
**Primary Editor/Contact Person:** Garrick Davis
**Address:** P.O. Box 5222
Arlington, VA 22205
**Web Site Address:** http://www.cprw.com
**Publishes:** reviews
**Editorial Focus:** The CPR is the largest archive of poetry criticism in the world.
**Representative Authors:** Ernest Hilbert, Peter Campion, and Justin Quinn
**Submissions Policy:** The CPR only publishes criticism on poets and poetry. It does not print poetry.
**Simultaneous Subs:** no
**Reading Period:** Year-round
**Reporting Time:** 1 to 4 weeks
**Author Payment:** cash
**Contests:** Contributors are paid $50 per article.
**Founded:** 1998
**Non Profit:** yes
**Paid Staff:** 25
**Unpaid Staff:** 0
**Average Page Views per Month:** 30,000
**Average Unique Visitors per Month:** 15,000
**Frequency per Year:** 12
**Publish Print Anthology:** no
**Average Percentage of Pages per Category:** Reviews 100%
**Ad Rates:** See Web Site for Details.

# CONTEXT

**Type:** online
**CLMP member:** no
**Primary Editor/Contact Person:** Editor
**Address:** Center for Book Culture
ISU 8905
Normal, IL 61790-8905
**Web Site Address:** http://www.readcontext.com
**Publishes:** essays, nonfiction, reviews, and translation

**Editorial Focus:** Creating a historical and cultural context in which to read modern and contemporary literature.
**Representative Authors:** Gilbert Sorrentino, Jaimy Gordon, and Robert Creeley
**Submissions Policy:** no unsolicited submissions
**Simultaneous Subs:** no
**Reading Period:** Year-round
**Reporting Time:** 1 to 3 months
**Author Payment:** cash
**Founded:** 1981
**Non Profit:** yes
**Paid Staff:** 15
**Unpaid Staff:** 2
**Distributors:** Center for Book Culture
**Average Page Views per Month:** 2,000
**Average Unique Visitors per Month:** 300
**Frequency per Year:** 2
**Publish Print Anthology:** no
**Average Percentage of Pages per Category:** Fiction 10%, Nonfiction 35%, Reviews 5%, Essays 35%, Translation 15%
**Ads:** no

# Contrary

**Type:** online
**CLMP member:** yes
**Primary Editor/Contact Person:** Jeff McMahon
**Address:** P.O. Box 4044
Merchandise Mart
Chicago, IL 60654-4044
**Web Site Address:**
http://www.contrarymagazine.com
**Publishes:** essays, fiction, nonfiction, poetry, and art
**Editorial Focus:** We seek contrary work that confronts entities, voids, and the edges of its type, genre, or category.
**Representative Authors:** poetry like Mark Strand, commentary like Heywood Broun, and fiction like Michel Houellebec
**Submissions Policy:** We accept only electronic submissions, sent by e-mail to submissions@contrary-magazine.com. If not brief, then breathless.
**Simultaneous Subs:** yes
**Reading Period:** Year-round
**Reporting Time:** 1 to 3 months
**Author Payment:** none
**Founded:** 2003
**Non Profit:** yes
**Paid Staff:** 0

**Unpaid Staff:** 7
**ISSN Number/ISBN Number:** ISSN 1549-7038
**Average Page Views per Month:** untracked
**Average Unique Visitors per Month:** 1,200
**Frequency per Year:** 4
**Average Percentage of Pages per Category:** Fiction 33%, Nonfiction 20%, Poetry 33%, Essays 10%, Art 4%
**Ads:** no

## Cool Grove Publishing

**Type:** press
**CLMP member:** yes
**Address:** 512 Argyle Road
Brooklyn, NY 11218
**Web Site Address:** http://www.coolgrove.com
**Publishes:** fiction, nonfiction, art, and translation
**Reading Period:** Year-round
**Reporting Time:** 1 to 2 months
**Author Payment:** none
**Non Profit:** yes
**Average Percentage Printed:** Hardcover 100%
**Backfile Available:** yes

## Copper Canyon Press

**Type:** press
**CLMP member:** yes
**Primary Editor/Contact Person:** Michael Wiegers
**Address:** P.O. Box 271
Port Townsend, WA 98368
**Web Site Address:**
http://www.coppercanyonpress.org/
**Publishes:** poetry
**Editorial Focus:** CCP publishes contemporary American poetry and poetry in translation.
**Recent Awards Received:** Pulitzer Prize, National Book Award, Lenore Marshall Award, Macarthur Fellowship
**Representative Authors:** W.S. Merwin, Ted Kooser, and C.D. Wright
**Submissions Policy:** We do not accept unsolicited manuscripts. First through third books should be submitted to our annual Hayden Carruth Award.
**Simultaneous Subs:** no
**Reading Period:** Year-round
**Reporting Time:** 2 to 3 months
**Author Payment:** none and royalties
**Contests:** See Web Site for Contest Guidelines.
**Founded:** 1972

**Non Profit:** yes
**Paid Staff:** 7
**Unpaid Staff:** 2
**Distributors:** Consortium
**Wholesalers:** Ingram, Baker & Taylor, SPD
**ISSN Number/ISBN Number:** ISBN 1-55659
**Number of Books Published per Year:** 14-18
**Titles in Print:** 300
**Average Print Run:** 2,500
**Average Percentage Printed:** Hardcover 10%, Paperback 90%
**Average Price:** $16

## The Cortland Review

**Type:** online
**CLMP member:** yes
**Primary Editor/Contact Person:** Guy Shahar
**Address:** 527 Third Ave. #279
New York, NY 10016
**Web Site Address:** http://www.cortlandreview.com
**Publishes:** essays, fiction, nonfiction, poetry, reviews, art, translation, and audio
**Representative Authors:** R.T. Smith, John Kinsella, and David Lehman
**Submissions Policy:** Varies, please see our submission page on website.
**Simultaneous Subs:** no
**Reading Period:** 9/1 to 5/31
**Reporting Time:** 6 to 12 months
**Author Payment:** none
**Founded:** 1997
**Non Profit:** yes
**Paid Staff:** 0
**Unpaid Staff:** 12
**ISSN Number/ISBN Number:** ISSN 1524-6744
**Backfile Available:** no
**Average Page Views per Month:** 250,000
**Average Unique Visitors per Month:** 30,000
**Frequency per Year:** 8
**Publish Print Anthology:** no
**Average Percentage of Pages per Category:** Fiction 5%, Nonfiction 5%, Poetry 30%, Reviews 5%, Essays 5%, Audio 50%
**Ads:** no

## Coteau Books

**Type:** press
**CLMP member:** yes
**Primary Editor/Contact Person:** Nik L. Burton,

Managing Editor
**Address:** 2517 Victoria Ave.
Regina, SK S4P 0T2
**Web Site Address:** http://www.coteaubooks.com
**Publishes:** fiction, nonfiction, and poetry
**Editorial Focus:** Canadian works of Literary Art, with an emphasis on western Canada
**Representative Authors:** J. Jill Robinson, Linda Smith, and Terrence Heath
**Submissions Policy:** Canadian or landed immigrant authors only. Complete manuscript or query/sample, hard copy submissions only. No simultaneous.
**Simultaneous Subs:** no
**Reading Period:** Year-round
**Reporting Time:** 2 to 3 months
**Author Payment:** royalties
**Founded:** 1975
**Non Profit:** yes
**Paid Staff:** 6
**Unpaid Staff:** 0
**Distributors:** Fitzhenry & Whiteside
**Wholesalers:** As many as possible
**ISSN Number/ISBN Number:** ISBN 978-1-55050-
**Number of Books Published per Year:** 16
**Titles in Print:** 150
**Average Print Run:** 2,000
**Average Percentage Printed:** Paperback 100%
**Average Price:** $18.95

# Cottonwood Magazine and Press

**Type:** magazine
**CLMP member:** yes
**Primary Editor/Contact Person:** Tom Lorenz, Editor
**Address:** 1301 Jayhawk Blvd. Rm. 400 Kansas Union
Kansas Union, Univ. of Kansas
Lawrence, KS 66045
**Publishes:** essays, fiction, poetry, and reviews
**Editorial Focus:** We publish fiction and poetry with clear images and interesting narratives. Submissions from throughout the US considered.
**Representative Authors:** Rita Dove, Virgil Suarez, and Cris Mazza
**Submissions Policy:** Submit 4-6 poems and 1 story (1,000 to 7,000 words); include SASE
**Simultaneous Subs:** yes
**Reading Period:** Year-round
**Reporting Time:** 3 to 6 months
**Author Payment:** copies
**Founded:** 1965
**Non Profit:** yes

**Paid Staff:** 0
**Unpaid Staff:** 14
**Total Circulation:** 500
**Paid Circulation:** 150
**Average Print Run:** 600
**Subscription Rate:** Individual $15/Institution $10.50
**Single Copy Price:** $8.50
**Current Volume/Issue:** Issue 63
**Frequency per Year:** 2
**Backfile Available:** yes
**Unsolicited Ms. Received:** yes
**% of Unsolicited Ms. Published per Year:** 1%
**Format:** perfect
**Size:** H 9" W 6"
**Average Pages:** 104
**Ads:** no

# Crab Creek Review

**Type:** magazine
**CLMP member:** yes
**Primary Editor/Contact Person:** Emily Bedard
**Address:** P.O. Box 85088
Seattle, WA 98145-1088
**Web Site Address:** http://www.crabcreekreview.org
**Publishes:** fiction, poetry, and art
**Editorial Focus:** Eclectic poetry and dynamic short fiction. Memorable voices and canny cover art.
**Representative Authors:** Martha Silano, Kathleen Flenniken, and Gregory Hischak
**Submissions Policy:** Up to 5 poems. Short shorts and stories up to 6,000 words.
**Simultaneous Subs:** no
**Reading Period:** Year-round
**Reporting Time:** 4 to 5 months
**Author Payment:** copies
**Contests:** See Web Site for Contest Guidelines.
**Founded:** 1983
**Non Profit:** yes
**Paid Staff:** 0
**Unpaid Staff:** 4
**Distributors:** Ubiquity, Small Changes
**Wholesalers:** EBSCO
**ISSN Number/ISBN Number:** ISSN 0738-7008
**Total Circulation:** 400
**Paid Circulation:** 200
**Average Print Run:** 600
**Subscription Rate:** Individual $12/Institution $20
**Single Copy Price:** $7
**Current Volume/Issue:** XIX/1
**Frequency per Year:** 2

**Backfile Available:** yes
**Unsolicited Ms. Received:** yes
**% of Unsolicited Ms. Published per Year:** 5%
**Format:** perfect
**Size:** H 9" W 6"
**Average Pages:** 100
**Ads:** no

## Crab Orchard Review

**Type:** magazine
**CLMP member:** yes
**Primary Editor/Contact Person:** Allison Joseph/Jon Tribble
**Address:** Department of English, Mail Code 4503 SIUC, 1000 Faner Dr.
Carbondale, IL 62901
**Web Site Address:** http://www.siu.edu/~crborchd/
**Publishes:** essays, fiction, nonfiction, and poetry
**Editorial Focus:** A biannual journal of new works by writers from across the nation and around the world.
**Recent Awards Received:** 2005 Illinois Arts Literary Awards
**Representative Authors:** Cathy Song, Anthony Butts, and Jean Thompson
**Submissions Policy:** Simultaneous submissions welcome with notice. No e-mail submissions. Check the website for complete guidelines.
**Simultaneous Subs:** yes
**Reading Period:** 9/05 to 4/06
**Reporting Time:** 1 to 7 months
**Author Payment:** cash, copies, and subscription
**Contests:** See Web Site for Contest Guidelines.
**Founded:** 1995
**Non Profit:** yes
**Paid Staff:** 9
**Unpaid Staff:** 16
**ISSN Number/ISBN Number:** ISSN 1083-5571
**Total Circulation:** 2,600
**Paid Circulation:** 2,200
**Average Print Run:** 3,200
**Subscription Rate:** Individual $15/Institution $16
**Single Copy Price:** $10
**Current Volume/Issue:** 11/1
**Frequency per Year:** 2
**Backfile Available:** yes
**Unsolicited Ms. Received:** yes
**% of Unsolicited Ms. Published per Year:** 1%
**Format:** perfect
**Size:** H 8 1/2" W 5 1/2"
**Average Pages:** 304

**Ads:** no

## Cranky Literary Journal

**Type:** magazine
**CLMP member:** no
**Primary Editor/Contact Person:** Amber Curtis
**Address:** 322 10th Ave. E. C-5
Seattle, WA 98102
**Web Site Address:** http://www.failedpromise.org
**Publishes:** essays, fiction, poetry, and reviews
**Editorial Focus:** Cranky Literary Journal is like a kid let out for recess: small, but with a big shouting voice.
**Representative Authors:** Olena Kalytiak Davis, Kary Wayson, and Matthew Zapruder
**Submissions Policy:** We only accept submissions via e-mail. Your submission must be accompanied by a brief cover letter and a bio of less than 50 words. Send 3-5 poems or 1-2 prose pieces under 2,000 words each. Paste your submission into the body of an e-mail and send to submissions@failedpromise.org. Please write either Poetry Submission or Fiction Submission in the subject line. We do not accept attachments.
**Simultaneous Subs:** yes
**Reading Period:** Year-round
**Reporting Time:** 6 to 8 weeks
**Author Payment:** copies
**Contests:** No contests.
**Founded:** 2003
**Non Profit:** yes
**Paid Staff:** 0
**Unpaid Staff:** 5
**ISSN Number/ISBN Number:** ISSN 1550-0330
**Total Circulation:** 500
**Paid Circulation:** 100
**Average Print Run:** 500
**Subscription Rate:** Individual $20/Institution $20
**Single Copy Price:** $8
**Current Volume/Issue:** 1/6
**Frequency per Year:** 3
**Backfile Available:** yes
**Unsolicited Ms. Received:** yes
**% of Unsolicited Ms. Published per Year:** 95%
**Format:** perfect
**Size:** H 9" W 6"
**Average Pages:** 110
**Ads:** no

# Crazyhorse

**Type:** magazine
**CLMP member:** yes
**Primary Editor/Contact Person:** Garrett Doherty
**Address:** English Dept., College of Charleston
66 George St.
Charleston, SC 29424
**Web Site Address:** http://crazyhorse.cofc.edu
**Publishes:** essays, fiction, nonfiction, poetry, art, and translation
**Editorial Focus:** Today's fiction, essays, and poetry: from the mainstream to the avant-garde, from the established to the undiscovered writer.
**Recent Awards Received:** Best American Poetry 2005, 2004 Pushcart Prize, reprinted in Harper's
**Representative Authors:** Dean Young, Michael Martone, and Nance Van Winckel
**Submissions Policy:** Send up to 25 pages of prose or 3-5 poems. Send with SASE.
**Simultaneous Subs:** yes
**Reading Period:** Year-round
**Reporting Time:** 3 to 4 months
**Author Payment:** cash, copies, and subscription
**Contests:** See Web Site for Contest Guidelines.
**Founded:** 1960
**Non Profit:** yes
**Paid Staff:** 3
**Unpaid Staff:** 4
**Distributors:** Ingram, DeBoer
**ISSN Number/ISBN Number:** ISSN 0011-0841
**Total Circulation:** 1,500
**Paid Circulation:** 1,300
**Average Print Run:** 2,500
**Subscription Rate:** Individual $15/Institution $15
**Single Copy Price:** $8.50
**Current Volume/Issue:** Issue 68
**Frequency per Year:** 2
**Backfile Available:** yes
**Unsolicited Ms. Received:** yes
**% of Unsolicited Ms. Published per Year:** 3%
**Format:** perfect
**Size:** H 8.75" W 8.25"
**Average Pages:** 160
**Ads:** yes
**Ad Rates:** $200/full page
See Web Site for Details.

# Creative Nonfiction

**Type:** magazine
**CLMP member:** yes
**Primary Editor/Contact Person:** Lee Gutkind
**Address:** 5501 Walnut St, Ste. 202
Ste. 202
Pittsburgh, PA 15232-2329
**Web Site Address:** http://www.creativenonfiction.org
**Publishes:** essays and nonfiction
**Editorial Focus:** First journal devoted exclusively to literary nonfiction. Publishes personal essay, memoir, and literary journalism.
**Representative Authors:** Richard Rodriguez, Tracy Kidder, and Annie Dillard
**Submissions Policy:** Accepts hard copy only. SASE and cover letter required for reply. No queries. No reprints.
**Simultaneous Subs:** yes
**Reading Period:** Year-round
**Reporting Time:** 3 to 5 months
**Author Payment:** cash and copies
**Contests:** See Web Site for Contest Guidelines.
**Founded:** 1993
**Non Profit:** yes
**Paid Staff:** 3
**Unpaid Staff:** 2
**Distributors:** Ingram, Media Solutions
**ISSN Number/ISBN Number:** ISSN 1070-0714
**Total Circulation:** 3,500
**Paid Circulation:** 2,100
**Average Print Run:** 4,500
**Subscription Rate:** Individual $29.95/Institution $40
**Single Copy Price:** $10
**Current Volume/Issue:** Issue 26
**Frequency per Year:** 3
**Backfile Available:** yes
**Unsolicited Ms. Received:** yes
**% of Unsolicited Ms. Published per Year:** 10%
**Format:** perfect
**Size:** H 8" W 5.5"
**Average Pages:** 144
**Ads:** yes
**Ad Rates:** See Web Site for Details.

# Creative Nonfiction

**Type:** press
**CLMP member:** yes
**Primary Editor/Contact Person:** Lee Gutkind
**Address:** 5501 Walnut St, Ste. 202
Ste. 202
Pittsburgh, PA 15232-2329
**Web Site Address:** http://www.creativenonfiction.org
**Publishes:** essays and nonfiction

**Editorial Focus:** First journal devoted exclusively to literary nonfiction. Publishes personal essay, memoir, and literary journalism.
**Representative Authors:** Richard Rodriguez, Tracy Kidder, and Annie Dillard
**Submissions Policy:** Accepts hard copy only. SASE and cover letter required for reply. No queries. No reprints.
**Simultaneous Subs:** yes
**Reading Period:** Year-round
**Reporting Time:** 3 to 5 months
**Author Payment:** cash, copies, and subscription
**Contests:** Has sponsored essay contests with awards of up to $10,000.
See Web Site for Contest Guidelines.
**Founded:** 1993
**Non Profit:** yes
**Paid Staff:** 2
**Unpaid Staff:** 1
**Distributors:** Ingram, Media Solutions
**ISSN Number/ISBN Number:** ISSN 1070-0714
**Number of Books Published per Year:** 3
**Titles in Print:** 21
**Average Percentage Printed:** Paperback 100%
**Backfile Available:** yes

## Creosote: A Journal of Poetry and Prose

**Type:** magazine
**CLMP member:** no
**Primary Editor/Contact Person:** Ken Raines
**Address:** Dept. of English, Mohave Community Coll.
1977 W. Acoma Blvd.
Lake Havasu City, AZ 86403
**Publishes:** essays, fiction, nonfiction, and poetry
**Editorial Focus:** We have a slight bias in favor of traditional forms and verse. However, all quality work is considered.
**Representative Authors:** Ruth Moose, Charles Springer, and Ryan G. Van Cleave
**Submissions Policy:** Up to 5 poems or 5,000 words of prose considered in each submission. No previously published material.
**Simultaneous Subs:** yes
**Reading Period:** 8/1 to 3/1
**Reporting Time:** 2 to 6 months
**Author Payment:** copies
**Founded:** 1999
**Non Profit:** yes
**Paid Staff:** no

**Unpaid Staff:** yes
**Total Circulation:** 400
**Paid Circulation:** 45
**Subscription Rate:** Individual $4/Institution $4
**Single Copy Price:** $4
**Current Volume/Issue:** 4/1
**Frequency per Year:** 1
**Backfile Available:** yes
**Unsolicited Ms. Received:** yes
**% of Unsolicited Ms. Published per Year:** 3-5%
**Format:** stapled
**Size:** H 8.5" W 5.5"
**Average Pages:** 48
**Ads:** no

## CROWD

**Type:** magazine
**CLMP member:** yes
**Primary Editor/Contact Person:** Aimee Kelley
**Address:** P.O. Box 1373
New York, NY 10276
**Web Site Address:** http://www.crowdmagazine.com
**Publishes:** essays, fiction, nonfiction, poetry, and art
**Editorial Focus:** CROWD publishes visual art and writing from all genres.
**Representative Authors:** Shelley Jackson, Paul Muldoon, and Lyn Hejinian
**Submissions Policy:** Please include SASE for reply. We encourage purchasing a copy or subscription prior to submitting work.
**Simultaneous Subs:** yes
**Reading Period:** 9/15 to 5/15
**Reporting Time:** 1 to 4 months
**Author Payment:** copies
**Founded:** 2001
**Non Profit:** yes
**Paid Staff:** 0
**Unpaid Staff:** 4
**Distributors:** DeBoer, Ingram, Ubiquity
**Total Circulation:** 1,000
**Paid Circulation:** 125
**Average Print Run:** 1,000
**Subscription Rate:** Individual $18/Institution $25
**Single Copy Price:** $10
**Current Volume/Issue:** Issue 5/6
**Frequency per Year:** 2
**Backfile Available:** yes
**Unsolicited Ms. Received:** yes
**% of Unsolicited Ms. Published per Year:** 65%
**Format:** perfect

**Size:** H 9" W 6.75"
**Average Pages:** 130
**Ads:** yes
**Ad Rates:** $150 per full page

## Crying Sky: Poetry and Conversation

**Type:** magazine
**CLMP member:** yes
**Primary Editor/Contact Person:** W.E. Butts and S. Stephanie
**Address:** 164 Maple St. Unit 1
Manchester, NH 03103
**Publishes:** essays and poetry
**Editorial Focus:** Features established and emerging poets, and interviews. Seeks well-crafted poetry reflecting the human condition.
**Representative Authors:** David Wojahn, Betsy Sholl, and Robert Wrigley
**Submissions Policy:** Submit 3-5 typed poems, bio and SASE.
**Simultaneous Subs:** no
**Reading Period:** Year-round
**Reporting Time:** 1 to 2 months
**Author Payment:** copies
**Contests:** Occasionally sponsors judged contests.
**Founded:** 2004
**Non Profit:** no
**Paid Staff:** 0
**Unpaid Staff:** 2
**Distributors:** DeBoer
**ISSN Number/ISBN Number:** ISSN 1551-9848
**Total Circulation:** 500
**Paid Circulation:** 60
**Average Print Run:** 500
**Subscription Rate:** Individual $16/Institution $12.80
**Single Copy Price:** $9
**Current Volume/Issue:** 1/2
**Frequency per Year:** 2
**Backfile Available:** yes
**Unsolicited Ms. Received:** yes
**% of Unsolicited Ms. Published per Year:** 5%
**Format:** stapled
**Size:** H 8 1/2" W 5 1/2"
**Average Pages:** 84
**Ads:** no

## Curbstone Press

**Type:** press
**CLMP member:** yes

**Primary Editor/Contact Person:** Alexander Taylor
**Address:** 321 Jackson St.
Willimantic, CT 06226
**Web Site Address:** http://www.curbstone.org
**Publishes:** essays, fiction, poetry, and translation
**Editorial Focus:** literature that reflects a commitment to human rights and intercultural understanding.
**Representative Authors:** Claribel Alegr,a, Marnie Mueller, and Luis J. Rodr,guez
**Submissions Policy:** Please make sure your ms. fits Curbstone's mission. Then send query letter, author info, publication history, and sample of ms.
**Simultaneous Subs:** yes
**Reading Period:** Year-round
**Reporting Time:** 1 to 3 months
**Author Payment:** royalties
**Contests:** See Web Site for Contest Guidelines.
**Founded:** 1975
**Non Profit:** yes
**Paid Staff:** 4
**Unpaid Staff:** 2
**Distributors:** Consortium
**Wholesalers:** most of them
**ISSN Number/ISBN Number:** ISBN 1-880684/1-931896
**Number of Books Published per Year:** 8-10
**Titles in Print:** 154
**Average Print Run:** 2,000
**Average Percentage Printed:** Hardcover 7%, Paperback 93%
**Average Price:** $14

## Cutbank

**Type:** magazine
**CLMP member:** no
**Primary Editor/Contact Person:** Jason McMackin
**Address:** Department of English
University of Montana
Missoula, MT 59812
**Web Site Address:**
http://www.umt.edu/cutbank/default.htm
**Publishes:** essays, fiction, nonfiction, and poetry
**Submissions Policy:** up to 40 pp prose, five poems.
**Simultaneous Subs:** yes
**Reading Period:** 8/15 to 4/15
**Reporting Time:** 1 to 2 months
**Author Payment:** copies
**Founded:** 1973
**Non Profit:** yes
**Paid Staff:** 0

**Unpaid Staff:** 6
**Total Circulation:** 500
**Paid Circulation:** 150
**Subscription Rate:** Individual $6. per/Institution $6
**Single Copy Price:** $7.95
**Current Volume/Issue:** Issue 62
**Frequency per Year:** 2
**Backfile Available:** yes
**Unsolicited Ms. Received:** yes
**% of Unsolicited Ms. Published per Year:** 1-2%
**Format:** perfect
**Average Pages:** 125
**Ads:** yes

# Dalkey Archive Press

**Type:** press
**CLMP member:** yes
**Primary Editor/Contact Person:** Editor
**Address:** Center for Book Culture
ISU 8905
Normal, IL 61790-8905
**Web Site Address:** http://www.dalkeyarchive.com
**Publishes:** fiction and translation
**Editorial Focus:** Modern and contemporary works of innovative world literature.
**Representative Authors:** Flann O'Brien, Gilbert Sorrentino, and Nicholas Mosley
**Simultaneous Subs:** yes
**Reading Period:** Year-round
**Reporting Time:** 2 to 6 months
**Author Payment:** royalties, cash, and copies
**Founded:** 1984
**Non Profit:** yes
**Paid Staff:** 15
**Unpaid Staff:** 2
**Distributors:** University of Nebraska Press
**Wholesalers:** SPD, Ingram, Baker & Taylor
**ISSN Number/ISBN Number:** ISBN 1-56478-, 0-916583-
**Number of Books Published per Year:** 25
**Titles in Print:** 300
**Average Percentage Printed:** Hardcover 10%, Paperback 90%

# Dan River Press

**Type:** press
**CLMP member:** no
**Primary Editor/Contact Person:** Richard S. Danbury, III

**Address:** P.O. Box 298
Thomaston, ME 04861
**Web Site Address:** http://www.americanletters.org
**Publishes:** fiction and nonfiction
**Editorial Focus:** Fiction and biography only.
**Representative Authors:** Jim Ainsworth, Andrew Laszlo, and James R. Clifford
**Submissions Policy:** No electronic submissions, nothing previously published. Send personal marketing plan.
**Simultaneous Subs:** yes
**Reading Period:** Year-round
**Reporting Time:** 1 to 2 weeks
**Author Payment:** royalties
**Founded:** 1976
**Non Profit:** yes
**Paid Staff:** 1
**Unpaid Staff:** 1
**Distributors:** Ingram, Baker & Taylor, Barnes & Noble, amazon.com
**ISSN Number/ISBN Number:** ISBN 0-89754-xxx-x
**Number of Books Published per Year:** 8
**Titles in Print:** 30
**Average Percentage Printed:** Hardcover 5%, Paperback 95%

# David Paul Books

**Type:** press
**CLMP member:** no
**Primary Editor/Contact Person:** David Paul
**Address:** 25 Methuen Park
London
England, UK N10 2JR
**Web Site Address:** http://www.davidpaulbooks.com
**Publishes:** fiction, nonfiction, and translation
**Editorial Focus:** Good quality cutting edge fiction, translations, focus on themes of Jewish or intercultural interest
**Recent Awards Received:** International PEN Tucholsky Award to Palestinian writer Samir El Youssef for his novella in Gaza Blues.
**Representative Authors:** Etgar Keret, Esther Singer Kreitman, and Samir El Youssef
**Submissions Policy:** Will only take submissions from previously published authors
**Simultaneous Subs:** no
**Reading Period:** Year-round
**Reporting Time:** 2 to 4 weeks
**Author Payment:** royalties and copies
**Founded:** 2001

**Non Profit:** no
**Paid Staff:** 1
**Unpaid Staff:** 1
**Distributors:** Central Books (not N America)
**Wholesalers:** Gardners, Bertrams
**Number of Books Published per Year:** 3
**Titles in Print:** 9
**Average Print Run:** 1,500
**Average Percentage Printed:** Hardcover 25%, Paperback 75%
**Average Price:** $16

# DC Books

**Type:** press
**CLMP member:** no
**Primary Editor/Contact Person:** Steve Luxton
**Address:** Box 662
950 Decarie
Montreal, QC H4L4V9
**Web Site Address:** http://www.dcbooks.ca
**Publishes:** essays, fiction, nonfiction, poetry, and translation
**Editorial Focus:** Literary publisher of Canadian fiction, drama, and poetry. Some foreign English language work also considered.
**Representative Authors:** Robert Allen, Todd Swift, and Louis Dudek
**Submissions Policy:** Query first.
**Simultaneous Subs:** yes
**Reading Period:** Year-round
**Reporting Time:** 6 to 12 months
**Author Payment:** royalties, cash, and copies
**Founded:** 1974
**Non Profit:** no
**Paid Staff:** 0
**Unpaid Staff:** 3
**Distributors:** LitDistCo
**ISSN Number/ISBN Number:** ISBN 0919688, 1897190
**Number of Books Published per Year:** 6
**Titles in Print:** 50
**Average Percentage Printed:** Hardcover 10%, Paperback 90%

# Del Sol Press

**Type:** press
**CLMP member:** no
**Primary Editor/Contact Person:** Joan Houlihan
**Address:** 2020 Pennsylvania Ave.
Ste. 443
Washington, DC 20006
**Web Site Address:** http://webdelsol.com/DelSolPress
**Publishes:** fiction and poetry
**Editorial Focus:** DSP seeks to publish exceptional work by both new and recognized writers, as well as republish literary works that we consider extremely significant and that have gone out of print.
**Representative Authors:** Michael Brodksy, Kimberly Nichols, and Joan Houlihan
**Submissions Policy:** Currently, DSP is not taking unsolicited submissions, synopses, or outlines in any form, however, query letters and all other communications, including requests for review copies can be sent to dspress@webdelsol.com. In your query letter, please include a bio, publishing history for this project (if any), and other previous publications. Poetry queries should be sent to dsp-poetry@webdelsol.com.
**Simultaneous Subs:** yes
**Reading Period:** Year-round
**Reporting Time:** 2 to 6 weeks
**Author Payment:** copies
**Contests:** Del Sol Press Poetry Prize: http://webdelsol.com/DelSolPress/con1test.htm
**Founded:** 2003
**Non Profit:** yes
**Paid Staff:** 0
**Unpaid Staff:** 3
**Distributors:** Ingram, Baker & Taylor
**Number of Books Published per Year:** 4-5
**Titles in Print:** 4
**Average Percentage Printed:** Paperback 100%

# The Del Sol Review

**Type:** online
**CLMP member:** no
**Primary Editor/Contact Person:** Michael Neff
**Address:** 2020 Pennsylvania Ave., NW
Ste. 443
Washington, DC 20006
**Web Site Address:** http://webdelsol.com/Del_Sol_Review
**Publishes:** essays, fiction, nonfiction, poetry, and reviews
**Editorial Focus:** Strong original fiction, experimental fiction, all types of poetry except for language poetry.
**Representative Authors:** Forrest Gander, Paul West, and Luisa Costa Gomes
**Submissions Policy:** See our site at: http://webdelsol.com/Del_Sol_ReviewTheme issues upcoming.

**Simultaneous Subs:** yes
**Reading Period:** Year-round
**Reporting Time:** 1 to 4 weeks
**Author Payment:** none
**Founded:** 1997
**Non Profit:** yes
**Paid Staff:** 0
**Unpaid Staff:** 6
**Average Page Views per Month:** 8,000
**Average Unique Visitors per Month:** 2,000
**Frequency per Year:** 3
**Publish Print Anthology:** no
**Average Percentage of Pages per Category:** Fiction 60%, Nonfiction 5%, Poetry 20%, Reviews 10%, Essays 5%
**Ads:** no

# Denver Quarterly

**Type:** magazine
**CLMP member:** yes
**Primary Editor/Contact Person:** Danielle Dutton
**Address:** University of Denver
2000 E Asbury
Denver, CO 80208
**Web Site Address:** http://www.denverquarterly.com
**Publishes:** essays, fiction, poetry, reviews, art, and translation
**Simultaneous Subs:** yes
**Reading Period:** 9/15 to 5/15
**Reporting Time:** 3 to 4 months
**Author Payment:** cash, copies, and subscription
**Founded:** 1964
**Non Profit:** yes
**Paid Staff:** 2
**Unpaid Staff:** 1
**Total Circulation:** 1,500
**Paid Circulation:** 1,000
**Average Print Run:** 1,500
**Subscription Rate:** Individual $22/Institution $25
**Single Copy Price:** $6
**Current Volume/Issue:** 40/1
**Frequency per Year:** 4
**Backfile Available:** yes
**Unsolicited Ms. Received:** yes
**% of Unsolicited Ms. Published per Year:** 85%
**Format:** perfect
**Average Pages:** 200
**Ads:** no

# Descant

**Type:** magazine
**CLMP member:** yes
**Primary Editor/Contact Person:** Mary Newberry
**Address:** P.O. Box 314
Station P
Toronto, ON M5T1L4
**Web Site Address:** http://www.descant.on.ca
**Publishes:** essays, fiction, nonfiction, poetry, and art
**Editorial Focus:** We focus on poetry and short fiction from both emerging and established writers. We publish both themed and general issues.
**Recent Awards Received:** 3 National Magazine Award nominations
**Representative Authors:** Jane Urquhart, P.K. Page, and Mark Kingwell
**Submissions Policy:** We consider unpublished poetry, short stories, nonfiction and art. Please send postage or IRC for reply.
**Simultaneous Subs:** no
**Reading Period:** Year-round
**Reporting Time:** 9 to 12 months
**Author Payment:** cash
**Contests:** N/A
**Founded:** 1970
**Non Profit:** yes
**Paid Staff:** 3
**Unpaid Staff:** 5-6
**Distributors:** TTS Distribution
**Wholesalers:** Magazines Canada
**ISSN Number/ISBN Number:** 0382-909-X
**Total Circulation:** 1,200
**Paid Circulation:** 700
**Average Print Run:** 1,300
**Subscription Rate:** Individual $25/Institution $35
**Single Copy Price:** $15
**Current Volume/Issue:** 35/2
**Frequency per Year:** 4
**Backfile Available:** yes
**Unsolicited Ms. Received:** yes
**% of Unsolicited Ms. Published per Year:** 5%
**Format:** perfect
**Size:** H 9" W 6"
**Average Pages:** 220
**Ads:** yes
**Ad Rates:** full page $300, 1/2 page $150, 1/4 page $75

# Diagram

**Type:** online
**CLMP member:** yes
**Primary Editor/Contact Person:** Ander Monson
**Address:** 648 Crescent NE
Grand Rapids, MI 49503
**Web Site Address:** http://thediagram.com
**Publishes:** essays, fiction, nonfiction, poetry, reviews, art, translation, and audio
**Editorial Focus:** Schematic, literary fiction, poetry, short-shorts, and genre-bending or -transcending work. See website for examples.
**Representative Authors:** Medbh McGuckian, Ben Marcus, and Miranda July
**Submissions Policy:** Read year-round, e-mail submissions much preferred. See website for complete guidelines and mailing addresses.
**Simultaneous Subs:** yes
**Reading Period:** Year-round
**Reporting Time:** 1 to 6 weeks
**Author Payment:** none and copies
**Contests:** See Web Site for Contest Guidelines.
**Founded:** 2000
**Non Profit:** no
**Paid Staff:** 0
**Unpaid Staff:** 6
**Distributors:** Ingram (for periodic print edition)
**ISSN Number/ISBN Number:** ISSN 1543-5784
**Average Page Views per Month:** 140,000
**Average Unique Visitors per Month:** 10,000
**Frequency per Year:** 6
**Publish Print Anthology:** yes
Price: $15
**Average Percentage of Pages per Category:** Fiction 20%, Nonfiction 5%, Poetry 35%, Reviews 15%, Essays 5%, Art 15%, Audio 5%
**Ads:** no

# Dicey Brown

**Type:** magazine
**CLMP member:** yes
**Address:** 80 St. Mark's Place (#2GN)
Staten Island, NY 10301
**Web Site Address:** http://www.diceybrown.com
**Publishes:** fiction, poetry, and art
**Reading Period:** Year-round
**Reporting Time:** 1 to 2 months
**Author Payment:** none
**Founded:** 2002
**Non Profit:** no
**Backfile Available:** yes

# Diner

**Type:** magazine
**CLMP member:** yes
**Primary Editor/Contact Person:** Eve Rifkah
**Address:** P.O. Box 60676
Greendale Station
Worcester, MA 01606-2378
**Web Site Address:** http://www.spokenword.to/diner
**Publishes:** poetry, reviews, art, and translation
**Editorial Focus:** We are looking for a melding of sound and content-poets willing to take risks with language
**Representative Authors:** Sandra Kohler, Jeffrey Levine, and Rachel Zucker
**Submissions Policy:** max 5 poems with SASE, cover letter with brief bio.
**Simultaneous Subs:** yes
**Reading Period:** Year-round
**Reporting Time:** 1 to 6 months
**Author Payment:** copies
**Contests:** See Web Site for Contest Guidelines.
**Founded:** 2001
**Non Profit:** yes
**Paid Staff:** 0
**Unpaid Staff:** 4
**ISSN Number/ISBN Number:** ISSN 1533-7448
**Total Circulation:** 350
**Paid Circulation:** 150
**Average Print Run:** 500
**Subscription Rate:** Individual $18/Institution $18
**Single Copy Price:** $9.95
**Current Volume/Issue:** 5/2
**Frequency per Year:** 2
**Backfile Available:** yes
**Unsolicited Ms. Received:** yes
**% of Unsolicited Ms. Published per Year:** 2%
**Format:** perfect
**Size:** H 9.5" W 6"
**Average Pages:** 104
**Ads:** yes
**Ad Rates:** See Web Site for Details.

# Dirt Press

**Type:** press
**CLMP member:** yes
**Primary Editor/Contact Person:** Brian Lemond
**Address:** 15 N. Oxford St., 3rd Floor
Brooklyn, NY 11205
**Web Site Address:** http://www.dirtpress.com
**Publishes:** fiction, poetry, and art

**Representative Authors:** Derek Ableman, David J. Alworth, and Dewayne Washington
**Submissions Policy:** rolling, open call for submissions
**Simultaneous Subs:** yes
**Reading Period:** Year-round
**Reporting Time:** 1 to 2 months
**Author Payment:** none
**Contests:** Hendrickson Memorial Prize in Short Fiction and Poetry-alternates annually between the disciplines. $300 1st prize, $100 2nd prize See Web Site for Contest Guidelines.
**Founded:** 2002
**Non Profit:** no
**Paid Staff:** 0
**Unpaid Staff:** 5
**ISSN Number/ISBN Number:** 1553-2135/0-97633368-0-4
**Number of Books Published per Year:** 1
**Titles in Print:** 1
**Average Print Run:** 2,000
**Average Percentage Printed:** Paperback 100%
**Average Price:** $20

# The Dirty Goat

**Type:** magazine
**CLMP Member:** no
**Primary Editor/Contact Person:** Joe Bratcher and Elzbieta Szoka
**Address:** 1000 E. 7th St.
Ste. 201
Austin, TX 78702
**Web Site Address:** http://www.thedirtygoat.com
**Publishes:** essays, fiction, poetry, art, and translation
**Editorial Focus:** Bringing the world to the US, The Dirty Goat focuses on little known US literature and great works from around the world.
**Representative Authors:** Alexis Lykiard, Christopher Cook, and Ayyapa Paniker
**Submissions Policy:** Send work with SASE.
**Simultaneous Subs:** yes
**Reading Period:** Year-round
**Reporting Time:** 6 to 12 months
**Author Payment:** copies
**Founded:** 1989
**Non Profit:** no
**Paid Staff:** 3
**Unpaid Staff:** 0
**ISSN Number/ISBN Number:** ISSN 1042-4768
**Total Circulation:** 500

**Paid Circulation:** 200
**Average Print Run:** 750
**Subscription Rate:** Individual $10/Institution $20
**Single Copy Price:** $10
**Current Volume/Issue:** Issue 13
**Frequency per Year:** 1
**Backfile Available:** yes
**Unsolicited Ms. Received:** yes
**% of Unsolicited Ms. Published per Year:** 20%
**Format:** perfect
**Size:** H 10" W 8"
**Average Pages:** 150
**Ads:** no

# divide

**Type:** magazine
**CLMP member:** yes
**Primary Editor/Contact Person:** Steven Wingate
**Address:** Program for Writing and Rhetoric
Box 317, University of Colorado-Boulder
Boulder, CO 80309
**Web Site Address:** http://www.colorado.edu/journals/divide/
**Publishes:** essays, fiction, nonfiction, poetry, reviews, art, and translation
**Editorial Focus:** We are an annual literary journal of creative responses to contemporary social questions. See website for issue themes.
**Representative Authors:** Richard Rodriguez, Naomi Shihab Nye, and Joanne Greenberg
**Submissions Policy:** Submissions of all kinds are read during the academic year. We print all varieties of work and consider reprints if on theme.
**Simultaneous Subs:** yes
**Reading Period:** 10/1 to 3/31
**Reporting Time:** 2 to 3 months
**Author Payment:** copies
**Contests:** We do not currently have contests, but plan on inaugurating contests for the 2005-06 issue.
**Founded:** 2002
**Non Profit:** yes
**Paid Staff:** 3
**Unpaid Staff:** 7
**Distributors:** Kent News and other regional distributors TBD
**ISSN Number/ISBN Number:** ISSN 1542-6424
**Total Circulation:** 850
**Paid Circulation:** 150
**Subscription Rate:** Individual $8/issue/Institution $8/issue

**Single Copy Price:** $8
**Current Volume/Issue:** Issue 2
**Frequency per Year:** 1
**Backfile Available:** yes
**Unsolicited Ms. Received:** yes
**% of Unsolicited Ms. Published per Year:** 8%
**Format:** perfect
**Size:** H 11" W 8 1/2"
**Average Pages:** 96
**Ads:** no

# Doorjamb Press

**Type:** press
**CLMP member:** yes
**Primary Editor/Contact Person:** Christine Monhollen
**Address:** P.O. Box 1296
Royal Oak, MI 48069
**Web Site Address:** http://www.doorjambpress.org
**Publishes:** essays, fiction, nonfiction, poetry, art, and translation
**Editorial Focus:** Small press publishes Dispatch Detroit journal, poetry/prose of national/local writers. Non-traditional writing featured.
**Representative Authors:** George Tysh, Ted Pearson, and Carla Harryman
**Submissions Policy:** For Dispatch Detroit (annually), editor looks for original use of language, form and continuing body of work.
**Simultaneous Subs:** yes
**Reading Period:** Year-round
**Reporting Time:** 1 to 12 months
**Author Payment:** copies
**Founded:** 1998
**Non Profit:** yes
**Paid Staff:** 0
**Unpaid Staff:** 1
**Distributors:** SPD
**Wholesalers:** books can be ordered through Paypal
**ISSN Number/ISBN Number:** 1-884118-09-7/1-884118-02-X
**Number of Books Published per Year:** 1-2
**Titles in Print:** 10
**Average Print Run:** 500
**Average Percentage Printed:** Paperback 90%, Chapbook 10%
**Average Price:** $13

# The Dos Passos Review

**Type:** magazine
**CLMP member:** yes
**Primary Editor/Contact Person:** Mary Carroll-Hackett
**Address:** Department of English
Longwood University
Farmville, VA 23909
**Web Site Address:**
http://www.longwood.edu/dospassosreview
**Publishes:** fiction, nonfiction, and poetry
**Editorial Focus:** In the spirit of John Dos Passos, we seek innovative strong work in all genres written by emerging and established writers
**Representative Authors:** Simon Perchik, Robert Bausch, and Toni Jensen
**Submissions Policy:** Submit 3-5 poems, 1 story or essay no more than 3,000 words, disposable copies only, SASE for reply, no electronic subs
**Simultaneous Subs:** yes
**Reading Period:** 2/1 to 7/31
**Reporting Time:** 1 to 2 months
**Author Payment:** copies
**Contests:** Associated with Briery Creek Press and The Liam Rector First Book Prize for Poetry
**Founded:** 2003
**Non Profit:** yes
**Paid Staff:** 0
**Unpaid Staff:** 14
**ISSN Number/ISBN Number:** ISBN 0-9765110-1-0
**Total Circulation:** 200
**Paid Circulation:** 60
**Average Print Run:** 500
**Subscription Rate:** Individual $20/Institution $26
**Single Copy Price:** $8
**Current Volume/Issue:** 2/1
**Frequency per Year:** 2
**Backfile Available:** yes
**Unsolicited Ms. Received:** yes
**Format:** perfect
**Average Pages:** 96

# Double Room

**Type:** online
**CLMP member:** no
**Primary Editor/Contact Person:** Peter Conners/Mark Tursi
**Address:** 2020 Pennsylvania Ave.
Ste. 443
Washington, DC 20006
**Web Site Address:**

http://webdelsol.com/Double_Room
**Publishes:** essays, fiction, poetry, reviews, art, and translation
**Editorial Focus:** Double Room focuses exclusively on prose poetry and flash fiction. New writing, mini-essays, reviews, and original artwork.
**Representative Authors:** Rosmarie Waldrop, Russell Edson, and Sean Thomas Dougherty
**Submissions Policy:** Our submission policies vary between solicit-only and open submission periods. Visit our web site for current policy.
**Simultaneous Subs:** yes
**Reading Period:** Year-round
**Reporting Time:** 1 to 6 months
**Author Payment:** none
**Founded:** 2002
**Non Profit:** yes
**Paid Staff:** 0
**Unpaid Staff:** 5
**Distributors:** Web del Sol
**Average Page Views per Month:** 5,000
**Average Unique Visitors per Month:** 1,000
**Frequency per Year:** 2
**Publish Print Anthology:** no
**Average Percentage of Pages per Category:** Fiction 25%, Poetry 25%, Reviews 15%, Essays 25%, Art 10%
**Ads:** no

# Drexel Online Journal

**Type:** online
**CLMP member:** no
**Primary Editor/Contact Person:** Albert DiBartolomeo
**Address:** 3210 Cherry St.
Philadelphia, PA 19104
**Web Site Address:** http://www.drexel.edu/doj
**Publishes:** essays, fiction, nonfiction, poetry, reviews, art, translation, and audio
**Editorial Focus:** The arts, culture, current events, personalities, photography, medicine, science, technology, travel
**Representative Authors:** Gerald Stern, Henry Petroski, and Paula Cohen
**Submissions Policy:** Submit to the site or, in hard copy, to the address. We reply only to accepted material, unless ms. is accompanied by SASE.
**Simultaneous Subs:** yes
**Reading Period:** Year-round
**Reporting Time:** 4 to 6 weeks
**Author Payment:** cash

**Contests:** Successive Years: fiction-science/medicine-poetry-creative nonfiction
See Web Site for Contest Guidelines.
**Founded:** 1999
**Non Profit:** yes
**Paid Staff:** x
**Unpaid Staff:** x
**Distributors:** Drexel University
**Average Page Views per Month:** 2,500
**Average Unique Visitors per Month:** 1,200
**Frequency per Year:** 12
**Publish Print Anthology:** no
**Average Percentage of Pages per Category:** Fiction 10%, Nonfiction 25%, Poetry 15%, Reviews 10%, Essays 20%, Art 10%, Translation 5%, Audio 5%
**Ads:** no

# Drunken Boat

**Type:** online
**CLMP member:** yes
**Primary Editor/Contact Person:** Ravi Shankar
**Address:** 119 Main St.
Chester, CT 06412
**Web Site Address:** http://www.drunkenboat.com
**Publishes:** essays, fiction, nonfiction, poetry, reviews, art, translation, and audio
**Editorial Focus:** Publishing the best of more traditional forms of representation alongside works of art endemic to the medium of the web.
**Representative Authors:** Alice Fulton, Mark Amerika, and Suji Kwock Kim
**Submissions Policy:** We accept unsolicited submissions year-round. Work should be sent as an attachment AND pasted into e-mail (URLs are fine).
**Simultaneous Subs:** yes
**Reading Period:** Year-round
**Reporting Time:** 4 to 6 months
**Author Payment:** none
**Contests:** Drunken Boat plans to host a contest in 2005 for writers and new media artists. Details will appear on website.
**Founded:** 1998
**Non Profit:** yes
**Paid Staff:** 0
**Unpaid Staff:** 8
**ISSN Number/ISBN Number:** ISSN 1537-2812
**Backfile Available:** yes
**Average Page Views per Month:** 10,000
**Average Unique Visitors per Month:** 6,000
**Frequency per Year:** 1

**Publish Print Anthology:** no
**Average Percentage of Pages per Category:** Fiction 15%, Nonfiction 10%, Poetry 25%, Reviews 10%, Essays 10%, Art 15%, Translation 5%, Audio 10%
**Ads:** yes
**Ad Rates:** $250 per banner ad; ads will also be considered for exchange

# Ducky magazine

**Type:** online
**CLMP member:** no
**Primary Editor/Contact Person:** Tom Hartman
**Address:** 807 Almond St.
Philadelphia, PA 19125
**Web Site Address:** http://www.duckymag.com
**Publishes:** essays, fiction, nonfiction, poetry, and translation
**Editorial Focus:** Contemporary poetry, fiction, interviews and essays in English
**Representative Authors:** Russell Edson, Joe Wenderoth, and Matthew Rohrer
**Submissions Policy:** Send 3-5 poems, 1 story. Attach sub to e-mail, MS Word, please. Send one doc. No snail mail! Follow guides on site!
**Simultaneous Subs:** yes
**Reading Period:** Year-round
**Reporting Time:** 2 to 3 months
**Author Payment:** none
**Founded:** 2001
**Non Profit:** yes
**Paid Staff:** 0
**Unpaid Staff:** 5
**Average Page Views per Month:** 6,000+
**Average Unique Visitors per Month:** 3,000
**Frequency per Year:** 2
**Publish Print Anthology:** yes
Price: $TBD
**Average Percentage of Pages per Category:** Fiction 40%, Nonfiction 10%, Poetry 50%
**Ads:** no
**Ad Rates:** Happy to exchange with other journals-e-mail us!

# Ducts Webzine

**Type:** online
**CLMP member:** yes
**Primary Editor/Contact Person:** Jonathan Kravetz
**Address:** 158 Noble St., #2
Brooklyn, NY 10163

**Web Site Address:** http://ducts.org
**Publishes:** essays, fiction, nonfiction, poetry, reviews, art, and audio
**Editorial Focus:** Ducts was founded in 1999 with the intent of giving emerging writers a venue to regularly publish their compelling, personal work.
**Representative Authors:** Charles Salzberg, Tim Tomlinson, and Cindy Moore
**Submissions Policy:** Query via e-mail with attachment for works of fiction, art, poetry and nonfiction.
**Simultaneous Subs:** yes
**Reading Period:** Year-round
**Reporting Time:** 2 to 6 weeks
**Author Payment:** none
**Founded:** 1999
**Non Profit:** yes
**Paid Staff:** 0
**Unpaid Staff:** 8
**Backfile Available:** yes
**Average Page Views per Month:** 10,000
**Average Unique Visitors per Month:** 500
**Frequency per Year:** 2
**Average Percentage of Pages per Category:** Fiction 20%, Nonfiction 15%, Poetry 15%, Reviews 15%, Essays 15%, Art 15%, Audio 5%

# Eclipse

**Type:** magazine
**CLMP member:** yes
**Primary Editor/Contact Person:** Bart Edelman
**Address:** 1500 N. Verdugo Rd.
Glendale, CA 91208
**Publishes:** fiction and poetry
**Editorial Focus:** Eclipse publishes quality fiction and poetry. It encourages all writers to contribute their work. We read year-round.
**Representative Authors:** William Heyen, Dana Gioia, and Wanda Coleman
**Submissions Policy:** Submissions are limited to five poems-any length. Contributors can also submit one story, 6,000 words maximum.
**Simultaneous Subs:** yes
**Reading Period:** Year-round
**Reporting Time:** 1 to 3 months
**Author Payment:** copies
**Founded:** 1989
**Non Profit:** yes
**Paid Staff:** no
**Unpaid Staff:** yes
**Distributors:** Ingram

**ISSN Number/ISBN Number:** 1530-5066/0-9701938-3-1
**Total Circulation:** 1,800
**Paid Circulation:** ~100
**Subscription Rate:** Individual $6/Institution $6
**Single Copy Price:** $6
**Current Volume/Issue:** 15/one
**Frequency per Year:** 1
**Backfile Available:** yes
**Unsolicited Ms. Received:** yes
**% of Unsolicited Ms. Published per Year:** 90%
**Format:** perfect
**Size:** H 9" W 6"
**Average Pages:** 180
**Ads:** no
**Ad Rates:** none

# Edgar Literary Magazine
**Type:** magazine
**CLMP member:** yes
**Primary Editor/Contact Person:** S.M. Geiger
**Address:** P.O. Box 5776
San Leon, TX 77539
**Web Site Address:** http://www.edgarliterary-magazine.com
**Publishes:** essays, fiction, and poetry
**Editorial Focus:** Well-crafted literary prose
**Submissions Policy:** Please see our website: http://www.edgarliterarymagazine.com
**Simultaneous Subs:** yes
**Reading Period:** Year-round
**Reporting Time:** 3 to 6 months
**Author Payment:** copies
**Founded:** 2003
**Non Profit:** yes
**Paid Staff:** 0
**Unpaid Staff:** 4
**Total Circulation:** 10,000
**Average Print Run:** 3,000
**Single Copy Price:** N/A
**Current Volume/Issue:** Issue 12
**Frequency per Year:** 4
**Backfile Available:** yes
**Unsolicited Ms. Received:** yes
**Format:** Saddle-stitched
**Size:** H 11" W 8.5"
**Average Pages:** 30

# edifice WRECKED
**Type:** online
**CLMP member:** yes
**Primary Editor/Contact Person:** Leigh Hughes
**Address:** 3602 Melrose Ln.
Temple, TX 76502
**Web Site Address:** http://www.edificewrecked.com
**Publishes:** essays, fiction, nonfiction, poetry, reviews, and art
**Editorial Focus:** Our only requirement is that you fully express your creative vision in such a way that your reality becomes the only reality.
**Submissions Policy:** Submissions must be made via online submission form. Simultaneous submissions okay; multiple submissions not.
**Simultaneous Subs:** yes
**Reading Period:** Year-round
**Reporting Time:** 1 to 2 months
**Author Payment:** copies and subscription
**Contests:** Flash Fiction Contest
See Web Site for Contest Guidelines.
**Founded:** 2004
**Non Profit:** yes
**Paid Staff:** 0
**Unpaid Staff:** 6
**ISSN Number/ISBN Number:** ISSN 1552-2342
**Average Page Views per Month:** 45,000
**Average Unique Visitors per Month:** 2,500
**Frequency per Year:** 6
**Publish Print Anthology:** yes
Price: $15
**Average Percentage of Pages per Category:** Fiction 45%, Nonfiction 5%, Poetry 15%, Reviews 5%, Essays 5%, Art 25%
**Ad Rates:** See Web Site for Details.

# Ekstasis Editions
**Type:** press
**CLMP member:** no
**Primary Editor/Contact Person:** Richard Olafson
**Address:** Box 8474, Main Postal Outlet
Victoria, BC V8W 3S1
**Web Site Address:** http://www.ekstasiseditions.com
**Publishes:** essays, fiction, nonfiction, poetry, reviews, art, translation, and audio
**Editorial Focus:** Literary texts: from neoformalism to language poetry
**Representative Authors:** Jim Christy, Ted Joans, and Ludwig Zeller
**Submissions Policy:** SASE, neatly typed, no e-mail or

faxes, on hardcopy
**Simultaneous Subs:** yes
**Reading Period:** Year-round
**Reporting Time:** 2 to 8 months
**Author Payment:** royalties
**Contests:** Mocambo Prize
See Web Site for Contest Guidelines.
**Founded:** 1982
**Non Profit:** yes
**Paid Staff:** 3
**Unpaid Staff:** non
**Distributors:** Canadabooks Ltd.
**ISSN Number/ISBN Number:** 1896860/1894800
**Number of Books Published per Year:** 16
**Titles in Print:** 246
**Average Print Run:** 1,500
**Average Percentage Printed:** Hardcover 20%, Paperback 80%
**Average Price:** $16

# The Electronic Book Review

**Type:** online
**CLMP member:** no
**Primary Editor/Contact Person:** Joseph Tabbi/Dave Ciccoricco
**Address:** 601 S. Morgan St.
UIC Dept of English
Chicago, IL 60607
**Web Site Address:** http://www.electronicbookreview.com
**Publishes:** essays, reviews, art, and audio
**Editorial Focus:** Cutting-edge lit crit, theory and philosophy re: literary, theoretical, and artistic innovations in digital environments.
**Representative Authors:** Joseph McElroy, Raymond Federman, and Michael Berube
**Submissions Policy:** Send proposals and submissions in a plain-text e-mail to the editors, ebr@altx.com. Freestanding hypertexts considered also.
**Simultaneous Subs:** yes
**Reading Period:** Year-round
**Reporting Time:** 1 to 3 weeks
**Author Payment:** none
**Founded:** 1995
**Non Profit:** yes
**Paid Staff:** 6
**Unpaid Staff:** 4
**Distributors:** http://www.altx.com
**Average Page Views per Month:** 30,000

**Average Unique Visitors per Month:** 6,000
**Frequency per Year:** 1
**Publish Print Anthology:** no
**Average Percentage of Pages per Category:** Fiction 2%, Poetry 2%, Reviews 40%, Essays 50%, Art 5%, Audio 1%
**Ads:** no

# Emergency Press/The Emergency Almanac

**Type:** press
**CLMP member:** yes
**Primary Editor/Contact Person:** Scott Zieher, Bryan Tomasovich
**Address:** 531 W. 25th St.
New York, NY 10001
**Web Site Address:** http://www.emergencypress.org
**Publishes:** essays, fiction, nonfiction, poetry, and art
**Editorial Focus:** Emergency Collective writers report on issues using a craft that highlights facts/research/utility.
**Representative Authors:** Scott Zieher, Molly McQuade, and Bryan Tomasovich
**Submissions Policy:** Send a short letter that introduces you to us, and tells why, and what you would like to write for the Emergency Almanac.
**Simultaneous Subs:** no
**Reading Period:** Year-round
**Reporting Time:** 1 to 2 months
**Author Payment:** none
**Contests:** Emergency Press runs an annual book contest open to members who contribute to the Emergency Almanac the current year.
**Founded:** 2001
**Non Profit:** yes
**Paid Staff:** 0
**Unpaid Staff:** 40
**Distributors:** Ingram, Baker & Taylor
**ISSN Number/ISBN Number:** ISBN 0-9753623
**Number of Books Published per Year:** 1-2
**Titles in Print:** 3
**Average Print Run:** 300
**Average Percentage Printed:** Paperback 100%
**Average Price:** $15

# Emrys Foundation

**Type:** press
**CLMP member:** yes
**Primary Editor/Contact Person:** Lydia Dishman

**Address:** P.O. Box 8813
Greenville, SC 29604
**Web Site Address:** http://www.emrys.org
**Publishes:** essays, fiction, nonfiction, and poetry
**Editorial Focus:** Engaging poetry and short stories, creative nonfiction and essays.
**Representative Authors:** Ron Rash, Jan Bailey, and Rosa Shand
**Submissions Policy:** Please enclose SASE. Send no more than 5 poems. Short fiction, essay and nonfiction should be no more than 7,500 words.
**Simultaneous Subs:** yes
**Reading Period:** 8/15 to 12/1
**Reporting Time:** 6 to 8 weeks
**Author Payment:** copies
**Founded:** 1983
**Non Profit:** yes
**Paid Staff:** 5
**Unpaid Staff:** 10
**ISSN Number/ISBN Number:** ISBN 0960324674
**Number of Books Published per Year:** 1
**Titles in Print:** 3
**Average Percentage Printed:** Hardcover 45%, Paperback 45%, Other 10%

# The Emrys Journal

**Type:** magazine
**CLMP member:** yes
**Primary Editor/Contact Person:** L.B. Dishman
**Address:** P.O. Box 8813
Greenville, SC 29604
**Web Site Address:** http://www.emrys.org
**Publishes:** essays, fiction, and poetry
**Editorial Focus:** literary fiction, creative nonfiction and memoir, contemporary poetry
**Representative Authors:** Rosa Shand, Elizabeth Swados, and Jessica Goodfellow
**Submissions Policy:** submit five poems or two essays or short stories, max 5,000 words. No genre fiction. Please SASE for reply.
**Simultaneous Subs:** yes
**Reading Period:** 8/1 to 11/1
**Reporting Time:** 1 to 2 months
**Author Payment:** copies
**Contests:** One award for best of each category published in the annual Fiction, Creative Nonfiction, Poetry $250 prize for each winner
See Web Site for Contest Guidelines.
**Founded:** 1984
**Non Profit:** yes

**Paid Staff:** 3
**Unpaid Staff:** 6
**Distributors:** Emrys Foundation, Open Book, Barnes & Noble
**ISSN Number/ISBN Number:** 1068-7335
**Total Circulation:** 400
**Paid Circulation:** 150
**Average Print Run:** 400
**Subscription Rate:** Individual $50/Institution $50
**Single Copy Price:** $12
**Current Volume/Issue:** 22/1
**Frequency per Year:** 1
**Backfile Available:** yes
**Unsolicited Ms. Received:** yes
**% of Unsolicited Ms. Published per Year:** 100%
**Format:** perfect
**Average Pages:** 120
**Ad Rates:** no ads

# Epicenter: A Literary Magazine

**Type:** magazine
**CLMP member:** yes
**Primary Editor/Contact Person:** Jeff Green
**Address:** P.O. Box 367
Riverside, CA 92502
**Web Site Address:**
http://www.epicentermagazine.org
**Publishes:** essays, fiction, nonfiction, poetry, and art
**Editorial Focus:** We publish a variety of poetry, short stories, and nonfiction. We review submissions from any author, printing what we like.
**Representative Authors:** Virgil Suarez, Egon H.E. Lass, and James Grinwis
**Submissions Policy:** We review poetry, short stories, nonfiction, and artwork. We are open to a wide variety of styles, forms and subjects.
**Simultaneous Subs:** yes
**Reading Period:** Year-round
**Reporting Time:** 1 to 2 months
**Author Payment:** copies
**Founded:** 1994
**Non Profit:** yes
**Paid Staff:** 0
**Unpaid Staff:** 4
**Wholesalers:** Fiddlerdoubleday
**ISSN Number/ISBN Number:** ISSN 1552-9169
**Total Circulation:** 500
**Paid Circulation:** 20
**Average Print Run:** 500
**Subscription Rate:** Individual $28/Institution $28

**Single Copy Price:** $7
**Current Volume/Issue:** 9/1
**Frequency per Year:** 2
**Backfile Available:** yes
**Unsolicited Ms. Received:** yes
**% of Unsolicited Ms. Published per Year:** 5%
**Format:** perfect
**Size:** H 8.5" W 5.5"
**Average Pages:** 80
**Ads:** no

## Epiphany

**Type:** magazine
**CLMP member:** no
**Primary Editor/Contact Person:** Willard Cook, Editor
**Address:** 10 Astor Place, #502
New York, NY 10003
**Web Site Address:** http://www.epiphanyzine.com
**Publishes:** essays, fiction, nonfiction, and poetry
**Simultaneous Subs:** yes
**Reading Period:** Year-round
**Reporting Time:** 3 to 4 months
**Author Payment:** none
**Founded:** 2003
**Non Profit:** yes
**Paid Staff:** 2
**Unpaid Staff:** 4
**Total Circulation:** 2,000
**Paid Circulation:** 50
**Subscription Rate:** Individual $10/Institution $15
**Single Copy Price:** $10
**Current Volume/Issue:** 1/premier
**Frequency per Year:** 1
**Backfile Available:** yes
**Unsolicited Ms. Received:** yes
**% of Unsolicited Ms. Published per Year:** 75%
**Format:** perfect

## EPOCH

**Type:** magazine
**CLMP member:** yes
**Primary Editor/Contact Person:** Michael Koch
**Address:** 251 Goldwin Smith Hall
Cornell University
Ithaca, NY 14853-3201
**Publishes:** essays, fiction, nonfiction, poetry, and art
**Editorial Focus:** Literary fiction, poetry, essays, memoir. Graphic art.
**Submissions Policy:** SASE required. No electronic or

e-mail submissions accepted.
**Simultaneous Subs:** no
**Reading Period:** 9/15 to 4/15
**Reporting Time:** 1 to 2 months
**Author Payment:** cash and copies
**Founded:** 1947
**Non Profit:** yes
**Paid Staff:** 9
**Unpaid Staff:** 15
**Distributors:** Ubiquity Distributors
**ISSN Number/ISBN Number:** ISSN 0145-1391
**Total Circulation:** 1,000
**Paid Circulation:** 574
**Subscription Rate:** Individual $11/Institution $11
**Single Copy Price:** $5
**Current Volume/Issue:** 53/2
**Frequency per Year:** 3
**Backfile Available:** yes
**Unsolicited Ms. Received:** yes
**Format:** perfect
**Size:** H 9" W 6"
**Average Pages:** 128
**Ads:** yes
**Ad Rates:** write for details

## Essays on Canadian Writing

**Type:** magazine
**CLMP member:** no
**Primary Editor/Contact Person:** Kevin Flynn
**Address:** 2120 Queen St. East
Ste. 200
Toronto, ON M4E 1E2
**Web Site Address:** http://www.ecw.ca
**Publishes:** essays and reviews
**Editorial Focus:** ECW publishes scholarly essays on all aspects of Canadian literature, and from all theoretical perspectives.
**Submissions Policy:** Submissions must be made in triplicate, and must conform to the MLA Handbook, fifth edition. Please include SASE.
**Simultaneous Subs:** no
**Reading Period:** Year-round
**Reporting Time:** 9 to 12 weeks
**Author Payment:** none
**Contests:** See Web Site for Contest Guidelines.
**Founded:** 1974
**Non Profit:** yes
**Paid Staff:** 3
**Unpaid Staff:** 6
**ISSN Number/ISBN Number:**

03130300/2527405002
**Total Circulation:** 1,400
**Paid Circulation:** 900
**Subscription Rate:** Individual $25/Institution $50
**Single Copy Price:** $9
**Current Volume/Issue:** Issue 82
**Frequency per Year:** 3
**Backfile Available:** yes
**Unsolicited Ms. Received:** yes
**Format:** perfect
**Average Pages:** 230
**Ads:** no

## Etruscan Press

**Type:** press
**CLMP member:** no
**Primary Editor/Contact Person:** Cathy Jewell
**Address:** P.O. Box 9685
Silver Spring, MD 20906
**Web Site Address:** http://www.etruscanpress.org
**Publishes:** essays, fiction, nonfiction, and poetry
**Editorial Focus:** Etruscan is a cooperative of poets
producing books that nurture the dialogue among
genres and achieve a distinctive voice.
**Representative Authors:** H.L. Hix, William Heyen, and
Tom Bailey
**Submissions Policy:** Currently not accepting unso-
licited submissions.
**Simultaneous Subs:** yes
**Reading Period:** Year-round
**Reporting Time:** 1 to 3 months
**Author Payment:** royalties and copies
**Founded:** 2001
**Non Profit:** yes
**Paid Staff:** 1
**Unpaid Staff:** 4
**Distributors:** SPD, Mint Publishers Group
**ISSN Number/ISBN Number:** ISBN 0-9718228
**Number of Books Published per Year:** 3
**Titles in Print:** 5
**Average Percentage Printed:** Hardcover 15%,
Paperback 85%

## Euphony

**Type:** magazine
**CLMP member:** yes
**Primary Editor/Contact Person:** Joseph N. Liss
**Address:** 5706 S. University Ave.
Chicago, IL 60637

**Web Site Address:** http://euphony.uchicago.edu
**Publishes:** essays, fiction, poetry, reviews, and trans-
lation
**Editorial Focus:** Euphony is dedicated to publishing
the finest work currently being done by writers both
accomplished and aspiring.
**Representative Authors:** Charles Wright, Mark
Strand, and Adam Zagajewski
**Submissions Policy:** Unpublished work only. Mail
manuscripts or e-mail in MS Word attachments to
euphony@uchicago.edu.
**Simultaneous Subs:** yes
**Reading Period:** 9/15 to 5/15
**Reporting Time:** 2 to 3 months
**Author Payment:** copies
**Founded:** 2000
**Non Profit:** yes
**Paid Staff:** 0
**Unpaid Staff:** all
**Distributors:** Staff
**Total Circulation:** 3,500
**Paid Circulation:** N/A
**Subscription Rate:** Individual $12/Institution $24
**Single Copy Price:** free
**Current Volume/Issue:** 3/2
**Frequency per Year:** 2
**Backfile Available:** no
**Unsolicited Ms. Received:** yes
**% of Unsolicited Ms. Published per Year:** 80%
**Format:** perfect
**Size:** H 8.5" W 5.5"
**Average Pages:** 100
**Ads:** yes
**Ad Rates:** $100 for half-page, $250 for full page
See Web Site for Details.

## Exhibition

**Type:** magazine
**CLMP member:** no
**Primary Editor/Contact Person:** Victoria Josslin
**Address:** Bainbridge Island Arts and Humanities
Council
221 Winslow Way W., Ste. 201
Bainbridge Island, WA 98110
**Web Site Address:** http://www.artshum.org
**Publishes:** essays, fiction, nonfiction, poetry, and art
**Editorial Focus:** Exhibition publishes original art and
writing by people who live in or are connected to
Bainbridge Island. We value diversity
**Representative Authors:** John Willson, Richard M.

## Profile: Chris Fishbach, Senior Editor, Coffee House

**1) How did you arrive at your current position?**
I graduated from college, and took an internship with Coffee House Press. At the end of my internship, I kept showing up, and eventually, someone quit, and I interviewed for the job and got it. That was eleven years ago.

**2) What is the staff structure like at your press/magazine?**
We have a board of directors.
Our Founder and Publisher is Allan Kornblum
Senior Editor (me)
Marketing Director
Publicist
Designer/Production Manager
Office Manager/Development Assistant
Interns

**3) How do you keep your press/magazine running?**
The same as any nonprofit publisher: raising enough money, keeping sales up while sticking with our mission, keeping our authors happy, keeping our distributor and vendors happy, and keeping a good staff.

**4) What do or don't you hope to see in a cover letter?**
Do: Short, concise, no-nonsense, white paper, standard font, what they are sending me, and who they are.

Don't: Anything cutesy, self-deprecation, funny fonts, colored paper, irony.

**5) What do you look for in a submission?**
A list can answer this: Honesty, boldness, formal presentation, daring, humility

**6) How are submissions processed at your press/magazine?**
I open everything, and either reject it right away, or put it in a pile for either myself to read later, for for interns to read and report to me. When the interns report to me, I ask many questions, and then either reject it based on the answers to those questions, or put it in a pile to read myself.

**7) Do you have a favorite unsolicited submission discovery or story?**
Only that nearly all our fiction comes from the slush pile.

**8) Do you have any advice for first-time submitters?**
Communicate with other writers you trust about where to send your work, and ask them if they think it is ready. Buy more books and read more. Revise. Shorten. Revise.

West, and Margi Berger
**Submissions Policy:** Typed submissions, e-mail, or attached Word documents are welcome. 1,600 word limit.
**Simultaneous Subs:** yes
**Reading Period:** 1/1 to 12/31
**Reporting Time:** 3 to 6 months
**Author Payment:** none
**Founded:** 1985
**Non Profit:** yes
**Paid Staff:** 1
**Unpaid Staff:** 2
**Total Circulation:** 1,000
**Paid Circulation:** 0
**Subscription Rate:** N/A
**Single Copy Price:** $7
**Current Volume/Issue:** Issue 2004
**Frequency per Year:** 2
**Backfile Available:** no
**Unsolicited Ms. Received:** yes
**Format:** stapled
**Size:** H 11" W 8.5"
**Average Pages:** 36
**Ads:** yes
**Ad Rates:** See Web Site for Details.

## eye-rhyme

**Type:** magazine
**CLMP member:** yes
**Primary Editor/Contact Person:** Laura Brian
**Address:** 1003 SE Grant St.
Portland, OR 97214
**Web Site Address:** http://www.eye-rhyme.com
**Publishes:** fiction, poetry, and art
**Editorial Focus:** eye-rhyme: journal of experimental literature publishes new poetry and short fiction in beautiful biannual editions.
**Representative Authors:** Fiona Hile, Alan Catlin, and B.Z. Niditch
**Submissions Policy:** We consider previously unpublished poetry (6 poems max), short fiction (10,000 words max), and B&W art. Send w/bio and SASE.
**Simultaneous Subs:** yes
**Reading Period:** Year-round
**Reporting Time:** 4 to 16 weeks
**Author Payment:** copies
**Founded:** 1998
**Non Profit:** no
**Paid Staff:** 0
**Unpaid Staff:** 3

**Wholesalers:** Baker & Taylor
**ISSN Number/ISBN Number:** ISSN 1540-6113
**Total Circulation:** 1,000
**Paid Circulation:** 100
**Subscription Rate:** Individual $8/Institution $10
**Single Copy Price:** $5
**Current Volume/Issue:** Issue 6
**Frequency per Year:** 2
**Backfile Available:** no
**Unsolicited Ms. Received:** yes
**% of Unsolicited Ms. Published per Year:** 70%
**Format:** perfect
**Size:** H 6.5" W 4.5"
**Average Pages:** 104
**Ads:** no

## Factorial Press

**Type:** press
**CLMP member:** no
**Primary Editor/Contact Person:** Sawako Nakayasu
**Address:** (please see website)
San Francisco, CA 94118
**Web Site Address:** http://www.factorial.org
**Publishes:** essays, fiction, nonfiction, poetry, art, and translation
**Editorial Focus:** Factorial Press has a shifting editorial focus, including collaborations & translations. Please see website for more details.
**Representative Authors:** N. Cole, K. Bradshaw, and A. Howell
**Submissions Policy:** Please query first by e-mail regarding all book and project proposals.
**Simultaneous Subs:** no
**Reading Period:** Year-round
**Reporting Time:** 2 to 6 months
**Author Payment:** copies
**Founded:** 2001
**Non Profit:** yes
**Paid Staff:** 0
**Unpaid Staff:** 4
**Distributors:** amazon.com
**ISSN Number/ISBN Number:** ISSN 1541-2660
**Number of Books Published per Year:** 1
**Titles in Print:** 3
**Average Print Run:** 500
**Average Percentage Printed:** Paperback 100%
**Average Price:** $8

## failbetter

**Type:** online
**CLMP member:** yes
**Primary Editor/Contact Person:** Thom Didato
**Address:** 40 Montgomery Place, #2
Brooklyn, NY 11215
**Web Site Address:** http://www.failbetter.com
**Publishes:** fiction, poetry, and art
**Editorial Focus:** failbetter.com is a quarterly online magazine published in the spirit of a traditional literary journal.
**Representative Authors:** Jim Shepard, Terrance Hayes, and Lee Upton
**Submissions Policy:** Please read submission guidelines at: http://www.failbetter.com/Submit.html
**Simultaneous Subs:** yes
**Reading Period:** Year-round
**Reporting Time:** 3 to 5 months
**Author Payment:** none
**Founded:** 2000
**Non Profit:** yes
**Paid Staff:** 0
**Unpaid Staff:** 7
**Average Page Views per Month:** 55,000
**Average Unique Visitors per Month:** 15,000
**Frequency per Year:** 4
**Publish Print Anthology:** yes
Price: $TBD
**Average Percentage of Pages per Category:** Fiction 40%, Poetry 40%, Art 20%
**Ads:** no

## Faultline

**Type:** press
**CLMP member:** no
**Primary Editor/Contact Person:** Sarah Cohen/Sara J Robinson
**Address:** Dept. of English & Comp. Lit.
University of California, Irvine
Irvine, CA 92697-2650
**Web Site Address:**
http://www.humanities.uci.edu/faultline
**Publishes:** essays, fiction, nonfiction, poetry, art, and translation
**Editorial Focus:** High quality poetry and prose that speaks with an original and compelling voice.
**Representative Authors:** C.K. Williams, Larisa Szporluk, and Steve Almond
**Submissions Policy:** Up to 20 pages of prose and up to 5 pages of poetry. Note genre on envelope.
**Simultaneous Subs:** yes

**Reading Period:** 9/1 to 3/1
**Reporting Time:** 3 to 6 months
**Author Payment:** copies
**Founded:** 1993
**Non Profit:** yes
**Paid Staff:** 2
**Unpaid Staff:** 12
**Distributors:** Ingram, Armadillo
**ISSN Number/ISBN Number:** ISSN 1076-0776
**Number of Books Published per Year:** 1
**Titles in Print:** 14
**Average Print Run:** 900
**Average Percentage Printed:** Paperback 100%
**Average Price:** $5-10

## Faux Press

**Type:** press
**CLMP member:** no
**Primary Editor/Contact Person:** Jack Kimball
**Address:** 24 Dale
Newton, MA 02460-1902
**Web Site Address:** http://www.fauxpress.com
**Publishes:** poetry
**Representative Authors:** David Larsen, Brandon Downing, and Alice Notley
**Simultaneous Subs:** no
**Reading Period:** Year-round
**Reporting Time:** 1 to 2 months
**Author Payment:** copies
**Founded:** 2000
**Non Profit:** yes
**Distributors:** SPD
**Number of Books Published per Year:** 3-4
**Titles in Print:** 12
**Average Print Run:** 500
**Average Percentage Printed:** Paperback 100%
**Average Price:** $15

## FC2 (Fiction Collective Two)

**Type:** press
**CLMP member:** yes
**Primary Editor/Contact Person:** Brenda L. Mills
**Address:** Department of English
Florida State University
Tallahassee, FL 32306-1580
**Web Site Address:** http://fc2.org
**Publishes:** fiction
**Editorial Focus:** FC2 is devoted to publishing fiction considered too challenging, innovative, or heterodox

for the commercial milieu.
**Representative Authors:** Ronald Sukenick, Cris Mazza, and Brian Evenson
**Submissions Policy:** See submission guidelines at http://fc2.org.
**Simultaneous Subs:** yes
**Reading Period:** 9/5 to 1/31
**Reporting Time:** 4 to 9 months
**Author Payment:** royalties and cash
**Founded:** 1973
**Non Profit:** yes
**Paid Staff:** 2
**Unpaid Staff:** 4
**Distributors:** Northwestern University Press, SPD
**ISSN Number/ISBN Number:** 157366 . . . ./091459 . . .
**Number of Books Published per Year:** 6
**Titles in Print:** 150
**Average Print Run:** 1,800
**Average Percentage Printed:** Paperback 100%
**Average Price:** $13.95

## Feather Books

**Type:** press
**CLMP member:** no
**Primary Editor/Contact Person:** Revd. John Waddington-Feather
**Address:** P.O. Box 438
Shrewsbury, Shrop UK, SY3 0WN
**Web Site Address:**
http://www.waddysweb.freeuk.com/
**Publishes:** essays, fiction, nonfiction, and poetry
**Editorial Focus:** Christian literature, art, music. Publishes the poetry quarterly Poetry Church and poetry collections. Also the Quill novel
**Representative Authors:** Walter Nash, Susan Glyn, and Laurie Bates
**Submissions Policy:** Submissions must be typed and not more than three poems sent with SASE. Poems not more than 30 lines for magazine.
**Simultaneous Subs:** yes
**Reading Period:** Year-round
**Reporting Time:** 1 to 2 weeks
**Author Payment:** none
**Founded:** 1980
**Non Profit:** yes
**Paid Staff:** 2
**Unpaid Staff:** 5
**Distributors:** M-Y Books Ltd, Maidenhead Yard, Hertford SG14 3AW
**Wholesalers:** as above

**ISSN Number/ISBN Number:** 1 84175
**Number of Books Published per Year:** 50
**Titles in Print:** 254
**Average Percentage Printed:** Paperback 25%, Chapbook 75%

## The Feminist Press

**Type:** press
**CLMP member:** no
**Primary Editor/Contact Person:** Livia Tenzer
**Address:** at the City University of New York
365 Fifth Ave.
New York, NY 10016
**Web Site Address:** http://www.feministpress.org
**Publishes:** essays, nonfiction, and translation
**Editorial Focus:** The Feminist Press is a nonprofit literary and educational publisher dedicated to publishing work by and about women.
**Representative Authors:** Charlotte Perkins Gilman, Paule Marshall, and Dorothy Hughes
**Submissions Policy:** To submit a proposal or query, send an e-mail to jcasella@gc.cuny.edu with the word "Submission" in the subject line.
**Simultaneous Subs:** no
**Reading Period:** Year-round
**Reporting Time:** 1 to 12 months
**Author Payment:** royalties
**Founded:** 1970
**Non Profit:** yes
**Paid Staff:** 8
**Unpaid Staff:** 4
**Distributors:** Consortium
**Wholesalers:** Ingram, Baker & Taylor
**ISSN Number/ISBN Number:** 0732-/1-55861-
**Number of Books Published per Year:** 22
**Titles in Print:** 256
**Average Percentage Printed:** Hardcover 30%, Paperback 70%

## Feminist Studies

**Type:** magazine
**CLMP member:** no
**Primary Editor/Contact Person:** Claire G. Moses
**Address:** 0103 Taliaferro
University of Maryland
College Park, MD 20742
**Web Site Address:** http://www.feministstudies.org
**Publishes:** essays, fiction, poetry, reviews, and art
**Editorial Focus:** Founded to encourage analytic

responses to feminist issues and to open new areas of research, criticism, and speculation.

**Representative Authors:** Bernice L. Hausman, Leslie J. Reagan, and Susan K. Cahn

**Submissions Policy:** We will publish serious writing of a critical, scholarly, speculative, and political nature.

**Simultaneous Subs:** no

**Reading Period:** Year-round

**Reporting Time:** 3 to 4 months

**Author Payment:** none

**Founded:** 1973

**Non Profit:** yes

**Paid Staff:** 2

**Unpaid Staff:** 10

**ISSN Number/ISBN Number:** ISSN 0046-3663

**Total Circulation:** 5,000

**Paid Circulation:** 4,880

**Subscription Rate:** Individual $33/Institution $132

**Single Copy Price:** $15

**Current Volume/Issue:** 29/2

**Frequency per Year:** 3

**Backfile Available:** yes

**Unsolicited Ms. Received:** yes

**% of Unsolicited Ms. Published per Year:** 7%

**Format:** perfect

**Size:** H 9" W 6"

**Average Pages:** 240

**Ads:** yes

**Ad Rates:** $360

See Web Site for Details.

# Fence Books

**Type:** press

**CLMP member:** yes

**Primary Editor/Contact Person:** Rebecca Wolff

**Address:** 303 E. 8th St. #B1

New York, NY 10009

**Web Site Address:** http://www.fencebooks.com

**Publishes:** poetry

**Editorial Focus:** To provide expanded exposure to poets whose work is excellent, challenging, and truly original. (see website)

**Representative Authors:** Joyelle McSweeney, Anthony McCann, and Catherine Wagner

**Submissions Policy:** Fence Books is a self-selecting publisher; manuscripts come to our attention through our contests. (see website)

**Simultaneous Subs:** yes

**Reading Period:** 11/1 to 2/28

**Reporting Time:** 6 to 7 months

**Author Payment:** royalties, cash, and copies

**Contests:** See Web Site for Contest Guidelines.

**Founded:** 2001

**Non Profit:** yes

**Paid Staff:** 0

**Unpaid Staff:** 2

**Distributors:** UPNE (Univ. Press New England)

**Wholesalers:** SPD

**Number of Books Published per Year:** 4

**Titles in Print:** 13

**Average Percentage Printed:** Paperback 100%

# Fence

**Type:** magazine

**CLMP member:** yes

**Primary Editor/Contact Person:** Charles Valle

**Address:** 303 E. Eighth St., #B1

New York, NY 10009

**Web Site Address:** http://www.fencemag.com

**Publishes:** fiction, nonfiction, poetry, art, and translation

**Editorial Focus:** Fence publishes poetry, fiction, art and criticism distinguished by idiosyncrasy and intelligence.

**Representative Authors:** Anne Carson, Lynne Tillman, and Joyelle McSweeney

**Submissions Policy:** see http://www.fencemag.com

**Simultaneous Subs:** yes

**Reading Period:** 10/1 to 4/31

**Reporting Time:** 2 to 9 months

**Author Payment:** copies and subscription

**Contests:** See Web Site for Contest Guidelines.

**Founded:** 1998

**Non Profit:** yes

**Paid Staff:** 1

**Unpaid Staff:** 9

**Distributors:** DeBoer, Ingram

**Wholesalers:** SPD

**ISSN Number/ISBN Number:** 1097-9980/0-9713189-9-9

**Total Circulation:** 3,300

**Paid Circulation:** 1,500

**Average Print Run:** 3,000

**Subscription Rate:** Individual $17/Institution $25

**Single Copy Price:** $10

**Current Volume/Issue:** 8.1/15

**Frequency per Year:** 2

**Backfile Available:** yes

**Unsolicited Ms. Received:** yes

**% of Unsolicited Ms. Published per Year:** 5%

**Format:** perfect
**Size:** H 9" W 7"
**Average Pages:** 200
**Ads:** yes
**Ad Rates:** contact fence@angel.net

# Fiction

**Type:** magazine
**CLMP member:** yes
**Primary Editor/Contact Person:** Mark Jay Mirsky
**Address:** c/o English Department
138 St. and Convent Ave.
NY, NY 10031
**Web Site Address:** http://fictioninc.com
**Publishes:** fiction and translation
**Editorial Focus:** Fiction goes to terra incognita in the writing of the imagination and asks that modern fiction set itself serious questions.
**Representative Authors:** Joseph McElroy, Robert Musil, and Clarice Lispector
**Submissions Policy:** We take simultaneous submissions of Fiction. Manuscripts will not returned without SASEs.
**Simultaneous Subs:** yes
**Reading Period:** 9/15 to 4/15
**Reporting Time:** 6 to 9 months
**Author Payment:** cash and copies
**Contests:** Check website for contest announcements.
**Founded:** 1972
**Non Profit:** yes
**Paid Staff:** 4
**Unpaid Staff:** 20
**Distributors:** DeBoer Distributors, Ingram
**ISSN Number/ISBN Number:** ISSN 7447080497
**Total Circulation:** 600
**Paid Circulation:** 550
**Subscription Rate:** Individual $38/Institution $30
**Single Copy Price:** $10
**Current Volume/Issue:** 18/1
**Frequency per Year:** 2
**Backfile Available:** yes
**Unsolicited Ms. Received:** yes
**% of Unsolicited Ms. Published per Year:** 75%
**Format:** perfect
**Size:** H 9" W 5"
**Average Pages:** 200
**Ads:** yes
**Ad Rates:** See Web Site for Details.

# FIELD: Contemporary Poetry and Poetics

**Type:** magazine
**CLMP member:** yes
**Primary Editor/Contact Person:** Linda Slocum, Managing Editor
**Address:** 50 N. Professor St.
Peters G 08
Oberlin, OH 44074-1091
**Web Site Address:** http://www.oberlin.edu/ocpress
**Publishes:** essays and poetry
**Editorial Focus:** FIELD is published twice a year; features established and emerging poets, symposia on famous poets and poetry book reviews
**Representative Authors:** Carl Phillips, Jean Valentine, and C.D. Wright
**Submissions Policy:** Send 3-5 poems to Editors/FIELD, 50 N. Professor St. Oberlin, OH 44074. Enclose a SASE; allow six weeks for response.
**Simultaneous Subs:** no
**Reading Period:** Year-round
**Reporting Time:** 6 to 8 weeks
**Author Payment:** cash and copies
**Contests:** FIELD Poetry Prize held annually in May for manuscripts of 50 to 80 pages. $1,000 and publication.$22 reading fee.
See Web Site for Contest Guidelines.
**Founded:** 1969
**Non Profit:** yes
**Paid Staff:** .5
**Unpaid Staff:** 4
**Distributors:** Fulfillment through Cornell University Press Services
**Wholesalers:** Ingram; Baker & Taylor
**ISSN Number/ISBN Number:** ISSN 0015-0657
**Total Circulation:** 1,400
**Paid Circulation:** 1,250
**Average Print Run:** 1,500
**Subscription Rate:** Individual $14/Institution $14
**Single Copy Price:** $7
**Current Volume/Issue:** Issue 69
**Frequency per Year:** 2
**Backfile Available:** yes
**Unsolicited Ms. Received:** yes
**% of Unsolicited Ms. Published per Year:** .5%
**Format:** perfect
**Size:** H 8.5" W 5.25"
**Average Pages:** 100
**Ads:** no

## Fine Madness

**Type:** magazine
**CLMP member:** yes
**Primary Editor/Contact Person:** Sean Bentley
**Address:** 6809 Dayton Ave. N.
Seattle, WA 98103
**Web Site Address:** http://www.finemadness.org
**Publishes:** poetry
**Editorial Focus:** No particular bias. We seek poetry that is thoughtful, well crafted, and exciting to us. Check website for examples.
**Representative Authors:** Carolyn Knox, Albert Goldbarth, and Melinda Mueller
**Submissions Policy:** Three to six poems with SASE. We accept e-mail submissions only from writers outside the US.
**Simultaneous Subs:** no
**Reading Period:** Year-round
**Reporting Time:** 4 to 6 months
**Author Payment:** copies
**Contests:** See Web Site for Contest Guidelines.
**Founded:** 1982
**Non Profit:** yes
**Paid Staff:** 0
**Unpaid Staff:** 5
**Distributors:** Small Changes, DeBoer
**ISSN Number/ISBN Number:** ISSN 0737-4704
**Total Circulation:** 1,000
**Paid Circulation:** 100
**Subscription Rate:** Individual $12/Institution $14
**Single Copy Price:** $7
**Current Volume/Issue:** 28/28
**Frequency per Year:** 1
**Backfile Available:** yes
**Unsolicited Ms. Received:** yes
**% of Unsolicited Ms. Published per Year:** 2%
**Format:** perfect
**Size:** H 8" W 5"
**Average Pages:** 64
**Ads:** no

## Finishing Line Press

**Type:** press
**CLMP member:** yes
**Primary Editor/Contact Person:** Leah Maines
**Address:** P.O. Box 1626
Georgetown, KY 40324
**Web Site Address:** http://www.finishinglinepress.com
**Publishes:** poetry
**Editorial Focus:** At this time we are publishing mostly poetry chapbooks. However, we are open to short story and creative nonfiction chaps.
**Recent Awards Received:** San Diego Book Award for a book of poetry, National Federation of Press Women's annual competition, in category 75-creative verse
**Representative Authors:** Tony Crunk, George Held, and Abigail Gramig
**Submissions Policy:** Up to 26 pages, bio, SASE, acknowledgements (including book publication): e-mail FinishingBooks@aol.com for current guideline
**Simultaneous Subs:** yes
**Reading Period:** Year-round
**Reporting Time:** 3 to 6 months
**Author Payment:** cash and copies
**Contests:** See Web Site for Contest Guidelines.
**Founded:** 1998
**Non Profit:** no
**Paid Staff:** 2
**Unpaid Staff:** 4
**ISSN Number/ISBN Number:** yes/yes
**Number of Books Published per Year:** 75
**Titles in Print:** 41
**Average Print Run:** 500
**Average Percentage Printed:** Paperback 1%, Chapbook 99%
**Average Price:** $12

## Fire By Nite

**Type:** magazine
**CLMP member:** yes
**Address:** 120 E. FM 544
Ste. 72 PMB 354
Murphy, TX 75094
**Web Site Address:** http://www.firebynite.com
**Publishes:** fiction and reviews
**Reading Period:** Year-round
**Reporting Time:** 1 to 2 months
**Author Payment:** none
**Founded:** 2004
**Non Profit:** yes
**Backfile Available:** yes

## Firewheel Editions

**Type:** press
**CLMP member:** yes
**Primary Editor/Contact Person:** Brian Clements, Editor
**Address:** Box 7, Western Conn. St. University

181 White St.
Danbury, CT 06810
**Web Site Address:** http://firewheel-editions.org
**Publishes:** poetry
**Editorial Focus:** Poetry and innovative work, such as hybrid or experimental texts, that might not see print if we didn't publish it.
**Representative Authors:** Denise Duhamel, Joe Ahearn, and Charles Kesler
**Submissions Policy:** Check the website.
**Simultaneous Subs:** yes
**Reading Period:** Year-round
**Reporting Time:** 1 to 6 months
**Author Payment:** royalties and copies
**Contests:** Check the website.
See Web Site for Contest Guidelines.
**Founded:** 2002
**Non Profit:** yes
**Paid Staff:** 0
**Unpaid Staff:** 3
**Wholesalers:** DeBoer, Amazon
**Number of Books Published per Year:** 2-4
**Titles in Print:** 6
**Average Print Run:** 1,000
**Average Percentage Printed:** Paperback 80%, Chapbook 20%
**Average Price:** $10

# First Class

**Type:** magazine
**CLMP member:** no
**Primary Editor/Contact Person:** Christopher M.
**Address:** P.O. Box 86
Friendship, IN 47021
**Web Site Address:** http://www.four-sep.com
**Publishes:** fiction, poetry, and art
**Editorial Focus:** Belt out a graphic, uncommon, thought-provoking poem or short story that won't leave the reader thinking "so what?"
**Representative Authors:** spiel, John Bennett, and Gary Every
**Submissions Policy:** Please send disposable mss.with a cover letter and SASE. I respond within a week or two, then one week prior to publication.
**Simultaneous Subs:** yes
**Reading Period:** Year-round
**Reporting Time:** 1 to 2 weeks
**Author Payment:** copies
**Contests:** The "make me think about your message award" wins publication in First Class. Contests are a

scam to make $ for "editors."
**Founded:** 1995
**Non Profit:** yes
**Paid Staff:** 0
**Unpaid Staff:** 2
**Distributors:** Tower Magazines/Records
**Total Circulation:** 300ish
**Paid Circulation:** 50
**Average Print Run:** 300ish
**Subscription Rate:** Individual $11/Institution $11
**Single Copy Price:** $6
**Current Volume/Issue:** Issue 25
**Frequency per Year:** 2
**Backfile Available:** yes
**Unsolicited Ms. Received:** yes
**% of Unsolicited Ms. Published per Year:** 10%
**Format:** stapled
**Size:** H 11" W 4.25"
**Average Pages:** 52
**Ads:** no

# First Intensity

**Type:** magazine
**CLMP member:** no
**Primary Editor/Contact Person:** Lee Chapman
**Address:** P.O. Box 665
Lawrence, KS 66044
**Web Site Address:** http://www.FirstIntensity.com
**Publishes:** essays, fiction, nonfiction, poetry, reviews, and translation
**Editorial Focus:** To promote innovative writing through publishing the best in contemporary literature.
**Representative Authors:** Robert Kelly, Laura Moriarty, and Barry Gifford
**Submissions Policy:** Send up to 15 pp for fiction; up to five poems; no electronic submissions. Allow 8 weeks for response.
**Simultaneous Subs:** no
**Reading Period:** Year-round
**Reporting Time:** 8 to 10 weeks
**Author Payment:** copies
**Founded:** 1993
**Non Profit:** no
**Paid Staff:** 0
**Unpaid Staff:** 1
**Distributors:** SPD
**ISSN Number/ISBN Number:** ISSN 1540-8019
**Total Circulation:** 175
**Paid Circulation:** 50-80
**Average Print Run:** 250

**Subscription Rate:** Individual $28/Institution $32
**Single Copy Price:** $14
**Current Volume/Issue:** Issue 20
**Frequency per Year:** 1
**Backfile Available:** yes
**Unsolicited Ms. Received:** yes
**% of Unsolicited Ms. Published per Year:** 10%
**Format:** perfect
**Size:** H 9" W 6"
**Average Pages:** 220
**Ads:** yes
**Ad Rates:** $150/full page; $75/half page

## The First Line

**Type:** magazine
**CLMP member:** no
**Primary Editor/Contact Person:** David LaBounty
**Address:** P.O. Box 250382
Plano, TX 75025-0382
**Web Site Address:** http://www.thefirstline.com
**Publishes:** essays, fiction, and reviews
**Editorial Focus:** We print stories that stem from the same first line.
**Simultaneous Subs:** no
**Reading Period:** Year-round
**Reporting Time:** 2 to 6 weeks
**Author Payment:** cash and copies
**Founded:** 1999
**Non Profit:** no
**Paid Staff:** 2
**Unpaid Staff:** 1
**ISSN Number/ISBN Number:** ISSN 1525-9382
**Total Circulation:** 425
**Paid Circulation:** 150
**Average Print Run:** 475
**Subscription Rate:** Individual $10/Institution $10
**Single Copy Price:** $3
**Current Volume/Issue:** 7/4
**Frequency per Year:** 4
**Backfile Available:** yes
**Unsolicited Ms. Received:** yes
**% of Unsolicited Ms. Published per Year:** 95%
**Format:** perfect
**Size:** H 8" W 5"
**Average Pages:** 64
**Ads:** no

## Five Fingers Review

**Type:** magazine
**CLMP member:** yes
**Primary Editor/Contact Person:** Jaime Robles
**Address:** P.O. Box 4
San Leandro, CA 94577-0100
**Web Site Address:** http://www.fivefingersreview.org
**Publishes:** essays, fiction, poetry, reviews, art, and translation
**Editorial Focus:** We are interested in fresh, innovative writing and art that is not defined by aesthetic ideology. Each issue is theme based.
**Representative Authors:** Rosmarie Waldrop, Elizabeth Willis, and Rafael Campo
**Submissions Policy:** Include SASE.
**Simultaneous Subs:** yes
**Reading Period:** 6/1 to 8/31
**Reporting Time:** 3 to 4 months
**Author Payment:** copies
**Contests:** See Web Site for Contest Guidelines.
**Founded:** 1984
**Non Profit:** yes
**Paid Staff:** 0
**Unpaid Staff:** 8
**Distributors:** Ingram, SPD
**Total Circulation:** 800
**Paid Circulation:** 50-100
**Subscription Rate:** Individual $20/Institution $22
**Single Copy Price:** $12
**Current Volume/Issue:** Issue 21
**Frequency per Year:** 1
**Backfile Available:** yes
**Unsolicited Ms. Received:** yes
**Format:** perfect
**Size:** H 9" W 6"
**Average Pages:** 224
**Ads:** yes
**Ad Rates:** $500 full page; $300 half page; $150 quarter page

## Five Points

**Type:** magazine
**CLMP member:** yes
**Primary Editor/Contact Person:** Megan Sexton
**Address:** Five Points, Georgia State University
P.O. Box 3999
Atlanta, GA 30302-3999
**Web site Address:** http://webdelsol.com/Five_Points
**Publishes:** essays, fiction, poetry, art, and translation
**Editorial Focus:** Original poetry, fiction, essays, also

translations, art, and interviews rich in the craft of language and imagination.
**Representative Authors:** Billy Collins, Alice Hoffman, and Nancy Reisman
**Submissions Policy:** Two submissions per genre per reading period.
**Simultaneous Subs:** no
**Reading Period:** 9/1 to 4/30
**Reporting Time:** up to 3 months
**Author Payment:** cash and copies
**Founded:** 1996
**Non Profit:** yes
**Paid Staff:** 7
**Unpaid Staff:** 0
**Distributors:** Ingram, Media Solutions
**ISSN Number/ISBN Number:** ISSN 1088-8500
**Total Circulation:** 2,000
**Paid Circulation:** 800
**Average Print Run:** 2,000
**Subscription Rate:** Individual $20/Institution $54
**Single Copy Price:** $7
**Current Volume/Issue:** 3
**Frequency per Year:** 3
**Backfile Available:** yes
**Unsolicited Ms. Received:** yes
**% of Unsolicited Ms. Published per Year:** 5%
**Format:** perfect
**Size:** H 6.5" W 9"
**Average Pages:** 150
**Ads:** yes
**Ad Rates:** e-mail: info@langate.gsu.edu

## Flash!Point Literary Journal

**Type:** magazine
**CLMP member:** no
**Primary Editor/Contact Person:** Frances LeMoine
**Address:** P.O. Box 540
Merrimack, NH 03054
**Publishes:** essays, fiction, poetry, reviews, and translation
**Editorial Focus:** Largely poetry, but accept any and all writing considered excellent by editorial staff
**Representative Authors:** R.D. Armstrong, Cheryl Snell, and Corey Mesler
**Submissions Policy:** Up to five poems, 30 lines max. Fiction/essays up to 1,500 words max. No pornography. Send SASE for reply
**Simultaneous Subs:** yes
**Reading Period:** Year-round
**Reporting Time:** 1 to 6 months

**Author Payment:** copies and subscription
**Contests:** Annual poetry and short fiction contests, usually announced in Poets & Writers Magazine
**Founded:** 1998
**Non Profit:** yes
**Paid Staff:** 0
**Unpaid Staff:** 1
**Distributors:** Barnes & Noble, Nashua NH, Toadstool Books, Milford NH
**Total Circulation:** 300
**Paid Circulation:** 50
**Subscription Rate:** Individual $33/Institution $33
**Single Copy Price:** $11
**Current Volume/Issue:** 9/9
**Frequency per Year:** 3
**Backfile Available:** yes
**Unsolicited Ms. Received:** yes
**% of Unsolicited Ms. Published per Year:** 10%
**Format:** perfect
**Size:** H 8.5" W 5.5"
**Average Pages:** 90
**Ads:** no

## The Florida Review

**Type:** magazine
**CLMP member:** yes
**Primary Editor/Contact Person:** Jeanne Leiby
**Address:** The University of Central Florida
Department of English
Orlando, FL 32816-0115
**Web Site Address:** http://www.flreview.com
**Publishes:** essays, fiction, nonfiction, poetry, and reviews
**Editorial Focus:** Mainstream and experimental literary fiction, poetry, and nonfiction
**Representative Authors:** Lola Haskins, Billy Collins, and Wendell Mayo
**Submissions Policy:** Poetry, max 5 poems. Literary fiction and nonfiction up to 7,500 words. Short shorts okay. Include SASE.
**Simultaneous Subs:** yes
**Reading Period:** Year-round
**Reporting Time:** 1 to 3 months
**Author Payment:** none and copies
**Contests:** Annual Editors' award. $1,000 prize in fiction, nonfiction, and poetry. $15 reading fee. Reading from December to March 15th.
See Web Site for Contest Guidelines.
**Founded:** 1972
**Non Profit:** yes

**Paid Staff:** 3
**Unpaid Staff:** 15
**Distributors:** amazon.com
**Total Circulation:** 1,500
**Paid Circulation:** 1,100
**Average Print Run:** 2,000
**Subscription Rate:** Individual $15/Institution $20
**Single Copy Price:** $8
**Current Volume/Issue:** 30/1
**Frequency per Year:** 2
**Backfile Available:** yes
**Unsolicited Ms. Received:** yes
**% of Unsolicited Ms. Published per Year:** 90%
**Format:** perfect
**Size:** H 6" W 9"
**Average Pages:** 168
**Ads:** yes
**Ad Rates:** $200 page. Nonprofit discount and 1/2 and 1/4 pgs available

## Flume Press

**Type:** press
**CLMP member:** yes
**Primary Editor/Contact Person:** Casey Huff
**Address:** California State University, Chico
400 W. 1st St.
Chico, CA 95929-0830
**Web Site Address:**
http://www.csuchico.edu/engl/flumepress/
**Publishes:** fiction and poetry
**Editorial Focus:** Flume Press aims to help newer writers get the sort of exposure that can help them achieve the recognition they deserve.
**Representative Authors:** John Brehm, Sherrie Flick, and Luis Omar Salinas
**Submissions Policy:** Our annual chapbook contest deadline is December 1. Send for guidelines or see our website: http://www.csuchico.edu/engl/flume-press/
**Simultaneous Subs:** yes
**Reading Period:** 12/05 to 5/06
**Reporting Time:** 5 to 6 months
**Author Payment:** cash
**Contests:** See Web Site for Contest Guidelines.
**Founded:** 1983
**Non Profit:** yes
**Paid Staff:** 1
**Unpaid Staff:** 8
**ISSN Number/ISBN Number:** ISBN 1-886226
**Number of Books Published per Year:** 1

**Titles in Print:** 20
**Average Print Run:** 500
**Average Percentage Printed:** Chapbook 100%
**Average Price:** $8

## Flyway: A Literary Review

**Type:** magazine
**CLMP member:** no
**Primary Editor/Contact Person:** Steve Pett
**Address:** 206 Ross Hall
Iowa State University
Ames, IA 50011
**Web Site Address:** http://www.flyway.org
**Publishes:** essays, fiction, nonfiction, poetry, and art
**Editorial Focus:** We are looking for solid, quality writing regardless of an author's publishing history.
**Representative Authors:** Jane Smiley, Naomi Shihab Nye, and Gina Ochsner
**Simultaneous Subs:** yes
**Reading Period:** 9/06 to 4/07
**Reporting Time:** 3 to 6 weeks
**Author Payment:** copies
**Contests:** Sweet Corn Prize Contest
See Web Site for Contest Guidelines.
**Founded:** 1995
**Non Profit:** yes
**Paid Staff:** 0
**Unpaid Staff:** 4
**Total Circulation:** 500
**Paid Circulation:** 500
**Average Print Run:** 600
**Subscription Rate:** Individual $18/Institution $18
**Single Copy Price:** $6
**Current Volume/Issue:** 10/1
**Frequency per Year:** 3
**Backfile Available:** yes
**Unsolicited Ms. Received:** yes
**% of Unsolicited Ms. Published per Year:** 95%
**Format:** perfect
**Size:** H 9" W 6"
**Average Pages:** 120
**Ads:** yes
**Ad Rates:** Exchange Ads

## Folio, A Literary Journal at American U.

**Type:** magazine
**CLMP member:** no
**Primary Editor/Contact Person:** Lauren Fanelli

**Address:** Department of Literature
American University
Washington, DC 20016
**Web Site Address:** http://www.foliojournal.org
**Publishes:** fiction, nonfiction, poetry, and art
**Editorial Focus:** We are looking for work that ignites and endures, is artful, natural, daring, and elegant.
**Representative Authors:** Denise Duhamel, Alice Fulton, and E. Ethelbert Miller
**Submissions Policy:** Submit 4-6 poems; no more than 3,500 words for prose. SASE for response. Include cover letter with contact info. and bio.
**Simultaneous Subs:** yes
**Reading Period:** 8/15 to 3/1
**Reporting Time:** 1 to 3 months
**Author Payment:** copies
**Founded:** 1984
**Non Profit:** yes
**Paid Staff:** 9
**Unpaid Staff:** 0
**ISSN Number/ISBN Number:** ISSN 1547-4151
**Total Circulation:** 150
**Paid Circulation:** 25
**Average Print Run:** 200
**Subscription Rate:** Individual $12/Institution $24
**Single Copy Price:** $6
**Current Volume/Issue:** 20/1
**Frequency per Year:** 2
**Backfile Available:** yes
**Unsolicited Ms. Received:** yes
**% of Unsolicited Ms. Published per Year:** 20%
**Format:** perfect
**Average Pages:** 70
**Ads:** yes

## Foreword

**Type:** magazine
**CLMP member:** yes
**Primary Editor/Contact Person:** Alex Moore
**Address:** 129 1/2 E. Front St.
Traverse City, MI 49684
**Web Site Address:**
http://www.forewordmagazine.com/
**Publishes:** reviews
**Editorial Focus:** Reviews and feature stories focusing on great books from small presses.
**Recent Awards Received:** FOLIO Eddy Award for Editorial Excellence 2003/2004
**Submissions Policy:** please e-mail managing editor for details.

**Simultaneous Subs:** yes
**Reading Period:** Year-round
**Reporting Time:** 1 to 2 months
**Author Payment:** cash
**Contests:** Book of the Year Awards program for titles published in current year
See Web Site for Contest Guidelines.
**Founded:** 1998
**Non Profit:** no
**Paid Staff:** 5
**Unpaid Staff:** 0
**Distributors:** USPS
**ISSN Number/ISBN Number:** ISSN 1099-2642
**Total Circulation:** 8,500
**Paid Circulation:** 400
**Average Print Run:** 7,500
**Subscription Rate:** Individual $40/Institution $34
**Single Copy Price:** $10
**Current Volume/Issue:** 8/6
**Frequency per Year:** 6
**Backfile Available:** yes
**Unsolicited Ms. Received:** no
**Format:** perfect
**Average Pages:** 72
**Ad Rates:** See Web Site for Details.

## Four Way Books

**Type:** press
**CLMP member:** yes
**Primary Editor/Contact Person:** Martha Rhodes
**Address:** POB 535 Village Station
NY, NY 10014
**Web Site Address:** http://www.fourwaybooks.com
**Publishes:** fiction and poetry
**Editorial Focus:** We are primarily a poetry press although we publish short story collections and novellas.
**Representative Authors:** Catherine Bowman, Sarah Manguso, and Jeffrey Harrison
**Submissions Policy:** For contest and open reading period, check our website first as reading dates may change year-to-year.
**Simultaneous Subs:** yes
**Reading Period:** 6/1 to 6/30
**Reporting Time:** 1 to 5 months
**Author Payment:** royalties and cash
**Contests:** See Web Site for Contest Guidelines.
**Founded:** 1993
**Non Profit:** yes
**Paid Staff:** 5

**Unpaid Staff:** 2
**Distributors:** University Press of New England (UPNE)
**ISSN Number/ISBN Number:** ISBN 1884800
**Number of Books Published per Year:** 6-8
**Titles in Print:** 70
**Average Print Run:** 1,000
**Average Percentage Printed:** Paperback 100%
**Average Price:** $14.95

## Fourteen Hills

**Type:** magazine
**CLMP member:** yes
**Primary Editor/Contact Person:** Jason Snyder
**Address:** Creative Writing Dept.
1600 Holloway Ave.
San Francisco, CA 94132-1722
**Web Site Address:** http://www.14hills.net
**Publishes:** essays, fiction, nonfiction, poetry, art, and translation
**Editorial Focus:** Biannual journal committed to presenting experimental and progressive work by emerging, established, and cross-genre writers.
**Simultaneous Subs:** yes
**Reading Period:** Year-round
**Reporting Time:** 2 to 8 months
**Author Payment:** copies
**Contests:** Holmes Awards: $250 each; best poem, best prose published each year by emerging writers who have not yet published first book
**Founded:** 1994
**Non Profit:** yes
**Paid Staff:** 1
**Unpaid Staff:** 20
**Total Circulation:** 600
**Paid Circulation:** 50
**Subscription Rate:** Individual $12/Institution $18
**Single Copy Price:** $7
**Current Volume/Issue:** 10/1
**Frequency per Year:** 2
**Backfile Available:** yes
**Unsolicited Ms. Received:** yes
**% of Unsolicited Ms. Published per Year:** 2%
**Format:** perfect
**Size:** H 9" W 6"
**Average Pages:** 180
**Ads:** yes
**Ad Rates:** $50 half page; $80 full page

## Freefall Magazine

**Type:** magazine
**CLMP member:** no
**Primary Editor/Contact Person:** Vivian Hansen
**Address:** 922-9 Ave. SE
Calgary, AB T3G 1R2
**Web Site Address:** http://www.alexandrawriters.org
**Publishes:** essays, fiction, nonfiction, poetry, reviews, art, and translation
**Editorial Focus:** a journal committed to cutting edge literary work. We publish primarily poetry and fiction or nonfiction.
**Representative Authors:** Audrey Whitson, Robert Stallworthy, and Betty Jane Hegerat
**Submissions Policy:** 3 copies of submission, SASE required. 2,500 words for fiction, 3,000 words nonfiction. Essays 2,500 words, poetry 3-5 pieces
**Simultaneous Subs:** no
**Reading Period:** Year-round
**Reporting Time:** 6 to 8 months
**Author Payment:** cash
**Contests:** See Web Site for Contest Guidelines.
**Founded:** 1990
**Non Profit:** yes
**Paid Staff:** 1/2
**Unpaid Staff:** 3
**Distributors:** Alexandra Writers Centre
**ISSN Number/ISBN Number:** ISSN 1203-9586
**Total Circulation:** 500
**Paid Circulation:** 200
**Average Print Run:** 300
**Subscription Rate:** Individual $15/Institution $20
**Single Copy Price:** $7
**Current Volume/Issue:** XV/1
**Frequency per Year:** 2
**Backfile Available:** yes
**Unsolicited Ms. Received:** yes
**% of Unsolicited Ms. Published per Year:** 100%
**Format:** stapled
**Size:** H 11" W 8 1/2"
**Average Pages:** 35
**Ads:** yes
**Ad Rates:** See Web Site for Details.

## Frigate

**Type:** online
**CLMP member:** no
**Primary Editor/Contact Person:** Patricia Eakins
**Address:** 1200 Broadway
New York, NY 11021

**Web Site Address:** http://www.frigatezine.com
**Publishes:** essays, fiction, nonfiction, poetry, reviews, and art
**Editorial Focus:** We are multi-syncratic, with a spectrum of vivid voices. We like quirk and flavor. We read difficult writing for the sheer pleasure of its language. We are fond of all things experimental, innovative and playful. We loathe blandness, earnestness, and pious correctitude.
**Representative Authors:** Eric Darton, Elain Terranova, and Gerry Gomez Pearlberg
**Submissions Policy:** Solicited only.
**Simultaneous Subs:** yes
**Reading Period:** Year-round
**Reporting Time:** 2 to 4 months
**Author Payment:** none
**Founded:** 2000
**Non Profit:** yes
**Paid Staff:** 3
**Unpaid Staff:** 21
**Average Page Views per Month:** 10,000
**Average Unique Visitors per Month:** 3,000
**Frequency per Year:** 1
**Publish Print Anthology:** no
**Average Percentage of Pages per Category:** Fiction 5%, Nonfiction 10%, Poetry 5%, Reviews 35%, Essays 35%, Art 10%
**Ads:** no

# FRiGG: A Magazine of Fiction and Poetry

**Type:** online
**CLMP member:** yes
**Primary Editor/Contact Person:** Ellen Parker
**Address:** 9036 Evanston Ave. N.
Seattle, WA 98103
**Web Site Address:** http://www.friggmagazine.com
**Publishes:** fiction, nonfiction, poetry, and art
**Simultaneous Subs:** yes
**Reading Period:** Year-round
**Reporting Time:** 1 to 3 months
**Author Payment:** none
**Founded:** 2003
**Non Profit:** yes
**Paid Staff:** 0
**Unpaid Staff:** 5
**Average Page Views per Month:** varies
**Average Unique Visitors per Month:** varies
**Frequency per Year:** 4
**Average Percentage of Pages per Category:** Fiction

45%, Nonfiction 5%, Poetry 40%, Art 10%

# Fugue State Press

**Type:** press
**CLMP member:** no
**Primary Editor/Contact Person:** James Chapman
**Address:** P.O. Box 80, Cooper Station
New York, NY 10003
**Web Site Address:** http://www.fuguestatepress.com
**Publishes:** fiction
**Editorial Focus:** Experimental and advanced fiction: novels only
**Representative Authors:** Prakash Kona, Randie Lipkin, and James Chapman
**Submissions Policy:** We're looking for experimental novels that are ambitious, visionary, private, idiosyncratic, emotional.
**Simultaneous Subs:** yes
**Reading Period:** Year-round
**Reporting Time:** 1 to 2 weeks
**Author Payment:** copies
**Founded:** 1992
**Non Profit:** no
**Paid Staff:** 0
**Unpaid Staff:** 1
**Wholesalers:** Baker & Taylor
**ISSN Number/ISBN Number:** ISBN 1879193
**Number of Books Published per Year:** 3
**Titles in Print:** 15
**Average Print Run:** 1,000
**Average Percentage Printed:** Paperback 100%
**Average Price:** $12

# Fugue

**Type:** magazine
**CLMP member:** yes
**Primary Editor/Contact Person:** Sara Kaplan and Justin Jainchill
**Address:** University of Idaho, English Department
200 Brink Hall
Moscow, ID 83844-1102
**Web Site Address:**
http://www.class.uidaho.edu/Fugue/
**Publishes:** fiction, nonfiction, and poetry
**Editorial Focus:** Fugue brings together diverse modes of expression and voices within each issue.
**Representative Authors:** W.S. Merwin, Dean Young, and Maura Stanton
**Submissions Policy:** Prose: 6,000 words. Poetry: 3 to

5 poems, not more than 10 pages. Address to appropriate editor.
**Simultaneous Subs:** yes
**Reading Period:** 9/1 to 5/1
**Reporting Time:** 3 to 6 months
**Author Payment:** cash and copies
**Contests:** See Web Site for Contest Guidelines.
**Founded:** 1990
**Non Profit:** yes
**Paid Staff:** no
**Unpaid Staff:** 21
**Distributors:** DeBoer, Ingram
**ISSN Number/ISBN Number:** ISSN 10546014
**Total Circulation:** 1,000
**Paid Circulation:** no
**Average Print Run:** 800
**Subscription Rate:** Individual $14/Institution $22
**Single Copy Price:** $8
**Current Volume/Issue:** 1/27
**Frequency per Year:** 2
**Backfile Available:** yes
**Unsolicited Ms. Received:** yes
**% of Unsolicited Ms. Published per Year:** 80%
**Format:** perfect
**Size:** H 9" W 6"
**Average Pages:** 175
**Ads:** yes
**Ad Rates:** Inquire

## Full Circle Journal

**Type:** magazine
**CLMP member:** no
**Primary Editor/Contact Person:** Allegra Wong/Daniel Blasi
**Address:** P.O. Box 15554
Boston, MA 02215
**Web Site Address:** http://www.fullcirclejrnl.com
**Publishes:** essays, fiction, nonfiction, poetry, and translation
**Editorial Focus:** We seek outstanding literature.
**Representative Authors:** Robert Pinsky, Elizabeth Arnold, and Allan Peterson
**Submissions Policy:** We accept submissions via postal mail. Include a self-addressed stamped envelope and a brief bio.
**Simultaneous Subs:** yes
**Reading Period:** Year-round
**Reporting Time:** 3 to 5 months
**Author Payment:** copies
**Contests:** varies

See Web Site for Contest Guidelines.
**Founded:** 2002
**Non Profit:** yes
**Paid Staff:** 0
**Unpaid Staff:** 4
**ISSN Number/ISBN Number:** ISSN 1542-197X
**Total Circulation:** 1,000
**Paid Circulation:** 350
**Subscription Rate:** Individual $18/Institution $18
**Single Copy Price:** $10
**Current Volume/Issue:** one/two
**Frequency per Year:** 2
**Backfile Available:** yes
**Unsolicited Ms. Received:** yes
**% of Unsolicited Ms. Published per Year:** 3%
**Format:** perfect
**Size:** H 8" W 5.5"
**Average Pages:** 225
**Ads:** yes
**Ad Rates:** query for rates

## FuseBox

**Type:** online
**CLMP member:** yes
**Primary Editor/Contact Person:** Ram Devineni
**Address:** 532 La Guardia Place
Ste. 353
New York, NY 10012
**Web Site Address:** http://www.rattapallax.com/fusebox.htm
**Publishes:** essays, fiction, nonfiction, poetry, reviews, art, translation, and audio
**Editorial Focus:** Focus on international poetry and performance.
**Representative Authors:** Robert Creeley, Arnaldo Antunes, and AJA (Adisa Jelani Andwele)
**Submissions Policy:** Contact editor by e-mail.
**Simultaneous Subs:** yes
**Reading Period:** Year-round
**Reporting Time:** 1 to 2 months
**Author Payment:** none
**Founded:** 2003
**Non Profit:** yes
**Paid Staff:** 0
**Unpaid Staff:** 4
**Distributors:** online
**Average Page Views per Month:** 60
**Average Unique Visitors per Month:** 1,200
**Publish Print Anthology:** yes
Price: $24

**Average Percentage of Pages per Category:** Fiction 5%, Nonfiction 5%, Poetry 40%, Reviews 5%, Essays 5%, Art 5%, Translation 30%, Audio 5%
**Ad Rates:** See Web Site for Details.

## Future Tense Books

**Type:** press
**CLMP member:** no
**Primary Editor/Contact Person:** Kevin Sampsell
**Address:** P.O. Box 42416
Portland, OR 97242
**Web Site Address:** http://www.futuretensebooks.com
**Publishes:** essays, fiction, and poetry
**Editorial Focus:** We publish chapbooks and paperbacks from emerging and established writers, often dealing with work that other presses ignore.
**Representative Authors:** Eric Spitznagel, Susannah Breslin, and Magdalen Powers
**Submissions Policy:** Please send a query and SASE or an e-mail describing the work before submitting. Mostly interested in fiction or memoir.
**Simultaneous Subs:** yes
**Reading Period:** Year-round
**Reporting Time:** 2 to 8 weeks
**Author Payment:** copies
**Founded:** 1990
**Non Profit:** no
**Paid Staff:** 2
**Unpaid Staff:** 2
**Distributors:** Last Gasp
**Number of Books Published per Year:** 2-4
**Titles in Print:** 24
**Average Print Run:** 500
**Average Percentage Printed:** Paperback 25%, Chapbook 75%
**Average Price:** $5

## Futurepoem books

**Type:** press
**CLMP member:** yes
**Primary Editor/Contact Person:** Dan Machlin
**Address:** P.O. Box 34
New York, NY 10014
**Web Site Address:** http://www.futurepoem.com
**Publishes:** fiction and poetry
**Editorial Focus:** Innovative poetry and prose. Works that blur the line between literary genres.
**Recent Awards Received:** AIGA 50 Books/50 Covers for best Covers of 2004

**Representative Authors:** Jo Ann Wasserman, Shanxing Wang, and Rachel Levitsky
**Submissions Policy:** Unsolicited manuscripts are accepted only during open reading period. Please check Web site submission page for details.
**Simultaneous Subs:** yes
**Reading Period:** 9/1 to 9/30
**Reporting Time:** 5 to 6 months
**Author Payment:** royalties and copies
**Founded:** 2001
**Non Profit:** yes
**Paid Staff:** 0
**Unpaid Staff:** 5
**Distributors:** SPD Books
**ISSN Number/ISBN Number:** ISBN 0-9716800
**Number of Books Published per Year:** 2
**Titles in Print:** 2
**Average Print Run:** 750
**Average Percentage Printed:** Paperback 100%
**Average Price:** $14

## Gargoyle Magazine

**Type:** magazine
**CLMP member:** yes
**Primary Editor/Contact Person:** Richard Peabody
**Address:** 3819 N. 13th St.
Arlington, VA 22201
**Web Site Address:**
http://www.gargoylemagazine.com
**Publishes:** essays, fiction, nonfiction, poetry, art, translation, and audio
**Editorial Focus:** We tend to be edgy and bent. We collect books and mags, love to read and write, and actually believe lit matters. Silly us.
**Representative Authors:** John Dufresne, Nin Andrews, and Eileen Myles
**Submissions Policy:** Prefer electronic submissions in the body of an e-mail. If we like something we'll ask for a Word attachment. Snail mail OK.
**Simultaneous Subs:** yes
**Reading Period:** 5/30 to 9/4
**Reporting Time:** 1 to 3 months
**Author Payment:** copies
**Founded:** 1976
**Non Profit:** no
**Paid Staff:** 0
**Unpaid Staff:** 3
**Distributors:** DeBoer
**ISSN Number/ISBN Number:** ISSN 0162-1149
**Total Circulation:** 1,500

**Paid Circulation:** 25
**Average Print Run:** 1,500
**Subscription Rate:** Individual $30/Institution $40
**Single Copy Price:** $14.95
**Current Volume/Issue:** Issue 50
**Frequency per Year:** 1
**Backfile Available:** yes
**Unsolicited Ms. Received:** yes
**% of Unsolicited Ms. Published per Year:** 40%
**Format:** perfect
**Size:** H 9" W 6"
**Average Pages:** 300+
**Ads:** yes
**Ad Rates:** $100 full-page; $60 half page

# Geist Magazine

**Type:** magazine
**CLMP member:** yes
**Primary Editor/Contact Person:** Stephen Osborne
**Address:** 341 Water St., Ste. 200
Vancouver, BC V6B 1B8
**Web Site Address:** http://www.geist.com
**Publishes:** essays, fiction, nonfiction, poetry, and art
**Editorial Focus:** A literary magazine of Canadian Ideas and Culture.
**Recent Awards Received:** Magazine of the Year at the Western Magazine Awards 2001 and 2003.
**Submissions Policy:** Submissions should have a connection to Canada, either by content or author nationality.
**Simultaneous Subs:** yes
**Reading Period:** Year-round
**Reporting Time:** 1 to 5 months
**Author Payment:** cash and copies
**Contests:** Annual Literal Literary Postcard Contest (December deadline)
See Web Site for Contest Guidelines.
**Founded:** 1990
**Non Profit:** yes
**Paid Staff:** 2
**Unpaid Staff:** 12
**Distributors:** Magazines Canada, Disticor, Doormouse
**ISSN Number/ISBN Number:** ISSN 1181-6554
**Total Circulation:** 10,000
**Paid Circulation:** 4,691
**Average Print Run:** 12,000
**Subscription Rate:** Individual $20/Institution $25
**Single Copy Price:** $5.95
**Current Volume/Issue:** 14/57
**Frequency per Year:** 4

**Backfile Available:** yes
**Unsolicited Ms. Received:** yes
**Format:** stapled
**Size:** H 10.5" W 8"
**Average Pages:** 58
**Ads:** yes
**Ad Rates:** See Web Site for Details.

# Georgetown Review

**Type:** magazine
**CLMP member:** yes
**Primary Editor/Contact Person:** Steven Carter
**Address:** 400 E. College St.
P.O. Box 227
Georgetown, KY 40324
**Web Site Address:** http://georgetownreview.georgetowncollege.edu
**Publishes:** essays, fiction, nonfiction, and poetry
**Editorial Focus:** We're simply looking to publish quality fiction, poetry, creative nonfiction, and essays.
**Representative Authors:** David Allan Evans, Ben Brooks, and David Romtvedt
**Submissions Policy:** No page length limit for fiction or essays; please limit poetry submissions to 10 pages.
**Simultaneous Subs:** yes
**Reading Period:** 9/1 to 3/15
**Reporting Time:** 1 to 3 months
**Author Payment:** copies and subscription
**Contests:** Held yearly, $1,000 first prize, runners-up considered for publication.
See Web Site for Contest Guidelines.
**Founded:** 1992
**Non Profit:** yes
**Paid Staff:** no
**Unpaid Staff:** yes
**Distributors:** DeBoer, Ubiquity
**Total Circulation:** 1,000
**Paid Circulation:** 75
**Average Print Run:** 1,200
**Subscription Rate:** Individual $5/1 year/Institution $9/1 year
**Single Copy Price:** $5
**Current Volume/Issue:** 7/1
**Frequency per Year:** 1
**Backfile Available:** yes
**Unsolicited Ms. Received:** yes
**% of Unsolicited Ms. Published per Year:** 15%
**Format:** perfect
**Size:** H 9" W 6"

**Average Pages:** 192
**Ads:** yes
**Ad Rates:** See Web Site for Details.

## The Georgia Review

**Type:** magazine
**CLMP member:** yes
**Primary Editor/Contact Person:** T.R. Hummer
**Address:** 012 Gilbert Hall
The University of Georgia
Athens, GA 30602-9009
**Web Site Address:** http://www.uga.edu/garev
**Publishes:** essays, fiction, nonfiction, poetry, reviews, and art
**Editorial Focus:** A rich gathering of stories, essays, poems, book reviews and visual art orchestrated to invite and sustain repeated readings.
**Representative Authors:** Philip Levine, Barry Lopez, and Liza Ward
**Submissions Policy:** See website or send SASE. No electronic submissions.
**Simultaneous Subs:** no
**Reading Period:** 8/5 to 12/15
**Reporting Time:** 4 to 6 months
**Author Payment:** cash, copies, and subscription
**Founded:** 1947
**Non Profit:** yes
**Paid Staff:** 7
**Unpaid Staff:** 0-2
**Distributors:** DeBoer, Ingram, Media Solutions, Ubiquity
**ISSN Number/ISBN Number:** ISSN 0016-8386
**Total Circulation:** 4,358
**Paid Circulation:** 4,021
**Subscription Rate:** Individual $24/Institution $24
**Single Copy Price:** $9
**Current Volume/Issue:** LVII/3
**Frequency per Year:** 4
**Backfile Available:** yes
**Unsolicited Ms. Received:** yes
**% of Unsolicited Ms. Published per Year:** 1%
**Format:** perfect
**Size:** H 10" W 6.75"
**Average Pages:** 200
**Ads:** yes
**Ad Rates:** $425 cover, $350 page, $225 half page, $600 2-pg. spread
See Web Site for Details.

## The Germ: A Journal of Poetic Research

**Type:** magazine
**CLMP member:** yes
**Primary Editor/Contact Person:** Andrew Maxwell
**Address:** 1440 Allison Ave.
Los Angeles, CA 90026
**Web Site Address:** http://germspot.blogspot.com
**Publishes:** essays, fiction, poetry, and translation
**Editorial Focus:** Belles lettres. "The poem of the act of the mind." Translation, sidelong glances: "literalists of the imagination."
**Recent Awards Received:** The Arthur Symons Living Difficultly Inappropriate Endurance Award, 2005.
**Representative Authors:** Eugene Ostashevsky, Charles North, and Paul LaFarge
**Submissions Policy:** Check to see if we're reading first by e-mail. Warning: we're an occasional with sudden, unpredictable eruptions of activity.
**Simultaneous Subs:** no
**Reading Period:** Year-round
**Reporting Time:** 1 to 3 months
**Author Payment:** copies
**Contests:** See Web Site for Contest Guidelines.
**Founded:** 1996
**Non Profit:** yes
**Paid Staff:** 0
**Unpaid Staff:** 2
**Distributors:** SPD, Consortium, Armadillo
**ISSN Number/ISBN Number:** ISSN 1093-6610
**Total Circulation:** 400
**Paid Circulation:** 150
**Average Print Run:** 1,000
**Subscription Rate:** Individual $20/Institution $25
**Single Copy Price:** $10
**Current Volume/Issue:** Issue 7
**Frequency per Year:** 1
**Backfile Available:** yes
**Unsolicited Ms. Received:** yes
**% of Unsolicited Ms. Published per Year:** 40%
**Format:** perfect
**Size:** H 8.5" W 7"
**Average Pages:** 250
**Ads:** no

## The Gettysburg Review

**Type:** magazine
**CLMP member:** yes
**Primary Editor/Contact Person:** Peter Stitt
**Address:** Gettysburg College

300 N. Washington St.
Gettysburg, PA 17325-1491
**Web Site Address:** http://www.gettysburgreview.com
**Publishes:** essays, fiction, nonfiction, poetry, reviews, and art
**Editorial Focus:** Our central criterion is high literary quality; we seek writers who can shape the language in unique and beautiful ways.
**Recent Awards Received:** Best New Design, CLMP
**Representative Authors:** Scott Schrader, Pattiann Rogers, and Bret Lott
**Submissions Policy:** Please visit our web site at http://www.gettysburgreview.com for submission guidelines
**Simultaneous Subs:** yes
**Reading Period:** 9/1 to 5/31
**Reporting Time:** 3 to 6 months
**Author Payment:** cash, copies, and subscription
**Founded:** 1988
**Non Profit:** yes
**Paid Staff:** 6
**Unpaid Staff:** 1
**Distributors:** Ingram; Ubiquity Distributors
**ISSN Number/ISBN Number:** ISSN 0898-4557
**Total Circulation:** 2,250
**Paid Circulation:** 1,800
**Average Print Run:** 2,500
**Subscription Rate:** Individual $24/Institution $24
**Single Copy Price:** $7
**Current Volume/Issue:** 18/2
**Frequency per Year:** 4
**Backfile Available:** yes
**Unsolicited Ms. Received:** yes
**% of Unsolicited Ms. Published per Year:** 2%
**Format:** perfect
**Average Pages:** 168
**Ad Rates:** E-mail kkupperm@gettysburg.edu for information

# Gingko Tree Review

**Type:** magazine
**CLMP member:** no
**Primary Editor/Contact Person:** Randall Fuller
**Address:** Drury University
900 N. Benton Ave.
Springfield, MO 65802
**Web Site Address:** http://www.drury.edu/gingkotree/
**Publishes:** essays, fiction, nonfiction, and poetry
**Editorial Focus:** We strive to publish both new and established authors who captivate us with singular voices and exceptional language.

**Representative Authors:** Rick Moody, Ioanna Carlsen, and Roy Kesey
**Submissions Policy:** The Gingko Tree Review invites submissions of poetry, fiction and nonfiction. There are no length restrictions.
**Simultaneous Subs:** yes
**Reading Period:** Year-round
**Reporting Time:** 1 to 2 months
**Author Payment:** copies
**Contests:** The Annual Bob Shacochis Short Story Contest awards $1,000 and publication. See Web Site for Contest Guidelines.
**Founded:** 2001
**Non Profit:** yes
**Paid Staff:** 1
**Unpaid Staff:** 7
**Total Circulation:** 800
**Paid Circulation:** 500
**Subscription Rate:** Individual $14/Institution $14
**Single Copy Price:** $10
**Current Volume/Issue:** 2/1
**Frequency per Year:** 2
**Backfile Available:** yes
**Unsolicited Ms. Received:** yes
**% of Unsolicited Ms. Published per Year:** 70%
**Format:** perfect
**Size:** H 8" W 5"
**Average Pages:** 200
**Ads:** no

# Gival Press

**Type:** press
**CLMP member:** yes
**Primary Editor/Contact Person:** Robert L. Giron
**Address:** P.O. Box 3812
Arlington, VA 22203
**Web Site Address:** http://www.givalpress.com
**Publishes:** essays, fiction, nonfiction, poetry, and translation
**Editorial Focus:** We look for quality works that have a message, be it philosophical or social. Books are in English, Spanish, and French.
**Recent Awards Received:** 2004 Lambda Literary Award for Poetry; ForeWord Magazine Book of the Year for Translation (Silver in 2003; Bronze in 2001)
**Representative Authors:** David Garrett Izzo, Beverly Burch, and Carlos Rubio
**Submissions Policy:** Query 1st w/ info re: the project; say if simultaneous submission. Mss. sent per contests must follow the specific guidelines.
**Simultaneous Subs:** yes

**Reading Period:** 3/1 to 5/30
**Reporting Time:** 3 to 4 months
**Author Payment:** royalties, cash, and copies
**Contests:** See Web Site for Contest Guidelines.
**Founded:** 1998
**Non Profit:** no
**Paid Staff:** 2
**Unpaid Staff:** 0
**Distributors:** Ingram; Baker & Taylor; Whitaker
**Wholesalers:** BookMasters; Academic Book Center;
Blackwell's
**ISSN Number/ISBN Number:** ISSN 1-928589
**Number of Books Published per Year:** 5
**Titles in Print:** 26
**Average Print Run:** 500
**Average Percentage Printed:** Paperback 99%,
Chapbook 1%
**Average Price:** $15

## Glimmer Train Stories

**Type:** magazine
**CLMP member:** yes
**Primary Editor/Contact Person:** Linda Swanson-
Davies
**Address:** 1211 NW Glisan St., Ste. 207
Portland, OR 97209-3054
**Web Site Address:** http://www.glimmertrain.com
**Publishes:** fiction
**Editorial Focus:** Literary short stories by emerging
and established fiction writers. Unsolicited work is
welcomed.
**Representative Authors:** George Makana Clark,
Karen Outen, and Daniel Wallace
**Submissions Policy:** Payment and response time
vary by category. Check guidelines and submit online:
http://www.glimmertrain.com
**Simultaneous Subs:** no
**Reading Period:** Year-round
**Reporting Time:** 2 to 3 months
**Author Payment:** cash
**Contests:** See Web Site for Contest Guidelines.
**Founded:** 1991
**Non Profit:** no
**Paid Staff:** 0
**Unpaid Staff:** 2
**Distributors:** IPD, Ingram, Ubiquity
**ISSN Number/ISBN Number:** ISSN 1055-7520
**Total Circulation:** 10,000
**Paid Circulation:** 6,000
**Subscription Rate:** Individual $36/Institution $36
**Single Copy Price:** $12

**Current Volume/Issue:** Issue 52
**Frequency per Year:** 4
**Backfile Available:** yes
**Unsolicited Ms. Received:** yes
**Format:** perfect
**Size:** H 9-3/4" W 6-1/4"
**Average Pages:** 260
**Ads:** no

## Golden Handcuffs Review

**Type:** magazine
**CLMP member:** no
**Primary Editor/Contact Person:** Lou Rowan
**Address:** Box 20158
Seattle, WA 98102
**Web Site Address:** http://goldenhandcuffsreview.com
**Publishes:** essays, fiction, nonfiction, poetry, reviews,
art, and translation
**Editorial Focus:** Seek the new, fresh, experimental.
**Representative Authors:** Robert Coover, Toby Olson,
and Jerome Rothenberg
**Submissions Policy:** Prefer submissions in mail with
SASE.
**Simultaneous Subs:** yes
**Reading Period:** Year-round
**Reporting Time:** 1 to 12 weeks
**Author Payment:** copies
**Founded:** 2002
**Non Profit:** no
**Paid Staff:** 1
**Unpaid Staff:** 2
**Distributors:** Ingram; DeBoer
**ISSN Number/ISBN Number:** ISSN 1541-2547
**Total Circulation:** 2,300
**Paid Circulation:** 100
**Subscription Rate:** Individual $14/Institution $14
**Single Copy Price:** $6.95
**Current Volume/Issue:** 1/2
**Frequency per Year:** 2
**Backfile Available:** yes
**Unsolicited Ms. Received:** yes
**% of Unsolicited Ms. Published per Year:** 2%
**Format:** perfect
**Size:** H 9" W 5"
**Average Pages:** 120
**Ads:** yes
**Ad Rates:** $100/page
See Web Site for Details.

## Good Foot

**Type:** magazine
**CLMP member:** yes
**Primary Editor/Contact Person:** Carmine Simmons, Co-editor
**Address:** P.O. Box 681
Murray Hill Station
New York, NY 10156
**Web Site Address:**
http://www.goodfootmagazine.com
**Publishes:** poetry
**Editorial Focus:** Compelling, readable work from across the poetry spectrum.
**Representative Authors:** Ted Mathys, M.J. Bender, and Wilma Elizabeth McDaniels
**Submissions Policy:** Submit no more than three poems with 50-word bio and cover letter. See Web site for complete guidelines.
**Simultaneous Subs:** yes
**Reading Period:** 2/1 to 10/31
**Reporting Time:** 2 to 4 months
**Author Payment:** copies
**Contests:** To be announced. Visit Web site for details.
**Founded:** 2001
**Non Profit:** yes
**Paid Staff:** 0
**Unpaid Staff:** 4
**Distributors:** DeBoer
**ISSN Number/ISBN Number:** ISSN 1540-9708
**Total Circulation:** 0
**Paid Circulation:** 275
**Average Print Run:** 1,000
**Subscription Rate:** Individual $14/Institution $28
**Single Copy Price:** $8
**Current Volume/Issue:** Issue 7
**Frequency per Year:** 2
**Backfile Available:** yes
**Unsolicited Ms. Received:** yes
**% of Unsolicited Ms. Published per Year:** 85%
**Format:** perfect
**Average Pages:** 120
**Ads:** yes
**Ad Rates:** Full-page $150; half-page $85. Please inquire for details.

## Grain Magazine

**Type:** magazine
**CLMP member:** no
**Primary Editor/Contact Person:** Kent Bruyneel
**Address:** P.O. Box 67
Saskatoon, SK S7K 3K1
**Web Site Address:** http://www.grainmagazine.ca
**Publishes:** fiction, nonfiction, and poetry
**Editorial Focus:** New and original poetry and fiction from across North America and the world. Some creative nonfiction.
**Recent Awards Received:** Journey Prize for Fiction, 2003; National Magazine Awards; Western Magazine Awards (Canada)
**Representative Authors:** Yann Martel, Tim Lilburn, and Tom Wayman
**Submissions Policy:** Maximum 8 poems or 2 stories, paper copy only, SASE or e-mail response. No returns with insufficient Canadian postage or IRC.
**Simultaneous Subs:** no
**Reading Period:** 9/1 to 5/31
**Reporting Time:** 12 to 16 weeks
**Author Payment:** cash and copies
**Contests:** Short Grain Contest-various categories, $500 cash prize, deadline January 31.
See Web Site for Contest Guidelines.
**Founded:** 1973
**Non Profit:** yes
**Paid Staff:** 6
**Unpaid Staff:** 0
**Distributors:** Prairie Advertising, Magazines Canada
**ISSN Number/ISBN Number:** ISSN 1491-0497
**Total Circulation:** 1,400
**Paid Circulation:** 850
**Average Print Run:** 1,500
**Subscription Rate:** Individual $29.95/Institution $35
**Single Copy Price:** $9.95
**Current Volume/Issue:** 33/1
**Frequency per Year:** 4
**Backfile Available:** yes
**Unsolicited Ms. Received:** yes
**% of Unsolicited Ms. Published per Year:** 3%
**Format:** perfect
**Size:** H 9" W 6"
**Average Pages:** 125
**Ads:** yes
**Ad Rates:** $225 per full page; $150 per half page; $275 inside front

## Grand Street

**Type:** magazine
**CLMP member:** no
**Primary Editor/Contact Person:** Jean Stein
**Address:** 214 Sullivan St., Ste. 6C
New York, NY 10012
**Web Site Address:** http://www.grandstreet.com
**Publishes:** essays, fiction, nonfiction, poetry, art, and translation
**Editorial Focus:** We showcase the best of innovative fiction, poetry, essays, and visual art, from writers and artists around the world.
**Representative Authors:** William T. Vollmann, Shelley Jackson, and Victor Pelevin
**Submissions Policy:** The size of our staff prevents us from accepting unsolicited fiction submissions. For poetry guidelines, visit our website.
**Simultaneous Subs:** yes
**Reading Period:** Year-round
**Reporting Time:** 2 to 3 months
**Author Payment:** cash
**Founded:** 1981
**Non Profit:** yes
**Paid Staff:** 4
**Unpaid Staff:** 3
**Distributors:** D.A.P., Ingram, DeBoer, Ubiquity
**Total Circulation:** 4,000
**Paid Circulation:** 1,500
**Subscription Rate:** Individual $25/Institution $30
**Single Copy Price:** $15
**Current Volume/Issue:** Issue 72
**Frequency per Year:** 2
**Backfile Available:** yes
**Unsolicited Ms. Received:** no
**Format:** perfect
**Size:** H 9.5" W 8.25"
**Average Pages:** 236
**Ads:** yes
**Ad Rates:** full page: $450; some swap ads available

## Graywolf Press

**Type:** press
**CLMP member:** yes
**Primary Editor/Contact Person:** Katie Dublinski
**Address:** 2402 University Ave, Ste. 203
St. Paul, MN 55114
**Web Site Address:** http://www.graywolfpress.org/
**Publishes:** essays, fiction, nonfiction, poetry, and translation
**Editorial Focus:** Graywolf publishes work that combines a distinct voice with a distinct vision.
**Submissions Policy:** Graywolf does not accept unsolicited manuscripts, we ask that you first send a query letter by regular mail.
**Simultaneous Subs:** no
**Reading Period:** Year-round
**Reporting Time:** 3 to 4 months
**Author Payment:** none, royalties, cash, and copies
**Contests:** S. Mariella Gable Prize for fiction and the Graywolf Press Nonfiction Prize
See Web Site for Contest Guidelines.
**Founded:** 1974
**Non Profit:** yes
**Paid Staff:** 8
**Unpaid Staff:** 2
**Distributors:** Farrar, Straus & Giroux
**Number of Books Published per Year:** 21-23
**Titles in Print:** 300
**Average Percentage Printed:** Hardcover 10%, Paperback 90%
**Backfile Available:** no

## Great Marsh Press/The Reading Room

**Type:** magazine
**CLMP member:** yes
**Address:** P.O. Box 2144
Lenox Hill Station
New York, NY 10021
**Web Site Address:** http://www.greatmarshpress.com
**Publishes:** fiction, nonfiction, and translation
**Simultaneous Subs:** yes
**Reading Period:** Year-round
**Reporting Time:** 1 to 2 months
**Author Payment:** none
**Founded:** 1999
**Non Profit:** yes
**Unpaid Staff:** 5
**Wholesalers:** Ingram
**Backfile Available:** yes

## Great River Review

**Type:** magazine
**CLMP member:** yes
**Primary Editor/Contact Person:** Robert Hedin
**Address:** 163 Tower View Dr.
Red Wing, MN 55066
**Web Site Address:** http://www.andersoncenter.org
**Publishes:** essays, fiction, nonfiction, poetry, and

translation

**Editorial Focus:** To publish the best work.
**Representative Authors:** Ted Kooser, Linda Pastan, and Robert Bly
**Submissions Policy:** No e-mail Submissions
**Simultaneous Subs:** no
**Reading Period:** Year-round
**Reporting Time:** 1 to 2 months
**Author Payment:** copies
**Contests:** no
**Founded:** 1977
**Non Profit:** yes
**Paid Staff:** 0
**Unpaid Staff:** 2
**Total Circulation:** 1,000
**Paid Circulation:** 750
**Subscription Rate:** Individual $14/Institution $30
**Single Copy Price:** $6
**Current Volume/Issue:** Issue 40
**Frequency per Year:** 2
**Backfile Available:** yes
**Unsolicited Ms. Received:** yes
**% of Unsolicited Ms. Published per Year:** 10%
**Format:** perfect
**Size:** H 9" W 6"
**Average Pages:** 100
**Ads:** no

# The Green Hills Literary Lantern

**Type:** magazine
**CLMP member:** yes
**Primary Editor/Contact Person:** Adam Davis
**Address:** Truman State University, Lang. & Lit.
Kirksville, MO 63501
**Web Site Address:** http://ll.truman.edu/ghllweb
**Publishes:** essays, fiction, poetry, reviews, and translation
**Editorial Focus:** We're open to new writers as well as more established writers. Work must reflect strong awareness of craft.
**Representative Authors:** Jim Thomas, Francine Tolf, and Ian MacMillan
**Submissions Policy:** Submit 3-7 poems, typed, one poem per page. Free or formal verse. We accept stories up to 7,000 words and short-shorts.
**Simultaneous Subs:** yes
**Reading Period:** Year-round
**Reporting Time:** 1 to 4 months
**Author Payment:** copies
**Founded:** 1990

**Non Profit:** yes
**Paid Staff:** no
**Unpaid Staff:** yes
**ISSN Number/ISBN Number:** ISSN 1089-2060
**Total Circulation:** 300
**Paid Circulation:** 100
**Subscription Rate:** Individual $10/Institution $10
**Single Copy Price:** $10
**Current Volume/Issue:** Issue 15
**Frequency per Year:** 1
**Backfile Available:** yes
**Unsolicited Ms. Received:** yes
**% of Unsolicited Ms. Published per Year:** 2%
**Format:** perfect
**Size:** H 9" W 6"
**Average Pages:** 300-400
**Ads:** yes

# Greenboathouse Books

**Type:** press
**CLMP member:** no
**Primary Editor/Contact Person:** Jason Dewinetz
**Address:** #4-1404 Harrison St.
Victoria, BC V8S 3S2
**Web Site Address:** http://www.greenboathouse.com
**Publishes:** fiction and poetry
**Editorial Focus:** Greenboathouse Books is a small literary press focusing on poetry, fiction and mixed-form work by writers from across Canada.
**Recent Awards Received:** Recent publications have received 2 consecutive national book design awards.
**Representative Authors:** Shane Rhodes, Laisha Rosnau, and Matt Rader
**Submissions Policy:** Please visit our website for submission guidelines. Please do not submit without first reading those guidelines.
**Simultaneous Subs:** yes
**Reading Period:** 6/1 to 7/31
**Reporting Time:** 3 to 6 months
**Author Payment:** copies
**Founded:** 1999
**Non Profit:** no
**Paid Staff:** 1
**Unpaid Staff:** 1
**ISSN Number/ISBN Number:** ISBN 0-9685357 and 1-894744
**Number of Books Published per Year:** 2-5
**Titles in Print:** 4
**Average Print Run:** 120
**Average Percentage Printed:** Hardcover 10%,

Chapbook 90%
**Average Price:** $15-35

## The Greensboro Review

**Type:** magazine
**CLMP member:** yes
**Primary Editor/Contact Person:** Jim Clark
**Address:** English Dept. 134 McIver Building
P.O. Box 26170
Greensboro, NC 27402-6170
**Web Site Address:** http://www.uncg.edu/eng/mfa/
**Publishes:** fiction and poetry
**Editorial Focus:** We want to see the best being written, regardless of theme, subject, or style.
**Representative Authors:** George Singleton, Thomas Lux, and Daniel Wallace
**Submissions Policy:** No previously published works, works accepted for publication, or dual submissions. No e-mail or fax submissions.
**Simultaneous Subs:** no
**Reading Period:** Year-round
**Reporting Time:** 1 to 2 months
**Author Payment:** copies
**Contests:** Greensboro Review Literary Awards in Poetry and Fiction. Yearly Deadline Sept. 15th See Web Site for Contest Guidelines.
**Founded:** 1966
**Non Profit:** yes
**Paid Staff:** 3
**Unpaid Staff:** 4
**Distributors:** DeBoer
**Wholesalers:** Total Circulation Services
**ISSN Number/ISBN Number:** ISSN 0017-4084
**Total Circulation:** 800
**Paid Circulation:** 400
**Average Print Run:** 800
**Subscription Rate:** Individual $10/Institution $10
**Single Copy Price:** $5
**Current Volume/Issue:** Issue 78
**Frequency per Year:** 2
**Backfile Available:** yes
**Unsolicited Ms. Received:** yes
**% of Unsolicited Ms. Published per Year:** 90%
**Format:** perfect
**Size:** H 9" W 6"
**Average Pages:** 144
**Ads:** yes
**Ad Rates:** Exchange

## The Groundwater Press

**Type:** press
**CLMP member:** no
**Primary Editor/Contact Person:** Eugene Richie
**Address:** P.O. Box 704
Hudson, NY 12534
**Web site Address:**
http://webpage.pace.edu/erichie/groundwater
**Publishes:** poetry and translation
**Editorial Focus:** A non-profit press, we publish literature and sponsor readings and other cultural events and activities.
**Representative Authors:** Pierre Martory, Jaime Manrique, and Edward Barrett
**Submissions Policy:** We do not accept unsolicited material, except when we have a grant for an anthology. Material is not returned without SASE.
**Simultaneous Subs:** no
**Reading Period:** 10/1 to 3/31
**Reporting Time:** 1 to 2 months
**Author Payment:** copies
**Founded:** 1984
**Non Profit:** yes
**Paid Staff:** 0
**Unpaid Staff:** 3
**Distributors:** SPD
**Wholesalers:** All
**ISSN Number/ISBN Number:** none/1-877593
**Number of Books Published per Year:** 1
**Titles in Print:** 23
**Average Print Run:** 500
**Average Percentage Printed:** Paperback 100%
**Average Price:** $12.95

## The Grunge Papers

**Type:** press
**CLMP member:** no
**Primary Editor/Contact Person:** Grant Wilkins
**Address:** P.O. Box 20517
390 Rideau St.
Ottawa, ON K1N 1A3
**Web Site Address:** http://www.grungepapers.com
**Publishes:** essays, fiction, poetry, and translation
**Editorial Focus:** Mostly interested in reissuing old Canadian Lit and classic poetry, which we print as broadsheets by letterpress on handmade paper.
**Representative Authors:** Archibald Lampman, Isabella Valancy Crawford, and P.B. Shelley
**Submissions Policy:** Probably no point in submitting anything at the moment, unless you've been dead for a long while.

**Simultaneous Subs:** no
**Reading Period:** Year-round
**Reporting Time:** 1 to 3 months
**Author Payment:** cash and copies
**Founded:** 2000
**Non Profit:** no
**Paid Staff:** 0
**Unpaid Staff:** 1
**Number of Books Published per Year:** 1-3
**Titles in Print:** 6
**Average Print Run:** 50
**Average Percentage Printed:** Chapbook 20%, Other 80%
**Average Price:** $3 to $6

## Guernica: A Magazine of Art and Politics

**Type:** online
**CLMP member:** yes
**Primary Editor/Contact Person:** Elizabeth Onusko
**Address:** Fordham University
113 W. 60th St., Room 924I
New York, NY 10023
**Web Site Address:** http://www.guernicamag.com
**Publishes:** essays, fiction, nonfiction, poetry, art, translation, audio, and video
**Editorial Focus:** We believe that it's imperative for art and politics to be addressed as what they are areas that constantly collide and intersect instead of being regarded as autonomous subjects.
**Representative Authors:** Eamon Grennan, Elisabeth Frost, and Julian Rios
**Submissions Policy:** Please check the website for our complete submissions policy.
**Simultaneous Subs:** yes
**Reading Period:** Year-round
**Reporting Time:** 1 to 3 months
**Author Payment:** none
**Contests:** Coming soon.
See Web Site for Contest Guidelines.
**Founded:** 2004
**Non Profit:** yes
**Paid Staff:** 0
**Unpaid Staff:** 15
**Average Page Views per Month:** 100,000
**Average Unique Visitors per Month:** 25,000
**Frequency per Year:** 12
**Publish Print Anthology:** no
**Average Percentage of Pages per Category:** Audio 100%

**Ads:** no

## Gulf Coast: A Journal of Literature and Fine Arts

**Type:** magazine
**CLMP member:** yes
**Primary Editor/Contact Person:** Sasha West, Managing Editor
**Address:** Department of English
University of Houston
Houston, TX 77204-3013
**Web Site Address:** http://www.gulfcoastmag.org
**Publishes:** fiction, nonfiction, poetry, reviews, art, and translation
**Recent Awards Received:** Pushcart Prize, Best American Poetry
**Representative Authors:** Terrance Hayes, Anne Carson, and Karen An-Hwei Lee
**Submissions Policy:** Send 3-5 poems, one story, or one essay w/ cover letter and SASE. No entire manuscripts, novellas, or electronic submissions.
**Simultaneous Subs:** yes
**Reading Period:** 8/15 to 5/1
**Reporting Time:** 3 to 6 months
**Author Payment:** cash, copies, and subscription
**Contests:** See Web Site for Contest Guidelines.
**Founded:** 1986
**Non Profit:** yes
**Paid Staff:** PT
**Unpaid Staff:** 37-47
**Distributors:** Ingram, DeBoer
**ISSN Number/ISBN Number:** ISSN 0896-2551
**Total Circulation:** 2,500
**Paid Circulation:** 1,000
**Average Print Run:** 2,500
**Subscription Rate:** Individual $14/Institution $20
**Single Copy Price:** $8
**Current Volume/Issue:** 18/1
**Frequency per Year:** 2
**Backfile Available:** yes
**Unsolicited Ms. Received:** yes
**% of Unsolicited Ms. Published per Year:** 60%
**Format:** perfect
**Size:** H 9" W 7"
**Average Pages:** 300
**Ads:** no

## Gulf Stream

**Type:** magazine
**CLMP member:** yes
**Primary Editor/Contact Person:** John Dufresne
**Address:** English Dept, FIU
Biscayne Bay Campus, 3000 NE 151st St.
North Miami, FL 33181
**Web Site Address:** http://www.fiu.edu/~gulfstrm/
**Publishes:** essays, fiction, nonfiction, and poetry
**Editorial Focus:** Gulf Stream seeks writing that is intelligent, distinct, and establishes a strong bond with the reader.
**Representative Authors:** Dennis Lehane, David Kirby, and Richard Blanco
**Submissions Policy:** We accept fiction/nonfiction (5,000 words max) and up to 3 poems. Electronic submissions through FormSite okay, but no e-mails.
**Simultaneous Subs:** yes
**Reading Period:** 9/1 to 3/31
**Reporting Time:** 2 to 3 months
**Author Payment:** copies and subscription
**Contests:** See Web Site for Contest Guidelines.
**Founded:** 1989
**Non Profit:** yes
**Paid Staff:** yes
**Unpaid Staff:** 3
**Distributors:** purchase at w3.fiu.edu/gulfstrm
**Total Circulation:** 1,000
**Paid Circulation:** 550
**Average Print Run:** 1,000
**Subscription Rate:** Individual $15/Institution $15
**Single Copy Price:** $8
**Current Volume/Issue:** 24/24
**Frequency per Year:** 2
**Backfile Available:** yes
**Unsolicited Ms. Received:** yes
**% of Unsolicited Ms. Published per Year:** 50%
**Format:** perfect
**Size:** H 8 1/2" W 5 1/2"
**Average Pages:** 120
**Ads:** yes
**Ad Rates:** $400 for full page

## Haight Ashbury Literary Journal

**Type:** magazine
**CLMP member:** yes
**Primary Editor/Contact Person:** Alice E. Rogoff
**Address:** 558 Joost Ave.
San Francisco, CA 94127
**Web Site Address:**
http://www.haightashbury.org/poetry.html
**Publishes:** fiction and poetry
**Editorial Focus:** Personal and social, urban and nature, diverse cultures, leans towards realism, national but encourages local writers
**Representative Authors:** Lee Herrick, Adam David Miller, and Andrena Zawinski
**Submissions Policy:** Send 6 poems or less, with SASE, prefer poems under 2 pages. Fiction considered for next year.
**Simultaneous Subs:** yes
**Reading Period:** Year-round
**Reporting Time:** 4 to 6 months
**Author Payment:** none
**Founded:** 1980
**Non Profit:** yes
**Paid Staff:** 3
**Unpaid Staff:** 0
**Distributors:** Readmore, Yankee Book Peddler
**ISSN Number/ISBN Number:** ISBN 0-926664-0402
**Total Circulation:** 2,000
**Paid Circulation:** 200
**Subscription Rate:** Individual $6
**Single Copy Price:** $2
**Current Volume/Issue:** 22/1
**Frequency per Year:** 2
**Backfile Available:** yes
**Unsolicited Ms. Received:** yes
**% of Unsolicited Ms. Published per Year:** 10%
**Format:** tabloid
**Size:** H 8.5" W 11"
**Average Pages:** 16
**Ads:** yes

## Hanging Loose

**Type:** magazine
**CLMP member:** yes
**Primary Editor/Contact Person:** Robert Hershon
**Address:** 231 Wyckoff St.
Brooklyn, NY 11217
**Web Site Address:**
http://www.hangingloosepress.com
**Publishes:** fiction and poetry
**Editorial Focus:** Lively, humorous and non-academic poetry. We occasionally publish fiction, rarely nonfiction, but there are exceptions.
**Representative Authors:** Sherman Alexie, Ha Jin, and Hettie Jones
**Submissions Policy:** As a rule, send up to 6 poems or 1 story at a time. Enclose an SASE. We also have a

section of work by high school writers
**Simultaneous Subs:** no
**Reading Period:** Year-round
**Reporting Time:** 1 to 5 months
**Author Payment:** cash and copies
**Contests:** no
**Founded:** 1966
**Non Profit:** yes
**Distributors:** SPD
**Wholesalers:** Ingram, DeBoer
**ISSN Number/ISBN Number:** ISSN 0440-2316
**Total Circulation:** 2,000
**Paid Circulation:** 1,000
**Average Print Run:** N/A
**Subscription Rate:** Individual $22/Institution $27
**Single Copy Price:** $9
**Current Volume/Issue:** Issue 87
**Frequency per Year:** 2
**Backfile Available:** yes
**Unsolicited Ms. Received:** yes
**Format:** perfect
**Size:** H 7" W 8.5"
**Average Pages:** 120
**Ads:** no

## Harbour Publishing

**Type:** press
**CLMP member:** no
**Primary Editor/Contact Person:** Alicia Miller
**Address:** P.O. Box 219
4437 Rondeview Road
Madeira Park, BC V0N 2H0
**Web Site Address:**
http://www.harbourpublishing.com
**Publishes:** fiction, nonfiction, and poetry
**Editorial Focus:** Nonfiction, fiction and children's books with a focus on the Pacific Northwest and Pacific Northwest authors.
**Representative Authors:** Al Purdy, Stephen Hume, and Edith Iglauer
**Submissions Policy:** Accept unsolicited ms with SASE.
**Simultaneous Subs:** yes
**Reading Period:** Year-round
**Reporting Time:** 3 to 6 months
**Author Payment:** royalties and copies
**Founded:** 1974
**Non Profit:** no
**Paid Staff:** 10
**Unpaid Staff:** 0

**Distributors:** Canada: Harbour Publishing. USA: GACPC.
**ISSN Number/ISBN Number:** ISBN 1-55017-, 0-920080
**Number of Books Published per Year:** 24
**Titles in Print:** 400
**Average Percentage Printed:** Hardcover 50%, Paperback 50%

## Harpur Palate

**Type:** magazine
**CLMP member:** yes
**Primary Editor/Contact Person:** Catherine Dent
**Address:** Dept. of English, Binghamton University
P.O. Box 6000
Binghamton, NY 13902-6000
**Web Site Address:**
http://harpurpalate.binghamton.edu
**Publishes:** fiction, nonfiction, poetry, and art
**Editorial Focus:** We have no restrictions on subject matter or form. We are mainly interested in the highest-quality writing.
**Representative Authors:** Lee K. Abbott, Sascha Feinstein, and Stephen Corey
**Submissions Policy:** Fiction and CNF: 250-8,000 words; no more than 1 submission per author. Poetry: 3-5 poems; no more than 10 pages per author.
**Simultaneous Subs:** yes
**Reading Period:** Year-round
**Reporting Time:** 3 to 6 months
**Author Payment:** copies
**Contests:** John Gardner Memorial Prize for Fiction, $500 prize; Milton Kessler Memorial Prize for Poetry, $500 prize
See Web Site for Contest Guidelines.
**Founded:** 2000
**Non Profit:** yes
**Paid Staff:** 0
**Unpaid Staff:** 30
**Distributors:** DeBoer
**ISSN Number/ISBN Number:** ISSN 0-9749107-2-4
**Total Circulation:** 750
**Paid Circulation:** 100
**Average Print Run:** 1,000
**Subscription Rate:** Individual $16/Institution $20
**Single Copy Price:** $10
**Current Volume/Issue:** 5/1
**Frequency per Year:** 2
**Backfile Available:** yes
**Unsolicited Ms. Received:** yes

**% of Unsolicited Ms. Published per Year:** 70%
**Format:** perfect
**Size:** H 8.5" W 6"
**Average Pages:** 180
**Ads:** yes
**Ad Rates:** See Web Site for Details.

## Harvard Review

**Type:** magazine
**CLMP member:** yes
**Primary Editor/Contact Person:** Christina Thompson, Editor
**Address:** Lamont Library, level 5
Harvard University
Cambridge, MA 02138
**Web Site Address:** http://hcl.harvard.edu/harvardreview
**Publishes:** essays, fiction, poetry, reviews, art, and translation
**Recent Awards Received:** Best American Short Stories, 2005, 2003; Best American Essays, 2004, 2003; Best American Poetry, 2002.
**Simultaneous Subs:** yes
**Reading Period:** Year-round
**Reporting Time:** 2 to 4 months
**Author Payment:** none
**Founded:** 1992
**Non Profit:** yes
**Paid Staff:** 2
**Unpaid Staff:** 3
**Distributors:** Ingram
**Total Circulation:** 2,500
**Paid Circulation:** 500
**Average Print Run:** 2,500
**Subscription Rate:** Individual $16/Institution $24
**Single Copy Price:** $10
**Current Volume/Issue:** Issue 29
**Frequency per Year:** 2
**Backfile Available:** yes
**Unsolicited Ms. Received:** yes
**Format:** perfect

## Hawai'i Pacific Review

**Type:** magazine
**CLMP member:** no
**Primary Editor/Contact Person:** Ms. Patrice Wilson
**Address:** 1060 Bishop St., LB 402
Honolulu, HI 96813
**Web Site Address:** http://www.hpu.edu

**Publishes:** essays, fiction, and poetry
**Editorial Focus:** Open theme, open form, would like more experimental work
**Representative Authors:** Wendell Mayo, Bob Hicok, and Wendy Bishop
**Submissions Policy:** Sept 1-Dec 31, 5 poems or 5,000 words, one submission per issue, no previously published work, simultaneous submissions OK.
**Simultaneous Subs:** yes
**Reading Period:** 9/1 to 12/31
**Reporting Time:** 12 to 15 weeks
**Author Payment:** copies
**Contests:** none
**Founded:** 1987
**Non Profit:** yes
**Paid Staff:** 1
**Unpaid Staff:** 10
**Distributors:** Booklines Hawai'i
**ISSN Number/ISBN Number:** 1047-4331/0-9703239-3-X
**Total Circulation:** 500
**Paid Circulation:** 25
**Average Print Run:** 500
**Subscription Rate:** Individual $8.95/Institution $10
**Single Copy Price:** $5
**Current Volume/Issue:** 17/1
**Frequency per Year:** 1
**Backfile Available:** yes
**Unsolicited Ms. Received:** yes
**% of Unsolicited Ms. Published per Year:** 18%
**Format:** perfect
**Size:** H 9" W 6"
**Average Pages:** 100
**Ads:** yes
**Ad Rates:** Exchange

## Hayden's Ferry Review

**Type:** magazine
**CLMP member:** yes
**Primary Editor/Contact Person:** Salima Keegan
**Address:** Piper Center for Creative Writing
Box 875002 Arizona State University
Tempe, AZ 85287-5002
**Web Site Address:** http://www.asu.edu/pipercwcenter/publications
**Publishes:** essays, fiction, nonfiction, poetry, art, and translation
**Editorial Focus:** We publish the best quality poetry, creative nonfiction, fiction, and translations by emerging and established writers.

**Representative Authors:** David St. John, C.D. Wright, and Ron Carlson
**Submissions Policy:** Submit poetry and prose separately. Include SASE for response. Please, no e-mail submissions.
**Simultaneous Subs:** yes
**Reading Period:** Year-round
**Reporting Time:** 12 to 16 weeks
**Author Payment:** cash, copies, and subscription
**Founded:** 1986
**Non Profit:** yes
**Paid Staff:** 6
**Unpaid Staff:** 20
**Distributors:** Ingram
**ISSN Number/ISBN Number:** ISSN 0887-5170
**Total Circulation:** 1,200
**Paid Circulation:** 400
**Average Print Run:** 1,300
**Subscription Rate:** Individual $14/Institution $14
**Single Copy Price:** $6
**Current Volume/Issue:** Issue 36
**Frequency per Year:** 2
**Backfile Available:** yes
**Unsolicited Ms. Received:** yes
**% of Unsolicited Ms. Published per Year:** 80%
**Format:** perfect
**Size:** H 6 3/4" W 10"
**Average Pages:** 162
**Ads:** yes

# HazMat Review

**Type:** magazine
**CLMP member:** no
**Primary Editor/Contact Person:** Norm Davis
**Address:** P.O. Box 30507
Rochester, NY 14603-0507
**Web Site Address:** http://www.hazmatlitreview.org
**Publishes:** essays, fiction, nonfiction, poetry, reviews, art, and translation
**Editorial Focus:** Social consciousness, Women's consciousness a high priority, anti-imperialist, political writing welcome, want top quality.
**Representative Authors:** Lyn Lifshin, Marc Olmsted, and Koon Woon
**Submissions Policy:** No prose over 2,500 words. Send three poems plus SASE. Incarcerated writers need not send SASE. No Hallmark verse.
**Simultaneous Subs:** yes
**Reading Period:** Year-round
**Reporting Time:** 1 to 3 months

**Author Payment:** copies
**Founded:** 1996
**Non Profit:** yes
**Paid Staff:** 0
**Unpaid Staff:** 12
**Distributors:** Writers & Books, Rochester, New York
**ISSN Number/ISBN Number:** ISSN 1521-7639
**Total Circulation:** 150
**Paid Circulation:** 50
**Subscription Rate:** Individual $18/Institution $18
**Single Copy Price:** $12
**Current Volume/Issue:** 7/1
**Frequency per Year:** 2
**Backfile Available:** yes
**Unsolicited Ms. Received:** yes
**% of Unsolicited Ms. Published per Year:** 15%
**Format:** perfect
**Size:** H 8 1/2" W 5 1/2"
**Average Pages:** 110
**Ads:** no

# Heartlands

**Type:** magazine
**CLMP member:** no
**Primary Editor/Contact Person:** Larry Smith
**Address:** One University Road
Huron, OH 44839
**Web Site Address:**
http://www.theheartlandstoday.net/
**Publishes:** essays, fiction, nonfiction, poetry, reviews, and art
**Editorial Focus:** Midwest . . . themes for each issue . . . inquire
**Representative Authors:** Stephen Ostrander, Gary Snyder, and Larry Smith
**Simultaneous Subs:** yes
**Reading Period:** 1/1 to 6/6
**Reporting Time:** 1 to 2 months
**Author Payment:** cash and copies
**Founded:** 1990
**Non Profit:** yes
**Paid Staff:** 1
**Unpaid Staff:** 7
**Distributors:** Bottom Dog Press, SPD
**ISSN Number/ISBN Number:** ISSN 01066-6176
**Total Circulation:** 600
**Paid Circulation:** 150
**Average Print Run:** 600
**Subscription Rate:** Individual $6/Institution $6
**Single Copy Price:** $6

**Current Volume/Issue:** Issue 1
**Frequency per Year:** 2
**Backfile Available:** no
**Unsolicited Ms. Received:** yes
**% of Unsolicited Ms. Published per Year:** 75%
**Format:** perfect
**Size:** H 11" W 8.5"
**Average Pages:** 90
**Ads:** yes
**Ad Rates:** apply
See Web Site for Details.

# Heat Press

**Type:** press
**CLMP member:** yes
**Primary Editor/Contact Person:** Christopher Natale Peditto
**Address:** P.O. Box 26218
Los Angeles, CA 90026
**Publishes:** poetry
**Editorial Focus:** Poets close to the Beat Generation in their coming of age and oral sensibilities. Jazz and poetry.
**Representative Authors:** Eric Priestley, Charles Bivins, and Elliott Levin
**Submissions Policy:** No unsolicited manuscripts
**Simultaneous Subs:** no
**Reading Period:** Year-round
**Reporting Time:** 1 to 3 months
**Author Payment:** royalties
**Founded:** 1993
**Non Profit:** no
**Paid Staff:** 0
**Unpaid Staff:** 3
**Distributors:** SPD
**ISSN Number/ISBN Number:** ISSN 1-884773
**Number of Books Published per Year:** 1
**Titles in Print:** 4
**Average Print Run:** 1,500
**Average Percentage Printed:** Paperback 100%
**Average Price:** $9.95

# Heaven Bone Magazine

**Type:** magazine
**CLMP member:** no
**Primary Editor/Contact Person:** Steve Hirsch
**Address:** P.O. Box 486
Chester, NY 10918
**Publishes:** essays, fiction, nonfiction, poetry, reviews, art, and translation
**Editorial Focus:** Poetry, Fiction, Essays, Reviews and artwork with an emphasis on the experimental, surreal, "post-Beat" and Buddhist/Hindu.
**Representative Authors:** Anne Waldman, Stephen-Paul Martin, and Diane DiPrima
**Submissions Policy:** 10 Pages poetry max.; 7,500 words fiction max. Always include SASE. Simultaneous subs OK if notified. Read a sample issue!!!
**Simultaneous Subs:** yes
**Reading Period:** Year-round
**Reporting Time:** 3 to 15 months
**Author Payment:** copies
**Contests:** Bi-Annual Chapbook Contest welcomes manuscripts from all over the world. Watch Poets & Writers for announcements and deadlines.
**Founded:** 1986
**Non Profit:** yes
**Paid Staff:** 0
**Unpaid Staff:** 6
**Distributors:** SPD; Amazon.com
**ISSN Number/ISBN Number:** ISSN 1042-5381
**Total Circulation:** 2,500
**Paid Circulation:** 160
**Average Print Run:** 2,500
**Subscription Rate:** Individual $10/Institution $10
**Single Copy Price:** $10
**Current Volume/Issue:** Issue 13
**Frequency per Year:** 1
**Backfile Available:** yes
**Unsolicited Ms. Received:** yes
**% of Unsolicited Ms. Published per Year:** 3%
**Format:** perfect
**Size:** H 11" W 8.5"
**Average Pages:** 128
**Ads:** yes
**Ad Rates:** Query by e-mail for current rates

# The Heaven Bone Press

**Type:** press
**CLMP member:** no
**Primary Editor/Contact Person:** Steve Hirsch
**Address:** P.O. Box 486
Chester, NY 10918
**Publishes:** essays, fiction, nonfiction, poetry, reviews, art, and translation
**Editorial Focus:** Poetry and fiction with an emphasis on the surreal, experimental, "post-Beat" and Buddhist/Hindu. Chapbooks mostly.
**Representative Authors:** Anne Waldman, Stephen-

Paul Martin, and Diane DiPrima
**Submissions Policy:** Query first with sample. Simultaneous subs OK if notified. See a sample of our magazine, Heaven Bone.
**Simultaneous Subs:** yes
**Reading Period:** Year-round
**Reporting Time:** 3 to 15 months
**Author Payment:** copies
**Contests:** Bi-Annual Chapbook contest awards cash prize $500. Query for guidelines or watch Poets & Writers for announcement of deadline
**Founded:** 1986
**Non Profit:** no
**Paid Staff:** 0
**Unpaid Staff:** 6
**Distributors:** SPD; Amazon.com
**Number of Books Published per Year:** 1
**Titles in Print:** 16
**Average Percentage Printed:** Paperback 20%, Chapbook 80%

# Helen Marx Books

**Type:** press
**CLMP member:** yes
**Address:** 23 E. 69th St., #BF
New York, NY 10021
**Web Site Address:** http://www.turtlepoint.com/TurtlePointnew_content.html
**Publishes: fiction and nonfiction**
**Reading Period:** Year-round
**Reporting Time:** 1 to 2 months
**Author Payment:** none
**Non Profit:** yes
**Average Percentage Printed:** Hardcover 100%
**Backfile Available:** yes

# Helicon Nine Editions

**Type:** press
**CLMP member:** no
**Primary Editor/Contact Person:** Gloria Vando Hickok
**Address:** P.O. Box 22412
Kansas City, MO 64113
**Web Site Address:** http://heliconnine@aol.com
**Publishes:** essays, fiction, and poetry
**Representative Authors:** Sheila Kohler, novel, Philip Miller, poems, and Robert Stewart essays,
**Submissions Policy:** We are not accepting unsolicited manuscripts at this time.

**Simultaneous Subs:** no
**Reading Period:** Year-round
**Reporting Time:** 6 to 12 months
**Author Payment:** royalties and copies
**Founded:** 1977
**Non Profit:** yes
**Paid Staff:** 1
**Unpaid Staff:** 2
**Distributors:** Baker & Taylor, Brodart, Barnes & Noble
**ISSN Number/ISBN Number:** ISBN 1-884235-
**Number of Books Published per Year:** 2-3
**Titles in Print:** 46
**Average Percentage Printed:** Paperback 100%

# Heliotrope, a Journal of Poetry

**Type:** magazine
**CLMP member:** yes
**Primary Editor/Contact Person:** Susan Sindall, the Editors
**Address:** P.O. Box 456
Shady, NY 12409
**Web Site Address:** http://www.heliopoems.com
**Publishes:** poetry
**Editorial Focus:** High quality work by a broad range of poets. We encourage older women.
**Representative Authors:** Cortney Davis, David Dodd Lee, and Jean Monahan
**Submissions Policy:** 3-5 pages, single-spaced, with author's name and address on each page. SASE required.
**Simultaneous Subs:** yes
**Reading Period:** Year-round
**Reporting Time:** 8 to 10 months
**Author Payment:** copies
**Founded:** 2000
**Non Profit:** yes
**Paid Staff:** 0
**Unpaid Staff:** 3
**ISSN Number/ISBN Number:** ISSN 1533-0052
**Total Circulation:** 250
**Paid Circulation:** 75
**Subscription Rate:** Individual $22/Institution $ 22
**Single Copy Price:** $8
**Current Volume/Issue:** Issue #4
**Frequency per Year:** 1
**Backfile Available:** no
**Unsolicited Ms. Received:** yes
**% of Unsolicited Ms. Published per Year:** 5%
**Format:** perfect
**Average Pages:** 75

## Profile: Kathleen Volk Miller, Managing Editor, Painted Bride Quarterly

**1) How did you arrive at your current position?**
Kathleen Volk Miller came to Painted Bride Quarterly 15 years ago, while she was in graduate school. Marion Wrenn joined the staff next. After a few years, as editors came and went, Kathleen and Marion took the helm, and have been co-editors for more than 7 years.

**2) What is the staff structure like at your press/magazine?**
Marion runs an editorial staff in New York. Kathleen runs an editorial staff in Philadelphia, comprised of area writers and students at Drexel University. Drexel University houses the magazine, and provides administrative assistance.

**3) How do you keep your press/magazine running?**
Money. Simultaneous submissions.

**4) What do or don't you hope to see in a cover letter?**
"This is a simultaneous submission."

**5) What do you look for in a submission?**
Something fresh. Wake us up.

**6) How are submissions processed at your press/magazine?**
PBQ is dedicated to maintaining a democratic editorial policy: every submission is read by a minimum of three staff members. If even one member says "Yes," when others have said no, the work gets brought to an editorial meeting, real aloud, discussed, and voted on, with no "elder" members vote counting for more than the newest member. We believe this process retains our quality, yet eclectic publishing history.

**7) Do you have a favorite unsolicited submission discovery or story?**
So many: There are the times that literary agents found our authors online, contacted our authors, and got them book contracts, like Rita Welte Bourke. Or those who won one of our contests and were then contacted for book deals (and would even go on to win an award, like Elizabeth Oness). Or, the time we saw BJ Ward read a piece at a Writers Conference, which he then submitted to PBQ, which we ran and then it won a Pushcart? Something about PBQ acting as the conduit between the writer and the world at large: that's what redeems this job, what makes it all seem worth it.

**8) Do you have any advice for first-time submitters?**
The single most effective way to improve your own writing skills is—in my opinion—to read LOTS of the best of the kind of writing you want to do. (Also, take notice: What publications do you like to read? Those might be good places to start sending your work since you and the editors obviously have shared tastes.)

## Hobart

**Type:** magazine
**CLMP member:** yes
**Address:** 394 Waymarket
Ann Arbor, MI 48103
**Web Site Address:** http://www.hobartpulp.com
**Publishes:** fiction and nonfiction
**Reading Period:** Year-round
**Reporting Time:** 1 to 2 months
**Author Payment:** none
**Founded:** 2001
**Non Profit:** yes
**Backfile Available:** yes

## Hogtown Creek Review

**Type:** magazine
**CLMP member:** no
**Primary Editor/Contact Person:** Michael Martin
**Address:** 4736 Hummingbird Ln.
2601 SW 8th Dr., Gainesville, FL 32601
Valdosta, GA 31602
**Web Site Address:** http://www.hogtowncreek.org
**Publishes:** essays, fiction, nonfiction, poetry, reviews, art, and translation
**Editorial Focus:** HCR seeks the best in literature and art.
**Representative Authors:** Dean Paschal, Jack Butler, and Moira Crone
**Submissions Policy:** Best reviewed at our website.
**Simultaneous Subs:** yes
**Reading Period:** Year-round
**Reporting Time:** 1 to 3 months
**Author Payment:** copies
**Founded:** 1999
**Non Profit:** yes
**Paid Staff:** no
**Unpaid Staff:** yes
**Distributors:** Hogtown Press
**ISSN Number/ISBN Number:** ISSN 1533-7243
**Total Circulation:** 750
**Paid Circulation:** 150
**Subscription Rate:** Individual $10/Institution same
**Single Copy Price:** $10
**Current Volume/Issue:** Issue 4
**Frequency per Year:** 1
**Backfile Available:** yes
**Unsolicited Ms. Received:** yes
**% of Unsolicited Ms. Published per Year:** 5%
**Format:** perfect
**Size:** H 11.668" W 8.25"
**Average Pages:** 88

**Ads:** yes
**Ad Rates:** $200 full page, $100 1/2, $50 quarter page
See Web Site for Details.

## The Hollins Critic

**Type:** magazine
**CLMP member:** yes
**Primary Editor/Contact Person:** Amanda Cockwell
**Address:** P.O. Box 9538
Hollins University
Roanoke, VA 24020
**Web Site Address:** http://www.hollins.edu/academics/critic
**Publishes:** essays, poetry, and reviews
**Editorial Focus:** Essays on the work of contemporary poets, fiction writers and dramatists; poetry; brief book reviews
**Representative Authors:** George Garrett, Kelly Cherry, and Henry Taylor
**Submissions Policy:** Submit up to 5 poems with SASE. No e-mail submissions. Unsolicited essays not accepted. Unsolicited reviews rarely accepted.
**Simultaneous Subs:** yes
**Reading Period:** 9/1 to 12/15
**Reporting Time:** 1 to 2 months
**Author Payment:** cash and copies
**Founded:** 1964
**Non Profit:** yes
**Paid Staff:** 3
**Unpaid Staff:** 2
**ISSN Number/ISBN Number:** ISSN 0018-3644
**Total Circulation:** 500
**Paid Circulation:** 350
**Average Print Run:** 500
**Subscription Rate:** Individual $8/Institution $8
**Single Copy Price:** $2
**Current Volume/Issue:** XLIV/1
**Frequency per Year:** 5
**Backfile Available:** yes
**Unsolicited Ms. Received:** yes
**% of Unsolicited Ms. Published per Year:** 5%
**Format:** stapled
**Size:** H 10" W 7"
**Average Pages:** 24
**Ads:** no

## Home Planet News

**Type:** magazine
**CLMP member:** yes
**Primary Editor/Contact Person:** Donald Lev
**Address:** Home Planet Publications
P.O. Box 455

High Falls, NY 12440
**Web Site Address:** http://www.homeplanetnews.org
**Publishes:** essays, fiction, poetry, and reviews
**Editorial Focus:** Poetry
**Representative Authors:** Enid Dame, Andrew Glaze, and Hal Sirowitz
**Submissions Policy:** 3-5 poems w/SASE-fiction up to 3,000 words. Reviews and articles, please query.
**Simultaneous Subs:** no
**Reading Period:** Year-round
**Reporting Time:** 1 to 3 months
**Author Payment:** copies and subscription
**Founded:** 1979
**Non Profit:** yes
**Paid Staff:** 0
**Unpaid Staff:** 18
**Distributors:** Sunspot Distribution, Marina Penzner
**ISSN Number/ISBN Number:** ISSN 023-303x
**Total Circulation:** 3,000
**Paid Circulation:** 242
**Average Print Run:** 3,000
**Subscription Rate:** Individual $10/Institution same
**Single Copy Price:** $4
**Current Volume/Issue:** 13/53
**Frequency per Year:** 2-3
**Backfile Available:** yes
**Unsolicited Ms. Received:** yes
**% of Unsolicited Ms. Published per Year:** 2%
**Format:** tabloid
**Size:** H 14.5" W 10"
**Average Pages:** 24
**Ads:** yes
**Ad Rates:** $1 per square inch

## Horse & Buggy Press

**Type:** press
**CLMP member:** no
**Primary Editor/Contact Person:** Dave Wofford
**Address:** 2016 Englewood Ave.
Durham, NC 27705
**Web Site Address:**
http://www.antfarmstudios.org/dwofford/
**Publishes:** essays, fiction, nonfiction, and poetry
**Editorial Focus:** Short-length books (36-64) pages. Two editions are published, a trade edition, and a hand-printed letterpress edition.
**Representative Authors:** Allan Gurganus, Stephen Gibson, and John Lane
**Submissions Policy:** Manuscript accepted at all time but are not returned.
**Simultaneous Subs:** yes

**Reading Period:** Year-round
**Reporting Time:** 1 to 2 months
**Author Payment:** copies
**Contests:** Annual poetry chapbook contest begins 2004. 36-page book, printed letterpress and hand-bound. Winner receives 50 of 200 books
**Founded:** 1996
**Non Profit:** no
**Paid Staff:** 1
**Unpaid Staff:** 1
**Distributors:** SPD
**Number of Books Published per Year:** 2
**Titles in Print:** 9
**Average Percentage Printed:** Hardcover 10%, Paperback 40%, Other 50%

## Host Publications

**Type:** press
**CLMP member:** yes
**Primary Editor/Contact Person:** Susan Lesak
**Address:** 100 E. 7th St.
Ste. 201
Austin, TX 78702
**Web Site Address:** http://www.hostpublications.com
**Publishes:** fiction, poetry, and translation
**Editorial Focus:** International in scope, Host Publications brings literature from around the world to US readers.
**Representative Authors:** Pablo Neruda, Dave Oliphant, and Alfred Leslie
**Submissions Policy:** Send abstract of work with author CV. We will respond as quickly as possible.
**Simultaneous Subs:** yes
**Reading Period:** Year-round
**Reporting Time:** 6 to 12 months
**Author Payment:** cash and copies
**Founded:** 1988
**Non Profit:** no
**Paid Staff:** 3
**Unpaid Staff:** 0
**Distributors:** Ingram Distribution, Baker & Taylor
**ISSN Number/ISBN Number:** ISBN 0-924047
**Number of Books Published per Year:** 2
**Titles in Print:** 16
**Average Print Run:** 1,500
**Average Percentage Printed:** Hardcover 10%, Paperback 90%
**Average Price:** $15

# Hourglass Books

**Type:** press
**CLMP member:** yes
**Primary Editor/Contact Person:** W.C. Scheurer
**Address:** P.O. Box 132
Antioch, IL 60002-0132
**Web Site Address:** http://www.hourglassbooks.com
**Publishes:** fiction
**Editorial Focus:** Hourglass Books publishes themed anthologies of literary short stories for the general reading public.
**Representative Authors:** Pam Houston, Peter Ho Davies, and Aimee Bender
**Submissions Policy:** See http://www.hourglass-books.com for current theme. We accept previously published stories from literary magazines and collections.
**Simultaneous Subs:** yes
**Reading Period:** Year-round
**Reporting Time:** 2 to 6 months
**Author Payment:** royalties
**Founded:** 2003
**Non Profit:** yes
**Paid Staff:** 3
**Unpaid Staff:** 13
**Wholesalers:** Ingram; Baker & Taylor
**ISSN Number/ISBN Number:** ISBN 0972525424
**Number of Books Published per Year:** 2
**Titles in Print:** 2
**Average Percentage Printed:** Paperback 100%
**Backfile Available:** yes

# HOW2 Magazine

**Type:** online
**CLMP member:** no
**Primary Editor/Contact Person:** Kate Fagan
**Address:** 26 Iredale St.
Newtown, Sydney, AUS, 2042
**Web Site Address:** http://how2journal.com
**Publishes:** essays, poetry, reviews, art, translation, audio, and video
**Editorial Focus:** Contemporary innovative and modernist writing by women; non-traditional directions in scholarship.
**Representative Authors:** Redell Olsen, Leslie Scalapino, and Lola Ridge
**Submissions Policy:** Submissions must be by or about women innovators, with an emphasis on poetry. International focus.
**Simultaneous Subs:** yes

**Reading Period:** Year-round
**Reporting Time:** 1 to 2 months
**Author Payment:** none
**Contests:** none
**Founded:** 1999
**Non Profit:** yes
**Paid Staff:** 0
**Unpaid Staff:** 3-9
**Distributors:** Archives hosted by Arizona State University
**Average Page Views per Month:** 600
**Average Unique Visitors per Month:** 300
**Frequency per Year:** 2
**Publish Print Anthology:** no
**Average Percentage of Pages per Category:** Nonfiction 15%, Poetry 25%, Reviews 10%, Essays 25%, Art 10%, Translation 10%, Audio 5%
**Ads:** no

# Hub City Writers Project

**Type:** press
**CLMP member:** no
**Primary Editor/Contact Person:** Betsy Teter
**Address:** P.O. Box 8421
Spartanburg, SC 29305
**Web Site Address:** http://www.hubcity.org
**Publishes:** essays, fiction, nonfiction, and poetry
**Editorial Focus:** Hub City publishes books with a strong sense of place and is primarily interested in books by authors from the Carolinas.
**Representative Authors:** Ron Rash, John Lane, and Rosa Shand
**Submissions Policy:** We take 3-page book proposals with a sample chapter in March and September.
**Simultaneous Subs:** yes
**Reading Period:** 4/1 to 5/1
**Reporting Time:** 2 to 3 months
**Author Payment:** none, royalties, cash, and copies
**Founded:** 1995
**Non Profit:** yes
**Paid Staff:** 2
**Unpaid Staff:** 0
**Wholesalers:** Ingram, Baker & Taylor
**ISSN Number/ISBN Number:** ISBN 1891885
**Number of Books Published per Year:** 2-4
**Titles in Print:** 18
**Average Print Run:** 1,000
**Average Percentage Printed:** Hardcover 20%, Paperback 80%
**Average Price:** $15

# The Hudson Review

**Type:** magazine
**CLMP member:** yes
**Primary Editor/Contact Person:** Paula Deitz
**Address:** 684 Park Ave.
New York, NY 10021
**Web Site Address:** http://www.hudsonreview.com
**Publishes:** essays, fiction, nonfiction, poetry, reviews, and translation
**Editorial Focus:** A forum for the work of new writers and for exploration and development in literature and the arts.
**Submissions Policy:** Poetry: April 1 through June 30. Fiction: September 1 through November 30. Nonfiction: January 1 through March 31.
**Simultaneous Subs:** no
**Reading Period:** Year-round
**Reporting Time:** 4 to 7 months
**Author Payment:** cash
**Founded:** 1948
**Non Profit:** yes
**Paid Staff:** 4
**Unpaid Staff:** 2
**Total Circulation:** 4,500
**Paid Circulation:** 3,500
**Subscription Rate:** Individual $32/Institution $38
**Single Copy Price:** $9
**Current Volume/Issue:** LVII/2
**Frequency per Year:** 4
**Backfile Available:** yes
**Unsolicited Ms. Received:** yes
**Format:** perfect
**Ads:** yes
**Ad Rates:** See Web Site for Details.

# The Hudson Valley Writers' Center

**Type:** press
**CLMP member:** yes
**Primary Editor/Contact Person:** Margo Stever
**Address:** Slapering Hol Press
300 Riverside Dr.
Sleepy Hollow, NY 10591
**Web Site Address:** http://www.writerscenter.org
**Publishes:** poetry
**Editorial Focus:** SHP publishes chapbooks by poets who have not previously published a book or chapbook; and occasionally, thematic anthologies
**Representative Authors:** David Tucker, Dina Ben-Lev, and Rachel Loden
**Submissions Policy:** see web site (www.writerscen-

ter.org) for guidelines
**Simultaneous Subs:** yes
**Reading Period:** 2/1 to 5/15
**Reporting Time:** 2 to 3 months
**Author Payment:** cash and copies
**Contests:** See Web Site for Contest Guidelines.
**Founded:** 1990
**Non Profit:** yes
**Paid Staff:** 0
**Unpaid Staff:** 2
**Distributors:** applied to SPD; waiting to hear
**ISSN Number/ISBN Number:** ISBN 0-9700277
**Number of Books Published per Year:** 1-2
**Titles in Print:** 16
**Average Print Run:** 500
**Average Percentage Printed:** Paperback 5%, Chapbook 95%
**Average Price:** $12

# Hunger Mountain

**Type:** magazine
**CLMP member:** yes
**Primary Editor/Contact Person:** Caroline Mercurio
**Address:** 36 College St.
36 College St.
Montpelier, VT 05602
**Web Site Address:** http://www.hungermtn.org
**Publishes:** essays, fiction, nonfiction, poetry, art, and translation
**Editorial Focus:** The Vermont College Journal of Arts & Letters accepts unpublished work by both established and emerging writers and artists.
**Representative Authors:** Alice Hoffman, Maxine Kumin, and James Tate
**Submissions Policy:** Refer to submission guidelines on website. No genre fiction, reviews, or multiple submissions.
**Simultaneous Subs:** yes
**Reading Period:** 4/1 to 1/31
**Reporting Time:** 1 to 4 months
**Author Payment:** cash and copies
**Contests:** See Web Site for Contest Guidelines.
**Founded:** 2002
**Non Profit:** yes
**Paid Staff:** 3
**Unpaid Staff:** 25
**ISSN Number/ISBN Number:** ISSN 1539-9931
**Total Circulation:** 1,500
**Paid Circulation:** 700
**Average Print Run:** 1,600

**Subscription Rate:** Individual $17/Institution $17
**Single Copy Price:** $10
**Current Volume/Issue:** Issue 7
**Frequency per Year:** 2
**Backfile Available:** yes
**Unsolicited Ms. Received:** yes
**% of Unsolicited Ms. Published per Year:** 5%
**Format:** perfect
**Size:** H 10" W 7"
**Average Pages:** 200
**Ads:** yes
**Ad Rates:** contact Managing Editor
(hungermtn@tui.edu) for info

# IBEX Publishers

**Type:** press
**CLMP member:** no
**Primary Editor/Contact Person:** Farhad Shirzad
**Address:** P.O. Box 30087
Bethesda, MD 20824
**Web Site Address:** http://www.ibexpub.com
**Publishes:** fiction, nonfiction, poetry, translation, and
audio
**Editorial Focus:** IBEX Publishers publishes English
and Persian language books about Iran and the Middle
East.
**Representative Authors:** Hafez of Shiraz, E.G.
Browne, and Wheeler M. Thackston
**Submissions Policy:** Please send outline, synopsis
and CV. Books should have some relevance to the
Middle East.
**Simultaneous Subs:** no
**Reading Period:** Year-round
**Reporting Time:** 2 to 3 months
**Author Payment:** none, royalties, and copies
**Founded:** 1979
**Non Profit:** no
**Paid Staff:** 3
**Unpaid Staff:** 0
**Wholesalers:** Ingram, Baker & Taylor
**ISSN Number/ISBN Number:** ISBN 0-936347 1-
58814-
**Number of Books Published per Year:** 12
**Titles in Print:** 130
**Average Print Run:** 1,500
**Average Percentage Printed:** Hardcover 50%,
Paperback 50%
**Average Price:** depends

# Ibis Editions

**Type:** press
**CLMP member:** no
**Primary Editor/Contact Person:** Peter Cole, Adina
Hoffman
**Address:** P.O. Box 8074
German Colony
Jerusalem, Israel
**Web Site Address:** http://www.ibiseditions.com
**Publishes:** essays, fiction, nonfiction, poetry, and
translation
**Editorial Focus:** Literature of the Levant in Translation
from Arabic, Hebrew, French, Ladino, Greek, German,
and other languages.
**Representative Authors:** Muhyaddin Ibn al-Arabi,
Gershom Scholem, and Taha Muhammad Ali
**Submissions Policy:** query letters only
**Simultaneous Subs:** no
**Reading Period:** Year-round
**Reporting Time:** 1 to 3 months
**Author Payment:** copies
**Founded:** 1998
**Non Profit:** yes
**Paid Staff:** 0
**Unpaid Staff:** 3
**Distributors:** SPD, Reuben Mass
**Number of Books Published per Year:** 1-2
**Titles in Print:** 13
**Average Percentage Printed:** Paperback 100%

# The Ice Cube Press

**Type:** press
**CLMP member:** no
**Primary Editor/Contact Person:** S.H. Semken
**Address:** 205 N Front
North Liberty, IA 52317
**Web Site Address:** http://www.icecubepress.com
**Publishes:** essays and nonfiction
**Editorial Focus:** Regional and place-based writing on
the environment and spirit of the Midwest. S1tories,
biography and essays.
**Recent Awards Received:** Iowa Arts Council
Humanities Iowa (NEH)
**Submissions Policy:** If you think "everyone, or the
general public" will like it, don't send! We very very
rarely take on a new author, or unsolicited work.
**Simultaneous Subs:** yes
**Reading Period:** Year-round
**Reporting Time:** 2 to 3 months
**Author Payment:** copies

**Founded:** 1993
**Non Profit:** no
**Paid Staff:** 1
**Unpaid Staff:** 0
**Distributors:** the distributors, quality books
**ISSN Number/ISBN Number:** ISBN 1-888160
**Number of Books Published per Year:** 5
**Titles in Print:** 20
**Average Print Run:** 500
**Average Percentage Printed:** Hardcover 5%, Paperback 90%, Other 5%
**Average Price:** $11.95

# Iconoclast

**Type:** magazine
**CLMP member:** no
**Primary Editor/Contact Person:** Philip Wagner
**Address:** 1675 Amazon Road
Mohegan Lake, NY 10547-1804
**Publishes:** essays, fiction, nonfiction, poetry, reviews, art, and translation
**Editorial Focus:** original, creative work showing craft, intelligence, and more than a passing acquaintance with the world at large
**Submissions Policy:** send hard copy only, with SASE appropriate for reply and/or return of material
**Simultaneous Subs:** no
**Reading Period:** Year-round
**Reporting Time:** 3 to 5 weeks
**Author Payment:** cash and copies
**Founded:** 1992
**Non Profit:** no
**Paid Staff:** 0
**Unpaid Staff:** 8
**Distributors:** in house
**Wholesalers:** in house
**ISSN Number/ISBN Number:** ISSN 1064-1777
**Total Circulation:** 850
**Paid Circulation:** 425
**Average Print Run:** 3,000
**Subscription Rate:** Individual $16/8/Institution $16/8
**Single Copy Price:** $5
**Current Volume/Issue:** Issue 90
**Frequency per Year:** 5
**Backfile Available:** yes
**Unsolicited Ms. Received:** yes
**% of Unsolicited Ms. Published per Year:** 5%
**Format:** stapled
**Size:** H 10.5" W 8"
**Average Pages:** 96

**Ads:** yes
**Ad Rates:** $100 full page/$60 half page

# The Idaho Review

**Type:** magazine
**CLMP member:** yes
**Primary Editor/Contact Person:** Mitch Wieland, Editor
**Address:** Boise State University
1910 University Dr.
Boise, ID 83725
**Publishes:** essays, fiction, poetry, and reviews
**Editorial Focus:** High quality literary work.
**Representative Authors:** Joy Williams, Ann Beattie, and Richard Bausch
**Submissions Policy:** Fiction-no length requirement, one ms. per submission. Poetry-3 to 5 poems per submission.
**Simultaneous Subs:** yes
**Reading Period:** 9/1 to 12/1
**Reporting Time:** 3 to 5 months
**Author Payment:** cash and subscription
**Contests:** Annual Editor's Prize. Payment $1,000 plus publication. Deadline: October 1 of each year. See Web Site for Contest Guidelines.
**Founded:** 1998
**Non Profit:** yes
**Paid Staff:** 2
**Unpaid Staff:** 7
**ISSN Number/ISBN Number:** 1520-8389/0-9706392-4-4
**Total Circulation:** 1,000
**Paid Circulation:** 150
**Subscription Rate:** Individual $21.95/3 yr./Institution same
**Single Copy Price:** $10.95
**Current Volume/Issue:** 2004/VI
**Frequency per Year:** 1
**Backfile Available:** no
**Unsolicited Ms. Received:** yes
**% of Unsolicited Ms. Published per Year:** 50%
**Format:** perfect
**Size:** H 9 " W 6 "
**Average Pages:** 200
**Ads:** yes
**Ad Rates:** Exchange ads with literary journals

# Ig Publishing

**Type:** press
**CLMP member:** no
**Primary Editor/Contact Person:** Robert Lasner
**Address:** 178 Clinton Ave.
Brooklyn, NY 11205
**Web Site Address:** http://www.igpub.com
**Publishes:** fiction, nonfiction, and translation
**Editorial Focus:** Ig Publishing publishes literary fiction and political nonfiction.
**Representative Authors:** Robert Lasner, Edward Bernays, and Kirby Gann
**Submissions Policy:** Prefer e-mail submissions to igsubmissions@earthlink.net
**Simultaneous Subs:** yes
**Reading Period:** Year-round
**Reporting Time:** 3 to 6 months
**Author Payment:** royalties
**Founded:** 2000
**Non Profit:** no
**Paid Staff:** 2
**Unpaid Staff:** 0
**Distributors:** Consortium
**ISSN Number/ISBN Number:** ISBN 0-9703125
**Number of Books Published per Year:** 10
**Titles in Print:** 16
**Average Print Run:** 3,000
**Average Percentage Printed:** Hardcover 9%, Paperback 91%
**Average Price:** $12.95

# Image

**Type:** magazine
**CLMP member:** yes
**Primary Editor/Contact Person:** Gregory Wolfe
**Address:** 3307 Third Ave. W
Seattle, WA 98119
**Web Site Address:** http://www.imagejournal.org
**Publishes:** essays, fiction, nonfiction, poetry, reviews, art, and translation
**Editorial Focus:** Image is a unique forum for the best writing and artwork that are informed by-or grapple with-religious faith.
**Recent Awards Received:** Twice nominated by Utne Reader for Alternative Press Awards; work reprinted in Pushcart, Best American Essays, and others.
**Representative Authors:** Mark Jarman, Julia Kasdorf, and Robert Olen Butler
**Submissions Policy:** We welcome unsolicited submissions. Include SASE for response. No e-mail submissions, please.
**Simultaneous Subs:** yes
**Reading Period:** Year-round
**Reporting Time:** 2 to 3 months
**Author Payment:** cash and copies
**Founded:** 1989
**Non Profit:** yes
**Paid Staff:** 3
**Unpaid Staff:** 3-5
**Distributors:** Ingram
**ISSN Number/ISBN Number:** ISSN 1087-3503
**Total Circulation:** 5,100
**Paid Circulation:** 4,500
**Average Print Run:** 5,500
**Subscription Rate:** Individual $39.95/Institution $49.95
**Single Copy Price:** $12
**Current Volume/Issue:** Issue 47
**Frequency per Year:** 4
**Backfile Available:** yes
**Unsolicited Ms. Received:** yes
**% of Unsolicited Ms. Published per Year:** 3%
**Format:** perfect
**Size:** H 10" W 7"
**Average Pages:** 128
**Ads:** yes
**Ad Rates:** See Web Site for Details.

# Images For Media, Yefief

**Type:** press
**CLMP member:** no
**Primary Editor/Contact Person:** Ann Racuya-Robbins
**Address:** P.O. Box 8505
Santa Fe, NM 87504
**Web Site Address:** http://www.ifm.com, http://www.wkbank.com
**Publishes:** essays, fiction, nonfiction, poetry, art, translation, and audio
**Editorial Focus:** new forms, transcultural, quality work of all kinds
**Representative Authors:** Nicole Brossard, Xue Di, and Lucia Pavia Ticzon
**Simultaneous Subs:** yes
**Reading Period:** Year-round
**Reporting Time:** 1 to 3 months
**Author Payment:** copies
**Founded:** 1993
**Non Profit:** no
**Paid Staff:** 1
**Unpaid Staff:** 1

**Distributors:** Amazon.com, ifm.com
**ISSN Number/ISBN Number:** 1074-5629,/1-884432
**Number of Books Published per Year:** 0-6
**Titles in Print:** 9
**Average Percentage Printed:** Paperback 100%

# Impetus

**Type:** online
**CLMP member:** no
**Primary Editor/Contact Person:** Cheryl A Townsend
**Address:** 4975 Comanche Trail
Stow, OH 44224-1217
**Web Site Address:**
http://www.mipogallery.com/Impetus/
**Publishes:** essays, fiction, nonfiction, poetry, reviews, and art
**Editorial Focus:** Impetus wants poetry that screams. Poetry so real it hurts. No rhyme. No oatmeal. No taboos (other than isms)
**Representative Authors:** Ron Androla, Lyn Lifshin, and Jim Chandler
**Submissions Policy:** It is highly suggested that you first read an issue of Impetus before submitting to get a better idea of what we are looking for. All written text must be sent within the e-mail. No attachments will be opened other than jpgs or gifs of artwork. Please write "Submission" in subject line of e-mail.
**Simultaneous Subs:** yes
**Reading Period:** Year-round
**Reporting Time:** 1 to 2 months
**Author Payment:** none
**Founded:** 1984
**Non Profit:** yes
**Paid Staff:** 0
**Unpaid Staff:** 3
**Distributors:** Past print issues/anthology through Waterrow Books
**Wholesalers:** Via publisher
**ISSN Number/ISBN Number:** ISSN 1044-7490
**Frequency per Year:** 4
**Publish Print Anthology:** yes
Price: $10
**Average Percentage of Pages per Category:** Fiction 1%, Nonfiction 1%, Poetry 56%, Reviews 1%, Essays 1%, Art 40%
**Ads:** no

# Indian Bay Press

**Type:** press
**CLMP member:** yes
**Primary Editor/Contact Person:** W.R. Mayo, Publisher
**Address:** Delta House Publishing Company
Executive Square, One West Mountain
Fayetteville, AR 72701
**Web Site Address:** http://www.indianbaypress.com
**Publishes:** poetry and reviews
**Simultaneous Subs:** no
**Reading Period:** Year-round
**Reporting Time:** 1 to 2 months
**Author Payment:** none, cash, and copies
**Contests:** Oliver W. Browning Poetry Content, Annually See Web Site for Contest Guidelines.
**Founded:** 2003
**Non Profit:** no
**Paid Staff:** 0
**Unpaid Staff:** 4
**ISSN Number/ISBN Number:** ISSN 1547-448X
**Number of Books Published per Year:** 2,500
**Titles in Print:** Poesia
**Average Print Run:** 2,500
**Average Percentage Printed:** Chapbook 100%
**Average Price:** $ 3.75

# Indiana Review

**Type:** magazine
**CLMP member:** yes
**Primary Editor/Contact Person:** Grady Jaynes
**Address:** 465 Ballantine Hall
1020 E. Kirkwood Ave.
Bloomington, IN 47405-7103
**Web Site Address:** http://www.indiana.edu/~inreview
**Publishes:** essays, fiction, nonfiction, poetry, reviews, art, and translation
**Editorial Focus:** Showcasing talents of emerging and established writers, while offering the highest quality writing within a wide aesthetic.
**Recent Awards Received:** O'Henry Award 2006, O'Henry Award 2005, multiple Pushcart nominations
**Representative Authors:** Lucia Perillo, Denise Duhamel, and Michael Martone
**Submissions Policy:** See
http://www.indiana.edu/~inreview/general/guide-lines.html
**Simultaneous Subs:** yes
**Reading Period:** Year-round
**Reporting Time:** 2 to 4 months

**Author Payment:** cash, copies, and subscription
**Contests:** See Web Site for Contest Guidelines.
**Founded:** 1976
**Non Profit:** yes
**Paid Staff:** 4
**Unpaid Staff:** 15
**Distributors:** Ingram
**ISSN Number/ISBN Number:** ISSN 0738-386X
**Total Circulation:** 3,000
**Paid Circulation:** 2,000
**Average Print Run:** 5,000
**Subscription Rate:** Individual $17/Institution $20
**Single Copy Price:** $9
**Current Volume/Issue:** 27/2
**Frequency per Year:** 2
**Backfile Available:** yes
**Unsolicited Ms. Received:** yes
**% of Unsolicited Ms. Published per Year:** 1%
**Format:** perfect
**Size:** H 9" W 6"
**Average Pages:** 180
**Ads:** yes
**Ad Rates:** $300 for full page

## Ink Pot

**Type:** magazine
**CLMP member:** no
**Primary Editor/Contact Person:** Beverly Jackson
**Address:** 3909 Reche Road #132
Fallbrook, CA 92028
**Web Site Address:** http://www.litpotpress.com
**Publishes:** essays, fiction, nonfiction, poetry, and art
**Editorial Focus:** Quality literary journal with eclectic work from new as well as established artisans.
**Representative Authors:** Susan O'Neill, Joseph Young, and Karen Fitzgerald (art)
**Submissions Policy:** Guidelines at http://www.litpot.com
**Simultaneous Subs:** yes
**Reading Period:** Year-round
**Reporting Time:** 0 to 1 weeks
**Author Payment:** cash and copies
**Contests:** Contests for affiliated ezine, Lit Pot See Web Site for Contest Guidelines.
**Founded:** 2003
**Non Profit:** yes
**Paid Staff:** 0
**Unpaid Staff:** 10
**Distributors:** In process-websites: amazon.com
**Total Circulation:** 100

**Paid Circulation:** 35
**Subscription Rate:** Individual $30/Institution $25
**Single Copy Price:** $10
**Current Volume/Issue:** 100/1
**Frequency per Year:** 4
**Backfile Available:** yes
**Unsolicited Ms. Received:** yes
**% of Unsolicited Ms. Published per Year:** 100%
**Format:** perfect
**Size:** H 8.5" W 5.5"
**Average Pages:** 200
**Ads:** no

## Inkwell

**Type:** magazine
**CLMP member:** no
**Primary Editor/Contact Person:** Christine O. Adler
**Address:** Manhattanville College
2900 Purchase St.
Purchase, NY 10577
**Web Site Address:** http://www.inkwelljournal.org
**Publishes:** essays, fiction, nonfiction, poetry, and art
**Editorial Focus:** A platform for quality veteran and up-and-coming writers.
**Representative Authors:** Alice Elliott Dark, Mithran Somasundrum, and Benjamin Cheever
**Submissions Policy:** Guidelines available at our website.
**Simultaneous Subs:** yes
**Reading Period:** 8/1 to 11/30
**Reporting Time:** 2 to 6 months
**Author Payment:** cash and copies
**Contests:** See Web Site for Contest Guidelines.
**Founded:** 1995
**Non Profit:** yes
**Paid Staff:** 2
**Unpaid Staff:** 9
**Distributors:** DeBoer, Ingram
**ISSN Number/ISBN Number:** ISSN 1085-0287
**Total Circulation:** 400
**Paid Circulation:** 20
**Subscription Rate:** Individual $15 /Institution $15
**Single Copy Price:** $8
**Current Volume/Issue:** 15/2004
**Frequency per Year:** 2
**Backfile Available:** yes
**Unsolicited Ms. Received:** yes
**% of Unsolicited Ms. Published per Year:** 60%
**Format:** perfect
**Size:** H 8.5" W 5 3/8"

**Average Pages:** 150
**Ads:** yes
**Ad Rates:** Reciprocal available, or $200/full page, $100/half page

# insolent rudder

**Type:** online
**CLMP member:** no
**Primary Editor/Contact Person:** Tim Ljunggren
**Address:** P.O. Box 433
Bristol, IN 46507
**Web Site Address:** http://www.insolentrudder.org
**Publishes:** fiction and reviews
**Editorial Focus:** An electronic magazine dedicated to "furiously fresh flash fiction."
**Representative Authors:** Lisette Garcia, Paul A. Toth, and Susan Henderson
**Submissions Policy:** We accept stories of 500 words or less. For more information, please go to http://www.insolentrudder.org/submissions.
**Simultaneous Subs:** yes
**Reading Period:** 10/1 to 6/30
**Reporting Time:** 4 to 6 weeks
**Author Payment:** none
**Contests:** See Web Site for Contest Guidelines.
**Founded:** 2001
**Non Profit:** yes
**Paid Staff:** 0
**Unpaid Staff:** 5
**Average Page Views per Month:** 1,250
**Average Unique Visitors per Month:** 900
**Publish Print Anthology:** no
**Average Percentage of Pages per Category:** Fiction 95%, Reviews 5%
**Ads:** no

# Insurance

**Type:** magazine
**CLMP member:** no
**Primary Editor/Contact Person:** C. Tokar/K. Anaglnopoulos
**Address:** 132 N. 1st St. #11
Brooklyn, NY 11211
**Publishes:** essays, fiction, nonfiction, and poetry
**Editorial Focus:** Contemporary previously unpublished work; we lean toward experimental but seek work from a variety of "schools."
**Submissions Policy:** We read poetry, short fiction, and prose. We prefer submissions of at least 6 pages

of work (multiple pieces).
**Simultaneous Subs:** yes
**Reading Period:** Year-round
**Reporting Time:** 1 to 3 months
**Author Payment:** cash and copies
**Founded:** 1999
**Non Profit:** yes
**Paid Staff:** 0
**Unpaid Staff:** 2-4
**Distributors:** DeBoer
**Total Circulation:** 500
**Paid Circulation:** 75
**Subscription Rate:** Individual $18/Institution $18
**Single Copy Price:** $10
**Current Volume/Issue:** 3/3
**Frequency per Year:** 1
**Backfile Available:** yes
**Unsolicited Ms. Received:** yes
**% of Unsolicited Ms. Published per Year:** 70%
**Format:** perfect
**Average Pages:** 90
**Ads:** no

# Interlope Magazine

**Type:** magazine
**CLMP member:** no
**Primary Editor/Contact Person:** Summi Kaipa
**Address:** P.O. Box 423058
San Francisco, CA 94142-3058
**Web Site Address:** http://www.interlope.org
**Publishes:** essays, fiction, poetry, and art
**Editorial Focus:** Interlope publishes innovative writing by Asian Americans.
**Representative Authors:** Linh Dinh, Eileen Tabios, and Hoa Nguyen
**Submissions Policy:** 6-10 pages of unsolicited writing considered. Writers should familiarize themselves with Interlope before submitting.
**Simultaneous Subs:** yes
**Reading Period:** Year-round
**Reporting Time:** 6 to 12 weeks
**Author Payment:** copies
**Founded:** 1998
**Non Profit:** yes
**Paid Staff:** 0
**Unpaid Staff:** 1
**Total Circulation:** 50
**Paid Circulation:** 25
**Subscription Rate:** Individual $10/Institution $20
**Single Copy Price:** $5

**Current Volume/Issue:** Issue 9
**Frequency per Year:** 2
**Backfile Available:** yes
**Unsolicited Ms. Received:** yes
**% of Unsolicited Ms. Published per Year:** 30%
**Format:** stapled
**Size:** H 8.5" W 8.5"
**Average Pages:** 65
**Ads:** no

# International Poetry Review

**Type:** magazine
**CLMP member:** no
**Address:** U. of North Carolina at Greensboro
Dept. of Romance Languages
Greensboro, NC 27412-5001
**Publishes:** poetry and translation
**Reading Period:** Year-round
**Reporting Time:** 1 to 2 months
**Author Payment:** none
**Non Profit:** no

# Into the Teeth of the Wind

**Type:** magazine
**CLMP member:** no
**Primary Editor/Contact Person:** Amber Wallace
**Address:** College of Creative Studies
UCSB
Santa Barbara, CA 93106
**Web Site Address:** http://www.ccs.ucsb.edu/wind-steeth
**Publishes:** poetry
**Editorial Focus:** Into the Teeth of the Wind publishes a variety of poems from both well-known and previously unpublished poets.
**Representative Authors:** John Ridland and John Wilson
**Submissions Policy:** All manuscripts, up to eight pages of previously unpublished poetry, are considered. SASE required for response.
**Simultaneous Subs:** yes
**Reading Period:** Year-round
**Reporting Time:** 6 to 8 weeks
**Author Payment:** copies
**Contests:** none
**Founded:** 1999
**Non Profit:** yes
**Paid Staff:** 0
**Unpaid Staff:** 10

**Total Circulation:** 200
**Paid Circulation:** 25
**Subscription Rate:** Individual $18/Institution $18
**Single Copy Price:** $5.50
**Current Volume/Issue:** 3/4
**Frequency per Year:** 4
**Backfile Available:** yes
**Unsolicited Ms. Received:** yes
**% of Unsolicited Ms. Published per Year:** 20%
**Format:** perfect
**Size:** H 8.5" W 5.5"
**Average Pages:** 64
**Ads:** no

# iota

**Type:** magazine
**CLMP member:** no
**Primary Editor/Contact Person:** Janet Murch
**Address:** 1 Lodge Farm
Snitterfield
Stratford-on-Avon, UK CV37 0LR
**Web Site Address:** http://www.iotapoetry.co.uk
**Publishes:** poetry and reviews
**Editorial Focus:** Contemporary poetry with something interesting to say.
**Representative Authors:** Michael Kriesel, Jane Kinninmont, and Christopher James
**Submissions Policy:** Up to 6 poems by post (with SASE/IRC) or in main body of e-mail. State if previously published and detail when and where.
**Simultaneous Subs:** no
**Reading Period:** Year-round
**Reporting Time:** 3 to 6 weeks
**Author Payment:** copies
**Contests:** iota annual poetry competition. Deadline: April 15th.
See Web Site for Contest Guidelines.
**Founded:** 1987
**Non Profit:** yes
**Paid Staff:** 0
**Unpaid Staff:** 2
**ISSN Number/ISBN Number:** ISSN 0266-2922
**Total Circulation:** 290
**Paid Circulation:** 175
**Average Print Run:** 300
**Subscription Rate:** Individual £18 (US)/Institution £18 (US)
**Single Copy Price:** £4.50
**Current Volume/Issue:** Issue 71
**Frequency per Year:** 4

**Backfile Available:** yes
**Unsolicited Ms. Received:** yes
**% of Unsolicited Ms. Published per Year:** 100%
**Format:** perfect
**Size:** H 210mm W 148mm
**Average Pages:** 60
**Ads:** no
**Ad Rates:** See Web Site for Details.

## The Iowa Review

**Type:** magazine
**CLMP member:** yes
**Primary Editor/Contact Person:** David Hamilton
**Address:** 308 English/Philosophy Bldg.
University of Iowa
Iowa City, IA 52242
**Web Site Address:** http://www.uiowa.edu/~iareview
**Publishes:** essays, fiction, nonfiction, poetry, and reviews
**Editorial Focus:** Contemporary writing, the best we can find.
**Representative Authors:** Jill Osier, Marianne Boruch, and Lance Olsen
**Submissions Policy:** Only in hard copy, with SASE, and through the fall semester.
**Simultaneous Subs:** yes
**Reading Period:** 9/1 to 12/1
**Reporting Time:** 1 to 3 months
**Author Payment:** cash, copies, and subscription
**Contests:** See Web Site for Contest Guidelines.
**Founded:** 1970
**Non Profit:** yes
**Paid Staff:** 4
**Unpaid Staff:** 12
**Distributors:** Ingram and DeBoer
**ISSN Number/ISBN Number:** ISSN 0021-065X
**Total Circulation:** 2,500
**Paid Circulation:** 1,100
**Subscription Rate:** Individual $20/Institution $20
**Single Copy Price:** $7.95
**Current Volume/Issue:** 33/2
**Frequency per Year:** 3
**Backfile Available:** yes
**Unsolicited Ms. Received:** yes
**Format:** perfect
**Size:** H 8.5" W 5.5"
**Average Pages:** 192
**Ads:** yes

## iris

**Type:** magazine
**CLMP member:** no
**Primary Editor/Contact Person:** Annie Schutte
**Address:** The Women's Center
P.O. Box 800588-0588
Charlottesville, VA 22908
**Web Site Address:** http://iris.virginia.edu
**Publishes:** essays, fiction, nonfiction, poetry, and art
**Simultaneous Subs:** yes
**Reading Period:** 8/3 to 5/4
**Reporting Time:** 1 to 4 months
**Author Payment:** none
**Founded:** 1980
**Non Profit:** yes
**Paid Staff:** 3
**Unpaid Staff:** 13
**Total Circulation:** 2,500
**Paid Circulation:** yes $9
**Average Print Run:** 2,500
**Subscription Rate:** Individual $9/Institution $40
**Single Copy Price:** $5
**Current Volume/Issue:** Issue 51
**Frequency per Year:** 2
**Backfile Available:** yes
**Unsolicited Ms. Received:** yes
**Format:** stapled

## Iron Horse Literary Review

**Type:** magazine
**CLMP member:** no
**Primary Editor/Contact Person:** Jill Patterson
**Address:** English Dept., Texas Tech University
MS 43091
Lubbock, TX 79409-3091
**Web Site Address:** http://english.ttu.edu/ih
**Publishes:** fiction, nonfiction, poetry, reviews, and art
**Representative Authors:** Melanie Rae Thon, Lee Martin, and Li-Young Lee
**Submissions Policy:** Please let us respond to one manuscript before submitting another. We do not accept simultaneous submissions in poetry.
**Simultaneous Subs:** yes
**Reading Period:** Year-round
**Reporting Time:** 1 to 3 months
**Author Payment:** cash and copies
**Founded:** 1999
**Non Profit:** yes
**Paid Staff:** yes
**Unpaid Staff:** yes

**Total Circulation:** 472
**Paid Circulation:** 433
**Subscription Rate:** Individual $12/Institution $12
**Single Copy Price:** $6
**Current Volume/Issue:** 5/2
**Frequency per Year:** 2
**Backfile Available:** yes
**Unsolicited Ms. Received:** yes
**% of Unsolicited Ms. Published per Year:** 85%
**Format:** perfect
**Size:** H 6" W 9"
**Average Pages:** 200
**Ads:** yes
**Ad Rates:** ad swap program

## Isotope

**Type:** magazine
**CLMP member:** yes
**Primary Editor/Contact Person:** Christopher Cokinos
**Address:** Dept. of English, Utah State University
3200 Old Main Hill
Logan, UT 84322-3200
**Web Site Address:** http://isotope.usu.edu/
**Publishes:** essays, fiction, nonfiction, poetry, and art
**Editorial Focus:** Literary nonfiction, fiction, poetry and artwork that engages the varied relationships between the human and nonhuman worlds.
**Representative Authors:** Pattiann Rogers, D.K. McCutchen, and R.T. Smith
**Submissions Policy:** See website http://isotope.usu.edu/ for writer's guidelines.
**Simultaneous Subs:** yes
**Reading Period:** 8/1 to 11/15
**Reporting Time:** 4 to 6 months
**Author Payment:** cash, copies, and subscription
**Contests:** Yearly Editors' Prizes in Nonfiction, Fiction and Poetry
See Web Site for Contest Guidelines.
**Founded:** 2003
**Non Profit:** yes
**Paid Staff:** 3
**Unpaid Staff:** 0
**ISSN Number/ISBN Number:** ISSN 1544-8479
**Total Circulation:** 620
**Paid Circulation:** 400
**Average Print Run:** 900
**Subscription Rate:** Individual $10/Institution $10
**Single Copy Price:** $5
**Current Volume/Issue:** 3/1
**Frequency per Year:** 2

**Backfile Available:** yes
**Unsolicited Ms. Received:** yes
**% of Unsolicited Ms. Published per Year:** 5%
**Format:** stapled
**Size:** H 11" W 8.5"
**Average Pages:** 44

## Jane's Stories Press Foundation

**Type:** press
**CLMP member:** yes
**Primary Editor/Contact Person:** Linda Mowry
**Address:** 5500 N. 50 W
Fremont, IN 46737
**Web Site Address:** http://www.janespress.org
**Publishes:** essays, fiction, nonfiction, and poetry
**Editorial Focus:** women's literature, multicultural literary traditions
**Representative Authors:** M. Eliza Hamilton Abégúndé, Jan Kent, and Shobha Sharma
**Submissions Policy:** Submissions by invitation or contest entry only at this time. Send contact information to join our mailing list.
**Simultaneous Subs:** yes
**Reading Period:** Year-round
**Reporting Time:** 2 to 4 months
**Author Payment:** none
**Contests:** See Web Site for Contest Guidelines.
**Founded:** 2000
**Non Profit:** yes
**Paid Staff:** 0
**Unpaid Staff:** 2-4
**Distributors:** Baker & Taylor
**Number of Books Published per Year:** 1-3
**Titles in Print:** 10
**Average Print Run:** 750
**Average Percentage Printed:** Paperback 50%, Chapbook 50%
**Average Price:** $14

## Journal of New Jersey Poets

**Type:** magazine
**CLMP member:** yes
**Primary Editor/Contact Person:** Sander Zulauf, Editor
**Address:** County College of Morris
214 Center Grove Road
Randolph, NJ 07869
**Web Site Address:** http://www.ccm.edu
**Publishes:** essays, poetry, and reviews

**Editorial Focus:** The Journal of New Jersey Poets is dedicated to publishing the best new poetry, essays and reviews by poets from New Jersey.
**Recent Awards Received:** Excellence in Print Award from The Poet and the Poem, WPFW-FM, Washington, DC and the Library of Congress
**Representative Authors:** Joe Weil, Tina Kelley, and Ruth Moon Kempher
**Submissions Policy:** Annual deadline Sept. 1. Send up to three poems and SASE for acceptance or return, or instructions to recycle manuscripts.
**Simultaneous Subs:** yes
**Reading Period:** 9/1 to 10/15
**Reporting Time:** 6 to 12 months
**Author Payment:** copies and subscription
**Contests:** None.
**Founded:** 1976
**Non Profit:** yes
**Paid Staff:** 0
**Unpaid Staff:** 4
**Distributors:** DeBoer
**ISSN Number/ISBN Number:** ISSN 0363-4205
**Total Circulation:** 900
**Paid Circulation:** 360
**Average Print Run:** 1,000
**Subscription Rate:** Individual $16/2/Institution $16/1
**Single Copy Price:** $10
**Current Volume/Issue:** 2006/43
**Frequency per Year:** 1
**Backfile Available:** yes
**Unsolicited Ms. Received:** yes
**% of Unsolicited Ms. Published per Year:** 100%
**Format:** stapled
**Size:** H 8 1/2" W 5 1/2"
**Average Pages:** 78
**Ads:** yes
**Ad Rates:** Exchange.

## Journal of Ordinary Thought

**Type:** magazine
**CLMP member:** yes
**Primary Editor/Contact Person:** Annie Knepler
**Address:** Neighborhood Writing Alliance
1313 E. 60th St.
Chicago, IL 60637
**Web Site Address:** http://www.jot.org
**Publishes:** essays, fiction, and poetry
**Editorial Focus:** JOT publishes reflections people make on their personal histories and everyday experiences.

**Representative Authors:** Charlie Clements, Susan House, and Felicia Madlock
**Submissions Policy:** Only work produced in weekly workshops hosted by the Neighborhood Writing Alliance in Chicago neighborhoods are considered.
**Simultaneous Subs:** yes
**Reading Period:** Year-round
**Reporting Time:** 1 to 2 months
**Author Payment:** none
**Founded:** 1991
**Non Profit:** yes
**Paid Staff:** 3
**Unpaid Staff:** 6
**Distributors:** Neighborhood Writing Alliance
**ISSN Number/ISBN Number:** ISSN 1535-0614
**Total Circulation:** 2,500+
**Paid Circulation:** 500
**Average Print Run:** 2.5-4k
**Subscription Rate:** Individual $25/Institution $50
**Single Copy Price:** $10
**Current Volume/Issue:** 2005
**Frequency per Year:** 4
**Backfile Available:** yes
**Unsolicited Ms. Received:** no
**Format:** perfect
**Size:** H 9 1/2" W 6 1/2"
**Average Pages:** 75
**Ads:** no

## The Journal

**Type:** magazine
**CLMP member:** no
**Primary Editor/Contact Person:** Kathy Fagan
**Address:** Department of English
164 W. 17th Ave.
Columbus, OH 43210
**Web Site Address:**
http://english.osu.edu/journals/the_journal/
**Publishes:** essays, fiction, nonfiction, poetry, reviews, and art
**Representative Authors:** Bob Hicok, Mark Conway, and Lore Segal
**Submissions Policy:** Quality fiction, poetry, nonfiction and reviews of new books of poetry. No length restrictions. Submissions by mail only. Include e-mail address or SASE for response.
**Simultaneous Subs:** yes
**Reading Period:** Year-round
**Reporting Time:** 4 to 8 weeks
**Author Payment:** cash and copies

**Contests:** See Web Site for Contest Guidelines.
**Founded:** 1972
**Non Profit:** yes
**Paid Staff:** 4
**Unpaid Staff:** 10
**Distributors:** Ingram
**ISSN Number/ISBN Number:** ISSN 1045-084X
**Total Circulation:** 1,500
**Paid Circulation:** 800
**Average Print Run:** 1,200
**Subscription Rate:** Individual $12/Institution $14
**Single Copy Price:** $7
**Current Volume/Issue:** 28/2
**Frequency per Year:** 2
**Backfile Available:** yes
**Unsolicited Ms. Received:** yes
**Format:** perfect
**Size:** H 9" W 6"
**Average Pages:** 140
**Ads:** yes
**Ad Rates:** negotiable

# jubilat

**Type:** magazine
**CLMP member:** yes
**Primary Editor/Contact Person:** Jedediah Berry
**Address:** English Dept., Bartlett Hall
University of Massachusetts
Amherst, MA 01003-0515
**Web Site Address:** http://www.jubilat.org
**Publishes:** poetry, art, and translation
**Editorial Focus:** Contemporary poetry alongside art, translations, interviews, poetic prose, and found/forgotten pieces.
**Recent Awards Received:** Inclusion in multiple editions of Pushcart Prize and Best American Poetry anthologies
**Representative Authors:** Dean Young, C.D. Wright, and John Ashbery
**Submissions Policy:** Poetry and art, as well as other forms of writing on poetry, poetics, or subjects that have nothing to do with poetry.
**Simultaneous Subs:** yes
**Reading Period:** 9/1-5/1
**Reporting Time:** 3 to 6 months
**Author Payment:** copies and subscription
**Founded:** 1999
**Non Profit:** yes
**Paid Staff:** 1
**Unpaid Staff:** 7

**Distributors:** Ingram, DeBoer, SPD
**ISSN Number/ISBN Number:** ISSN 1529-0999
**Total Circulation:** 1,055
**Paid Circulation:** 480
**Subscription Rate:** Individual $14/Institution $28
**Single Copy Price:** $8
**Current Volume/Issue:** 4/1
**Frequency per Year:** 2
**Backfile Available:** yes
**Unsolicited Ms. Received:** yes
**Format:** perfect
**Size:** H 7.5" W 5.5"
**Average Pages:** 160
**Ads:** yes
**Ad Rates:** Full Page: $200

# Juked

**Type:** online
**CLMP member:** no
**Primary Editor/Contact Person:** J.W. Wang
**Address:** 2908 1/2 Hardy St. #3
Hattiesburg, MS 39401
**Web Site Address:** http://www.juked.com
**Publishes:** essays, fiction, nonfiction, and poetry
**Editorial Focus:** Stories, essays, and shorts.
**Recent Awards Received:** Honorable Mention, Writer's Digest National Zine Publishing Awards
**Simultaneous Subs:** yes
**Reading Period:** Year-round
**Reporting Time:** 1 to 4 weeks
**Author Payment:** none
**Contests:** Occasional fiction contests.
See Web Site for Contest Guidelines.
**Founded:** 1999
**Non Profit:** yes
**Paid Staff:** 0
**Unpaid Staff:** 3
**Average Page Views per Month:** 26,000
**Average Unique Visitors per Month:** 3,500
**Frequency per Year:** 12
**Publish Print Anthology:** yes
Price: $5
**Average Percentage of Pages per Category:** Fiction 75%, Nonfiction 10%, Poetry 5%, Essays 10%
**Ad Rates:** See Web Site for Details.

# Junction Press

**Type:** press
**CLMP member:** yes
**Primary Editor/Contact Person:** Mark Weiss
**Address:** P.O. Box 40537
San Diego, CA 92164-0537
**Publishes:** poetry
**Editorial Focus:** Modernist/Postmodernist US and Latin American poetry
**Representative Authors:** Rochelle Owens, Armand Schwerner, and Jos/Kozer
**Submissions Policy:** 10 pages with SASE
**Simultaneous Subs:** yes
**Reading Period:** Year-round
**Reporting Time:** 1 to 2 weeks
**Author Payment:** copies
**Founded:** 1992
**Non Profit:** yes
**Paid Staff:** 0
**Unpaid Staff:** 1
**Distributors:** SPD, Latin American Book Service
**Wholesalers:** Baker & Taylor, Brodart, Ingram, Midwest, Coutts
**ISSN Number/ISBN Number:** ISBN 1-881523
**Number of Books Published per Year:** 1
**Titles in Print:** 13
**Average Percentage Printed:** Paperback 100%
**Backfile Available:** yes

# Kaleidoscope Magazine

**Type:** magazine
**CLMP member:** yes
**Primary Editor/Contact Person:** Gail Willmott
**Address:** United Disability Services
701 S. Main St.
Akron, OH 44311-1019
**Web Site Address:** http://www.udsakron.org
**Publishes:** essays, fiction, nonfiction, poetry, reviews, and art
**Editorial Focus:** Explores the experience of disability from the perspective of individuals, families, professionals and society as a whole.
**Representative Authors:** Megan Sullivan, Linda A. Cronin, and Jeff Stimpson
**Submissions Policy:** Considers unsolicited material, accepts simultaneous submissions, publishes previously published work. Double space and SASE.
**Simultaneous Subs:** yes
**Reading Period:** Year-round
**Reporting Time:** 3 to 6 months

**Author Payment:** cash and copies
**Founded:** 1979
**Non Profit:** yes
**Paid Staff:** 4
**Unpaid Staff:** 1
**ISSN Number/ISBN Number:** ISSN 0748-8742
**Total Circulation:** 1,000
**Paid Circulation:** 350
**Average Print Run:** 1,000
**Subscription Rate:** Individual $10/Institution $15
**Single Copy Price:** $6
**Current Volume/Issue:** Issue 49
**Frequency per Year:** 2
**Backfile Available:** yes
**Unsolicited Ms. Received:** yes
**% of Unsolicited Ms. Published per Year:** 75%
**Format:** stapled
**Size:** H 11" W 8.5"
**Average Pages:** 64
**Ads:** no

# Kalliope, a Journal of Women's Literature & Art

**Type:** magazine
**CLMP member:** yes
**Primary Editor/Contact Person:** Mary Sue Koeppel
**Address:** 11901 Beach Blvd.
Jacksonville, FL 32246
**Web Site Address:** http://www.fccj.edu/kalliope
**Publishes:** fiction, poetry, reviews, and art
**Editorial Focus:** Kalliope publishes poetry, short fiction, Q&A interviews, and fine B&W art by established and excellent new writers.
**Representative Authors:** Marge Piercy, Leslie Schwartz, and Maxine Kumin
**Submissions Policy:** Send 3-5 poems, 1-2 short fiction under 3,500 words, query Q&A interviews. Send B&W photos of fine art. SASE and bio.
**Simultaneous Subs:** no
**Reading Period:** Year-round
**Reporting Time:** 6 to 9 months
**Author Payment:** copies and subscription
**Contests:** See Web Site for Contest Guidelines.
**Founded:** 1978
**Non Profit:** yes
**Paid Staff:** 1
**Unpaid Staff:** 20
**Distributors:** Ingram, Ubiquity, Armadillo
**ISSN Number/ISBN Number:** ISSN 0 74470 81705 5
**Total Circulation:** 1,600

**Paid Circulation:** 600
**Average Print Run:** 1,600
**Subscription Rate:** Individual $16/Institution $26.95
**Single Copy Price:** $9
**Current Volume/Issue:** 25/2
**Frequency per Year:** 2
**Backfile Available:** yes
**Unsolicited Ms. Received:** yes
**% of Unsolicited Ms. Published per Year:** 99%
**Format:** perfect
**Size:** H 8 1/2" W 7 1/4"
**Average Pages:** 120
**Ads:** no

## Karamu

**Type:** magazine
**CLMP member:** yes
**Primary Editor/Contact Person:** Olga Abella
**Address:** English Dept, Eastern Illinois Univ.
600 Lincoln Ave.
Charleston, IL 61920
**Web Site Address:** http://www.eiu.edu/~karamu/
**Publishes:** essays, fiction, nonfiction, poetry, and art
**Editorial Focus:** writing that builds around real experiences, real images, and real characters, avoiding overt philosophizing and preaching
**Recent Awards Received:** Illinois Arts Council Literary Award
**Representative Authors:** Maureen Tolman Flannery, Therese Halscheid, and Kevin Dobbs
**Submissions Policy:** poetry: 5 poems at a time. prose: 1 piece not longer than 3,500 words. All submissions must include SASE.
**Simultaneous Subs:** no
**Reading Period:** 9/1 to 2/15
**Reporting Time:** 4 to 6 months
**Author Payment:** copies
**Founded:** 1966
**Non Profit:** yes
**Paid Staff:** 0
**Unpaid Staff:** 7-8
**Distributors:** Canio's Books, Flessor's Candy Kitchen
**ISSN Number/ISBN Number:** ISBN 0022-8990
**Total Circulation:** 700
**Paid Circulation:** 150
**Average Print Run:** 500
**Subscription Rate:** Individual $8/Institution $8
**Single Copy Price:** $8
**Current Volume/Issue:** 19/2
**Frequency per Year:** 1

**Backfile Available:** yes
**Unsolicited Ms. Received:** yes
**% of Unsolicited Ms. Published per Year:** 100%
**Format:** perfect
**Size:** H 8" W 5"
**Average Pages:** 200
**Ads:** no

## Katabasis

**Type:** press
**CLMP member:** no
**Primary Editor/Contact Person:** Dinah Livingstone
**Address:** 10 St. Martin's Close
London, UK NW1 0HR
**Web Site Address:** http://www.katabasis.co.uk
**Publishes:** fiction, nonfiction, poetry, and translation
**Editorial Focus:** Katabasis publishes English and Latin American poetry and prose.
**Representative Authors:** Dinah Livingstone, Ernesto Cardenal, and Kathleen McPhilemy
**Submissions Policy:** No unsolicited manuscripts
**Simultaneous Subs:** no
**Reading Period:** Year-round
**Reporting Time:** 6 to 8 weeks
**Author Payment:** none
**Founded:** 1967
**Non Profit:** yes
**Paid Staff:** 0
**Unpaid Staff:** 1
**Distributors:** Central Books
**ISSN Number/ISBN Number:** ISBN 0904872
**Number of Books Published per Year:** 1-2
**Titles in Print:** 28
**Average Print Run:** 500
**Average Percentage Printed:** Paperback 100%
**Average Price:** £6.95

## Kaya Press

**Type:** press
**CLMP member:** yes
**Primary Editor/Contact Person:** Julie Koo
**Address:** 116 Pinehurst Ave. #E51
New York, NY 10033
**Web Site Address:** http://www.kaya.com
**Publishes:** fiction, nonfiction, poetry, art, and translation
**Editorial Focus:** Publisher of Asian, Pacific Islander, and API diasporic fiction, poetry, critical essays, art, and culture

**Representative Authors:** R. Zamora Linmark, Sesshu Foster, and Ishle Park
**Submissions Policy:** See http://www.kaya.com/submit.html
**Simultaneous Subs:** yes
**Reading Period:** 1/4 to 5/4
**Reporting Time:** 3 to 12 months
**Author Payment:** royalties and copies
**Founded:** 1994
**Non Profit:** yes
**Paid Staff:** 0
**Unpaid Staff:** 2
**Distributors:** DAP
**Wholesalers:** SPD
**ISSN Number/ISBN Number:** ISBN 1-885030
**Number of Books Published per Year:** 2
**Titles in Print:** 12
**Average Percentage Printed:** Hardcover 5%, Paperback 95%
**Backfile Available:** yes

# Kegedonce Press

**Type:** press
**CLMP member:** no
**Primary Editor/Contact Person:** Renee Abram
**Address:** Cape Croker First Nation
RR#5
Wiarton, ON N0H 2T0
**Web Site Address:** http://www.kegedonce.com
**Publishes:** fiction, nonfiction, and poetry
**Editorial Focus:** Indigenous Literature
**Recent Awards Received:** WordCraft Circle of Writers-2002
**Representative Authors:** Richard Van Camp, Basil Johnston, and Al Hunter
**Submissions Policy:** Publishing history, sample chapter or max. 30 pages, SASE if require return of materials
**Simultaneous Subs:** yes
**Reading Period:** Year-round
**Reporting Time:** 2 to 3 months
**Author Payment:** royalties and copies
**Founded:** 1993
**Non Profit:** no
**Paid Staff:** 1.5
**Unpaid Staff:** .5
**Distributors:** LitDistCo (The Literary Press Group Canada)
**ISSN Number/ISBN Number:** ISBN 0-9731396/0-9697120

**Number of Books Published per Year:** 2
**Titles in Print:** 9
**Average Print Run:** 1,500
**Average Percentage Printed:** Paperback 100%
**Average Price:** $15

# The Kelsey Review

**Type:** magazine
**CLMP member:** no
**Primary Editor/Contact Person:** Robin Schore
**Address:** Mercer County College
Trenton, NJ 08690
**Web Site Address:** http://www.mccc.edu
**Publishes:** essays, fiction, nonfiction, poetry, and art
**Editorial Focus:** Regional literary journal accepting contributions exclusively from people living and working in Mercer County, NJ
**Representative Authors:** Bruce Petronio, Janet Kirk, and Helen Gorenstein
**Submissions Policy:** Deadline: May 1; prose: max 2,000 words; poetry: max 6 poems. previously unpublished
**Simultaneous Subs:** no
**Reading Period:** 5/4 to 6/4
**Reporting Time:** 6 to 8 weeks
**Author Payment:** copies
**Contests:** none
**Founded:** 1988
**Non Profit:** yes
**Paid Staff:** 1
**Unpaid Staff:** 3
**Distributors:** Mercer County Community College
**ISSN Number/ISBN Number:** ISSN 0451-6338
**Total Circulation:** 1,800
**Paid Circulation:** 0
**Single Copy Price:** free
**Current Volume/Issue:** 23/1
**Frequency per Year:** 1
**Backfile Available:** no
**Unsolicited Ms. Received:** yes
**% of Unsolicited Ms. Published per Year:** 100%
**Format:** stapled
**Size:** H 11" W 7"
**Average Pages:** 88
**Ads:** no

## Kelsey Street Press

**Type:** press
**CLMP member:** yes
**Primary Editor/Contact Person:** Rena Rosenwasser
**Address:** 50 Northgate Ave.
Berkeley, CA 94708
**Web Site Address:** http://www.kelseyst.com
**Publishes:** poetry and art
**Editorial Focus:** The Press publishes poetry by contemporary women writers that challenges traditional notions about form, content, and expression, as well as collaborations between poets and visual artists.
**Recent Awards Received:** 7th Annual Asian American Award for Poetry, for Mei-mei Berssenbrugge's Nest
**Representative Authors:** Barbara Guest, Mei-mei Berssenbrugge, and Renee Gladman
**Submissions Policy:** Currently we are not accepting any unsolicited manuscripts. Check our websites for any changes regarding submissions.
**Simultaneous Subs:** yes
**Reading Period:** 6/1 to 8/30
**Reporting Time:** 2 to 3 months
**Author Payment:** royalties
**Contests:** See Web Site for Contest Guidelines.
**Founded:** 1974
**Non Profit:** yes
**Paid Staff:** 0
**Unpaid Staff:** 6
**Distributors:** SPD
**ISSN Number/ISBN Number:** none/0-932716
**Number of Books Published per Year:** 2
**Titles in Print:** 45
**Average Print Run:** 1,000
**Average Percentage Printed:** Hardcover .5%, Paperback 99.5%
**Average Price:** $12

## The Kent State University Press

**Type:** press
**CLMP member:** no
**Primary Editor/Contact Person:** Joanna Hildebrand Craig
**Address:** Box 5190
Kent, OH 44242-0001
**Web Site Address:**
http://kentstateuniversitypress.com
**Publishes:** essays and nonfiction
**Editorial Focus:** US history, US literature, regional (Ohio) studies, military history, fantasy literary criticism
**Representative Authors:** Verlyn Flieger, George Knepper, and Joe Harsh
**Submissions Policy:** letter of inquiry explaining or introducing proposal, outline or table of contents, 2 sample chapters, resume/CV
**Simultaneous Subs:** yes
**Reading Period:** Year-round
**Reporting Time:** 4 to 7 months
**Author Payment:** royalties
**Founded:** 1965
**Non Profit:** yes
**Paid Staff:** 10
**Unpaid Staff:** 2
**Distributors:** Bookmasters
**Wholesalers:** all
**ISSN Number/ISBN Number:** ISBN 87338
**Number of Books Published per Year:** 33
**Titles in Print:** 350
**Average Print Run:** Varies
**Average Percentage Printed:** Hardcover 30%, Paperback 60%, Chapbook 10%
**Average Price:** varies

## The Kenyon Review

**Type:** magazine
**CLMP member:** yes
**Primary Editor/Contact Person:** David Lynn, Editor
**Address:** Walton House
104 College Dr.
Gambier, OH 43022
**Web Site Address:** http://www.kenyonreview.org
**Publishes:** essays, fiction, nonfiction, poetry, reviews, and translation
**Editorial Focus:** International in scope, KR publishes innovative work from emerging and established writers.
**Representative Authors:** Alice Hoffman, Kellie Wells, and Ron Rash
**Submissions Policy:** Please see submissions guidelines on our web site:
http://www.kenyonreview.org/magazine/submission.asp
**Simultaneous Subs:** no
**Reading Period:** 9/1 to 3/31
**Reporting Time:** 3 to 4 months
**Author Payment:** cash and copies
**Founded:** 1939
**Non Profit:** yes
**Paid Staff:** 6
**Unpaid Staff:** 18
**Distributors:** Ingram; Media Solutions
**ISSN Number/ISBN Number:** ISSN 0163-075X

**Total Circulation:** 6,300
**Paid Circulation:** 3,380
**Subscription Rate:** Individual $30/Institution $35
**Single Copy Price:** $10
**Current Volume/Issue:** XXVI/4
**Frequency per Year:** 4
**Backfile Available:** yes
**Unsolicited Ms. Received:** yes
**Format:** perfect
**Size:** H 10" W 7"
**Average Pages:** 232
**Ads:** yes
**Ad Rates:** See Web Site for Details.

## The King's English

**Type:** online
**CLMP member:** yes
**Primary Editor/Contact Person:** Benjamin Chambers
**Address:** 3114 NE 47th Ave.
Portland, OR 97213
**Web Site Address:** http://www.thekingsenglish.org
**Publishes:** essays, fiction, poetry, and reviews
**Editorial Focus:** Novellas(11,000-48,000 words) and long personal essays (3,000-48,000 words). Also poetry and offbeat book reviews.
**Recent Awards Received:** Winner of the 2005 Million Writers Award for Best Publisher of Novella-Length Fiction
**Submissions Policy:** See guidelines at http://www.thekingsenglish.org. Electronic submission preferred.
**Simultaneous Subs:** yes
**Reading Period:** Year-round
**Reporting Time:** 1 to 2 months
**Author Payment:** none
**Contests:** Blodgett Waxwing Literary Prize in Fiction. $500 first prize, $100 second prize, $50 third prize See Web Site for Contest Guidelines.
**Founded:** 2003
**Non Profit:** yes
**Paid Staff:** 0
**Unpaid Staff:** 4
**Average Page Views per Month:** 1,112
**Average Unique Visitors per Month:** 574
**Frequency per Year:** 4
**Publish Print Anthology:** no
**Average Percentage of Pages per Category:** Fiction 70%, Poetry 5%, Reviews 5%, Essays 20%
**Ads:** no

## Knock

**Type:** magazine
**CLMP member:** yes
**Address:** 2326 6th Ave.
Seattle, WA 98121
**Web Site Address:** http://www.knockjournal.org
**Publishes:** essays, fiction, nonfiction, poetry, and art
**Reading Period:** Year-round
**Reporting Time:** 1 to 2 months
**Author Payment:** none
**Non Profit:** yes
**Backfile Available:** yes

## Konocti Books

**Type:** press
**CLMP member:** no
**Primary Editor/Contact Person:** Noel Peattie
**Address:** 23311 County Road 88
Winters, CA 95694
**Publishes:** poetry
**Editorial Focus:** Country poetry with depth.
**Representative Authors:** Doc Dachtler, Lynne Savitt, and Jane Blue
**Submissions Policy:** Presently inactive. Query with sample before sending.
**Simultaneous Subs:** no
**Reading Period:** Year-round
**Reporting Time:** 3 to 5 weeks
**Author Payment:** copies
**Founded:** 1973
**Non Profit:** yes
**Paid Staff:** 1
**Unpaid Staff:** 0
**ISSN Number/ISBN Number:** ISBN 0-914134
**Number of Books Published per Year:** 1
**Titles in Print:** 5
**Average Percentage Printed:** Paperback 100%

## Konundrum Engine Literary Review

**Type:** online
**CLMP member:** yes
**Primary Editor/Contact Person:** Pitchaya Sudbanthad
**Address:** 345 South End Ave, 6E
New York, NY 10280
**Web Site Address:** http://www.lit.konundrum.com
**Publishes:** essays, fiction, nonfiction, and poetry
**Editorial Focus:** Unique, kick-ass fiction and poetry by both new and established writers.

**Representative Authors:** Jim Shepard, Jonathan Lethem, and Oni Buchanan
**Submissions Policy:** Please visit our website for guidelines.
**Simultaneous Subs:** yes
**Reading Period:** Year-round
**Reporting Time:** 1 to 4 months
**Author Payment:** none
**Founded:** 2003
**Non Profit:** no
**Paid Staff:** 0
**Unpaid Staff:** 4
**Average Page Views per Month:** 45,000
**Average Unique Visitors per Month:** 15,000
**Frequency per Year:** 8
**Publish Print Anthology:** no
**Average Percentage of Pages per Category:** Fiction 40%, Nonfiction 10%, Poetry 40%, Essays 10%

# Kore Press

**Type:** press
**CLMP member:** yes
**Address:** P.O. Box 3044
Tucson, AZ 85702
**Web Site Address:** http://www.korepress.org
**Publishes:** poetry
**Reading Period:** Year-round
**Reporting Time:** 1 to 2 months
**Author Payment:** none
**Founded:** 1993
**Non Profit:** no
**Average Percentage Printed:** Hardcover 100%
**Backfile Available:** yes

# KRUPSKAYA

**Type:** press
**CLMP member:** no
**Primary Editor/Contact Person:** Jocelyn Saidenberg
**Address:** P.O. Box 420249
San Francisco, CA 94142-0249
**Web Site Address:** http://www.krupskayabooks.com
**Publishes:** fiction and poetry
**Editorial Focus:** Dedicated to publishing experimental poetry and prose KRUPSKAYA is structured as a collective .
**Representative Authors:** Kevin Killian, Renee Gladman, and Stacy Doris
**Submissions Policy:** See Web site for information.
**Simultaneous Subs:** yes
**Reading Period:** Year-round

**Reporting Time:** 4 to 6 months
**Author Payment:** copies
**Founded:** 1998
**Non Profit:** yes
**Paid Staff:** 0
**Unpaid Staff:** 3
**Distributors:** SPD
**ISSN Number/ISBN Number:** ISBN 1-928650-##-#
**Number of Books Published per Year:** 4
**Titles in Print:** 25
**Average Print Run:** 750
**Average Percentage Printed:** Paperback 100%
**Average Price:** $14

# La Alameda Press

**Type:** press
**CLMP member:** no
**Primary Editor/Contact Person:** JB Bryan
**Address:** 9636 Guadalupe Tr. NW
Albuquerque, NM 87114
**Web Site Address:** http://www.laalamedapress.com
**Publishes:** essays, fiction, nonfiction, and poetry
**Editorial Focus:** A micro-press. Beautiful books of artistic and cultural merit. Many, not all, titles are poetry-an essential art form.
**Recent Awards Received:** Anselm Hollo: Academy American Poet's 2004 Harold Morton Landon Translation Award, for Pentti Saarikoski's Trilogy (2003)
**Representative Authors:** Anselm Hollo, Kate Horsley, and Miriam Sagan
**Submissions Policy:** Sorry, we are not accepting manuscripts.
**Simultaneous Subs:** no
**Author Payment:** copies
**Founded:** 1991
**Non Profit:** no
**Paid Staff:** 2
**Unpaid Staff:** 0
**Distributors:** U of New Mexico Press, SPD
**Wholesalers:** Ingram's, Baker & Taylor, Blackwell's, etc
**ISSN Number/ISBN Number:** ISBN 0-9631909, 1-888809
**Number of Books Published per Year:** 2
**Titles in Print:** 48
**Average Print Run:** 1,000
**Average Percentage Printed:** Paperback 75%, Chapbook 25%
**Average Price:** $14

# La Petite Zine

**Type:** online
**CLMP member:** yes
**Primary Editor/Contact Person:** Jeffrey Salane/Danielle Pafunda
**Address:** 270 5th St. #2E
Brooklyn, NY 11215
**Web Site Address:** http://lapetitezine.org
**Publishes:** essays, fiction, nonfiction, reviews, art, and translation
**Editorial Focus:** Established and new voices, which might be defined as "edgy," "rocking out," or "brilliant." To editors' subjective tastes.
**Representative Authors:** Heidi Lynn Staples, Joyelle McSweeney, and David Lehman
**Submissions Policy:** Submit via e-mail to lapetitezine@yahoo.com. For greater detail, see lapetitezine.org.
**Simultaneous Subs:** yes
**Reading Period:** Year-round
**Reporting Time:** 6 to 10 weeks
**Author Payment:** none
**Founded:** 1998
**Non Profit:** yes
**Paid Staff:** no
**Unpaid Staff:** 2
**Backfile Available:** yes
**Average Page Views per Month:** 100+
**Average Unique Visitors per Month:** 50+
**Frequency per Year:** 3
**Price:** 0
**Average Percentage of Pages per Category:** Fiction 20%, Nonfiction 5%, Poetry 60%, Reviews 5%, Art 10%
**Ads:** no

# Lactuca

**Type:** magazine
**CLMP member:** no
**Primary Editor/Contact Person:** Mike Selender
**Address:** 159 Jewett Ave.
Jersey City, NJ 07304-2003
**Publishes:** fiction, poetry, reviews, art, and translation
**Editorial Focus:** Work with an sense of place or experience coming from an honest emotional depth.
**Submissions Policy:** Currently dormant. Query before sending work

**Simultaneous Subs:** no
**Reading Period:** Year-round
**Author Payment:** copies
**Founded:** 1983
**Non Profit:** no
**Paid Staff:** 0
**Unpaid Staff:** 1
**ISSN Number/ISBN Number:** ISSN 0896-8705
**Frequency per Year:** 1
**Backfile Available:** yes
**Unsolicited Ms. Received:** yes
**Format:** stapled
**Size:** H 11 1/2" W 7"
**Average Pages:** 60
**Ads:** no

# Lake Effect

**Type:** magazine
**CLMP member:** yes
**Primary Editor/Contact Person:** George Looney
**Address:** Penn State Erie
5091 Station Rd.
Erie, PA 16563-1501
**Publishes:** essays, fiction, nonfiction, and poetry
**Editorial Focus:** Writing that uses language with precision and a knowledge of craft to forge a genuine and rewarding experience.
**Representative Authors:** Edith Pearlman, T.R. Hummer, and David Kirby
**Submissions Policy:** Send 3-5 poems, 1 story (or several short shorts) or nonfiction piece to appropriate editor. Include SASE and cover letter.
**Simultaneous Subs:** yes
**Reading Period:** Year-round
**Reporting Time:** 1 to 4 months
**Author Payment:** copies
**Founded:** 1978
**Non Profit:** yes
**Paid Staff:** 1
**Unpaid Staff:** 19
**ISSN Number/ISBN Number:** ISSN 1538-3105
**Total Circulation:** 800
**Paid Circulation:** 170
**Average Print Run:** 800
**Subscription Rate:** Individual $6/Institution $6
**Single Copy Price:** $6
**Current Volume/Issue:** 9

**Frequency per Year:** 1
**Backfile Available:** no
**Unsolicited Ms. Received:** yes
**% of Unsolicited Ms. Published per Year:** 7%
**Format:** perfect
**Size:** H 8 1/2" W 5 1/2"
**Average Pages:** 150
**Ads:** no

# The Land-Grant College Review

**Type:** magazine
**CLMP member:** yes
**Primary Editor/Contact Person:** Dave Koch and Josh Melrod
**Address:** P.O. Box 1164
New York, NY 10159-1164
**Web Site Address:** http://www.lgcr.org
**Publishes:** fiction and art
**Editorial Focus:** The Land-Grant College Review publishes contemporary short stories.
**Recent Awards Received:** Utne Independent Press Award
**Representative Authors:** Aimee Bender, Frederick Barthelme, and Joan Silber
**Submissions Policy:** Send us only your very best work. Familiarize yourself with past issues to get an idea of the type of stories we like.
**Simultaneous Subs:** yes
**Reading Period:** Year-round
**Reporting Time:** 4 to 6 months
**Author Payment:** cash and copies
**Contests:** See Web Site for Contest Guidelines.
**Founded:** 2002
**Non Profit:** yes
**Paid Staff:** 2
**Unpaid Staff:** 10
**Distributors:** DeBoer, Ingram
**ISSN Number/ISBN Number:** ISSN 0972867805
**Total Circulation:** 2,500
**Paid Circulation:** 750
**Average Print Run:** 2,500
**Subscription Rate:** Individual $18/Institution $18
**Single Copy Price:** $12
**Current Volume/Issue:** Issue 3
**Frequency per Year:** 1
**Backfile Available:** yes
**Unsolicited Ms. Received:** yes
**% of Unsolicited Ms. Published per Year:** 5%
**Format:** perfect

**Size:** H 9" W 6"
**Average Pages:** 200
**Ads:** no

# Latin American Literary Review Press

**Type:** press
**CLMP member:** yes
**Primary Editor/Contact Person:** Yvette E. Miller
**Address:** P.O. Box 17660
Pittsburgh, PA 15235
**Web Site Address:** http://www.lalrp.org
**Publishes:** translation
**Editorial Focus:** Translations of Latin American Literature into English
**Representative Authors:** Pablo Neruda, Luisa Valenzuela, and Mempo Giardinelli
**Submissions Policy:** Translated Manuscripts Only.
**Simultaneous Subs:** yes
**Reading Period:** Year-round
**Reporting Time:** 1 to 12 months
**Author Payment:** royalties and copies
**Founded:** 1980
**Non Profit:** yes
**Paid Staff:** 3
**Unpaid Staff:** 0
**Distributors:** Bilingual Press
**ISSN Number/ISBN Number:** ISBN 1-891270
**Number of Books Published per Year:** 4
**Titles in Print:** 146
**Average Print Run:** 1,500
**Average Percentage Printed:** Hardcover 10%, Paperback 90%
**Average Price:** $15

# Latin American Literary Review

**Type:** magazine
**CLMP member:** yes
**Primary Editor/Contact Person:** Yvette E. Miller
**Address:** P.O. Box 17660
Pittsburgh, PA 15235
**Web Site Address:** http://www.lalrp.org
**Publishes:** nonfiction
**Editorial Focus:** Critical journal for Latin American Literature
**Submissions Policy:** MLA Style, three hardcopies plus 3.5" Mac diskette, Word 4.0 and up
**Simultaneous Subs:** no
**Reading Period:** Year-round
**Reporting Time:** 4 to 7 months

**Author Payment:** none
**Founded:** 1980
**Non Profit:** yes
**Paid Staff:** 3
**Unpaid Staff:** 1
**ISSN Number/ISBN Number:** ISSN 0047
**Total Circulation:** 1,000
**Paid Circulation:** 750
**Subscription Rate:** Individual $26/Institution $46
**Single Copy Price:** $20
**Current Volume/Issue:** 32/63
**Frequency per Year:** 2
**Backfile Available:** yes
**Unsolicited Ms. Received:** yes
**% of Unsolicited Ms. Published per Year:** 100%
**Format:** perfect
**Size:** H 9" W 6"
**Average Pages:** 100
**Ads:** yes
**Ad Rates:** Full Page, $260; Half Page, $150; Quarter Page, $90

# The Laurel Review

**Type:** magazine
**CLMP member:** yes
**Primary Editor/Contact Person:** John Gallaher/Rebecca Aronson
**Address:** GreenTower Press
NW Missouri State U, Dept. of English
Maryville, MO 64468
**Web Site Address:** http://info.nwmissouri.edu/~m500025/index.htm
**Publishes:** essays, fiction, nonfiction, poetry, reviews, and translation
**Editorial Focus:** Our focus is to present an eclectic mix of the best work.
**Representative Authors:** Angie Estes, Mary Ruefle, and Bin Ramke
**Simultaneous Subs:** no
**Reading Period:** 9/1 to 5/1
**Reporting Time:** 1 to 3 months
**Author Payment:** copies and subscription
**Contests:** See Web Site for Contest Guidelines.
**Founded:** 1960
**Non Profit:** yes
**Paid Staff:** 4
**Unpaid Staff:** 4
**Total Circulation:** 600
**Paid Circulation:** 458
**Average Print Run:** 700

**Subscription Rate:** Individual $10/Institution $10
**Single Copy Price:** $7
**Current Volume/Issue:** 39/2
**Frequency per Year:** 2
**Backfile Available:** yes
**Unsolicited Ms. Received:** yes
**% of Unsolicited Ms. Published per Year:** 3%
**Format:** perfect
**Size:** H 9" W 6"
**Average Pages:** 128
**Ads:** yes
**Ad Rates:** See Web Site for Details.

# Lazara Press

**Type:** press
**CLMP member:** no
**Primary Editor/Contact Person:** Penny Goldsmith
**Address:** Box 2269
VMPO
Vancouver, BC V5B 3W2
**Web Site Address:** http://www.lazarapress.ca
**Publishes:** essays, fiction, nonfiction, and poetry
**Editorial Focus:** Alternative, progressive literature and essays.
**Representative Authors:** Marusya Bociurkiw, Helen Potrebenko, and Elise Goldsmith
**Simultaneous Subs:** yes
**Reading Period:** Year-round
**Reporting Time:** 3 to 6 months
**Author Payment:** royalties
**Founded:** 1982
**Non Profit:** yes
**Paid Staff:** 0
**Unpaid Staff:** 1
**ISSN Number/ISBN Number:** ISBN 0-920999
**Number of Books Published per Year:** 2
**Titles in Print:** 14
**Average Print Run:** 500
**Average Percentage Printed:** Paperback 20%, Chapbook 60%, Other 20%
**Average Price:** $12

# Leaping Dog Press/Asylum Arts Press

**Type:** press
**CLMP member:** yes
**Primary Editor/Contact Person:** Jordan Jones
**Address:** P.O. Box 3316
San Jose, CA 95156-3316

**Web Site Address:** http://www.leapingdogpress.com/
**Publishes:** essays, fiction, nonfiction, poetry, translation, audio, and video
**Editorial Focus:** Literature with bark and bite.
**Representative Authors:** Rikki Ducornet, Greg Boyd, and Stephen Dixon
**Submissions Policy:** We will not be accepting submissions until Fall 2006. Submissions and queries should be made by snail mail, not e-mail.
**Simultaneous Subs:** yes
**Reading Period:** 9/1 to 5/31
**Reporting Time:** 1 to 6 months
**Author Payment:** royalties and copies
**Founded:** 1985
**Non Profit:** no
**Paid Staff:** 1
**Unpaid Staff:** 1
**Distributors:** Biblio Distribution, SPD
**Wholesalers:** Ingram, Baker & Taylor
**ISSN Number/ISBN Number:** ISBN 1-58775, 1-878580-
**Number of Books Published per Year:** 8
**Titles in Print:** 50
**Average Print Run:** 1,200
**Average Percentage Printed:** Hardcover 10%, Paperback 40%, Chapbook 50%
**Average Price:** $14.95

## The Left Curve Publications

**Type:** magazine
**CLMP member:** yes
**Primary Editor/Contact Person:** Csaba Polony
**Address:** P.O. Box 472
Oakland, CA 94604
**Web Site Address:** http://www.leftcurve.org
**Publishes:** essays, fiction, nonfiction, poetry, reviews, art, and translation
**Editorial Focus:** Artist-produced cultural journal that encourages non-institutional defetishized work (all forms) from a radical perspective.
**Representative Authors:** Amiri Baraka, Jack Hirschman, and devorah major
**Simultaneous Subs:** no
**Reading Period:** Year-round
**Reporting Time:** 1 to 6 months
**Author Payment:** copies
**Founded:** 1974
**Non Profit:** yes
**Paid Staff:** 0
**Unpaid Staff:** 10

**Distributors:** Ingram, DeBoer, Ubiquity
**ISSN Number/ISBN Number:** ISSN 0160-1857
**Total Circulation:** 2,000
**Paid Circulation:** 150
**Subscription Rate:** Individual $30/Institution $45
**Single Copy Price:** $10
**Current Volume/Issue:** Issue 28
**Frequency per Year:** 1
**Backfile Available:** yes
**Unsolicited Ms. Received:** yes
**% of Unsolicited Ms. Published per Year:** 25%
**Format:** perfect
**Size:** H 11.5" W 8"
**Average Pages:** 144
**Ads:** yes
**Ad Rates:** 200 full page, 150 half, 75, quarter

## Lichen Arts & Letters Preview

**Type:** magazine
**CLMP member:** no
**Primary Editor/Contact Person:** The Editorial Board
**Address:** 234-701 Rossland Road East
Whitby, ON L1N 9K3
**Web Site Address:** http://www.lichenjournal.ca
**Publishes:** essays, fiction, nonfiction, poetry, reviews, and art
**Editorial Focus:** Each spring and fall, Lichen brings the best of new writing and artwork from Canada and abroad to readers, first.
**Recent Awards Received:** Grants from the Ontario Arts Council as well as The Ontario Trillium Foundation.
**Representative Authors:** George Elliott Clarke, Steven Heighton, and Robyn Sarah
**Submissions Policy:** Submit unpublished, original work in English:3-6 poems, or 1 short story (max. 3,000 words), or 1 essay (max. 1,500 words)
**Simultaneous Subs:** no
**Reading Period:** Year-round
**Reporting Time:** 4 to 6 months
**Author Payment:** copies and subscription
**Contests:** "Tracking A Serial Poet" competition: Dec. 31 deadline. "Writing Between The Lines" fiction competition: July 31 deadline.
See Web Site for Contest Guidelines.
**Founded:** 1999
**Non Profit:** yes
**Paid Staff:** 1
**Unpaid Staff:** 11
**Distributors:** Disticor Direct Inc.

**ISSN Number/ISBN Number:** ISSN 1488-1829
**Total Circulation:** 1,000
**Paid Circulation:** 400
**Average Print Run:** 1,000
**Subscription Rate:** Individual $19/Institution $19
**Single Copy Price:** $12
**Current Volume/Issue:** 7.2/Fall
**Frequency per Year:** 2
**Backfile Available:** yes
**Unsolicited Ms. Received:** yes
**% of Unsolicited Ms. Published per Year:** 10%
**Format:** perfect
**Size:** H 8.25" W 5.25"
**Average Pages:** 144
**Ads:** yes
**Ad Rates:** Full: $200, 1/2: $110, 1/4: $60 (discounts available)
See Web Site for Details.

## The Licking River Review

**Type:** magazine
**CLMP member:** no
**Primary Editor/Contact Person:** P. Andrew Miller, Advisor
**Address:** Box 66 University Center
Northern Kentucky University
Highland Heights, KY 41099
**Publishes:** fiction and poetry
**Editorial Focus:** We take quality contemporary fiction and poetry. Seldom publish genre work like romance, of SF/F.
**Representative Authors:** Mary Winters, Henryk Skwar, and Sam Vargo
**Submissions Policy:** Submit stories up to 25 pages and no more than 5 poems, 75 lines max, between 9/1-12/1 of each year.
**Simultaneous Subs:** no
**Reading Period:** 9/1 to 12/1
**Reporting Time:** 3 to 4 months
**Author Payment:** copies
**Founded:** 1990
**Non Profit:** yes
**Paid Staff:** 3
**Unpaid Staff:** 6
**Distributors:** Northern Kentucky University
**Total Circulation:** 1,000
**Paid Circulation:** 20
**Subscription Rate:** Individual $5/Institution $5
**Single Copy Price:** $5
**Current Volume/Issue:** 34

**Frequency per Year:** 1
**Backfile Available:** yes
**Unsolicited Ms. Received:** yes
**% of Unsolicited Ms. Published per Year:** 5%
**Format:** perfect
**Average Pages:** 96

## Light Quarterly

**Type:** magazine
**CLMP member:** yes
**Primary Editor/Contact Person:** John Mella
**Address:** P.O. Box 7500
Chicago, IL 60680
**Web Site Address:** http://www.lightquarterly.com
**Publishes:** essays, nonfiction, poetry, reviews, and art
**Editorial Focus:** Light Quarterly is the only publication in America to print Light Verse on an exclusive, regular basis.
**Representative Authors:** John Updike, X.J. Kennedy, and Tom Disch
**Submissions Policy:** 1-6 poems with SASE.
**Simultaneous Subs:** no
**Reading Period:** Year-round
**Reporting Time:** 1 to 6 months
**Author Payment:** copies
**Founded:** 1992
**Non Profit:** no
**Paid Staff:** 2
**Unpaid Staff:** 0
**Distributors:** DeBoer
**ISSN Number/ISBN Number:** ISSN 1064-8186
**Total Circulation:** 1,000
**Paid Circulation:** 650
**Subscription Rate:** Individual $20/Institution $20
**Single Copy Price:** $6
**Current Volume/Issue:** Issue 41
**Frequency per Year:** 4
**Unsolicited Ms. Received:** yes
**% of Unsolicited Ms. Published per Year:** 8%
**Format:** perfect
**Size:** H 5-1/2" W 9"
**Average Pages:** 64
**Ads:** yes
**Ad Rates:** 1 page: $100, 1/2 page: $50

# Lilies and Cannonballs Review

**Type:** magazine
**CLMP member:** yes
**Primary Editor/Contact Person:** Daniel Connor
**Address:** P.O. Box 702
Bowling Green Station
New York, NY 10274-0702
**Web Site Address:**
http://www.liliesandcannonballs.com
**Publishes:** essays, fiction, nonfiction, poetry, art, and translation
**Editorial Focus:** Aesthetically driven and socially conscious; traditional and experimental; crazy-man conservative and bleeding liberal
**Representative Authors:** John Bradley, James Doyle, and Lynn Crawford
**Submissions Policy:** Poetry: no more than four poems. Prose: 8,000 words max. Include SASE.
**Simultaneous Subs:** yes
**Reading Period:** Year-round
**Reporting Time:** 1 to 6 months
**Author Payment:** copies
**Founded:** 2003
**Non Profit:** no
**Paid Staff:** 0
**Unpaid Staff:** 7
**Distributors:** DeBoer
**ISSN Number/ISBN Number:** ISSN 1548-8365
**Total Circulation:** 475
**Paid Circulation:** 75
**Average Print Run:** 550
**Subscription Rate:** Individual $23/Institution $28
**Single Copy Price:** $12
**Current Volume/Issue:** 2/1
**Frequency per Year:** 2
**Backfile Available:** yes
**Unsolicited Ms. Received:** yes
**% of Unsolicited Ms. Published per Year:** 50%
**Format:** perfect
**Size:** H 9" W 6"
**Average Pages:** 96
**Ads:** yes
**Ad Rates:** See Web Site for Details.

# Lilith Magazine

**Type:** University Press
**CLMP member:** yes
**Address:** 250 W. 57th St., Ste. 2432
New York, NY 10107
**Web Site Address:** http://www.lilith.org

**Publishes:** essays, fiction, and nonfiction
**Reading Period:** Year-round
**Reporting Time:** 1 to 2 months
**Author Payment:** none
**Non Profit:** no
**Backfile Available:** yes

# Lips

**Type:** magazine
**CLMP member:** yes
**Primary Editor/Contact Person:** Laura Boss
**Address:** 7002 Blvd., #2-26G
Guttenberg, NJ 07093
**Publishes:** poetry
**Editorial Focus:** Strong poetry that is accessible and has impact
**Representative Authors:** Allen Ginsberg, Ruth Stone, and Michael Benedikt
**Submissions Policy:** Send 5 poems, SASE
**Simultaneous Subs:** no
**Reading Period:** 9/4 to 3/5
**Reporting Time:** 3 to 6 months
**Author Payment:** copies
**Founded:** 1981
**Non Profit:** no
**Paid Staff:** 0
**Unpaid Staff:** 1
**ISSN Number/ISBN Number:** ISSN 0278-0933
**Total Circulation:** 2,000
**Average Print Run:** 2,000
**Subscription Rate:** Individual $15/Institution $18
**Single Copy Price:** $10
**Current Volume/Issue:** Issue 25
**Frequency per Year:** 2
**Backfile Available:** yes
**Unsolicited Ms. Received:** yes
**% of Unsolicited Ms. Published per Year:** 5%
**Format:** perfect
**Size:** H 8.5" W 5.5"
**Average Pages:** 154
**Ads:** yes
**Ad Rates:** $300

# Lit Magazine

**Type:** magazine
**CLMP member:** yes
**Address:** New School Writing Program Rm. 508
66 W. 12th St.
New York, NY 10011

**Publishes:** poetry, fiction, nonfiction, and essays
**Reading Period:** Year-round
**Reporting Time:** 1 to 2 months
**Author Payment:** none
**Founded:** 1999
**Non Profit:** no
**Backfile Available:** yes

# Lit Pot Press

**Type:** press
**CLMP member:** no
**Primary Editor/Contact Person:** Beverly A. Jackson
**Address:** 3909 Reche Rd #132
Fallbrook, CA 92028
**Web Site Address:** http://www.litpotpress.com
**Publishes:** essays, fiction, nonfiction, poetry, and art
**Editorial Focus:** We specialize in literary prose and poetry in a potpourri of classic to outsider work, beginners to veterans in the arts.
**Representative Authors:** Tom Sheehan, Terri Brown-Davidson, and Michael Spring
**Submissions Policy:** Collections of poetry, short stories or novellas should be queried first. We solicit authors normally, but read samples.
**Simultaneous Subs:** yes
**Reading Period:** Year-round
**Reporting Time:** 1 to 2 weeks
**Author Payment:** royalties and copies
**Founded:** 2001
**Non Profit:** yes
**Paid Staff:** 0
**Unpaid Staff:** 2
**Distributors:** Website/Amazon.com
**Number of Books Published per Year:** 8
**Titles in Print:** 15
**Average Percentage Printed:** Paperback 100%

# Lit Pot

**Type:** online
**CLMP member:** no
**Primary Editor/Contact Person:** Beverly A. Jackson
**Address:** 3909 Reche Rd #132
Fallbrook, CA 92028
**Web Site Address:** http://www.literarypotpourri.com
**Publishes:** essays, fiction, nonfiction, poetry, and art
**Editorial Focus:** This is an online version of material taken from the print journal Ink Pot. A potpourri of poetry, prose and creative NF

**Representative Authors:** Roger Weingarten, Nancy McCabe, and Joseph Young
**Submissions Policy:** See Website for guidelines-online submissions by e-mail preferred
**Simultaneous Subs:** yes
**Reading Period:** Year-round
**Reporting Time:** 0 to 1 weeks
**Author Payment:** cash and copies
**Contests:** Contest deadline 11/3 for Ink Pot and Lit Pot entries-short stories and flash fiction
See Web Site for Contest Guidelines.
**Founded:** 2001
**Non Profit:** yes
**Paid Staff:** 0
**Unpaid Staff:** 10
**Distributors:** Website/Amazon.com
**Average Page Views per Month:** Unknown
**Average Unique Visitors per Month:** 1,000
**Publish Print Anthology:** no
**Average Percentage of Pages per Category:** Fiction 30%, Nonfiction 10%, Poetry 30%, Essays 10%, Art 20%
**Ads:** no

# Literal Latte

**Type:** press
**CLMP member:** yes
**Primary Editor/Contact Person:** Jenine Gordon Bockman
**Address:** 61 E. 8th St., Ste. 240
New York, NY 10003
**Web Site Address:** http://www.literal-latte.com
**Publishes:** essays, fiction, nonfiction, poetry, reviews, and art
**Editorial Focus:** Mind stimulating words-all styles and subjects.
**Submissions Policy:** Stories/essays up to 6,000 words. Poems/plays up to 2,000 words. Send with SASE or e-mail for reply.
**Simultaneous Subs:** yes
**Reading Period:** Year-round
**Reporting Time:** 3 to 6 months
**Author Payment:** copies and subscription
**Contests:** Fiction Awards; Poetry Awards; Essay Awards; Food Verse Contest; Short Shorts Contest
See Web Site for Contest Guidelines.
**Founded:** 1994
**Non Profit:** no
**Paid Staff:** xx

**Unpaid Staff:** xx
**Number of Books Published per Year:** 0
**Titles in Print:** 0
**Average Percentage Printed:** Other 100%
**Backfile Available:** yes

## Literal, Latin American Voices

**Type:** magazine
**CLMP member:** yes
**Primary Editor/Contact Person:** Rose Mary Salum
**Address:** 770 S. Post Oak Ln., Ste. 530
Houston, TX 77056
**Web Site Address:** http://www.literalmagazine.com
**Publishes:** essays, fiction, nonfiction, poetry, reviews, art, and translation
**Recent Awards Received:** A Lone Star Award For Best PR Magazine, a Lone Star Award For Layout, a Maggie Award Nomination for best semi-annual
**Representative Authors:** Mario Vargas Llosa, Ilan Stavans, and Sandra Cisneros
**Submissions Policy:** Via regular mail. Only articles accepted will get notified.
**Simultaneous Subs:** no
**Reading Period:** Year-round
**Reporting Time:** 1 to 6 months
**Author Payment:** copies and subscription
**Founded:** 2004
**Non Profit:** no
**Paid Staff:** 2
**Unpaid Staff:** 6
**Distributors:** Ingram and Ubiquity in the US and Alieri in Mexico
**Total Circulation:** 5,000
**Paid Circulation:** 200
**Average Print Run:** 5,000
**Subscription Rate:** Individual $18/Institution $20
**Single Copy Price:** $4.50
**Current Volume/Issue:** 1/3
**Frequency per Year:** 4
**Backfile Available:** yes
**Unsolicited Ms. Received:** yes
**% of Unsolicited Ms. Published per Year:** 20%
**Format:** perfect
**Average Pages:** 54
**Ad Rates:** $300, 600 and 1,200
See Web Site for Details.

## Literary Imagination

**Type:** magazine
**CLMP member:** yes
**Primary Editor/Contact Person:** Sarah Spence, Editor
**Address:** Classics, 221 Park Hall
University of Georgia
Athens, GA 30602-6203
**Web Site Address:** http://www.bu.edu/literary
**Publishes:** essays, fiction, poetry, reviews, and translation
**Editorial Focus:** Works that explore and celebrate the literary imagination.
**Recent Awards Received:** 2005 Pushcart to Geoffrey Hill, contributor to 6.2 (Spring 2004) "On the Reality of the Symbol" (poem)
**Representative Authors:** Clare Cavanagh, Anne Ferry, and Karl Kirchwey
**Submissions Policy:** Cannot consider submissions sent by fax or e-mail.
**Simultaneous Subs:** no
**Reading Period:** Year-round
**Reporting Time:** 1 to 2 months
**Author Payment:** none
**Contests:** none
**Founded:** 1999
**Non Profit:** yes
**Paid Staff:** 3
**Unpaid Staff:** 0
**Distributors:** Ingram
**ISSN Number/ISBN Number:** 1523-9012
**Total Circulation:** 1,604
**Paid Circulation:** 121
**Average Print Run:** 2,133
**Subscription Rate:** Individual $25/Institution $60 in US
**Single Copy Price:** $8.95+
**Current Volume/Issue:** 7/2
**Frequency per Year:** 3
**Backfile Available:** yes
**Unsolicited Ms. Received:** yes
**% of Unsolicited Ms. Published per Year:** 85%
**Format:** perfect
**Size:** H 10" W 7"
**Average Pages:** 160
**Ads:** yes
**Ad Rates:** Advertising available to members and their publishers.
See Web Site for Details.

## Literary Mama

**Type:** online
**CLMP member:** yes
**Address:** University of South Carolina
Department of English
Columbia, SC 29208
**Web Site Address:** http://www.literarymama.com
**Publishes:** essays, fiction, nonfiction, poetry, and reviews
**Reading Period:** Year-round
**Reporting Time:** 1 to 2 months
**Author Payment:** none
**Founded:** 2003
**Non Profit:** yes
**Backfile Available:** yes
**Average Percentage of Pages per Category:** Audio 100%

## Literary Potpourri

**Type:** online
**CLMP member:** no
**Address:** 3909 Reche Rd. Ste. 132
Fallbrook, CA 92028
**Web Site Address:** http://www.literarypotpourri.com
**Publishes:** essays, fiction, nonfiction, poetry, and art
**Reading Period:** Year-round
**Reporting Time:** 1 to 2 months
**Author Payment:** none
**Founded:** 2001
**Non Profit:** no
**Average Percentage of Pages per Category:** Audio 100%

## The Literary Review

**Type:** magazine
**CLMP member:** yes
**Primary Editor/Contact Person:** Rene Steinke
**Address:** 285 Madison Ave.
Madison, NJ 07940
**Web Site Address:** http://www.theliteraryreview.org/
**Publishes:** essays, fiction, nonfiction, poetry, reviews, and translation
**Editorial Focus:** We publish writing from around the world in translation, as well as new contemporary American authors.
**Representative Authors:** Jeffery Allen, Thomas E. Kennedy, and Douglas A. Martin

**Submissions Policy:** Poetry: submit up to 6 poems at a time; Fiction: one story 10-20 pgs; contemporary reviews and essays
**Simultaneous Subs:** yes
**Reading Period:** 9/1 to 5/30
**Reporting Time:** 3 to 4 months
**Author Payment:** copies and subscription
**Founded:** 1957
**Non Profit:** yes
**Paid Staff:** 4
**Unpaid Staff:** 6
**Distributors:** Ingram; Media Solutions
**Total Circulation:** 2,000
**Paid Circulation:** 800
**Average Print Run:** 2,000
**Subscription Rate:** Individual $18/Institution $18
**Single Copy Price:** $7
**Current Volume/Issue:** 48/1
**Frequency per Year:** 4
**Backfile Available:** yes
**Unsolicited Ms. Received:** yes
**% of Unsolicited Ms. Published per Year:** 1.5%
**Format:** perfect
**Size:** H 9" W 6"
**Average Pages:** 175
**Ads:** no

## Litmus Press

**Type:** press
**CLMP member:** yes
**Primary Editor/Contact Person:** E. Tracy Grinnell
**Address:** P.O. Box 25526
Brooklyn, NY 11202-5526
**Web Site Address:** http://www.litmuspress.org
**Publishes:** essays, nonfiction, and poetry
**Editorial Focus:** Established and emerging poets in the experimental tradition and poetry/writing in translation.
**Representative Authors:** Keith Waldrop, Danielle Collobert (in trans.), and Stacy Szymaszek
**Submissions Policy:** MS must be accompanied by cover letter and current contact information. Please query before submitting MS.
**Simultaneous Subs:** yes
**Reading Period:** Year-round
**Reporting Time:** 1 to 3 months
**Author Payment:** copies
**Founded:** 2000
**Non Profit:** yes
**Paid Staff:** 0

**Unpaid Staff:** 1
**Distributors:** SPD
**Number of Books Published per Year:** 2
**Titles in Print:** 11
**Average Print Run:** 700
**Average Percentage Printed:** Paperback 100%
**Average Price:** $12

## Living Forge

**Type:** magazine
**CLMP member:** yes
**Primary Editor/Contact Person:** Jerod Sikorskyj
**Address:** c/o Jerod J. Sikorskyj
43 Crescent Ave, Upper
Buffalo, NY 14214
**Web Site Address:** http://www.livingforge.com
**Publishes:** essays, fiction, nonfiction, poetry, reviews, art, audio, and video
**Editorial Focus:** Creative and critical work focusing on: Rustbelt, Rustbelt Diaspora, Great Lakes, industrial United States, developing world.
**Recent Awards Received:** N/A
**Representative Authors:** Will Watson, Mark Nowak, and Carolyn Kraus
**Submissions Policy:** E-mail submissions (MS Word or Rich Text Document) to submissions@livingforge.com. Artwork = 300dpi min. Hardcopy accepted, SASE
**Simultaneous Subs:** no
**Reading Period:** Year-round
**Reporting Time:** 1 to 2 months
**Author Payment:** copies
**Founded:** 2002
**Non Profit:** yes
**Paid Staff:** 0
**Unpaid Staff:** 3
**Distributors:** Distributed privately to Rustbelt region
**ISSN Number/ISBN Number:** 1545-7176/1-932-583-(05/22)-x
**Total Circulation:** 500
**Paid Circulation:** N/A
**Average Print Run:** 500
**Subscription Rate:** Individual $10/Institution $15
**Single Copy Price:** $10
**Current Volume/Issue:** 3/1
**Frequency per Year:** 1
**Backfile Available:** yes
**Unsolicited Ms. Received:** yes
**% of Unsolicited Ms. Published per Year:** 50%
**Format:** perfect
**Size:** H 8.5" W 5.5"

**Average Pages:** 150
**Ads:** no

## Living Forge

**Type:** press
**CLMP member:** yes
**Primary Editor/Contact Person:**
K.Ernst/J.Senchyne/J.Sikorskyj
**Address:** c/o Jerod J. Sikorskyj
43 Crescent Ave, Upper
Buffalo, NY 14214
**Web Site Address:** http://www.livingforge.com
**Publishes:** essays, fiction, nonfiction, poetry, reviews, art, audio, and video
**Editorial Focus:** Class studies (Creative/critical work): Rustbelt, Rustbelt Diaspora, Great Lakes, industrial United States, developing world
**Recent Awards Received:** N/A
**Representative Authors:** Will Watson, Mark Nowak, and Carolyn Kraus
**Submissions Policy:** E-mail submissions to submissions@livingforge.com(MS Word or Rich Text Document). Artwork = 300dpi min. Hardcopy accepted, SASE
**Simultaneous Subs:** no
**Reading Period:** Year-round
**Reporting Time:** 1 to 2 months
**Author Payment:** copies
**Contests:** N/A
**Founded:** 2002
**Non Profit:** yes
**Paid Staff:** 0
**Unpaid Staff:** 3
**Distributors:** Distributed privately to Rustbelt region
**ISSN Number/ISBN Number:** 1545-7176/1-932-583-(05/22)-x
**Number of Books Published per Year:** 1
**Titles in Print:** 2
**Average Print Run:** 500
**Average Percentage Printed:** Paperback 100%
**Average Price:** $10 w/CD

## Livingston Press

**Type:** press
**CLMP member:** yes
**Primary Editor/Contact Person:** Joe Taylor
**Address:** Station 22
University of West Alabama
Livingston, AL 35470

**Web Site Address:**
http://www.livingstonpress.uwa.edu
**Publishes:** fiction
**Editorial Focus:** We are especially interested in form as it affects novels and story collections.
**Representative Authors:** Suzanne Hudson, Tom Abrams, and Corey Mesler
**Submissions Policy:** Send only in May, except for Tartt Award entries. If familiar with our line, send entire work; otherwise, send 30 pages.
**Simultaneous Subs:** yes
**Reading Period:** 5/1 to 6/1
**Reporting Time:** 3 to 5 months
**Author Payment:** royalties and copies
**Contests:** Tartt First Fiction Award for story collections by an author who has yet to publish such. See Web Site for Contest Guidelines.
**Founded:** 1982
**Non Profit:** yes
**Paid Staff:** 4
**Unpaid Staff:** 5
**Wholesalers:** Ingram, Baker & Taylor, Brodart, Blackwell, Yankee
**ISSN Number/ISBN Number:** ISBN 1-931982
**Number of Books Published per Year:** 11
**Titles in Print:** 85
**Average Print Run:** 2,000
**Average Percentage Printed:** Hardcover 15%, Paperback 85%
**Average Price:** $20

## The Long Story

**Type:** magazine
**CLMP member:** no
**Primary Editor/Contact Person:** R.P. Burnham
**Address:** 18 Eaton St.
Lawrence, MA 01843
**Web Site Address:**
homepage.mac.com/rpburnham/longstory.html
**Publishes:** fiction and poetry
**Editorial Focus:** stories 8,000-20,000 words with thematic emphasis
**Submissions Policy:** include SASE, no electronic submissions; no unsolicited poetry
**Simultaneous Subs:** yes
**Reading Period:** Year-round
**Reporting Time:** 6 to 8 weeks
**Author Payment:** none
**Founded:** 1982
**Non Profit:** yes

**Paid Staff:** x
**Unpaid Staff:** 2
**Distributors:** Ingram
**ISSN Number/ISBN Number:** ISSN 0741-4242
**Total Circulation:** 800
**Paid Circulation:** 50
**Average Print Run:** 1,000
**Subscription Rate:** Individual $12/Institution $14
**Single Copy Price:** $7
**Current Volume/Issue:** Issue 23
**Frequency per Year:** 1
**Backfile Available:** yes
**Unsolicited Ms. Received:** yes
**% of Unsolicited Ms. Published per Year:** 2%
**Format:** perfect
**Size:** H 8.5" W 5.5"
**Average Pages:** 160
**Ads:** no

## Lost Horse Press

**Type:** press
**CLMP member:** yes
**Primary Editor/Contact Person:** Christine Holbert
**Address:** 105 Lost Horse Ln.
Sandpoint, ID 83864-8609
**Web Site Address:** http://www.losthorsepress.org
**Publishes:** essays, fiction, and poetry
**Editorial Focus:** The independent, nonprofit Lost Horse Press publishes poetry, fiction and creative nonfiction titles of high literary merit.
**Representative Authors:** Valerie Martin, Robert Pack, and Donald Junkins
**Submissions Policy:** Please check submissions policy at the LHP web site at http://www.losthorsepress.org.
**Simultaneous Subs:** yes
**Reading Period:** Year-round
**Reporting Time:** 9 to 12 months
**Author Payment:** cash
**Contests:** See Web Site for Contest Guidelines.
**Founded:** 1998
**Non Profit:** yes
**Paid Staff:** 1
**Unpaid Staff:** 2
**Distributors:** EWU Press, SPD
**ISSN Number/ISBN Number:** 0-9717265-/0-9668612-
**Number of Books Published per Year:** 4-6
**Titles in Print:** 21
**Average Print Run:** 1,000

**Average Percentage Printed:** Hardcover 2%, Paperback 98%
**Average Price:** $16.95

# Lotus Press

**Type:** press
**CLMP member:** yes
**Primary Editor/Contact Person:** Naomi Madgett
**Address:** P.O. Box 21607
Detroit, MI 48221-0607
**Web Site Address:** http://www.lotuspress.org
**Publishes:** poetry
**Editorial Focus:** No preference in style or subject matter. Literary excellence and good taste are only criteria.
**Representative Authors:** Anthony A. Lee, Naomi Long Madgett, and Mendi Lewis Obadike
**Submissions Policy:** No unsolicited manuscripts except award entries. Guidelines available on web site, by e-mail, or SASE
**Simultaneous Subs:** no
**Reading Period:** 1/2 to 3/31
**Reporting Time:** 2 to 3 months
**Author Payment:** cash and copies
**Contests:** Naomi Long Madgett Poetry Awards open to African American poets. Judge varies annually. Winner receives $500 and publication. No fee.
**Founded:** 1972
**Non Profit:** yes
**Paid Staff:** 0
**Unpaid Staff:** 3
**Distributors:** various
**Wholesalers:** various
**ISSN Number/ISBN Number:** ISBN 0-916418
**Number of Books Published per Year:** 1-2
**Titles in Print:** 65
**Average Print Run:** 800
**Average Percentage Printed:** Hardcover 1%, Paperback 98%, Other 1%
**Average Price:** $17

# Louisiana Literature

**Type:** magazine
**CLMP member:** yes
**Primary Editor/Contact Person:** Jack B. Bedell
**Address:** SLU Box 10792
Hammond, LA 70402-0792
**Web Site Address:** http://www.louisianaliterature.org
**Publishes:** fiction, poetry, and reviews

**Editorial Focus:** We strive to publish the highest quality creative work we receive. Our readers' focus is always on craft.
**Representative Authors:** Robert Olen Butler, Vivian Shipley, and Virgil Suarez
**Submissions Policy:** Submission guidelines are available on our website.
**Simultaneous Subs:** no
**Reading Period:** Year-round
**Reporting Time:** 1 to 2 months
**Author Payment:** copies and subscription
**Contests:** See Web Site for Contest Guidelines.
**Founded:** 1984
**Non Profit:** yes
**Paid Staff:** 5
**Unpaid Staff:** 2
**ISSN Number/ISBN Number:** ISSN 0890-0477
**Total Circulation:** 1,200
**Paid Circulation:** 400
**Subscription Rate:** Individual $12/Institution $18
**Single Copy Price:** $8
**Current Volume/Issue:** 20/1
**Frequency per Year:** 2
**Backfile Available:** yes
**Unsolicited Ms. Received:** yes
**% of Unsolicited Ms. Published per Year:** 5%
**Format:** perfect
**Size:** H 9" W 6"
**Average Pages:** 146
**Ads:** yes
**Ad Rates:** By exchange only.

# The Louisville Review/Fleur-de-Lis Press

**Type:** magazine
**CLMP member:** yes
**Primary Editor/Contact Person:** Kathleen Driskell
**Address:** Spalding University
851 S. Fourth St.
Louisville, KY 40203
**Web Site Address:** http://www.louisvillereview.org
**Publishes:** essays, fiction, nonfiction, and poetry
**Submissions Policy:** Unpublished manuscripts w/ self-addressed, stamped envelope for reply only. No electronic submissions. Guidelines on website.
**Simultaneous Subs:** yes
**Reading Period:** Year-round
**Reporting Time:** 4 to 6 months
**Author Payment:** none
**Founded:** 1976

# Profile: Hilda Raz, Editor, Prairie Schooner

## 1) How did you arrive at your current position?

I began as a book reviewer and manuscript reader for Bernice Slote, who was the third editor in *Prairie Schooner*'s seventy-nine years of continuous publication (I'm the fifth); then she asked me to write a quarterly column called "Seen in Series" and I did. When I left Nebraska, Bernice sent me a telegram offering me a paid position on the magazine. I came back as a contributing editor, became poetry editor, then editor in chief..

## 2) What is the staff structure like at your press/magazine?

The Managing Editor and the Editor in Chief are full time paid staff positions, although in fact I'm a Professor of English so Kelly Grey Carlisle as Managing Editor is the full-time paid staffer. We have a half-time Book Series Coordinator for our annual Prize Book Series in Poetry and Short Fiction ($3,000 prize for each of two book manuscripts, one poetry, one short fiction, published by the University of Nebraska Press) and many volunteer readers from the wider community of writers, the graduate program in creative writing, the graduate faculty in the Department of English at the University of Nebraska, as well as advanced undergraduate student interns who are paid by a university-wide research initiative called UCARE.

## 3) How do you keep your press/magazine running?

Time and money. With the expansion of *Prairie Schooner*'s programs to include graduate education and the Prize Book Series, staff time is stretched. Thanks to the philanthropy of Glenna Luschei, *Prairie Schooner* magazine is endowed in perpetuity, as is its editor. Now that the magazine's future is secure, we hope to expand opportunities and rewards for our contributors and fix firmly the future of the book series.

## 4) What do or don't you hope to see in a cover letter?

Basic information about previous publications and interests.

## 5) What do you look for in a submission?

Brilliant writing; work that takes chances in order to extend literary conventions; passionate commitment to subject, narrative, form, and voice.

## 6) How are submissions processed at your press/magazine?

As quickly as possible. The volume of mail is huge. A student intern opens the mail, sorts the envelopes into business matters and submissions, enters basic information (name, date, genre) into a data base, and passes on the sorted mail for appropriate action. Submissions are read and sent back or passed along to senior readers in each genre, sent back or passed on to me for final decision. We publish a mix of fiction, poetry, essays, and book reviews.

## 7) Do you have a favorite unsolicited submission discovery or story?

Three, in fact, to stand for many more: In my first year at *Prairie Schooner*, I read the submissions of a new writer, J.C. Oates. The mail opener knew I was eager to read the stories and poems and sent them straight to my desk. I first recommended a story called, "A View of the Enemy," which we published. Much later, Joyce Carol Oates was keynote speaker for our 75th Anniversary Conference and Celebration. As a young poetry editor with a challenging life, I opened an unsolicited manuscript from Amy Clampitt. The elegance and courage of her poems lifted my spirits. We published her work early in her career and I believe her poems shaped my life.

I was alone in the office during a hot Nebraska summer and answered the phone to hear Tennessee Williams ask for copies of his work we'd published. He'd lost them and his publishers were angry. I found them in our files and we became telephone friends

## 8) Do you have any advice for first-time submitters?

Be fierce and self-absorbed. Read the journals you submit to. Send out your work until a journal is smart enough to publish it. Resolve to write a lot and be patient Know an entire force of publishers and editors spend their short lives as advocates for your work. Put manuscripts into the mail at regular intervals. Keep copies. Work with other writers in summer workshops, classes, and informal groups. Read a lot and subscribe to journals.

**Non Profit:** yes
**Paid Staff:** N/A
**Unpaid Staff:** 5
**Total Circulation:** 1,000
**Paid Circulation:** 85%
**Average Print Run:** 700
**Subscription Rate:** Individual $14/Institution $14
**Single Copy Price:** $8
**Current Volume/Issue:** Issue 58
**Frequency per Year:** 2
**Backfile Available:** yes
**Unsolicited Ms. Received:** yes
**% of Unsolicited Ms. Published per Year:** 95%
**Format:** perfect
**Size:** H 8.5" W 5.5"
**Average Pages:** 160+

## Lullwater Review

**Type:** press
**CLMP member:** no
**Primary Editor/Contact Person:** Nina Wainwright
**Address:** P.O. Box 22036
Emory University
Atlanta, GA 30322
**Publishes:** essays, fiction, and poetry
**Editorial Focus:** none
**Representative Authors:** Lyn Lifshin, Arthur Gottlieb, and Julian Edney
**Submissions Policy:** No more than 6 poems, of any length or subject. No genre writing. Fiction must be limited to 5,000 words
**Simultaneous Subs:** yes
**Reading Period:** 8/5 to 3/4
**Reporting Time:** 3 to 5 months
**Author Payment:** copies
**Founded:** 1990
**Non Profit:** yes
**Paid Staff:** 0
**Unpaid Staff:** 15
**ISSN Number/ISBN Number:** ISSN 1051-5968
**Number of Books Published per Year:** 2
**Titles in Print:** 25
**Average Percentage Printed:** Paperback 100%

## LUNGFULL!magazine

**Type:** magazine
**CLMP member:** yes
**Primary Editor/Contact Person:** Brendan Lorber
**Address:** 316 23rd St.
Brooklyn, NY 11215
**Web Site Address:** http://lungfull.org
**Publishes:** poetry and art
**Editorial Focus:** We print the rough draft of contributors' writing in addition to the final version so you can see the creative process.
**Representative Authors:** Alice Notley, Noelle Kocot, and Bill Kushner
**Submissions Policy:** Please read a copy before sending. Mentioning in your cover letter why you want to be in the journal is always nice.
**Simultaneous Subs:** yes
**Reading Period:** Year-round
**Reporting Time:** 6 to 12 months
**Author Payment:** copies
**Founded:** 1994
**Non Profit:** no
**Paid Staff:** 0
**Unpaid Staff:** 9
**Distributors:** Ubiquity, DeBoer
**Total Circulation:** 1,000
**Paid Circulation:** 150
**Average Print Run:** 1,000
**Subscription Rate:** Individual $35.80/Institution $45
**Single Copy Price:** $10.50
**Current Volume/Issue:** Issue 14
**Frequency per Year:** 1
**Backfile Available:** yes
**Unsolicited Ms. Received:** yes
**% of Unsolicited Ms. Published per Year:** 2%
**Format:** perfect
**Size:** H 8.5" W 7"
**Average Pages:** 210
**Ads:** yes
**Ad Rates:** See Web Site for Details.

## Lyric Poetry Review

**Type:** magazine
**CLMP member:** yes
**Primary Editor/Contact Person:** Mira Rosenthal
**Address:** P.O. Box 2494
Bloomington, IN 47403
**Web Site Address:** http://www.lyricreview.org
**Publishes:** essays, poetry, and translation
**Editorial Focus:** Independent international journal of

poetry and creative exchange.
**Recent Awards Received:** Best American Poetry 2004, Pushcart Prize
**Representative Authors:** Mark Doty, Lucille Clifton, and Marilyn Hacker
**Submissions Policy:** We work hard to present newer writers along with more established figures. Unpublished work only.
**Simultaneous Subs:** yes
**Reading Period:** Year-round
**Reporting Time:** 1 to 4 months
**Author Payment:** copies
**Founded:** 2000
**Non Profit:** yes
**Paid Staff:** 0
**Unpaid Staff:** 5
**Distributors:** DeBoer
**ISSN Number/ISBN Number:** ISSN 1533-1776
**Total Circulation:** 400
**Paid Circulation:** 100
**Average Print Run:** 1,000
**Subscription Rate:** Individual $14/Institution $30
**Single Copy Price:** $8
**Current Volume/Issue:** Issue 8
**Frequency per Year:** 2
**Backfile Available:** yes
**Unsolicited Ms. Received:** yes
**% of Unsolicited Ms. Published per Year:** 10%
**Format:** perfect
**Size:** H 8.5" W 5"
**Average Pages:** 96
**Ads:** yes
**Ad Rates:** Swap with other Lit Mags See Web Site for Details.

# The MacGuffin

**Type:** magazine
**CLMP member:** yes
**Primary Editor/Contact Person:** Steven A. Dolgin
**Address:** 18600 Haggerty Road
Livonia, MI 48152-2696
**Web Site Address:** http://www.macguffin.org
**Publishes:** essays, fiction, nonfiction, poetry, and art
**Editorial Focus:** No religious, inspirations, juvenile, romance, horror, pornography
**Representative Authors:** Terry Blackhawk, Conrad Hilberry, and Laurence Lieberman
**Submissions Policy:** enclose a self-addressed, stamped envelope (SASE) or sufficient International Reply Coupons for reply only.

**Simultaneous Subs:** yes
**Reading Period:** 8/15 to 6/1
**Reporting Time:** 12 to 16 weeks
**Author Payment:** copies
**Founded:** 1984
**Non Profit:** yes
**Paid Staff:** 2
**Unpaid Staff:** 12
**ISSN Number/ISBN Number:** ISSN 1527-234 6
**Total Circulation:** 600
**Paid Circulation:** 150
**Average Print Run:** 500
**Subscription Rate:** Individual $22/Institution $22
**Single Copy Price:** $9
**Current Volume/Issue:** 21/3
**Frequency per Year:** 3
**Backfile Available:** yes
**Unsolicited Ms. Received:** yes
**% of Unsolicited Ms. Published per Year:** 90%
**Format:** perfect
**Size:** H 9" W 6"
**Average Pages:** 200
**Ads:** no

# Mad Hatters' Review

**Type:** online
**CLMP member:** yes
**Primary Editor/Contact Person:** Carol Novack
**Address:** http://www.madhattersreview.com
New York, NY 10011-7841
**Web Site Address:**
http://www.madhattersreview.com
**Publishes:** fiction, nonfiction, poetry, reviews, art, translation, audio, and video
**Editorial Focus:** Weâre particularly interested in "edgy," experimental, gutsy, thematically broad, psychologically and philosophically sophisticated writings. Black/dark humor, whimsy, wise satire, erotica, irony, magic realism and surrealism are welcome.
**Submissions Policy:**
http://www.madhattersreview.com/submit.shtml
**Simultaneous Subs:** yes
**Reading Period:** Year-round
**Reporting Time:** 1 to 4 weeks
**Author Payment:** none
**Contests:** See Web Site for Contest Guidelines.
**Founded:** 2005
**Non Profit:** no
**Paid Staff:** 1
**Unpaid Staff:** 16

**ISSN Number/ISBN Number:** ISSN 1556-147X
**Average Page Views per Month:** 13,680
**Average Unique Visitors per Month:** 2,160
**Frequency per Year:** 3
**Average Percentage of Pages per Category:** Audio 100%
**Ad Rates:** http://www.madhattersreview.com/sponsorship.shtml
See Web Site for Details.

# Maelstrom

**Type:** magazine
**CLMP member:** no
**Primary Editor/Contact Person:** Christine L. Reed
**Address:** HC#1 Box 1624
Blakeslee, pa 18610
**Web Site Address:** http://www.geocities.com/~read-maelstrom
**Publishes:** essays, fiction, poetry, reviews, art, and translation
**Editorial Focus:** Tight, well-crafted poetry and gripping fiction.
**Representative Authors:** Mekeel McBride, Edgar Silex, and Grace Cavalieri
**Submissions Policy:** Send 4 poems or fiction 3,000 words or less. Art is held over for consideration in future issues unless otherwise requested.
**Simultaneous Subs:** yes
**Reading Period:** Year-round
**Reporting Time:** 1 to 4 months
**Author Payment:** copies
**Founded:** 1997
**Non Profit:** yes
**Paid Staff:** 0
**Unpaid Staff:** 4
**ISSN Number/ISBN Number:** ISSN 1096-3820
**Total Circulation:** 500
**Paid Circulation:** 50
**Subscription Rate:** Individual $20/Institution $20
**Single Copy Price:** $5
**Current Volume/Issue:** 4/3
**Frequency per Year:** 4
**Backfile Available:** yes
**Unsolicited Ms. Received:** yes
**% of Unsolicited Ms. Published per Year:** 2%
**Format:** stapled
**Size:** H 8 1/2" W 5 1/2"
**Average Pages:** 42
**Ads:** yes
**Ad Rates:** send query

# Main Street Rag

**Type:** magazine
**CLMP member:** no
**Primary Editor/Contact Person:** M. Scott Douglass
**Address:** 4416 Shea Ln.
Charlotte, NC 28227
**Web Site Address:** http://www.MainStreetRag.com
**Publishes:** essays, fiction, nonfiction, poetry, reviews, and art
**Editorial Focus:** We like things that are alive with an edge whether serious, humorous, political, satirical. Not interested in garden poetry.
**Representative Authors:** David Chorlton, Joy Harjo, and David Slavitt
**Submissions Policy:** Up to 6 PAGES of poetry, 6,000 words for short fiction, 2,000 words for essays. See website for reviews and/or interviews.
**Simultaneous Subs:** no
**Reading Period:** Year-round
**Reporting Time:** 3 to 6 weeks
**Author Payment:** copies
**Contests:** Chapbook, full-length poetry, short fiction
See Web Site for Contest Guidelines.
**Founded:** 1996
**Non Profit:** no
**Paid Staff:** 3
**Unpaid Staff:** 0
**Distributors:** Ingram
**Total Circulation:** 800
**Paid Circulation:** 200
**Average Print Run:** 800
**Subscription Rate:** Individual $20/Institution $20
**Single Copy Price:** $7
**Current Volume/Issue:** 10/3
**Frequency per Year:** 4
**Backfile Available:** yes
**Unsolicited Ms. Received:** yes
**% of Unsolicited Ms. Published per Year:** 10%
**Format:** perfect
**Size:** H 9" W 6"
**Average Pages:** 96
**Ads:** yes
**Ad Rates:** vary according to size, but cheap-mostly swap ads

# Maisonneuve

**Type:** magazine
**CLMP member:** no
**Primary Editor/Contact Person:** Derek Webster/Kena Herod

**Address:** 400 de Maisonneuve Blvd.
Ste. 655
Montreal, QC H3A 1L4
**Web Site Address:** http://www.maisonneuve.org
**Publishes:** essays, fiction, nonfiction, poetry, reviews, art, translation, and audio
**Editorial Focus:** Eclectic Curiosity. The magazine balances diverse perspectives and topics, and aims to present it coherently and provocatively.
**Recent Awards Received:** Among many honors: the President's Medal and other awards from the National Magazine Awards and 2 Canadian Newsstand Awards.
**Representative Authors:** Jon Mooallem, Mona Awad, and Paul Winner
**Submissions Policy:** Anything else that demonstrates curiosity, energy or elegance across all fields of human endeavor. See website for details.
**Simultaneous Subs:** yes
**Reading Period:** Year-round
**Reporting Time:** 1 to 4 months
**Author Payment:** cash
**Contests:** See website.
See Web Site for Contest Guidelines.
**Founded:** 2002
**Non Profit:** yes
**Paid Staff:** 7
**Unpaid Staff:** 3
**Distributors:** LMPI
**ISSN Number/ISBN Number:** ISSN 1703-0056
**Total Circulation:** 14,000
**Paid Circulation:** 2,900
**Average Print Run:** 12,000
**Subscription Rate:** Individual $24/Institution $32
**Single Copy Price:** $6.95CAD
**Current Volume/Issue:** 2/4
**Frequency per Year:** 6
**Backfile Available:** yes
**Unsolicited Ms. Received:** yes
**% of Unsolicited Ms. Published per Year:** 20%
**Format:** stapled
**Size:** H 11" W 8.5"
**Average Pages:** 96
**Ads:** yes
**Ad Rates:** See Web Site for Details.

## The Malahat Review
**Type:** magazine
**CLMP member:** no
**Primary Editor/Contact Person:** John Barton
**Address:** University of Victoria

Box 1700, Stn CSC
Victoria, BC V8V 2E6
**Web Site Address:** http://www.malahatreview.ca
**Publishes:** fiction, poetry, and reviews
**Editorial Focus:** Publish mainstream and experimental poetry and fiction by emerging and established writers from Canada and around the world.
**Recent Awards Received:** Journey Prize, 2004; O'Henry Award, 2001; National Magazine Award, 1995; Magazine of the Year, Western Magazine Awards, 1995
**Representative Authors:** Bill Gaston, Patricia Young, and Elisabeth Harvor
**Submissions Policy:** We invite submissions of previously unpublished one short story or five to eight poems for first world rights.
**Simultaneous Subs:** no
**Reading Period:** Year-round
**Reporting Time:** 1 to 10 months
**Author Payment:** cash and subscription
**Contests:** Novella Contest; Long Poem Contest; Far Horizons Award for Short Fiction; Far Horizons Award for Poetry
**Founded:** 1967
**Non Profit:** yes
**Paid Staff:** 3
**Unpaid Staff:** 10
**Distributors:** Magazines Canada
**ISSN Number/ISBN Number:** ISSN 0025-1216
**Total Circulation:** 1,000
**Paid Circulation:** 800
**Average Print Run:** 1,500
**Subscription Rate:** Individual $45/Institution $55
**Single Copy Price:** $11.95
**Current Volume/Issue:** Issue 152
**Frequency per Year:** 4
**Backfile Available:** yes
**Unsolicited Ms. Received:** yes
**% of Unsolicited Ms. Published per Year:** 2%
**Format:** perfect
**Size:** H 9" W 6"
**Average Pages:** 112
**Ads:** yes
**Ad Rates:** See Web Site for Details.

## MAMMOTH books
**Type:** press
**CLMP member:** yes
**Primary Editor/Contact Person:** Antonio Vallone
**Address:** MAMMOTH press Inc.

7 Juniata St.
DuBois, PA 15801
**Publishes:** essays, fiction, nonfiction, and poetry
**Representative Authors:** William Heyen, Liz Rosenberg, and Dinty W. Moore
**Submissions Policy:** We've ended our contests. No manuscripts are being accepted at this time.
**Simultaneous Subs:** no
**Reading Period:** Year-round
**Reporting Time:** 11 to 12 months
**Author Payment:** copies
**Contests:** We've ended our contests.
**Founded:** 1997
**Non Profit:** yes
**Paid Staff:** 1
**Unpaid Staff:** 2
**Distributors:** SPD
**Number of Books Published per Year:** 4/5
**Titles in Print:** 25
**Average Print Run:** 300
**Average Percentage Printed:** Paperback 100%
**Average Price:** $11-20

## Mandorla: New Writing from the Americas

**Type:** magazine
**CLMP member:** yes
**Primary Editor/Contact Person:** Kristin Dykstra
**Address:** Dept. of English, Illinois State University
Campus Box 4240
Normal, IL 61790-4240
**Web Site Address:** http://www.litline.org/Mandorla/
**Publishes:** essays, fiction, nonfiction, poetry, art, and translation
**Editorial Focus:** innovative writing in its original language-usually English or Spanish-and new translations; visual art; critical essays.
**Representative Authors:** Jay Wright, Tamara Kamenszain, and Antonio José Ponte
**Simultaneous Subs:** no
**Reading Period:** 7/15 to 10/15
**Reporting Time:** 2 to 4 months
**Author Payment:** none
**Founded:** 1991
**Non Profit:** yes
**Paid Staff:** 2
**Unpaid Staff:** 3
**ISSN Number/ISBN Number:** ISSN 1550-7432
**Total Circulation:** 900
**Paid Circulation:** 400

**Average Print Run:** 1,000
**Subscription Rate:** Individual $12.50/Institution $18
**Single Copy Price:** $12.50
**Current Volume/Issue:** Issue 7
**Frequency per Year:** 1
**Backfile Available:** yes
**Unsolicited Ms. Received:** no
**Format:** perfect
**Average Pages:** 215
**Ad Rates:** full page $500. half page $250.

## Mangrove

**Type:** magazine
**CLMP member:** yes
**Primary Editor/Contact Person:** Neil de la Flor
**Address:** University of Miami, English Dept.
Box 248145
Miami, FL 33124-4632
**Web Site Address:** http://www.mangroveonline.org
**Publishes:** fiction, nonfiction, poetry, art, translation, audio, and video
**Representative Authors:** Terese Svoboda, Richard Grayson, and Denise Duhamel
**Simultaneous Subs:** yes
**Reading Period:** 8/1 to 4/30
**Reporting Time:** 1 to 2 months
**Author Payment:** none
**Contests:** $500 Mangrove Literary Award alternates between fiction and poetry. Check mangroveonline.org for details.
See Web Site for Contest Guidelines.
**Founded:** 1994
**Non Profit:** yes
**Paid Staff:** 0
**Unpaid Staff:** 8
**Total Circulation:** 500
**Paid Circulation:** 50
**Average Print Run:** 50
**Subscription Rate:** Individual $28/Institution $20
**Single Copy Price:** $10
**Current Volume/Issue:** 1/15
**Frequency per Year:** 2
**Backfile Available:** yes
**Unsolicited Ms. Received:** yes
**% of Unsolicited Ms. Published per Year:** 50%
**Format:** perfect
**Ads:** yes

# The Manhattan Review

**Type:** magazine
**CLMP member:** yes
**Primary Editor/Contact Person:** Philip Fried
**Address:** 440 Riverside Dr. #38
New York, NY 10027
**Web Site Address:**
http://www.themanhattanreview.com
**Publishes:** essays, poetry, reviews, and translation
**Editorial Focus:** contemporary poetry in the US and abroad.
**Representative Authors:** D. Nurkse, Jeanne Marie Beaumont, and Baron Wormser
**Submissions Policy:** 3-5 poems. Brief bio. Notification if simultaneous.
**Simultaneous Subs:** yes
**Reading Period:** Year-round
**Reporting Time:** 3 to 5 months
**Author Payment:** none
**Founded:** 1980
**Non Profit:** no
**Paid Staff:** no
**Unpaid Staff:** no
**Distributors:** DeBoer
**ISSN Number/ISBN Number:** ISSN 275-6889
**Total Circulation:** 500
**Paid Circulation:** 400
**Average Print Run:** 500
**Subscription Rate:** Individual $15/Institution $20
**Single Copy Price:** $7.50
**Current Volume/Issue:** 12/1
**Frequency per Year:** 2
**Backfile Available:** yes
**Unsolicited Ms. Received:** yes
**% of Unsolicited Ms. Published per Year:** .5%
**Format:** perfect
**Size:** H 8-1/2" W 5-1/2"
**Average Pages:** 200
**Ads:** yes
**Ad Rates:** $50/page

# Manic D Press

**Type:** press
**CLMP member:** yes
**Primary Editor/Contact Person:** Jennifer Joseph
**Address:** P.O. Box 410804
San Francisco, CA 94141
**Web Site Address:** http://www.manicdpress.com
**Publishes:** essays, fiction, nonfiction, poetry, and art
**Editorial Focus:** Engrossing narrative fiction, stunningly good poetry, thought-provoking nonfiction and brilliantly original art.
**Representative Authors:** Jeffrey McDaniel, Adrienne Su, and Justin Chin
**Submissions Policy:**
http://www.manicdpress.com/submissions.html
**Simultaneous Subs:** yes
**Reading Period:** 1/1 to 1/31
**Reporting Time:** 1 to 6 months
**Author Payment:** royalties
**Founded:** 1984
**Non Profit:** no
**Paid Staff:** 2
**Unpaid Staff:** 3
**Distributors:** Consortium, Publishers Group Canada
**Wholesalers:** SPD, Last Gasp, Ingram, Baker & Taylor, et al.
**ISSN Number/ISBN Number:** ISBN 0-916397, 1-933149
**Number of Books Published per Year:** 10
**Titles in Print:** 80
**Average Print Run:** 3,500
**Average Percentage Printed:** Hardcover 5%, Paperback 95%
**Average Price:** $13.95

# Manifold Press

**Type:** press
**CLMP member:** yes
**Primary Editor/Contact Person:** Carol Frome
**Address:** 102 Bridge St.
Plattsburgh, NY 12901
**Web Site Address:** http://www.manifoldpress.com
**Publishes:** poetry
**Editorial Focus:** Well-crafted lyric poetry by known and unknown poets.
**Representative Authors:** N/A
**Submissions Policy:** We accept manuscripts year-round. Please include $20 reading fee and business-size SASE. Manuscripts will be recycled.
**Simultaneous Subs:** yes
**Reading Period:** Year-round
**Reporting Time:** 3 to 4 months
**Author Payment:** royalties and cash
**Contests:** We are trying to avoid running contests.
**Founded:** 2003
**Non Profit:** no
**Paid Staff:** no
**Unpaid Staff:** yes
**Distributors:** SPD Books

**Number of Books Published per Year:** 1-4
**Titles in Print:** 0
**Average Percentage Printed:** Paperback 100%
**Backfile Available:** yes

## Manoa

**Type:** magazine
**CLMP member:** yes
**Primary Editor/Contact Person:** Frank Stewart, Editor
**Address:** c/o UH English Dept.
1733 Donaghho Road
Honolulu, HI 96822
**Web Site Address:** http://manoajournal.hawaii.edu
**Publishes:** essays, fiction, nonfiction, poetry, reviews, art, and translation
**Editorial Focus:** New writing from Asia, the Pacific, and America
**Representative Authors:** Arthur Sze, Tony Barnstone, and Leza Lowitz
**Simultaneous Subs:** yes
**Reading Period:** Year-round
**Reporting Time:** 1 to 6 months
**Author Payment:** cash and copies
**Founded:** 1988
**Non Profit:** yes
**Paid Staff:** 6
**Unpaid Staff:** 2
**ISSN Number/ISBN Number:** ISSN 1045-7909
**Total Circulation:** 3,000
**Paid Circulation:** 1,300
**Average Print Run:** 1,300
**Subscription Rate:** Individual $22/Institution $40
**Single Copy Price:** $20
**Current Volume/Issue:** 17/1
**Frequency per Year:** 2
**Backfile Available:** yes
**Unsolicited Ms. Received:** yes
**% of Unsolicited Ms. Published per Year:** 1%
**Format:** perfect
**Size:** H 7" W 10"
**Average Pages:** 220
**Ads:** yes

## Many Mountains Moving

**Type:** magazine
**CLMP member:** yes
**Primary Editor/Contact Person:** Naomi Horii
**Address:** 420 22nd St.

Boulder, CO 80302
**Web Site Address:** http://www.mmminc.org
**Publishes:** essays, fiction, nonfiction, poetry, reviews, art, and translation
**Editorial Focus:** Top-notch work from authors and artists from all walks of life.
**Representative Authors:** Isabel Allende, Sherman Alexie, and Ursula K. Le Guin
**Submissions Policy:** Read May through August only. Send unpublished manuscript with SASE. Simultaneous submissions OK with notification.
**Simultaneous Subs:** yes
**Reading Period:** 5/1 to 8/30
**Reporting Time:** 1 to 3 months
**Author Payment:** copies
**Founded:** 1994
**Non Profit:** yes
**Paid Staff:** 0
**Unpaid Staff:** 3
**Distributors:** SPD
**ISSN Number/ISBN Number:** ISSN 1080-6474
**Total Circulation:** 3,000
**Paid Circulation:** 300
**Subscription Rate:** Individual $29/Institution $29
**Single Copy Price:** $9.25
**Current Volume/Issue:** 6/1
**Frequency per Year:** 2
**Backfile Available:** yes
**Unsolicited Ms. Received:** yes
**% of Unsolicited Ms. Published per Year:** 1%
**Format:** perfect
**Size:** H 11" W 8.5"
**Average Pages:** 50
**Ads:** yes
**Ad Rates:** See Web Site for Details.

## Many Names Press

**Type:** press
**CLMP member:** no
**Primary Editor/Contact Person:** Kate Hitt
**Address:** 1961 Main St. #244
Watsonville, CA 95076
**Web Site Address:** http://www.manynamespress.com
**Publishes:** essays, fiction, nonfiction, poetry, and art
**Editorial Focus:** Poignant Creative Writing, Poetry, Environmental and Social Justice, Nonfiction, Quality, Lasting Publications, Book Arts.
**Recent Awards Received:** Writers Almanac: Keillor read author on NPR. Western Books award for book design

**Representative Authors:** Andrea Rich, Amber Coverdale Sumrall, and Maude Meehan
**Submissions Policy:** Do not submit manuscripts. Grant fuel welcome for poets. Distinguished and liberal. Gay and Lesbian authors.
**Simultaneous Subs:** no
**Reading Period:** 6/06 to 9/06
**Reporting Time:** 4 to 8 weeks
**Author Payment:** copies
**Founded:** 1993
**Non Profit:** no
**Paid Staff:** 0
**Unpaid Staff:** 1
**Distributors:** SPD, manynamespress.com
**ISSN Number/ISBN Number:** ISBN 09652575
**Number of Books Published per Year:** 1-4
**Titles in Print:** 10
**Average Print Run:** 1,000
**Average Percentage Printed:** Paperback 75%, Chapbook 25%
**Average Price:** $15

# Margin: Exploring Modern Magical Realism

**Type:** online
**CLMP member:** yes
**Primary Editor/Contact Person:** Tamara Kaye Sellman
**Address:** 321 High School Road NE
PMB 204
Bainbridge Island, WA 98110
**Web Site Address:** http://www.magical-realism.com
**Publishes:** essays, fiction, nonfiction, poetry, reviews, and translation
**Editorial Focus:** The world's only continuous survey of magical realism. Exists to answer the question, "What is literary magical realism?"
**Recent Awards Received:** Arete Wave of a Site
**Representative Authors:** Dr. Gregory Rabassa, Sondra Kelly-Green, and Michelle Cliff
**Submissions Policy:** Indefinite hiatus in 2006-07 due to backlog and site improvements; check site in June 2006 for progress report and details
**Simultaneous Subs:** yes
**Reading Period:** 9/4 to 4/5
**Reporting Time:** up to 6 months
**Author Payment:** cash and subscription
**Contests:** See web site for contest guidelines or visit http://www.angelfire.com/wa2/margin/periphery.html
**Founded:** 1999

**Non Profit:** yes
**Paid Staff:** 0
**Unpaid Staff:** 5
**Distributors:** Web; we also offer Periphery, a print zine annual
**Average Page Views per Month:** 3,800
**Average Unique Visitors per Month:** 2,200
**Frequency per Year:** 3
**Publish Print Anthology:** yes
Price: $6
**Average Percentage of Pages per Category:** Fiction 48%, Nonfiction 10%, Poetry 20%, Reviews 10%, Essays 10%, Art 1%, Translation 1%
**Ad Rates:** sponsorship rates online, trades discussed See Web Site for Details.

# Marion Boyars Publishers

**Type:** press
**CLMP member:** no
**Primary Editor/Contact Person:** Catheryn Kilgarriff
**Address:** 24 Lacy Road
London, UK SW15 1NL
**Web Site Address:** http://www.marionboyars.co.uk
**Publishes:** fiction, nonfiction, and translation
**Editorial Focus:** Unusual fiction, written to arouse public interest and publicity. Nonfiction in the fields of cinema, drama and culture
**Representative Authors:** Hubert Selby Jr., Hong Ying, and Pauline Kael
**Submissions Policy:** Fiction via a literary agent. Nonfiction-synopsis and return postage.
**Simultaneous Subs:** yes
**Reading Period:** Year-round
**Reporting Time:** 6 to 8 weeks
**Author Payment:** royalties and cash
**Founded:** 1975
**Non Profit:** no
**Paid Staff:** 4
**Unpaid Staff:** 0
**Distributors:** Consortium
**ISSN Number/ISBN Number:** ISBN 0 7145
**Number of Books Published per Year:** 20
**Titles in Print:** 250
**Average Print Run:** 5,000
**Average Percentage Printed:** Hardcover 10%, Paperback 90%
**Average Price:** $14.95

# mark(s)

**Type:** online

**CLMP member:** no
**Primary Editor/Contact Person:** Deb King
**Address:** 332 W. Woodland
Ferndale, MI 48220
**Web Site Address:** http://www.markszine.com
**Publishes:** essays, fiction, poetry, and art
**Editorial Focus:** mark(s) consistently presents new work across a wide variety of artistic practices.
**Representative Authors:** Nathaniel Mackey, Rachel Blau DuPlessis, and Harryette Mullen
**Submissions Policy:** At this time we can not accept unsolicited submissions.
**Simultaneous Subs:** no
**Reading Period:** Year-round
**Reporting Time:** 1 to 3 months
**Author Payment:** none
**Founded:** 1999
**Non Profit:** yes
**Paid Staff:** 0
**Unpaid Staff:** 3
**Average Page Views per Month:** 30,000
**Average Unique Visitors per Month:** 2,200
**Frequency per Year:** 4
**Publish Print Anthology:** no
**Average Percentage of Pages per Category:** Poetry 40%, Essays 15%, Art 45%
**Ads:** no

# The Marlboro Review

**Type:** magazine
**CLMP member:** yes
**Address:** P.O. Box 243
Marlboro, VT 05344
**Web Site Address:** http://www.marlbororeview.com
**Publishes:** essays, fiction, nonfiction, poetry, and reviews
**Reading Period:** Year-round
**Reporting Time:** 1 to 2 months
**Author Payment:** none
**Founded:** 1995
**Non Profit:** no
**Unpaid Staff:** 5
**Backfile Available:** yes

# Marsh Hawk Press

**Type:** press
**CLMP member:** yes
**Primary Editor/Contact Person:** Sandy McIntosh
**Address:** P.O. Box 206

East Rockaway, NY 11518
**Web Site Address:** http://www.marshhawkpress.org
**Publishes:** poetry
**Editorial Focus:** Poetry with affiliations to the visual arts.
**Representative Authors:** Eileen Tabios, Jane Augustine, and Edward Foster
**Submissions Policy:** Only through annual contest. Please see website for details.
**Simultaneous Subs:** no
**Reading Period:** Year-round
**Reporting Time:** 1 to 2 months
**Author Payment:** royalties
**Contests:** See Web Site for Contest Guidelines.
**Founded:** 2001
**Non Profit:** yes
**Paid Staff:** 0
**Unpaid Staff:** 6
**Distributors:** Small Press Distributors
**Wholesalers:** Baker & Taylor
**Number of Books Published per Year:** 6
**Titles in Print:** 29
**Average Print Run:** 1,000
**Average Percentage Printed:** Paperback 100%
**Average Price:** $12.50

# The Massachusetts Review

**Type:** magazine
**CLMP member:** yes
**Primary Editor/Contact Person:** Corwin Ericson, Managing Editor
**Address:** South College
University of Massachusetts
Amherst, MA 01003
**Web Site Address:** http://www.massreview.org
**Publishes:** essays, fiction, nonfiction, poetry, art, and translation
**Editorial Focus:** We publish interesting, well-written, creative, topical, enduring, fascinating fiction, essays, poetry and artwork.
**Representative Authors:** Ilan Stavans, Adrienne Rich, and Valerie Martin
**Submissions Policy:** All submissions must include an SASE. No queries are necessary. No e-mail submissions. See Web site for further guidelines.
**Simultaneous Subs:** no
**Reading Period:** 10/1 to 5/31
**Reporting Time:** 2 to 4 months
**Author Payment:** cash and subscription
**Founded:** 1959

**Non Profit:** yes
**Paid Staff:** 1
**Unpaid Staff:** 15
**Distributors:** Ubiquity, DeBoer
**ISSN Number/ISBN Number:** ISSN 0025-4878
**Total Circulation:** 1,500
**Paid Circulation:** 1,300
**Average Print Run:** 1,500
**Subscription Rate:** Individual $25/Institution $35
**Single Copy Price:** $8
**Current Volume/Issue:** 45/2
**Frequency per Year:** 7
**Backfile Available:** yes
**Unsolicited Ms. Received:** yes
**% of Unsolicited Ms. Published per Year:** 5%
**Format:** perfect
**Size:** H 9" W 6"
**Average Pages:** 200
**Ads:** yes
**Ad Rates:** See Web Site for Details.

# Matrix Magazine

**Type:** magazine
**CLMP member:** no
**Primary Editor/Contact Person:** Jon Paul Fiorentino
**Address:** 1400 de Maisonneuve Blvd LB 502
Montreal, QC H3G1S5
**Web Site Address:** http://alcor.concordia.ca/~matrix
**Publishes:** essays, fiction, nonfiction, poetry, reviews, art, and translation
**Editorial Focus:** Based in Montreal, Matrix is the most innovative, eclectic, and irreverent literary magazine in Canada.
**Representative Authors:** Christian B"k, David McGimpsey, and Mary di Michele
**Submissions Policy:** Text should be double-spaced on one-side of the paper, while poetry can be single-spaced. Please include an SASE.
**Simultaneous Subs:** no
**Reading Period:** Year-round
**Reporting Time:** 4 to 6 months
**Author Payment:** cash, copies, and subscription
**Contests:** See Web Site for Contest Guidelines.
**Founded:** 1975
**Non Profit:** yes
**Paid Staff:** 6
**Unpaid Staff:** 4
**Distributors:** CMPA, Benjamin News, Ubiquity (USA)
**ISSN Number/ISBN Number:** ISSN 0318-3610
**Total Circulation:** 1,500

**Paid Circulation:** 500
**Subscription Rate:** Individual $21/Institution $25
**Single Copy Price:** $8
**Current Volume/Issue:** Issue 68
**Frequency per Year:** 3
**Backfile Available:** yes
**Unsolicited Ms. Received:** yes
**% of Unsolicited Ms. Published per Year:** 10%
**Format:** perfect
**Size:** H 10" W 8"
**Average Pages:** 64
**Ads:** yes
**Ad Rates:** $300 Full Page, $150 Half Page, $100 $75 Quarter Page

# Matter Magazine

**Type:** magazine
**CLMP member:** no
**Primary Editor/Contact Person:** Leigh Money/Emily Pedder
**Address:** 48 Beechwood Road
London, UK E8 3DY
**Web Site Address:** http://www.mattermagazine.co.uk
**Publishes:** fiction and poetry
**Editorial Focus:** Matter brings together the best of new writing, alongside the work of established guest authors
**Representative Authors:** Michel Faber, Ali Smith, and Toby Litt
**Submissions Policy:** No unsolicited submissions
**Simultaneous Subs:** no
**Reading Period:** 3/30 to 5/30
**Reporting Time:** 1 to 2 months
**Author Payment:** copies
**Founded:** 2001
**Non Profit:** yes
**Paid Staff:** 0
**Unpaid Staff:** 6
**Distributors:** INK Publishing
**Wholesalers:** Amazon.co.uk
**ISSN Number/ISBN Number:** ISBN 0954315014
**Total Circulation:** 1,000
**Paid Circulation:** 200
**Subscription Rate:** Individual £3.99/Institution £3.99
**Single Copy Price:** £4.99
**Current Volume/Issue:** 2003/3
**Frequency per Year:** 1
**Backfile Available:** yes
**Unsolicited Ms. Received:** no
**Format:** perfect

**Size:** H 6.5" W 4.75"
**Average Pages:** 170
**Ads:** yes
**Ad Rates:** £150 full page

## McPherson & Company, Publishers

**Type:** press
**CLMP member:** yes
**Primary Editor/Contact Person:** Bruce McPherson
**Address:** P.O. Box 1126
Kingston, NY 12402
**Web Site Address:** http://www.mcphersonco.com
**Publishes:** fiction, nonfiction, and translation
**Editorial Focus:** American and British fiction; Italian, French and Spanish fiction in translation; art theory, filmmaking, cultural studies
**Recent Awards Received:** ForeWord Magazine, Book of the Year 2004: Historical Fiction, gold medal for John Shors's Beneath a Marble Sky
**Representative Authors:** Thomas McEvilley, Jaimy Gordon, and Robert Kelly
**Submissions Policy:** Query first. No unsolicited manuscripts.
**Simultaneous Subs:** no
**Reading Period:** Year-round
**Reporting Time:** 1 to 3 months
**Author Payment:** royalties
**Founded:** 1974
**Non Profit:** yes
**Paid Staff:** 2
**Unpaid Staff:** 0
**Distributors:** McPherson & Co.
**Wholesalers:** New Leaf, Central Books (London), Ingram
**ISSN Number/ISBN Number:** ISBN 0929701-, 0914232-
**Number of Books Published per Year:** 5
**Titles in Print:** 120
**Average Print Run:** 1,200
**Average Percentage Printed:** Hardcover 50%, Paperback 50%
**Average Price:** $18

## McSweeney's Publishing

**Type:** press
**CLMP member:** yes
**Primary Editor/Contact Person:** Eli Horowitz/Andrew Leland
**Address:** 826 Valencia St.
San Francisco, CA 94110
**Web Site Address:** http://www.mcsweeneys.net
**Publishes:** fiction, nonfiction, reviews, and art
**Editorial Focus:** McSweeney's is committed to finding new voices, printing gifted but underappreciated writers, and pushing form forward.
**Representative Authors:** Paul Collins, Lydia Davis, and Rick Moody
**Submissions Policy:** Please visit our web sites, http://www.mcsweeneys.net and http://www.believer-mag.com, for current submissions guidelines.
**Simultaneous Subs:** yes
**Reading Period:** Year-round
**Reporting Time:** 1 to 5 months
**Author Payment:** cash and copies
**Founded:** 1998
**Non Profit:** no
**Paid Staff:** 5
**Unpaid Staff:** 0
**Number of Books Published per Year:** 10-20
**Titles in Print:** 50
**Average Print Run:** varies
**Average Percentage Printed:** Hardcover 80%, Paperback 20%
**Average Price:** $22

## The Melic Review

**Type:** online
**CLMP member:** no
**Primary Editor/Contact Person:** C.E. Chaffin
**Address:** c/o CE 220 N. Zapata Hwy #11A-179
Laredo, TX 78043
**Web Site Address:** http://www.melicreview.com
**Publishes:** essays, fiction, poetry, reviews, art, translation, and audio
**Editorial Focus:** After six years The Melic Review continues to publish the highest quality fiction, criticism, and poetry online.
**Representative Authors:** Scott Murphy, Alfred Corn, and C.E. Chaffin
**Submissions Policy:** Poetry under 50 lines, fiction approx. 1,000 words, exceptions made for longer works of merit and critical essays.
**Simultaneous Subs:** no

**Reading Period:** Year-round
**Reporting Time:** 1 to 3 months
**Author Payment:** none
**Founded:** 1998
**Non Profit:** yes
**Paid Staff:** 0
**Unpaid Staff:** 10
**ISSN Number/ISBN Number:** ISSN pending
**Average Page Views per Month:** 15,000
**Average Unique Visitors per Month:** 1,500
**Publish Print Anthology:** yes
**Average Percentage of Pages per Category:** Fiction 25%, Poetry 50%, Essays 25%
**Ads:** no

## Memorious: A Forum for New Verse and Poetics

**Type:** online
**CLMP member:** yes
**Primary Editor/Contact Person:** Robert Arnold
**Address:** 1 Stinson Ct. #3
Cambridge, MA 02139
**Web Site Address:** http://www.memorious.org
**Publishes:** essays, fiction, nonfiction, poetry, reviews, art, translation, and audio
**Editorial Focus:** Outstanding poetry and fiction by both established and emerging writers.
**Representative Authors:** Sean Singer, David Rivard, and Maggie Dietz
**Submissions Policy:** Accepts e-mail submissions, simultaneous submissions if notified. Check website for guidelines.
**Simultaneous Subs:** yes
**Reading Period:** Year-round
**Reporting Time:** 1 to 3 months
**Author Payment:** none
**Founded:** 2003
**Non Profit:** yes
**Paid Staff:** 0
**Unpaid Staff:** 3
**Average Page Views per Month:** 4,500
**Average Unique Visitors per Month:** 900
**Frequency per Year:** 4
**Publish Print Anthology:** no
**Average Percentage of Pages per Category:** Fiction 20%, Nonfiction 5%, Poetry 60%, Reviews 5%, Essays 5%, Art 1%, Translation 3%, Audio 1%
**Ads:** no

## Mercury House

**Type:** press
**CLMP member:** no
**Primary Editor/Contact Person:** K. Janene-Nelson
**Address:** P.O. Box 192850
San Francisco, CA 94119-2850
**Web Site Address:** http://www.mercuryhouse.org
**Publishes:** essays, fiction, nonfiction, and translation
**Editorial Focus:** We are a nonprofit press guided by a dedication to literary values and works of social significance.
**Representative Authors:** Leonard Michaels, William Kittredge, and Bill Porter/Red Pine
**Submissions Policy:** We are not currently accepting submissions.
**Simultaneous Subs:** no
**Author Payment:** royalties and cash
**Founded:** 1985
**Non Profit:** yes
**Paid Staff:** 1
**Unpaid Staff:** 5
**Distributors:** Consortium
**Wholesalers:** various
**ISSN Number/ISBN Number:** ISBN 1-56279-
**Number of Books Published per Year:** 1
**Titles in Print:** 85
**Average Percentage Printed:** Hardcover 10%, Paperback 90%

## The Mercury Press

**Type:** press
**CLMP member:** no
**Primary Editor/Contact Person:** Beverley Daurio
**Address:** 22 Prince Rupert Ave.
Toronto, ON M6P 2A7
**Web Site Address:** http://www.themercurypress.ca
**Publishes:** fiction, nonfiction, poetry, and translation
**Editorial Focus:** The Mercury Press publishes poetry, fiction, murder mysteries, and culturally significant nonfiction by Canadian authors.
**Representative Authors:** Nicole Brossard, Sandra Shamas, and bp nichol
**Submissions Policy:** Manuscripts must be word typewritten on one side of page, double spaced. SASE. Only Canadian authors.
**Simultaneous Subs:** yes
**Reading Period:** Year-round
**Reporting Time:** 4 to 6 weeks
**Author Payment:** royalties
**Founded:** 1978
**Non Profit:** no

**Paid Staff:** 2
**Unpaid Staff:** 0
**Distributors:** LitDistCo
**ISSN Number/ISBN Number:** ISBN 1-55128
**Number of Books Published per Year:** 9
**Titles in Print:** 140
**Average Percentage Printed:** Paperback 100%

# Meridian

**Type:** magazine
**CLMP member:** no
**Primary Editor/Contact Person:** James Livingood
**Address:** P.O. Box 400145
University of Virginia
Charlottesville, VA 22904-4145
**Web Site Address:** http://www.readmeridian.org
**Publishes:** essays, fiction, nonfiction, reviews, art, and translation
**Editorial Focus:** Ambitious, well-crafted literary fiction and poetry. We publish Nobel Prize-winners and first-time authors.
**Representative Authors:** Seamus Heaney, Ann Beattie, and Heather McHugh
**Submissions Policy:** Electronic submissions begin 10/1/05. If postal, include SASE. If simultaneous submission, mention in cover letter.
**Simultaneous Subs:** yes
**Reading Period:** 9/1 to 5/1
**Reporting Time:** 2 to 3 months
**Author Payment:** cash and copies
**Contests:** Annual $1,000 prizes in poetry and fiction; Dec. due date. See Web site.
**Founded:** 1998
**Non Profit:** yes
**Paid Staff:** 3
**Unpaid Staff:** 5
**Distributors:** Ingram
**ISSN Number/ISBN Number:** ISSN 1527-3555
**Total Circulation:** 1,000
**Paid Circulation:** 660
**Average Print Run:** 1,100
**Subscription Rate:** Individual $10/Institution $15
**Single Copy Price:** $7
**Current Volume/Issue:** Issue 14
**Frequency per Year:** 2
**Backfile Available:** yes
**Unsolicited Ms. Received:** yes
**% of Unsolicited Ms. Published per Year:** 3%
**Format:** perfect
**Size:** H 9.25" W 6.5"

**Average Pages:** 150
**Ads:** yes
**Ad Rates:** $150/page

# Michigan State University Press

**Type:** press
**CLMP member:** no
**Primary Editor/Contact Person:** Martha A. Bates
**Address:** 1405 S. Harrison Road, Ste. 25
East Lansing, MI 48823
**Web Site Address:** http://www.msupress. msu.edu
**Publishes:** essays, fiction, nonfiction, and poetry
**Editorial Focus:** Scholarly nonfiction, memoir, fiction, and poetry: Great Lakes, Environment, Rhetoric, Native American, Black American
**Representative Authors:** Valerie Miner, Martin J. Medhurst, and Gordon Henry
**Submissions Policy:** Query letter with sample chapters to Acquisitions Editor
**Simultaneous Subs:** no
**Reading Period:** Year-round
**Reporting Time:** 4 to 6 months
**Author Payment:** royalties
**Contests:** Kohr-Campbell book award for Rhetoric and Public Affairs
See Web Site for Contest Guidelines.
**Founded:** 1948
**Non Profit:** yes
**Paid Staff:** 13
**Unpaid Staff:** 5
**Number of Books Published per Year:** 35
**Titles in Print:** 468
**Average Percentage Printed:** Hardcover 35%, Paperback 65%

# Mid-American Review

**Type:** magazine
**CLMP member:** yes
**Primary Editor/Contact Person:** Michael Czyzniejewski
**Address:** Department of English
Bowling Green State University
Bowling Green, OH 43403
**Web Site Address:** http://www.bgsu.edu/midamericanreview
**Publishes:** essays, fiction, nonfiction, poetry, reviews, and translation
**Editorial Focus:** Our goal is to put the best contemporary work in front of the largest audience, including

both new and established writers.

**Representative Authors:** Robin Becker, David Kirby, and Steve Almond

**Submissions Policy:** Send previously unpublished work and a cover letter, 2-6 poems or 6,000 words of prose. See web site for more information.

**Simultaneous Subs:** yes

**Reading Period:** Year-round

**Reporting Time:** 1 to 4 months

**Author Payment:** copies and subscription

**Contests:** See Web Site for Contest Guidelines.

**Founded:** 1981

**Non Profit:** yes

**Paid Staff:** 2

**Unpaid Staff:** 25-30

**Distributors:** DeBoer

**Wholesalers:** Swets

**ISSN Number/ISBN Number:** ISSN 0747-8895

**Total Circulation:** 2,200

**Paid Circulation:** 1,100

**Average Print Run:** 2,500

**Subscription Rate:** Individual $12/Institution $9.60

**Single Copy Price:** $9

**Current Volume/Issue:** XXVI/1

**Frequency per Year:** 2

**Backfile Available:** yes

**Unsolicited Ms. Received:** yes

**% of Unsolicited Ms. Published per Year:** 85%

**Format:** perfect

**Size:** H 9" W 6"

**Average Pages:** 224

**Ads:** yes

**Ad Rates:** free exchange ads, or $250 per page See Web Site for Details.

## Midnight Mind Magazine

**Type:** magazine

**CLMP member:** no

**Primary Editor/Contact Person:** Brett Van Emst

**Address:** P.O. Box 146912
Chicago, IL 60614

**Web Site Address:** http://www.midnightmind.com

**Publishes:** essays, fiction, nonfiction, poetry, reviews, and art

**Editorial Focus:** Midnight Mind Magazine is a cultural review magazine

**Representative Authors:** Denis Johnson, Jim Harrison, and Rick Moody

**Submissions Policy:** Send it to us. If it is something for our columns, let us know that. If it is a submission

for the magazine in general (features) check the web site for theme.

**Simultaneous Subs:** yes

**Reading Period:** Year-round

**Reporting Time:** 1 to 52 weeks

**Author Payment:** copies

**Founded:** 2000

**Non Profit:** no

**Paid Staff:** 2

**Unpaid Staff:** 2

**Distributors:** DeBoer, Ingram, Tower Records

**ISSN Number/ISBN Number:** ISBN 1540-3130

**Total Circulation:** 1,600

**Paid Circulation:** 120

**Subscription Rate:** Individual $12/Institution $12

**Single Copy Price:** $7.95

**Current Volume/Issue:** 1/5

**Frequency per Year:** 2

**Backfile Available:** yes

**Unsolicited Ms. Received:** yes

**% of Unsolicited Ms. Published per Year:** 70%

**Format:** perfect

**Size:** H 10" W 8"

**Average Pages:** 160

**Ads:** yes

**Ad Rates:** contact advert@midnightmind.com See Web Site for Details.

## Milkweed Editions

**Type:** press

**CLMP member:** yes

**Primary Editor/Contact Person:** Sid Farrar

**Address:** 1011 Washington Ave. S., Ste. 300
Minneapolis, MN 55415-1246

**Web Site Address:** http://www.milkweed.org

**Publishes:** essays, fiction, nonfiction, and poetry

**Editorial Focus:** Milkweed Editions publishes literary writing with the intention of making a humane impact on society.

**Representative Authors:** Seth Kantner, Faith Sullivan, and Bill Holm

**Submissions Policy:** Please visit our submission guidelines at http://www.milkweed.org.

**Simultaneous Subs:** yes

**Reading Period:** Year-round

**Reporting Time:** 1 to 6 months

**Author Payment:** royalties

**Contests:** Milkweed National Fiction Prize and Milkweed Prize for Children's Literature See Web Site for Contest Guidelines.

**Founded:** 1979
**Non Profit:** yes
**Paid Staff:** 10
**Unpaid Staff:** 6
**Distributors:** Publishers Group West
**ISSN Number/ISBN Number:** ISBN 1-57131
**Number of Books Published per Year:** 15
**Titles in Print:** 200
**Average Percentage Printed:** Hardcover 25%, Paperback 75%
**Backfile Available:** yes

## the minnesota review

**Type:** magazine
**CLMP member:** yes
**Primary Editor/Contact Person:** Jeff Williams
**Address:** Carnegie Mellon University
Department of English
Pittsburgh, PA 15213-3890
**Web Site Address:** http://theminnesotareview.org
**Publishes:** essays, fiction, nonfiction, poetry, reviews, and translation
**Editorial Focus:** Cultural politics
**Representative Authors:** Bruce Robbins, Barbara Foley, and Jim Daniels
**Simultaneous Subs:** yes
**Reading Period:** Year-round
**Reporting Time:** 2 to 4 months
**Author Payment:** copies
**Founded:** 1960
**Non Profit:** yes
**Paid Staff:** 3
**Unpaid Staff:** 3
**Distributors:** Ubiquity, DeBoer
**Total Circulation:** 1,500
**Paid Circulation:** 600
**Subscription Rate:** Individual $30/Institution $55
**Single Copy Price:** $15
**Current Volume/Issue:** Issue 63
**Frequency per Year:** 2
**Backfile Available:** yes
**Unsolicited Ms. Received:** yes
**% of Unsolicited Ms. Published per Year:** 5%
**Format:** perfect
**Size:** H 8.5" W 5.5"
**Ads:** yes

## MiPo Magazine

**Type:** online
**CLMP member:** no
**Primary Editor/Contact Person:** Didi Menendez
**Address:** 9240 SW 44 St.
Miami, FL 33165
**Web Site Address:** http://www.mipoesias.com
**Publishes:** essays, fiction, nonfiction, poetry, reviews, art, and audio
**Editorial Focus:** Our mission is to make digital publications the standard. We promote established and new writers via the Internet.
**Representative Authors:** David Trinidad, Denise Duhamel, and Lyn Lifshin
**Submissions Policy:** We accept submission via e-mail to editor@mipoesias.com. We do not accept previously published works.
**Simultaneous Subs:** yes
**Reading Period:** Year-round
**Reporting Time:** 1 to 3 months
**Author Payment:** none
**Contests:** Bonsai Project. Our poetry board participates in the IBPC and PBL.
See Web Site for Contest Guidelines.
**Founded:** 2000
**Non Profit:** yes
**Paid Staff:** 0
**Unpaid Staff:** 6
**ISSN Number/ISBN Number:** ISSN 1543-6063
**Average Page Views per Month:** 9,000
**Average Unique Visitors per Month:** 2,500
**Frequency per Year:** 10
**Publish Print Anthology:** no
**Average Percentage of Pages per Category:** Fiction 10%, Nonfiction 10%, Poetry 40%, Essays 5%, Art 30%, Audio 5%
**Ads:** no

## Mississippi Review

**Type:** magazine
**CLMP member:** yes
**Primary Editor/Contact Person:** Frederick Barthelme
**Address:** 118 College Dr., #5144
Hattiesburg, MS 39406-5144
**Web Site Address:** http://www.mississippireview.com
**Publishes:** fiction and poetry
**Editorial Focus:** Contemporary fiction and poetry.
**Representative Authors:** Marlys West, Lisa Glatt, and Stacey Richter
**Submissions Policy:** Reading only for MR Prize com-

petition. Not reading unsolicited work at this time.
**Simultaneous Subs:** yes
**Reading Period:** 4/1 to 10/1
**Reporting Time:** 2 to 3 months
**Author Payment:** copies
**Contests:** See Web Site for Contest Guidelines.
**Founded:** 1971
**Non Profit:** yes
**Paid Staff:** 3
**Unpaid Staff:** 6
**Distributors:** DeBoer
**ISSN Number/ISBN Number:** ISSN 0047-7559
**Total Circulation:** 2,000
**Paid Circulation:** 200
**Average Print Run:** 2,000
**Subscription Rate:** Individual $15/27/40/Institution same
**Single Copy Price:** $12
**Current Volume/Issue:** 32/3
**Frequency per Year:** 2
**Backfile Available:** yes
**Unsolicited Ms. Received:** no
**Format:** perfect
**Size:** H 8.5" W 5.5"
**Average Pages:** 170
**Ads:** yes
**Ad Rates:** $100/page

# Mississippireview.com

**Type:** online
**CLMP member:** no
**Primary Editor/Contact Person:** Frederick Barthelme
**Address:** Box 5144
Hattiesburg, MS 39402
**Web Site Address:** http://mississippireview.com
**Publishes:** essays, fiction, nonfiction, poetry, reviews, art, and translation
**Editorial Focus:** Not reprints and not an ad for our print mag, we publish new literary work selected by our editors. See site for details.
**Representative Authors:** Stacey Richter, Rick Bass, and David Kirby
**Submissions Policy:** See web site. We have guest editors for each issue.
**Simultaneous Subs:** yes
**Reading Period:** Year-round
**Reporting Time:** 1 to 12 weeks
**Author Payment:** none
**Contests:** See Mississippi Review Prize, annual contest associated with our print magazine.

See Web Site for Contest Guidelines.
**Founded:** 1995
**Non Profit:** yes
**Paid Staff:** 1
**Unpaid Staff:** 14
**Distributors:** online
**Average Page Views per Month:** 42,641
**Average Unique Visitors per Month:** 15,662
**Frequency per Year:** 4
**Publish Print Anthology:** no
**Average Percentage of Pages per Category:** Fiction 50%, Nonfiction 10%, Poetry 30%, Essays 10%
**Ad Rates:** See Web Site for Details.

# The Missouri Review

**Type:** magazine
**CLMP member:** yes
**Primary Editor/Contact Person:** Hoa Ngo
**Address:** 1507 Hillcrest Hall, UMC
Columbia, MO 65211
**Web Site Address:** http://www.missourireview.com
**Publishes:** essays, fiction, nonfiction, poetry, reviews, and art
**Editorial Focus:** For over twenty-five years we've upheld a reputation for finding and publishing the very best writers first.
**Representative Authors:** Andrea Barrett, Robert Olen Butler, and Talvikki Ansel
**Simultaneous Subs:** yes
**Reading Period:** Year-round
**Reporting Time:** 6 to 8 weeks
**Author Payment:** cash and copies
**Contests:** Editors' Prize in Fiction and Essay, Larry Levis Prize in Poetry. $2,000 and publication in each category. Deadline Oct 15.
See Web Site for Contest Guidelines.
**Founded:** 1978
**Non Profit:** yes
**Paid Staff:** 6
**Unpaid Staff:** 14
**Distributors:** Ingram
**ISSN Number/ISBN Number:** ISBN 7447081278
**Total Circulation:** 6,500
**Paid Circulation:** 5,000
**Subscription Rate:** Individual $22/Institution $40
**Single Copy Price:** $7.95
**Current Volume/Issue:** 26/2
**Frequency per Year:** 3
**Backfile Available:** yes
**Unsolicited Ms. Received:** yes

**% of Unsolicited Ms. Published per Year:** 90%
**Format:** perfect
**Size:** H 9" W 6"
**Average Pages:** 208
**Ads:** yes
**Ad Rates:** $500 per page or exchange
See Web Site for Details.

# The Mochila Review

**Type:** magazine
**CLMP member:** no
**Primary Editor/Contact Person:** Bill Church
**Address:** Missouri Western State College
4525 Downs Dr.
St. Joseph, MO 64507
**Web Site Address:** http://www.mwsc.edu/eflj/mochila/index.h
**Publishes:** essays, fiction, nonfiction, and poetry
**Editorial Focus:** Seeking quality writing in all genres. Fresh voices, fresh topics, fresh treatments.
**Representative Authors:** Ron McFarland, Murzban Shroff, and Sandra Kohler
**Submissions Policy:** Please specify genre on envelope and submit genres separately.
**Simultaneous Subs:** yes
**Reading Period:** 9/1 to 11/1
**Reporting Time:** 2 to 3 months
**Author Payment:** copies
**Contests:** John Gilgun Literary Awards annually in fiction and poetry.
See Web Site for Contest Guidelines.
**Founded:** 1998
**Non Profit:** yes
**Paid Staff:** 2
**Unpaid Staff:** 10
**Distributors:** Missouri Western State College
**Total Circulation:** 300
**Paid Circulation:** 25
**Subscription Rate:** Individual $6/Institution $6
**Single Copy Price:** $6
**Current Volume/Issue:** 4/1
**Frequency per Year:** 1
**Backfile Available:** yes
**Unsolicited Ms. Received:** yes
**% of Unsolicited Ms. Published per Year:** 5%
**Format:** perfect
**Size:** H 9" W 6"
**Average Pages:** 152
**Ads:** no

# Montemayor Press

**Type:** press
**CLMP member:** yes
**Primary Editor/Contact Person:** Edward Myers
**Address:** P.O. Box 526
Millburn, NJ 07041
**Web Site Address:**
http://www.montemayorpress.com
**Publishes:** fiction and nonfiction
**Editorial Focus:** literary fiction, young-adult fiction, general nonfiction, books about the Latino experience in America
**Recent Awards Received:** Silver Award, Young-Adult Fiction category, 2004 ForeWord Magazine Book of the Year Awards (for ICE)
**Representative Authors:** Joanne Greenberg, Meredith Sue Willis, and Adrian Rodriguez
**Submissions Policy:** by invitation only; no unsolicited manuscripts accepted until further notice
**Simultaneous Subs:** no
**Reading Period:** Year-round
**Reporting Time:** 1 to 2 months
**Author Payment:** royalties and copies
**Founded:** 1999
**Non Profit:** no
**Paid Staff:** 1
**Unpaid Staff:** 0
**Wholesalers:** Ingram, Baker & Taylor, Quality Books Inc., Follett
**ISSN Number/ISBN Number:** ISBN 0-9674477-, 1-932727
**Number of Books Published per Year:** 2-3
**Titles in Print:** 12
**Average Print Run:** 2,000
**Average Percentage Printed:** Paperback 100%
**Average Price:** $12.95

# Moon City Review

**Type:** magazine
**CLMP member:** yes
**Address:** English Dept., Southwest Missouri State University
901 S. National Ave.
Springfield, MO 65804
**Web Site Address:**
http://www.smsu.edu/English/moon_city_review.htm
**Publishes:** essays, fiction, nonfiction, poetry, and reviews
**Reading Period:** Year-round
**Reporting Time:** 1 to 2 months

**Author Payment:** none
**Founded:** 1905
**Non Profit:** yes
**Backfile Available:** yes

## The Moonwort Review

**Type:** online
**CLMP member:** yes
**Primary Editor/Contact Person:** Robert Rutherford
**Address:** 1160 Buckeye Rd.
Elk Park, NC 28622
**Web Site Address:**
http://www.themoonwortreview.com
**Publishes:** essays, fiction, poetry, reviews, art, and translation
**Editorial Focus:** TMR is interested in well written, cutting edge fiction. Stories that go somewhere. Poetry that contains interesting word choices. Thought provoking images. Essays on almost any subject but, we favor thoughts on writing. We are interested in book reviews. A query to the editors is a good idea for reviews. We also consider book promotion by publishers and authors.
**Representative Authors:** Lee Upton, Sara Claytor, and Tom Sheehan
**Submissions Policy:** We accept both snail-mail and electronic submissions. Best if electronic submissions are in the body of your e-mail message. We will open attachments if the information about your submission is clearly defined in your message. Include something about yourself as well as previously published credits. Who you are is less important than the writing quality.
**Simultaneous Subs:** yes
**Reading Period:** Year-round
**Reporting Time:** 8 to 16 weeks
**Author Payment:** none
**Founded:** 2001
**Non Profit:** yes
**Paid Staff:** non
**Unpaid Staff:** 2-3
**Average Page Views per Month:** 5,000
**Average Unique Visitors per Month:** 5,000
**Frequency per Year:** 4
**Publish Print Anthology:** no
**Average Percentage of Pages per Category:** Fiction 40%, Poetry 40%, Reviews 10%, Essays 10%
**Ads:** no

## Mosaic Literary Magazine

**Type:** magazine
**CLMP member:** yes
**Primary Editor/Contact Person:** Ron Kavanaugh
**Address:** 314 W 231st St, Ste 470
#470
Bronx, NY 10463
**Web Site Address:** http://www.mosaicbooks.com
**Publishes:** essays, fiction, nonfiction, poetry, and reviews
**Editorial Focus:** Mosaic Literary Magazine showcases and critiques Black and Latino literature.
**Representative Authors:** Nelly Rosario, Major Jackson, and Colson Whitehead
**Submissions Policy:** Mosaic considers unsolicited essays and criticism. We do not consider unsolicited book reviews.
**Simultaneous Subs:** yes
**Reading Period:** Year-round
**Reporting Time:** 8 to 12 weeks
**Author Payment:** cash and copies
**Founded:** 1997
**Non Profit:** yes
**Paid Staff:** 0
**Unpaid Staff:** 3
**ISSN Number/ISBN Number:** ISSN 1531-0388
**Total Circulation:** 1,500
**Paid Circulation:** 600
**Average Print Run:** 1,500
**Subscription Rate:** Individual $12/Institution $25
**Single Copy Price:** $4
**Current Volume/Issue:** Issue 14
**Frequency per Year:** 4
**Backfile Available:** yes
**Unsolicited Ms. Received:** no
**% of Unsolicited Ms. Published per Year:** 50%
**Format:** stapled
**Size:** H 10.5" W 8"
**Average Pages:** 50
**Ads:** yes
**Ad Rates:** $600/full page
See Web Site for Details.

## Mslexia

**Type:** magazine
**CLMP member:** no
**Primary Editor/Contact Person:** Debbie Taylor
**Address:** P.O. Box 656
Newcastle Upon Tyne, UK NE1 4XF
**Web Site Address:** http://www.mslexia.co.uk

**Publishes:** fiction, poetry, reviews, and art
**Editorial Focus:** The magazine for women who write. Advice and inspiration; news, reviews, interviews; competitions and grants.
**Representative Authors:** Wendy Cope (Guest Editor), Carol Ann Duffy (Guest Editor), and Helen Dunmore (Guest Editor)
**Submissions Policy:** Article proposal by e-mail. Up to 4 poems of up to 40 lines; up to 2 stories of up to 3,000 words on our current themes.
**Simultaneous Subs:** yes
**Reading Period:** Year-round
**Reporting Time:** 0 to 3 months
**Author Payment:** cash and copies
**Contests:** Women's Poetry Competition, Entry fee: Up to 5 poems for £5. Deadline each April. £1,000 first prize. £500 2nd, £250 3rd.
See Web Site for Contest Guidelines.
**Founded:** 1999
**Non Profit:** yes
**Paid Staff:** 6
**Unpaid Staff:** 0
**Distributors:** Jordans & Company International Limited
**Total Circulation:** 20,000
**Paid Circulation:** 10,500
**Average Print Run:** 300
**Subscription Rate:** Individual £30
**Single Copy Price:** £7.50
**Current Volume/Issue:** Issue 27
**Frequency per Year:** 4
**Backfile Available:** yes
**Unsolicited Ms. Received:** yes
**% of Unsolicited Ms. Published per Year:** 10%
**Format:** stapled
**Size:** H 12" W 8.5"
**Average Pages:** 67
**Ads:** yes
**Ad Rates:** £330 half page, £165 quarter page
See Web Site for Details.

# Mudlark

**Type:** online
**CLMP member:** yes
**Primary Editor/Contact Person:** William Slaughter
**Address:** Department of English
4567 St. Johns Bluff Rd., S.
Jacksonville, FL 32224-2645
**Web Site Address:** http://www.unf.edu/mudlark
**Publishes:** poetry

**Editorial Focus:** Accomplished work that locates itself anywhere on the spectrum of contemporary practice.
**Representative Authors:** Ian Randall Wilson, Jesse Lee Kercheval, and Michael Ruby
**Submissions Policy:** To submit or not to submit? Have a look at Mudlark and then decide.
**Simultaneous Subs:** yes
**Reading Period:** Year-round
**Reporting Time:** 1 to 4 weeks
**Author Payment:** none
**Founded:** 1995
**Non Profit:** yes
**Paid Staff:** 0
**Unpaid Staff:** 1
**ISSN Number/ISBN Number:** ISSN 1081-3500
**Backfile Available:** yes
**Average Page Views per Month:** 75,000
**Average Unique Visitors per Month:** 5,000
**Frequency per Year:** 12
**Publish Print Anthology:** no
**Average Percentage of Pages per Category:** Poetry 100%
**Ads:** no

# Murderous Signs

**Type:** magazine
**CLMP member:** no
**Primary Editor/Contact Person:** Grant Wilkins
**Address:** P.O. Box 20517
390 Rideau St.
Ottawa, ON K1N 1A3
**Web Site Address:**
http://www.grungepapers.com/msigns
**Publishes:** essays, fiction, nonfiction, and poetry
**Editorial Focus:** Dedicated to the notion that the printed word, well crafted and aimed, can be used as a weapon.
**Representative Authors:** Stan Rogal, jw curry, and George Elliott Clarke
**Submissions Policy:** Looking for prose, poetry and comment in any style or format.
**Simultaneous Subs:** yes
**Reading Period:** Year-round
**Reporting Time:** 6 to 12 months
**Author Payment:** cash and copies
**Founded:** 2000
**Non Profit:** yes
**Paid Staff:** 0
**Unpaid Staff:** 1
**ISSN Number/ISBN Number:** ISSN 1499-6006

**Total Circulation:** 400
**Paid Circulation:** 50
**Average Print Run:** 400
**Subscription Rate:** Individual $8/4/Institution $8/4
**Single Copy Price:** $2.50
**Current Volume/Issue:** Issue 9
**Frequency per Year:** 2
**Backfile Available:** yes
**Unsolicited Ms. Received:** yes
**% of Unsolicited Ms. Published per Year:** 10%
**Format:** stapled
**Size:** H 8.5" W 5.5"
**Average Pages:** 28
**Ads:** no

## Mystery Scene Magazine

**Type:** magazine
**CLMP member:** yes
**Primary Editor/Contact Person:** Kate Stine
**Address:** 331 W. 57th St., Ste. 148
New York, NY 10019
**Web Site Address:**
http://www.mysteryscenemag.com
**Publishes:** essays, nonfiction, and reviews
**Editorial Focus:** Covers the entire crime and mystery genre-books, TV, films, audio, reference, adult and kids.
**Recent Awards Received:** 2004 Anthony Award "Best Mystery Magazine"
**Submissions Policy:** See website. Query first. No fiction.
**Simultaneous Subs:** no
**Reading Period:** Year-round
**Reporting Time:** 1 to 2 months
**Author Payment:** cash and copies
**Contests:** no
**Founded:** 1985
**Non Profit:** no
**Paid Staff:** 4
**Unpaid Staff:** 0
**Distributors:** Ingram, Ubiquity, Disticor, Small Changes, Kent
**ISSN Number/ISBN Number:** ISSN 1087-674X
**Total Circulation:** 10,000
**Paid Circulation:** 6,000
**Average Print Run:** 12,000
**Subscription Rate:** Individual $32/Institution $32
**Single Copy Price:** $7.50
**Current Volume/Issue:** 21/91
**Frequency per Year:** 5

**Backfile Available:** yes
**Unsolicited Ms. Received:** yes
**% of Unsolicited Ms. Published per Year:** 30%
**Format:** e-mail
**Average Pages:** 80
**Ad Rates:** See Web Site for Details.

## n+1 Research

**Type:** magazine
**CLMP member:** yes
**Address:** P.O. Box 20688
Park West Finance Station
New York, NY 10025
**Web Site Address:** http://www.nplusonemag.com
**Publishes:** essays, fiction, nonfiction, and reviews
**Reading Period:** Year-round
**Reporting Time:** 1 to 2 months
**Author Payment:** none
**Founded:** 2004
**Non Profit:** yes
**Backfile Available:** yes

## Nanny Fanny Poetry Magazine

**Type:** magazine
**CLMP member:** no
**Primary Editor/Contact Person:** Lou Hertz
**Address:** 2524 Stockbridge Dr #15
Indianapolis, IN 46268-2670
**Publishes:** poetry and reviews
**Editorial Focus:** "Nanny Fanny" publishes mostly character studies with a preference for accessible, upbeat poems.
**Representative Authors:** John Grey, Ellaraine Lockie, and Edward Michael Supranowicz
**Submissions Policy:** Prefer 3-8 poems at a time, 8 to 30 lines. A cover letter is preferred, SASE is a must.
**Simultaneous Subs:** no
**Reading Period:** Year-round
**Reporting Time:** 6 to 10 weeks
**Author Payment:** copies
**Founded:** 1998
**Non Profit:** no
**Paid Staff:** 0
**Unpaid Staff:** 1
**ISSN Number/ISBN Number:** ISSN 1529-434X
**Total Circulation:** 150
**Paid Circulation:** 40
**Subscription Rate:** Individual $10/Institution $10
**Single Copy Price:** $4

**Current Volume/Issue:** Issue 20
**Frequency per Year:** 3
**Backfile Available:** yes
**Unsolicited Ms. Received:** yes
**% of Unsolicited Ms. Published per Year:** 8%
**Format:** stapled
**Size:** H 8 1/2" W 5 1/2"
**Average Pages:** 40
**Ads:** Not using advertising currently but would consider it

## Natural Bridge

**Type:** magazine
**CLMP member:** no
**Primary Editor/Contact Person:** Steven Schreiner
**Address:** University of Missouri-St. Louis
One University Blvd.
St. Louis, MO 63121
**Web Site Address:** http://www.umsl.edu/~natural
**Publishes:** essays, fiction, nonfiction, poetry, and translation
**Editorial Focus:** Eclectic mix of quality contemporary literature, no specific genre expectations.
**Representative Authors:** Beckian Fritz Goldberg, Timothy Liu, and Mark Jay Mirsky
**Submissions Policy:** Regular mail. Submit in one genre only. Enclose SASE. 2 reading periods: 11/1-12/31 and 7/1-8/31. Check website for guidelines.
**Simultaneous Subs:** yes
**Reading Period:** 11/1 to 12/31
**Reporting Time:** 3 to 5 months
**Author Payment:** copies and subscription
**Contests:** no
**Founded:** 1998
**Non Profit:** yes
**Paid Staff:** 0
**Unpaid Staff:** 12
**Distributors:** Ubiquity
**ISSN Number/ISBN Number:** ISSN 1525-9897
**Total Circulation:** 900
**Paid Circulation:** 200
**Average Print Run:** 900
**Subscription Rate:** Individual $12/Institution $18
**Single Copy Price:** $8
**Current Volume/Issue:** Issue 16
**Frequency per Year:** 2
**Backfile Available:** yes
**Unsolicited Ms. Received:** yes
**% of Unsolicited Ms. Published per Year:** 3%
**Format:** perfect

**Size:** H 8" W 6"
**Average Pages:** 225
**Ads:** no
**Ad Rates:** exchange only

## Neshui

**Type:** press
**CLMP member:** no
**Primary Editor/Contact Person:** Bradley Hodge
**Address:** 8029 Forsyth Blvd. Ste. 204
St. Louis, MO 63105
**Web Site Address:** http://www.neshui.com
**Publishes:** fiction, nonfiction, poetry, and translation
**Editorial Focus:** fiction and nonfiction books and 10 books of poetry and three books of translations
**Representative Authors:** Qiu Xiaolong, Michael Castro, and Ryan Jones
**Submissions Policy:** please send hard copy
**Simultaneous Subs:** yes
**Reading Period:** Year-round
**Reporting Time:** 6- to 8 weeks
**Author Payment:** royalties
**Founded:** 1995
**Non Profit:** no
**Paid Staff:** 3
**Unpaid Staff:** 40
**Distributors:** Baker & Taylor, Ingram
**ISSN Number/ISBN Number:** 1931190/1931190
**Number of Books Published per Year:** 25
**Titles in Print:** 50
**Average Percentage Printed:** Paperback 100%

## New American Writing

**Type:** magazine
**CLMP member:** no
**Primary Editor/Contact Person:** Paul Hoover
**Address:** 369 Molino Ave.
Mill Valley, CA 94941
**Web Site Address:**
http://www.newamericanwriting.com
**Publishes:** essays, fiction, poetry, and translation
**Editorial Focus:** contemporary American poetry, with emphasis on the innovative, and poetry in translation
**Representative Authors:** Ann Lauterbach, Charles Bernstein, and Nathaniel Mackey
**Submissions Policy:** Send 3-5 poems and stories no longer than 15 pages, with accompanying SASE.
**Simultaneous Subs:** yes
**Reading Period:** Year-round

**Reporting Time:** 2 to 3 weeks
**Author Payment:** copies
**Founded:** 1986
**Non Profit:** yes
**Paid Staff:** 0
**Unpaid Staff:** 2
**Distributors:** Ingram
**ISSN Number/ISBN Number:** 0893-7842/none
**Total Circulation:** 3,500
**Paid Circulation:** 202
**Average Print Run:** 3,500
**Subscription Rate:** Individual $27/Institution $36
**Single Copy Price:** $10
**Current Volume/Issue:** Issue 23
**Frequency per Year:** 1
**Backfile Available:** yes
**Unsolicited Ms. Received:** yes
**% of Unsolicited Ms. Published per Year:** 5%
**Format:** perfect
**Size:** H 5.5" W 8.5"
**Average Pages:** 175
**Ads:** yes
**Ad Rates:** $250/page; $200/page for two or more ads.

## The New Compass: A Critical Review

**Type:** online
**CLMP member:** no
**Primary Editor/Contact Person:** Michael John DiSanto
**Address:** 35 Flannery Ln.
Thorold, ON L2V 4V8
**Web Site Address:** http://www.thenewcompass.ca
**Publishes:** essays, fiction, nonfiction, poetry, reviews, and translation
**Editorial Focus:** We are interested in ethics and aesthetics and we invite critical essays on literature in English from a range of periods.
**Submissions Policy:** Electronic submissions are preferred. Use MS Word (.doc) attachment. Please include short abstract and biographical note.
**Simultaneous Subs:** no
**Reading Period:** Year-round
**Reporting Time:** 1 to 3 months
**Author Payment:** none
**Founded:** 2002
**Non Profit:** yes
**Paid Staff:** 0
**Unpaid Staff:** 5
**ISSN Number/ISBN Number:** ISSN 1708-3133

**Average Page Views per Month:** 250
**Average Unique Visitors per Month:** 100
**Frequency per Year:** 2
**Publish Print Anthology:** no
**Average Percentage of Pages per Category:** Fiction 3%, Nonfiction 2%, Poetry 10%, Reviews 25%, Essays 60%
**Ads:** no

## New Delta Review

**Type:** magazine
**CLMP member:** no
**Address:** Department of English
Louisiana State University
Baton Rouge, LA 70803-5001
**Web Site Address:** http://english.lsu.edu/journals/ndr
**Publishes:** essays, fiction, nonfiction, poetry, art, and translation
**Reading Period:** Year-round
**Reporting Time:** 1 to 2 months
**Author Payment:** none
**Founded:** 1984
**Non Profit:** no

## New Directions Publishing

**Type:** press
**CLMP member:** no
**Primary Editor/Contact Person:** Peggy Fox
**Address:** 80 8th Ave, 19th Fl
NYC, NY 10011
**Web Site Address:** http://www.ndpublishing.com
**Publishes:** essays, fiction, poetry, and translation
**Editorial Focus:** Contemporary literary fiction and poetry.
**Representative Authors:** W.G. Sebald, Hilda Doolittle, and Ezra Pound
**Simultaneous Subs:** no
**Reading Period:** Year-round
**Reporting Time:** 3 to 4 months
**Author Payment:** royalties, cash, and copies
**Founded:** 1934
**Non Profit:** no
**Paid Staff:** 10
**Unpaid Staff:** 0
**Number of Books Published per Year:** 30
**Titles in Print:** 900
**Average Percentage Printed:** Hardcover 15%, Paperback 85%

# New England Review

**Type:** magazine
**CLMP member:** yes
**Primary Editor/Contact Person:** Carolyn Kuebler
**Address:** Middlebury College
Middlebury, VT 05753
**Web Site Address:** http://go.middlebury.edu/nereview
**Publishes:** essays, fiction, nonfiction, poetry, reviews, and translation
**Editorial Focus:** Committed to all forms of contemporary cultural expression in the US and abroad.
**Representative Authors:** Brigit Pegeen Kelly, Janet Kauffman, and Paul Muldoon
**Submissions Policy:** see submission guidelines at http://www.middlebury.edu/~nereview.guidelines.html
**Simultaneous Subs:** yes
**Reading Period:** 9/1 to 5/31
**Reporting Time:** 10 to 12 weeks
**Author Payment:** cash and copies
**Founded:** 1978
**Non Profit:** yes
**Paid Staff:** 3
**Unpaid Staff:** 0
**Distributors:** Ingram, Ubiquity, DeBoer
**ISSN Number/ISBN Number:** ISSN 1053-1297
**Total Circulation:** 2,000
**Paid Circulation:** 1,000
**Average Print Run:** 2,000
**Subscription Rate:** Individual $25/Institution $40
**Single Copy Price:** $8
**Current Volume/Issue:** 26/3
**Frequency per Year:** 4
**Backfile Available:** yes
**Unsolicited Ms. Received:** yes
**% of Unsolicited Ms. Published per Year:** 95%
**Format:** perfect
**Size:** H 10" W 7"
**Average Pages:** 230
**Ads:** yes
**Ad Rates:** call for information

# New Letters Magazine

**Type:** magazine
**CLMP member:** yes
**Primary Editor/Contact Person:** Robert Stewart
**Address:** University House
5101 Rockhill Road
Kansas City, MO 64110
**Web Site Address:** http://www.newletters.org

**Publishes:** essays, fiction, poetry, reviews, art, and translation
**Editorial Focus:** To continue the 70-year tradition of finding the best writing that is fresh and on the cutting edge in style and content.
**Representative Authors:** Sherman Alexie, Naomi Shihab Nye, and Albert Goldbarth
**Submissions Policy:** Please see our website for complete writer's and artist's guidelines.
**Simultaneous Subs:** yes
**Reading Period:** 5/1 to 10/1
**Reporting Time:** 4 to 18 weeks
**Author Payment:** cash and copies
**Contests:** See Web Site for Contest Guidelines.
**Founded:** 1934
**Non Profit:** yes
**Paid Staff:** 3
**Unpaid Staff:** 4
**Distributors:** Ingram and DeBoer
**ISSN Number/ISBN Number:** ISSN 0146-4930
**Total Circulation:** varies
**Paid Circulation:** 2,000
**Average Print Run:** 3,500
**Subscription Rate:** Individual $22/Institution $30
**Single Copy Price:** $10
**Current Volume/Issue:** 72/1
**Frequency per Year:** 4
**Backfile Available:** yes
**Unsolicited Ms. Received:** yes
**% of Unsolicited Ms. Published per Year:** 90%
**Format:** perfect
**Size:** H 9" W 6"
**Average Pages:** 150
**Ads:** yes
**Ad Rates:** exchange ads offered; paid ads start at $150.

# New Michigan Press

**Type:** press
**Primary Editor/Contact Person:** Ander Monson
**Address:** 648 Crescent NE
Grand Rapids, MI 49503
**Web Site Address:**
http://newmichiganpress.com/nmp
**Publishes:** fiction, nonfiction, and poetry
**Editorial Focus:** Literary fiction, poetry, and especially genre-bending or -transcending work.
**Representative Authors:** Simone Muench, Arielle Greenberg, and G C Waldrep
**Submissions Policy:** We read unsolicited submissions

only through our yearly chapbook contest (guidelines on site), deadline in spring.
**Simultaneous Subs:** yes
**Reading Period:** Year-round
**Reporting Time:** 1 to 4 months
**Author Payment:** cash and copies
**Contests:** See Web Site for Contest Guidelines.
**Founded:** 1999
**Non Profit:** no
**Paid Staff:** 1
**Unpaid Staff:** 8
**ISSN Number/ISBN Number:** ISBN 0-9725095
**Number of Books Published per Year:** 4-6
**Titles in Print:** 10
**Average Print Run:** 500
**Average Percentage Printed:** Paperback 10%, Chapbook 90%
**Average Price:** $8

## The New Press

**Type:** press
**CLMP member:** no
**Primary Editor/Contact Person:** Colin Robinson
**Address:** 38 Greene St.
4th Floor
New York, NY 10013
**Web Site Address:** http://thenewpress.com
**Publishes:** essays, nonfiction, and translation
**Editorial Focus:** Contemporary social issues, immigration, human rights, labor and popular economics, education, law, international literature.
**Representative Authors:** Studs Terkel, Mike Davis, and David Cole
**Submissions Policy:** Unsolicited manuscripts and proposals must be submitted with SASE.
**Simultaneous Subs:** yes
**Reading Period:** Year-round
**Reporting Time:** 3 to 6 weeks
**Author Payment:** royalties, cash, and copies
**Founded:** 1984
**Non Profit:** yes
**Paid Staff:** 20
**Unpaid Staff:** 3
**Distributors:** W.W. Norton
**Wholesalers:** Ingram, Baker & Taylor
**ISSN Number/ISBN Number:** ISBN 1-56584-
**Number of Books Published per Year:** 50
**Titles in Print:** 600
**Average Percentage Printed:** Hardcover 54%, Paperback 46%

**Backfile Available:** yes

## New Rivers Press

**Type:** press
**CLMP member:** yes
**Primary Editor/Contact Person:** Donna Carlson, Managing Editor
**Address:** New Rivers Press, MSUM
1104 Seventh Ave. S.
Moorhead, MN 56563
**Web Site Address:** http://www.newriverspress.com
**Publishes:** essays, fiction, nonfiction, poetry, and translation
**Editorial Focus:** We consider work of every character from new and emerging writers, and are especially interested in upper Midwest writers.
**Representative Authors:** Cezarija Abartis, Ron Rindo, and Ronna Wineberg
**Submissions Policy:** We publish 3 books each year in our MVP contest. For information on it and other submissions, go to http://www.newriverspress.com
**Simultaneous Subs:** yes
**Reading Period:** Year-round
**Reporting Time:** 1 to 2 months
**Author Payment:** royalties, cash, and copies
**Contests:** See Web Site for Contest Guidelines.
**Founded:** 1968
**Non Profit:** yes
**Paid Staff:** 3
**Unpaid Staff:** 15+
**Distributors:** Consortium
**ISSN Number/ISBN Number:** ISBN 0-89823-
**Number of Books Published per Year:** 4-6
**Titles in Print:** 314
**Average Print Run:** 1,500
**Average Percentage Printed:** Paperback 100%
**Average Price:** $13.95

## New Star Books

**Type:** press
**CLMP member:** no
**Primary Editor/Contact Person:** Carellin Brooks
**Address:** 107-3477 Commercial St.
Vancouver, BC V5K 1K8
**Web Site Address:** http://www.newstarbooks.com
**Publishes:** fiction, nonfiction, and poetry
**Editorial Focus:** Books on social issues, politics, British Columbia and the West, and literary works. Details on our website.

**Representative Authors:** Andrew Struthers, Brian Fawcett, and Noam Chomsky
**Submissions Policy:** Considers unsolicited fiction MS; does not consider unsolicited poetry. For nonfiction, send query first.
**Simultaneous Subs:** yes
**Reading Period:** Year-round
**Reporting Time:** 4 to 6 months
**Author Payment:** royalties and copies
**Founded:** 1969
**Non Profit:** no
**Paid Staff:** 3
**Unpaid Staff:** 0
**Distributors:** New Star Books
**Number of Books Published per Year:** 12
**Titles in Print:** 76
**Average Print Run:** 1,000
**Average Percentage Printed:** Paperback 100%
**Average Price:** $18

## The New York Quarterly

**Type:** magazine
**CLMP member:** yes
**Primary Editor/Contact Person:** Raymond Hammond
**Address:** P.O. Box 693
Old Chelsea Station
New York, NY 10113
**Web Site Address:** http://www.nyquarterly.com
**Publishes:** essays and poetry
**Editorial Focus:** NYQ is devoted to excellence in the publication of the best cross-section of contemporary poetry.
**Representative Authors:** Charles Bukowski, W.D. Snodgrass, and X.J. Kennedy
**Submissions Policy:** Enclose a SASE and no more than 3-5 typewritten poems.
**Simultaneous Subs:** yes
**Reading Period:** Year-round
**Reporting Time:** 6 to 8 weeks
**Author Payment:** copies
**Founded:** 1969
**Non Profit:** yes
**Paid Staff:** 0
**Unpaid Staff:** 12
**Distributors:** DeBoer, Ubiquity
**ISSN Number/ISBN Number:** ISSN 0028-7482
**Total Circulation:** 1,000
**Paid Circulation:** 800
**Average Print Run:** 1,500
**Subscription Rate:** Individual $20/Institution $28

**Single Copy Price:** $8
**Current Volume/Issue:** Issue 60
**Frequency per Year:** 3
**Backfile Available:** yes
**Unsolicited Ms. Received:** yes
**% of Unsolicited Ms. Published per Year:** 5%
**Format:** perfect
**Size:** H 9" W 6"
**Average Pages:** 128
**Ads:** yes
**Ad Rates:** See Web Site for Details.

## New York Stories

**Type:** magazine
**CLMP member:** yes
**Primary Editor/Contact Person:** Daniel Caplice Lynch
**Address:** 31-10 Thomson Ave. (E-103)
LIC, NY 11101
**Web Site Address:** http://newyorkstories.org
**Publishes:** essays and fiction
**Editorial Focus:** New York Stories seeks to publish the best contemporary short fiction set anywhere and nonfiction with a New York City focus
**Representative Authors:** John Updike, Thomas Beller, and G.K. Wuori
**Submissions Policy:** No more than 6,000 words. Include a brief bio. No genre fiction. Send a query for nonfiction.
**Simultaneous Subs:** yes
**Reading Period:** Year-round
**Reporting Time:** 2 to 6 months
**Author Payment:** cash
**Contests:** See Web Site for Contest Guidelines.
**Founded:** 1998
**Non Profit:** yes
**Paid Staff:** 1
**Unpaid Staff:** 3
**Distributors:** Ingram
**ISSN Number/ISBN Number:** ISSN 1096-2956
**Total Circulation:** 1,200
**Paid Circulation:** 300
**Average Print Run:** 1,500
**Subscription Rate:** Individual $13.40/Institution $16
**Single Copy Price:** $5.95
**Current Volume/Issue:** Fall/2004
**Frequency per Year:** 3
**Backfile Available:** yes
**Unsolicited Ms. Received:** yes
**% of Unsolicited Ms. Published per Year:** 2%
**Format:** stapled

Size: H 11" W 8.5"
Average Pages: 48
Ads: yes
Ad Rates: $300 for a full page or trade
See Web Site for Details.

## The New York Theatre Experience, Inc

Type: press
CLMP member: no
Primary Editor/Contact Person: Martin Denton
Address: P.O. Box 1606
Murray Hill Station
New York, NY 10156
Web Site Address: http://www.nyte.org
Publishes: fiction
Editorial Focus: An annual anthology of plays by emerging playwrights recently produced.
Representative Authors: Paul Knox, Brian Sloan, and Joe Godfrey
Submissions Policy: Plays must be seen live by the editor and staff. No submissions
Simultaneous Subs: no
Reading Period: Year-round
Reporting Time: 1 to 12 months
Author Payment: copies
Founded: 1999
Non Profit: yes
Paid Staff: 1
Unpaid Staff: 1
Distributors: Baker & Taylor Books
Wholesalers: Amazon.com, Drama Bookshop, Barnes & Noble
ISSN Number/ISBN Number: 1546-1319/09670234xx
Number of Books Published per Year: 1
Titles in Print: 5
Average Print Run: 1,500
Average Percentage Printed: Paperback 100%
Average Price: $16

## NeWest Press

Type: press
CLMP member: no
Primary Editor/Contact Person: Amber Rider
Address: 201-8540-109 St.
Edmonton, AB T6G 1E6
Web Site Address: http://www.newestpress.ccom
Publishes: fiction, nonfiction, and poetry

Editorial Focus: The role of NeWest Press in Canadian publishing is to publish the voices of western Canada.
Recent Awards Received: 2005 Alberta Book Awards Trade Fiction Book of the year for Displaced Persons by Margie Taylor
Simultaneous Subs: yes
Reading Period: Year-round
Reporting Time: 6 to 9 months
Author Payment: royalties
Founded: 1977
Non Profit: yes
Paid Staff: 3
Unpaid Staff: 0
Distributors: LitDistCo, Gazelle Book Services
ISSN Number/ISBN Number: ISBN 1896300, 0920897,
Number of Books Published per Year: 12
Titles in Print: 120
Average Print Run: 1,500
Average Percentage Printed: Paperback 100%
Average Price: $20

## Newtopia Magazine

Type: online
CLMP member: no
Primary Editor/Contact Person: Charles Shaw
Address: 4410 N. Wolcott 2S
Chicago, IL 60640
Web Site Address: http://www.newtopiamagazine.net
Publishes: essays, fiction, nonfiction, poetry, reviews, art, and audio
Editorial Focus: a journal of countercultural thought covering alternative art, culture, economics, history, politics, and social movements.
Recent Awards Received: 2005 Democratic Media Award
Representative Authors: Charles Shaw, David Ray Griffin, and Kevin Zeese
Submissions Policy: Guidelines posted on the website.
Simultaneous Subs: yes
Reading Period: Year-round
Reporting Time: 1 to 2 months
Author Payment: none
Founded: 2002
Non Profit: yes
Paid Staff: 0
Unpaid Staff: 35
ISSN Number/ISBN Number: none/none

**Average Page Views per Month:** 813,000
**Average Unique Visitors per Month:** 200,000
**Frequency per Year:** 12
**Publish Print Anthology:** yes
**Average Percentage of Pages per Category:** Fiction 10%, Nonfiction 10%, Poetry 10%, Reviews 10%, Essays 50%, Art 10%
**Ad Rates:** Usually our ads are free endorsements for friends and allies
See Web Site for Details.

# Night Train Publications/Night Train

**Type:** magazine
**CLMP member:** yes
**Primary Editor/Contact Person:** Rusty Barnes
**Address:** 212 Bellingham Ave.
#2
Revere, MA 02151-4106
**Web Site Address:**
http://www.nighttrainmagazine.com
**Publishes:** fiction
**Editorial Focus:** Night Train focuses on Short Fiction exclusively.
**Representative Authors:** Robert Boswell, Edward Falco, and Dylan Landis
**Submissions Policy:** Send one story at a time to submission@nighttrainmagazine.com. No snail-mail submissions.
**Simultaneous Subs:** yes
**Reading Period:** Year-round
**Reporting Time:** 4 to 8 weeks
**Author Payment:** copies and subscription
**Contests:** See Web Site for Contest Guidelines.
**Founded:** 2002
**Non Profit:** yes
**Paid Staff:** 0
**Unpaid Staff:** 10
**Distributors:** DeBoer, Ingram
**ISSN Number/ISBN Number:** ISSN 1540-5494
**Total Circulation:** 2,000
**Paid Circulation:** 300
**Average Print Run:** 2250
**Subscription Rate:** Individual $17.95/Institution $24.95
**Single Copy Price:** $9.95
**Current Volume/Issue:** Issue 5
**Frequency per Year:** 2
**Backfile Available:** yes
**Unsolicited Ms. Received:** yes
**% of Unsolicited Ms. Published per Year:** 90%

**Format:** perfect
**Size:** H 9" W 6"
**Average Pages:** 200
**Ads:** no
**Ad Rates:** See Web Site for Details.

# Nightboat Books

**Type:** press
**CLMP member:** yes
**Primary Editor/Contact Person:** Kazim Ali and Jennifer Chapis
**Address:** P.O. Box 656
Beacon, NY 12508
**Web Site Address:** http://www.nightboat.org
**Publishes:** fiction and poetry
**Editorial Focus:** Innovative poetry, prose, and mixed genre (or anti-genre!) work.
**Representative Authors:** Fanny Howe, Juliet Patterson, and Katherine Dimma
**Submissions Policy:** Poetry: please see website for guidelines. Prose: no unsolicited mss. at this time. Please query with sample chapter.
**Simultaneous Subs:** yes
**Reading Period:** 9/1 to 11/30
**Reporting Time:** 1 to 2 months
**Author Payment:** royalties, cash, and copies
**Contests:** See Web Site for Contest Guidelines.
**Founded:** 2003
**Non Profit:** yes
**Paid Staff:** 0
**Unpaid Staff:** 6
**Wholesalers:** Baker & Taylor
**ISSN Number/ISBN Number:** ISBN 0-9767185
**Number of Books Published per Year:** 2
**Titles in Print:** 5
**Average Print Run:** 1,000
**Average Percentage Printed:** Paperback 100%
**Average Price:** $16

# Nightshade Press

**Type:** press
**CLMP member:** yes
**Primary Editor/Contact Person:** Lynn Marie Petrillo
**Address:** Keystone College
One College Green
La Plume, PA 18440
**Publishes:** fiction, nonfiction, and poetry
**Editorial Focus:** Has been poetry; currently literary work relating to the "Keystone Culture"-education,

diversity, nature, art, enlightenment
**Representative Authors:** Karen Blomain, Martha Silano, and David Watts
**Submissions Policy:** will accept open submissions from authors living in PA, NY, and other areas of the Northeastern US within reading period
**Simultaneous Subs:** yes
**Reading Period:** 4/1 to 9/30
**Reporting Time:** 4 to 10 months
**Author Payment:** copies
**Founded:** 1988
**Non Profit:** yes
**Paid Staff:** 2
**Unpaid Staff:** ~6
**Number of Books Published per Year:** 1
**Titles in Print:** 59
**Average Percentage Printed:** Paperback 100%
**Backfile Available:** yes

# Nimrod International Journal

**Type:** magazine
**CLMP member:** yes
**Primary Editor/Contact Person:** Francine Ringold
**Address:** The University of Tulsa
600 S. College Ave.
Tulsa, OK 74104
**Web Site Address:** http://www.utulsa.edu/nimrod
**Publishes:** fiction, nonfiction, poetry, art, and translation
**Editorial Focus:** We are looking for writing of quality and vigor.
**Representative Authors:** Gina Ochsner, Don Welch, and Virgil Suarez
**Submissions Policy:** Open submissions all year. E-mails only from writers living overseas. Theme information for spring issue available in fall.
**Simultaneous Subs:** yes
**Reading Period:** Year-round
**Reporting Time:** 1 to 3 months
**Author Payment:** copies
**Contests:** See Web Site for Contest Guidelines.
**Founded:** 1956
**Non Profit:** yes
**Paid Staff:** 3
**Unpaid Staff:** 21
**ISSN Number/ISBN Number:** 0029-053X/changes
**Total Circulation:** 2,000
**Paid Circulation:** 1,400
**Average Print Run:** 2,500
**Subscription Rate:** Individual $17.50/Institution $30

**Single Copy Price:** $10
**Current Volume/Issue:** 47/1
**Frequency per Year:** 2
**Backfile Available:** yes
**Unsolicited Ms. Received:** yes
**% of Unsolicited Ms. Published per Year:** 85%
**Format:** perfect
**Size:** H 9" W 6"
**Average Pages:** 200
**Ads:** yes
**Ad Rates:** exchange

# Ninth Letter

**Type:** magazine
**CLMP member:** yes
**Primary Editor/Contact Person:** Jodee Stanley
**Address:** Dept. of English, Univ. of Illinois
608 S. Wright St.
Urbana, IL 61801
**Web Site Address:** http://www.ninthletter.com
**Publishes:** fiction, nonfiction, poetry, and translation
**Recent Awards Received:** Illinois Arts Council Literary Awards, Best American Short Stories, Best New Poets Anthology
**Representative Authors:** Ron Carlson, Ann Beattie, and T.R. Hummer
**Submissions Policy:** Please submit only one prose submission or up to 6 poems at a time.
**Simultaneous Subs:** yes
**Reading Period:** 9/1 to 4/30
**Reporting Time:** 8 to 10 weeks
**Author Payment:** cash and copies
**Founded:** 2003
**Non Profit:** yes
**Paid Staff:** 6
**Unpaid Staff:** 10
**Distributors:** Ingram
**ISSN Number/ISBN Number:** ISSN 1547-8440
**Total Circulation:** 2,500
**Paid Circulation:** 300
**Average Print Run:** 3,500
**Subscription Rate:** Individual $19.95/Institution $19.95
**Single Copy Price:** $12.95
**Current Volume/Issue:** 2/2
**Frequency per Year:** 2
**Backfile Available:** yes
**Unsolicited Ms. Received:** yes
**% of Unsolicited Ms. Published per Year:** 75%
**Format:** perfect

**Size:** H 9" W 12"
**Average Pages:** 192
**Ads:** no

# No: a journal of the arts

**Type:** magazine
**CLMP member:** yes
**Primary Editor/Contact Person:** Deb Klowden
**Address:** 39 W. 29th St. Ste. 11A
New York, NY 10001
**Web Site Address:** http://www.nojournal.com
**Publishes:** essays, poetry, reviews, art, and translation
**Submissions Policy:** Submissions should be sent through post, SASE included. Electronic submissions are not accepted.
**Simultaneous Subs:** yes
**Reading Period:** Year-round
**Reporting Time:** 1 to 2 months
**Author Payment:** none
**Founded:** 2003
**Non Profit:** yes
**Paid Staff:** yes
**Unpaid Staff:** yes
**Distributors:** SPD, DeBoer, Ingram
**Total Circulation:** 1,800
**Paid Circulation:** 350
**Subscription Rate:** Individual $20/Institution $28
**Single Copy Price:** $12
**Current Volume/Issue:** Issue 3
**Frequency per Year:** 2
**Backfile Available:** yes
**Unsolicited Ms. Received:** yes
**Format:** perfect
**Size:** H 9" W 6"
**Average Pages:** 230
**Ads:** no

# Non Serviam Press

**Type:** press
**CLMP member:** no
**Primary Editor/Contact Person:** Patrick Walsh
**Address:** 101 Stanton St, Apt 8
New York, NY 10009
**Web Site Address:** http://www.nonserviamnyc.com
**Publishes:** essays, fiction, and poetry
**Editorial Focus:** NSP seeks original styles and bold ideas.
**Representative Authors:** Alan Lockwood, Roger

Ludwig, and Patrick Walsh
**Submissions Policy:** Send a sample of any kind of writing to the address above. Include SASE
**Simultaneous Subs:** yes
**Reading Period:** Year-round
**Reporting Time:** 4 to 6 weeks
**Author Payment:** none
**Contests:** no contests
**Founded:** 2001
**Non Profit:** yes
**Paid Staff:** 0
**Unpaid Staff:** 5
**Number of Books Published per Year:** 2
**Titles in Print:** 2
**Average Percentage Printed:** Paperback 90%, Chapbook 10%

# NOON

**Type:** magazine
**CLMP member:** yes
**Primary Editor/Contact Person:** Diane Williams
**Address:** PMB 298
1369 Madison Ave.
New York, NY 10128
**Publishes:** essays, fiction, nonfiction, art, and translation
**Submissions Policy:** Include SASE and necessary postage.
**Simultaneous Subs:** yes
**Reading Period:** Year-round
**Reporting Time:** 1 to 3 months
**Author Payment:** none
**Founded:** 2000
**Non Profit:** yes
**Paid Staff:** 4
**Unpaid Staff:** 8
**Distributors:** DeBoer and Ingram and SPD
**ISSN Number/ISBN Number:** ISSN 15268055
**Total Circulation:** 5,000
**Paid Circulation:** 500
**Average Print Run:** 5,000
**Subscription Rate:** Individual $9/Institution $9
**Single Copy Price:** $9
**Current Volume/Issue:** Volume 5
**Frequency per Year:** 1
**Backfile Available:** yes
**Unsolicited Ms. Received:** yes
**% of Unsolicited Ms. Published per Year:** 85%
**Format:** perfect
**Average Pages:** 140

**Ads:** yes

# North American Review

**Type:** magazine
**CLMP member:** yes
**Primary Editor/Contact Person:** Grant Tracey
**Address:** University of Northern Iowa
1222 W. 27th St.
Cedar Falls, IA 50614-0516
**Web Site Address:**
http://webdelsol.com/NorthAmReview/NAR
**Publishes:** essays, fiction, nonfiction, poetry, reviews,
art, and translation
**Editorial Focus:** We are interested in high-quality
poetry, fiction, nonfiction, and art on any subject.
**Representative Authors:** Gary Gildner, Maxine Hong
Kingston, and Marilyn Hacker
**Submissions Policy:** Address Submissions to: Fiction
Editor or Poetry Editor or Nonfiction Editor or Book
Review Editor
**Simultaneous Subs:** no
**Reading Period:** Year-round
**Reporting Time:** 3 to 6 months
**Author Payment:** cash and copies
**Contests:** See Web Site for Contest Guidelines.
**Founded:** 1815
**Non Profit:** yes
**Paid Staff:** 3
**Unpaid Staff:** 5-8
**ISSN Number/ISBN Number:** ISSN 0029-2397
**Total Circulation:** 2,500
**Paid Circulation:** 2,000
**Subscription Rate:** Individual $22/Institution $22
**Single Copy Price:** $5
**Current Volume/Issue:** 289/5
**Frequency per Year:** 5
**Backfile Available:** yes
**Unsolicited Ms. Received:** yes
**% of Unsolicited Ms. Published per Year:** 99%
**Format:** stapled
**Size:** H 10 7/8" W 8 1/8"
**Average Pages:** 54
**Ads:** yes
**Ad Rates:** Request from managing editor.
See Web Site for Details.

# The North Atlantic Review

**Type:** magazine
**CLMP member:** yes

**Primary Editor/Contact Person:** John Gill
**Address:** 15 Arbutus Ln.
Stony Brook, NY 11790-1408
**Web Site Address:** http://www.johnedwardgill.com
**Publishes:** essays, fiction, nonfiction, poetry, reviews,
and art
**Editorial Focus:** Looking for quality fiction, poetry and
or prose.
**Representative Authors:** Stephen Lewis, Margaret
Genovese, and Kim Tilbury
**Submissions Policy:** Manuscripts should be typed
and double-spaced. All correspondence must be
accompanied by a self-addressed, stamped envelope.
**Simultaneous Subs:** yes
**Reading Period:** Year-round
**Reporting Time:** 5 to 6 months
**Author Payment:** copies
**Founded:** 1982
**Non Profit:** yes
**Paid Staff:** 0
**Unpaid Staff:** 4
**Distributors:** http://www.johnedwardgill.com
**ISSN Number/ISBN Number:** ISSN 1040-7324
**Total Circulation:** 5,000
**Paid Circulation:** 100
**Subscription Rate:** Individual $18/Institution $18
**Single Copy Price:** $10
**Current Volume/Issue:** 16/2004
**Frequency per Year:** 1
**Backfile Available:** yes
**Unsolicited Ms. Received:** yes
**% of Unsolicited Ms. Published per Year:** 35%
**Format:** perfect
**Size:** H 9.75" W 6.75"
**Average Pages:** 300
**Ads:** yes
**Ad Rates:** complimentary

# North Carolina Literary Review

**Type:** magazine
**CLMP member:** yes
**Primary Editor/Contact Person:** Margaret Bauer
**Address:** Dept. of English
East Carolina University
Greenville, NC 27858
**Web Site Address:** http://www.ecu.edu/nclr
**Publishes:** essays, fiction, nonfiction, poetry, reviews,
and art
**Editorial Focus:** North Carolina literature and writers
**Recent Awards Received:** Council of Editors of

Learned Journals Best Design Award (1999) and Best New Journal (1994); numerous design awards.
**Representative Authors:** Fred Chappell and James Applewhite
**Submissions Policy:** see our website for submission guidelines
**Simultaneous Subs:** no
**Reading Period:** Year-round
**Reporting Time:** 1 to 6 months
**Author Payment:** copies and subscription
**Founded:** 1992
**Non Profit:** yes
**Paid Staff:** 1
**Unpaid Staff:** 10
**Distributors:** NC bookstores
**Wholesalers:** the NCLR office
**ISSN Number/ISBN Number:** ISSN 1063-00724
**Total Circulation:** 750
**Paid Circulation:** 325
**Average Print Run:** 1,000
**Subscription Rate:** Individual $20/2years/Institution $20/2years
**Single Copy Price:** $15
**Current Volume/Issue:** 13/2004
**Frequency per Year:** 1
**Backfile Available:** yes
**Unsolicited Ms. Received:** yes
**% of Unsolicited Ms. Published per Year:** 10%
**Format:** perfect
**Size:** H 10" W 7"
**Average Pages:** 200
**Ads:** yes
**Ad Rates:** $200 full-page, $125 half-page, $75 quarter-page.

## North Dakota Quarterly

**Type:** magazine
**CLMP member:** yes
**Primary Editor/Contact Person:** Robert W. Lewis
**Address:** Box 7209
University of North Dakota
Grand Forks, ND 58202-7209
**Web Site Address:** http://www.und.nodak.edu/org/ndq
**Publishes:** essays, fiction, nonfiction, poetry, reviews, and art
**Editorial Focus:** Ethnic/multicultural, historical, literary, especially interested in work by and about Native American writers.
**Representative Authors:** Kathleen Norris, Peter

Nabokov, and Ted Kooser
**Submissions Policy:** Hard copies only. No simultaneous poetry or essay submissions.
**Simultaneous Subs:** yes
**Reading Period:** Year-round
**Reporting Time:** 2 to 4 months
**Author Payment:** copies
**Founded:** 1911
**Non Profit:** yes
**Paid Staff:** .5
**Unpaid Staff:** 2-3
**Distributors:** EBSCO, SWETS, North American Library Services
**ISSN Number/ISBN Number:** ISSN 0029-277X
**Total Circulation:** 600
**Paid Circulation:** 450
**Subscription Rate:** Individual $25/Institution $30
**Single Copy Price:** $8
**Current Volume/Issue:** 71/3
**Frequency per Year:** 4
**Backfile Available:** yes
**Unsolicited Ms. Received:** yes
**% of Unsolicited Ms. Published per Year:** 60%
**Format:** perfect
**Size:** H 9" W 6"
**Average Pages:** 160
**Ads:** yes
**Ad Rates:** Full page $150; half-page$100

## Northeast African Studies

**Type:** magazine
**CLMP member:** no
**Primary Editor/Contact Person:** Carol Cole
**Address:** Michigan State University Press
1405 S. Harrison Rd., Ste. 25
East Lansing, MI 48823-5245
**Web Site Address:** http://msupress.msu.edu/journals/neas/
**Publishes:** essays and reviews
**Editorial Focus:** Interdisciplinary scholarly journal focusing on Ethiopia, Sudan, Eritrea, Somalia, and Djibouti
**Representative Authors:** Jon Abbink, Ludwien Kapteijns, and Donald Donham
**Submissions Policy:** Consult MSU Press before preparing manuscripts. Follow Chicago style 15th ed., endnote reference system or author-date system
**Simultaneous Subs:** yes
**Reading Period:** Year-round
**Reporting Time:** 3 to 6 months

**Author Payment:** none
**Founded:** 1994
**Non Profit:** yes
**Paid Staff:** 1
**Unpaid Staff:** 2
**Distributors:** Michigan State University Press
**ISSN Number/ISBN Number:** ISSN 0740-9133
**Total Circulation:** 150
**Paid Circulation:** 120
**Average Print Run:** 350
**Subscription Rate:** Individual $40/Institution $55
**Single Copy Price:** $20
**Current Volume/Issue:** 8/2
**Frequency per Year:** 3
**Backfile Available:** yes
**Unsolicited Ms. Received:** yes
**Format:** perfect
**Size:** H 9" W 6"
**Average Pages:** 125
**Ads:** yes
**Ad Rates:** See Web Site for Details.

## Northwest Review

**Type:** magazine
**CLMP member:** no
**Primary Editor/Contact Person:** John Witte
**Address:** 369 PLC
Eugene, OR 97403
**Web Site Address:**
http://www.uoregon.edu/~engl/deptinfo/NWR.html
**Publishes:** essays, fiction, nonfiction, poetry, reviews, art, and translation
**Editorial Focus:** "Eclectic, but not promiscuous," is how Carolyn Kizer describes Northwest Review. One of America's oldest and most esteemed.
**Recent Awards Received:** Our authors have recently been included in the Best American Poetry, Pushcart Prize, and Best American Essays anthologies.
**Representative Authors:** Ted Kooser, Lucia Perillo, and Charles Bukowski
**Submissions Policy:** Invites submissions of original poems, stories and essays.
**Simultaneous Subs:** no
**Reading Period:** Year-round
**Reporting Time:** 8 to 10 weeks
**Author Payment:** copies and subscription
**Founded:** 1957
**Non Profit:** yes
**Paid Staff:** 3
**Unpaid Staff:** 15

**Distributors:** DeBoer
**ISSN Number/ISBN Number:** ISSN 0029 3423
**Total Circulation:** 1,400
**Paid Circulation:** 1,000
**Average Print Run:** 1,400
**Subscription Rate:** Individual $22/Institution $28
**Single Copy Price:** $8
**Current Volume/Issue:** 43/3
**Frequency per Year:** 3
**Backfile Available:** yes
**Unsolicited Ms. Received:** yes
**% of Unsolicited Ms. Published per Year:** 100%
**Format:** perfect
**Size:** H 9" W 6"
**Average Pages:** 140
**Ads:** yes
**Ad Rates:** $165/full page
See Web Site for Details.

## The Northwoods Journal, a mag for writers

**Type:** magazine
**CLMP member:** no
**Primary Editor/Contact Person:** Robert Olmsted
**Address:** PO BOX 298
Thomaston, ME 04861
**Web Site Address:** http://www.americanletters.org
**Publishes:** essays, fiction, nonfiction, poetry, and reviews
**Editorial Focus:** Good stuff that might otherwise be lost. Real guidance to writers.
**Representative Authors:** J.F. Pytko, Richard Vaughn, and Mary Wallace
**Submissions Policy:** No electronic submission. Nothing previously published. Reading guidelines before submitting. #10 SASE.
**Simultaneous Subs:** no
**Reading Period:** Year-round
**Reporting Time:** 1 to 13 weeks
**Author Payment:** cash
**Founded:** 1974
**Non Profit:** yes
**Paid Staff:** 1
**Unpaid Staff:** 2
**Total Circulation:** 200
**Paid Circulation:** 200
**Average Print Run:** 225
**Subscription Rate:** Individual $18/Institution $18
**Single Copy Price:** $6.50
**Current Volume/Issue:** XI/1

**Frequency per Year:** 4
**Backfile Available:** yes
**Unsolicited Ms. Received:** yes
**% of Unsolicited Ms. Published per Year:** 50%
**Format:** stapled
**Size:** H 8.5" W 5.5"
**Average Pages:** 36-40
**Ads:** yes
**Ad Rates:** $70 page, 38 1/2 page $20 1/4 page.
Almost none sold.
See Web Site for Details.

# Northwoods Press

**Type:** press
**CLMP member:** no
**Primary Editor/Contact Person:** Robert W. Olmsted
**Address:** PO BOX 298
Thomaston, ME 04861
**Web Site Address:** http://www.americanletters.org
**Publishes:** nonfiction and poetry
**Editorial Focus:** Poetry and local/family history
**Representative Authors:** Robert Johnson, Diana
Durham, and Paul Bellerive
**Submissions Policy:** Start with a personal marketing
plan. Book must be 104 pages or more.
**Simultaneous Subs:** yes
**Reading Period:** Year-round
**Reporting Time:** 1 to 2 weeks
**Author Payment:** royalties
**Contests:** See Web Site for Contest Guidelines.
**Founded:** 1972
**Non Profit:** yes
**Paid Staff:** 1
**Unpaid Staff:** 1
**Distributors:** Ingram, Baker & Taylor, Barnes & Noble,
amazon.com
**ISSN Number/ISBN Number:** ISBN 0-89002-xxx-x
**Number of Books Published per Year:** 5
**Titles in Print:** 20
**Average Percentage Printed:** Hardcover 5%,
Paperback 90%, Other 5%

# The Notre Dame Review

**Type:** magazine
**CLMP member:** yes
**Primary Editor/Contact Person:** Kathleen Canavan
**Address:** 840 Flanner Hall
University of Notre Dame
Notre Dame, IN 46556
**Web Site Address:**
http://www.nd.edu/~ndr/review.htm

**Publishes:** fiction, poetry, and reviews
**Editorial Focus:** an independent, non-commercial
magazine of contemporary American and international
fiction, poetry, criticism and art.
**Representative Authors:** Seamus Heaney, Czeslaw
Milosz, and Emer Martin
**Submissions Policy:** Submit best fiction and poetry.
All themes. We only read submissions from
September through November and January through
April.
**Simultaneous Subs:** yes
**Reading Period:** 9/3 to 11/3
**Reporting Time:** 2 to 4 months
**Author Payment:** cash, copies, and subscription
**Contests:** See Web Site for Contest Guidelines.
**Founded:** 1994
**Non Profit:** yes
**Paid Staff:** yes
**Unpaid Staff:** 12
**Distributors:** Ingram, IPD, Media Solutions, Ubiquity
**ISSN Number/ISBN Number:** 1082-1864/1-892492-
15-6
**Total Circulation:** 1,500
**Paid Circulation:** 220
**Subscription Rate:** Individual $15/Institution $20
**Single Copy Price:** $8
**Current Volume/Issue:** Issue 16
**Frequency per Year:** 2
**Backfile Available:** yes
**Unsolicited Ms. Received:** yes
**Format:** perfect
**Size:** H 9" W 6"
**Average Pages:** 195
**Ads:** yes
**Ad Rates:** Exchange

# Nuvein Magazine

**Type:** online
**CLMP member:** no
**Primary Editor/Contact Person:** Enrique Diaz
**Address:** 4522 N. Jerry Ave.
Baldwin Park, CA 91706
**Web Site Address:** http://www.nuvein.com
**Publishes:** essays, fiction, nonfiction, poetry, reviews,
art, translation, and audio
**Editorial Focus:** Nuvein's editorial focus is on writing
which is just off the mainstream path, publishing voic-
es rarely heard.
**Representative Authors:** Tom Sheehan, Elaine
Hatfield, and Paul A. Toth

**Submissions Policy:** Submit by e-mail or postal mail. There is no limit on the number of words per work or the number of works submitted.
**Simultaneous Subs:** no
**Reading Period:** Year-round
**Reporting Time:** 1 to 3 months
**Author Payment:** none and subscription
**Contests:** See Web Site for Contest Guidelines.
**Founded:** 1982
**Non Profit:** yes
**Paid Staff:** 0
**Unpaid Staff:** 6
**ISSN Number/ISBN Number:** ISSN 1523-7877
**Average Page Views per Month:** 8,000
**Average Unique Visitors per Month:** 3,500
**Frequency per Year:** 4
**Publish Print Anthology:** yes
**Average Percentage of Pages per Category:** Fiction 40%, Nonfiction 4%, Poetry 40%, Reviews 2%, Essays 10%, Art 1%, Translation 1%, Audio 2%
**Ad Rates:** See Web Site for Details.

## Oasis

**Type:** magazine
**CLMP member:** no
**Primary Editor/Contact Person:** Neal Storrs
**Address:** P.O. Box 626
Largo, FL 33779-0626
**Publishes:** essays, fiction, nonfiction, poetry, and translation
**Editorial Focus:** looking for work of literary distinction
**Representative Authors:** James Sallis, Caroline Stoloff, and Simon Perchik
**Submissions Policy:** Send complete work to POB 626 Largo FL 33779-0626. Include SASE. Or send to oasislit@aol.com
**Simultaneous Subs:** yes
**Reading Period:** Year-round
**Reporting Time:** 0 to 1 weeks
**Author Payment:** copies
**Contests:** no contest
**Founded:** 1992
**Non Profit:** no
**Paid Staff:** no
**Unpaid Staff:** no
**Distributors:** EBSCO Subscription Services
**ISSN Number/ISBN Number:** ISSN 1064-6299
**Total Circulation:** 300
**Paid Circulation:** 50
**Subscription Rate:** Individual $20/Institution $20

**Single Copy Price:** $6
**Current Volume/Issue:** XI/II
**Frequency per Year:** 4
**Backfile Available:** yes
**Unsolicited Ms. Received:** yes
**% of Unsolicited Ms. Published per Year:** 0.5%
**Format:** perfect
**Average Pages:** 70
**Ads:** no

## Oberlin College Press

**Type:** press
**CLMP member:** yes
**Primary Editor/Contact Person:** Linda Slocum, Managing Editor
**Address:** 50 N. Professor St.
Peters G23
Oberlin, OH 44074-1091
**Web Site Address:** http://www.oberlin.edu/ocpress
**Publishes:** essays, poetry, and translation
**Editorial Focus:** The FIELD Translation Series, FIELD Poetry Series, and FIELD Editions (anthologies) make world's best poetry available.
**Representative Authors:** Franz Wright, Miroslav Holub, and Beckian Fritz Goldberg
**Submissions Policy:** Submit English manuscripts to FIELD Poetry Prize in May. Send translation inquiry/samples to Editor David Young any time.
**Simultaneous Subs:** yes
**Reading Period:** 5/1 to 5/31
**Reporting Time:** 2 to 3 months
**Author Payment:** royalties, cash, and copies
**Contests:** See Web Site for Contest Guidelines.
**Founded:** 1969
**Non Profit:** yes
**Paid Staff:** .5
**Unpaid Staff:** 4
**Distributors:** Orders filled by Cornell University Press Services
**ISSN Number/ISBN Number:** ISBN 0932440—
**Number of Books Published per Year:** 3
**Titles in Print:** 46
**Average Print Run:** 1,000
**Average Percentage Printed:** Paperback 100%
**Average Price:** $16.95

## Omnidawn Publishing

**Type:** press
**CLMP member:** yes

**Primary Editor/Contact Person:** Rusty Morrison
**Address:** 1632 Elm Ave.
Richmond, CA 94805-1614
**Web Site Address:** http://www.omnidawn.com
**Publishes:** fiction and poetry
**Editorial Focus:** Publishers of innovative poetry and new wave fabulist fiction.
**Recent Awards Received:** 2005 PEN USA Award in Poetry for Martha Ronk's poetry collection: In A Landscape of Having To Repeat
**Representative Authors:** Lyn Hejinian, Rosmarie Waldrop, and Elizabeth Robinson
**Submissions Policy:** See our website for full details.
**Simultaneous Subs:** yes
**Reading Period:** Year-round
**Reporting Time:** 3 to 4 months
**Author Payment:** royalties, cash, and copies
**Founded:** 1999
**Non Profit:** no
**Paid Staff:** 1
**Unpaid Staff:** 1
**Wholesalers:** SPD
**ISSN Number/ISBN Number:** ISBN 1-890650
**Number of Books Published per Year:** 3
**Titles in Print:** 15
**Average Print Run:** varies
**Average Percentage Printed:** Paperback 100%
**Average Price:** varies

# OnceWritten.com

**Type:** online
**CLMP member:** no
**Primary Editor/Contact Person:** Monica Poling
**Address:** 1850 N. Whitley Ave. #404
Hollywood, CA 90028
**Web Site Address:** http://www.oncewritten.com
**Publishes:** essays, fiction, nonfiction, poetry, and reviews
**Editorial Focus:** Focuses on works by new authors including novels, fiction and poetry.
**Submissions Policy:** Inquiries may be sent to monica@oncewritten.com
**Simultaneous Subs:** yes
**Reading Period:** Year-round
**Reporting Time:** 4 to 6 weeks
**Author Payment:** cash
**Contests:** See Web Site for Contest Guidelines.
**Founded:** 2003
**Non Profit:** no
**Paid Staff:** 0

**Unpaid Staff:** 0
**Average Page Views per Month:** 40,000
**Average Unique Visitors per Month:** 1,000
**Frequency per Year:** 12
**Publish Print Anthology:** no
**Average Percentage of Pages per Category:** Fiction 25%, Nonfiction 20%, Poetry 10%, Reviews 40%, Essays 5%
**Ad Rates:** Varies depending on size of ad See Web Site for Details.

# One Story

**Type:** magazine
**CLMP member:** yes
**Primary Editor/Contact Person:** Hannah Tinti
**Address:** P.O. Box 150618
Brooklyn, NY 11215
**Web Site Address:** http://www.one-story.com
**Publishes:** fiction
**Editorial Focus:** Publishes one short story every 3 weeks. Seeks literary fiction of any style. Stories must be brave enough to stand alone.
**Representative Authors:** Kelly Link, Judy Budnitz, and Karl Iagnemma
**Submissions Policy:** Stories must be between 3,000 and 8,000 words. We have an online submission tool and do not accept paper submissions.
**Simultaneous Subs:** yes
**Reading Period:** 9/06 to 5/07
**Reporting Time:** 2 to 6 months
**Author Payment:** cash and copies
**Contests:** See Web Site for Contest Guidelines.
**Founded:** 2001
**Non Profit:** yes
**Paid Staff:** 0
**Unpaid Staff:** 7
**Distributors:** Subscription Only
**Wholesalers:** Subscription Only
**Total Circulation:** 3,500
**Paid Circulation:** 3,200
**Average Print Run:** 3,800
**Subscription Rate:** Individual $21/Institution $21
**Single Copy Price:** $2
**Current Volume/Issue:** 4/8
**Frequency per Year:** 18
**Backfile Available:** yes
**Unsolicited Ms. Received:** yes
**% of Unsolicited Ms. Published per Year:** 50%
**Format:** stapled
**Size:** H 7" W 5"

**Average Pages:** 24
**Ads:** no

## Ontario Review

**Type:** magazine
**CLMP member:** no
**Address:** 9 Honey Brook Dr.
Princeton, NJ 8540
**Web Site Address:**
http://www.ontarioreviewpress.com
**Publishes:** essays, fiction, nonfiction, poetry, and art
**Reading Period:** Year-round
**Reporting Time:** 1 to 2 months
**Author Payment:** none
**Founded:** 1974
**Non Profit:** no

## Open City Books

**Type:** press
**CLMP member:** yes
**Primary Editor/Contact Person:** Thomas Beller and
Joanna Yas
**Address:** 270 Lafayette St.
Ste. 1412
New York, NY 10012
**Web Site Address:** http://www.opencity.org
**Publishes:** essays, fiction, and poetry
**Editorial Focus:** Unusual voices and great story-
telling-by new writers as well as undiscovered talents
from the past.
**Representative Authors:** David Berman, Edward St.
Aubyn, and Meghan Daum
**Submissions Policy:** No unsolicited manuscripts. We
find books by reading submissions to Open City mag-
azine; please follow those guidelines.
**Simultaneous Subs:** no
**Reading Period:** 9/1 to 5/31
**Reporting Time:** 2 to 5 months
**Author Payment:** royalties and cash
**Founded:** 1999
**Non Profit:** yes
**Paid Staff:** 1
**Unpaid Staff:** 4
**Distributors:** Publishers Group West
**Wholesalers:** Ingram, Koen, Baker & Taylor
**ISSN Number/ISBN Number:** ISBN 1890447
**Number of Books Published per Year:** 1-2
**Titles in Print:** 5
**Average Print Run:** 6,000

**Average Percentage Printed:** Paperback 100%
**Average Price:** $14

## Open City

**Type:** magazine
**CLMP member:** yes
**Primary Editor/Contact Person:** Joanna Yas and
Thomas Beller
**Address:** 270 Lafayette St.
Ste. 1412
New York, NY 10012-3327
**Web Site Address:** http://www.opencity.org
**Publishes:** essays, fiction, poetry, art, and translation
**Editorial Focus:** Poetry and prose with a daring,
youthful, spirit.
**Recent Awards Received:** Poems selected for Best
American Poetry
**Representative Authors:** Alicia Erian, Rachel
Sherman, and James Lasdun
**Submissions Policy:** One story, essay, or novel
excerpt at a time, up to 5,000 words; up to 5 poems;
no unsolicited artwork.
**Simultaneous Subs:** yes
**Reading Period:** 9/1 to 5/31
**Reporting Time:** 3 to 6 months
**Author Payment:** cash and copies
**Contests:** See Web Site for Contest Guidelines.
**Founded:** 1990
**Non Profit:** yes
**Paid Staff:** 1
**Unpaid Staff:** 4
**Distributors:** Publishers Group West, Ubiquity, DeBoer
**Wholesalers:** Ingram, Koen, Baker & Taylor
**ISSN Number/ISBN Number:** ISSN 10895523
**Total Circulation:** 5,000
**Paid Circulation:** 3,000
**Average Print Run:** 5,000
**Subscription Rate:** Individual $30/Institution $40
**Single Copy Price:** $10
**Current Volume/Issue:** Issue 22
**Frequency per Year:** 3
**Backfile Available:** yes
**Unsolicited Ms. Received:** yes
**% of Unsolicited Ms. Published per Year:** 1%
**Format:** perfect
**Size:** H 9" W 6"
**Average Pages:** 250
**Ads:** yes
**Ad Rates:** $600/full page; discounts for arts-oriented
organizations.

# Open Spaces Publications

**Type:** magazine
**CLMP member:** no
**Primary Editor/Contact Person:** Anne Bradley
**Address:** 6327-C SW Capitol Hwy.
Portland, OR 97239
**Web Site Address:** http://www.open-spaces.com
**Publishes:** essays, fiction, nonfiction, poetry, reviews, and art
**Editorial Focus:** Creative writing and nonfiction articles on science, history, politics, international relations, law, medicine and the arts.
**Representative Authors:** Robert Sullivan, Rick Bass, and Jane Lubchenco
**Submissions Policy:** On our website at http://www.open-spaces.com
**Simultaneous Subs:** yes
**Reading Period:** Year-round
**Reporting Time:** 1 to 6 months
**Author Payment:** cash, copies, and subscription
**Founded:** 1997
**Non Profit:** no
**Paid Staff:** 5
**Unpaid Staff:** 22
**Distributors:** Small Changes, Anderson, IPD, etc.
**ISSN Number/ISBN Number:** ISSN 1096-3901
**Total Circulation:** 10,000
**Paid Circulation:** 5,500
**Subscription Rate:** Individual $25/Institution $25.
**Single Copy Price:** $7.95
**Current Volume/Issue:** 6/4
**Frequency per Year:** 4
**Backfile Available:** yes
**Unsolicited Ms. Received:** yes
**% of Unsolicited Ms. Published per Year:** 25%
**Format:** perfect
**Size:** H 11" W 81/2"
**Average Pages:** 64
**Ads:** yes
**Ad Rates:** Call 1-800-448-5271
See Web Site for Details.

# Opium Magazine

**Type:** online
**CLMP member:** yes
**Address:** 586 Dean St.
Brooklyn, NY 11238
**Web Site Address:** http://www.opiummagazine.com

**Publishes:** fiction, poetry, art, and reviews
**Reading Period:** Year-round
**Reporting Time:** 1 to 2 months
**Author Payment:** none
**Founded:** 2001
**Non Profit:** yes
**Backfile Available:** yes
**Average Percentage of Pages per Category:** Audio 100%

# Orchid: A Literary Review

**Type:** magazine
**CLMP member:** yes
**Primary Editor/Contact Person:** Keith Hood
**Address:** P.O. Box 131457
Ann Arbor, MI 48113-1457
**Web Site Address:** http://www.orchidlit.org
**Publishes:** fiction and art
**Editorial Focus:** Orchid celebrates stories and the art of storytelling. We welcome submissions of fiction and interviews on fiction craft.
**Representative Authors:** Sarah Gerkensmeyer, Keya Mitra, and Daniel Mueller
**Submissions Policy:** We consider fiction of all lengths: including novellas and novel excerpts. We do not consider unsolicited poetry.
**Simultaneous Subs:** yes
**Reading Period:** Year-round
**Reporting Time:** 6 to 12 months
**Author Payment:** cash and copies
**Contests:** See Web Site for Contest Guidelines.
**Founded:** 2001
**Non Profit:** yes
**Paid Staff:** 0
**Unpaid Staff:** 11
**ISSN Number/ISBN Number:** ISSN 1537-0763
**Total Circulation:** 1,000
**Paid Circulation:** 350
**Average Print Run:** 2,000
**Subscription Rate:** Individual $16/Institution $16
**Single Copy Price:** $8
**Current Volume/Issue:** Issue 6
**Frequency per Year:** 2
**Backfile Available:** yes
**Unsolicited Ms. Received:** yes
**% of Unsolicited Ms. Published per Year:** 95%
**Format:** perfect
**Size:** H 9" W 6"
**Average Pages:** 200
**Ads:** yes

**Ad Rates:** Full Page Ad-$100, Half Page Ad-$50

## Orchises Press

**Type:** press
**CLMP member:** no
**Primary Editor/Contact Person:** Roger Lathbury
**Address:** P.O. Box 20602
Alexandria, VA 22320-1602
**Web Site Address:** http://mason.gmu.edu/~rlathbur
**Publishes:** nonfiction and poetry
**Editorial Focus:** A literary press, Orchises does four books yearly, including reprints. No fiction, children's books, or cookbooks.
**Representative Authors:** David Kirby, Stephen Akey, and L.S. Asekoff
**Submissions Policy:** We receive 300 submissions, publish 4-5 titles a year. We prefer to seek out poetry rather than receive blind submissions.
**Simultaneous Subs:** yes
**Reading Period:** Year-round
**Reporting Time:** 4 to 12 weeks
**Author Payment:** royalties
**Founded:** 1983
**Non Profit:** no
**Paid Staff:** 1
**Unpaid Staff:** 1
**Distributors:** Washington Book Distributors
**ISSN Number/ISBN Number:** ISBN 0914061, 1932535
**Number of Books Published per Year:** 5
**Titles in Print:** 100
**Average Print Run:** 750
**Average Percentage Printed:** Hardcover 20%, Paperback 77%, Chapbook 3%
**Average Price:** $14.95

## Osiris

**Type:** magazine
**CLMP member:** yes
**Primary Editor/Contact Person:** Andrea Moorhead
**Address:** P.O. Box 297
Deerfield, MA 01342
**Publishes:** poetry
**Editorial Focus:** Multi-lingual contemporary poetry journal.
**Representative Authors:** Prospero Saiz, Yves Broussard, and Madeleine Gagnon
**Submissions Policy:** Four to five poems, short biography and SASE

**Simultaneous Subs:** no
**Reading Period:** Year-round
**Reporting Time:** 2 to 4 weeks
**Author Payment:** copies and subscription
**Founded:** 1972
**Non Profit:** yes
**Paid Staff:** 0
**Unpaid Staff:** 3
**ISSN Number/ISBN Number:** ISSN 0095-019X
**Total Circulation:** 500
**Paid Circulation:** 125
**Average Print Run:** 500
**Subscription Rate:** Individual $15/Institution $15
**Single Copy Price:** $7.50
**Current Volume/Issue:** 60/60
**Frequency per Year:** 2
**Backfile Available:** yes
**Unsolicited Ms. Received:** yes
**% of Unsolicited Ms. Published per Year:** 10%
**Format:** perfect
**Size:** H 9" W 6"
**Average Pages:** 54
**Ads:** yes
**Ad Rates:** 150 full page

## Other Press

**Type:** press
**CLMP member:** yes
**Primary Editor/Contact Person:** Sarah Russo, Dir. of Publicity
**Address:** 307 7th Ave.
New York, NY 10001
**Web Site Address:** http://www.otherpress.com
**Publishes:** fiction, nonfiction, poetry, reviews, and translation
**Editorial Focus:** Literary criticism, poetry, literature in translation, and contemporary American literature.
**Representative Authors:** Leslie Epstein, Daniel Dorman, M.D., and Arnon Grunberg
**Submissions Policy:** CV, one-page abstract of the work or a query letter, an outline of the entire manuscript if appropriate, and sample chapter
**Simultaneous Subs:** no
**Reading Period:** Year-round
**Reporting Time:** 2 to 6 months
**Author Payment:** royalties
**Founded:** 1998
**Non Profit:** no
**Paid Staff:** 20
**Unpaid Staff:** 0

**Distributors:** Commission sales reps.
**Wholesalers:** Baker & Taylor, Ingram
**ISSN Number/ISBN Number:** ISBN 159051, 1892746
**Number of Books Published per Year:** 40
**Titles in Print:** 150
**Average Percentage Printed:** Hardcover 60%,
Paperback 40%
**Backfile Available:** yes

## Other Voices

**Type:** magazine
**CLMP member:** yes
**Primary Editor/Contact Person:** Gina Frangello,
Exec. Ed.
**Address:** University of IL-Chicago, English Dept.
601 S. Morgan
Chicago, IL 60607-7120
**Web Site Address:** http://www.othervoices-
magazine.org
**Publishes:** fiction and reviews
**Editorial Focus:** diverse, original literary short fiction,
novel excerpts, one-act plays, interviews, book
reviews.
**Recent Awards Received:** Illinois Arts Council
Literary Awards, Pushcart Prize nominations, inclusion
in Best American Short Stories of the Century.
**Representative Authors:** Pam Houston, Aimee Liu,
and Dan Chaon
**Submissions Policy:** Submit entire manuscript with
brief cover letter. We read between Oct 1 and April 1
only. 6,500 word max.
**Simultaneous Subs:** yes
**Reading Period:** 10/1 to 4/1
**Reporting Time:** 4 to 16 weeks
**Author Payment:** cash and copies
**Contests:** See Web Site for Contest Guidelines.
**Founded:** 1985
**Non Profit:** yes
**Paid Staff:** 0
**Unpaid Staff:** 35
**Distributors:** Ingram, DeBoer
**ISSN Number/ISBN Number:**
87564696/7447079831
**Total Circulation:** 2,000
**Paid Circulation:** 650
**Average Print Run:** 2,000
**Subscription Rate:** Individual $26/Institution $28
**Single Copy Price:** $9
**Current Volume/Issue:** Issue 43
**Frequency per Year:** 2

**Backfile Available:** yes
**Unsolicited Ms. Received:** yes
**% of Unsolicited Ms. Published per Year:** 2%
**Format:** perfect
**Size:** H 9" W 6"
**Average Pages:** 200
**Ads:** yes
**Ad Rates:** primarily through exchange

## Out of Line

**Type:** magazine
**CLMP member:** yes
**Primary Editor/Contact Person:** Sam Longmire
**Address:** 843 Ashley Ct.
Trenton, OH 45067
**Web Site Address:** http://www.readoutofline.com
**Publishes:** essays, fiction, nonfiction, poetry, and
translation
**Editorial Focus:** Issues of Peace and Justice. Focus
on tolerance, nonviolence, diversity, healthy relation-
ships, human rights and peace.
**Representative Authors:** Maureen Tolman Flannery,
Lyn Lifshin, and Leza Lowitz
**Submissions Policy:** Manuscripts should not exceed
4,000 words. SASE for return. Open to all writers.
Publication one year after acceptance.
**Simultaneous Subs:** yes
**Reading Period:** Year-round
**Reporting Time:** 1 to 3 months
**Author Payment:** copies
**Founded:** 1998
**Non Profit:** no
**Paid Staff:** 0
**Unpaid Staff:** 6
**Distributors:** Out of Line staff promote and distribute.
**Wholesalers:** Selected bookstores.
**ISSN Number/ISBN Number:** ISSN 1526-6109
**Total Circulation:** 500
**Paid Circulation:** 140
**Subscription Rate:** Individual $12.50/Institution
$12.50
**Single Copy Price:** $12.50
**Current Volume/Issue:** 2004/2004
**Frequency per Year:** 1
**Backfile Available:** yes
**Unsolicited Ms. Received:** yes
**% of Unsolicited Ms. Published per Year:** 25%
**Format:** perfect
**Size:** H 8" W 5"
**Average Pages:** 130

**Ads:** no

## Outlaw Editions

**Type:** press
**CLMP member:** no
**Primary Editor/Contact Person:** Jay Ruzesky
**Address:** 2829 Dysart Road
Victoria, BC V9A 2J7
**Web site Address:**
http://web.mala.bc.ca/ruzeskyj/Outlaw/outlawe
**Publishes:** essays, fiction, nonfiction, poetry, translation, and audio
**Editorial Focus:** Top quality, innovative, excellent work written for the chapbook form by groovy cats.
**Representative Authors:** P.K. Page, John Harley, and Michael Ondaatje
**Submissions Policy:** Query first.
**Simultaneous Subs:** no
**Reading Period:** 5/1 to 8/31
**Reporting Time:** 1 to 3 months
**Author Payment:** copies
**Founded:** 1993
**Non Profit:** yes
**Paid Staff:** N/A
**Unpaid Staff:** 2
**Number of Books Published per Year:** 2
**Titles in Print:** 12
**Average Print Run:** 100
**Average Percentage Printed:** Chapbook 95%, Other 5%
**Average Price:** $7

## The Owl Press

**Type:** press
**CLMP member:** no
**Primary Editor/Contact Person:** Albert Flynn DeSilver
**Address:** P.O. Box 126
Woodacre, CA 94973
**Web Site Address:** http://www.theowlpress.com
**Publishes:** poetry
**Editorial Focus:** Innovative Poetry and Poetic Collaboration
**Representative Authors:** Frank O'Hara, Bernadette Mayer, and Edmund Berrigan
**Submissions Policy:** No unsolicited submissions at this time!
**Simultaneous Subs:** no
**Reading Period:** Year-round
**Reporting Time:** 2 to 8 weeks

**Author Payment:** copies
**Founded:** 1997
**Non Profit:** yes
**Paid Staff:** 0
**Unpaid Staff:** 1
**Distributors:** SPD, Baker & Taylor, Amazon
**Number of Books Published per Year:** 2
**Titles in Print:** 7
**Average Print Run:** 750
**Average Percentage Printed:** Paperback 80%, Chapbook 20%
**Average Price:** $12

## Oyster Boy Review

**Type:** magazine
**CLMP member:** no
**Primary Editor/Contact Person:** Damon Sauve
**Address:** Post Office Box 77842
San Francisco, CA 94107-0842
**Web Site Address:** http://www.oysterboyreview.com
**Publishes:** essays, fiction, nonfiction, poetry, reviews, and art
**Editorial Focus:** Fiction and poetry by new and upcoming authors.
**Representative Authors:** Kevin McGowin, C.A. Conrad, and Corvin Thomas
**Submissions Policy:** Submissions are open from January through September. Prior to sending work, read the guidelines available on the website.
**Simultaneous Subs:** no
**Reading Period:** 1/1 to 9/30
**Reporting Time:** 3 to 6 months
**Author Payment:** copies
**Founded:** 1994
**Non Profit:** no
**Paid Staff:** 0
**Unpaid Staff:** 7
**ISSN Number/ISBN Number:** ISSN 1085-2727
**Total Circulation:** 250
**Paid Circulation:** 50
**Subscription Rate:** Individual $20/Institution $20
**Single Copy Price:** $5
**Current Volume/Issue:** 10/1
**Frequency per Year:** 4
**Unsolicited Ms. Received:** yes
**% of Unsolicited Ms. Published per Year:** 100%
**Format:** stapled
**Size:** H 11" W 6"
**Average Pages:** 72
**Ads:** no

## Paintbrush: A Journal of Poetry & Translation

**Type:** magazine
**CLMP member:** yes
**Primary Editor/Contact Person:** Dr. Ben Bennani
**Address:** College of Humanities & Social Sciences
UAE University, P.O. Box 17771
Al Ain, AD U.A.E.
**Web Site Address:** http://www.paintbrush.org
**Publishes:** essays, poetry, reviews, and translation
**Editorial Focus:** Any theme is welcome, but work must reflect a genuine commitment to, and expertise in new technique and style.
**Representative Authors:** Ruth Stone, Charles E. Eaton, and Bruce Bennett
**Submissions Policy:** 3-5 poems in hard copy and/or electronically. Include cover letter and short bio.
**Simultaneous Subs:** no
**Reading Period:** 9/1 to 5/1
**Reporting Time:** 4 to 6 weeks
**Author Payment:** copies
**Contests:** Periodically announced.
See Web Site for Contest Guidelines.
**Founded:** 1974
**Non Profit:** yes
**Paid Staff:** 0
**Unpaid Staff:** 1
**Distributors:** DeBoer
**ISSN Number/ISBN Number:** 0094-1964
**Total Circulation:** 500
**Paid Circulation:** 100
**Average Print Run:** 1,000
**Subscription Rate:** Individual $15/Institution $20
**Single Copy Price:** $15
**Current Volume/Issue:** XXX
**Frequency per Year:** 1
**Backfile Available:** yes
**Unsolicited Ms. Received:** yes
**% of Unsolicited Ms. Published per Year:** 80%
**Format:** perfect
**Size:** H 8.5" W 5.5"
**Average Pages:** 200
**Ads:** yes
**Ad Rates:** $150/full page; $100/half page

## The Painted Bride Quarterly

**Type:** online
**CLMP member:** yes
**Primary Editor/Contact Person:** Marion Wrenn/Kathy Volk Miller
**Address:** Rutgers University-Camden
311 N. Fifth St.
Camden, NJ 08102
**Web Site Address:** http://pbq.rutgers.edu
**Publishes:** essays, fiction, nonfiction, poetry, reviews, art, and translation
**Editorial Focus:** The writers PBQ has published over the last three decades extend from the most traditional to language school explorations
**Representative Authors:** Ruth Stone, Nick Flynn, and Stephen Dunn
**Submissions Policy:** Accepts up to 5 poems, fiction up to 5,000 words, essays and reviews up to 3,000 words, art also. No electronic submissions.
**Simultaneous Subs:** yes
**Reading Period:** Year-round
**Reporting Time:** 3 to 6 months
**Author Payment:** copies
**Contests:** See Web Site for Contest Guidelines.
**Founded:** 1973
**Non Profit:** yes
**Paid Staff:** 0
**Unpaid Staff:** 12
**Distributors:** Ingram and DeBoer
**ISSN Number/ISBN Number:** ISBN 0-9728565-0-1
**Average Page Views per Month:** 5,000
**Average Unique Visitors per Month:** 500
**Frequency per Year:** 4
**Publish Print Anthology:** yes
**Price:** $15
**Average Percentage of Pages per Category:** Fiction 20%, Nonfiction 10%, Poetry 35%, Reviews 10%, Essays 10%, Art 10%, Translation 5%
**Ad Rates:** See Web Site for Details.

## Paper Street

**Type:** magazine
**CLMP member:** yes
**Primary Editor/Contact Person:** Arlan Hess
**Address:** P.O. Box 14786
Pittsburgh, PA 15234-0786
**Web Site Address:** http://www.paperstreetpress.org
**Publishes:** fiction, poetry, and reviews
**Editorial Focus:** Character driven fiction and narrative poetry: "Fiction sure of its history and footing; poetry unencumbered by distraction."
**Representative Authors:** Sandra Kohler, Sandra Ahrens, and Sean Padriac McCarthy
**Submissions Policy:** See web site.

**Simultaneous Subs:** yes
**Reading Period:** 5/1 to 8/31
**Reporting Time:** 1 to 3 months
**Author Payment:** copies and subscription
**Founded:** 2003
**Non Profit:** yes
**Paid Staff:** no
**Unpaid Staff:** yes
**ISSN Number/ISBN Number:** ISSN 1547-2922
**Total Circulation:** 500
**Paid Circulation:** 200
**Average Print Run:** 500
**Subscription Rate:** Individual $16/Institution $16
**Single Copy Price:** $9
**Current Volume/Issue:** 2/2
**Frequency per Year:** 2
**Backfile Available:** yes
**Unsolicited Ms. Received:** yes
**% of Unsolicited Ms. Published per Year:** 100%
**Format:** perfect
**Size:** H 9" W 6"
**Average Pages:** 160
**Ads:** no

## Parakeet

**Type:** magazine
**CLMP member:** yes
**Primary Editor/Contact Person:** Deb Olin Unferth
**Address:** 515 Indiana #A
Lawrence, KS 66044
**Publishes:** essays, fiction, nonfiction, and poetry
**Editorial Focus:** Innovative and experimental writing
**Simultaneous Subs:** yes
**Reading Period:** Year-round
**Reporting Time:** 2 to 3 months
**Author Payment:** none
**Founded:** 2004
**Non Profit:** yes
**Paid Staff:** 0
**Unpaid Staff:** 2
**Total Circulation:** 750
**Paid Circulation:** 100
**Average Print Run:** 1,000
**Subscription Rate:** Individual $10/Institution $10
**Single Copy Price:** $10
**Current Volume/Issue:** 2/1
**Frequency per Year:** 1
**Backfile Available:** yes
**Unsolicited Ms. Received:** yes
**Format:** perfect

## Paris Press

**Type:** press
**CLMP member:** yes
**Primary Editor/Contact Person:** Jan Freeman
**Address:** P.O. Box 487
1117 West Rd.
Ashfield, MA 01330
**Web Site Address:** http://www.parispress.org
**Publishes:** fiction, nonfiction, poetry, and audio
**Editorial Focus:** Paris Press publishes daring literature by women that has been neglected or misrepresented by the commercial publishing world
**Representative Authors:** Ruth Stone, Muriel Rukeyser, and Virginia Woolf
**Submissions Policy:** Submit a 10-20 page excerpt, along with a resume and an SASE, between November and February.
**Simultaneous Subs:** yes
**Reading Period:** 11/3 to 2/4
**Reporting Time:** 6 to 18 months
**Author Payment:** royalties
**Founded:** 1995
**Non Profit:** yes
**Paid Staff:** 1
**Unpaid Staff:** 2
**Distributors:** Consortium
**Wholesalers:** Ingram, Baker & Taylor, etc.
**ISSN Number/ISBN Number:** ISBN 0-9638183 ; 1-930464
**Number of Books Published per Year:** 1-2
**Titles in Print:** 13
**Average Percentage Printed:** Hardcover 30%, Paperback 90%, Chapbook 5%, Other 5%
**Backfile Available:** yes

## The Paris Review

**Type:** magazine
**CLMP member:** yes
**Primary Editor/Contact Person:** Editor (see below)
**Address:** 62 White St.
New York, NY 10013
**Web Site Address:** http://www.theparisreview.org
**Publishes:** essays, fiction, nonfiction, poetry, art, and translation
**Editorial Focus:** The Paris Review publishes the finest in original new fiction, poetry, interviews, essays, and art in its quarterly issues.
**Submissions Policy:** Fiction should be sent to the attention of the Fiction Editor, poetry to the Poetry Editor, at the address above.

**Simultaneous Subs:** yes
**Reading Period:** Year-round
**Reporting Time:** 2 to 3 months
**Author Payment:** cash and copies
**Contests:** See Web Site for Contest Guidelines.
**Founded:** 1953
**Non Profit:** yes
**Paid Staff:** 7
**Unpaid Staff:** 4
**Distributors:** Ingram, DeBoer, Small Changes
**Wholesalers:** Total Circulation Services, Kent News
**ISSN Number/ISBN Number:** ISSN 0031-2037
**Total Circulation:** 6,000
**Paid Circulation:** 4,500
**Subscription Rate:** Individual $40/Institution $49
**Single Copy Price:** $12
**Current Volume/Issue:** 46/170
**Frequency per Year:** 4
**Backfile Available:** yes
**Unsolicited Ms. Received:** yes
**Format:** perfect
**Size:** H 8.5" W 5.50"
**Average Pages:** 300
**Ads:** yes
**Ad Rates:** Full Page, $1,000. 1/2 Page, $600.
See Web Site for Details.

# Parnassus: Poetry in Review

**Type:** magazine
**CLMP member:** yes
**Primary Editor/Contact Person:** Herbert Leibowitz
**Address:** 205 W. 89th St., #8F
New York, NY 10024
**Web Site Address:** http://www.parnassuspoetry.com
**Publishes:** essays, fiction, nonfiction, poetry, reviews, art, and translation
**Editorial Focus:** Critical essays and reviews of poetry written in stylish prose. Poems that employ complex syntax, rhythm, and subject matter.
**Recent Awards Received:** Poets House 2002 Elizabeth Kray Award for "service to poetry."
**Representative Authors:** David Barber, Mary Karr, and Eric Ormsby
**Submissions Policy:** We read all unsolicited work. Authors should read Parnassus before submitting poems or prose for an idea of our taste.
**Simultaneous Subs:** yes
**Reading Period:** Year-round
**Reporting Time:** 1 to 3 months
**Author Payment:** cash, copies, and subscription

**Founded:** 1972
**Non Profit:** yes
**Paid Staff:** 5
**Unpaid Staff:** 1-2
**ISSN Number/ISBN Number:** ISBN 0048-3028
**Total Circulation:** 2,500
**Paid Circulation:** 1,200
**Average Print Run:** 1,800
**Subscription Rate:** Individual $24/Institution $46
**Single Copy Price:** $12-15
**Current Volume/Issue:** 28/1/2
**Frequency per Year:** 2
**Backfile Available:** yes
**Unsolicited Ms. Received:** yes
**% of Unsolicited Ms. Published per Year:** 2-5%
**Format:** perfect
**Average Pages:** 350
**Ads:** yes
**Ad Rates:** See Web Site for Details.

# Parthenon West Review

**Type:** magazine
**CLMP member:** yes
**Primary Editor/Contact Person:** David Holler, Chad Sweeney
**Address:** 15 Littlefield Terrace
San Francisco, CA 94107
**Web Site Address:**
http://www.ParthenonWestReview.com
**Publishes:** poetry
**Simultaneous Subs:** yes
**Reading Period:** Year-round
**Reporting Time:** 1 to 4 months
**Author Payment:** none
**Founded:** 2004
**Non Profit:** yes
**Paid Staff:** 0
**Unpaid Staff:** 2
**Total Circulation:** 300
**Paid Circulation:** 50
**Average Print Run:** 500
**Subscription Rate:** Individual $20/Institution $20
**Single Copy Price:** $12
**Current Volume/Issue:** Issue 3
**Frequency per Year:** 2
**Backfile Available:** yes
**Unsolicited Ms. Received:** yes
**Format:** perfect

## Passager

**Type:** magazine
**CLMP member:** yes
**Primary Editor/Contact Person:** Kendra Kopelke
**Address:** University of Baltimore
1420 N. Charles St.
Baltimore, MD 21201
**Web Site Address:** http://www.raven.ubalt.edu/features/passager
**Publishes:** fiction, nonfiction, and poetry
**Simultaneous Subs:** yes
**Reading Period:** Year-round
**Reporting Time:** 2 to 4 months
**Author Payment:** copies
**Contests:** Poetry Contest for Writers over 50. **Reading period:** Sept. 1-Feb.15. Reading fee: $20, includes 1-year subscription.
See Web Site for Contest Guidelines.
**Founded:** 1990
**Non Profit:** no
**Paid Staff:** 0
**Unpaid Staff:** 5
**Total Circulation:** 1,400
**Paid Circulation:** 1,200
**Average Print Run:** 2,000
**Subscription Rate:** Individual $20/Institution $20
**Single Copy Price:** $6
**Current Volume/Issue:** Issue 40
**Frequency per Year:** 2
**Backfile Available:** yes
**Unsolicited Ms. Received:** yes
**% of Unsolicited Ms. Published per Year:** 100%
**Format:** perfect
**Ads:** no

## Paterson Literary Review

**Type:** magazine
**CLMP member:** yes
**Primary Editor/Contact Person:** Maria Mazziotti Gillan
**Address:** at Poetry Center at Passaic County Community College
1 College Blvd.
Paterson, NJ 07505-1179
**Web Site Address:** http://www.pccc.edu/poetry
**Publishes:** essays, fiction, nonfiction, poetry, reviews, art, and translation
**Editorial Focus:** High quality literary magazine with work that is not esoteric or intended for an audience of post-modern individuals.
**Representative Authors:** Diane di Prima, Marge Piercy, and Ruth Stone

**Submissions Policy:** Send 5 poems or one story, essay, nonfiction piece. Reviews are assigned.
**Simultaneous Subs:** yes
**Reading Period:** 11/05 to 3/06
**Reporting Time:** 3 to 6 months
**Author Payment:** copies
**Contests:** See Web Site for Contest Guidelines.
**Founded:** 1977
**Non Profit:** yes
**Paid Staff:** 6
**Unpaid Staff:** 0
**ISSN Number/ISBN Number:** ISSN 0743-2259
**Total Circulation:** 2,000
**Paid Circulation:** 756
**Average Print Run:** 1,000
**Subscription Rate:** Individual $15./Institution $15.
**Single Copy Price:** $15
**Current Volume/Issue:** 39/34
**Frequency per Year:** 1
**Backfile Available:** yes
**Unsolicited Ms. Received:** yes
**% of Unsolicited Ms. Published per Year:** 10%
**Format:** perfect
**Size:** H 9" W 6"
**Average Pages:** 350
**Ads:** yes
**Ad Rates:** $400 full page; $200 half page

## Pathwise Press

**Type:** press
**CLMP member:** no
**Primary Editor/Contact Person:** Christopher Harter
**Address:** P.O. Box 178
Erie, PA 16512
**Web Site Address:** http://www.bluemarble.net/~charter/btgin.htm
**Publishes:** essays, fiction, and poetry
**Editorial Focus:** Strong emphasis on imagery. Nothing overly academic or Bukowski-esque
**Representative Authors:** Mark Terrill, Kell Robertson, and Mike James
**Submissions Policy:** Query first. Then send complete manuscript hardcopy if press is accepting manuscripts.
**Simultaneous Subs:** yes
**Reading Period:** Year-round
**Reporting Time:** 4 to 6 weeks
**Author Payment:** royalties and copies
**Founded:** 1997
**Non Profit:** yes

**Paid Staff:** 0
**Unpaid Staff:** 1
**Distributors:** via website and catalogs
**Wholesalers:** Baker & Taylor
**ISSN Number/ISBN Number:** ISBN 0-9675226
**Number of Books Published per Year:** 2-3
**Titles in Print:** 11
**Average Print Run:** 300
**Average Percentage Printed:** Chapbook 100%
**Average Price:** $5.95

## Paul Dry Books

**Type:** press
**CLMP member:** no
**Primary Editor/Contact Person:** Paul Dry
**Address:** 117 S. 17th St. (1102)
Philadelphia, PA 19103
**Web Site Address:** http://www.pauldrybooks.com
**Publishes:** essays, fiction, and nonfiction
**Editorial Focus:** We are a small literary press, publishing new work, translations, and reprints.
**Representative Authors:** Eva Brann, James McConkey, and Peter Cashwell
**Submissions Policy:** Request submissions guidelines via our website.
**Simultaneous Subs:** yes
**Reading Period:** Year-round
**Reporting Time:** 2 to 4 weeks
**Author Payment:** royalties
**Founded:** 1998
**Non Profit:** no
**Paid Staff:** 3
**Unpaid Staff:** 0
**Distributors:** Consortium
**Wholesalers:** All major wholesales through our distributor
**Number of Books Published per Year:** 6
**Titles in Print:** 35
**Average Print Run:** 2,500
**Average Percentage Printed:** Hardcover 20%, Paperback 80%
**Average Price:** $15

## Pavement Saw Press

**Type:** press
**CLMP member:** no
**Primary Editor/Contact Person:** David Baratier
**Address:** P.O. Box 6291
Columbus, OH 43206
**Web Site Address:** http://pavementsaw.org
**Publishes:** poetry
**Editorial Focus:** A wide range of poetry, from collected poems of recognizable authors to experimental book length poems written in 7 languages
**Representative Authors:** Simon Perchik, Sofia Starnes, and Alan Catlin
**Submissions Policy:** We have a yearly first book contest and a open chapbook contest. Otherwise books are chosen through journal contributors.
**Simultaneous Subs:** yes
**Reading Period:** Year-round
**Reporting Time:** 2 to 4 months
**Author Payment:** royalties and copies
**Contests:** See Web Site for Contest Guidelines.
**Founded:** 1992
**Non Profit:** yes
**Paid Staff:** 1
**Unpaid Staff:** 8
**Distributors:** Baker & Taylor, SPD, Brodart,
**ISSN Number/ISBN Number:** ISBN 1-886-350
**Number of Books Published per Year:** 7
**Titles in Print:** 51
**Average Print Run:** 1,000
**Average Percentage Printed:** Paperback 86%, Chapbook 14%
**Average Price:** $12

## Pavement Saw

**Type:** magazine
**CLMP member:** no
**Primary Editor/Contact Person:** David Baratier
**Address:** P.O. Box 6291
Columbus, OH 43206
**Web Site Address:** http://pavementsaw.org
**Publishes:** poetry
**Editorial Focus:** Each has a name. #8 The All Male Unfinished Interview, Issue #7 The Ultimate Issue, #6 The Minty Fresh Pirate Issue etcetera
**Representative Authors:** There are no 3 authors useful, to understand our great, and wonderously variable taste
**Submissions Policy:** We only publish good poetry. If you write good poetry, please send some. Guidelines regularly change. Inside each issue $7pp
**Simultaneous Subs:** no
**Reading Period:** Year-round
**Reporting Time:** 3 to 8 weeks
**Author Payment:** copies
**Founded:** 1992

**Non Profit:** yes
**Paid Staff:** 1
**Unpaid Staff:** 8
**Distributors:** Baker & Taylor, SPD, Brodart
**ISSN Number/ISBN Number:** ISBN 1-886350
**Total Circulation:** 551
**Average Print Run:** 551
**Subscription Rate:** Individual $12/Institution $14
**Single Copy Price:** $7
**Current Volume/Issue:** 1/8
**Frequency per Year:** 1
**Backfile Available:** yes
**Unsolicited Ms. Received:** yes
**% of Unsolicited Ms. Published per Year:** 100%
**Format:** perfect
**Size:** H 7" W 10"
**Average Pages:** 88
**Ads:** no

## Pearl Editions

**Type:** press
**CLMP member:** yes
**Primary Editor/Contact Person:** Marilyn Johnson
**Address:** 3030 E. Second St.
Long Beach, CA 90803
**Web Site Address:** http://www.pearlmag.com
**Publishes:** poetry
**Editorial Focus:** Specializes in books of reader-friendly poetry that are as readable, dramatic, and entertaining as a good novel or memoir.
**Representative Authors:** Lisa Glatt, Donna Hilbert, and Andrew Kaufman
**Submissions Policy:** Only accepts submissions to the annual Pearl Poetry Prize. All others are by invitation only.
**Simultaneous Subs:** yes
**Reading Period:** 5/1 to 7/15
**Reporting Time:** 5 to 6 months
**Author Payment:** royalties and copies
**Contests:** See Web Site for Contest Guidelines.
**Founded:** 1974
**Non Profit:** no
**Paid Staff:** 0
**Unpaid Staff:** 3
**Wholesalers:** Baker & Taylor
**ISSN Number/ISBN Number:** ISBN 1888219
**Number of Books Published per Year:** 3
**Titles in Print:** 25
**Average Print Run:** 1,000
**Average Percentage Printed:** Paperback 70%,

Chapbook 30%
**Average Price:** $12

## Pearl

**Type:** magazine
**CLMP member:** yes
**Primary Editor/Contact Person:** Marilyn Johnson
**Address:** 3030 E. 2nd St.
Long Beach, CA 90803
**Web Site Address:** http://www.pearlmag.com
**Publishes:** fiction, poetry, and art
**Editorial Focus:** Accessible, humanistic poetry and fiction that communicates and is related to real life. No taboos. Humor and wit welcome.
**Representative Authors:** Jim Daniels, Lisa Glatt, and Charles Harper Webb
**Submissions Policy:** Submit 3-5 poems, up to 40 lines, and short-short stories, up to 1,200 words, with SASE. No e-mail submissions.
**Simultaneous Subs:** yes
**Reading Period:** 9/1 to 5/31
**Reporting Time:** 6 to 8 weeks
**Author Payment:** copies
**Contests:** See Web Site for Contest Guidelines.
**Founded:** 1974
**Non Profit:** no
**Paid Staff:** 0
**Unpaid Staff:** 3
**Total Circulation:** 700
**Paid Circulation:** 150
**Subscription Rate:** Individual $18/Institution $20
**Single Copy Price:** $8
**Current Volume/Issue:** Issue 33
**Frequency per Year:** 2
**Backfile Available:** yes
**Unsolicited Ms. Received:** yes
**% of Unsolicited Ms. Published per Year:** 5%
**Format:** perfect
**Size:** H 8.5" W 5.5"
**Average Pages:** 148
**Ads:** no

## Pecan Grove Press

**Type:** press
**CLMP member:** yes
**Primary Editor/Contact Person:** H. Palmer Hall
**Address:** Box AL, St. Mary's University
1 Camino Santa Maria
San Antonio, TX 78228

**Web Site Address:**
http://library.stmarytx.edu/pgpress/
**Publishes:** poetry
**Editorial Focus:** Fresh, original poetry, with each poem acting as a kind of art exhibit: poems gaining strength through interrelationships.
**Representative Authors:** Edward Byrne, Patricia Fargnoli, and Trinidad Sanchez
**Submissions Policy:** Prefers complete manuscript of from 34 to 56 pages; inc. SASE, prefers recycling Mss. Submissions read all year.
**Simultaneous Subs:** yes
**Reading Period:** Year-round
**Reporting Time:** 2 to 4 months
**Author Payment:** copies
**Contests:** See Web Site for Contest Guidelines.
**Founded:** 1985
**Non Profit:** yes
**Paid Staff:** 0
**Unpaid Staff:** 2
**Distributors:** Baker & Taylor, Amazon.com
**ISSN Number/ISBN Number:** ISBN 1-931247-
**Number of Books Published per Year:** 6-9
**Titles in Print:** 57
**Average Print Run:** 500
**Average Percentage Printed:** Paperback 67%, Chapbook 33%
**Average Price:** $9-$12

# The Pedestal Magazine.com

**Type:** online
**CLMP member:** yes
**Primary Editor/Contact Person:** John Amen
**Address:** 228 E. Park Ave.
Charlotte, NC 28203
**Web Site Address:**
http://www.ThePedestalMagazine.com
**Publishes:** fiction, nonfiction, poetry, reviews, and art
**Editorial Focus:** New and established writers and visual artists.
**Representative Authors:** Philip Levine, W.S. Merwin, and Maxine Kumin
**Submissions Policy:** Submissions via website only. See guidelines and reading periods on website.
**Simultaneous Subs:** yes
**Reading Period:** Year-round
**Reporting Time:** 6 to 8 weeks
**Author Payment:** cash
**Founded:** 2000
**Non Profit:** yes

**Paid Staff:** 3
**Unpaid Staff:** 0
**Average Page Views per Month:** 70,000
**Average Unique Visitors per Month:** 11,500
**Frequency per Year:** 6
**Publish Print Anthology:** no
**Average Percentage of Pages per Category:** Fiction 7%, Poetry 60%, Reviews 10%, Art 23%
**Ad Rates:** See Web Site for Details.

# Pen & Inc Press

**Type:** press
**CLMP member:** no
**Primary Editor/Contact Person:** Sarah Gooderson
**Address:** School of Literature & Creative Writing
University of East Anglia
Norwich, Norfolk, UK NR4 7TJ
**Web Site Address:**
http://www.inpressbooks.co.uk/penandinc
**Publishes:** essays, fiction, nonfiction, poetry, and translation
**Editorial Focus:** Literary magazine Pretext features short fiction, nonfiction and poetry. Reactions anthology features contemporary poetry.
**Representative Authors:** Seamus Heaney, Michael Holroyd, and J G Ballard
**Submissions Policy:** Work must be original and unpublished. Prose up to 6,000 words. Up to 10 poems. Must be typed and sent by post.
**Simultaneous Subs:** yes
**Reading Period:** Year-round
**Reporting Time:** 4 to 6 months
**Author Payment:** cash and copies
**Founded:** 1999
**Non Profit:** no
**Paid Staff:** 2
**Unpaid Staff:** 2
**Distributors:** Central Books
**Number of Books Published per Year:** 4
**Titles in Print:** 22
**Average Print Run:** 700
**Average Percentage Printed:** Paperback 100%
**Average Price:** £7.99

# PEN America: A Journal for Writers and Readers

**Type:** magazine
**CLMP member:** yes
**Address:** 568 Broadway, Ste. 401
New York, NY 10012-3225
**Web Site Address:** http://www.pen.org/journal/
**Publishes:** essays, fiction, nonfiction, poetry, reviews, and translation
**Simultaneous Subs:** no
**Reading Period:** Year-round
**Reporting Time:** 1 to 2 months
**Author Payment:** none
**Founded:** 2000
**Non Profit:** no
**Unpaid Staff:** 6
**Backfile Available:** yes

# Pennsylvania English

**Type:** magazine
**CLMP member:** no
**Primary Editor/Contact Person:** Antonio Vallone
**Address:** Penn State DuBois
College Place
DuBois, PA 15801
**Publishes:** essays, fiction, nonfiction, poetry, and translation
**Editorial Focus:** We look at all genres, all styles.
**Representative Authors:** Phil Terman, Henry Hughes, and William Heyen
**Submissions Policy:** We have no restrictions.
**Simultaneous Subs:** yes
**Reading Period:** Year-round
**Reporting Time:** 11 to 12 months
**Author Payment:** copies
**Contests:** We do not have contests.
**Founded:** 1979
**Non Profit:** yes
**Paid Staff:** 0
**Unpaid Staff:** 5
**Wholesalers:** EBSCO
**ISSN Number/ISBN Number:** ISSN 0741805
**Total Circulation:** 300
**Paid Circulation:** 200
**Average Print Run:** 350
**Subscription Rate:** Individual $10/Institution $10
**Single Copy Price:** $10
**Current Volume/Issue:** 28/1/2
**Frequency per Year:** 1
**Backfile Available:** yes

**Unsolicited Ms. Received:** yes
**% of Unsolicited Ms. Published per Year:** 20%
**Format:** perfect
**Size:** H 8.25" W 5.25"
**Average Pages:** 200
**Ads:** no

# Pequod

**Type:** press
**CLMP member:** no
**Primary Editor/Contact Person:** Mark Rudman
**Address:** 817 West End Ave.
Ste. 4A
New York, NY 10025
**Publishes:** essays, fiction, poetry, art, and translation
**Editorial Focus:** Most of the work in Pequod is solicited. We publish mainly poetry and fiction.
**Representative Authors:** Alan Warner, Lucia Perillo, and Rika Lesser
**Submissions Policy:** SASE and double spaced fiction.
**Simultaneous Subs:** yes
**Reading Period:** Year-round
**Reporting Time:** 2 to 24 months
**Author Payment:** cash and subscription
**Contests:** no
**Founded:** 1974
**Non Profit:** yes
**Paid Staff:** 0
**Unpaid Staff:** 3
**Distributors:** Ingram, DeBoer
**ISSN Number/ISBN Number:** ISSN 0419-0516
**Number of Books Published per Year:** 0
**Titles in Print:** 0
**Average Percentage Printed:** Paperback 100%

# Peregrine

**Type:** press
**CLMP member:** yes
**Primary Editor/Contact Person:** Nancy Rose
**Address:** P O Box 1076
Amherst, MA 01004-1076
**Web Site Address:** http://www.amherstwriters.com
**Publishes:** fiction and poetry
**Editorial Focus:** Peregrine is committed to finding exceptional work by new as well as established writers. We are open to all styles, forms, and subjects (except greeting card verse), but we do not accept work for or by children.
**Representative Authors:** Gerald Wheeler, Dianna Hunter, and Earl Maxwell Coleman
**Submissions Policy:** No electronic submissions. Prose: 3,000 word limit. Double space. Indicate word count on first page. Poetry: 3-5 poems, each poem limited to 60 lines and spaces. Short poems, 30 lines max., have a better chance. Include cover letter with current address, spring and summer addresses, day and evening phone numbers, and a 40 word (max) bio. Enclose #10 SASE for our response or sufficient postage and packaging for return of manuscript.
**Simultaneous Subs:** yes
**Reading Period:** 10/1 to 4/1
**Reporting Time:** 6 to 9 months
**Author Payment:** copies
**Contests:** no contest
**Founded:** 1983
**Non Profit:** yes
**Paid Staff:** 0
**Unpaid Staff:** 15
**Distributors:** Amherst Writers & Artists Press
**ISSN Number/ISBN Number:** ISSN 0890-622x
**Number of Books Published per Year:** 6
**Titles in Print:** 32
**Average Percentage Printed:** Hardcover 10%, Paperback 30%, Chapbook 60%

# Perihelion

**Type:** online
**CLMP member:** no
**Primary Editor/Contact Person:** Joan Houlihan
**Address:** 2020 Pennsylvania Ave.
Ste. 443
Washington, DC 20006
**Web site Address:** http://webdelsol.com/Perihelion
**Publishes:** poetry, reviews, and translation
**Editorial Focus:** To publish the best in contemporary poetry and poetry translations. To present articles, reviews and interviews that provide insights into the theory, style and content of contemporary poetry.
**Representative Authors:** Nick Flynn, Martha Zweig, and Larissa Szporluk
**Simultaneous Subs:** yes
**Reading Period:** Year-round
**Reporting Time:** 1 to 3 months
**Author Payment:** none
**Founded:** 1996
**Non Profit:** yes
**Paid Staff:** 0
**Unpaid Staff:** 4
**Average Page Views per Month:** 4,250
**Average Unique Visitors per Month:** 1,200
**Publish Print Anthology:** no
**Average Percentage of Pages per Category:** Poetry 50%, Reviews 25%, Translation 25%

# Perugia Press

**Type:** press
**CLMP member:** yes
**Primary Editor/Contact Person:** Susan Kan
**Address:** P.O. Box 60364
Florence, MA 01062
**Web Site Address:** http://www.perugiapress.com
**Publishes:** poetry
**Editorial Focus:** We publish one 1st or 2nd book by a woman each year. Each book is the winner of our annual Intro Award Contest.
**Recent Awards Received:** ABA's Top 10 Poetry Book, 2005; Ohioana Book of the Year; Pushcart Prize; Weatherford Prize Finalist; Greenwall Fund Grant
**Representative Authors:** Diane Gilliam Fisher, Carol Edelstein, and Melanie Braverman
**Submissions Policy:** Women can submit first or second book mss. to our annual Intro Award Contest. Guidelines are available online.
**Simultaneous Subs:** yes
**Reading Period:** 8/1 to 11/15
**Reporting Time:** 3 to 6 months
**Author Payment:** royalties, cash, and copies
**Contests:** See Web Site for Contest Guidelines.
**Founded:** 1997
**Non Profit:** yes
**Paid Staff:** 1/2
**Unpaid Staff:** 1/2
**Wholesalers:** Baker & Taylor
**ISSN Number/ISBN Number:** ISBN 0-9660459
**Number of Books Published per Year:** 1

**Titles in Print:** 8
**Average Print Run:** 650
**Average Percentage Printed:** Paperback 100%
**Average Price:** $14

## Phantasmagoria

**Type:** magazine
**CLMP member:** yes
**Primary Editor/Contact Person:** Abigail Allen
**Address:** English Dept, Century College
3300 Century Ave. N.
White Bear Lake, MN 55110
**Publishes:** essays, fiction, and poetry
**Representative Authors:** Kim Chinquee, Greg Mulcahy, and B.Z. Niditch
**Submissions Policy:** No previously published work. Include SASE for return/notification.
**Simultaneous Subs:** no
**Reading Period:** Year-round
**Reporting Time:** 2 to 4 months
**Author Payment:** copies
**Founded:** 2001
**Non Profit:** yes
**Paid Staff:** 3
**Unpaid Staff:** 8
**Distributors:** Ingram
**ISSN Number/ISBN Number:** ISSN 1534-6129
**Total Circulation:** 950
**Paid Circulation:** 53
**Average Print Run:** 1,000
**Subscription Rate:** Individual $15/Institution $20
**Single Copy Price:** $9
**Current Volume/Issue:** 5/1
**Frequency per Year:** 2
**Backfile Available:** yes
**Unsolicited Ms. Received:** yes
**% of Unsolicited Ms. Published per Year:** 97%
**Format:** perfect
**Average Pages:** 160
**Ad Rates:** $100/pg

## Philos Press

**Type:** press
**CLMP member:** no
**Primary Editor/Contact Person:** Laura Beausoleil
**Address:** 8038A N. Bicentennial Loop S.E.
Lacey, WA 98503
**Publishes:** essays, fiction, poetry, and art
**Editorial Focus:** Publish primarily poetry.

**Representative Authors:** George Hitchcock, Dino Siotis, and Gary Amdahl
**Submissions Policy:** No submissions accepted.
**Simultaneous Subs:** no
**Reading Period:** Year-round
**Author Payment:** cash and copies
**Contests:** none
**Founded:** 1999
**Non Profit:** yes
**Paid Staff:** 1
**Unpaid Staff:** 2
**Distributors:** SPD, Amazon.com
**Wholesalers:** Blackwell's
**Number of Books Published per Year:** 1
**Titles in Print:** 5
**Average Percentage Printed:** Paperback 100%

## The Pikestaff Press

**Type:** press
**CLMP member:** yes
**Primary Editor/Contact Person:** Robert D. Sutherland
**Address:** P.O. Box 127
Normal, IL 61761
**Publishes:** fiction and poetry
**Representative Authors:** Lucia C. Getsi, J.W. Rivers, and Jeff Gundy
**Submissions Policy:** Send query letter first, with SASE.
**Simultaneous Subs:** yes
**Reading Period:** Year-round
**Reporting Time:** 2 to 6 weeks
**Author Payment:** copies
**Founded:** 1977
**Non Profit:** yes
**Paid Staff:** 0
**Unpaid Staff:** 1
**ISSN Number/ISBN Number:** ISBN 0-936044
**Number of Books Published per Year:** 1
**Titles in Print:** 6
**Average Print Run:** varies
**Average Percentage Printed:** Hardcover 20%, Paperback 80%
**Average Price:** varies

## Pilgrimage

**Type:** magazine
**CLMP member:** yes
**Primary Editor/Contact Person:** Peter Anderson
**Address:** Box 696

Crestone, CO 81131
**Web Site Address:** http://www.pilgrimagepress.org
**Publishes:** essays, nonfiction, and poetry
**Editorial Focus:** Reflective autobiographical writings; place, spirit, peace and justice; in and beyond the American Southwest.
**Representative Authors:** Kim Stafford, Parker Palmer, and Nancy Mairs
**Submissions Policy:** Welcomes autobiographical nonfiction and poetry; tell the truth and "tell it hot." Occasional fiction. Black and white art.
**Simultaneous Subs:** yes
**Reading Period:** Year-round
**Reporting Time:** 3 to 4 months
**Author Payment:** copies and subscription
**Contests:** See Web Site for Contest Guidelines.
**Founded:** 1974
**Non Profit:** yes
**Paid Staff:** yes
**Unpaid Staff:** yes
**Distributors:** Kent News
**Wholesalers:** EBSCO, Harrasowitz
**Total Circulation:** 600
**Paid Circulation:** 400
**Average Print Run:** 700
**Subscription Rate:** Individual $22/Institution $40
**Single Copy Price:** $8
**Current Volume/Issue:** 30/3
**Frequency per Year:** 3
**Backfile Available:** yes
**Unsolicited Ms. Received:** yes
**% of Unsolicited Ms. Published per Year:** 20%
**Format:** perfect
**Size:** H 6" W 8"
**Average Pages:** 100

## Pima Press

**Type:** press
**CLMP member:** yes
**Primary Editor/Contact Person:** Meg Files
**Address:** Pima Community College
2202 W. Anklam Road
Tucson, AZ 85709-0170
**Publishes:** fiction and poetry
**Representative Authors:** Dan Gilmore, Barrie Ryan, and Robert Longoni
**Submissions Policy:** by invitation only
**Simultaneous Subs:** yes
**Reading Period:** Year-round
**Reporting Time:** 1 to 2 months

**Author Payment:** none
**Founded:** 1997
**Non Profit:** yes
**Paid Staff:** 0
**Unpaid Staff:** 6
**Distributors:** Baker & Taylor, Ingram
**Number of Books Published per Year:** 2
**Titles in Print:** 6
**Average Print Run:** 500
**Average Percentage Printed:** Paperback 100%
**Average Price:** $12

## Pinball Publishing

**Type:** press
**CLMP member:** yes
**Primary Editor/Contact Person:** Laura Brian
**Address:** 2621 SE Clinton St.
Portland, OR 97202
**Web Site Address:** http://www.pinballpublishing.com
**Publishes:** fiction, nonfiction, and poetry
**Editorial Focus:** We independently publish exceptional editions of contemporary poetry and fiction.
**Representative Authors:** Casey Kwang, David Harrison Horton, and Fiona Hile
**Submissions Policy:** We consider poetry, fiction, and creative nonfiction manuscripts. Send 30-page sample and bio w/query letter.
**Simultaneous Subs:** yes
**Reading Period:** Year-round
**Reporting Time:** 4 to 16 weeks
**Author Payment:** royalties and copies
**Founded:** 2001
**Non Profit:** no
**Paid Staff:** 2
**Unpaid Staff:** 1
**Wholesalers:** Baker & Taylor
**ISSN Number/ISBN Number:** 1540-6113/0-9721926
**Number of Books Published per Year:** 2
**Titles in Print:** 6
**Average Percentage Printed:** Paperback 80%, Chapbook 20%
**Backfile Available:** yes

## Pindeldyboz

**Type:** online
**CLMP member:** yes
**Primary Editor/Contact Person:** Whitney Pastorek
**Address:** 23-55 38th St.
Astoria, NY 11105

**Web Site Address:** http://www.pindeldyboz.com

**Publishes:** essays, fiction, nonfiction, poetry, and art

**Editorial Focus:** Write something that has to be told. Show us something familiar in a different light. Kick ass. Surprise us.

**Recent Awards Received:** some stuff here and there. hey, check out our website for more specific info about us, no? yes!

**Submissions Policy:** We only accept unpublished work. If what you're sending can be found anywhere else, don't send it. We like shiny things.

**Simultaneous Subs:** yes

**Reading Period:** 9/1 to 2/1

**Reporting Time:** 2 to 4 months

**Author Payment:** copies

**Founded:** 2000

**Non Profit:** no

**Paid Staff:** 0

**Unpaid Staff:** 6

**Distributors:** Ingram, DeBoer

**Average Page Views per Month:** 22,000

**Average Unique Visitors per Month:** 12,000

**Frequency per Year:** 18

**Publish Print Anthology:** yes

**Price:** $12

**Average Percentage of Pages per Category:** Fiction 80%, Nonfiction 5%, Poetry 5%, Essays 5%, Art 5%

**Ads:** no

## Pleiades Press/LMWT Poetry Series

**Type:** press

**CLMP member:** yes

**Primary Editor/Contact Person:** Kevin Prufer and Susan Ludvigson

**Address:** Department of English
Central Missouri State University
Warrensburg, MO 64093

**Web Site Address:**
http://www.cmsu.edu/englphil/pleiades

**Publishes:** poetry

**Editorial Focus:** Poetry books by American authors.

**Representative Authors:** Nils Michals, Kathleen Jesme, and Matthew Cooperman

**Submissions Policy:** Books are selected only through our annual competition.

**Simultaneous Subs:** yes

**Reading Period:** 7/9 to 30/30

**Reporting Time:** 3 to 6 months

**Author Payment:** cash

**Founded:** 1998

**Non Profit:** yes

**Paid Staff:** 2

**Unpaid Staff:** 5

**Distributors:** Louisiana State University Press

**Number of Books Published per Year:** 1

**Titles in Print:** 6

**Average Percentage Printed:** Paperback 100%

## Pleiades: A Journal of New Writing

**Type:** magazine

**CLMP member:** yes

**Primary Editor/Contact Person:** Kevin Prufer

**Address:** Dept. of English
Central Missouri State University
Warrensburg, MO 64093

**Web Site Address:**
http://www.cmsu.edu/englphil/pleiades

**Publishes:** essays, fiction, nonfiction, poetry, reviews, and translation

**Editorial Focus:** We publish poetry, fiction, essays, and reviews of important small and university press books.

**Representative Authors:** James Tate, Carl Phillips, and Chris Offutt

**Submissions Policy:** Send submissions with SASE. We read all year, though are a little slower in the summer.

**Simultaneous Subs:** yes

**Reading Period:** Year-round

**Reporting Time:** 1 to 3 months

**Author Payment:** none

**Contests:** See Web Site for Contest Guidelines.

**Founded:** 1991

**Non Profit:** yes

**Paid Staff:** 3

**Unpaid Staff:** 2

**Distributors:** Ingram, DeBoer, Media Solutions

**ISSN Number/ISBN Number:** ISSN 1063-3391

**Total Circulation:** 3,000

**Paid Circulation:** 1,000

**Average Print Run:** 4,500

**Subscription Rate:** Individual $12/Institution $12

**Single Copy Price:** $6

**Current Volume/Issue:** 26/1

**Frequency per Year:** 2

**Backfile Available:** yes

**Unsolicited Ms. Received:** yes

**% of Unsolicited Ms. Published per Year:** .5%

**Format:** perfect

**Size:** H 8.5" W 5"

**Average Pages:** 160
**Ads:** yes
**Ad Rates:** on request

# Pleasure Boat Studio: A Literary Press

**Type:** press
**CLMP member:** yes
**Primary Editor/Contact Person:** Jack Estes
**Address:** 201 W. 89th St., +6F
New York, NY 10024
**Web Site Address:**
http://www.pleasureboatstudio.com
**Publishes:** essays, fiction, nonfiction, and poetry
**Editorial Focus:** High quality literary works, usually with sociological or philosophical inclinations.
**Recent Awards Received:** Excellent reviews in key journal.
**Representative Authors:** Mary Lou Sanelli, Frances Driscoll, and Mike O'Connor
**Submissions Policy:** Query first, via e-mail. Include a brief description of your book.
**Simultaneous Subs:** yes
**Reading Period:** Year-round
**Reporting Time:** 1 to 6 months
**Author Payment:** royalties and copies
**Founded:** 1996
**Non Profit:** no
**Paid Staff:** 2
**Unpaid Staff:** 1
**Distributors:** SPD
**Wholesalers:** Ingram, Baker & Taylor, Partners/West
**ISSN Number/ISBN Number:** ISBN 1-929355
**Number of Books Published per Year:** 3-4
**Titles in Print:** 30
**Average Print Run:** 500
**Average Percentage Printed:** Paperback 85%, Chapbook 15%
**Average Price:** $15

# Ploughshares

**Type:** magazine
**CLMP member:** yes
**Primary Editor/Contact Person:** Don Lee and David Daniel
**Address:** Emerson College
120 Boylston St.
Boston, MA 02116
**Web Site Address:** http://www.pshares.org

**Publishes:** fiction, nonfiction, and poetry
**Editorial Focus:** Guest-edited serially by prominent writers who explore different visions, aesthetics, and literary circles.
**Representative Authors:** Antonya Nelson, Toi Derricotte, and Jonah Winter
**Submissions Policy:** 1 story or 1-3 poems
**Simultaneous Subs:** yes
**Reading Period:** 8/1 to 3/31
**Reporting Time:** 3 to 5 months
**Author Payment:** cash, copies, and subscription
**Founded:** 1971
**Non Profit:** yes
**Paid Staff:** 4
**Unpaid Staff:** 20
**Distributors:** Ingram
**ISSN Number/ISBN Number:** ISSN 0048-4474
**Total Circulation:** 6,000
**Paid Circulation:** 3,600
**Average Print Run:** 7,500
**Subscription Rate:** Individual $24/Institution $27
**Single Copy Price:** $10.95
**Current Volume/Issue:** 30/2 and 3
**Frequency per Year:** 3
**Backfile Available:** yes
**Unsolicited Ms. Received:** yes
**% of Unsolicited Ms. Published per Year:** 1%
**Format:** perfect
**Size:** H 8.5" W 5.375"
**Average Pages:** 220
**Ads:** yes
**Ad Rates:** $400 full/$275 half
See Web Site for Details.

# PMS poemmemoirstory

**Type:** magazine
**CLMP member:** yes
**Primary Editor/Contact Person:** Linda Frost
**Address:** University of Alabama at Birmingham
HOH 1530 3rd Ave. South
Birmingham, AL 35294-4450
**Web Site Address:** http://www.pms-journal.org
**Publishes:** essays, fiction, nonfiction, and poetry
**Editorial Focus:** Top quality literary work by women; one memoir by a woman who shares her historically significant experience.
**Recent Awards Received:** Best American Poetry 2003, 2004; New Stories from the South 2005; Best American Essays 2005
**Representative Authors:** Ruth Stone, Amy Gerstler,

and Sonia Sanchez

**Submissions Policy:** 5 poems or 15 pages of prose with SASE.
**Simultaneous Subs:** yes
**Reading Period:** 9/1 to 11/30
**Reporting Time:** 4 to 6 weeks
**Author Payment:** copies and subscription
**Founded:** 2001
**Non Profit:** yes
**Paid Staff:** 0
**Unpaid Staff:** 10
**ISSN Number/ISBN Number:** 1535-1335/0-89732-578-8
**Total Circulation:** 500
**Paid Circulation:** 150
**Average Print Run:** 750
**Subscription Rate:** Individual $7/Institution $7
**Single Copy Price:** $6
**Current Volume/Issue:** Issue 5
**Frequency per Year:** 1
**Backfile Available:** yes
**Unsolicited Ms. Received:** yes
**% of Unsolicited Ms. Published per Year:** 80%
**Format:** perfect
**Size:** H 9" W 6"
**Average Pages:** 120
**Ads:** no

# Poem

**Type:** magazine
**CLMP member:** yes
**Primary Editor/Contact Person:** Rebecca Harbor
**Address:** P.O. Box 2006
Huntsville, AL 35804
**Web Site Address:** http://www.hla-hsv.org
**Publishes:** poetry
**Editorial Focus:** mostly lyric poetry; traditional and free verse; compact language, precise diction, apt imagery," a tuned ear and practiced pen"
**Representative Authors:** Robert Cooperman, Kathryn Kirkpatrick, and T. Alan Broughton
**Submissions Policy:** no translations, previously published works, or simultaneous submissions; 3-5 poems with cover letter and SASE
**Simultaneous Subs:** no
**Reading Period:** Year-round
**Reporting Time:** 1 to 2 months
**Author Payment:** copies
**Founded:** 1967
**Non Profit:** yes

**Paid Staff:** 0
**Unpaid Staff:** 5
**Total Circulation:** 475
**Paid Circulation:** 300
**Average Print Run:** 500
**Subscription Rate:** Individual $20/Institution $20
**Single Copy Price:** $10
**Current Volume/Issue:** Issue 94
**Frequency per Year:** 2
**Backfile Available:** yes
**Unsolicited Ms. Received:** yes
**% of Unsolicited Ms. Published per Year:** 5-6%
**Format:** perfect
**Size:** H 7 1/4" W 4 3/8"
**Average Pages:** 90
**Ads:** no

# Poems & Plays

**Type:** magazine
**CLMP member:** no
**Primary Editor/Contact Person:** Gaylord Brewer
**Address:** English Department
Middle Tennessee State University
Murfreesboro, TN 37132
**Web Site Address:**
http://www.middleenglish.org/poemsandplays
**Publishes:** poetry
**Editorial Focus:** Poems and short plays.
**Representative Authors:** Julie Lechevsky, David Kirby, and Charles Harper Webb
**Submissions Policy:** We read submissions Oct.-Dec. for subsequent spring issue.
**Simultaneous Subs:** yes
**Reading Period:** 10/1 to 12/31
**Reporting Time:** 6 to 8 weeks
**Author Payment:** copies
**Founded:** 1993
**Non Profit:** yes
**Paid Staff:** 0
**Unpaid Staff:** 2-3
**ISSN Number/ISBN Number:** ISSN 1073-1172
**Total Circulation:** 900
**Paid Circulation:** N/A
**Average Print Run:** 900
**Subscription Rate:** Individual $10/Institution $20
**Single Copy Price:** $6
**Current Volume/Issue:** Issue 10
**Frequency per Year:** 1
**Backfile Available:** yes
**Unsolicited Ms. Received:** yes

**% of Unsolicited Ms. Published per Year:** 1%
**Format:** perfect
**Size:** H 9" W 6"
**Average Pages:** 88
**Ads:** no

# Poesy

**Type:** magazine
**CLMP member:** yes
**Primary Editor/Contact Person:** Brian Morrisey
**Address:** P.O. Box 7823
Santa Cruz, CA 95061
**Web Site Address:** http://www.poesy.org
**Publishes:** poetry and art
**Editorial Focus:** Poesy is an anthology for poets across the country. Poesy's main concentration is Boston, MA and Santa Cruz, CA
**Representative Authors:** Diane di Prima, Jack Hirschman, and A.D. Winans
**Submissions Policy:** Requested but not limited to: 32 lines or less, 5-7 poems may be considered for each issue.
**Simultaneous Subs:** yes
**Reading Period:** Year-round
**Reporting Time:** 5 to 7 weeks
**Author Payment:** copies
**Founded:** 1990
**Non Profit:** yes
**Paid Staff:** 0
**Unpaid Staff:** 3
**Distributors:** Bound Together Books, City Lights, Quimby's
**ISSN Number/ISBN Number:** ISSN 1541-8162
**Total Circulation:** 1,000
**Paid Circulation:** 55
**Subscription Rate:** Individual $12/Institution $15
**Single Copy Price:** $1
**Current Volume/Issue:** Issue 22
**Frequency per Year:** 4
**Backfile Available:** yes
**Unsolicited Ms. Received:** yes
**% of Unsolicited Ms. Published per Year:** 10%
**Format:** glued
**Size:** H 8.125" W 10.5"
**Average Pages:** 16-20
**Ads:** yes
**Ad Rates:** $10, $25, $40, $70
See Web Site for Details.

# Poet Lore

**Type:** magazine
**CLMP member:** yes
**Primary Editor/Contact Person:** Sunil Freeman
**Address:** The Writer's Center
4508 Walsh St.
Bethesda, MD 20815-8006
**Web Site Address:** http://www.writer.org/poetlore
**Publishes:** essays and poetry
**Editorial Focus:** Inviting all types of poetry, the editors look for a high level of craftsmanship, and imaginative use of language and image
**Representative Authors:** David Wagoner, Fleda Brown, and Linda Pastan
**Submissions Policy:** You may submit three to five poems. All poems must be typed with name and address on each poem. If a poem is more than one page, please indicate if the second page begins with a new stanza. Reviewers: Please query the editors with a sample of your writing. We ask you let us know in your cover letter if poems are simultaneously submitted, and notify us immediately if the work is accepted elsewhere.
**Simultaneous Subs:** yes
**Reading Period:** Year-round
**Reporting Time:** 1 to 3 months
**Author Payment:** copies
**Founded:** 1889
**Non Profit:** yes
**Paid Staff:** 1
**Unpaid Staff:** 4
**Distributors:** EBSCO, Swets Blackwell, Harrassowitz
**ISSN Number/ISBN Number:** ISSN 0032-1966
**Total Circulation:** 800
**Paid Circulation:** 450
**Subscription Rate:** Individual $18/Institution $26.60
**Single Copy Price:** $9
**Current Volume/Issue:** 99/3/4
**Frequency per Year:** 2
**Backfile Available:** yes
**Unsolicited Ms. Received:** yes
**% of Unsolicited Ms. Published per Year:** 5%
**Format:** perfect
**Size:** H 9" W 6"
**Average Pages:** 120
**Ads:** yes
**Ad Rates:** full page $100, half page $50

## The Poetry Church

**Type:** magazine
**CLMP member:** no
**Primary Editor/Contact Person:** Rev. John Waddington-Feather
**Address:** P.O. Box 438
nil
Shrewsbury UK, Sa SY3 0WN
**Web Site Address:** http://www.waddysweb.freeuk.com
**Publishes:** poetry and reviews
**Editorial Focus:** The current state of Christian art, music and writing. Often in the form of a sermonette.
**Representative Authors:** Walter Nash, Susan Glyn, and Laurie Bates
**Submissions Policy:** Poems must be 30 lines or less. Longer for our bi-annual Collections winter and summer. Typed and with SASE.
**Simultaneous Subs:** yes
**Reading Period:** Year-round
**Reporting Time:** 1 to 2 weeks
**Author Payment:** none
**Contests:** None. But poetry contests are listed in our News section each quarter.
**Founded:** 1985
**Non Profit:** yes
**Paid Staff:** 2
**Unpaid Staff:** 5
**Distributors:** Feather Books, P.O. Box 438, Shrewsbury SY3 0WN
**ISSN Number/ISBN Number:** none/1 84175
**Total Circulation:** 1,000
**Paid Circulation:** 280
**Subscription Rate:** Individual $25/Institution $30
**Single Copy Price:** $6
**Current Volume/Issue:** 9/3
**Frequency per Year:** 4
**Backfile Available:** yes
**Unsolicited Ms. Received:** yes
**% of Unsolicited Ms. Published per Year:** 50%
**Format:** stapled
**Size:** H 8" W 6"
**Average Pages:** 40
**Ads:** no

## Poetry Daily

**Type:** online
**CLMP member:** yes
**Primary Editor/Contact Person:** Don Selby
**Address:** P.O. Box 1306
Charlottesville, VA 22902-1306
**Web Site Address:** http://www.poems.com
**Publishes:** essays, poetry, and reviews
**Editorial Focus:** Poems, news, essays, reviews, and special editorial features selected from current books and journals; weekly e-mail newsletter
**Representative Authors:** Rita Dove, Bob Hicok, and W.S. Merwin
**Submissions Policy:** We do not take original submissions
**Simultaneous Subs:** no
**Author Payment:** none
**Founded:** 1997
**Non Profit:** yes
**Paid Staff:** 1
**Unpaid Staff:** 1
**Backfile Available:** no
**Average Page Views per Month:** 1.1 million
**Average Unique Visitors per Month:** 17,000
**Frequency per Year:** 18
**Publish Print Anthology:** yes
Price: $14.95
**Average Percentage of Pages per Category:** Poetry 98%, Reviews 1%, Essays 1%
**Ad Rates:** See Web Site for Details.

## Poetry Flash

**Type:** magazine
**CLMP member:** yes
**Primary Editor/Contact Person:** Joyce Jenkins
**Address:** 1450 Fourth St., #4
Berkeley, CA 94710
**Web Site Address:** http://www.poetryflash.org
**Publishes:** essays and reviews
**Simultaneous Subs:** yes
**Reading Period:** Year-round
**Reporting Time:** 1 to 2 months
**Author Payment:** none
**Founded:** 1972
**Non Profit:** no
**Unpaid Staff:** 3 +
**Backfile Available:** yes

## Poetry International

**Type:** magazine
**CLMP member:** yes
**Primary Editor/Contact Person:** Fred Moramarco
**Address:** Dept. of English
San Diego State University

San Diego, CA 92182
**Web Site Address:** http://poetryinternational.sdsu.edu
**Publishes:** essays, nonfiction, poetry, reviews, and art
**Editorial Focus:** Quality poetry and translations from throughout the world
**Representative Authors:** Billy Collins, Kim Addonizio, and Adrienne Rich
**Submissions Policy:** Read manuscripts only between Sept. 1 and Dec. 30 of each year. Send no more than five poems at that time.
**Simultaneous Subs:** yes
**Reading Period:** 9/1 to 12/31
**Reporting Time:** 3 to 4 months
**Author Payment:** copies
**Founded:** 1997
**Non Profit:** yes
**Paid Staff:** 4
**Unpaid Staff:** 3
**Distributors:** Ingham Periodicals
**ISSN Number/ISBN Number:** 1093-054-X/varies
**Total Circulation:** 1,000
**Paid Circulation:** 400
**Average Print Run:** 1,500
**Subscription Rate:** Individual $45/Institution $54
**Single Copy Price:** $15
**Current Volume/Issue:** Issue 10
**Frequency per Year:** 1
**Backfile Available:** yes
**Unsolicited Ms. Received:** yes
**% of Unsolicited Ms. Published per Year:** 7%
**Format:** perfect
**Average Pages:** 200
**Ad Rates:** See Web Site for Details.

# Poetry

**Type:** magazine
**CLMP member:** yes
**Primary Editor/Contact Person:** Christian Wiman
**Address:** The Poetry Foundation
1030 N. Clark St., Ste. 420
Chicago, IL 60610
**Web Site Address:** http://www.poetrymagazine.org
**Publishes:** essays, poetry, reviews, and translation
**Editorial Focus:** To print the best poetry written today, in whatever style, genre, or approach.
**Representative Authors:** W.S. Di Piero, Kay Ryan, and August Kleinzahler
**Submissions Policy:** Submissions must be made by mail and accompanied by a SASE. We do not take e-mail submissions. Please refer to website.

**Simultaneous Subs:** no
**Reading Period:** Year-round
**Reporting Time:** 2 to 8 weeks
**Author Payment:** cash and copies
**Contests:** See Web Site for Contest Guidelines.
**Founded:** 1912
**Non Profit:** yes
**Paid Staff:** 6
**Unpaid Staff:** 0
**Distributors:** DeBoer, Ingram, Ubiquity
**ISSN Number/ISBN Number:** 0032-2032
**Total Circulation:** 20,500
**Paid Circulation:** 18,000
**Average Print Run:** 23,000
**Subscription Rate:** Individual $35/Institution $38
**Single Copy Price:** $3.75
**Current Volume/Issue:** 186/5
**Frequency per Year:** 12
**Backfile Available:** yes
**Unsolicited Ms. Received:** yes
**% of Unsolicited Ms. Published per Year:** 100%
**Format:** perfect
**Size:** H 9" W 5.5"
**Average Pages:** 72
**Ads:** yes
**Ad Rates:** $800 per page
See Web Site for Details.

# Poetry Midwest

**Type:** online
**CLMP member:** no
**Primary Editor/Contact Person:** Matthew W. Schmeer
**Address:** 5915 W. 100th Terrace
Overland Park, KS 66207
**Web Site Address:** http://www.poetrymidwest.org
**Publishes:** fiction, nonfiction, and poetry
**Editorial Focus:** We look for highly literary pieces that capture the essence of experience with vivid imagery while avoiding didacticism.
**Representative Authors:** John Grey, Rhoda Janzen, and Roger Pfingston
**Submissions Policy:** E-mail submissions only. Send 3 poems or 1 piece of prose. No prose over 300 words. E-mail to submit@poetrymidwest.org.
**Simultaneous Subs:** yes
**Reading Period:** Year-round
**Reporting Time:** 1 to 6 months
**Author Payment:** none
**Founded:** 2000

**Non Profit:** yes
**Paid Staff:** 0
**Unpaid Staff:** 2
**ISSN Number/ISBN Number:** ISSN 1536-870X
**Average Page Views per Month:** 1,500
**Average Unique Visitors per Month:** 1,200
**Frequency per Year:** 3
**Publish Print Anthology:** no
**Average Percentage of Pages per Category:** Fiction 10%, Nonfiction 10%, Poetry 80%
**Ads:** no

## Poetry Miscellany

**Type:** magazine
**CLMP member:** no
**Primary Editor/Contact Person:** Richard Jackson
**Address:** English Dept. UT-Chattanooga
Chattanooga, TN 37411
**Web Site Address:**
http://www.utc.edu/~engldept/pm/pmhp.html
**Publishes:** essays, fiction, poetry, and reviews
**Editorial Focus:** Poetry from all schools and tastes; chapbook series of European writers in translation
**Representative Authors:** William Olsen, Maxine Kumin, and Marvin Bell
**Submissions Policy:** 3-5 poems; query for prose
**Simultaneous Subs:** no
**Reading Period:** Year-round
**Reporting Time:** 5 to 6 months
**Author Payment:** none
**Founded:** 1970
**Non Profit:** yes
**Paid Staff:** 1
**Unpaid Staff:** 5
**Total Circulation:** 500
**Paid Circulation:** 100
**Subscription Rate:** Individual $5/Institution $5
**Single Copy Price:** $5
**Current Volume/Issue:** Issue 29
**Frequency per Year:** 1
**Backfile Available:** yes
**Unsolicited Ms. Received:** yes
**% of Unsolicited Ms. Published per Year:** 1%
**Format:** Saddle Stitched
**Size:** H 8" W 12"
**Average Pages:** 45
**Ads:** yes
**Ad Rates:** $100 (full page)

## The Poetry Project Newsletter

**Type:** magazine
**CLMP member:** yes
**Primary Editor/Contact Person:** A. Berrigan/Brendan Lorber
**Address:** 131 E. 10th St.
at St. Mark's Church
New York, NY 10003
**Web Site Address:** http://www.thepoetryproject.com
**Publishes:** essays, poetry, and reviews
**Editorial Focus:** A bimonthly newsletter devoted to innovative poetry and poetics by way of essays, reviews, debate, and experimental writing.
**Representative Authors:** Brenda Coultas, Edwin Torres, and Ron Padgett
**Submissions Policy:** For potential book reviews, please send one copy of book and cover letter, attn: Brendan Lorber.
**Simultaneous Subs:** no
**Reading Period:** Year-round
**Reporting Time:** 1 to 6 weeks
**Author Payment:** none
**Founded:** 1973
**Non Profit:** yes
**Paid Staff:** 5
**Unpaid Staff:** 5
**Distributors:** SPD
**Total Circulation:** 5,800
**Paid Circulation:** 1,950
**Average Print Run:** 5,800
**Subscription Rate:** Individual $25/Institution $25
**Single Copy Price:** $5
**Current Volume/Issue:** Issue 196
**Frequency per Year:** 5
**Backfile Available:** yes
**Unsolicited Ms. Received:** no
**Format:** stapled
**Ads:** yes
**Ad Rates:** Please contact info@poetryproject.com for ad inquiries.

## The Poetz Group

**Type:** online
**CLMP member:** yes
**Primary Editor/Contact Person:** Jackie Sheeler
**Address:** P.O. Box 1401
New York, NY 10026
**Web Site Address:** http://www.poetz.com
**Publishes:** poetry
**Editorial Focus:** Crafted yet risky work that addresses

the human, usually urban, experience.
**Representative Authors:** Martin Espada, Eileen McDermott, and Clara Sala
**Submissions Policy:** By invitation only. We hope to open submissions further during 2004. Check the website for policy changes.
**Simultaneous Subs:** yes
**Reading Period:** Year-round
**Reporting Time:** 1 to 3 months
**Author Payment:** none
**Founded:** 1999
**Non Profit:** yes
**Paid Staff:** 0
**Unpaid Staff:** 1
**Backfile Available:** yes
**Average Page Views per Month:** 10,000
**Average Unique Visitors per Month:** unknown
**Publish Print Anthology:** no
**Average Percentage of Pages per Category:** Poetry 90%, Reviews 10%
**Ads:** no

## Poltroon Press

**Type:** press
**CLMP member:** no
**Primary Editor/Contact Person:** Alastair Johnston
**Address:** P.O. Box 5476
Berkeley, CA 94705
**Web Site Address:** http://www.poltroonpress.com
**Publishes:** fiction, nonfiction, poetry, and translation
**Representative Authors:** Mark Coggins, Lucia Berlin, and Philip Whalen
**Submissions Policy:** Do not read unsolicited work
**Simultaneous Subs:** yes
**Reading Period:** Year-round
**Reporting Time:** 12 to 24 months
**Author Payment:** royalties
**Founded:** 1975
**Non Profit:** yes
**Paid Staff:** 0
**Unpaid Staff:** 2
**Distributors:** SPD
**ISSN Number/ISBN Number:** ISBN 0-918395-
**Number of Books Published per Year:** 2
**Titles in Print:** 30
**Average Percentage Printed:** Hardcover 100%

## POOL: A Journal of Poetry

**Type:** magazine

**CLMP member:** yes
**Primary Editor/Contact Person:** Judith Taylor
**Address:** P.O. Box 49738
Los Angeles,, CA 90049
**Web Site Address:** http://www.poolpoetry.com
**Publishes:** poetry and reviews
**Editorial Focus:** POOL is a national journal published in Los Angeles, featuring fresh and unexpected poetry.
**Recent Awards Received:** The Best American Poetry 2004 and 2005
**Representative Authors:** Amy Gerstler, Jane Miller, and Michael Burkard
**Submissions Policy:** See website for guidelines.
**Simultaneous Subs:** yes
**Reading Period:** 12/1 to 2/28
**Reporting Time:** 2 to 3 months
**Author Payment:** copies
**Founded:** 2000
**Non Profit:** yes
**Paid Staff:** 0
**Unpaid Staff:** 2
**Distributors:** DeBoer; Armadillo
**ISSN Number/ISBN Number:** ISBN 0-9721088-3-1
**Total Circulation:** 850
**Paid Circulation:** 80
**Average Print Run:** 900
**Subscription Rate:** Individual $10/18/24/Institution $12
**Single Copy Price:** $10
**Current Volume/Issue:** Issue 4
**Frequency per Year:** 1
**Backfile Available:** yes
**Unsolicited Ms. Received:** yes
**% of Unsolicited Ms. Published per Year:** 50%
**Format:** perfect
**Size:** H 9" W 6"
**Average Pages:** 120
**Ads:** yes
**Ad Rates:** Exchange ads only.

## Portable Press at Yo-Yo Labs

**Type:** press
**CLMP member:** yes
**Primary Editor/Contact Person:** Brenda Iijima
**Address:** 596 Bergen St.
Brooklyn, NY 11238
**Publishes:** poetry and art
**Editorial Focus:** experimental poetry, emergent hybridized writing, work that fuses the political, socio-

logical, lingual and emotional realms.

**Representative Authors:** Peter Lamborn Wilson, Jill Magi, and Christina Strong

**Submissions Policy:** open submission policy, although most works are solicited.

**Simultaneous Subs:** yes

**Reading Period:** Year-round

**Reporting Time:** 1 to 2 months

**Author Payment:** none

**Founded:** 2002

**Non Profit:** yes

**Paid Staff:** 0

**Unpaid Staff:** 1

**Number of Books Published per Year:** 5

**Titles in Print:** 25

**Average Print Run:** 150

**Average Percentage Printed:** Paperback 5%, Chapbook 90%, Other 5%

**Average Price:** $6

# Portals Press

**Type:** press

**CLMP member:** no

**Primary Editor/Contact Person:** John P. Travis

**Address:** 4411 Fontainebleau Dr.
New Orleans, LA 70125

**Web Site Address:** http://www.portalspress.com

**Publishes:** fiction and poetry

**Representative Authors:** John Gery, Kay Murphy, and Grace Bauer

**Submissions Policy:** Query first.

**Simultaneous Subs:** yes

**Reading Period:** Year-round

**Reporting Time:** 1 to 6 months

**Author Payment:** royalties and copies

**Founded:** 1993

**Non Profit:** no

**Paid Staff:** 1

**Unpaid Staff:** 5

**Distributors:** Baker & Taylor; http://www.portals-press.com; Amazon

**ISSN Number/ISBN Number:** ISBN 0-916620-

**Number of Books Published per Year:** 2

**Titles in Print:** 20

**Average Print Run:** 750

**Average Percentage Printed:** Hardcover 10%, Paperback 90%

**Average Price:** $15

# Post Road

**Type:** magazine

**CLMP member:** yes

**Primary Editor/Contact Person:** Mary Cotton, Publisher

**Address:** P.O. Box 400951
Cambridge, MA 02139

**Web Site Address:** http://www.postroadmag.com

**Publishes:** essays, fiction, nonfiction, poetry, art, and translation

**Editorial Focus:** Post Road seeks to publish new and original work by those writers and artists not represented in the mainstream.

**Representative Authors:** Nelly Reifler, Maile Chapman, and Stoney Conley

**Submissions Policy:** Post Road accepts submissions in the following genres: fiction, nonfiction, poetry. See website for submission guidelines.

**Simultaneous Subs:** yes

**Reading Period:** Year-round

**Reporting Time:** 2 to 3 months

**Author Payment:** none

**Founded:** 2000

**Non Profit:** yes

**Paid Staff:** no

**Unpaid Staff:** 13

**Distributors:** Ingram; DeBoer

**Total Circulation:** 2,000

**Paid Circulation:** 100

**Subscription Rate:** Individual $16/Institution $32

**Single Copy Price:** $10.99

**Current Volume/Issue:** Issue 9

**Frequency per Year:** 2

**Backfile Available:** yes

**Unsolicited Ms. Received:** yes

**% of Unsolicited Ms. Published per Year:** 50%

**Format:** perfect

**Size:** H 8.5" W 4.25"

**Average Pages:** 208

**Ads:** yes

**Ad Rates:** swap

# The Post-Apollo Press

**Type:** press

**CLMP member:** yes

**Primary Editor/Contact Person:** Simone Fattal

**Address:** 35 Marie St.
Sausalito, CA 94965

**Publishes:** essays, fiction, and poetry

**Editorial Focus:** Experimental poetry and prose, with

an emphasis on international literature.

**Representative Authors:** Etel Adnan, Lyn Hejinian, and Jalal Toufic

**Submissions Policy:** TPAP both solicits and accepts unsolicited manuscripts. We are not accepting fiction at this time.

**Simultaneous Subs:** yes

**Reading Period:** Year-round

**Reporting Time:** 4 to 8 months

**Author Payment:** copies

**Founded:** 1982

**Non Profit:** no

**Paid Staff:** 1

**Unpaid Staff:** 0

**Distributors:** SPD, New Leaf

**Number of Books Published per Year:** 3

**Titles in Print:** 41

**Average Print Run:** 1,000

**Average Percentage Printed:** Paperback 100%

**Average Price:** $12

# Potomac Review

**Type:** magazine

**CLMP member:** yes

**Primary Editor/Contact Person:** Christa Watters

**Address:** Peck Humanities Inst., Montgomery Coll.
51 Mannake St.
Rockville, MD 20850

**Web Site Address:**
http://www.montgomerycollege.edu/potomacreview

**Publishes:** essays, fiction, nonfiction, poetry, reviews, art, and translation

**Editorial Focus:** Via original prose, poetry and art-work, to explore the inner and outer terrain of the Mid-Atlantic region and beyond.

**Representative Authors:** Hilary Tham, Doreen Baingana, and Jo Neace Krause

**Submissions Policy:** Poetry: Up to three poems/5 pages; Prose: Up to 5,000 words. Art, copies or on disk, no originals.

**Simultaneous Subs:** yes

**Reading Period:** Year-round

**Reporting Time:** 2 to 6 months

**Author Payment:** copies

**Contests:** See Web Site for Contest Guidelines.

**Founded:** 1993

**Non Profit:** yes

**Paid Staff:** 0

**Unpaid Staff:** 2

**ISSN Number/ISBN Number:** ISSN 10073-1989

**Total Circulation:** 1,200

**Paid Circulation:** 650

**Subscription Rate:** Individual $18/Institution $18

**Single Copy Price:** $10

**Current Volume/Issue:** Issue 37

**Frequency per Year:** 2

**Backfile Available:** yes

**Unsolicited Ms. Received:** yes

**% of Unsolicited Ms. Published per Year:** 10%

**Format:** perfect

**Size:** H 8 1/2" W 5 3/8"

**Average Pages:** 248

**Ads:** yes

**Ad Rates:** Exchanges
See Web Site for Details.

# Prairie Schooner

**Type:** magazine

**CLMP member:** yes

**Primary Editor/Contact Person:** Hilda Raz/Erin Flanagan

**Address:** 201 Andrews Hall
The University of Nebraska
Lincoln, NE 68588-0334

**Web Site Address:**
http://www.unl.edu/schooner/psmain.htm

**Publishes:** essays, fiction, nonfiction, poetry, reviews, and translation

**Editorial Focus:** In our 77th year of continuous publi-cation, we seek new work from established, mid-career, and beginning prose writers and poets.

**Representative Authors:** Judith Ortiz Cofer, Lee Martin, and Constance Merritt

**Submissions Policy:** From Sept. through May only. SASE required; no simultaneous submissions; 8 poems or 2 stories/essays maximum per submission.

**Simultaneous Subs:** no

**Reading Period:** 9/1 to 5/31

**Reporting Time:** 2 to 3 months

**Author Payment:** royalties and copies

**Contests:** $6,000+ in prizes for best prose and poetry published each year. Yearly Prize Book Series in fiction and poetry, two $3,00 prizes

**Founded:** 1926

**Non Profit:** yes

**Paid Staff:** 2

**Unpaid Staff:** 13

**Distributors:** Ingram

**Wholesalers:** call direct: 1.800.715.2387

**ISSN Number/ISBN Number:** ISSN 0032-6682

**Total Circulation:** 2,000
**Paid Circulation:** 1,000
**Subscription Rate:** Individual $26/Institution $30
**Single Copy Price:** $9
**Current Volume/Issue:** 77/3
**Frequency per Year:** 4
**Backfile Available:** yes
**Unsolicited Ms. Received:** yes
**% of Unsolicited Ms. Published per Year:** 100%
**Format:** perfect
**Size:** H 9" W 6"
**Average Pages:** 200
**Ads:** yes
**Ad Rates:** $250 commercial publishers, discount to university presses

## PREP Publishing

**Type:** press
**CLMP member:** yes
**Primary Editor/Contact Person:** Anne McKinney
**Address:** 1110 1/2 Hay St., Ste. C
Fayetteville, NC 28305
**Web Site Address:** http://www.prep-pub.com
**Publishes:** fiction and nonfiction
**Editorial Focus:** Primary emphasis is nonfiction and biographies, and some fiction.
**Representative Authors:** Gordon Beld, Anne McKinney, and Patty Sleem
**Submissions Policy:** Send self-addressed stamped envelope (.60 postage) for submissions info or visit website at http://www.prep-pub.com
**Simultaneous Subs:** yes
**Reading Period:** Year-round
**Reporting Time:** 2 to 10 weeks
**Author Payment:** royalties
**Founded:** 1994
**Non Profit:** no
**Paid Staff:** 5
**Unpaid Staff:** 0
**Distributors:** publisher
**Wholesalers:** Ingram, Baker & Taylor, Unique, Quality, others
**ISSN Number/ISBN Number:** ISBN 1-885288
**Number of Books Published per Year:** 12
**Titles in Print:** 38
**Average Percentage Printed:** Hardcover 5%, Paperback 95%
**Backfile Available:** yes

## PRISM international

**Type:** magazine
**CLMP member:** no
**Primary Editor/Contact Person:** Editors
**Address:** Creative Writing Program, UBC
Buch E462-1866 Main Mall
Vancouver, BC V6T 1Z1
**Web Site Address:** http://prism.arts.ubc.ca
**Publishes:** fiction, nonfiction, poetry, art, and translation
**Submissions Policy:** See our website for submissions guidelines.
**Simultaneous Subs:** no
**Reading Period:** Year-round
**Reporting Time:** 2 to 6 months
**Author Payment:** cash, copies, and subscription
**Contests:** See Web Site for Contest Guidelines.
**Founded:** 1959
**Non Profit:** yes
**Paid Staff:** 4
**Unpaid Staff:** 0
**Distributors:** CMPA
**ISSN Number/ISBN Number:** ISSN 0032.8790
**Total Circulation:** 1,200
**Paid Circulation:** 700
**Average Print Run:** 1250
**Subscription Rate:** Individual $25/Institution $32
**Single Copy Price:** $9
**Current Volume/Issue:** 44/1
**Frequency per Year:** 4
**Backfile Available:** yes
**Unsolicited Ms. Received:** yes
**% of Unsolicited Ms. Published per Year:** 3%
**Format:** perfect
**Average Pages:** 80
**Ads:** yes
**Ad Rates:** See Web Site for Details.

## Prose Ax

**Type:** press
**CLMP member:** no
**Primary Editor/Contact Person:** J. Salazar
**Address:** P.O. Box 22643
Honolulu, HI 96823
**Web Site Address:** http://www.proseax.com
**Publishes:** fiction, nonfiction, poetry, and art
**Editorial Focus:** Edgy and stimulating prose and poetry from emerging and established artists.
**Representative Authors:** Cyril Wong, Nathalie Chicha, and Justin Barrett

**Submissions Policy:** Flash fiction, short stories up to 2,000 words, poetry, black and white art. Check website for guidelines.
**Simultaneous Subs:** yes
**Reading Period:** Year-round
**Reporting Time:** 2 to 4 months
**Author Payment:** copies
**Contests:** Potent Prose Ax Prize
See Web Site for Contest Guidelines.
**Founded:** 2000
**Non Profit:** yes
**Paid Staff:** 0
**Unpaid Staff:** 2
**ISSN Number/ISBN Number:** ISSN 1533-824x
**Number of Books Published per Year:** 0
**Titles in Print:** 0
**Average Percentage Printed:** Other 100%

# Pudding House Publications

**Type:** press
**CLMP member:** no
**Primary Editor/Contact Person:** Jennifer Bosveld
**Address:** 81 Shadymere Ln.
Columbus, OH 43213
**Web Site Address:** http://www.puddinghouse.com
**Publishes:** essays, fiction, poetry, and reviews
**Editorial Focus:** Poetry (some short short stories and essays), any style/subject. Make words dance together that haven't danced together before
**Representative Authors:** Roy Bentley, Charlene Fix, and David Chorlton
**Submissions Policy:** Standard professionalism, include SASE and e-mail, don't individually fold, no simultaneous, conserve by resending rejected work.
**Simultaneous Subs:** no
**Reading Period:** Year-round
**Reporting Time:** 1 to 1 weeks
**Author Payment:** copies
**Contests:** See Web Site for Contest Guidelines.
**Founded:** 1979
**Non Profit:** yes
**Paid Staff:** 2
**Unpaid Staff:** 9
**Distributors:** direct mail, web, phone directly to Pudding House
**Wholesalers:** We sell directly to bookstores, educational orgs
**ISSN Number/ISBN Number:** 0196-5913/many series
**Number of Books Published per Year:** 130

**Titles in Print:** 600
**Average Print Run:** 300
**Average Percentage Printed:** Paperback 2%, Chapbook 97%, Other 1%
**Average Price:** $8.95 chap

# Puerto del Sol/Nightjar Press

**Type:** magazine
**CLMP member:** yes
**Address:** New Mexico State University
Box 30001, Dept. 3E, English Bldg
Las Cruces, NM 88003-8001
**Web Site Address:**
http://www.nmsu.edu/~puerto/welcome.html
**Publishes:** essays, fiction, nonfiction, and poetry
**Reading Period:** Year-round
**Reporting Time:** 1 to 2 months
**Author Payment:** none
**Founded:** 1960
**Non Profit:** no
**Backfile Available:** yes

# PulpLit.com

**Type:** online
**CLMP member:** no
**Primary Editor/Contact Person:** Jason Clarke
**Address:** 411A Highland Ave. #376
Somerville, MA 02144
**Web Site Address:** http://www.pulplit.com
**Publishes:** essays, fiction, nonfiction, poetry, reviews, and art
**Editorial Focus:** We're love genre fiction that transcends genre, literary analysis that goes beyond mundane formalism and exciting poetry.
**Simultaneous Subs:** yes
**Reading Period:** Year-round
**Reporting Time:** 1 to 6 months
**Author Payment:** cash
**Founded:** 2002
**Non Profit:** no
**Paid Staff:** 0
**Unpaid Staff:** 5
**ISSN Number/ISBN Number:** ISSN 1547-9374
**Average Page Views per Month:** 15,000
**Average Unique Visitors per Month:** 2,500
**Frequency per Year:** 4
**Publish Print Anthology:** yes
Price: free
**Average Percentage of Pages per Category:** Audio

100%
**Ad Rates:** $1 per thousand views
See Web Site for Details.

## QRL

**Type:** press
**CLMP member:** no
**Primary Editor/Contact Person:** Renee Weiss
**Address:** 26 Haslet Ave.
Princeton, NJ 08540
**Web Site Address:** http://www.princeton.edu/~qrl
**Publishes:** essays, fiction, poetry, reviews, and translation
**Editorial Focus:** QRL is no longer publishing new work. But it will remain active to distribute its very large list of still available volumes.
**Representative Authors:** Ezra Pound, William Carlos Williams, Wallace Stevens
**Submissions Policy:** none
**Simultaneous Subs:** yes
**Reading Period:** Year-round
**Author Payment:** none
**Contests:** See web site for list of books still available: www.princeton.edu/~qrl
See Web Site for Contest Guidelines.
**Founded:** 1943
**Non Profit:** yes
**Paid Staff:** Non
**Unpaid Staff:** 3
**Distributors:** QRL
**Wholesalers:** QRL
**ISSN Number/ISBN Number:** 1-888 545-43-7/1-888 545-44-5
**Titles in Print:** 70
**Average Percentage Printed:** Hardcover 60%, Paperback 40%

## Quale Press

**Type:** press
**CLMP member:** yes
**Primary Editor/Contact Person:** Gian Lombardo
**Address:** 93 Main St.
Florence, MA 01062
**Web Site Address:** http://www.quale.com
**Publishes:** fiction, nonfiction, poetry, and translation
**Editorial Focus:** Prose poetry, political poetry (leftist), translations, experimental fiction, reissues.
**Representative Authors:** Dennis Barone, Arturo Giovannitti, and Holly Iglesias

**Submissions Policy:** No unsolicited work. By invitation only.
**Simultaneous Subs:** yes
**Author Payment:** royalties
**Founded:** 1997
**Non Profit:** no
**Paid Staff:** 2
**Unpaid Staff:** 1
**Distributors:** SPD
**ISSN Number/ISBN Number:** ISBN 0-9700663
**Number of Books Published per Year:** 5
**Titles in Print:** 15
**Average Print Run:** POD
**Average Percentage Printed:** Paperback 100%
**Average Price:** $14

## Quarterly West

**Type:** magazine
**CLMP member:** no
**Primary Editor/Contact Person:** David C. Hawkins
**Address:** 255 S. Central Campus Dr.
Dept. of English, LNCO 3500
Salt Lake City, UT 84112-9109
**Web Site Address:** http://www.utah.edu/quarterly-west
**Publishes:** essays, fiction, nonfiction, poetry, reviews, art, and translation
**Editorial Focus:** Quarterly West seeks original and accomplished literary verse, fiction, and creative nonfiction; also translations and reviews.
**Representative Authors:** Albert Goldbarth, George Saunders, and Eleanor Wilner
**Submissions Policy:** Submit 3-5 poems or short-shorts, or 1 story or essay. Translations should be accompanied by original.
**Simultaneous Subs:** yes
**Reading Period:** 9/1 to 5/1
**Reporting Time:** 4 to 6 months
**Author Payment:** cash and copies
**Contests:** QW sponsors a biennial novella competition. Two winners receive a cash prize and publication. See Web Site for Contest Guidelines.
**Founded:** 1976
**Non Profit:** yes
**Paid Staff:** 7
**Unpaid Staff:** 22
**Distributors:** Ingram, DeBoer, Small Press Dist.
**ISSN Number/ISBN Number:** ISSN 0194-4231
**Total Circulation:** 1,400
**Paid Circulation:** 500

**Subscription Rate:** Individual $14/Institution $15 ( US)
**Single Copy Price:** $8.50
**Current Volume/Issue:** 56/1
**Frequency per Year:** 2
**Backfile Available:** yes
**Unsolicited Ms. Received:** yes
**% of Unsolicited Ms. Published per Year:** 1%
**Format:** perfect
**Size:** H 10" W 7"
**Average Pages:** 176
**Ads:** yes
**Ad Rates:** Ad cards available upon request.

# Queer Ramblings

**Type:** magazine
**CLMP member:** yes
**Primary Editor/Contact Person:** Sandra R. Garcia
**Address:** 392 14th St., Apt. 1A
Ste. 1A
Brooklyn, NY 11215
**Web Site Address:** http://www.queerramblings.com
**Publishes:** essays, fiction, nonfiction, poetry, reviews, and art
**Editorial Focus:** Writing, art, photography by queer women and transgender folk.
**Submissions Policy:** Please visit our website, http://www.queerramblings.com for details.
**Simultaneous Subs:** yes
**Reading Period:** Year-round
**Reporting Time:** 1 to 2 months
**Author Payment:** copies
**Founded:** 2000
**Non Profit:** yes
**Paid Staff:** 0
**Unpaid Staff:** 1-5
**Distributors:** DeBoer
**ISSN Number/ISBN Number:** ISSN 1552-4701
**Total Circulation:** 20,000
**Paid Circulation:** 100
**Subscription Rate:** Individual $26/Institution $26
**Single Copy Price:** $4.50
**Current Volume/Issue:** 1/1
**Frequency per Year:** 4
**Backfile Available:** yes
**Unsolicited Ms. Received:** yes
**% of Unsolicited Ms. Published per Year:** 50%
**Format:** perfect
**Size:** H 11" W 8.5"
**Average Pages:** 48

**Ads:** yes
**Ad Rates:** See Web Site for Details.

# Quercus Review

**Type:** magazine
**CLMP member:** no
**Primary Editor/Contact Person:** Sam Pierstorff
**Address:** 435 College Ave.
Modesto Junior College
Modesto, CA 95350
**Web Site Address:** http://www.quercusreview.com
**Publishes:** fiction, poetry, and art
**Editorial Focus:** Poetry and fiction with a strong pulse.
**Representative Authors:** Amiri Baraka, Charles Harper Webb, and Dorianne Laux
**Submissions Policy:** We accept submissions year-round. Send 3-5 previously unpublished poems with cover letter, brief bio, and SASE.
**Simultaneous Subs:** no
**Reading Period:** Year-round
**Reporting Time:** 1 to 2 months
**Author Payment:** copies
**Contests:** Quercus Review Poetry Series Annual Book Award
See Web Site for Contest Guidelines.
**Founded:** 1999
**Non Profit:** no
**Paid Staff:** 1
**Unpaid Staff:** 5
**ISSN Number/ISBN Number:** ISSN 1543-4532
**Total Circulation:** 250
**Paid Circulation:** 50
**Average Print Run:** 500
**Subscription Rate:** Individual $20/Institution $20
**Single Copy Price:** $8
**Current Volume/Issue:** 1/5
**Frequency per Year:** 2
**Backfile Available:** yes
**Unsolicited Ms. Received:** yes
**% of Unsolicited Ms. Published per Year:** 1%
**Format:** perfect
**Average Pages:** 112

# Quick Fiction

**Type:** magazine
**CLMP member:** yes
**Primary Editor/Contact Person:** Jennifer Pieroni
**Address:** P.O. Box

Salem, MA 01970
**Web Site Address:** http://quickfiction.org/
**Publishes:** fiction
**Editorial Focus:** stories and narrative prose poems under 500 words
**Representative Authors:** Mark Yakich, Wayne Sullins, and Dan Kaplan
**Submissions Policy:** 25-500 words. No more than five stories at a time. Send cover letter and SASE. No e-mail submissions and no certified mail.
**Simultaneous Subs:** no
**Reading Period:** Year-round
**Reporting Time:** 3 to 6 months
**Author Payment:** copies
**Contests:** See Web Site for Contest Guidelines.
**Founded:** 2001
**Non Profit:** yes
**Paid Staff:** 0
**Unpaid Staff:** 3
**Distributors:** DeBoer
**ISSN Number/ISBN Number:** 1543-8376/0-9724776
**Total Circulation:** 750
**Paid Circulation:** 250
**Average Print Run:** 1,500
**Subscription Rate:** Individual $11/Institution $11
**Single Copy Price:** $6.50
**Current Volume/Issue:** Issue 8
**Frequency per Year:** 2
**Backfile Available:** no
**Unsolicited Ms. Received:** yes
**% of Unsolicited Ms. Published per Year:** 3%
**Format:** perfect
**Size:** H 6" W 6"
**Average Pages:** 55
**Ads:** no

# Radical Society

**Type:** magazine
**CLMP member:** no
**Primary Editor/Contact Person:** Kira Brunner
**Address:** P.O. Box 2329, Times Square Station
editors@radicalsociety.org
New York, NY 10108-2329
**Publishes:** essays, fiction, nonfiction, poetry, reviews, and art
**Editorial Focus:** is a forum for radical and progressive politics, cultural dissent, political economy and international relations to be debate
**Representative Authors:** Winifred Tate, William H. Thornton, and Tomaz Salamun

**Simultaneous Subs:** no
**Reading Period:** Year-round
**Reporting Time:** 1 to 2 months
**Author Payment:** cash
**Founded:** 2001
**Non Profit:** yes
**Paid Staff:** 5
**Unpaid Staff:** 15
**Distributors:** Routledge
**ISSN Number/ISBN Number:** ISSN 1476-0851
**Total Circulation:** 800
**Paid Circulation:** 400
**Subscription Rate:** Individual $39/Institution $180
**Single Copy Price:** $12
**Current Volume/Issue:** Issue 4
**Frequency per Year:** 4
**Backfile Available:** yes
**Unsolicited Ms. Received:** yes
**% of Unsolicited Ms. Published per Year:** 30%
**Format:** perfect
**Ads:** yes

# Ragged Raven Press

**Type:** press
**CLMP member:** no
**Primary Editor/Contact Person:** Janet Murch
**Address:** 1 Lodge Farm
Snitterfield
Stratford-on-Avon, UK CV37 0LR
**Web Site Address:** http://www.raggedraven.co.uk
**Publishes:** poetry
**Editorial Focus:** Contemporary poetry with something interesting to say.
**Representative Authors:** Chris Kinsey, Jane Kinninmont, and Christopher James
**Submissions Policy:** By post (with SASE/IRC) or in main body of e-mail. State if previously published and detail when and where.
**Simultaneous Subs:** no
**Reading Period:** Year-round
**Reporting Time:** 6 to 8 weeks
**Author Payment:** royalties, cash, and copies
**Contests:** Ragged Raven Press annual poetry competition and anthology. Deadline: October 31st. See Web Site for Contest Guidelines.
**Founded:** 1998
**Non Profit:** yes
**Paid Staff:** 0
**Unpaid Staff:** 2
**Number of Books Published per Year:** 3

**Titles in Print:** 12
**Average Print Run:** 400
**Average Percentage Printed:** Paperback 100%
**Average Price:** £6

## Rain Taxi Review of Books

**Type:** magazine
**CLMP member:** yes
**Primary Editor/Contact Person:** Eric Lorberer
**Address:** P.O. Box 3840
Minneapolis, MN 55403
**Web Site Address:** http://www.raintaxi.com
**Publishes:** essays and reviews
**Editorial Focus:** Reviews of fiction, poetry, art, photography, cultural studies, and other titles that might otherwise get overlooked.
**Recent Awards Received:** Utne Alternative Press Award
**Representative Authors:** Stephen Burt, Peter Gizzi, and Joyelle McSweeney
**Submissions Policy:** Visit http://www.raintaxi.com for complete submission guideline
**Simultaneous Subs:** no
**Reading Period:** Year-round
**Reporting Time:** 1 to 2 months
**Author Payment:** none
**Founded:** 1995
**Non Profit:** yes
**Paid Staff:** 2
**Unpaid Staff:** 1
**Total Circulation:** 18,000
**Paid Circulation:** 900
**Average Print Run:** 18,000
**Subscription Rate:** Individual $12/Institution $12
**Single Copy Price:** $4
**Current Volume/Issue:** 10/4
**Frequency per Year:** 4
**Backfile Available:** yes
**Unsolicited Ms. Received:** yes
**% of Unsolicited Ms. Published per Year:** 15%
**Format:** stapled
**Size:** H 10.25" W 8.25"
**Average Pages:** 56
**Ads:** yes
**Ad Rates:** 1/2: $375; 1/3: $275; 1/4: $225; 1/5: $175; 1/8: $125

## Rainbow Curve

**Type:** magazine
**CLMP member:** yes
**Primary Editor/Contact Person:** Julianne Bonnet/Daphne Young
**Address:** P.O. Box 93206
Las Vegas, NV 89193-3206
**Web Site Address:** http://www.rainbowcurve.com
**Publishes:** fiction, poetry, and art
**Editorial Focus:** RC has been described as publishing work that is "hard hitting and somewhat uncomfortable to read."
**Representative Authors:** Catherine Ryan Hyde, Virgil Suárez, and Terry Ehret
**Submissions Policy:** For complete guidelines visit http://www.rainbowcurve.com
**Simultaneous Subs:** yes
**Reading Period:** Year-round
**Reporting Time:** 2 to 3 months
**Author Payment:** copies
**Founded:** 2001
**Non Profit:** yes
**Paid Staff:** 0
**Unpaid Staff:** 2
**ISSN Number/ISBN Number:** 1538-2826/0 74470 05514
**Total Circulation:** 350
**Paid Circulation:** N/A
**Average Print Run:** 500
**Subscription Rate:** Individual $16/Institution $16
**Single Copy Price:** $8
**Current Volume/Issue:** Issue 7
**Frequency per Year:** 2
**Backfile Available:** yes
**Unsolicited Ms. Received:** yes
**% of Unsolicited Ms. Published per Year:** 2%
**Format:** perfect
**Ads:** yes

## Raritan

**Type:** magazine
**CLMP member:** no
**Address:** Rutgers/The State U. of New Jersey
31 Mine St.
New Brunswick, NJ 8903
**Publishes:** essays, fiction, poetry, and art
**Reading Period:** Year-round
**Reporting Time:** 1 to 2 months
**Author Payment:** none
**Founded:** 1981

**Non Profit:** no

# Rattapallax Press

**Type:** press
**CLMP member:** yes
**Primary Editor/Contact Person:** Ram Devineni
**Address:** 532 La Guardia Place
Ste. 353
New York, NY 10012
**Web Site Address:** http://www.rattapallax.com
**Publishes:** poetry and audio
**Editorial Focus:** International poetry.
**Representative Authors:** Willie Perdomo and Mark Nickels
**Submissions Policy:** Please contact editor before sending work.
**Simultaneous Subs:** no
**Reading Period:** Year-round
**Reporting Time:** 1 to 2 months
**Author Payment:** royalties, cash, and copies
**Founded:** 2002
**Non Profit:** yes
**Paid Staff:** 1
**Unpaid Staff:** 3
**Distributors:** Biblodistribution
**Wholesalers:** Baker & Taylor
**ISSN Number/ISBN Number:** ISBN 1-892494
**Number of Books Published per Year:** 2
**Titles in Print:** 20
**Average Percentage Printed:** Hardcover 5%, Paperback 90%, Other 5%

# Rattapallax

**Type:** magazine
**CLMP member:** yes
**Primary Editor/Contact Person:** Ram Devineni
**Address:** 532 La Guardia Place, Ste 353
Ste. 353
New York, NY 10012
**Web Site Address:** http://www.rattapallax.com
**Publishes:** essays, fiction, nonfiction, poetry, art, translation, and audio
**Editorial Focus:** Modern work that reflects the diversity of world cultures and is relevant to our society.
**Representative Authors:** MC Solaar, Glyn Maxwell, and Sonia Sanchez
**Submissions Policy:** Submit no more than five poems or two short stories. Translations are welcome.
**Simultaneous Subs:** no

**Reading Period:** Year-round
**Reporting Time:** 1 to 2 months
**Author Payment:** copies
**Founded:** 1998
**Non Profit:** yes
**Paid Staff:** 0
**Unpaid Staff:** 15
**Distributors:** Ingram, Editora34 (Brazil), Plagio (Chile)
**ISSN Number/ISBN Number:** ISSN 1521-2483
**Total Circulation:** 2,500
**Paid Circulation:** 300
**Subscription Rate:** Individual $14/Institution $14
**Single Copy Price:** $7.95
**Current Volume/Issue:** Issue 10
**Frequency per Year:** 2
**Backfile Available:** yes
**Unsolicited Ms. Received:** yes
**% of Unsolicited Ms. Published per Year:** 5%
**Format:** perfect
**Size:** H 9.25" W 7.375"
**Average Pages:** 112
**Ads:** yes
**Ad Rates:** See Web Site for Details.

# Rattle, Poetry for the 21st Century

**Type:** magazine
**CLMP member:** yes
**Primary Editor/Contact Person:** Stellasue Lee/Poetry Editor
**Address:** 12411 Ventura Blvd.
Studio City, CA 91604
**Web Site Address:** http://www.rattle.com
**Publishes:** essays, poetry, reviews, art, and translation
**Editorial Focus:** Quality work, accessible, image, moment. Please submit a cover letter, a short bio, along with all contact information.
**Representative Authors:** Robert Creeley, Gerald Stern, and Philip Levine
**Submissions Policy:** up to 6 poems, SASE, name and contact information in upper right-hand corner. Will consider e-mails submissions.
**Simultaneous Subs:** no
**Reading Period:** Year-round
**Reporting Time:** 6 to 8 weeks
**Author Payment:** copies
**Founded:** 1995
**Non Profit:** yes
**Paid Staff:** yes
**Unpaid Staff:** no

**Distributors:** Ingram/SPD/DeBoer/Armadillo
**ISSN Number/ISBN Number:** ISBN 1-931307-07-5
**Total Circulation:** 4,000
**Paid Circulation:** 1,200
**Subscription Rate:** Individual $3yr. 34/Institution $34
**Single Copy Price:** $8
**Current Volume/Issue:** 10/22
**Frequency per Year:** 2
**Backfile Available:** yes
**Unsolicited Ms. Received:** yes
**% of Unsolicited Ms. Published per Year:** 1-2%
**Format:** perfect
**Size:** H 9" W 6"
**Average Pages:** 200
**Ads:** no
**Ad Rates:** See Web Site for Details.

# The Raven Chronicles

**Type:** magazine
**CLMP member:** no
**Primary Editor/Contact Person:** Phoebe Bosch/
**Address:** Richard Hugo House
1634-11th Ave.
Seattle, WA 98122-2419
**Web Site Address:** http://www.ravenchronicles.org
**Publishes:** essays, fiction, nonfiction, poetry, reviews, art, and translation
**Editorial Focus:** Raven publishes uncommon poetry, fiction, essays, reviews, black/white art, and interviews. In each issue we feature poetics, memorials, odes to places/things, beyond borders, The Pacific Northwest, food/culture, nature writing.
**Representative Authors:** Kathleen Alcalá, Haunani-Kay Trask, and John Olson
**Submissions Policy:** Emerging and established writers. 3 poems or 2-15 pgs fiction. Online guidelines, www.ravenchronicles.org/raven/rvsubm/html
**Simultaneous Subs:** yes
**Reading Period:** 1/1 to 9/15
**Reporting Time:** 2 to 12 weeks
**Author Payment:** cash and copies
**Founded:** 1991
**Non Profit:** yes
**Paid Staff:** 2
**Unpaid Staff:** 8
**Distributors:** Small Changes
**ISSN Number/ISBN Number:** ISSN 1066-1883
**Total Circulation:** 2,000
**Paid Circulation:** 200
**Subscription Rate:** Individual $20/Institution $20

**Single Copy Price:** $7
**Current Volume/Issue:** 11/1
**Frequency per Year:** 3
**Backfile Available:** yes
**Unsolicited Ms. Received:** yes
**% of Unsolicited Ms. Published per Year:** 35%
**Format:** stapled
**Size:** H 8.5" W 11"
**Average Pages:** 96
**Ads:** yes
**Ad Rates:** See Web Site for Details.

# The Reading Room/Great Marsh Press

**Type:** magazine
**CLMP member:** yes
**Primary Editor/Contact Person:** Barbara Probst Solomon
**Address:** P.O. Box 2144
Lenox Hill Station
New York, NY 10021
**Web Site Address:** http://www.greatmarshpress.com
**Publishes:** essays, fiction, nonfiction, poetry, art, and translation
**Editorial Focus:** The best in contemporary writing.
**Representative Authors:** Saul Bellow, Alan Kaufman, and Daphne Merkin
**Submissions Policy:** Must be sent with SASE to: Great Marsh Press, P.O. Box, 2144 Lenox Hill Station, NY, NY 10021. No Web submissions.
**Simultaneous Subs:** yes
**Reading Period:** Year-round
**Reporting Time:** 3 to 5 months
**Author Payment:** none
**Founded:** 2000
**Non Profit:** yes
**Paid Staff:** 2
**Unpaid Staff:** 4
**Distributors:** Ingram, Barnes & Noble, Amazon.com
**Wholesalers:** Ingram
**ISSN Number/ISBN Number:** 1535-6728/1-928863-09-4
**Total Circulation:** 8,000
**Paid Circulation:** 1,000
**Average Print Run:** 5,000
**Subscription Rate:** Individual $65 for 4/Institution $65 for 4
**Single Copy Price:** $17.95
**Current Volume/Issue:** 1/4
**Frequency per Year:** 2

**Backfile Available:** yes
**Unsolicited Ms. Received:** yes
**% of Unsolicited Ms. Published per Year:** 25%
**Format:** Book Form
**Size:** H 9" W 6"
**Average Pages:** 315
**Ads:** yes
**Ad Rates:** $1,000 for full page

# Red Hen Press

**Type:** press
**CLMP member:** no
**Primary Editor/Contact Person:** Mark E. Cull
**Address:** P.O. Box 3537
Granada Hills, CA 91344
**Web Site Address:** http://redhen.org
**Publishes:** fiction and poetry
**Representative Authors:** Chris Abani, Stephen Dixon, and Tom Hayden
**Submissions Policy:** No unsolicited material. Send query letters only.
**Simultaneous Subs:** yes
**Reading Period:** 1/1 to 5/31
**Reporting Time:** 1 to 2 months
**Author Payment:** royalties
**Contests:** Benjamin Saltman Award, Short Fiction Award, Ruskin Poetry Award.
See Web Site for Contest Guidelines.
**Founded:** 1994
**Non Profit:** yes
**Paid Staff:** 4
**Unpaid Staff:** 4
**Distributors:** SPD
**Wholesalers:** Baker & Taylor
**ISSN Number/ISBN Number:** 1543-3536/1888996, 159709
**Number of Books Published per Year:** 16
**Titles in Print:** 100
**Average Print Run:** 1,000
**Average Percentage Printed:** Hardcover 2%, Paperback 98%
**Average Price:** $14.95

# Red Morning Press

**Type:** press
**CLMP member:** yes
**Primary Editor/Contact Person:** Andy Brown, Partner
**Address:** 1140 Connecticut Ave., Ste. 700
Washington, DC 20036

**Web Site Address:** http://www.redmorningpress.com
**Publishes:** poetry
**Representative Authors:** Sean Norton
**Submissions Policy:** Red Morning Press accepts unsolicited manuscripts year-round. We do not sponsor a contest, and there are no reading fees.
**Simultaneous Subs:** yes
**Reading Period:** Year-round
**Reporting Time:** 1 to 2 months
**Author Payment:** royalties
**Contests:** Red Morning Press does not sponsor a contest or charge reading fees.
**Founded:** 2004
**Non Profit:** no
**Paid Staff:** 0
**Unpaid Staff:** 3
**Number of Books Published per Year:** 1-2
**Titles in Print:** 1
**Average Print Run:** 1,000
**Average Percentage Printed:** Paperback 100%
**Average Price:** $11.95

# Red Rock Review

**Type:** magazine
**CLMP member:** yes
**Primary Editor/Contact Person:** Rich Logsdon, Sr. Editor
**Address:** 3200 E. Cheyenne Ave.
N. Las Vegas, NV 89030
**Web Site Address:** http://www.ccsn.nevada.edu/english/
**Publishes:** essays, fiction, nonfiction, poetry, and reviews
**Editorial Focus:** RRR seeks to publish the best in fiction and poetry. Essays, nonfiction, reviews welcome. Emphasis on Southwestern writers.
**Representative Authors:** Marge Piercy, Charles Harper Webb, and Adrian C. Louis
**Submissions Policy:** Stories: up to 7,500 words. Essays: up to 5,000 words. Reviews: up to 1,500 words. Poetry: any length. Include SASE.
**Simultaneous Subs:** no
**Reading Period:** 9/1 to 5/31
**Reporting Time:** 4 to 5 months
**Author Payment:** copies
**Contests:** See Web Site for Contest Guidelines.
**Founded:** 1995
**Non Profit:** yes
**Paid Staff:** 4
**Unpaid Staff:** 5

**Distributors:** DeBoer
**Wholesalers:** Borders
**ISSN Number/ISBN Number:** 1086-4342
**Total Circulation:** 750
**Paid Circulation:** 25
**Average Print Run:** 750
**Subscription Rate:** Individual $9.50/Institution $9.50
**Single Copy Price:** $5.50
**Current Volume/Issue:** 500/17
**Frequency per Year:** 2
**Backfile Available:** yes
**Unsolicited Ms. Received:** yes
**% of Unsolicited Ms. Published per Year:** 85%
**Format:** perfect
**Size:** H 9" W 6"
**Average Pages:** 140
**Ads:** yes
**Ad Rates:** inquire

# Red Wheelbarrow Literary Magazine

**Type:** magazine
**CLMP member:** no
**Primary Editor/Contact Person:** Randolph Splitter
**Address:** De Anza College
21250 Stevens Creek Blvd.
Cupertino, CA 95014
**Web Site Address:** http://www.deanza.edu/redwheelbarrow
**Publishes:** essays, fiction, poetry, art, and translation
**Editorial Focus:** A diverse range of styles and voices from around the country and the world.
**Representative Authors:** Mark Brazaitis, Mario Susko, and J. Lorraine Brown
**Submissions Policy:** Poetry: max. 5 poems. Prose: max. 4,000 words. Art: max. 5 submissions.
**Simultaneous Subs:** yes
**Reading Period:** 9/1 to 1/31
**Reporting Time:** 2 to 4 months
**Author Payment:** copies
**Founded:** 1976
**Non Profit:** yes
**Paid Staff:** 1
**Unpaid Staff:** 12
**ISSN Number/ISBN Number:** 1543-1983/1-932133-79-8
**Total Circulation:** 300
**Paid Circulation:** 1
**Subscription Rate:** Individual $7.50/Institution $7.50
**Single Copy Price:** $7.50
**Current Volume/Issue:** 4/1

**Frequency per Year:** 1
**Backfile Available:** yes
**Unsolicited Ms. Received:** yes
**% of Unsolicited Ms. Published per Year:** 98%
**Format:** perfect
**Size:** H 9" W 6"
**Average Pages:** 140
**Ads:** yes
**Ad Rates:** inquire

# RedBone Press

**Type:** press
**CLMP member:** yes
**Primary Editor/Contact Person:** Lisa C. Moore
**Address:** P.O. Box 15571
Washington, DC 20003
**Web Site Address:** http://www.redbonepress.com
**Publishes:** essays, fiction, and nonfiction
**Editorial Focus:** work that celebrates black lesbian culture, and that facilitates discussion between black gays/lesbians and black mainstream.
**Recent Awards Received:** Lambda Literary Awards, 1997, 1998
**Representative Authors:** Sharon Bridgforth, Marvin K. White, and Samiya Bashir
**Submissions Policy:** Send query letter with proposal first. Do not send your original manuscript.
**Simultaneous Subs:** yes
**Reading Period:** Year-round
**Reporting Time:** 2 to 6 months
**Author Payment:** royalties, cash, and copies
**Founded:** 1997
**Non Profit:** no
**Paid Staff:** 0
**Unpaid Staff:** 1
**Distributors:** SPD (Small Press Dist.), Marginal, Turnaround
**ISSN Number/ISBN Number:** ISBN 0-9656659
**Number of Books Published per Year:** 2
**Titles in Print:** 8
**Average Print Run:** 2,000
**Average Percentage Printed:** Paperback 100%
**Average Price:** $15

# Redivider

**Type:** magazine
**CLMP member:** yes
**Primary Editor/Contact Person:** Dara Cerv
**Address:** Emerson College, Writing, Lit. & Publishing Dept.
120 Boylston St.
Boston, MA 2116
**Web Site Address:** http://pages.emerson.edu/publications/redivider/
**Publishes:** essays, fiction, nonfiction, poetry, art, and translation
**Editorial Focus:** Darkly comic and at times hauntingly sad, we are eclectic, yet entirely readable.
**Submissions Policy:** Please see our website for submissions guidelines.
**Simultaneous Subs:** yes
**Reading Period:** Year-round
**Reporting Time:** 1 to 5 months
**Author Payment:** copies
**Founded:** 2004
**Non Profit:** yes
**Paid Staff:** 0
**Unpaid Staff:** all
**ISSN Number/ISBN Number:** ISSN 1551-9244
**Total Circulation:** 75
**Paid Circulation:** 50
**Average Print Run:** 2,000
**Subscription Rate:** Individual $10/Institution $10
**Single Copy Price:** $6
**Current Volume/Issue:** 2/2
**Frequency per Year:** 2
**Backfile Available:** yes
**Unsolicited Ms. Received:** yes
**% of Unsolicited Ms. Published per Year:** 75%
**Format:** perfect
**Average Pages:** 160

# Regent Press

**Type:** press
**CLMP member:** no
**Primary Editor/Contact Person:** Mark Weiman
**Address:** 6020-A Adeline
Oakland, CA 94608
**Web Site Address:** http://regentpress.net
**Publishes:** essays, fiction, nonfiction, poetry, reviews, art, translation, and audio
**Editorial Focus:** We are a broad based Press doing everything from intense literary short stories to vegan cookbooks.

**Representative Authors:** Claire Burch, William Crossman, and Patricia Leslie
**Submissions Policy:** Query letter please
**Simultaneous Subs:** yes
**Reading Period:** Year-round
**Reporting Time:** 2 to 4 weeks
**Author Payment:** royalties
**Founded:** 1978
**Non Profit:** no
**Paid Staff:** 5
**Unpaid Staff:** 0
**Wholesalers:** Baker & Taylor; Ingram
**Number of Books Published per Year:** 25
**Titles in Print:** 120
**Average Percentage Printed:** Hardcover 2%, Paperback 90%, Chapbook 2%, Other 6%

# The Rejected Quarterly

**Type:** magazine
**CLMP member:** no
**Primary Editor/Contact Person:** Daniel Weiss
**Address:** P.O. Box 1351
bplankton@juno.com
Cobb, CA 95426
**Web Site Address:** http://rejectedq.com
**Publishes:** essays, fiction, poetry, reviews, and art
**Editorial Focus:** We are looking for quality offbeat fiction. Only rejection-related poetry and essays. Always looking for cover art.
**Representative Authors:** Vera Searles, Jessica Anya Blau, and Lane Cohen
**Submissions Policy:** Five rejection slips must accompany each manuscript. Fiction to 8,000 words.
**Simultaneous Subs:** no
**Reading Period:** Year-round
**Reporting Time:** 1 to 6 months
**Author Payment:** cash and copies
**Founded:** 1998
**Non Profit:** no
**Paid Staff:** 0
**Unpaid Staff:** 4
**ISSN Number/ISBN Number:** ISSN 1525-2671
**Total Circulation:** 100
**Paid Circulation:** 60
**Average Print Run:** 180
**Subscription Rate:** Individual $20 per 4/Institution $20 per 4
**Single Copy Price:** $6
**Current Volume/Issue:** 3/11
**Frequency per Year:** 3

# Profile: Ravi Shankar, Editor, Drunken Boat

## How did you arrive at your current position?

*Drunken Boat* was founded by visual artist, Michael Mills and I in the summer of 2000. The apocryphal story, which happens to be true, was that we were languishing on a rooftop in Brooklyn one sultry night, after finishing graduate school, lamenting the possible venues for contemporary art and literature, for us and for other artists we knew. Since he happened to be a graphic designer and I a poet, we decided, on a whim, to begin a journal dedicated to arts online. We put out a small call for submissions and solicited work from a few folks, and within a year were awash in works hewn on six different continents.

## What is the staff structure like at your magazine?

Right now there are two founding editors, a managing editor, Aaron Hawn, a technical director, John Joynt, two associate editors, Catherine Daly and Sina Queyras, and a staff of about eight or so who help us with reading work, generating ideas, and publicizing events. Being a 501 (c)(3k) non-profit organization, we're also incorporated in the state of New York and have an advisory board whom we meet with periodically.

## How do you keep your magazine running?

First, the times cannot keep up with the means, so I fear we've arrived early on the leading edge of what will be a revolution as pronounced and unpronounceable as the invention of the printing press. What this means is that there's very little funding—no one cares to pay for content online, we don't service any particular geographic region per se, grant writing would be a full time job in itself—and there's a lot of competition. Our niche is in publishing works of art that might not normally be juxtaposed, so short films alongside hypertextual meditations, narrative poems alongside new elliptical narratives, photography alongside interactive web art, published in such a way to be accessible to as wide an audience as possible. Somehow the multiplicity of our vision does not translate well to very narrowly circumscribed grant givers. Finally, one of our editorial benefits is also a shortcoming: we have staff dispersed around the country, so have to work electronically instead of in person most of the time.

## What do or don't you hope to see in a cover letter?

It's useful to know your credentials, past publishing credits, and even a succinct writing philosophy; it's not useful to be smug, or font-happy, or excessively self-aggrandizing. If you've read our journal and responded to it in some way, let us know that. Was there a work that piqued your interest, an argument you took a side on, a theme you'd like to see enlarged upon? Identify yourself as one of our readers, show you support our publishing endeavor by making even a minute donation, write a note that we can forward on to one of our artists. We'll take the work you submit on its own merits, irrespective of any of this of course, but a cover letter can give us a better sense of your personality, and seriousness/inclinations as an artist.:

## What do you look for in a submission?

We want to see art works and writing that is at its fullest, most mature point of realization. Please don't send us first drafts or workshop poems. We have no preordained aesthetic restrictions, that is we're as open to lyric poetry as we are to language poetry, and we are as moved by literary realism as by magic nihilism. The only criterion is excellence. We'll take your work on its own terms, but we'll also question the necessity of your choices. There's no space for the arbitrary in the creative process unless out of it comes something necessary, and the constant pressure your work will be under is whether the decisions you've made help create something cohesive and exemplary.

## How are submissions processed at your magazine?

We respond to work in the order it was rec'd, but because our journal is run mainly as a labor of love, sometimes this can take up to six months. We read every submission that we receive though, even if we don't have the time to respond to everyone. The volume of submissions sometimes curtails our wish to communicate with every writer/artist who has sent us something, and because of this fact, we encourage simultaneous submissions so long as you let us know if something has been accepted elsewhere. The normal procedure is that the work is appraised by an editorial team of three readers and work that strikes two out of the three will be passed on to one of the genre editors, who in addition to judging this submitted work also solicits work from artists and authors particularly germane to the current issue. Please note that we have certain themed issues, such as the Ethnopoetics issue or the Aphasia issue, and during those periods, we will only read work that engages the theme, however overtly or obliquely.

## Do you have a favorite unsolicited submission discovery or story?

My personal favorite story is receiving a lengthy, serialized poem from one Mark, no last name given, in whose work we saw a lot of promise but also a lot of structural flaws. I corresponded with this person, detailing where we saw strengths and where the momentum of the piece seemed to cannibalize itself, offering a lot of minute suggestions as well as some more macroscopic ones. Turns out the poet in question was Mark Rudman, whose work I had studied in graduate school!

Turned out that he was very open to our suggestions, revising the work and sending it back to us. We published the piece in our second issue. Of course we've also published Suji Kwock Kim's poetry before she won the Walt Whitman Award, and Yael Kanarek before she was included in the Whitney Biennial, and Zoe Beloff before she won the Nam June Paik Award. But I prefer the story of how we tracked down Donald Green, an itinerant poet and former janitor who would stroll around the West Fourth Subway station with a sandwich board proclaiming he would write a poem on demand for a nominal fee. We spent an afternoon with him in Washington Square Park, recording an interview and poems with him, hearing his fascinating stories of how he worked as a janitor at Columbia University and spent time with Langston Hughes. Last I heard, his publishing credit on *Drunken Boat* was listed on the sandwich board.

**Do you have any advice for first-time submitters?**
Take time with the journal to glean the kind of work we're looking for. Don't over-saturate us with work, but send no more than 3-5 pieces at one time. We're very open to work that might not have a home elsewhere, manifestos and collaborations, so if you're doing something that's not traditional or linear, send it along. We're especially interested in work that uses the medium of the web as part of its compositional strategy. Remember we're not trying to replicate the efforts of a print journal online, but rather we're creating a new space, one where the paradigm of the page has flagged and one of relative boundlessness has opened up. Think about how you might use the possibilities inherent in publishing online to construct a work. We're almost always under-represented in sound, video, photo, and web art, so if you have work in those genres, we encourage you to send it along. Of course that's not to diminish our love of literature, which we're always happy to see.

**Backfile Available:** yes
**Unsolicited Ms. Received:** yes
**% of Unsolicited Ms. Published per Year:** 5%
**Format:** Saddle Stitched
**Size:** H 11" W 8 1/2"
**Average Pages:** 40
**Ads:** no

# Review: Latin American Literature & Arts

**Type:** magazine
**CLMP member:** no
**Primary Editor/Contact Person:** Daniel Shapiro
**Address:** The Americas Society
680 Park Ave.
New York, NY 10021
**Web Site Address:** http://www.americas-society.org
**Publishes:** essays, fiction, nonfiction, poetry, reviews, art, and translation
**Editorial Focus:** Contemporary literature in English/English translation by Caribbean, Latin American, and Canadian authors. Coverage of arts.
**Representative Authors:** Mario Vargas Llosa, Carmen Boullosa, and Gioconda Belli
**Submissions Policy:** We do not accept unsolicited submissions. Please send a query letter.
**Simultaneous Subs:** no
**Reading Period:** Year-round
**Reporting Time:** 2 to 3 months
**Author Payment:** cash and copies
**Contests:** no
**Founded:** 1968
**Non Profit:** yes
**Paid Staff:** 5
**Unpaid Staff:** 2
**Distributors:** Desert Moon, Ingram, Total, Ubiquity
**ISSN Number/ISBN Number:** ISSN 0890-5762
**Total Circulation:** 2,000
**Paid Circulation:** 1,200
**Subscription Rate:** Individual $22/Institution $32
**Single Copy Price:** $12
**Current Volume/Issue:** Fall/67
**Frequency per Year:** 2
**Backfile Available:** yes
**Unsolicited Ms. Received:** no
**Format:** perfect
**Size:** H 11" W 8 1/2"
**Average Pages:** 100
**Ads:** yes
**Ad Rates:** See Web Site for Details.

# Review of Contemporary Fiction

**Type:** magazine
**CLMP member:** no
**Primary Editor/Contact Person:** Editor
**Address:** Center for Book Culture
ISU 8905
Normal, IL 61790-8905
**Web Site Address:**
http://www.centerforbookculture.org
**Publishes:** essays, nonfiction, and reviews
**Editorial Focus:** Discussion of modern and contemporary writers, particularly those whose work is of an innovative or challenging nature.
**Representative Authors:** Gilbert Sorrentino, Ishmael Reed, and Ann Quin
**Submissions Policy:** No unsolicited submissions.
**Simultaneous Subs:** yes
**Reading Period:** Year-round
**Reporting Time:** 2 to 6 months
**Author Payment:** cash and copies
**Contests:** none
**Founded:** 1981
**Non Profit:** yes
**Paid Staff:** 15
**Unpaid Staff:** 2
**Distributors:** Ingram, University of Nebraska Press
**Wholesalers:** SPD
**ISSN Number/ISBN Number:** 0276-0045/1-56478-
**Total Circulation:** 2,500
**Paid Circulation:** 1,750
**Subscription Rate:** Individual $17/Institution $26
**Single Copy Price:** $8
**Current Volume/Issue:** 23/2
**Frequency per Year:** 3
**Backfile Available:** yes
**Unsolicited Ms. Received:** no
**Format:** perfect
**Size:** H 9" W 6"
**Average Pages:** 200
**Ads:** yes
**Ad Rates:** $250 full page

# RFD Press

**Type:** magazine
**CLMP member:** yes
**Address:**
P.O. Box 68
Liberty, TN 37095
**Web Site Address:** http://www.rfdmag.org/
**Publishes:** essays, fiction, nonfiction, poetry, and art

**Reading Period:** Year-round
**Reporting Time:** 1 to 2 months
**Author Payment:** none
**Founded:** 1974
**Non Profit:** no
**Backfile Available:** yes

# Rhapsody Magazine

**Type:** online
**CLMP member:** yes
**Primary Editor/Contact Person:** John Riddick
**Address:** P.O. Box 2443
Durham, NC 27715
**Web Site Address:**
http://www.rhapsodymagazine.com
**Publishes:** essays, fiction, poetry, reviews, and art
**Editorial Focus:** Creativity in all literary forms
**Representative Authors:** Linda Dominique Grosvenor
and Monda Webb
**Submissions Policy:** please e-mail or send hard
copy, be sure to include your contact information. Also
include your "15 min. of Fame" info.
**Simultaneous Subs:** yes
**Reading Period:** Year-round
**Reporting Time:** 1 to 3 months
**Author Payment:** copies
**Contests:** See Web Site for Contest Guidelines.
**Founded:** 1997
**Non Profit:** yes
**Paid Staff:** 2
**Unpaid Staff:** 5
**ISSN Number/ISBN Number:** ISSN 1094-2041
**Average Page Views per Month:** 300
**Average Unique Visitors per Month:** 120
**Frequency per Year:** 4
**Publish Print Anthology:** no
**Average Percentage of Pages per Category:** Fiction
15%, Poetry 50%, Reviews 15%, Essays 10%, Art
10%
**Ad Rates:** See Web Site for Details.

# RHINO

**Type:** magazine
**CLMP member:** yes
**Primary Editor/Contact Person:** Alice George,
Kathleen Kirk
**Address:** P.O. Box 591
Evanston, IL 60204
**Web Site Address:** http://www.rhinopoetry.org/

**Publishes:** essays, fiction, poetry, and reviews
**Simultaneous Subs:** yes
**Reading Period:** 4/1 to 10/1
**Reporting Time:** 3 to 6 months
**Author Payment:** none
**Founded:** 1976
**Non Profit:** yes
**Paid Staff:** 0
**Unpaid Staff:** 8
**ISSN Number/ISBN Number:** ISSN 1521-8414
**Total Circulation:** 1,000
**Paid Circulation:** 200
**Average Print Run:** 1,000
**Subscription Rate:** Individual $10/Institution $10
**Single Copy Price:** $10
**Current Volume/Issue:** Issue 2005
**Frequency per Year:** 1
**Backfile Available:** yes
**Unsolicited Ms. Received:** yes
**Format:** perfect
**Average Pages:** 150
**Ad Rates:** Exchange ads

# Rive Gauche

**Type:** magazine
**CLMP member:** yes
**Address:** Delgado Community College, West Bank
Campus
2600 General Meyer
New Orleans, LA 70114
**Web Site Address:** http://www.dcc.edu/rivegauche/
**Publishes:** essays, fiction, nonfiction, poetry, and art
**Reading Period:** Year-round
**Reporting Time:** 1 to 2 months
**Author Payment:** none
**Founded:** 2003
**Non Profit:** yes
**Backfile Available:** yes

# Rivendell Journal

**Type:** magazine
**CLMP member:** no
**Primary Editor/Contact Person:** Sebastian Matthews
**Address:** P.O. Box 9594
Asheville, NC 28815
**Web Site Address:**
http://www.greenmanwalking.com
**Publishes:** essays, fiction, nonfiction, poetry, reviews,
and art

**Editorial Focus:** Rivendell is a literary journal with an emphasis on place. Each issue focuses on a new locale, either geographic or thematic.

**Representative Authors:** David Budbill (New England), Peter J. Harris (Los Angeles), and Jean Pedrick (Workshop)

**Submissions Policy:** We accept submissions year-round. But we recommend you look at our website for guidelines. We take work that fits our theme.

**Simultaneous Subs:** yes

**Reading Period:** Year-round

**Reporting Time:** 3 to 6 weeks

**Author Payment:** copies

**Contests:** We are starting an Emerging Writers contest. More on this soon. (Check our website for updated info.)

**Founded:** 1999

**Non Profit:** yes

**Paid Staff:** 0

**Unpaid Staff:** 5

**Distributors:** we do it ourselves, working with ind. bookstores

**ISSN Number/ISBN Number:** ISSN different for each

**Total Circulation:** 500

**Paid Circulation:** 250

**Subscription Rate:** Individual $14/Institution same

**Single Copy Price:** $10

**Current Volume/Issue:** 1/3

**Frequency per Year:** 2

**Backfile Available:** yes

**Unsolicited Ms. Received:** yes

**% of Unsolicited Ms. Published per Year:** 5%

**Format:** perfect

**Size:** H 9" W 61/2"

**Average Pages:** 225

**Ads:** yes

**Ad Rates:** barter
See Web Site for Details.

# River City Publishing

**Type:** press

**CLMP member:** yes

**Primary Editor/Contact Person:** Jim Gilbert

**Address:** 1719 Mulberry St.
Montgomery, AL 36106

**Web Site Address:**
http://www.rivercitypublishing.com

**Publishes:** fiction and nonfiction

**Editorial Focus:** novels, short stories, literary travel, social history, and illustrated children's; works that focus on the South

**Recent Awards Received:** 2005 IPPY winner, 2004 IPPY finalist, 2004 ForeWord bronze, BookSense 76 selection, SEBA Award nominees

**Representative Authors:** Carolyn Haines, William Hoffman, and Wayne Greenhaw

**Submissions Policy:** Unsolicited/unagented OK. No electronic submissions. Include SASE for response, short bio, at least first 5 chapters.

**Simultaneous Subs:** yes

**Reading Period:** Year-round

**Reporting Time:** 1 to 3 months

**Author Payment:** royalties

**Contests:** Fred Bonnie Memorial Award-contest for best first novel
See Web Site for Contest Guidelines.

**Founded:** 1990

**Non Profit:** no

**Paid Staff:** 7

**Unpaid Staff:** 0

**Number of Books Published per Year:** 8-12

**Titles in Print:** 140

**Average Print Run:** 5,000

**Average Percentage Printed:** Hardcover 85%, Paperback 15%

**Average Price:** $25

# River City

**Type:** magazine

**CLMP member:** no

**Primary Editor/Contact Person:** Dr. Mary Leader

**Address:** 467 Patterson Hall
Memphis, TN 38152-3510

**Web Site Address:**
http://www.people.memphis.edu/~rivercity/

**Publishes:** fiction, nonfiction, poetry, and art

**Editorial Focus:** We publish both seasoned writers and new work that we think has promise.

**Representative Authors:** Paul Muldoon, Heidy Steidlmayer, and Connie Voisine

**Submissions Policy:** All typed manuscripts. Include SASE. About 7,000 words for fiction. About six or fewer poems.

**Simultaneous Subs:** yes

**Reading Period:** 8/25 to 3/15

**Reporting Time:** 1 to 3 months

**Author Payment:** none and subscription

**Contests:** Entries postmarked by 3/1. Reading fee: $12 per story, $5 per poem.
See Web Site for Contest Guidelines.

**Founded:** 1988
**Non Profit:** yes
**Paid Staff:** 4
**Unpaid Staff:** 25
**Distributors:** Ingram
**ISSN Number/ISBN Number:** 1048-129X
**Total Circulation:** 800
**Paid Circulation:** 200
**Subscription Rate:** Individual $12/Institution $12
**Single Copy Price:** $7
**Current Volume/Issue:** 22/2
**Frequency per Year:** 2
**Backfile Available:** yes
**Unsolicited Ms. Received:** yes
**% of Unsolicited Ms. Published per Year:** 50%
**Format:** perfect
**Average Pages:** 120
**Ads:** no

# River Teeth

**Type:** magazine
**CLMP member:** no
**Primary Editor/Contact Person:** Joe Mackall and Dan Lehman
**Address:** 401 College Ave.,
Ashland University
Ashland, OH 44805
**Web Site Address:** http://www.nebraskapress.unl.edu
**Publishes:** essays and nonfiction
**Editorial Focus:** Creative nonfiction, including essays, memoir, narrative journalism and critical essays about creative nonfiction
**Representative Authors:** David James Duncan, Chris Offutt, and Jon Franklin
**Submissions Policy:** We read year-round. Submissions must be typed and double-spaced. Include a brief bio with your submission.
**Simultaneous Subs:** yes
**Reading Period:** Year-round
**Reporting Time:** 1 to 3 months
**Author Payment:** copies
**Contests:** See Web Site for Contest Guidelines.
**Founded:** 1999
**Non Profit:** yes
**Paid Staff:** 0
**Unpaid Staff:** 5
**Distributors:** University of Nebraska Press
**ISSN Number/ISBN Number:** 1544-1849/none
**Total Circulation:** 1,000
**Paid Circulation:** 750

**Subscription Rate:** Individual $20/Institution $40
**Single Copy Price:** $12
**Current Volume/Issue:** 5/1
**Frequency per Year:** 2
**Backfile Available:** yes
**Unsolicited Ms. Received:** yes
**% of Unsolicited Ms. Published per Year:** 2%
**Format:** perfect
**Size:** H 9" W 5"
**Average Pages:** 200
**Ads:** yes
**Ad Rates:** Contact University of Nebraska Press

# Roof Books

**Type:** press
**CLMP member:** no
**Primary Editor/Contact Person:** James Sherry
**Address:** 300 Bowery
New York, NY 10012
**Web Site Address:** http://roofbooks.com
**Publishes:** essays and poetry
**Editorial Focus:** Since 1976 Roof Books has published innovative poetries and the writing around them.
**Representative Authors:** Ron Silliman, Charles Bernstein, and Nicole Brossard
**Submissions Policy:** Inquiries only, no mss., to geck044@earthlink.net.
**Simultaneous Subs:** no
**Reading Period:** Year-round
**Reporting Time:** 3 to 6 months
**Author Payment:** royalties and copies
**Founded:** 1976
**Non Profit:** yes
**Paid Staff:** 3
**Unpaid Staff:** 1
**Distributors:** SPD
**Wholesalers:** SPD
**ISSN Number/ISBN Number:** ISBN 937804
**Number of Books Published per Year:** 4
**Titles in Print:** 100
**Average Percentage Printed:** Paperback 100%

# The Rose & Thorn Literary E-zine

**Type:** online
**CLMP member:** yes
**Primary Editor/Contact Person:** Barbara Quinn
**Address:** theroseandthornezine.com
Rockland, NY 10901

**Web Site Address:** http://www.therose-andthornezine.com
**Publishes:** essays, fiction, nonfiction, poetry, reviews, and art
**Editorial Focus:** Award-winning zine showcases fiction, nonfiction, poetry, art, interviews. Offers free newsletter w/ markets, contests and tips.
**Recent Awards Received:** Named an Internet Envy site by Writer's Digest. Listed as one of Writer's Digest's top 100 sites for writers.
**Representative Authors:** Janet Buck, Emily Hanlon, and Troy Morash
**Submissions Policy:** Guidelines posted at the site. 2,000 word maximum for stories and essays.
**Simultaneous Subs:** yes
**Reading Period:** Year-round
**Reporting Time:** 2 to 14 weeks
**Author Payment:** none
**Founded:** 1997
**Non Profit:** yes
**Paid Staff:** 0
**Unpaid Staff:** 20
**Average Page Views per Month:** 135,000
**Average Unique Visitors per Month:** 8,000
**Frequency per Year:** 4
**Publish Print Anthology:** no
**Average Percentage of Pages per Category:** Fiction 50%, Nonfiction 20%, Poetry 15%, Essays 10%, Art 5%
**Ad Rates:** Start at $20
See Web Site for Details.

# Round Magazine

**Type:** online
**CLMP member:** yes
**Primary Editor/Contact Person:** Georg Pedersen and Beth Bayley
**Address:** 140 2nd St. Apt. C
Brooklyn, NY 11231
**Web Site Address:** http://www.roundonline.com
**Publishes:** essays, fiction, nonfiction, poetry, art, audio, and video
**Representative Authors:** Marcella Hammer and Nayiri Krikorian
**Submissions Policy:** Please see our website: http://roundonline.com/submit.shtml
**Simultaneous Subs:** yes
**Reading Period:** Year-round
**Reporting Time:** 1 to 2 months
**Author Payment:** none

**Founded:** 2002
**Non Profit:** yes
**Paid Staff:** 0
**Unpaid Staff:** 3
**Average Page Views per Month:** 19,000
**Average Unique Visitors per Month:** 3,000
**Frequency per Year:** 4
**Average Percentage of Pages per Category:** Fiction 25%, Nonfiction 7%, Poetry 7%, Essays 25%, Art 35%, Video 1%

# The Runaway Spoon Press

**Type:** press
**CLMP member:** no
**Primary Editor/Contact Person:** Bob Grumman
**Address:** Box 495597
Port Charlotte, FL 33949
**Publishes:** poetry
**Editorial Focus:** Xenovernacular Poetry, particularly litagraphy (i.e. "experimental" poetry, particularly "visual" poetry)
**Recent Awards Received:** 18 years in business and no awards, something I'm quite proud of.
**Representative Authors:** John M. Bennett, Geof Huth, and Gregory Vincent St. Thomasino
**Submissions Policy:** Standard-but presently overloaded with titles to publish so not open for submissions
**Simultaneous Subs:** yes
**Reading Period:** Year-round
**Reporting Time:** 1 to 50 months
**Author Payment:** copies
**Contests:** My press is not out to take poets.
**Founded:** 1987
**Non Profit:** no
**Paid Staff:** 0
**Unpaid Staff:** 1
**ISSN Number/ISBN Number:** ISBN 1-57141
**Number of Books Published per Year:** 4
**Titles in Print:** 150
**Average Print Run:** 100
**Average Percentage Printed:** Paperback 50%, Chapbook 50%
**Average Price:** $5

## RUNES/Arctos Press

**Type:** magazine
**CLMP member:** yes
**Primary Editor/Contact Person:** C.B. Follett
**Address:** P.O. Box 401
Sausalito, CA 94966
**Web Site Address:** http://members.aol.com/Runes
**Publishes:** nonfiction, art, and translation
**Editorial Focus:** The best 100 poems on the annual theme.
**Representative Authors:** David St. John, W.S. Merwin, and Philip Levine
**Submissions Policy:** up to 5 poems on theme, with SASE, unpublished. See guidelines on website.
**Simultaneous Subs:** yes
**Reading Period:** 4/1 to 5/31
**Reporting Time:** 3 to 4 months
**Author Payment:** copies
**Contests:** Annual RUNES Award on theme of hearth. National judge for '06 is Mark Doty. Up to 3 poems $15, additional poems $3 each.
See Web Site for Contest Guidelines.
**Founded:** 2001
**Non Profit:** yes
**Paid Staff:** 0
**Unpaid Staff:** 4
**Distributors:** SPD or Arctos Press
**Wholesalers:** SPD, Arctos Press
**ISSN Number/ISBN Number:** ISBN 0-9725384
**Total Circulation:** 1,200
**Paid Circulation:** 900
**Average Print Run:** 1,200
**Subscription Rate:** Individual $12/Institution $12
**Single Copy Price:** $12
**Current Volume/Issue:** 2005/1
**Frequency per Year:** 1
**Backfile Available:** yes
**Unsolicited Ms. Received:** yes
**% of Unsolicited Ms. Published per Year:** 1%
**Format:** perfect
**Average Pages:** 160

## SableLitMag

**Type:** magazine
**CLMP member:** no
**Primary Editor/Contact Person:** Kadija Sesay
**Address:** P.O. Box 33504
London, UK E97YE
**Web Site Address:** http://www.sablelitmag.org
**Publishes:** essays, fiction, nonfiction, poetry, reviews, translation, and audio
**Editorial Focus:** Showcasing creative writing by writers of color. Work by new authors and new work by established authors. Plus interview with major author.
**Representative Authors:** Ngugi wa Thiongo, Jhumpa Lahiri, and Marita Golden
**Submissions Policy:** All details are on the website- http://www.sablelitmag.org/submissions/html. No e-mail submissions accepted except for micro fiction.
**Simultaneous Subs:** yes
**Reading Period:** Year-round
**Reporting Time:** 1 to 3 months
**Author Payment:** none
**Contests:** Sable/Arvon creative writing residential course for writers of color at the Arvon Foundation in England.
**Founded:** 2000
**Non Profit:** yes
**Paid Staff:** no
**Unpaid Staff:** yes
**Distributors:** Ingram International
**ISSN Number/ISBN Number:** ISSN TBA
**Total Circulation:** 750
**Subscription Rate:** Individual $40/Institution $45
**Single Copy Price:** $12
**Current Volume/Issue:** Issue 5
**Frequency per Year:** 4
**Backfile Available:** yes
**Unsolicited Ms. Received:** yes
**% of Unsolicited Ms. Published per Year:** 85%
**Format:** perfect
**Size:** H A4" W A4"
**Average Pages:** 128
**Ads:** yes
**Ad Rates:** from $100 qtr; $175 half; $500 ROP; $750 cover
See Web Site for Details.

## Sacramento Poetry Center

**Type:** magazine
**CLMP member:** no
**Primary Editor/Contact Person:** Heather Hutcheson/Luke Breit
**Address:** 1631 K St.
Sacramento, CA 95814
**Web Site Address:** http://www.sacramentopoetrycenter.org
**Publishes:** poetry
**Representative Authors:** Gary Snyder, Dennis Schmitz, and Sandra McPherson

**Submissions Policy:** Submissions of poems, artwork, literary criticism, and other work of interest to the Sacramento poetry community are welcome. Work must be accompanied by a SASE for return. B&W or high contrast color photos & brief bios of submitters are encouraged. Please note that submissions to any of the Sacramento Poetry Center's publications may appear on the Center's website. Please submit to address above or e-mail poetrynow@sacramentopoetrycenter.org.

**Simultaneous Subs:** yes
**Reading Period:** Year-round
**Reporting Time:** 4 to 6 weeks
**Author Payment:** copies
**Contests:** See Web Site for Contest Guidelines.
**Founded:** 1979
**Non Profit:** yes
**Paid Staff:** 1
**Unpaid Staff:** 22
**Total Circulation:** 1,000
**Paid Circulation:** 220
**Subscription Rate:** Individual $25
**Single Copy Price:** $3
**Current Volume/Issue:** 9/10
**Frequency per Year:** 12
**Backfile Available:** yes
**Unsolicited Ms. Received:** yes
**% of Unsolicited Ms. Published per Year:** 20%
**Format:** 2 11x17 pages folded to 8.5x11
**Size:** H 8.5" W 11"
**Average Pages:** 8
**Ads:** yes
**Ad Rates:** See Web Site for Details.

# The Sage of Consciousness

**Type:** online
**CLMP member:** yes
**Primary Editor/Contact Person:** Michelle Williams
**Address:** P.O. Box 1209
Ocala, FL 34478-1209
**Web Site Address:** http://www.sageofcon.com
**Publishes:** essays, fiction, nonfiction, poetry, and art
**Editorial Focus:** To publish a diverse magazine with many different genres of art, poetry, nonfiction, articles, and new media.
**Recent Awards Received:** Hot Point Site of the Day. Webbie World top 10 People's Pick award. Webbie World Top 20 People's Pick award.
**Representative Authors:** Rob Rosen, Jennifer Thompson, and Janet Butler

**Submissions Policy:** Submissions accepted year-round. E-mail submissions in Word format. Through post, please include a disk in Word format.
**Simultaneous Subs:** yes
**Reading Period:** Year-round
**Reporting Time:** 1 to 2 months
**Author Payment:** none
**Founded:** 2004
**Non Profit:** yes
**Paid Staff:** 0
**Unpaid Staff:** 7
**ISSN Number/ISBN Number:** 1555-192X/none
**Average Page Views per Month:** 30,000
**Average Unique Visitors per Month:** 5,000
**Frequency per Year:** 4
**Publish Print Anthology:** no
**Average Percentage of Pages per Category:** Fiction 30%, Nonfiction 5%, Poetry 35%, Essays 5%, Art 25%
**Ad Rates:** See Web Site for Details.

# The Saint Ann's Review

**Type:** magazine
**CLMP member:** yes
**Primary Editor/Contact Person:** Beth Bosworth
**Address:** Saint Ann's School/129 Pierrepont St. Brooklyn, NY 11201
**Web Site Address:** http://www.saintannsreview.com
**Publishes:** essays, fiction, nonfiction, poetry, reviews, art, and translation
**Editorial Focus:** Well-crafted work that stands out.
**Representative Authors:** Diane Greco, Jane Avrich, and Anthony Calypso
**Submissions Policy:** The longer it is, the better-crafted and more unusual it has to be. See an issue or our website for details.
**Simultaneous Subs:** yes
**Reading Period:** Year-round
**Reporting Time:** 2 to 4 months
**Author Payment:** cash and copies
**Contests:** For now, we prefer not to conduct contests.
**Founded:** 2000
**Non Profit:** yes
**Paid Staff:** 5
**Unpaid Staff:** 3
**Distributors:** Ingram, Ubiquity
**ISSN Number/ISBN Number:** ISSN 25274
**Total Circulation:** 1,500
**Paid Circulation:** 400
**Subscription Rate:** Individual $18/Institution $18
**Single Copy Price:** $9

**Current Volume/Issue:** 4/1
**Frequency per Year:** 2
**Backfile Available:** yes
**Unsolicited Ms. Received:** yes
**% of Unsolicited Ms. Published per Year:** 25%
**Format:** perfect
**Size:** H 9.5" W 7"
**Average Pages:** 160
**Ads:** yes
**Ad Rates:** Ad rates may vary.

# Salamander

**Type:** magazine
**CLMP member:** yes
**Primary Editor/Contact Person:** Jennifer Barber
**Address:** Suffolk University/English Department
41 Temple St.
Boston, MA 02114-4280
**Web Site Address:** http://www.salamandermag.org
**Publishes:** essays, fiction, nonfiction, poetry, reviews, art, and translation
**Editorial Focus:** Salamander specializes in publishing highly accomplished work by writers who deserve a wider audience.
**Representative Authors:** Jessica Greenbaum, Fred Marchant, and Sandra Shea
**Submissions Policy:** Simultaneous submissions are accepted but we ask that you keep us informed
**Simultaneous Subs:** yes
**Reading Period:** 9/1 to 5/30
**Reporting Time:** 1 to 2 months
**Author Payment:** cash, copies, and subscription
**Founded:** 1992
**Non Profit:** yes
**Paid Staff:** 1
**Unpaid Staff:** 6
**Distributors:** DeBoer
**ISSN Number/ISBN Number:** ISSN 1063-3359
**Total Circulation:** 1,000
**Paid Circulation:** 350
**Average Print Run:** 1,000
**Subscription Rate:** Individual $23 (2 yr)/Institution $23
**Single Copy Price:** $7
**Current Volume/Issue:** 11/1-2
**Frequency per Year:** 2
**Backfile Available:** yes
**Unsolicited Ms. Received:** yes
**% of Unsolicited Ms. Published per Year:** 5%
**Format:** perfect

**Size:** H 5 1/2" W 8 1/2"
**Average Pages:** 90
**Ads:** yes
**Ad Rates:** $150 (full page)

# Salmagundi

**Type:** magazine
**CLMP member:** yes
**Primary Editor/Contact Person:** Peg Boyers/Robert Boyers
**Address:** Skidmore College
815 N. Broadway
Saratoga Springs, NY 12866
**Web Site Address:** in progress
**Publishes:** essays, fiction, nonfiction, poetry, reviews, and translation
**Editorial Focus:** We seek to publish work of quality in a variety of genres. It's impossible to define the 'focus' beyond this general goal
**Representative Authors:** Nadine Gordimer, Marilynne Robinson, and George Steiner
**Submissions Policy:** From Oct 15-May 1send mss. as attachments in Microsoft word to pboyers@skidmore.edu. or send hard copy to above address.
**Simultaneous Subs:** yes
**Reading Period:** 10/15 to 5/1
**Reporting Time:** 4 to 6 months
**Author Payment:** copies and subscription
**Founded:** 1965
**Non Profit:** yes
**Paid Staff:** 2
**Unpaid Staff:** 1
**Distributors:** DeBoer, Ingram
**Wholesalers:** not applicable
**ISSN Number/ISBN Number:** ISSN 0036-3529
**Total Circulation:** 4,800
**Paid Circulation:** 3,500
**Average Print Run:** 5,000
**Subscription Rate:** Individual $20/Institution $32
**Single Copy Price:** $8
**Current Volume/Issue:** 148/148
**Frequency per Year:** 4
**Backfile Available:** yes
**Unsolicited Ms. Received:** yes
**% of Unsolicited Ms. Published per Year:** 5%
**Format:** perfect
**Size:** H 8" W 5"
**Average Pages:** 200
**Ads:** yes
**Ad Rates:** $300 full page/175 for 1/2 page

# Salt Hill

**Type:** magazine
**CLMP member:** no
**Primary Editor/Contact Person:** Ellen Litman
**Address:** Salt Hill/Department of English
Syracuse University
Syracuse, NY 13244
**Web Site Address:** http://students.syr.edu/salthill
**Publishes:** essays, fiction, nonfiction, poetry, reviews, art, and translation
**Editorial Focus:** We have an open aesthetic and revolving editorship. We are equally committed to publishing experimental and traditional work.
**Representative Authors:** Dean Young, Brian Evenson, and Steve Almond
**Submissions Policy:** Send manuscript, cover letter, and SASE with sufficient postage. We do not accept electronic submissions.
**Simultaneous Subs:** yes
**Reading Period:** 8/1 to 4/1
**Reporting Time:** 2 to 6 months
**Author Payment:** copies
**Contests:** Poetry and short short fiction (1,500 words max) contests. Deadline-January 15. Reading fee-$10. Prizes: $500, $250, and $100
See Web Site for Contest Guidelines.
**Founded:** 1995
**Non Profit:** yes
**Paid Staff:** 0
**Unpaid Staff:** 20
**Distributors:** Ingram
**ISSN Number/ISBN Number:** ISSN 1078-8689
**Total Circulation:** 1,000
**Paid Circulation:** 20
**Subscription Rate:** Individual $15/Institution $20
**Single Copy Price:** $8
**Current Volume/Issue:** Issue 14
**Frequency per Year:** 2
**Backfile Available:** yes
**Unsolicited Ms. Received:** yes
**% of Unsolicited Ms. Published per Year:** 80%
**Format:** perfect
**Average Pages:** 130
**Ads:** yes
**Ad Rates:** See Web Site for Details.

# Sarabande Books

**Type:** press
**CLMP member:** yes
**Primary Editor/Contact Person:** Sarah Gorham
**Address:** 2234 Dundee Rd, Ste. 200
Louisville, KY 40205
**Web Site Address:** http://www.SarabandeBooks.org
**Publishes:** essays, fiction, nonfiction, and poetry
**Editorial Focus:** Sarabande publishes only the best literature, an eclectic mix of new and established writers both experimental and formal.
**Recent Awards Received:** National Jewish Book Award, Finalist Pulitzer Prize, Norma Farber First Book Award
**Representative Authors:** Cate Marvin, Ralph Angel, and Marjorie Sandor
**Submissions Policy:** Kathryn A. Morton Prize in Poetry, Mary McCarthy Prize in Short Fiction. Otherwise by invitation and recommendation.
**Simultaneous Subs:** yes
**Reading Period:** 1/1 to 2/15
**Reporting Time:** 12 to 15 weeks
**Author Payment:** royalties, cash, and copies
**Contests:** See Web Site for Contest Guidelines.
**Founded:** 1994
**Non Profit:** yes
**Paid Staff:** 6
**Unpaid Staff:** 2
**Distributors:** Consortium
**Wholesalers:** Baker & Taylor, Ingram
**ISSN Number/ISBN Number:** 889330/9641151
**Number of Books Published per Year:** 10-12
**Titles in Print:** 85
**Average Print Run:** 3,000
**Average Percentage Printed:** Hardcover 20%, Paperback 70%, Chapbook 10%
**Average Price:** $13

# Seal Press

**Type:** press
**CLMP member:** no
**Primary Editor/Contact Person:** Ingrid Emerick
**Address:** 300 Queen Anne Ave. N #375
Seattle, WA 98109
**Web Site Address:** http://www.sealpress.com
**Publishes:** fiction and nonfiction
**Editorial Focus:** Seal Press has a long, distinguished reputation for publishing books by women of incredible variety and depth.
**Representative Authors:** Ariel Gore and Ginny

NiCarthy

**Submissions Policy:** Please send either a query letter or proposal, with SASE, to our address. No e-mail or phone calls, please.

**Simultaneous Subs:** yes

**Reading Period:** Year-round

**Reporting Time:** 2 to 3 months

**Author Payment:** royalties, cash, and copies

**Founded:** 1976

**Non Profit:** no

**Paid Staff:** 4

**Unpaid Staff:** 0

**Number of Books Published per Year:** 21

**Titles in Print:** 125-50

**Average Percentage Printed:** Hardcover 5%, Paperback 95%

# The Seattle Review

**Type:** magazine

**CLMP member:** yes

**Primary Editor/Contact Person:** Colleen J. McElroy

**Address:** University of Washington

Padelford Hall, P. O. Box 354330

Seattle, WA 98195-4330

**Web Site Address:** http://www.seattlereview.org

**Publishes:** fiction, nonfiction, and poetry

**Editorial Focus:** See Website

**Representative Authors:** Sharon Olds, Yusef Komunyakaa, and Daniel Orozco

**Submissions Policy:** See Website

**Simultaneous Subs:** no

**Reading Period:** 10/1 to 5/31

**Reporting Time:** 2 to 4 months

**Author Payment:** none

**Contests:** Annual Poetry and Fiction Prize. Submissions accepted between January 1st and March 31st. Please visit website for details. See Web Site for Contest Guidelines.

**Founded:** 1978

**Non Profit:** yes

**Paid Staff:** 2

**Unpaid Staff:** 15

**Total Circulation:** 800

**Paid Circulation:** 184

**Average Print Run:** 800

**Subscription Rate:** Individual $20-32/Institution $20-32

**Single Copy Price:** $8

**Current Volume/Issue:** 27/2

**Frequency per Year:** 2

**Backfile Available:** yes

**Unsolicited Ms. Received:** yes

**Format:** perfect

**Average Pages:** 150

**Ads:** yes

**Ad Rates:** See Web Site for Details.

# Second Story Books

**Type:** press

**CLMP member:** yes

**Primary Editor/Contact Person:** Mary Burger

**Address:** 591 63rd St.

Oakland, CA 94609

**Web Site Address:** http://www.2ndstorybooks.com

**Publishes:** fiction, nonfiction, and poetry

**Editorial Focus:** Cross-genre works of experimental narrative, using elements of fiction, poetry, memoir, philosophy, and other forms.

**Representative Authors:** Renee Gladman, Brenda Coultas, and Camille Roy

**Submissions Policy:** Second Story Books usually publishes solicited works. Requests for submissions will be posted on our web site.

**Simultaneous Subs:** no

**Reading Period:** Year-round

**Reporting Time:** 1 to 6 months

**Author Payment:** copies

**Contests:** Future contests will be announced on our web site.

**Founded:** 1998

**Non Profit:** no

**Paid Staff:** 1/2

**Unpaid Staff:** 1

**Distributors:** SPD

**Number of Books Published per Year:** 1

**Titles in Print:** 7

**Average Print Run:** 500

**Average Percentage Printed:** Paperback 100%

**Average Price:** $12

# Seneca Review

**Type:** magazine

**CLMP member:** yes

**Primary Editor/Contact Person:** Deborah Tall

**Address:** Hobart and William Smith Colleges

Geneva, NY 14456

**Web Site Address:**

http://www.hws.edu/SenecaReview

**Publishes:** essays, poetry, and translation

**Editorial Focus:** Seneca Review publishes a wide variety of ambitious poetry and lyric essays, and we have great interest in translations of modern poetry. We regularly publish both established figures and emerging writers.
**Representative Authors:** Fanny Howe, Carl Phillips, and Dionisio D. Martinez
**Submissions Policy:** Note that we do not publish fiction. Due to the great number of manuscripts we receive, we ask that you limit yourself to just one submission during our annual reading period. We do not accept manuscripts electronically. All submissions must be accompanied by a SASE.
**Simultaneous Subs:** no
**Reading Period:** 9/1 to 5/1
**Reporting Time:** 10 to 12 weeks
**Author Payment:** copies and subscription
**Founded:** 1970
**Non Profit:** yes
**Paid Staff:** 2
**Unpaid Staff:** 2
**ISSN Number/ISBN Number:** ISSN 0037-2145
**Total Circulation:** 1,000
**Paid Circulation:** 400
**Average Print Run:** 1,200
**Subscription Rate:** Individual $11/Institution $11
**Single Copy Price:** $7
**Current Volume/Issue:** 35/2
**Frequency per Year:** 2
**Backfile Available:** yes
**Unsolicited Ms. Received:** yes
**% of Unsolicited Ms. Published per Year:** 1-2%
**Format:** perfect
**Size:** H 7.5" W 5.5"
**Average Pages:** 100
**Ads:** yes
**Ad Rates:** $75 full page

# Sentence

**Type:** magazine
**CLMP member:** yes
**Primary Editor/Contact Person:** Brian Clements, Editor
**Address:** Box 7, Western Connecticut State University 181 White St. Danbury, CT 06810
**Web Site Address:** http://firewheel-editions.org
**Publishes:** essays, poetry, reviews, and translation
**Editorial Focus:** Sentence publishes prose poems and work on the boundary of the prose poem, as well as reviews and essays on poetics
**Recent Awards Received:** Work selected for Best American Poetry 2005
**Submissions Policy:** Hard copy w/SASE or e-mail address. Electronic on CD, diskette, or in a SINGLE e-mail attachment (.doc, .pdf, .rtf, or .txt)
**Simultaneous Subs:** yes
**Reading Period:** Year-round
**Reporting Time:** 1 to 3 months
**Author Payment:** copies
**Founded:** 2002
**Non Profit:** yes
**Paid Staff:** 0
**Unpaid Staff:** 3
**Wholesalers:** DeBoer, Amazon
**ISSN Number/ISBN Number:** ISSN 1545-5378
**Total Circulation:** 1,000
**Paid Circulation:** 350
**Average Print Run:** 1,000
**Subscription Rate:** Individual $22/30/Institution $12/issue
**Single Copy Price:** $12
**Current Volume/Issue:** Issue 3
**Frequency per Year:** 2
**Backfile Available:** yes
**Unsolicited Ms. Received:** yes
**Format:** perfect
**Size:** H 7" W 5"
**Average Pages:** 200
**Ads:** yes
**Ad Rates:** $100 for full page or ad exchange See Web Site for Details.

# The Sewanee Review

**Type:** magazine
**CLMP member:** yes
**Primary Editor/Contact Person:** Bob Jones
**Address:** 735 University Ave. Sewanee, TN 37383-1000
**Web Site Address:** http://www.sewanee.edu/sreview/home.html
**Publishes:** essays, fiction, nonfiction, poetry, and reviews
**Editorial Focus:** High quality fiction, poetry, essays, and book reviews. Literary criticism without jargon or particular critical theories.
**Representative Authors:** Wendell Berry, George Garrett, and Sam Pickering
**Submissions Policy:** Poetry: 40 lines or less, no more than 6. Fiction: 3,500-7,500 words, 1 per submission.

Essays: 3,500-7,500, 1 per submission.
**Simultaneous Subs:** no
**Reading Period:** 9/1 to 5/31
**Reporting Time:** 5 to 6 weeks
**Author Payment:** royalties, cash, and copies
**Contests:** Four annual awards: short story, poem(s), essay, book reviewing. Chosen by the board of editors; may not be applied for.
**Founded:** 1892
**Non Profit:** yes
**Paid Staff:** 3
**Unpaid Staff:** 0
**Distributors:** Ingram
**ISSN Number/ISBN Number:** ISSN 0037-3052
**Total Circulation:** 3,070
**Paid Circulation:** 2,700
**Subscription Rate:** Individual $24/Institution $30
**Single Copy Price:** $8.50
**Current Volume/Issue:** 112/1
**Frequency per Year:** 4
**Backfile Available:** yes
**Unsolicited Ms. Received:** yes
**% of Unsolicited Ms. Published per Year:** 1%
**Format:** perfect
**Size:** H 6" W 9"
**Average Pages:** 192
**Ads:** yes
**Ad Rates:** $250/page; $180/half-page
See Web Site for Details.

# Shampoo

**Type:** online
**CLMP member:** no
**Primary Editor/Contact Person:** Del Ray Cross
**Address:** 903 Pine St., Apt. 35
San Francisco, CA 94108
**Web Site Address:** http://shampoopoetry.com
**Publishes:** poetry and art
**Submissions Policy:** always open. please attach .doc or .rtf files. previously unpublished. 3-10 pages of work is sufficient.
**Simultaneous Subs:** yes
**Reading Period:** Year-round
**Reporting Time:** 0 to 4 months
**Author Payment:** none
**Founded:** 2000
**Non Profit:** yes
**Paid Staff:** 0
**Unpaid Staff:** 1
**Frequency per Year:** 4

**Publish Print Anthology:** no
**Average Percentage of Pages per Category:** Poetry 99%, Art 1%
**Ads:** no

# The Sheep Meadow Press

**Type:** press
**CLMP member:** no
**Primary Editor/Contact Person:** Stanley Moss
**Address:** P.O. Box 1345
Riverdale, NY 10471
**Publishes:** fiction, nonfiction, poetry, art, and translation
**Editorial Focus:** Poetry, literary translations, cultural history, art history.
**Representative Authors:** Stanley Kunitz, Paul Celan, and Yehuda Amichai
**Submissions Policy:** We have a very small list and rarely accept unsolicited manuscripts.
**Simultaneous Subs:** yes
**Reading Period:** Year-round
**Reporting Time:** 4 to 6 months
**Author Payment:** royalties
**Contests:** Multiple.
**Founded:** 1976
**Non Profit:** yes
**Paid Staff:** 2
**Unpaid Staff:** 0
**Distributors:** University Presses of New England
**Number of Books Published per Year:** 10
**Titles in Print:** 150
**Average Percentage Printed:** Hardcover 5%, Paperback 95%

# Shenandoah: The Washington & Lee University Review

**Type:** magazine
**CLMP member:** yes
**Primary Editor/Contact Person:** Lynn Leech, Man. Ed.
**Address:** Washington and Lee University
Mattingly House/204 W Washington St.
Lexington, VA 24450-2116
**Web Site Address:** http://shenandoah.wlu.edu
**Publishes:** essays, fiction, nonfiction, poetry, reviews, and art
**Editorial Focus:** Work characterized by both formal and extemporaneous spirits.
**Representative Authors:** Mary Oliver, Pam Durban,

and Rick Bass
**Submissions Policy:** Short stories and essays (1 per submission), poems (5 per submission).
**Simultaneous Subs:** yes
**Reading Period:** 9/1 to 5/30
**Reporting Time:** 3 to 4 weeks
**Author Payment:** cash, copies, and subscription
**Founded:** 1950
**Non Profit:** yes
**Paid Staff:** 1.5
**Unpaid Staff:** 1
**Distributors:** Total Circulation, Ubiquity
**ISSN Number/ISBN Number:** ISSN 0037-3588
**Total Circulation:** 1,800
**Paid Circulation:** 1,360
**Average Print Run:** 2,100
**Subscription Rate:** Individual $22/Institution $25
**Single Copy Price:** $10
**Current Volume/Issue:** 55/1-3
**Frequency per Year:** 3
**Backfile Available:** yes
**Unsolicited Ms. Received:** yes
**% of Unsolicited Ms. Published per Year:** 2%
**Format:** perfect
**Size:** H 9" W 6"
**Average Pages:** 176
**Ads:** yes
**Ad Rates:** $300/full page; $150/half page
See Web Site for Details.

## Sí, Señor

**Type:** magazine
**CLMP member:** yes
**Address:** 1110 Canton Ave., Apt. 6
Brooklyn, NY 11218
**Web Site Address:** http://www.sisenor.info
**Publishes:** fiction, nonfiction, poetry, and art
**Reading Period:** Year-round
**Reporting Time:** 1 to 2 months
**Author Payment:** none
**Founded:** 2001
**Non Profit:** yes
**Backfile Available:** yes

## Silverfish Review Press

**Type:** press
**CLMP member:** yes
**Primary Editor/Contact Person:** Rodger Moody
**Address:** P.O. Box 3541

Eugene, OR 97403
**Web Site Address:**
http://www.silverfishreviewpress.com
**Publishes:** poetry
**Editorial Focus:** SRP publishes a book by winner of annual contest and other titles as well.
**Recent Awards Received:** Washington State Book Award for Breaking Ground by Paul Hunter
**Representative Authors:** Nin Andrews, Mark Conway, and Beth Gylys
**Submissions Policy:** We read manuscripts outside of the annual contest during the summer months only. Check web site for deadlines.
**Simultaneous Subs:** yes
**Reading Period:** 6/1 to 10/15
**Reporting Time:** 2 to 3 months
**Author Payment:** cash and copies
**Contests:** Gerald Cable Book Award is given annually for a first book.
See Web Site for Contest Guidelines.
**Founded:** 1978
**Non Profit:** yes
**Paid Staff:** 1
**Unpaid Staff:** 3
**Distributors:** SPD and Spring Church Book Company.
**ISSN Number/ISBN Number:** ISBN 1-878851
**Number of Books Published per Year:** 2
**Titles in Print:** 15
**Average Print Run:** 1,000
**Average Percentage Printed:** Paperback 100%
**Average Price:** $ $14.95

## Sixteen Rivers Press

**Type:** press
**CLMP member:** yes
**Primary Editor/Contact Person:** Terry Ehret
**Address:** P.O. Box 640663
San Francisco, CA 94164-0663
**Web Site Address:** http://www.sixteenrivers.com
**Publishes:** poetry
**Editorial Focus:** Sixteen Rivers is a shared-work poetry publishing collective for the S.F. Bay Area. Members make a 3-year work commitment.
**Representative Authors:** Margaret Kaufman, Lynn Trombetta, and Diane Lutovich
**Submissions Policy:** Manuscript of 60-80 pgs. may be submitted. Two new members are selected from these manuscripts each year.
**Simultaneous Subs:** yes
**Reading Period:** 1/1 to 3/1

**Reporting Time:** 6 to 8 months
**Author Payment:** copies
**Founded:** 1999
**Non Profit:** yes
**Paid Staff:** 0
**Unpaid Staff:** 7
**Distributors:** SPD
**Number of Books Published per Year:** 2
**Titles in Print:** 6
**Average Percentage Printed:** Paperback 100%
**Backfile Available:** yes

## SLAB: Sound and Literary Art Book

**Type:** magazine
**CLMP member:** yes
**Primary Editor/Contact Person:** Mark O'Connor
**Address:** 312-I, SWC
Slippery Rock University
Slippery Rock, PA 16057
**Web Site Address:** http://www.slablitmag.com
**Publishes:** essays, fiction, nonfiction, poetry, and art
**Editorial Focus:** Contemporary fiction, poetry, nonfiction, and web-based art.
**Representative Authors:** Tom Whalen, Ryan Van Cleave, and Kelli Russell Agadon
**Submissions Policy:** Multiple, surface, and online submissions are accepted
**Simultaneous Subs:** yes
**Reading Period:** Year-round
**Reporting Time:** 2 to 3 months
**Author Payment:** copies
**Contests:** Annual Poetry and Creative Nonfiction Contest.
See Web Site for Contest Guidelines.
**Founded:** 1975
**Non Profit:** yes
**Paid Staff:** 0
**Unpaid Staff:** 30
**Total Circulation:** 900
**Paid Circulation:** 100
**Average Print Run:** 1,000
**Subscription Rate:** Individual $10-2 years/Institution $10-2 years
**Single Copy Price:** $5
**Current Volume/Issue:** 1/1
**Frequency per Year:** 1
**Backfile Available:** yes
**Unsolicited Ms. Received:** yes
**% of Unsolicited Ms. Published per Year:** 100%
**Format:** perfect

**Size:** H 8" W 6"
**Average Pages:** 154
**Ads:** no

## Slapering Hol Press

**Type:** press
**CLMP member:** yes
**Primary Editor/Contact Person:** Margo Stever
**Address:** Hudson Valley Writers' Center
300 Riverside Dr.
Sleepy Hollow, NY 10591
**Web Site Address:** http://www.writerscenter.org
**Publishes:** poetry
**Editorial Focus:** SHP publishes chapbooks by poets who have not previously published a book or chapbook; and occasionally, thematic anthologies
**Representative Authors:** David Tucker, Dina Ben-Lev, and Rachel Loden
**Submissions Policy:** see web site for guidelines
**Simultaneous Subs:** yes
**Reading Period:** 2/1 to 5/15
**Reporting Time:** 2 to 3 months
**Author Payment:** cash and copies
**Contests:** See Web Site for Contest Guidelines.
**Founded:** 1990
**Non Profit:** yes
**Paid Staff:** 0
**Unpaid Staff:** 2
**Distributors:** applied to SPD-waiting to hear
**ISSN Number/ISBN Number:** ISBN 0-9700277
**Number of Books Published per Year:** 1-2
**Titles in Print:** 16
**Average Print Run:** 500
**Average Percentage Printed:** Paperback 5%, Chapbook 95%
**Average Price:** $12

## Slidingpillar

**Type:** magazine
**CLMP member:** no
**Primary Editor/Contact Person:** Will Goodman
**Address:** 143 S. Waverly St.
Orange, CA 92866
**Web Site Address:** http://www.slidingpillar.com
**Publishes:** essays, fiction, nonfiction, and poetry
**Editorial Focus:** Original, intelligent, creative content.
**Submissions Policy:** Anything, so long as it is less then 10 pages.
**Simultaneous Subs:** yes

**Reading Period:** Year-round
**Reporting Time:** 1 to 3 months
**Author Payment:** copies
**Founded:** 1999
**Non Profit:** no
**Paid Staff:** 1
**Unpaid Staff:** 0
**ISSN Number/ISBN Number:** ISSN 1530-4124
**Total Circulation:** 1,000
**Paid Circulation:** 3
**Subscription Rate:** Individual $5/Institution $5
**Single Copy Price:** $1
**Current Volume/Issue:** 4/1
**Frequency per Year:** 5
**Backfile Available:** yes
**Unsolicited Ms. Received:** yes
**% of Unsolicited Ms. Published per Year:** 50%
**Format:** stapled
**Size:** H 8.5" W 5.5"
**Average Pages:** 40
**Ads:** yes
**Ad Rates:** See Web Site for Details.

## Slipstream Publications

**Type:** press
**CLMP member:** no
**Primary Editor/Contact Person:** Dan Sicoli
**Address:** P.O. Box 2071
Niagara Falls, NY 14301
**Web Site Address:** http://www.slipstreampress.org
**Publishes:** poetry and art
**Representative Authors:** Gerald Locklin, David
Chorlton, and Terry Godbey
**Submissions Policy:** Please refer to guidelines on
web page.
**Simultaneous Subs:** yes
**Reading Period:** Year-round
**Reporting Time:** 1 to 3 months
**Author Payment:** copies
**Contests:** Annual Poetry Chapbook Competition has a
December 1st deadline. See Web page for complete
guidelines for submissions.
See Web Site for Contest Guidelines.
**Founded:** 1980
**Non Profit:** yes
**Paid Staff:** no
**Unpaid Staff:** yes
**Number of Books Published per Year:** 1
**Titles in Print:** 18
**Average Print Run:** 700

**Average Percentage Printed:** Chapbook 100%
**Average Price:** $7

## Slipstream

**Type:** magazine
**CLMP member:** no
**Primary Editor/Contact Person:** Dan Sicoli
**Address:** P.O. Box 2071
Niagara Falls, NY 14301
**Web Site Address:** http://www.slipstreampress.org
**Publishes:** poetry and art
**Representative Authors:** Johnny Cordova, Robert
Cooperman, and Lyn Lifshin
**Submissions Policy:** Please refer to guidelines on
web page.
**Simultaneous Subs:** yes
**Reading Period:** Year-round
**Reporting Time:** 1 to 3 months
**Author Payment:** copies
**Contests:** See Web Site for Contest Guidelines.
**Founded:** 1980
**Non Profit:** yes
**Paid Staff:** no
**Unpaid Staff:** yes
**Total Circulation:** 700
**Paid Circulation:** 450
**Average Print Run:** 700
**Subscription Rate:** Individual $20/Institution $20
**Single Copy Price:** $7
**Current Volume/Issue:** Issue 25
**Frequency per Year:** 1
**Backfile Available:** no
**Unsolicited Ms. Received:** yes
**% of Unsolicited Ms. Published per Year:** 7%
**Format:** perfect
**Size:** H 8.5" W 7"
**Average Pages:** 80-100
**Ads:** no

## Slope Editions

**Type:** press
**CLMP member:** no
**Primary Editor/Contact Person:** Ethan Paquin
**Address:** 340 Richmond Ave.
Buffalo, NY 14222
**Web Site Address:** http://www.slopeeditions.org
**Publishes:** poetry
**Editorial Focus:** Eclectic poetry
**Representative Authors:** Jenny Boully, Jonah Winter,

and William Waltz
**Submissions Policy:** See web site for guidelines.
**Simultaneous Subs:** no
**Reading Period:** Year-round
**Reporting Time:** 4 to 12 months
**Author Payment:** royalties and copies
**Contests:** See Web Site for Contest Guidelines.
**Founded:** 2001
**Non Profit:** yes
**Paid Staff:** 0
**Unpaid Staff:** 8
**Distributors:** Baker & Taylor, SPD
**Number of Books Published per Year:** 3
**Titles in Print:** 5
**Average Percentage Printed:** Paperback 100%

# Slope

**Type:** online
**CLMP member:** no
**Primary Editor/Contact Person:** Ethan Paquin
**Address:** 340 Richmond Ave.
Buffalo, NY 14222
**Web Site Address:** http://www.slope.org
**Publishes:** essays, poetry, reviews, translation, and audio
**Editorial Focus:** Eclectic
**Representative Authors:** Forrest Gander, James Tate, and Charles Bernstein
**Submissions Policy:** See web site for guidelines.
**Simultaneous Subs:** no
**Reading Period:** Year-round
**Reporting Time:** 1 to 6 months
**Author Payment:** none
**Founded:** 1999
**Non Profit:** yes
**Paid Staff:** 0
**Unpaid Staff:** 6
**Average Page Views per Month:** 1,000s
**Average Unique Visitors per Month:** 10,000s
**Frequency per Year:** 4
**Publish Print Anthology:** no
**Average Percentage of Pages per Category:** Poetry 85%, Reviews 15%
**Ads:** no

# Slovo/Word

**Type:** magazine
**CLMP member:** no
**Address:** Cultural Center for Soviet Refugees
139 E. 33rd St., Ste. 9M
New York, NY 10016

**Publishes:** essays and fiction
**Reading Period:** Year-round
**Reporting Time:** 1 to 2 months
**Author Payment:** none
**Founded:** 1986
**Non Profit:** no

# Small Beer Press

**Type:** magazine
**CLMP member:** yes
**Address:** 176 Prospect Ave.
Northampton, MA 01060
**Web Site Address:** http://www.lcrw.net
**Publishes:** essays
**Reading Period:** Year-round
**Reporting Time:** 1 to 2 months
**Author Payment:** none
**Founded:** 1996
**Non Profit:** yes
**Backfile Available:** yes

# Small Beer Press

**Type:** press
**CLMP member:** yes
**Primary Editor/Contact Person:** Gavin Grant
**Address:** 176 Prospect Ave.
Northampton, MA 01060
**Web Site Address:** http://www.lcrw.net
**Publishes:** fiction and nonfiction
**Representative Authors:** Kelly Link, Maureen F. McHugh, and Carol Emshwiller
**Simultaneous Subs:** no
**Reading Period:** Year-round
**Reporting Time:** 1 to 2 months
**Author Payment:** royalties and cash
**Founded:** 1996
**Non Profit:** no
**Paid Staff:** 0
**Unpaid Staff:** 2
**Distributors:** SCB Distributors
**Wholesalers:** Ingram, Baker & Taylor, etc.
**ISSN Number/ISBN Number:** 1544-7782/1931520
**Number of Books Published per Year:** 3
**Titles in Print:** 14
**Average Print Run:** 3,000
**Average Percentage Printed:** Hardcover 48%, Paperback 48%, Chapbook 4%
**Average Price:** $16

# Small Spiral Notebook

**Type:** magazine
**CLMP member:** yes
**Primary Editor/Contact Person:** Felicia C. Sullivan
**Address:** 172 5th Ave. #104
Brooklyn, NY 11217
**Web Site Address:**
http://www.smallspiralnotebook.com
**Publishes:** fiction, nonfiction, poetry, and reviews
**Editorial Focus:** Small Spiral Notebook seeks the very best in literary fiction, nonfiction and poetry with a focus on emerging writers.
**Representative Authors:** Judy Budnitz, Lisa Glatt, and Ken Foster
**Submissions Policy:** Please view our submission guidelines at
http://www.smallspiralnotebook.com/newsubmission.s html
**Simultaneous Subs:** yes
**Reading Period:** Year-round
**Reporting Time:** 1 to 3 months
**Author Payment:** copies
**Founded:** 2001
**Non Profit:** yes
**Paid Staff:** 0
**Unpaid Staff:** 10
**Distributors:** Ingram, DeBoer
**ISSN Number/ISBN Number:** ISSN 1557-1068
**Total Circulation:** 1,500
**Paid Circulation:** 200
**Average Print Run:** 1,500
**Subscription Rate:** Individual $18/Institution $18
**Single Copy Price:** $10
**Current Volume/Issue:** 2/2
**Frequency per Year:** 2
**Backfile Available:** yes
**Unsolicited Ms. Received:** yes
**% of Unsolicited Ms. Published per Year:** 60%
**Format:** perfect
**Size:** H 6" W 9"
**Average Pages:** 150
**Ads:** yes
**Ad Rates:** e-mail editor@smallspiralnotebook.com for details.

# Small Spiral Notebook

**Type:** online
**CLMP member:** yes
**Primary Editor/Contact Person:** Felicia C. Sullivan
**Address:** 248 W. 17th St. Ste. 307
New York, NY 10011
**Web Site Address:**
http://www.smallspiralnotebook.com
**Publishes:** fiction, nonfiction, poetry, and reviews
**Editorial Focus:** Small Spiral Notebook seeks the very best in literary fiction, nonfiction and poetry. Submissions accepted year-round.
**Representative Authors:** Aimee Bender, Gary Lutz, and Jonathan Ames
**Submissions Policy:** Please view our submission guidelines at
http://www.smallspiralnotebook.com/newsubmission.s html
**Simultaneous Subs:** yes
**Reading Period:** Year-round
**Reporting Time:** 1 to 3 months
**Author Payment:** none
**Founded:** 2001
**Non Profit:** yes
**Paid Staff:** 0
**Unpaid Staff:** 7
**Backfile Available:** yes
**Average Page Views per Month:** 16,000
**Average Unique Visitors per Month:** 8,500
**Publish Print Anthology:** yes
Price: $10
**Average Percentage of Pages per Category:** Fiction 40%, Nonfiction 10%, Poetry 40%, Reviews 10%
**Ads:** yes
**Ad Rates:** Ad swap. Contact Editor for details

# The Snail's Pace Press

**Type:** press
**CLMP member:** no
**Primary Editor/Contact Person:** Ken Denberg and Darby Renney
**Address:** 85 Darwin Rd
Cambridge, NY 12816
**Web Site Address:** none
**Publishes:** fiction and poetry
**Editorial Focus:** We publish full-length volumes of poetry and fiction.
**Representative Authors:** Aimee Nezhukumatathil, Gene Garber, and Gaylord Brewer
**Submissions Policy:** Solicited manuscripts only
**Simultaneous Subs:** no
**Reading Period:** Year-round
**Reporting Time:** 2 to 5 months
**Author Payment:** copies
**Contests:** none
**Founded:** 1990

**Non Profit:** yes
**Paid Staff:** 0
**Unpaid Staff:** 2
**Distributors:** Syracuse University Press, SPD
**ISSN Number/ISBN Number:** ISBN 0-9675273
**Number of Books Published per Year:** 1-2
**Titles in Print:** 6
**Average Percentage Printed:** Paperback 75%,
Chapbook 25%

## The SNReview

**Type:** online
**CLMP member:** yes
**Primary Editor/Contact Person:** Joseph Conlin
**Address:** 197 Fairchild Ave.
Fairfield, CT 06825-4856
**Web Site Address:** http://www.snreview.org
**Publishes:** essays, fiction, nonfiction, and poetry
**Editorial Focus:** Quality writing conveying stimulating themes.
**Representative Authors:** Margaret Karmazin, Adrian Louis, and Jeanne Mackin
**Submissions Policy:** SNReview accepts only e-mailed submissions. Paste your work into the e-mail and send to editor@snreview.org. No attachments.
**Simultaneous Subs:** yes
**Reading Period:** Year-round
**Reporting Time:** 1 to 2 months
**Author Payment:** none
**Contests:** No reading fees, no contests.
**Founded:** 1999
**Non Profit:** yes
**Paid Staff:** 0
**Unpaid Staff:** 3
**ISSN Number/ISBN Number:** ISSN 1527-344X
**Average Page Views per Month:** 2,497
**Average Unique Visitors per Month:** 1,290
**Frequency per Year:** 4
**Average Percentage of Pages per Category:** Fiction 45%, Nonfiction 5%, Poetry 45%, Essays 5%
**Ads:** yes
**Ad Rates:** Won't turn down a reasonable offer.

## So to Speak: A Feminist Journal of Language and Art

**Type:** magazine
**CLMP member:** yes
**Primary Editor/Contact Person:** Heather Holliger
**Address:** George Mason University
4400 University Dr.
Fairfax, VA 22030
**Web Site Address:**
http://www.gmu.edu/org/sts/masthead.htm
**Publishes:** essays, fiction, nonfiction, poetry, and art
**Editorial Focus:** Publishes work that addresses issues of significance to women's lives and movements for women's equality.
**Simultaneous Subs:** yes
**Reading Period:** 9/05 to 3/06
**Reporting Time:** 4 to 5 months
**Author Payment:** none
**Contests:** Poetry and Fiction Contests. See Web Site for Contest Guidelines.
**Founded:** 1993
**Non Profit:** yes
**Paid Staff:** 4
**Unpaid Staff:** 0
**Total Circulation:** 750
**Paid Circulation:** 50
**Average Print Run:** 1,000
**Subscription Rate:** Individual $12/Institution $12
**Single Copy Price:** $7
**Current Volume/Issue:** 14/2
**Frequency per Year:** 2
**Backfile Available:** yes
**Unsolicited Ms. Received:** yes
**% of Unsolicited Ms. Published per Year:** 80%
**Format:** perfect
**Ads:** yes

## Soft Skull Press

**Type:** press
**CLMP member:** yes
**Primary Editor/Contact Person:** Richard Nash
**Address:** 55 Washington St.
Ste. 804
Brooklyn, NY 11201
**Web Site Address:** http://www.softskull.com
**Publishes:** essays, fiction, nonfiction, poetry, and translation
**Editorial Focus:** Check out our catalog on our website
**Representative Authors:** William Upski Wimsatt, Eileen Myles, and Matthew Sharpe
**Submissions Policy:** Check out our submissions' guidelines on our website
**Simultaneous Subs:** yes
**Reading Period:** Year-round
**Reporting Time:** 2 to 18 months

**Author Payment:** royalties
**Founded:** 1993
**Non Profit:** no
**Paid Staff:** 4
**Unpaid Staff:** 6
**Distributors:** Publishers Group West
**Wholesalers:** All
**ISSN Number/ISBN Number:** ISBN 1-887128, 1-932360
**Number of Books Published per Year:** 50
**Titles in Print:** 150
**Average Print Run:** 3,500
**Average Percentage Printed:** Hardcover 8%, Paperback 90%, Other 2%
**Average Price:** $16

## Soho Press

**Type:** press
**CLMP member:** no
**Primary Editor/Contact Person:** Laura M.C. Hruska
**Address:** 853 Broadway
New York, NY 10003
**Web Site Address:** http://www.sohopress.com
**Publishes:** fiction and nonfiction
**Editorial Focus:** We want to publish good books well. Gorgeous novels, mysteries, memoirs-whatever is interesting, moving, and well-written.
**Representative Authors:** Edwidge Danticat, Peter Lovesey, and Robert Hellenga
**Submissions Policy:** We prefer that a query letter precede any submission. We do consider unsolicited material.
**Simultaneous Subs:** yes
**Reading Period:** Year-round
**Reporting Time:** 1 to 2 months
**Author Payment:** royalties and cash
**Founded:** 1986
**Non Profit:** no
**Paid Staff:** 4
**Unpaid Staff:** 1
**Distributors:** Consortium Book Sales and Distribution
**ISSN Number/ISBN Number:** ISBN 1-56947-
**Number of Books Published per Year:** 30-40
**Titles in Print:** 220+
**Average Percentage Printed:** Hardcover 70%, Paperback 30%

## SOLO: A Journal of Poetry

**Type:** magazine
**CLMP member:** yes
**Primary Editor/Contact Person:** Glenna Luschei
**Address:** 5146 Foothill Road
Carpinteria, CA 93013-3017
**Web Site Address:** http://www.solopress.org
**Publishes:** poetry, reviews, and translation
**Editorial Focus:** SOLO celebrates great poetry, with a special interest in translations from Spanish and Portuguese.
**Representative Authors:** Marjorie Agosin, Ron Koertge, and Charles Harper Webb
**Submissions Policy:** Send up to four poems at a time. Translations must include permission by original poet.
**Simultaneous Subs:** no
**Reading Period:** Year-round
**Reporting Time:** 8 to 12 weeks
**Author Payment:** copies
**Contests:** See Web Site for Contest Guidelines.
**Founded:** 1967
**Non Profit:** yes
**Paid Staff:** 0
**Unpaid Staff:** 5
**ISSN Number/ISBN Number:** ISSN 1088-3495
**Total Circulation:** 500
**Paid Circulation:** 50
**Subscription Rate:** Individual $20/Institution $60
**Single Copy Price:** $10
**Current Volume/Issue:** Issue 7
**Frequency per Year:** 2
**Backfile Available:** yes
**Unsolicited Ms. Received:** yes
**% of Unsolicited Ms. Published per Year:** 10%
**Format:** perfect
**Size:** H 9" W 6"
**Average Pages:** 124
**Ads:** yes

## Sona Books

**Type:** press
**CLMP member:** yes
**Primary Editor/Contact Person:** Jill Magi
**Address:** 7825 Fourth Ave., F10
Brooklyn, NY 11209
**Web Site Address:** http://www.sonaweb.net
**Publishes:** essays, fiction, nonfiction, poetry, art, and audio
**Editorial Focus:** Risky and quiet works, project-

based, inter-genre works, collaborations, audio and performance, art sized to fit the hands.
**Representative Authors:** Alicia Askenase, Jennifer Firestone, and Cecilia Vicuna
**Submissions Policy:** Unfortunately, no unsolicited submissions. Please query if you have a project in mind after seeing a Sona book or work.
**Simultaneous Subs:** no
**Reading Period:** Year-round
**Reporting Time:** 1 to 2 months
**Author Payment:** none
**Founded:** 2002
**Non Profit:** yes
**Paid Staff:** no
**Unpaid Staff:** no
**Distributors:** by subscription, web-site, St. Mark's books in NYC
**Number of Books Published per Year:** 2-4
**Titles in Print:** 10
**Average Print Run:** 150
**Average Percentage Printed:** Chapbook 70%, Other 30%
**Average Price:** $6

## Sou'wester

**Type:** magazine
**CLMP member:** no
**Address:** Dept. of Eng, Box 1438
Southern Illinois University
Edwardsville, IL 62026-1438
**Web Site Address:**
http://www.webhounds.com/wdorman/souwester/
**Publishes:** essays
**Reading Period:** Year-round
**Reporting Time:** 1 to 2 months
**Author Payment:** none
**Founded:** 1960
**Non Profit:** no
**Unpaid Staff:** 10
**Backfile Available:** yes

## Soundings

**Type:** magazine
**CLMP member:** yes
**Primary Editor/Contact Person:** Marian Blue
**Address:** Whidbey Island Writers Association
P.O. Box 1289
Langley, WA 98260
**Web Site Address:** http://www.writeonwhidbey.org

**Publishes:** essays, fiction, and poetry
**Editorial Focus:** We seek accessible poetry in any genre, style, voice; we want writers and readers to connect.
**Representative Authors:** Andrena Zawinski, Christopher Howell, and Brian Ames
**Submissions Policy:** SASE required; double space (except for poetry); up to 8,000 words prose; poetry under 100 lines
**Simultaneous Subs:** yes
**Reading Period:** Year-round
**Reporting Time:** 1 to 2 months
**Author Payment:** copies
**Founded:** 2004
**Non Profit:** yes
**Distributors:** Subscription
**ISSN Number/ISBN Number:** not yet/not yet
**Total Circulation:** 300
**Paid Circulation:** 0
**Subscription Rate:** Individual $9/Institution $9
**Single Copy Price:** $10
**Current Volume/Issue:** Issue 1
**Frequency per Year:** 1
**Backfile Available:** yes
**Unsolicited Ms. Received:** yes
**% of Unsolicited Ms. Published per Year:** 80%
**Format:** perfect
**Size:** H 9" W 6"
**Average Pages:** 200
**Ads:** yes
**Ad Rates:** See Web Site for Details.

## South Dakota Review

**Type:** magazine
**CLMP member:** yes
**Primary Editor/Contact Person:** Brian Bedard
**Address:** University of South Dakota/English
414 E. Clark St.
Vermillion, SD 57069-2390
**Web Site Address:** http://www.usd.edu/sdreview
**Publishes:** essays, fiction, nonfiction, and poetry
**Editorial Focus:** A literary, scholarly journal for new and established writers. Primary interests: American West and Great Plains themes.
**Representative Authors:** Kent Meyers, Gary Fincke, and Debra Marquart
**Submissions Policy:** Manuscripts with SASE, MLA style. No previously published works. No electronic submissions.
**Simultaneous Subs:** yes

**Reading Period:** Year-round
**Reporting Time:** 8 to 12 weeks
**Author Payment:** copies and subscription
**Founded:** 1963
**Non Profit:** yes
**Paid Staff:** 2
**Unpaid Staff:** 6
**ISSN Number/ISBN Number:** ISBN 0038-3368
**Total Circulation:** 550
**Paid Circulation:** 450
**Subscription Rate:** Individual $30/Institution $28
**Single Copy Price:** $10
**Current Volume/Issue:** 42/2
**Frequency per Year:** 4
**Backfile Available:** yes
**Unsolicited Ms. Received:** yes
**% of Unsolicited Ms. Published per Year:** 10%
**Format:** perfect
**Size:** H 9" W 6"
**Average Pages:** 160
**Ads:** no

# The Southeast Review

**Type:** magazine
**CLMP member:** yes
**Primary Editor/Contact Person:** Sara Pennington, Senior Editor
**Address:** Dept. of English
Florida State University
Tallahassee, FL 32306
**Web Site Address:** http://www.southeastreview.org
**Publishes:** essays, fiction, nonfiction, poetry, and reviews
**Editorial Focus:** We aim to discover exciting new writers of literary poetry and prose and to publish them alongside national award winners.
**Representative Authors:** Charles Wright, Tim O'Brien, and Ai
**Submissions Policy:** Type all submissions. Send 3-5 poems. Fiction and nonfiction: up to 7,500 words. Include a brief cover letter and SASE.
**Simultaneous Subs:** yes
**Reading Period:** Year-round
**Reporting Time:** 1 to 2 months
**Author Payment:** copies
**Contests:** World's Best Short Short Story Contest and The Southeast Review Poetry Contest. Prize: $500 and publication. Deadline: Feb. 15
See Web Site for Contest Guidelines.
**Founded:** 1980

**Non Profit:** yes
**Paid Staff:** 2
**Unpaid Staff:** 25
**ISSN Number/ISBN Number:** ISSN 1543-1363
**Total Circulation:** 1,000
**Paid Circulation:** 400
**Average Print Run:** 1,000
**Subscription Rate:** Individual $10/Institution $10
**Single Copy Price:** $5
**Current Volume/Issue:** 24/1/2
**Frequency per Year:** 2
**Backfile Available:** yes
**Unsolicited Ms. Received:** yes
**% of Unsolicited Ms. Published per Year:** 60%
**Format:** perfect
**Size:** H 9" W 6"
**Average Pages:** 160
**Ads:** yes
**Ad Rates:** We primarily deal in trade advertising. See Web Site for Details.

# Southern Humanities Review

**Type:** magazine
**CLMP member:** yes
**Primary Editor/Contact Person:** Dan Latimer
**Address:** 9088 Haley Center
Auburn University, AL 36849
**Web Site Address:**
http://www.auburn.edu/english/shr/home.htm
**Publishes:** essays, fiction, nonfiction, poetry, reviews, and translation
**Editorial Focus:** general humanities, scholarly
**Representative Authors:** Sheryl St. Germain, Kent Nelson, and Lynne Knight
**Submissions Policy:** SASE; one copy; double-space ms. 15,000 word max. for fiction and essays, 2-3 pgs. for poems. See web site for further info.
**Simultaneous Subs:** no
**Reading Period:** Year-round
**Reporting Time:** 1 to 3 months
**Author Payment:** copies
**Founded:** 1967
**Non Profit:** yes
**Paid Staff:** 4
**Unpaid Staff:** 2
**ISSN Number/ISBN Number:** ISSN 0038-4186
**Total Circulation:** ~650
**Paid Circulation:** ~550
**Average Print Run:** 800
**Subscription Rate:** Individual $15/Institution $15

**Single Copy Price:** $5
**Current Volume/Issue:** 39/4
**Frequency per Year:** 4
**Backfile Available:** yes
**Unsolicited Ms. Received:** yes
**Format:** perfect
**Size:** H 9" W 6"
**Average Pages:** 104
**Ads:** yes
**Ad Rates:** IBC full page vertical only, with sufficient notice

# Southern Indiana Review

**Type:** magazine
**CLMP member:** no
**Primary Editor/Contact Person:** Jim McGarrah
**Address:** University of Southern Indiana
8600 University Blvd.
Evansville, In 47712
**Web Site Address:** http://www.southernindianareview.org
**Publishes:** essays, fiction, nonfiction, poetry, reviews, art, and translation
**Editorial Focus:** New and established artists who strive for literary excellence, particularly when work conveys the character of the region.
**Representative Authors:** Robery Wrigley, Kevin McIlvoy, and Erin McGraw
**Simultaneous Subs:** yes
**Reading Period:** 9/12 to 1/31
**Reporting Time:** 2 to 3 months
**Author Payment:** copies
**Founded:** 1992
**Non Profit:** yes
**Paid Staff:** 2
**Unpaid Staff:** 6
**ISSN Number/ISBN Number:** ISSN 1-903508-04-2
**Total Circulation:** 500
**Paid Circulation:** 125
**Subscription Rate:** Individual $16/Institution $16
**Single Copy Price:** $10
**Current Volume/Issue:** 10/1
**Frequency per Year:** 2
**Backfile Available:** yes
**Unsolicited Ms. Received:** yes
**% of Unsolicited Ms. Published per Year:** 60%
**Format:** perfect
**Size:** H 9" W 6"
**Average Pages:** 100
**Ads:** no

# Southern Poetry Review

**Type:** magazine
**CLMP member:** yes
**Primary Editor/Contact Person:** Robert Parham
**Address:** Department of Lang., Lit., & Phil
Armstrong Atlantic State University
Savannah, GA 31419-1997
**Web Site Address:** http://www.spr.armstrong.edu
**Publishes:** poetry
**Editorial Focus:** The best contemporary poetry by established and new poets; editorially eclectic.
**Recent Awards Received:** Two 2005 Pushcart Prizes, one Honorable Mention
**Submissions Policy:** 5-7 unpublished poems (10 pgs. max) with SASE; no electronic or disk submissions; indicate simultaneous submission.
**Simultaneous Subs:** yes
**Reading Period:** Year-round
**Reporting Time:** 2 to 3 months
**Author Payment:** copies
**Contests:** See Web Site for Contest Guidelines.
**Founded:** 1958
**Non Profit:** yes
**Paid Staff:** 2
**Unpaid Staff:** 3
**ISSN Number/ISBN Number:** ISSN 0038-447X
**Total Circulation:** 800
**Paid Circulation:** 600
**Average Print Run:** 1,000
**Subscription Rate:** Individual $12/Institution $15
**Single Copy Price:** $6
**Current Volume/Issue:** 43/2
**Frequency per Year:** 2
**Backfile Available:** yes
**Unsolicited Ms. Received:** yes
**% of Unsolicited Ms. Published per Year:** 4%
**Format:** perfect
**Size:** H 6" W 9"
**Average Pages:** 80
**Ads:** yes
**Ad Rates:** Contact Associate Editor
See Web Site for Details.

## The Southern Review

**Type:** magazine
**CLMP member:** yes
**Primary Editor/Contact Person:** Bret Lott
**Address:** Old President's House
Louisiana State University
Baton Rouge, LA 70803
**Web Site Address:** http://www.lsu.edu/thesouthernreview
**Publishes:** essays, fiction, nonfiction, poetry, and reviews
**Editorial Focus:** Contemporary literature in the US and abroad with special interest in Southern culture and history.
**Recent Awards Received:** Four works from 2004's volume were selected for Pushcart Prizes; two stories were selected for Best Stories from the South
**Representative Authors:** Mary Oliver, R.T. Smith, and Denis Donoghue
**Submissions Policy:** See website or send SASE for guidelines
**Simultaneous Subs:** yes
**Reading Period:** 9/1 to 5/31
**Reporting Time:** 4 to 8 weeks
**Author Payment:** cash, copies, and subscription
**Contests:** See Web Site for Contest Guidelines.
**Founded:** 1935
**Non Profit:** yes
**Paid Staff:** 8
**Unpaid Staff:** 0
**Distributors:** Ingram Periodicals
**ISSN Number/ISBN Number:** ISSN 0038-4534
**Total Circulation:** 2,500
**Paid Circulation:** 2,000
**Average Print Run:** 2,500
**Subscription Rate:** Individual $25/Institution $50
**Single Copy Price:** $8
**Current Volume/Issue:** 42/4
**Frequency per Year:** 4
**Backfile Available:** yes
**Unsolicited Ms. Received:** yes
**% of Unsolicited Ms. Published per Year:** 2%
**Format:** perfect
**Size:** H 10" W 6.75"
**Average Pages:** 225
**Ads:** yes
**Ad Rates:** 250/full page; 150/half page
See Web Site for Details.

## Southwest Review

**Type:** magazine
**CLMP member:** no
**Primary Editor/Contact Person:** Willard Spiegelman
**Address:** P.O. Box 750374
6404 Hilltop Ln., Rm. 307
Dallas, TX 75275-0374
**Web Site Address:** http://www.southwestreview.org
**Publishes:** essays, fiction, and poetry
**Editorial Focus:** Discover works by new writers and publish them beside those of more established authors.
**Representative Authors:** John Hollander, Rachel Hadas, and Sandra Cisneros
**Submissions Policy:** Please see web site for complete guidelines.
**Simultaneous Subs:** no
**Reading Period:** 9/4 to 4/5
**Reporting Time:** 1 to 2 months
**Author Payment:** cash and copies
**Contests:** See Web Site for Contest Guidelines.
**Founded:** 1915
**Non Profit:** yes
**Paid Staff:** 3
**Unpaid Staff:** 0
**Distributors:** DeBoer; Total Circulation
**ISSN Number/ISBN Number:** ISSN 0038-4712
**Total Circulation:** 1,500
**Paid Circulation:** 700
**Subscription Rate:** Individual $24/Institution $30
**Single Copy Price:** $6
**Current Volume/Issue:** 89/2/3
**Frequency per Year:** 4
**Backfile Available:** yes
**Unsolicited Ms. Received:** yes
**% of Unsolicited Ms. Published per Year:** 90%
**Format:** perfect
**Size:** H 9" W 6"
**Average Pages:** 175
**Ads:** yes
**Ad Rates:** Call for information.

## Speakeasy

**Type:** magazine
**CLMP member:** yes
**Primary Editor/Contact Person:** Bart Schneider
**Address:** The Loft Literary Center
1011 Washington Ave. South
Minneapolis, MN 55415
**Web Site Address:**

http://www.speakeasymagazine.org

**Publishes:** essays, fiction, nonfiction, poetry, and reviews

**Editorial Focus:** To offer a Literary Look at Life, presenting a wide range of voices on intriguing themes.

**Representative Authors:** Sven Birkerts, Naomi Shihab Nye, and Gerald Early

**Submissions Policy:** We only consider unsolicited manuscripts for fiction and poetry. Essays and book reviews are solicited by the editor.

**Simultaneous Subs:** yes

**Reading Period:** Year-round

**Reporting Time:** 1 to 3 months

**Author Payment:** cash

**Contests:** See Web Site for Contest Guidelines.

**Founded:** 2002

**Non Profit:** yes

**Paid Staff:** 2

**Unpaid Staff:** 2

**Distributors:** Ingram and several independent distributors

**ISSN Number/ISBN Number:** ISSN 1540-9422

**Total Circulation:** 6,200

**Paid Circulation:** 3,500

**Subscription Rate:** Individual $19.99/Institution $19.99

**Single Copy Price:** $5.95

**Current Volume/Issue:** 2/2

**Frequency per Year:** 4

**Backfile Available:** yes

**Unsolicited Ms. Received:** yes

**Format:** stapled

**Size:** H 8" W 10"

**Average Pages:** 56

**Ads:** yes

**Ad Rates:** $1,210 Full page, B&W See Web Site for Details.

## Spillway

**Type:** magazine

**CLMP member:** yes

**Primary Editor/Contact Person:** Mifanwy Kaiser

**Address:** P.O. Box 7887
Huntington Beach, CA 92615-7887

**Web Site Address:** http://www.tebotbach.org

**Publishes:** essays and poetry

**Representative Authors:** Eleanor Wilner, Richard Jones, and Jeanette Clough

**Submissions Policy:** 6 poems, 10 pages max for poems, 5-15 pages for essays and reviews. SASE with correct postage

**Simultaneous Subs:** yes

**Reading Period:** Year-round

**Reporting Time:** 1 to 4 months

**Author Payment:** copies

**Founded:** 1993

**Non Profit:** yes

**Paid Staff:** 0

**Unpaid Staff:** 3

**Distributors:** Ingram, Small Press, Armadillo, DeBoer

**ISSN Number/ISBN Number:** 1096-7389/1-893670-12-0

**Total Circulation:** 1,000

**Paid Circulation:** 100

**Average Print Run:** 1,000

**Subscription Rate:** Individual $16/Institution $24

**Single Copy Price:** $9

**Current Volume/Issue:** Issue 11

**Frequency per Year:** 2

**Backfile Available:** yes

**Unsolicited Ms. Received:** yes

**Format:** perfect

**Size:** H 6" W 9"

**Average Pages:** 176

**Ads:** yes

**Ad Rates:** $50 one half page, 100 full page, $25 quarter page

## Spindrift

**Type:** magazine

**CLMP member:** yes

**Primary Editor/Contact Person:** Deborah Handrich

**Address:** 16101 Greenwood Ave. N.
Shoreline, WA 98133

**Web Site Address:** http://www.shoreline.edu/spindrift/home.html

**Publishes:** fiction, poetry, and art

**Submissions Policy:** Check website for details.

**Simultaneous Subs:** no

**Reading Period:** 10/1 to 2/1

**Reporting Time:** 1 to 2 months

**Author Payment:** none

**Founded:** 1966

**Non Profit:** yes

**Paid Staff:** 3

**Unpaid Staff:** 10

**Total Circulation:** Varies

**Paid Circulation:** Varies

**Average Print Run:** 500

**Single Copy Price:** $12

**Current Volume/Issue:** Issue 39
**Frequency per Year:** 1
**Backfile Available:** yes
**Unsolicited Ms. Received:** no
**Format:** perfect

# Spinning Jenny

**Type:** magazine
**CLMP member:** yes
**Primary Editor/Contact Person:** C.E. Harrison
**Address:** P.O. Box 1373
New York, NY 10276
**Web Site Address:** http://www.blackdresspress.com
**Publishes:** fiction and poetry
**Editorial Focus:** Poetry, fiction, drama, experimental work.
**Representative Authors:** Tony Tost, Karla Kelsey, and John Colburn
**Submissions Policy:** By mail or e-mail. See full guidelines at http://www.blackdresspress.com.
**Simultaneous Subs:** no
**Reading Period:** 9/1 to 5/31
**Reporting Time:** 3 to 4 months
**Author Payment:** copies
**Founded:** 1994
**Non Profit:** yes
**Paid Staff:** 0
**Unpaid Staff:** 2
**Distributors:** DeBoer
**ISSN Number/ISBN Number:** 1082-1406/1-887872-07-9
**Total Circulation:** 1,000
**Paid Circulation:** 200
**Subscription Rate:** Individual $15/Institution $15
**Single Copy Price:** $8
**Current Volume/Issue:** Issue 8
**Frequency per Year:** 1
**Backfile Available:** yes
**Unsolicited Ms. Received:** yes
**% of Unsolicited Ms. Published per Year:** 2%
**Format:** perfect
**Size:** H 9.5" W 5.5"
**Average Pages:** 112
**Ads:** no

# Spire Press

**Type:** magazine
**CLMP member:** yes
**Primary Editor/Contact Person:** Shelly Reed

**Address:** 532 LaGuardia Place, Ste. 298
New York, NY 11217
**Web Site Address:** http://www.spirepress.org
**Publishes:** essays, fiction, nonfiction, poetry, and reviews
**Representative Authors:** Gayle Elen Harvey, Jennifer MacPherson, and Ann E. Michael
**Simultaneous Subs:** yes
**Reading Period:** Year-round
**Reporting Time:** 1 to 2 months
**Author Payment:** copies
**Contests:** See Web Site for Contest Guidelines.
**Founded:** 2002
**Non Profit:** yes
**Paid Staff:** 0
**Unpaid Staff:** 3
**ISSN Number/ISBN Number:** 1541-4582/0-9740701
**Total Circulation:** 1,200
**Paid Circulation:** 200
**Subscription Rate:** Individual $24/Institution $12
**Single Copy Price:** $10
**Current Volume/Issue:** Issue 5
**Frequency per Year:** 2
**Backfile Available:** yes
**Unsolicited Ms. Received:** yes
**% of Unsolicited Ms. Published per Year:** 2-3%
**Format:** perfect
**Size:** H 11" W 8.5"
**Average Pages:** 60
**Ads:** yes
**Ad Rates:** The only ads are free or author's. Author's prices <$30

# Spire Press

**Type:** press
**CLMP member:** yes
**Primary Editor/Contact Person:** Shelly Reed
**Address:** 532 LaGuardia Place, Ste. 298
New York, NY 10012
**Web Site Address:** http://www.spirepress.org
**Publishes:** essays, fiction, nonfiction, poetry, and reviews
**Representative Authors:** Gayle Elen Harvey, Jennifer MacPherson, and Ann E. Michael
**Submissions Policy:** We only accept book submissions through contests, but see the website for journal guidelines.
**Simultaneous Subs:** yes
**Reading Period:** Year-round
**Reporting Time:** 2 to 3 months

**Author Payment:** royalties, cash, and copies
**Contests:** Yearly poetry contest in the Fall. Please see the website for details.
See Web Site for Contest Guidelines.
**Founded:** 2002
**Non Profit:** yes
**Paid Staff:** 0
**Unpaid Staff:** 3
**ISSN Number/ISBN Number:** 1541-4582/0-9740701
**Number of Books Published per Year:** 4-5
**Titles in Print:** 5
**Average Print Run:** 500+
**Average Percentage Printed:** Paperback 50%, Chapbook 50%
**Average Price:** $14.95

# The Spoon River Poetry Review

**Type:** magazine
**CLMP member:** yes
**Primary Editor/Contact Person:** Dr. Lucia Cordell Getsi
**Address:** Department of English
Illinois State University, Box 4240
Normal, IL 61790-4241
**Web Site Address:** http://www.litline.org//spoon
**Publishes:** poetry, reviews, and translation
**Editorial Focus:** Contemporary poetry in English and English translation; review essays on poetry and poetics.
**Representative Authors:** Alicia Ostriker, Haki Madhubuti, and Karen An-Hwei Lee
**Submissions Policy:** Three to five unpublished poems, SASE. Translations, send poems in original language.
**Simultaneous Subs:** yes
**Reading Period:** 9/15 to 4/15
**Reporting Time:** 2 to 3 months
**Author Payment:** copies and subscription
**Contests:** Editors' Prize Contest, April 15, $1,000 for winner, $100 each for two runners-up. Fee, $16, includes subscription.
See Web Site for Contest Guidelines.
**Founded:** 1974
**Non Profit:** yes
**Paid Staff:** 2
**Unpaid Staff:** 2
**Distributors:** Ingram; Ubiquity
**Wholesalers:** EBSCO, Blackwells
**ISSN Number/ISBN Number:** ISSN 0738-8993
**Total Circulation:** 1,200

**Paid Circulation:** 750
**Subscription Rate:** Individual $15/Institution $18
**Single Copy Price:** $10
**Current Volume/Issue:** 29/2
**Frequency per Year:** 2
**Backfile Available:** no
**Unsolicited Ms. Received:** yes
**% of Unsolicited Ms. Published per Year:** 1%
**Format:** perfect
**Size:** H 5 1/2" W 8 1/2"
**Average Pages:** 128
**Ads:** yes
**Ad Rates:** $150 per page
See Web Site for Details.

# Spout

**Type:** magazine
**CLMP member:** yes
**Address:** P.O. Box 581067
Minneapolis, MN 55458-1067
**Web Site Address:** http://www.spoutpress.com
**Publishes:** essays, fiction, nonfiction, poetry, and art
**Reading Period:** Year-round
**Reporting Time:** 1 to 2 months
**Author Payment:** none
**Founded:** 1989
**Non Profit:** yes
**Backfile Available:** yes

# Spring, Journal of the E.E. Cummings Society

**Type:** magazine
**CLMP member:** no
**Primary Editor/Contact Person:** Michael Webster
**Address:** 129 Lake Huron Hall
Grand Valley State University
Allendale, MI 49401-9403
**Web Site Address:**
http://www.gvsu.edu/english/cummings/Index.html
**Publishes:** essays and poetry
**Editorial Focus:** E.E. Cummings and his contemporaries, along with visual poetry in the Cummings tradition.
**Representative Authors:** Norman Friedman, Michael Dylan Welch, and Bernard V. Stehle
**Submissions Policy:** Essay submissions should follow MLA Style Manual; send them in rtf format (PC).
**Simultaneous Subs:** no
**Reading Period:** Year-round

**Reporting Time:** 1 to 2 months
**Author Payment:** none
**Founded:** 1992
**Non Profit:** yes
**Paid Staff:** 0
**Unpaid Staff:** 5
**Distributors:** DeBoer
**ISSN Number/ISBN Number:** ISSN 0735-6889
**Total Circulation:** 250
**Paid Circulation:** 200
**Average Print Run:** 500
**Subscription Rate:** Individual $17.50/Institution $22.50
**Single Copy Price:** $17.50
**Current Volume/Issue:** 2003/12
**Frequency per Year:** 1
**Backfile Available:** yes
**Unsolicited Ms. Received:** yes
**% of Unsolicited Ms. Published per Year:** 30?%
**Format:** perfect
**Size:** H 8 1/2" W 5 1/2"
**Average Pages:** 175-200
**Ads:** yes
**Ad Rates:** negotiable

# The Square Table

**Type:** online
**CLMP member:** no
**Primary Editor/Contact Person:** Dina Di Maio
**Address:** 3115 Blue Ridge Road
Raleigh, NC 27612
**Web Site Address:** http://www.thesquaretable.com
**Publishes:** essays, fiction, nonfiction, poetry, reviews, and art
**Editorial Focus:** The Square Table showcases today's top talent in writing, art, photography, music, design and more. Take a seat.
**Representative Authors:** Bob Mustin, Cheryl Diane Kidder, and Tom Sheehan
**Submissions Policy:** Send all submissions to editor@thesquaretable.com with the section you are submitting to in the subject line.
**Simultaneous Subs:** yes
**Reading Period:** Year-round
**Reporting Time:** 2 to 4 weeks
**Author Payment:** none
**Founded:** 2002
**Non Profit:** yes
**Paid Staff:** 0
**Unpaid Staff:** 3

**Average Page Views per Month:** 15,000
**Average Unique Visitors per Month:** 2,000
**Frequency per Year:** 2
**Publish Print Anthology:** no
**Average Percentage of Pages per Category:** Fiction 20%, Nonfiction 20%, Poetry 1%, Reviews 20%, Essays 20%, Art 19%
**Ads:** no

# St. Andrews College Press

**Type:** press
**CLMP member:** no
**Primary Editor/Contact Person:** Pete Dulgar
**Address:** 1700 Dogwood Mile
Laurinburg, NC 28352
**Web Site Address:** http://www.sapc.edu/sapress
**Publishes:** fiction, nonfiction, and poetry
**Editorial Focus:** We offer book publication to authors selected from our literary magazine, Cairn, and our college reading series.
**Representative Authors:** Barry Gifford, Anthony Abbott, and Judy Goldman
**Submissions Policy:** No unsolicited manuscripts. Submit work to Cairn magazine and, if selected there, inquire about book publication.
**Simultaneous Subs:** no
**Reading Period:** Year-round
**Reporting Time:** 2 to 4 months
**Author Payment:** copies and subscription
**Founded:** 1969
**Non Profit:** yes
**Paid Staff:** 2
**Unpaid Staff:** 4
**Number of Books Published per Year:** 3-4
**Titles in Print:** 80
**Average Percentage Printed:** Hardcover 2%, Paperback 73%, Chapbook 25%

# Star Cloud Press

**Type:** press
**CLMP member:** yes
**Primary Editor/Contact Person:** Steven E. Swerdfeger, Ph.D.
**Address:** 6137 E. Mescal St.
Scottsdale, AZ 85254-5418
**Web Site Address:** http://StarCloudPress.com
**Publishes:** fiction, nonfiction, and poetry
**Editorial Focus:** We are a small, independent press committed to publishing poetry, fiction, and creative

nonfiction of vision and enduring excellence.
**Submissions Policy:** Currently the submission of manuscripts is solely by invitation.
**Simultaneous Subs:** no
**Reading Period:** Year-round
**Reporting Time:** 3 to 6 months
**Author Payment:** royalties and copies
**Founded:** 1995
**Non Profit:** no
**Paid Staff:** 1
**Unpaid Staff:** 0
**Distributors:** Ingram
**ISSN Number/ISBN Number:** ISBN 9651835, 1-932842
**Number of Books Published per Year:** 4-5
**Titles in Print:** 4
**Average Percentage Printed:** Hardcover 50%, Paperback 50%
**Backfile Available:** yes

## Starcherone Books

**Type:** press
**CLMP member:** yes
**Primary Editor/Contact Person:** Ted Pelton
**Address:** P.O. Box 303
Buffalo, NY 14201
**Web Site Address:** http://www.starcherone.com
**Publishes:** fiction
**Editorial Focus:** Innovative fiction.
**Representative Authors:** Raymond Federman, Aimee Parkison, and Nina Shope
**Submissions Policy:** Query first. Most manuscripts come to us through our contest.
**Simultaneous Subs:** yes
**Reading Period:** 8/15 to 9/30
**Reporting Time:** 3 to 6 months
**Author Payment:** royalties and copies
**Contests:** See Web Site for Contest Guidelines.
**Founded:** 2,000
**Non Profit:** yes
**Paid Staff:** 0
**Unpaid Staff:** 6
**Distributors:** SPD
**Wholesalers:** Baker & Taylor
**ISSN Number/ISBN Number:** ISBN 09703165
**Number of Books Published per Year:** 4
**Titles in Print:** 10
**Average Print Run:** 750
**Average Percentage Printed:** Paperback 100%
**Average Price:** $17

## Stone Buzzard Press

**Type:** press
**CLMP member:** yes
**Primary Editor/Contact Person:** Mike Selender
**Address:** 159 Jewett Ave.
Jersey City, NJ 07304-2003
**Publishes:** fiction and poetry
**Editorial Focus:** Poetry and fiction.
**Representative Authors:** Joe Cardillo
**Submissions Policy:** Not looking for new material. Query before sending anything.
**Simultaneous Subs:** no
**Reading Period:** Year-round
**Author Payment:** copies
**Contests:** none
**Founded:** 1986
**Non Profit:** no
**Paid Staff:** 0
**Unpaid Staff:** 1
**ISSN Number/ISBN Number:** ISBN 0-9624082
**Number of Books Published per Year:** 0-1
**Titles in Print:** 2
**Average Percentage Printed:** Paperback 100%
**Backfile Available:** yes

## StoryQuarterly

**Type:** magazine
**CLMP member:** yes
**Primary Editor/Contact Person:** M.M.M. Hayes
**Address:** 431 Sheridan Road
Kenilworth, IL 60043-1220
**Web Site Address:** http://www.storyquarterly.com
**Publishes:** fiction and translation
**Editorial Focus:** High quality literary fiction, no genre. Short-shorts, long stories, all styles and subjects. Look for new insights and ideas
**Representative Authors:** T.C. Boyle, Steve Almond, and Stephen Dixon
**Submissions Policy:** Accept manuscripts online only (except authors with no Internet). Go to http://www.storyquarterly.com and click Submissions link.
**Simultaneous Subs:** yes
**Reading Period:** 10/1 to 3/31
**Reporting Time:** 6 to 12 weeks
**Author Payment:** copies and subscription
**Contests:** Robie Macauley Award for Fiction; independently judged from fiction already accepted for

magazine
See Web Site for Contest Guidelines.
**Founded:** 1975
**Non Profit:** yes
**Paid Staff:** 0
**Unpaid Staff:** 45
**Distributors:** Ingram, DeBoer
**ISSN Number/ISBN Number:** 0361-0144/0-9722444-1-7
**Total Circulation:** 5,500
**Paid Circulation:** 2,000
**Subscription Rate:** Individual $10/Institution $10
**Single Copy Price:** $10
**Current Volume/Issue:** Issue 39
**Frequency per Year:** 1
**Backfile Available:** yes
**Unsolicited Ms. Received:** yes
**% of Unsolicited Ms. Published per Year:** 95%
**Format:** perfect
**Size:** H 8.25" W 5.5"
**Average Pages:** 550
**Ads:** yes
**Ad Rates:** $300/pg
See Web Site for Details.

## the strange fruit

**Type:** magazine
**CLMP member:** yes
**Primary Editor/Contact Person:** Jessica Star Rockers, Editor
**Address:** 300 Lenora St., #250
Seattle, WA 98121
**Web Site Address:** http://www.thestrangefruit.com
**Publishes:** essays, fiction, nonfiction, and poetry
**Editorial Focus:** We aim to present poetry and prose that examine personal experiences for their commonly strange synchronicity.
**Submissions Policy:** Up to 6 poems or 6,000 words of prose. Include SASE.
**Simultaneous Subs:** yes
**Reading Period:** Year-round
**Reporting Time:** 1 to 3 months
**Author Payment:** copies
**Founded:** 2005
**Non Profit:** no
**Paid Staff:** 0
**Unpaid Staff:** 4
**ISSN Number/ISBN Number:** ISSN 1555-550X
**Total Circulation:** 300
**Paid Circulation:** 100

**Average Print Run:** 500
**Subscription Rate:** Individual $11/Institution $10
**Single Copy Price:** $6
**Current Volume/Issue:** 1/2
**Frequency per Year:** 2
**Backfile Available:** yes
**Unsolicited Ms. Received:** yes
**% of Unsolicited Ms. Published per Year:** 100%
**Format:** perfect
**Size:** H 8.5" W 5.5"
**Average Pages:** 100
**Ads:** yes
**Ad Rates:** See Web Site for Details.

## Studio: a Journal of Christians writing

**Type:** magazine
**CLMP member:** no
**Primary Editor/Contact Person:** Paul Grover
**Address:** 727 Peel St.
Albury NSW Australia
Albury, NS 2640
**Publishes:** essays, fiction, nonfiction, poetry, and reviews
**Editorial Focus:** Studio publishes prose and poetry of literary merit: a venue for previously published, new and aspiring writers.
**Representative Authors:** Andrew Lansdown, Les Murray, and Warren Breninger
**Submissions Policy:** Via e-mail or postal service-A4 one side double-spaced. Address and name on each submission. International Reply Coupons.
**Simultaneous Subs:** yes
**Reading Period:** Year-round
**Reporting Time:** 1 to 3 weeks
**Author Payment:** copies
**Contests:** Bi-annual Studio Award for poetry and prose. Special Contests for specific themes or events. Details in Studio journals.
**Founded:** 1980
**Non Profit:** yes
**Paid Staff:** 0
**Unpaid Staff:** 3
**ISSN Number/ISBN Number:** ISSN 0729-4042
**Total Circulation:** 300
**Paid Circulation:** 250
**Average Print Run:** 300
**Subscription Rate:** Individual $60 (AUD)/Institution $60 (AUD)
**Single Copy Price:** $10(AUD)

**Current Volume/Issue:** Issue 99
**Frequency per Year:** 4
**Backfile Available:** yes
**Unsolicited Ms. Received:** yes
**% of Unsolicited Ms. Published per Year:** 95%
**Format:** stapled
**Size:** H 8" W 5"
**Average Pages:** 36
**Ads:** yes
**Ad Rates:** $50 (AUD) half page; $100 (AUD) full page; $50 (AUD) insert

## subTerrain magazine

**Type:** magazine
**CLMP member:** no
**Primary Editor/Contact Person:** Brian Kaufman
**Address:** P.O. Box 3008, Main Post Office
Vancouver, BC V6B3X5
**Web Site Address:** http://www.subterrain.ca
**Publishes:** essays, fiction, nonfiction, poetry, reviews, and art
**Editorial Focus:** "Strong words for a Polite Nation." subTerrain publishes fiction, commentary, poetry, and art from Canada and abroad.
**Submissions Policy:** No unsolicited poetry. Enclose reply SASE or postage for ms return. No e-mail submissions. Read mag. first. Sample copy- $5.
**Simultaneous Subs:** yes
**Reading Period:** Year-round
**Reporting Time:** 2 to 4 months
**Author Payment:** cash and copies
**Contests:** See Web Site for Contest Guidelines.
**Founded:** 1988
**Non Profit:** yes
**Paid Staff:** 3
**Unpaid Staff:** 5
**ISSN Number/ISBN Number:** ISSN 0840-7533
**Total Circulation:** 3,000
**Paid Circulation:** 880
**Average Print Run:** 1,200
**Subscription Rate:** Individual $15/Institution $18
**Single Copy Price:** $4.95
**Current Volume/Issue:** 4/37
**Frequency per Year:** 3
**Backfile Available:** yes
**Unsolicited Ms. Received:** yes
**% of Unsolicited Ms. Published per Year:** 10%
**Format:** stapled
**Size:** H 11" W 8.5"
**Average Pages:** 56

**Ads:** yes
**Ad Rates:** half-page: $250; full-page: $450
See Web Site for Details.

## Subtropics

**Type:** magazine
**CLMP member:** yes
**Primary Editor/Contact Person:** Mark Mitchell, David Leavitt
**Address:** P.O. Box 112075
University of Florida
Gainesville, FL 32611-2075
**Web Site Address:** http://www.english.ufl.edu/sub-tropics
**Publishes:** essays, fiction, nonfiction, poetry, and translation
**Editorial Focus:** Some longer pieces, excerpts from longer works, works in translation, important works that are out of print, short shorts.
**Representative Authors:** John Barth, Anne Carson, and Joanna Scott
**Submissions Policy:** Submit in hard copy to address above. Submissions accepted August through May. Submissions cannot be returned.
**Simultaneous Subs:** yes
**Reading Period:** 8/15 to 5/15
**Reporting Time:** 4 to 6 weeks
**Author Payment:** cash
**Founded:** 2005
**Non Profit:** yes
**Paid Staff:** 5
**Unpaid Staff:** 4
**Distributors:** In process
**Wholesalers:** In process
**ISSN Number/ISBN Number:** ISSN In process
**Total Circulation:** N/A
**Paid Circulation:** N/A
**Average Print Run:** 2,500
**Current Volume/Issue:** 1/1
**Frequency per Year:** 3
**Backfile Available:** yes
**Unsolicited Ms. Received:** yes
**Format:** perfect
**Size:** H 9" W 6"
**Average Pages:** 148
**Ads:** yes
**Ad Rates:** Contact for trades.

# Sugar Mule

**Type:** online
**CLMP member:** no
**Primary Editor/Contact Person:** M.L. Weber
**Address:** 2 N. 24th St.
Colorado Springs, CO 80904
**Web Site Address:** http://www.sugarmule.com
**Publishes:** essays, fiction, nonfiction, poetry, reviews, art, and translation
**Editorial Focus:** A literary magazine with eccentric Buddhist leanings, we accept all forms of prose and poetry.
**Representative Authors:** Andrei Codrescu, Paul Hoover, Pierre Joris, and Rochelle Ratner
**Submissions Policy:** Please check the schedule of upcoming issues (on the 2nd page of the website) before sending work.
**Simultaneous Subs:** yes
**Reading Period:** Year-round
**Reporting Time:** 1 to 2 weeks
**Author Payment:** none
**Founded:** 1990
**Non Profit:** yes
**Paid Staff:** 0
**Unpaid Staff:** 2
**Average Page Views per Month:** 600
**Average Unique Visitors per Month:** 300
**Frequency per Year:** 3
**Publish Print Anthology:** no
**Average Percentage of Pages per Category:** Fiction 60%, Nonfiction 5%, Poetry 30%, Reviews 2%, Essays 1%, Art 1%, Translation 1%
**Ad Rates:** negotiable
See Web Site for Details.

# The Summerset Review

**Type:** online
**CLMP member:** yes
**Primary Editor/Contact Person:** Joseph Levens
**Address:** 25 Summerset Dr.
Smithtown, NY 11787
**Web Site Address:** http://www.summersetreview.org
**Publishes:** essays, fiction, nonfiction, and art
**Editorial Focus:** Contemporary literary fiction and nonfiction
**Submissions Policy:** Guidelines are on the site at: http://www.summersetreview.org
**Simultaneous Subs:** yes
**Reading Period:** Year-round
**Reporting Time:** 4 to 6 weeks
**Author Payment:** none
**Founded:** 2002
**Non Profit:** yes
**Paid Staff:** 0
**Unpaid Staff:** 3
**Average Page Views per Month:** 5,000
**Average Unique Visitors per Month:** 2,200
**Frequency per Year:** 4
**Publish Print Anthology:** no
**Average Percentage of Pages per Category:** Fiction 60%, Nonfiction 10%, Essays 20%, Art 10%
**Ads:** no

# The Sundry: A Journal of the Arts

**Type:** magazine
**CLMP member:** yes
**Primary Editor/Contact Person:** Peter L. Riesbeck, Director
**Address:** 109 Jepson Ave.
St. Clairsville, OH 43950
**Web Site Address:** http://www.sundryjournal.com
**Publishes:** essays, fiction, nonfiction, poetry, reviews, and art
**Editorial Focus:** Open to all genres, especially experimental. Eager to work with new and unpublished writers.
**Representative Authors:** Donna Vitucci, Nora Beck, and Josh Wallaert
**Submissions Policy:** Send complete manuscripts to attn: Fiction Editor. Send poetry to attn: Poetry. All other submissions send to attn: Director
**Simultaneous Subs:** yes
**Reading Period:** Year-round
**Reporting Time:** 1 to 3 months
**Author Payment:** copies
**Contests:** None Currently
See Web Site for Contest Guidelines.
**Founded:** 1993
**Non Profit:** yes
**Paid Staff:** 0
**Unpaid Staff:** 4
**ISSN Number/ISBN Number:** none/none
**Total Circulation:** 500
**Paid Circulation:** 50
**Subscription Rate:** Individual $11.99/6 mo/Institution same
**Single Copy Price:** $3.50
**Current Volume/Issue:** 500/3
**Frequency per Year:** 12
**Backfile Available:** no

**Unsolicited Ms. Received:** yes
**% of Unsolicited Ms. Published per Year:** 90%
**Format:** stapled
**Size:** H 8.5" W 5.5"
**Average Pages:** 50
**Ads:** yes
**Ad Rates:** See Web Site for Details.

# The Sun

**Type:** magazine
**CLMP member:** no
**Primary Editor/Contact Person:** Sy Safransky, Editor
**Address:** 107 N. Roberson St.
Chapel Hill, NC 27516
**Web Site Address:** http://www.thesunmagazine.org
**Publishes:** essays, fiction, nonfiction, and poetry
**Editorial Focus:** We tend to favor personal writing, but we're also looking for thoughtful, well-written essays on political, cultural, and philosophical themes. Please, no journalistic features, academic works, or opinion pieces.
**Representative Authors:** Alison Luterman, Poe Ballantine, and Genie Zeiger
**Submissions Policy:** Submissions should be typed, double-spaced, and accompanied by a self-addressed, stamped envelope. Your work will not be returned without sufficient postage. Do not send your only copy. Please do not e-mail your submissions to us.
**Simultaneous Subs:** yes
**Reading Period:** Year-round
**Reporting Time:** 4 to 6 months
**Author Payment:** cash, copies, and subscription
**Contests:** None.
**Founded:** 1974
**Non Profit:** yes
**Paid Staff:** 15
**Unpaid Staff:** 0
**Distributors:** Armadillo, Bear Family, Desert Moon, Don Olson
**ISSN Number/ISBN Number:** ISSN 0744-9666
**Total Circulation:** 65,000
**Paid Circulation:** 59,000
**Subscription Rate:** Individual $34/Institution $34
**Single Copy Price:** $3.95
**Current Volume/Issue:** Issue 333
**Frequency per Year:** 12
**Backfile Available:** yes
**Unsolicited Ms. Received:** yes
**% of Unsolicited Ms. Published per Year:** 1%

**Format:** stapled
**Size:** H 11" W 8.5"
**Average Pages:** 48
**Ads:** no

# Swan Scythe Press

**Type:** press
**CLMP member:** no
**Primary Editor/Contact Person:** Sandra McPherson
**Address:** 2052 Calaveras Ave.
Davis, CA 95616-3021
**Web Site Address:** http://www.swanscythe.com
**Publishes:** poetry
**Editorial Focus:** Poetry chapbooks; multi-ethnic; primarily emerging authors.
**Representative Authors:** Emmy Perez, John Olivares Espinoza, and Pos Moua
**Submissions Policy:** By solicitation only until we have another annual contest (we've had 4). Sorry, no contest in 2004. $15 reading fee; 36 pp. ms.
**Simultaneous Subs:** yes
**Reading Period:** Year-round
**Reporting Time:** 6 to 10 weeks
**Author Payment:** cash and copies
**Contests:** See Web Site for Contest Guidelines.
**Founded:** 1999
**Non Profit:** no
**Paid Staff:** 0
**Unpaid Staff:** 5
**Distributors:** ourselves
**Wholesalers:** ourselves
**ISSN Number/ISBN Number:** ISBN 1-930454-
**Number of Books Published per Year:** 4
**Titles in Print:** 22
**Average Percentage Printed:** Paperback 100%

# Swerve

**Type:** magazine
**CLMP member:** no
**Primary Editor/Contact Person:** Fred Schmalz
**Address:** 1405 8th Ave. #4D
Brooklyn, NY 11215
**Web Site Address:** http://www.swervemag.com
**Publishes:** poetry
**Editorial Focus:** swerve is a little magazine of contemporary poetry and art. Issues are hand-made in small editions (125-150 copies).
**Representative Authors:** Samantha Hunt, G.E. Patterson, and Ted Mathys

**Submissions Policy:** Swerve does not accept submissions. writing and artwork are solicited. See website.
**Simultaneous Subs:** no
**Reading Period:** Year-round
**Author Payment:** copies
**Founded:** 1999
**Non Profit:** yes
**Paid Staff:** 0
**Unpaid Staff:** 2
**Total Circulation:** 145
**Paid Circulation:** 90
**Average Print Run:** 145
**Subscription Rate:** Individual $30/Institution $30
**Current Volume/Issue:** Issue 14
**Frequency per Year:** 2
**Backfile Available:** no
**Unsolicited Ms. Received:** no
**Format:** hand-bound, each issue different
**Average Pages:** 40
**Ads:** no

# Swink

**Type:** magazine
**CLMP member:** yes
**Primary Editor/Contact Person:** Leelila Strogov
**Address:** 244 5th Ave. #2722
New York, NY 10001
**Web Site Address:** http://www.swinkmag.com
**Publishes:** essays, fiction, nonfiction, poetry, art, and translation
**Editorial Focus:** Swink publishes the highest caliber fiction, essays and poetry from established and emerging writers.
**Submissions Policy:** Prose should be mailed to the address above. Poetry should be sent to 5042 Wilshire Blvd. #628, Los Angeles, CA 90036.
**Simultaneous Subs:** yes
**Reading Period:** Year-round
**Reporting Time:** 1 to 4 months
**Author Payment:** cash and copies
**Contests:** See Web Site for Contest Guidelines.
**Founded:** 2003
**Non Profit:** yes
**Paid Staff:** 0
**Unpaid Staff:** 14
**Distributors:** Ingram, DeBoer, Armadillo, Doormouse
**Total Circulation:** 4,000
**Paid Circulation:** 1,500
**Average Print Run:** 4,500

**Subscription Rate:** Individual $16/Institution $16
**Single Copy Price:** $10
**Current Volume/Issue:** Issue 3
**Frequency per Year:** 2
**Backfile Available:** yes
**Unsolicited Ms. Received:** yes
**% of Unsolicited Ms. Published per Year:** .5%
**Format:** perfect
**Size:** H 9" W 7"
**Average Pages:** 224
**Ads:** yes
**Ad Rates:** Full page: $400

# Sycamore Review

**Type:** magazine
**CLMP member:** no
**Primary Editor/Contact Person:** Rebekah Silverman
**Address:** Purdue University, Dept. of English
500 Oval Dr.
West Lafayette, IN 47907
**Web Site Address:**
http://www.cla.purdue.edu/sycamore/
**Publishes:** fiction, nonfiction, poetry, reviews, art, and translation
**Editorial Focus:** The highest quality work. Particularly interested in work that pushes the limits of the form and still succeeds.
**Representative Authors:** Dean Young, Patricia O'Hara, and Denise Levertov
**Submissions Policy:** No electronic submissions.
**Simultaneous Subs:** yes
**Reading Period:** 8/1 to 3/31
**Reporting Time:** 2 to 3 months
**Author Payment:** copies
**Contests:** Wabash Prize for Poetry. Please visit website for more information.
**Founded:** 1988
**Non Profit:** yes
**Paid Staff:** yes
**Unpaid Staff:** yes
**Distributors:** Ingram
**ISSN Number/ISBN Number:** ISSN 1043-1497
**Total Circulation:** 800
**Paid Circulation:** 60
**Average Print Run:** 800-10
**Subscription Rate:** Individual $12/Institution $12
**Single Copy Price:** $7
**Current Volume/Issue:** 17/2
**Frequency per Year:** 2
**Backfile Available:** yes

**Unsolicited Ms. Received:** yes
**% of Unsolicited Ms. Published per Year:** 5%
**Format:** perfect
**Size:** H 9" W 5.5"
**Average Pages:** 100
**Ads:** yes
**Ad Rates:** See Web Site for Details.

# Tacenda

**Type:** magazine
**CLMP member:** yes
**Primary Editor/Contact Person:** Penny Lynn Dunn, Editor
**Address:** P.O. Box 1205
Port Angeles, WA 98362
**Publishes:** essays, fiction, nonfiction, poetry, reviews, art, and translation
**Editorial Focus:** Special interest in environmental and political themes. "Arts for the Environment! Environment for the Arts!"
**Representative Authors:** Robert Cooperman, Simon Perchik, and Leonard J. Cirino
**Submissions Policy:** SASE Required. Snail-mail submissions preferred. No gratuitous profanity, please. Name/address on each page. 3-5 poems.
**Simultaneous Subs:** yes
**Reading Period:** 9/1 to 5/31
**Reporting Time:** 2 to 4 months
**Author Payment:** copies and subscription
**Founded:** 1989
**Non Profit:** no
**Paid Staff:** 0
**Unpaid Staff:** 4-6
**Distributors:** Pending
**Wholesalers:** Pending (Member IPA)
**ISSN Number/ISBN Number:** ISSN 1059-8553
**Total Circulation:** 1,000
**Paid Circulation:** 25
**Subscription Rate:** Individual $20/Institution $22
**Single Copy Price:** $7
**Current Volume/Issue:** VII/II
**Frequency per Year:** 4
**Backfile Available:** yes
**Unsolicited Ms. Received:** yes
**% of Unsolicited Ms. Published per Year:** 80%
**Format:** Stapled and perfect-depends
**Size:** H 11" W 8"
**Average Pages:** 64
**Ads:** yes
**Ad Rates:** E-mail for rates.

# taint

**Type:** online
**CLMP member:** no
**Address:** 529 Carroll St. #4F
Brooklyn, NY 11215
**Web Site Address:** http://www.taintmagazine.com
**Publishes:** essays, fiction, and poetry
**Reading Period:** Year-round
**Reporting Time:** 1 to 2 months
**Author Payment:** none
**Founded:** 2001
**Non Profit:** no
**Average Percentage of Pages per Category:** Audio 100%

# Talon Books Ltd.

**Type:** press
**CLMP member:** no
**Primary Editor/Contact Person:** Sarah Warren
**Address:** P.O. Box 2076
Vancouver, BC V6B 3S3
**Web Site Address:** http://www.talonbooks.com
**Publishes:** fiction, nonfiction, poetry, and translation
**Editorial Focus:** Talonbooks is dedicated to the publication of premier Canadian literature that engages in key social and political issues.
**Recent Awards Received:** Governor General's Award for Drama for Girl in a Goldfish Bowl by Morris Panych.
**Representative Authors:** Michel Tremblay, bill bissett, and Morris Panych
**Submissions Policy:** No unsolicited poetry. Drama must first be professionally produced. Literary fiction and nonfiction. See talonbooks.com.
**Simultaneous Subs:** no
**Reading Period:** Year-round
**Reporting Time:** 3 to 6 months
**Author Payment:** royalties
**Founded:** 1967
**Non Profit:** no
**Paid Staff:** 5
**Unpaid Staff:** 1
**Distributors:** PGC in Canada, Northwestern University Press in US
**ISSN Number/ISBN Number:** ISSN 0-88922-
**Number of Books Published per Year:** 20
**Titles in Print:** 347
**Average Print Run:** N/A
**Average Percentage Printed:** Hardcover 1%, Paperback 99%

## Tampa Review

**Type:** magazine
**CLMP member:** yes
**Primary Editor/Contact Person:** Richard Mathews, Editor
**Address:** University of Tampa Press
401 W. Kennedy Blvd.
Tampa, FL 33606-1490
**Web Site Address:** http://tampareview.ut.edu
**Publishes:** essays, fiction, nonfiction, poetry, art, and translation
**Editorial Focus:** Dedicated to the integration of contemporary literature and visual arts featuring work from Florida and the world.
**Representative Authors:** Peter Meinke, Samrat Upadhyah, and Derek Walcott
**Submissions Policy:** Please send previously unpublished work accompanied by SASE. No e-mail submissions at this time. See guidelines on the Web
**Simultaneous Subs:** no
**Reading Period:** 9/1 to 12/31
**Reporting Time:** 2 to 6 months
**Author Payment:** cash and copies
**Contests:** See Web Site for Contest Guidelines.
**Founded:** 1988
**Non Profit:** yes
**Paid Staff:** 1
**Unpaid Staff:** 5
**ISSN Number/ISBN Number:** 0896-064X/1-879852-
**Total Circulation:** 700
**Paid Circulation:** 225
**Average Print Run:** 800
**Subscription Rate:** Individual $15/Institution $15
**Single Copy Price:** $9.95
**Current Volume/Issue:** Issue 28
**Frequency per Year:** 2
**Backfile Available:** yes
**Unsolicited Ms. Received:** yes
**Format:** Hardcover with color dust jacket
**Size:** H 10 1/2" W 7 1/2"
**Average Pages:** 80
**Ads:** no

## TamTam Books

**Type:** press
**CLMP member:** no
**Primary Editor/Contact Person:** Tosh Berman
**Address:** 2601 Waverly Dr.
Los Angeles, CA 90039-2724
**Web Site Address:** http://www.tamtambooks.com

**Publishes:** essays, fiction, nonfiction, and translation
**Editorial Focus:** Focus on French literature from 1946 to 1980s. Specifically the works of Boris Vian.
**Representative Authors:** Boris Vian, Serge Gainsbourg, and Guy Debord
**Submissions Policy:** If you are a translator interested in the above three authors, you may write to me.
**Simultaneous Subs:** yes
**Reading Period:** Year-round
**Reporting Time:** 2 to 6 months
**Author Payment:** cash and copies
**Founded:** 1998
**Non Profit:** no
**Paid Staff:** no
**Unpaid Staff:** yes
**Distributors:** SPD, AK Distribution, Marginal
**Wholesalers:** Ingram
**Number of Books Published per Year:** 2
**Titles in Print:** 4
**Average Percentage Printed:** Paperback 100%

## Tar River Poetry

**Type:** magazine
**CLMP member:** yes
**Primary Editor/Contact Person:** Peter Mackuk
**Address:** Department of English
East Carolina University
Greenville, NC 27834
**Web Site Address:** http://www.ecu.edu/english.journals
**Publishes:** poetry and reviews
**Editorial Focus:** No haiku. Narrative and short image poems, open or closed forms. We publish both newcomers and established poets.
**Representative Authors:** Gary Jacobik, Louis Simpson, and Henry Taylor
**Submissions Policy:** 4-5 poems per submission.
**Simultaneous Subs:** no
**Reading Period:** 9/1 to 4/30
**Reporting Time:** 4 to 7 weeks
**Author Payment:** copies
**Contests:** no
**Founded:** 1965
**Non Profit:** yes
**Paid Staff:** 2
**Unpaid Staff:** 2
**Wholesalers:** Sold in a number of North Carolina stores.
**ISSN Number/ISBN Number:** ISSN 0740-9141
**Total Circulation:** 650

**Paid Circulation:** 240
**Subscription Rate:** Individual $12/Institution $8
**Single Copy Price:** $6
**Current Volume/Issue:** 43/2
**Frequency per Year:** 2
**Backfile Available:** yes
**Unsolicited Ms. Received:** yes
**Format:** stapled
**Size:** H 9" W 6"
**Average Pages:** 64
**Ads:** yes
**Ad Rates:** exchange

## TCG Books

**Type:** press
**CLMP member:** yes
**Primary Editor/Contact Person:** Terry Nemeth, Publisher
**Address:** Theatre Communications Group
520 Eighth Ave. 24th Floor
New York, NY 10018-4156
**Web Site Address:** http://www.tcg.org/
**Publishes:** essays and fiction
**Editorial Focus:** Plays, translations, theatre resource books
**Recent Awards Received:** Recent publication "Doubt" by John Patrick Shanley received 2005 Pulitzer Prize for Drama
**Representative Authors:** Tony Kushner, Suzan-Lori Parks, and Eric Bogosian
**Simultaneous Subs:** yes
**Reading Period:** Year-round
**Reporting Time:** 1 to 2 months
**Author Payment:** royalties
**Founded:** 1961
**Non Profit:** yes
**Paid Staff:** 50
**Unpaid Staff:** 0
**Distributors:** Consortium Books Sales and Distribution
**Number of Books Published per Year:** 16
**Titles in Print:** 200
**Average Print Run:** 4,000
**Average Percentage Printed:** Paperback 100%
**Average Price:** $14.95

## Tebot Bach, Inc

**Type:** press
**CLMP member:** yes
**Primary Editor/Contact Person:** Mifanwy Kaiser
**Address:** Box 7887
Huntington Beach, CA 92615-7887
**Web Site Address:** http://www.tebotbach.org
**Publishes:** poetry
**Editorial Focus:** to provide national and international poets a venue to publish their poetry
**Representative Authors:** Robin S. Chapman, Richard Jones, and M. L. Liebler
**Submissions Policy:** Query first for full length books See Spillway for submission policy for the magazine
**Simultaneous Subs:** yes
**Reading Period:** Year-round
**Reporting Time:** 1 to 4 months
**Author Payment:** copies
**Founded:** 1993
**Non Profit:** yes
**Paid Staff:** 0
**Unpaid Staff:** 3
**Distributors:** Ingram, Small Press, Armadillo, DeBoer
**Number of Books Published per Year:** 3
**Titles in Print:** 6
**Average Print Run:** 1,000
**Average Percentage Printed:** Paperback 100%
**Average Price:** $13

## Ten Penny Players

**Type:** press
**CLMP member:** no
**Primary Editor/Contact Person:** Richard Spiegel/Barbara Fisher
**Address:** 393 Saint Pauls Ave.
Staten Island, NY 10304-2127
**Web Site Address:** http://www.tenpennyplayers.org
**Publishes:** essays, fiction, nonfiction, poetry, and art
**Editorial Focus:** Ten Penny Players publishes child, young adult and adult artists in print and online at our web site.
**Representative Authors:** Albert Huffstickler, Joy Hewitt Mann, and Robert Cooperman
**Submissions Policy:** TPP, the press, only accepts submissions from students; adults are by invitation only. Adults submit to Waterways magazine.
**Simultaneous Subs:** yes
**Reading Period:** Year-round
**Reporting Time:** 1 to 4 weeks
**Author Payment:** none and copies

**Founded:** 1967
**Non Profit:** yes
**Paid Staff:** 3
**Unpaid Staff:** 0
**ISSN Number/ISBN Number:** 0197-4777/0-934830
**Number of Books Published per Year:** 70
**Titles in Print:** 500
**Average Percentage Printed:** Paperback 2%,
Chapbook 98%

## Tender Buttons press
**Type:** press
**CLMP member:** no
**Primary Editor/Contact Person:** Lee Ann Brown
**Address:** P.O. Box 13, Cooper Station
New York, NY 10276
**Publishes:** poetry
**Editorial Focus:** Experimental poetry by women
under the vast sign of Stein
**Representative Authors:** Bernadette Mayer, Harryette
Mullen, and Jennifer Moxley
**Submissions Policy:** we usually don't take unsolicit-
ed manuscripts-send letter of inquiry with short sam-
ple.
**Simultaneous Subs:** yes
**Reading Period:** 6/1 to 9/1
**Reporting Time:** 1 to 3 months
**Author Payment:** copies
**Contests:** none
**Founded:** 1989
**Non Profit:** yes
**Paid Staff:** 0
**Unpaid Staff:** 3
**Distributors:** SPD
**Number of Books Published per Year:** 1-2
**Titles in Print:** 5
**Average Percentage Printed:** Paperback 90%,
Chapbook 10%

## Terminus: A Magazine of the Arts
**Type:** magazine
**CLMP member:** no
**Primary Editor/Contact Person:** Travis Denton or
Katie Chaple
**Address:** 1034 Hill St.
Atlanta, GA 30315
**Web Site Address:**
http://www.terminusmagazine.com
**Publishes:** essays, fiction, nonfiction, poetry, reviews,

art, translation, and audio
**Editorial Focus:** Writing that pushes boundaries but
endures-not trendy for its own sake. Accessible.
Metaphoric over metonymic.
**Representative Authors:** Denise Duhamel, Louis
Jenkins, and Christopher Buckley
**Submissions Policy:** Short and sweet is better than
long and self-congratulatory for cover letters. Need
more great fiction and nonfiction.
**Simultaneous Subs:** yes
**Reading Period:** 8/1 to 4/30
**Reporting Time:** 1 to 4 months
**Author Payment:** copies
**Contests:** See Web Site for Contest Guidelines.
**Founded:** 2001
**Non Profit:** yes
**Paid Staff:** no
**Unpaid Staff:** yes
**Distributors:** Desert Moon Periodicals and DeBoer
**ISSN Number/ISBN Number:** ISSN 1540-1871
**Total Circulation:** 1,000
**Paid Circulation:** 100
**Subscription Rate:** Individual $18/Institution $28
**Single Copy Price:** $9
**Current Volume/Issue:** Issue 4/5
**Frequency per Year:** 2
**Backfile Available:** yes
**Unsolicited Ms. Received:** yes
**% of Unsolicited Ms. Published per Year:** 70%
**Format:** perfect
**Size:** H 6.75" W 9.75"
**Average Pages:** 200
**Ads:** yes
**Ad Rates:** $50/half page, $100/full page, negotiates
ad-exchanges
See Web Site for Details.

## Terra Incognita
**Type:** magazine
**CLMP member:** yes
**Primary Editor/Contact Person:** Alexandra van de
Kamp
**Address:** P.O. Box 150585
Brooklyn, NY 11215-0585
**Web Site Address:** http://www.terra-incognita.com
**Publishes:** essays, fiction, nonfiction, poetry, art,
translation, and audio
**Editorial Focus:** Terra Incognita is an international lit-
erary and cultural journal published in English and
Spanish.

**Representative Authors:** Jos/Saramago, Billy Collins, and Ray Gonzalez
**Submissions Policy:** Fiction to 5,000 words. Nonfiction to 3,000 words. No poetry in English. Poetry in Spanish okay. See Web Site for more info.
**Simultaneous Subs:** yes
**Reading Period:** 9/1 to 5/1
**Reporting Time:** 2 to 3 months
**Author Payment:** copies
**Founded:** 1998
**Non Profit:** yes
**Paid Staff:** 0
**Unpaid Staff:** 10
**Total Circulation:** 900
**Paid Circulation:** 100
**Average Print Run:** 1,000
**Subscription Rate:** Individual $9/$17/Institution $9/$17
**Single Copy Price:** $7.5
**Current Volume/Issue:** Issue 6
**Frequency per Year:** 1
**Backfile Available:** yes
**Unsolicited Ms. Received:** yes
**% of Unsolicited Ms. Published per Year:** 2%
**Format:** perfect
**Size:** H 11.69" W 8.27"
**Average Pages:** 84
**Ads:** yes
**Ad Rates:** See Web Site for Details.

# Terra Nova
**Type:** press
**CLMP member:** no
**Primary Editor/Contact Person:** Wandee Pryor/Managing Editor
**Address:** New Jersey Institute of Technology Humanities Dept. NJIT Newark, NY 07102
**Web Site Address:** http://www.terranovabooks.org
**Publishes:** essays, fiction, nonfiction, poetry, and art
**Editorial Focus:** Terra Nova anthologies encourage innovative writing and art on nature and culture, presented in a serious and engaging way.
**Representative Authors:** Ellen Dissanayake, Edie Meidav, and John O'Grady
**Submissions Policy:** Visit Terra Nova's web-site for current information on submission deadlines and themes.
**Simultaneous Subs:** no
**Reading Period:** Year-round

**Reporting Time:** 6 to 12 months
**Author Payment:** copies
**Founded:** 1996
**Non Profit:** yes
**Paid Staff:** 2
**Unpaid Staff:** 0
**Distributors:** MIT Press
**ISSN Number/ISBN Number:** 0-262-18230-0/0-262-68136-6
**Number of Books Published per Year:** 1
**Titles in Print:** 6
**Average Percentage Printed:** Hardcover 60%, Paperback 40%

# Texas Poetry Journal
**Type:** magazine
**CLMP member:** yes
**Primary Editor/Contact Person:** Steven Ray Smith
**Address:** P.O. Box 90635 Austin, TX 78709-0635
**Web Site Address:** http://www.texaspoetryjournal.com
**Publishes:** essays and poetry
**Editorial Focus:** We publish poetry, interviews, and photography. We are especially focused on formal poetry but will consider all styles.
**Representative Authors:** Rhina P. Espaillat, Timothy Murphy, and Deborah Warren
**Submissions Policy:** Submit 3-5 poems. Prefer max of 20 lines. No previously published. Submit by mail with SASE or e-mail.
**Simultaneous Subs:** yes
**Reading Period:** Year-round
**Reporting Time:** 2 to 3 months
**Author Payment:** copies
**Founded:** 2004
**Non Profit:** no
**Paid Staff:** 0
**Unpaid Staff:** 2
**Distributors:** DeBoer
**ISSN Number/ISBN Number:** ISSN 1554-4931
**Total Circulation:** 450
**Paid Circulation:** 35
**Average Print Run:** 500
**Subscription Rate:** Individual $12/Institution $12
**Single Copy Price:** $7.50
**Current Volume/Issue:** 1/2
**Frequency per Year:** 2
**Backfile Available:** yes
**Unsolicited Ms. Received:** yes

**% of Unsolicited Ms. Published per Year:** 5%
**Format:** perfect
**Size:** H 8.5" W 5.5"
**Average Pages:** 100
**Ads:** yes
**Ad Rates:** See Web Site for Details.

## THEMA Literary Society

**Type:** magazine
**CLMP member:** yes
**Primary Editor/Contact Person:** Virginia Howard
**Address:** Box 8747
Metairie, LA 70011-8747
**Web Site Address:** http://members.cox.net/thema
**Publishes:** essays, fiction, nonfiction, poetry, and art
**Editorial Focus:** Each issue revolves around an unusual theme . . . we're looking for the most original, clever interpretations of the theme.
**Representative Authors:** M.L. Krueger, Penny Perry, and Richard Vaughn
**Submissions Policy:** We do not accept electronic submissions. Submission for which no THEMA theme has been indicated will not be considered.
**Simultaneous Subs:** yes
**Reading Period:** Year-round
**Reporting Time:** 3 to 4 months
**Author Payment:** cash and copies
**Founded:** 1988
**Non Profit:** yes
**Paid Staff:** 0
**Unpaid Staff:** 12
**Distributors:** EBSCO
**ISSN Number/ISBN Number:** ISSN 1041-4851
**Total Circulation:** 350
**Paid Circulation:** 220
**Average Print Run:** 500
**Subscription Rate:** Individual $16/Institution $16
**Single Copy Price:** $8
**Current Volume/Issue:** 15/3
**Frequency per Year:** 3
**Backfile Available:** yes
**Unsolicited Ms. Received:** yes
**% of Unsolicited Ms. Published per Year:** 100%
**Format:** perfect
**Size:** H 8.5" W 5.5"
**Average Pages:** 150
**Ads:** no

## Third Coast

**Type:** magazine
**CLMP member:** yes
**Primary Editor/Contact Person:** Peter Geye
**Address:** Dept. of English, Western Michigan Univ.
Sprau Tower
Kalamazoo, MI 49008
**Web Site Address:** http://www.wmich.edu/thirdcoast
**Publishes:** essays, fiction, nonfiction, poetry, reviews, and translation
**Editorial Focus:** Established and emerging writers' superior work. Recent anthologization: Best American Poetry, Pushcart fiction, elsewhere
**Representative Authors:** Trudy Lewis, John McNally, and Marvin Bell
**Submissions Policy:** Prose: We accept up to 9,000 words/30 pgs. For more info regarding all genres, please see our website.
**Simultaneous Subs:** yes
**Reading Period:** Year-round
**Reporting Time:** 1 to 6 months
**Author Payment:** copies and subscription
**Contests:** 1st place: $1,000.
See Web Site for Contest Guidelines.
**Founded:** 1995
**Non Profit:** yes
**Paid Staff:** 1
**Unpaid Staff:** 15
**Distributors:** Ingram
**ISSN Number/ISBN Number:** ISSN 1520-8206
**Total Circulation:** 2,775
**Paid Circulation:** 1,000
**Average Print Run:** 3,500
**Subscription Rate:** Individual $14/Institution $14
**Single Copy Price:** $8
**Current Volume/Issue:** Issue 21
**Frequency per Year:** 2
**Backfile Available:** yes
**Unsolicited Ms. Received:** yes
**% of Unsolicited Ms. Published per Year:** 1%
**Format:** perfect
**Size:** H 9" W 6"
**Average Pages:** 192
**Ads:** no

# Third Woman Press

**Type:** press
**CLMP member:** no
**Address:** 1435 4th St.
Berkeley, CA 94710
**Web Site Address:** http://www.thirdwomanpress.com
**Publishes:** essays, fiction, and poetry
**Reading Period:** Year-round
**Reporting Time:** 1 to 2 months
**Author Payment:** none
**Founded:** 1979
**Non Profit:** no
**Average Percentage Printed:** Hardcover 100%

# This Magazine

**Type:** magazine
**CLMP member:** no
**Primary Editor/Contact Person:** Lisa Whittington-Hill
**Address:** 396-401 Richmond St. W
Toronto, ON M5V 3A8
**Web Site Address:** http://www.thismagazine.ca
**Publishes:** essays, fiction, nonfiction, poetry, reviews, and art
**Editorial Focus:** This Magazine is Canada's leading independent magazine of politics, pop culture, and the arts.
**Representative Authors:** Clive Thompson, Gordon Laird, and Alex Roslin
**Submissions Policy:** Submissions by query only. We do not accept unsolicited fiction or poetry. Guidelines are available at http://www.thismagazine.ca
**Simultaneous Subs:** no
**Reading Period:** Year-round
**Reporting Time:** 8 to 12 weeks
**Author Payment:** cash and copies
**Contests:** See Web Site for Contest Guidelines.
**Founded:** 1966
**Non Profit:** yes
**Paid Staff:** 2.0
**Unpaid Staff:** 10
**Distributors:** CMPA, Disticor
**ISSN Number/ISBN Number:** ISSN 1491-2678
**Total Circulation:** 5,000
**Paid Circulation:** 3,500
**Average Print Run:** 7,500
**Subscription Rate:** Individual $25/Institution $37
**Single Copy Price:** $5
**Current Volume/Issue:** 39/2
**Frequency per Year:** 6
**Backfile Available:** yes

**Unsolicited Ms. Received:** no
**Format:** stapled
**Size:** H 8.5" W 11"
**Average Pages:** 48
**Ads:** yes
**Ad Rates:** 995 single page b/w
See Web Site for Details.

# The Threepenny Review

**Type:** magazine
**CLMP member:** no
**Primary Editor/Contact Person:** Wendy Lesser
**Address:** P.O. Box 9131
Berkeley, CA 94709
**Web Site Address:** http://www.threepennyreview.com
**Publishes:** essays, fiction, nonfiction, poetry, reviews, art, and translation
**Editorial Focus:** Essays on literature, theater, film, television, music, dance, and visual arts as well as new poetry and original fiction.
**Representative Authors:** Anne Carson, David Mamet, and Javier Marias
**Submissions Policy:** Please check submissions guidelines and sample articles on our website before sending work. Always include SASE.
**Simultaneous Subs:** no
**Reading Period:** 1/1 to 8/31
**Reporting Time:** 3 to 8 weeks
**Author Payment:** cash and subscription
**Founded:** 1980
**Non Profit:** yes
**Paid Staff:** 3
**Unpaid Staff:** 0
**Distributors:** Ingram; Ubiquity
**ISSN Number/ISBN Number:** ISSN 0275-1410
**Total Circulation:** 10,000
**Paid Circulation:** N/A
**Average Print Run:** 10,000
**Subscription Rate:** Individual $25/Institution $22
**Single Copy Price:** $12
**Current Volume/Issue:** XXVI/3
**Frequency per Year:** 4
**Backfile Available:** yes
**Unsolicited Ms. Received:** yes
**% of Unsolicited Ms. Published per Year:** 1%
**Format:** tabloid
**Average Pages:** 32
**Ads:** yes
**Ad Rates:** See Web Site for Details.

## Tia Chucha Press

**Type:** press
**CLMP member:** no
**Primary Editor/Contact Person:** Luis Rodriguez
**Address:** 12737 Glenoaks Blvd.
No. 20
Sylmar, CA 91342
**Web Site Address:** http://www.tiachucha.com
**Publishes:** poetry
**Editorial Focus:** Exclusively poetry, first books, writers of color, women writers
**Representative Authors:** A. Van Jordan, Angela Shannon, and Elizabeth Alexander
**Submissions Policy:** Please submit 3 to 5 poems that are the best examples of your work along with a letter of introduction.
**Simultaneous Subs:** yes
**Reading Period:** Year-round
**Reporting Time:** 4 to 12 months
**Author Payment:** royalties
**Founded:** 1989
**Non Profit:** yes
**Paid Staff:** 0
**Unpaid Staff:** 0
**Distributors:** Northwestern University Press
**ISSN Number/ISBN Number:** ISBN 1-882688
**Number of Books Published per Year:** 2-4
**Titles in Print:** 40
**Average Percentage Printed:** Paperback 90%, Chapbook 10%

## Tiferet: A Journal of Spiritual Literature

**Type:** magazine
**CLMP member:** yes
**Primary Editor/Contact Person:** Cynthia Brown, Managing Editor
**Address:** P.O. Box 659
Peapack, NJ 07977
**Web Site Address:** http://www.tiferetjournal.com
**Publishes:** essays, fiction, nonfiction, poetry, art, and translation
**Editorial Focus:** Tiferet Journal publishes poetry, prose, and commentary that reveal Spirit in the human experience.
**Representative Authors:** Robert Bly, Mary Hays, and Ray Bradbury
**Submissions Policy:** Submit hardcopies or electronically through our website. Include the genre and author's name and contact info on each submission.

**Simultaneous Subs:** yes
**Reading Period:** Year-round
**Reporting Time:** 3 to 4 months
**Author Payment:** copies
**Contests:** See Web Site for Contest Guidelines.
**Founded:** 2003
**Non Profit:** yes
**Paid Staff:** 2
**Unpaid Staff:** 3
**Distributors:** Ingram, New Leaf
**ISSN Number/ISBN Number:** ISSN 1547-2906
**Total Circulation:** 1,000
**Paid Circulation:** 400
**Average Print Run:** 1,000
**Subscription Rate:** Individual $22/Institution $22
**Single Copy Price:** $14.95
**Current Volume/Issue:** 1/2
**Frequency per Year:** 2
**Backfile Available:** yes
**Unsolicited Ms. Received:** yes
**% of Unsolicited Ms. Published per Year:** 85%
**Format:** perfect
**Size:** H 10" W 7"
**Average Pages:** 176
**Ads:** yes
**Ad Rates:** $100-$300
See Web Site for Details.

## Tilbury House, Publishers

**Type:** press
**CLMP member:** no
**Primary Editor/Contact Person:** Jennifer Bunting
**Address:** 2 Mechanic St., Ste. 3
Gardiner, ME 04345
**Web Site Address:** http://www.tilburyhouse.com
**Publishes:** nonfiction
**Editorial Focus:** Maine, maritime, and New England books, children's picture books, and teacher's guides.
**Representative Authors:** Neil Rolde, Mary Cerullo, and Pegi Deitz Shea
**Submissions Policy:** Please read our guidelines on our website. Do not send e-mail attachments. Please enclose SASE with submission.
**Simultaneous Subs:** yes
**Reading Period:** Year-round
**Reporting Time:** 4 to 6 weeks
**Author Payment:** royalties
**Founded:** 1970
**Non Profit:** no
**Paid Staff:** 6

**Unpaid Staff:** 0
**Wholesalers:** Ingram, Baker & Taylor, etc.
**ISSN Number/ISBN Number:** ISSN 0-88448
**Number of Books Published per Year:** 8
**Titles in Print:** 70
**Average Percentage Printed:** Hardcover 50%,
Paperback 50%

## Time Being Books

**Type:** press
**CLMP member:** no
**Primary Editor/Contact Person:** Trilogy Brodsky,
Office Manger
**Address:** 10411 Clayton Rd.
Ste.s 201-203
Frontenac, MO 63131
**Web Site Address:** http://www.timebeing.com
**Publishes:** poetry
**Editorial Focus:** We specialize in adult contemporary
poetry and short fiction.
**Representative Authors:** William Heyen, Albert
Goldbarth, and Rodger Kamenetz
**Submissions Policy:** We do not accept unsolicited
submissions.
**Simultaneous Subs:** no
**Author Payment:** royalties
**Founded:** 1988
**Non Profit:** yes
**Paid Staff:** 3
**Unpaid Staff:** 0
**Distributors:** Baker & Taylor, Blackwell's, Follett,
Amazon
**Wholesalers:** Baker & Taylor
**ISSN Number/ISBN Number:** ISBN 187777, 156809
**Number of Books Published per Year:** 5
**Titles in Print:** 78
**Average Print Run:** 200
**Average Percentage Printed:** Hardcover 2%,
Paperback 98%
**Average Price:** $14.95

## Tin House

**Type:** magazine
**CLMP member:** yes
**Primary Editor/Contact Person:** Rob Spillman
**Address:** 2601 NW Thurman St.
Portland, OR 97210
**Web Site Address:** http://www.tinhouse.com
**Publishes:** essays, fiction, nonfiction, poetry, reviews,
and translation
**Representative Authors:** Stacey Richter, James
Salter, and Ron Carlson
**Simultaneous Subs:** yes
**Reading Period:** 9/4 to 6/20
**Reporting Time:** 1 to 2 months
**Author Payment:** none
**Founded:** 1998
**Non Profit:** no
**Paid Staff:** 7
**Unpaid Staff:** 4
**Distributors:** Ingram, Eastern News, Desert Moon,
Small Changes.
**Total Circulation:** 10,500
**Paid Circulation:** 3,800
**Subscription Rate:** Individual $29.90/Institution
$29.90
**Single Copy Price:** $12.95
**Current Volume/Issue:** 5/4
**Frequency per Year:** 4
**Backfile Available:** yes
**Unsolicited Ms. Received:** yes
**Format:** perfect
**Average Pages:** 224
**Ads:** yes
**Ad Rates:** $400 for a full page

## Tool: A Magazine

**Type:** online
**CLMP member:** no
**Primary Editor/Contact Person:** Erik Sweet
**Address:** http://www.toolamagazine.com
Albany, NY 12208
**Web Site Address:** http://toolamagazine.com
**Publishes:** essays, fiction, nonfiction, poetry, reviews,
art, translation, and audio
**Editorial Focus:** We publish a range of things, from
poetry and prose to book and reading reviews. Our
main goal is to support what we like.
**Representative Authors:** Brenda Coultas, Eileen
Myles, and Eleni Sikelianos
**Submissions Policy:** Send submission queries via e-
mail to esweet01 at nycap.rr.com Thanks!
**Simultaneous Subs:** yes
**Reading Period:** Year-round
**Reporting Time:** 1 to 2 months
**Author Payment:** none
**Founded:** 1998
**Non Profit:** yes
**Paid Staff:** 0

**Unpaid Staff:** 0
**Distributors:** us
**Wholesalers:** us
**Average Page Views per Month:** unknown
**Average Unique Visitors per Month:** unknown
**Frequency per Year:** 1
**Average Percentage of Pages per Category:** Fiction 10%, Poetry 80%, Reviews 10%
**Ads:** no

## Topic Magazine

**Type:** magazine
**CLMP member:** no
**Primary Editor/Contact Person:** David Haskell
**Address:** P.O. Box 502
New York, NY 10014
**Web Site Address:** http://www.topicmag.com
**Publishes:** essays and nonfiction
**Editorial Focus:** First-person, nonfiction essays that explore each chosen topic.
**Recent Awards Received:** Nominated for Best New Title, Best Design: Independent Press Awards. Regional Design Annual: Print Magazine
**Representative Authors:** Amy Bloom, Lee Aaron Blair, and Kenneth Hartman
**Submissions Policy:** Must be first-person, nonfiction and on topic at hand. Contact submissions@topic-mag.com for information on future topics.
**Simultaneous Subs:** yes
**Reading Period:** Year-round
**Reporting Time:** 2 to 3 weeks
**Author Payment:** none
**Founded:** 2001
**Non Profit:** yes
**Paid Staff:** 0
**Unpaid Staff:** 40
**Distributors:** Ingram, Source Interlink, Comag, Ubiquity
**ISSN Number/ISBN Number:** ISSN 1477-5762
**Total Circulation:** 20,000
**Paid Circulation:** 8,000
**Average Print Run:** 20,000
**Subscription Rate:** Individual $35/Institution $35
**Single Copy Price:** $8
**Current Volume/Issue:** Issue 8
**Frequency per Year:** 4
**Backfile Available:** yes
**Unsolicited Ms. Received:** yes
**% of Unsolicited Ms. Published per Year:** 15%
**Format:** perfect

**Size:** H 10" W 8"
**Average Pages:** 96
**Ads:** yes
**Ad Rates:** varies
See Web Site for Details.

## The Transcendental Friend

**Type:** online
**CLMP member:** no
**Primary Editor/Contact Person:** Garrett Kalleberg
**Address:** 80 Skillman Ave., 2nd fl.
Brooklyn, NY 11211
**Web Site Address:**
http://www.morningred.com/friend
**Publishes:** essays, fiction, poetry, reviews, art, and translation
**Editorial Focus:** Contemporary poetry and poetics, art and criticism.
**Representative Authors:** Laird Hunt, Heather Ramsdell, and Eleni Sikelianos
**Submissions Policy:** Section-specific: "Physiology," "Schizmatics," "Critical Dictionary," etc. See site for details.
**Simultaneous Subs:** no
**Reading Period:** Year-round
**Reporting Time:** 2 to 6 weeks
**Author Payment:** none
**Founded:** 1998
**Non Profit:** yes
**Paid Staff:** 0
**Unpaid Staff:** 1
**ISSN Number/ISBN Number:** ISSN 1526-6559
**Average Page Views per Month:** 6,793
**Average Unique Visitors per Month:** 1,267
**Frequency per Year:** 4
**Average Percentage of Pages per Category:** Fiction 15%, Poetry 50%, Reviews 5%, Essays 10%, Art 5%, Translation 15%
**Ads:** no

## Transfer Magazine

**Type:** magazine
**CLMP member:** no
**Primary Editor/Contact Person:** Editor-in-chief
**Address:** Creative Writing Department, HUM 380
1600 Holloway Ave.
San Francisco, CA 94132
**Web Site Address:**
http://www.transfermagazine.sfsu.edu

**Publishes:** fiction, nonfiction, and poetry
**Editorial Focus:** Fiction, drama, poetry, and creative nonfiction of San Francisco State University students
**Representative Authors:** Anne Rice and Ernest J. Gaines
**Submissions Policy:** Writers of submissions must be enrolled in San Francisco State University
**Simultaneous Subs:** yes
**Reading Period:** Year-round
**Reporting Time:** 1 to 6 months
**Author Payment:** none
**Founded:** 1956
**Non Profit:** yes
**Paid Staff:** 0
**Unpaid Staff:** 4
**ISSN Number/ISBN Number:** ISSN 1533-3043
**Total Circulation:** 700
**Paid Circulation:** 5-25
**Subscription Rate:** Individual $7/issue/Institution $7/issue
**Single Copy Price:** $6
**Current Volume/Issue:** Issue 87
**Frequency per Year:** 2
**Backfile Available:** yes
**Unsolicited Ms. Received:** yes
**% of Unsolicited Ms. Published per Year:** 95%
**Format:** perfect
**Size:** H 8.5" W 5.5"
**Average Pages:** 130
**Ads:** no

## Translation Review

**Type:** magazine
**CLMP member:** yes
**Primary Editor/Contact Person:** Rainer Schulte
**Address:** American Literary Translators Association Box 830688-JO51, U. of Texas at Dallas Richardson, TX 75083-0688
**Web Site Address:** http://www.literarytranslators.org
**Publishes:** essays
**Editorial Focus:** Essays, articles, and interviews on the art, theory, and practice of literary translation.
**Simultaneous Subs:** no
**Reading Period:** Year-round
**Reporting Time:** 1 to 2 months
**Author Payment:** none
**Founded:** 1978
**Non Profit:** yes
**Paid Staff:** 0
**Unpaid Staff:** 1

**ISSN Number/ISBN Number:** ISSN 0737-4836
**Total Circulation:** 1,300
**Paid Circulation:** 600
**Subscription Rate:** Individual $60/Institution $90
**Current Volume/Issue:** Issue 67
**Frequency per Year:** twice yearly with membership to ALTA
**Backfile Available:** yes
**Unsolicited Ms. Received:** yes
**% of Unsolicited Ms. Published per Year:** 80%
**Format:** perfect
**Size:** H 11" W 8"
**Average Pages:** 80
**Ads:** yes
**Ad Rates:** See Web Site for Details.

## Transom & Gully

**Type:** press
**CLMP member:** no
**Primary Editor/Contact Person:** Jennifer Foster
**Address:** 620 W. Olympic Place #408 Seattle, WA 98119
**Web Site Address:** http://transomandgully.org
**Publishes:** fiction and poetry
**Editorial Focus:** We wish to bring inimitable, moving poetry and fiction into the world-books we love and admire and are taken to pieces by.
**Submissions Policy:** Submit via standard mail 5 poems not to exceed 10 pages from manuscript with a bio and list of recent publications.
**Simultaneous Subs:** yes
**Reading Period:** 9/05 to 5/06
**Reporting Time:** 2 to 4 months
**Author Payment:** royalties and copies
**Founded:** 2005
**Non Profit:** yes
**Paid Staff:** 0
**Unpaid Staff:** 4
**Number of Books Published per Year:** 3
**Titles in Print:** 0
**Average Print Run:** 1,000
**Average Percentage Printed:** Paperback 100%
**Average Price:** $15.95

## Trinity University Press

**Type:** press
**CLMP member:** yes
**Primary Editor/Contact Person:** Barbara Ras
**Address:** One Trinity Place

San Antonio, TX 78212
**Web Site Address:** http://www.trinity.edu/tupress
**Publishes:** nonfiction
**Editorial Focus:** landscape; regional books; the art and craft of writing, including the series the Writer's World, edited by Edward Hirsch
**Representative Authors:** Barry Lopez, Rebecca Solnit, and Peter Turchi
**Submissions Policy:** Send proposal, sample chapter, with CV, by US mail with a SASE for return of materials
**Simultaneous Subs:** yes
**Reading Period:** Year-round
**Reporting Time:** 3 to 4 months
**Author Payment:** none
**Founded:** 2002
**Non Profit:** yes
**Paid Staff:** 4
**Unpaid Staff:** 0
**Distributors:** Publishers Group West
**ISSN Number/ISBN Number:** ISBN 1-59534
**Number of Books Published per Year:** 6-8
**Titles in Print:** 15
**Average Print Run:** 2,500
**Average Percentage Printed:** Hardcover 50%, Paperback 50%
**Average Price:** $28

# TriQuarterly

**Type:** magazine
**CLMP member:** yes
**Primary Editor/Contact Person:** Susan Firestone Hahn
**Address:** 629 Noyes St.
Evanston, IL 60208
**Web Site Address:** http://www.triquarterly.org
**Publishes:** essays, fiction, nonfiction, poetry, and art
**Editorial Focus:** TriQuarterly publishes fiction and poetry, including longer works, contemporary and classical translation.
**Recent Awards Received:** Reprints in: Best American Poetry, Short Stories, and Mystery Stories; The Pushcart Prizes; and Stories of the New South.
**Representative Authors:** Stuart Dybek, David Ferry, and Susan Stewart
**Submissions Policy:** TriQuarterly accepts unsolicited work of all genres with SASE.
**Simultaneous Subs:** yes
**Reading Period:** 10/1 to 3/31
**Reporting Time:** 2 to 4 months
**Author Payment:** cash and copies

**Founded:** 1957
**Non Profit:** yes
**Paid Staff:** 2
**Unpaid Staff:** 2
**Distributors:** Ingram, Armadillo, Ubiquity
**ISSN Number/ISBN Number:** ISSN 0041 3097
**Total Circulation:** 3,000
**Paid Circulation:** 1,500
**Average Print Run:** 2,000
**Subscription Rate:** Individual $24/Institution $36
**Single Copy Price:** $11.95
**Current Volume/Issue:** Issue 117
**Frequency per Year:** 3
**Backfile Available:** yes
**Unsolicited Ms. Received:** yes
**% of Unsolicited Ms. Published per Year:** 30%
**Format:** perfect
**Size:** H 9 1/4" W 6"
**Average Pages:** 256
**Ads:** yes
**Ad Rates:** $250/page, $150/half page

# Truman State Univ. Press

**Type:** press
**CLMP member:** no
**Primary Editor/Contact Person:** Nancy Rediger
**Address:** 100 E. Normal St.
Kirksville, MO 63501
**Web Site Address:** http://tsup.truman.edu
**Publishes:** nonfiction and poetry
**Editorial Focus:** Regional studies, early modern studies, poetry
**Representative Authors:** Alfred Runte, Mona Lisa Saloy, and Joseph Schwieterman
**Submissions Policy:** Proposal letter, table of contents, and sample chapters.
**Simultaneous Subs:** no
**Reading Period:** Year-round
**Reporting Time:** 3 to 6 months
**Author Payment:** royalties and copies
**Contests:** See Web Site for Contest Guidelines.
**Founded:** 1986
**Non Profit:** yes
**Paid Staff:** 3
**Unpaid Staff:** 0
**Distributors:** Gazelle Book Services (Europe)
**Wholesalers:** Ingram, Baker & Taylor, Midwest Library Service
**ISSN Number/ISBN Number:** ISBN 1931112
**Number of Books Published per Year:** 10

**Titles in Print:** 90
**Average Print Run:** 1,000
**Average Percentage Printed:** Hardcover 40%,
Paperback 60%
**Average Price:** $25-$30

## Tupelo Press
**Type:** press
**CLMP member:** yes
**Primary Editor/Contact Person:** Margaret Donovan
**Address:** P.O. Box 539
Dorset, VT 05251
**Web Site Address:** http://tupelopress.org
**Publishes:** essays, fiction, nonfiction, and poetry
**Editorial Focus:** To publish stimulating works of poetry, literary fiction, and creative nonfiction by emerging and established writers.
**Representative Authors:** Jennifer Michael Hecht, Natasha Saje, and Alvin Greenberg
**Submissions Policy:** Two annual competitions for poetry and a biennial competition for prose, in addition to general submissions.
**Simultaneous Subs:** yes
**Reading Period:** Year-round
**Reporting Time:** 1 to 3 months
**Author Payment:** royalties
**Contests:** Annual first book prize for poetry, annual open poetry competition (Dorset Prize), biennial chapbook and prose competitions
See Web Site for Contest Guidelines.
**Founded:** 1999
**Non Profit:** yes
**Paid Staff:** 4
**Unpaid Staff:** 2
**Distributors:** Consortium
**Wholesalers:** Baker & Taylor, Ingram, SPD
**Number of Books Published per Year:** 6-10
**Titles in Print:** 18
**Average Percentage Printed:** Hardcover 15%,
Paperback 85%
**Backfile Available:** yes

## Turtle Point Press
**Type:** press
**CLMP member:** yes
**Address:** 233 Broadway Rm. 946
New York, NY 10279
**Web Site Address:** http://www.TurtlePoint.com
**Primary Editor/Contact person:** Jonathan D.

Rabinowitz
**Publishes:** essays, fiction, and poetry
**Recent Awards Received:** Lambda, Robert Frost Medeal, Bay Area Booksellers Award
**Representative Authors:** Richard Howard, George Stade, and Joe Ashby Porter
**Submissions Policy:** Full mss. only, SASE
**Reading Period:** Year-round
**Reporting Time:** 1 to 2 months
**Author Payment:** advance varies
**Founded:** 1991
**Non Profit:** yes
**Distributors:** Consortium
**Wholesalers:** Ingram, Baker & Taylor, SPD
**Number of Books Published per Year:** 7
**Titles in Print:** 60 plus
**Average Print Run:** 2,500
**Average Percentage Printed:** Paperback 90%,
Chapbook 10%
**Average Price:** $16.95

## Twelfth Street Review
**Type:** magazine
**CLMP member:** yes
**Address:** 388 13th St., 2R
Brooklyn, NY 11215
**Web Site Address:** http://www.twelfthstreet.org
**Publishes:** fiction, poetry, and art
**Reading Period:** Year-round
**Reporting Time:** 1 to 2 months
**Author Payment:** none
**Founded:** 2000
**Non Profit:** yes
**Backfile Available:** yes

## Two Lines: A Journal of Translation
**Type:** magazine
**CLMP member:** yes
**Primary Editor/Contact Person:** Zack Rogow
**Address:** Center for the Art of Translation
35 Stillman St., Ste. 201
San Francisco, CA 94107
**Web Site Address:** http://www.catranslation.org
**Publishes:** essays and translation
**Editorial Focus:** Publishes translations into English from every language and literary genre. Each issue has a theme. See web for details.
**Representative Authors:** Marilyn Hacker, Tess Gallagher, and John Felstiner

**Submissions Policy:** Publishes previously unpublished translations only. Translator cannot be the author. Include original language and intro.
**Simultaneous Subs:** no
**Reading Period:** 8/1 to 11/15
**Reporting Time:** 2 to 4 months
**Author Payment:** cash
**Founded:** 1994
**Non Profit:** yes
**Paid Staff:** 1
**Unpaid Staff:** 3
**Distributors:** SPD, amazon.com, BN.com
**ISSN Number/ISBN Number:** ISBN 1-931883
**Total Circulation:** 1,500
**Paid Circulation:** N/A
**Average Print Run:** 1,500
**Subscription Rate:** Individual $13.45/Institution $13.45
**Single Copy Price:** $10.95
**Current Volume/Issue:** 12/1
**Frequency per Year:** 1
**Backfile Available:** yes
**Unsolicited Ms. Received:** yes
**% of Unsolicited Ms. Published per Year:** 80%
**Format:** perfect
**Size:** H 5.5" W 8.5"
**Average Pages:** 240
**Ad Rates:** By exchange with other journals See Web Site for Details.

# Two Rivers Review

**Type:** magazine
**CLMP member:** yes
**Primary Editor/Contact Person:** Philip Memmer
**Address:** P.O. Box 300
Clinton, NY 13323
**Web Site Address:** http://trrpoetry.tripod.com
**Publishes:** fiction and poetry
**Editorial Focus:** Two Rivers Review prints contemporary poetry and short fiction, along with occasional works in translation.
**Representative Authors:** Baron Wormser, Reginald Shepherd, and Deena Linett
**Submissions Policy:** Previously unpublished work only. All submissions must include an SASE. Maximum of 4 poems or 1 story per submission.
**Simultaneous Subs:** no
**Reading Period:** Year-round
**Reporting Time:** 4 to 8 weeks
**Author Payment:** copies

**Contests:** See Web Site for Contest Guidelines.
**Founded:** 1997
**Non Profit:** yes
**Paid Staff:** 0
**Unpaid Staff:** 2
**ISSN Number/ISBN Number:** ISSN 1524-2749
**Total Circulation:** 400
**Paid Circulation:** 200
**Average Print Run:** 400
**Subscription Rate:** Individual $10/Institution $10
**Single Copy Price:** $6
**Current Volume/Issue:** 5/2
**Frequency per Year:** 2
**Backfile Available:** yes
**Unsolicited Ms. Received:** yes
**% of Unsolicited Ms. Published per Year:** 1%
**Format:** stapled
**Size:** H 8.5" W 5.5"
**Average Pages:** 44
**Ads:** no

# Uccelli Press

**Type:** press
**CLMP member:** no
**Primary Editor/Contact Person:** Toni Bennett
**Address:** P.O. Box 85394
Seattle, WA 98145-1394
**Web Site Address:** http://www.uccellipress.com
**Publishes:** essays, fiction, nonfiction, poetry, art, translation, and audio
**Editorial Focus:** Sophisticated fiction, poetry, art, photography, chapbooks, anthologies.
**Representative Authors:** John Amen and Nathan Leslie
**Submissions Policy:** Query via e-mail (preferred) or mail with sample of work.
**Simultaneous Subs:** yes
**Reading Period:** Year-round
**Reporting Time:** 3 to 6 months
**Author Payment:** royalties, cash, and copies
**Contests:** See Web Site for Contest Guidelines.
**Founded:** 2001
**Non Profit:** no
**Paid Staff:** 0
**Unpaid Staff:** 1
**Distributors:** Baker & Taylor
**ISSN Number/ISBN Number:** ISBN 0-9723231-1-2
**Number of Books Published per Year:** 1-2
**Titles in Print:** 4
**Average Percentage Printed:** Paperback 90%,

Chapbook 10%

## Ugly Duckling Presse

**Type:** press
**CLMP member:** yes
**Primary Editor/Contact Person:** Anna Moschovakis
**Address:** 106 Ferris St.
Second Floor
Brooklyn, NY 11231
**Web Site Address:**
http://www.uglyducklingpresse.org
**Publishes:** essays, fiction, poetry, art, translation, and audio
**Editorial Focus:** A non-profit arts and publishing collective, focused on non-commercial work, collaboration, and innovative book forms.
**Representative Authors:** Brent Cunningham, Jen Bervin, and Arkadii Dragomoshchenko
**Submissions Policy:** Not accepting unsolicited manuscripts. See website for guidelines and query procedure. Post is preferred.
**Simultaneous Subs:** yes
**Reading Period:** Year-round
**Reporting Time:** 1 to 4 months
**Author Payment:** copies
**Founded:** 2002
**Non Profit:** yes
**Paid Staff:** 0
**Unpaid Staff:** 10
**Distributors:** SPD
**ISSN Number/ISBN Number:** ISBN 1-933254-
**Number of Books Published per Year:** 10
**Titles in Print:** 15
**Average Print Run:** 500
**Average Percentage Printed:** Paperback 40%, Chapbook 50%, Other 10%
**Average Price:** $9

## United Artists Books

**Type:** press
**CLMP member:** no
**Primary Editor/Contact Person:** Lewis Warsh
**Address:** 114 W. 16th St., 5C
New York, NY 10011
**Web Site Address:** http://www.mindspring.com/-/warsh/uab/
**Publishes:** fiction and poetry
**Editorial Focus:** Experimental writing
**Recent Awards Received:** none
**Representative Authors:** Reed Bye, Bernadette Mayer, and Chris Tysh
**Submissions Policy:** Unsolicited mss. discouraged
**Simultaneous Subs:** yes
**Reading Period:** Year-round
**Reporting Time:** 2 to 4 weeks
**Author Payment:** copies
**Contests:** none
**Founded:** 1977
**Non Profit:** yes
**Paid Staff:** 0
**Unpaid Staff:** 1
**Distributors:** SPD
**ISSN Number/ISBN Number:** none/0-935992
**Number of Books Published per Year:** 2
**Titles in Print:** 25
**Average Print Run:** 1,000
**Average Percentage Printed:** Paperback 100%
**Average Price:** $14

## University College of Cape Breton Press

**Type:** press
**CLMP member:** no
**Primary Editor/Contact Person:** Mike R. Hunter
**Address:** P.O. Box 5300
Sydney, NS B1P 6L2
**Web Site Address:** http://www.uccbpress.ca
**Publishes:** fiction, nonfiction, and poetry
**Editorial Focus:** UCCB Press publishes works with a primary focus on Cape Breton Island and works of a broader academic nature.
**Representative Authors:** A.J.B. Johnston, Carol Corbin, and Jim Lotz
**Simultaneous Subs:** yes
**Reading Period:** Year-round
**Reporting Time:** 2 to 4 months
**Author Payment:** royalties
**Founded:** 1974
**Non Profit:** yes
**Paid Staff:** 3
**Unpaid Staff:** 3
**ISSN Number/ISBN Number:** ISBN 0920336; 1897009
**Number of Books Published per Year:** 4
**Titles in Print:** 75
**Average Percentage Printed:** Paperback 100%

# The University of Georgia Press

**Type:** press
**CLMP member:** no
**Primary Editor/Contact Person:** Andrew Berzanskis
**Address:** 330 Research Dr.
Athens, GA 30602-4901
**Web Site Address:** http://www.ugapress.uga.edu
**Publishes:** fiction, nonfiction, and poetry
**Editorial Focus:** Scholarly nonfiction; poetry, short fiction, regional studies, environmental studies, American studies
**Representative Authors:** Roy Hoffman, Ted Levin, and James C. Cobb
**Submissions Policy:** Please visit our Web site for our submissions policy
**Simultaneous Subs:** yes
**Reading Period:** Year-round
**Reporting Time:** 3 to 4 weeks
**Author Payment:** royalties
**Contests:** Flannery O'Connor Award for Short Fiction; Contemporary Poetry Series
See Web Site for Contest Guidelines.
**Founded:** 1938
**Non Profit:** yes
**Paid Staff:** 30
**Unpaid Staff:** 5
**ISSN Number/ISBN Number:** ISBN 0-8203
**Number of Books Published per Year:** 70
**Titles in Print:** 915
**Average Percentage Printed:** Hardcover 60%, Paperback 40%

# University of Massachusetts Press

**Type:** press
**CLMP member:** no
**Primary Editor/Contact Person:** Bruce Wilcox
**Address:** Box 429
Amherst, MA 01004
**Web Site Address:** http://www.umass.edu/umpress
**Publishes:** essays, fiction, nonfiction, and poetry
**Editorial Focus:** Scholarly books and serious nonfiction, with an emphasis on American studies, broadly construed.
**Recent Awards Received:** 2005 American Book Award; 2005 Eugene M. Kayden Award; 2004 New England Historical Association Book Award.
**Representative Authors:** Tom Engelhardt, Daniel Horowitz, and Doreen Baingana
**Submissions Policy:** For nonfiction, submit letter, table of contents, and introduction. Send poetry and

fiction to Juniper Prize competitions.
**Simultaneous Subs:** yes
**Reading Period:** Year-round
**Reporting Time:** 1 to 4 weeks
**Author Payment:** royalties and copies
**Contests:** See Web Site for Contest Guidelines.
**Founded:** 1963
**Non Profit:** yes
**Paid Staff:** 8
**Unpaid Staff:** 4
**Distributors:** Hopkins Fulfillment Services
**Wholesalers:** all major wholesalers
**ISSN Number/ISBN Number:** ISBN 1-55849-000-0
**Number of Books Published per Year:** 30-40
**Titles in Print:** 900
**Average Print Run:** 1,500
**Average Percentage Printed:** Hardcover 50%, Paperback 50%
**Average Price:** $19.95 paperback

# University of Tampa Press

**Type:** press
**CLMP member:** yes
**Primary Editor/Contact Person:** Richard Mathews, Director
**Address:** 401 W. Kennedy Blvd.
Tampa, FL 33606
**Web Site Address:** http://utpress.ut.edu
**Publishes:** nonfiction and poetry
**Editorial Focus:** Contemporary literature, with an emphasis on poetry and drama. We also publish regional history and some academic titles.
**Representative Authors:** Richard Chess, Jordan Smith, and Julia B. Levine
**Submissions Policy:** Unsolicited book manuscripts are accepted only through Tampa Review Prize or Pinter Review Prize competitions.
**Simultaneous Subs:** no
**Reading Period:** Year-round
**Reporting Time:** 8 to 16 weeks
**Author Payment:** royalties and copies
**Contests:** Tampa Review Prize for Poetry-http://tampareview.ut.edu/tr_prize.html and Pinter Review Prize for Drama (http://pinter.edu)
See Web Site for Contest Guidelines.
**Founded:** 1952
**Non Profit:** yes
**Paid Staff:** 1
**Unpaid Staff:** 14
**ISSN Number/ISBN Number:** 0896-064X/1-879852-

**Number of Books Published per Year:** 5-10
**Titles in Print:** 39
**Average Print Run:** 1,000
**Average Percentage Printed:** Hardcover 80%,
Paperback 20%
**Average Price:** $25

## University of Wisconsin Press

**Type:** press
**CLMP member:** no
**Primary Editor/Contact Person:** Raphael Kadushin,
Editor
**Address:** 1930 Monroe St., 3rd floor
Madison, WI 53711
**Web Site Address:** http://www.wisc.edu/wisconsin-
press
**Publishes:** fiction, nonfiction, and poetry
**Editorial Focus:** Scholarly, regional, and literary works
of enduring value. Biography, memoir, selected fiction,
Latino, GLBT, Wisconsin.
**Recent Awards Received:** 2004 Society of Midland
Authors Book Award for Adult Nonfiction, 2004 Winner
of the Triangle Award for Gay Poetry from the
Publishing Triangle
**Representative Authors:** Will Fellows, Sara Rath, and
Marilyn Ann Moss
**Submissions Policy:** see website for instructions on
submitting prospectus
**Simultaneous Subs:** yes
**Reading Period:** Year-round
**Reporting Time:** 1 to 3 months
**Author Payment:** royalties and copies
**Contests:** The annual Brittingham and Felix Pollak
prizes for poetry http://www.wisc.edu/wisconsin-
press/poetryguide.html
See Web Site for Contest Guidelines.
**Founded:** 1937
**Non Profit:** yes
**Paid Staff:** 25
**Unpaid Staff:** 15
**Distributors:** Chicago Distribution Center
**Wholesalers:** Ingram, Baker & Taylor, NACS, Partners,
others
**ISSN Number/ISBN Number:** ISBN 0-229
**Number of Books Published per Year:** 65
**Titles in Print:** 2,800
**Average Print Run:** 1,000
**Average Percentage Printed:** Hardcover 40%,
Paperback 55%, Other 5%
**Average Price:** $30

## Unpleasant Event Schedule

**Type:** online
**CLMP member:** yes
**Primary Editor/Contact Person:** Daniel Nester
**Address:** 2705th St. #2E
Brooklyn, NY 11215
**Web Site Address:** http://www.unpleasan-
teventschedule.com
**Publishes:** essays, fiction, nonfiction, poetry, art,
translation, and audio
**Editorial Focus:** UES publishes risk-taking work in a
decidedly ungenteel context that is still intelligent.
**Representative Authors:** David Trinidad, Jennifer
Knox, and Matthew Wascovich
**Submissions Policy:** E-mail submissions-pasted into
body of message-to editor@unpleasanteventsched-
ule.com.
**Simultaneous Subs:** no
**Reading Period:** Year-round
**Reporting Time:** 1 to 3 months
**Author Payment:** none
**Founded:** 2003
**Non Profit:** yes
**Paid Staff:** 0
**Unpaid Staff:** 3
**ISSN Number/ISBN Number:** ISBN coming soon
**Backfile Available:** yes
**Average Page Views per Month:** 2,000
**Average Unique Visitors per Month:** 400
**Frequency per Year:** 18
**Publish Print Anthology:** no
**Average Percentage of Pages per Category:** Fiction
5%, Nonfiction 5%, Poetry 75%, Essays 5%, Art 5%,
Translation 5%
**Ads:** no

## UpSet Press

**Type:** press
**CLMP member:** yes
**Primary Editor/Contact Person:** Robert Booras
**Address:** 7214 6th Ave., Apt. 2
P.O. Box 200340, Brooklyn, NY 11220
Brooklyn, NY 11209
**Web Site Address:** http://www.upsetpress.org
**Publishes:** fiction and poetry
**Representative Authors:** Nicholas Powers
**Simultaneous Subs:** yes
**Reading Period:** Year-round

**Reporting Time:** 2 to 4 months
**Author Payment:** none
**Contests:** none
**Founded:** 2000
**Non Profit:** yes
**Paid Staff:** 0
**Unpaid Staff:** 3
**ISSN Number/ISBN Number:** ISBN 0-9760142-0-3
**Number of Books Published per Year:** 1
**Titles in Print:** 1
**Average Print Run:** 1,000
**Average Percentage Printed:** Paperback 100%
**Average Price:** $10.95

# Urban Spaghetti

**Type:** magazine
**CLMP member:** no
**Primary Editor/Contact Person:** Cheryl Dodds
**Address:** P.O. Box 5186
Mansfield, OH 44901-5186
**Web Site Address:** http://www.urban-spaghetti.com
**Publishes:** essays, fiction, nonfiction, poetry, art, and audio
**Editorial Focus:** The current focus tends to be on women's issues, on defining and surviving individuality through lifecycles, and music culture
**Representative Authors:** Marge Piercy, David Citino, and Andrea Potos
**Submissions Policy:** Mostly solicited, relevant to focus, no e-mail attachments without approval, SASE, no stories larger than 2,500, unpublished.
**Simultaneous Subs:** yes
**Reading Period:** Year-round
**Reporting Time:** 2 to 6 months
**Author Payment:** copies
**Founded:** 1998
**Non Profit:** yes
**Paid Staff:** 0
**Unpaid Staff:** 3-7
**Distributors:** Barnes & Noble, Little Prof, online at web site
**ISSN Number/ISBN Number:** ISBN 1521-1371
**Total Circulation:** 500
**Paid Circulation:** N/A
**Subscription Rate:** Individual $0/Institution $0
**Single Copy Price:** $10
**Current Volume/Issue:** Issue 5
**Frequency per Year:** 1
**Backfile Available:** yes
**Unsolicited Ms. Received:** yes

**% of Unsolicited Ms. Published per Year:** 10%
**Format:** perfect
**Size:** H 8.5" W 5.5"
**Average Pages:** 150
**Ads:** no

# Vallum: contemporary poetry

**Type:** magazine
**CLMP member:** yes
**Primary Editor/Contact Person:** Joshua Auerbach, Eleni Auerbach
**Address:** P.O. Box 48003
Montreal, QC H2V 4S8
**Web Site Address:** http://www.vallummag.com
**Publishes:** essays, poetry, reviews, art, and translation
**Editorial Focus:** Vallum's focus is on the edgy and avant-garde, as well as on the best mainstream poetry. Publishes new and established poets.
**Representative Authors:** Paul Muldoon, Stephen Dunn, and Charles Bernstein
**Submissions Policy:** Send by regular mail, with SASE/IRC. 4 to 7 poems at a time. See website for theme guidelines.
**Simultaneous Subs:** no
**Reading Period:** OC/1 to MR/31
**Reporting Time:** 9 to 12 months
**Author Payment:** cash and copies
**Contests:** The Vallum Award for Poetry, an annual international competition. Two prizes of cash and publication.
See Web Site for Contest Guidelines.
**Founded:** 2001
**Non Profit:** yes
**Paid Staff:** 5
**Unpaid Staff:** 3
**Distributors:** Ingram, DeBoer, Disticor, Gordon and Gotch
**ISSN Number/ISBN Number:** ISSN 1496-5178
**Total Circulation:** 9,000
**Paid Circulation:** 200
**Average Print Run:** 3,000
**Subscription Rate:** Individual $14 in USA/Institution $20 in USA
**Single Copy Price:** $5.95
**Current Volume/Issue:** 3/2
**Frequency per Year:** 2
**Backfile Available:** yes
**Unsolicited Ms. Received:** yes
**% of Unsolicited Ms. Published per Year:** 1%

**Format:** perfect
**Size:** H 8.5" W 6.75"
**Average Pages:** 100
**Ads:** yes
**Ad Rates:** See Web Site for Details.

## Véhicule Press

**Type:** press
**CLMP member:** yes
**Primary Editor/Contact Person:** Simon Dardick
**Address:** P.O.B. 125
Place du Parc Station
Montreal, QC H2X 4A3
**Web Site Address:** http://www.vehiculepress.com
**Publishes:** essays, fiction, nonfiction, poetry, and translation
**Editorial Focus:** Prize-winning publications within the context of social history.
**Recent Awards Received:** Governor Generalâs Award for Translation, EJ Pratt Poetry Award, Quebec Writersâ Federation McAuslan First Book Prize
**Representative Authors:** Don Bell, Pierre Nepveu, and Elise Partridge
**Submissions Policy:** Send a profile, list of publications, SASE, and excerpt (25-30 pages double spaced). We mostly publish Canadian authors.
**Simultaneous Subs:** yes
**Reading Period:** Year-round
**Reporting Time:** 2 to 3 months
**Author Payment:** royalties
**Founded:** 1973
**Non Profit:** no
**Paid Staff:** 3
**Unpaid Staff:** 0
**Distributors:** Independent Publishers Group
**ISSN Number/ISBN Number:** ISBN 1-55065
**Number of Books Published per Year:** 12
**Titles in Print:** 250
**Average Print Run:** 1,200
**Average Percentage Printed:** Paperback 100%
**Average Price:** $16.95

## Verb

**Type:** magazine
**CLMP member:** yes
**Primary Editor/Contact Person:** Daren Wang
**Address:** P.O. Box 2684
Decatur, GA 30031
**Web Site Address:** http://www.verb.org
**Publishes:** fiction, poetry, and audio
**Editorial Focus:** New fiction, poetry, and music exclusively in audio
**Representative Authors:** Robert Olen Butler, Ha Jin, and Thomas Lux
**Submissions Policy:** No unsolicited manuscripts-contact before submitting
**Simultaneous Subs:** no
**Reading Period:** Year-round
**Reporting Time:** 1 to 2 months
**Author Payment:** cash, copies, and subscription
**Founded:** 2004
**Non Profit:** no
**Paid Staff:** 2
**Unpaid Staff:** 3
**Distributors:** University of Georgia Press, Audible.com
**Total Circulation:** 10,000
**Paid Circulation:** 1,500
**Average Print Run:** 5,000
**Subscription Rate:** Individual $50/Institution $50
**Single Copy Price:** $19.95
**Current Volume/Issue:** 1/1
**Frequency per Year:** 4
**Backfile Available:** yes
**Unsolicited Ms. Received:** no
**Format:** compact disc, download

## VERBATIM: The Language Quarterly

**Type:** magazine
**CLMP member:** yes
**Primary Editor/Contact Person:** Erin McKean
**Address:** 4907 N. Washtenaw Ave.
Chicago, IL 60625
**Web Site Address:** http://www.verbatimmag.com
**Publishes:** essays, nonfiction, poetry, and reviews
**Editorial Focus:** VERBATIM: The Language Quarterly is the only magazine of language and linguistics for the layperson.
**Representative Authors:** Nick Humez, Richard Lederer, and Paul McFedries
**Submissions Policy:** Please e-mail queries first, and check out our website. No poetry other than language-related light verse! No fiction!
**Simultaneous Subs:** yes
**Reading Period:** Year-round
**Reporting Time:** 2 to 3 months
**Author Payment:** cash and copies
**Founded:** 1974
**Non Profit:** yes
**Paid Staff:** 2
**Unpaid Staff:** 5
**Distributors:** DeBoer

**ISSN Number/ISBN Number:** ISSN 0162-0932
**Total Circulation:** 2,000
**Paid Circulation:** 1,600
**Average Print Run:** 2250
**Subscription Rate:** Individual $25/Institution $25
**Single Copy Price:** $6.50
**Current Volume/Issue:** 30/1
**Frequency per Year:** 4
**Backfile Available:** yes
**Unsolicited Ms. Received:** yes
**% of Unsolicited Ms. Published per Year:** 25%
**Format:** stapled
**Size:** H 11" W 8.5"
**Average Pages:** 32
**Ads:** yes
**Ad Rates:** please e-mail for details

# Verse

**Type:** magazine
**CLMP member:** no
**Primary Editor/Contact Person:** Brian Henry
**Address:** English Department
University of Richmond
Richmond, VA 23173
**Web Site Address:** http://versemag.blogspot.com
**Publishes:** essays, fiction, poetry, and reviews
**Representative Authors:** John Ashbery, Medbh
McGuckian, and John Kinsella
**Simultaneous Subs:** yes
**Reading Period:** 9/1 to 5/1
**Reporting Time:** 2 to 8 weeks
**Author Payment:** copies and subscription
**Founded:** 1984
**Non Profit:** yes
**Paid Staff:** 0
**Unpaid Staff:** 4
**Distributors:** DeBoer
**ISSN Number/ISBN Number:** ISSN 0268-3830
**Total Circulation:** 1,000
**Paid Circulation:** 800
**Average Print Run:** 1,000
**Subscription Rate:** Individual $18/Institution $36
**Single Copy Price:** $8-12
**Current Volume/Issue:** 22/1
**Frequency per Year:** 3
**Backfile Available:** yes
**Unsolicited Ms. Received:** yes
**Format:** perfect
**Size:** H 6" W 9"
**Ads:** no

# The Vincent Brothers Company

**Type:** press
**CLMP member:** no
**Primary Editor/Contact Person:** Kimberly Willardson
**Address:** 4566 Northern Circle
Riverside, OH 45424
**Web Site Address:** http://www.thevincentbrothersre-view.org
**Publishes:** fiction, poetry, and art
**Editorial Focus:** Quality, collectible chapbooks for
artists, and fiction and poetry writers.
**Representative Authors:** David Lee Garrison, Deanna
Pickard, and Jud Yalkut
**Submissions Policy:** Not open to unsolicited submis-
sions of manuscripts as of now.
**Simultaneous Subs:** no
**Reading Period:** Year-round
**Reporting Time:** 9 to 12 months
**Author Payment:** royalties and copies
**Contests:** We plan contests for the near future, but
none as of yet. Check our website.
See Web Site for Contest Guidelines.
**Founded:** 1988
**Non Profit:** yes
**Paid Staff:** 2
**Unpaid Staff:** 5
**Number of Books Published per Year:** 1
**Titles in Print:** 1
**Average Percentage Printed:** Chapbook 100%

# The Vincent Brothers Review

**Type:** magazine
**CLMP member:** no
**Primary Editor/Contact Person:** Kimberly A.
Willardson
**Address:** 4566 Northern Circle
Riverside, OH 45424
**Web Site Address:** http://www.thevincentbrothersre-view.org
**Publishes:** essays, fiction, nonfiction, poetry, reviews,
art, and translation
**Editorial Focus:** We seek original, creative work that
excites us so much that we feel it imperative to pass
the work along to our subscribers.
**Representative Authors:** Gordon Wilson, Deanna
Pickard, and Jared Carter
**Submissions Policy:** See our website for guidelines,
or send us a SASE.

**Simultaneous Subs:** yes
**Reading Period:** Year-round
**Reporting Time:** 4 to 9 months
**Author Payment:** cash and copies
**Contests:** Annual Fiction and Poetry Contests-see guidelines for specific themes.
See Web Site for Contest Guidelines.
**Founded:** 1988
**Non Profit:** yes
**Paid Staff:** 2
**Unpaid Staff:** 5
**ISSN Number/ISBN Number:** ISSN 1044-615X
**Total Circulation:** 450
**Paid Circulation:** 250
**Subscription Rate:** Individual $20/Institution $24
**Single Copy Price:** $11.50
**Current Volume/Issue:** IX/1
**Frequency per Year:** 2
**Backfile Available:** yes
**Unsolicited Ms. Received:** yes
**% of Unsolicited Ms. Published per Year:** 3%
**Format:** perfect
**Size:** H 8 and 1/2" W 5"
**Average Pages:** 164
**Ads:** no

# Virginia Quarterly Review

**Type:** magazine
**CLMP member:** yes
**Primary Editor/Contact Person:** Ted Genoways
**Address:** One West Range
P.O. Box 400223
Charlottesville, VA 22904-4223
**Web Site Address:** http://www.vqronline.org
**Publishes:** essays, fiction, nonfiction, poetry, reviews, art, and translation
**Editorial Focus:** A journal of literature and contemporary affairs.
**Recent Awards Received:** Finalist for 2 National Magazine Awards in 2005. 2005 Parnassus Award for Significant Editorial Achievement.
**Representative Authors:** Salmon Rushdie, Toni Morrison, and Michael Chabon
**Submissions Policy:** Five poems at a time, or 2 stories at once. Not in summer months. SASE for reply
**Simultaneous Subs:** no
**Reading Period:** 9/1 to 5/31
**Reporting Time:** 3 to 4 months
**Author Payment:** cash and copies
**Contests:** N/A

**Founded:** 1925
**Non Profit:** yes
**Paid Staff:** 4
**Unpaid Staff:** 25
**Distributors:** Ingram, DeBoer, Ubiquity
**ISSN Number/ISBN Number:** ISSN 0042-675X
**Total Circulation:** 5,500
**Paid Circulation:** 4,000
**Average Print Run:** 6,000
**Subscription Rate:** Individual $25/Institution $28
**Single Copy Price:** $11
**Current Volume/Issue:** 82/1
**Frequency per Year:** 4
**Backfile Available:** yes
**Unsolicited Ms. Received:** yes
**% of Unsolicited Ms. Published per Year:** 80%
**Format:** perfect
**Size:** H 6.75" W 10"
**Average Pages:** 288
**Ads:** yes
**Ad Rates:** full page: $300 B&W, $400 4C; 1/2 page: $180 B&W, $240 4C

# Void Magazine

**Type:** online
**CLMP member:** yes
**Primary Editor/Contact Person:** Chris Steib
**Address:** 410 E. 13th St., 5E
c/o Void Media, LLC
New York, NY 10009
**Web Site Address:** http://www.voidmagazine.com
**Publishes:** essays, fiction, nonfiction, poetry, and reviews
**Editorial Focus:** Impressive, creative, original and readable fiction, poetry, reviews and essays.
**Submissions Policy:** Submissions accepted on a rolling basis. See website for details.
**Simultaneous Subs:** yes
**Reading Period:** Year-round
**Reporting Time:** 1 to 2 months
**Author Payment:** none
**Contests:** Free contests-prizes and giveaways.
See Web Site for Contest Guidelines.
**Founded:** 2005
**Non Profit:** no
**Paid Staff:** 8
**Unpaid Staff:** 1
**Average Page Views per Month:** 12,000
**Average Unique Visitors per Month:** 5,000
**Frequency per Year:** 12

**Average Percentage of Pages per Category:** Fiction 35%, Poetry 30%, Reviews 25%, Essays 10%
**Ad Rates:** contact marketing@voidmagazine.com
See Web Site for Details.

# Vhicule Press

**Type:** press
**CLMP member:** no
**Primary Editor/Contact Person:** Simon Dardick
**Address:** P.O. Box 125, Place du Parc Station
Montreal, QC H2V 2P1
**Web Site Address:** http://www.vehiculepress.com
**Publishes:** fiction, nonfiction, and poetry
**Editorial Focus:** Vhicule Press publishes poetry, fiction, translations, and social history with a strong commitment to first-time authors.
**Submissions Policy:** Query first.
**Simultaneous Subs:** yes
**Reading Period:** Year-round
**Reporting Time:** 4 to 6 months
**Author Payment:** royalties and copies
**Founded:** 1973
**Non Profit:** no
**Paid Staff:** 3
**Unpaid Staff:** 0
**Distributors:** Independent Publishers Group ( US); LPG (Canada)
**ISSN Number/ISBN Number:** ISBN 1-55065-
**Number of Books Published per Year:** 12
**Titles in Print:** 300
**Average Percentage Printed:** Hardcover 2%, Paperback 98%

# War, Literature & the Arts

**Type:** magazine
**CLMP member:** yes
**Primary Editor/Contact Person:** Donald Anderson
**Address:** Dept. of English, US Air Force Academy
2354 Fairchild Dr., Ste. 6D207
USAF Academy, CO 80840-6242
**Web Site Address:** http://www.WLAjournal.com
**Publishes:** essays, fiction, nonfiction, poetry, reviews, art, and translation
**Editorial Focus:** From time immemorial, war and art have reflected one another, and it is this intersection that WLA seeks to illuminate.
**Representative Authors:** Philip Caputo, Carolyn Forche, and Paul West

**Submissions Policy:** See the website
**Simultaneous Subs:** no
**Reading Period:** Year-round
**Reporting Time:** 3 to 6 months
**Author Payment:** copies
**Founded:** 1989
**Non Profit:** yes
**Paid Staff:** yes
**Unpaid Staff:** 20
**ISSN Number/ISBN Number:** ISSN 1046-6967
**Total Circulation:** 500
**Paid Circulation:** 500
**Average Print Run:** 700
**Current Volume/Issue:** 16/1-2
**Frequency per Year:** 2
**Backfile Available:** yes
**Unsolicited Ms. Received:** yes
**% of Unsolicited Ms. Published per Year:** 10%
**Format:** perfect
**Size:** H 9" W 6"
**Average Pages:** 300+
**Ads:** no

# Washington Square

**Type:** magazine
**CLMP member:** no
**Primary Editor/Contact Person:** Maria Filippone
**Address:** 19 University Place
Room 219
New York, NY 10003
**Web Site Address:**
http://www.cwp.fas.nyu.edu/page/wsr
**Publishes:** fiction, nonfiction, poetry, and art
**Editorial Focus:** our tastes are diverse; well-written and of literary merit
**Representative Authors:** Rick Moody, Eamon Grennan, and Melissa Pritchard
**Submissions Policy:** short fiction or creative nonfiction twenty pages or less; up to three poems; submit no more than twice annually
**Simultaneous Subs:** yes
**Reading Period:** Year-round
**Reporting Time:** 1 to 3 months
**Author Payment:** none
**Contests:** See Web Site for Contest Guidelines.
**Founded:** 1996
**Non Profit:** yes
**Paid Staff:** 0
**Unpaid Staff:** 18
**Total Circulation:** 2,000

**Paid Circulation:** 200
**Subscription Rate:** Individual $10/Institution $12
**Single Copy Price:** $6
**Current Volume/Issue:** Issue 14
**Frequency per Year:** 2
**Backfile Available:** yes
**Unsolicited Ms. Received:** yes
**% of Unsolicited Ms. Published per Year:** 70%
**Format:** perfect
**Average Pages:** 132
**Ads:** yes

## Washington Writers' Publishing House

**Type:** press
**CLMP member:** yes
**Primary Editor/Contact Person:** Piotr Gwiazda
**Address:** English Department
University of Maryland, Baltimore County
Baltimore, MD 21250
**Web Site Address:** http://www.wwph.org
**Publishes:** fiction and poetry
**Editorial Focus:** Open to writers living in the Baltimore/Washington area.
**Representative Authors:** Moira Egan, Jane Satterfield, and Ned Balbo
**Submissions Policy:** Between July 1 and December 1 we accept manuscripts from Washington and Baltimore area writers for our annual competition.
**Simultaneous Subs:** yes
**Reading Period:** 7/1 to 12/1
**Reporting Time:** 2 to 3 months
**Author Payment:** royalties and copies
**Contests:** See Web Site for Contest Guidelines.
**Founded:** 1973
**Non Profit:** yes
**Paid Staff:** 0
**Unpaid Staff:** 5
**Distributors:** Baker & Taylor
**Number of Books Published per Year:** 2
**Titles in Print:** 2
**Average Print Run:** 1,000
**Average Percentage Printed:** Hardcover 10%, Paperback 90%
**Average Price:** $12

## Watchword

**Type:** magazine
**CLMP member:** yes

**Primary Editor/Contact Person:** Liz Lisle
**Address:** P.O. Box 5755
Berkeley, CA 94705
**Web Site Address:** http://www.watchwordpress.org
**Publishes:** essays, fiction, nonfiction, poetry, art, and translation
**Editorial Focus:** We're interested in work that offers a unique perspective, approach, or style. We also publish modern translations.
**Submissions Policy:** We only read a few times a year. The best thing to do is check our website for an update: http://www.watchwordpress.org.
**Simultaneous Subs:** yes
**Reading Period:** Year-round
**Reporting Time:** 2 to 4 months
**Author Payment:** copies
**Founded:** 2,000
**Non Profit:** yes
**Paid Staff:** 0
**Unpaid Staff:** 4
**Total Circulation:** 700
**Paid Circulation:** 400
**Average Print Run:** 1,000
**Subscription Rate:** Individual $40/Institution $40
**Single Copy Price:** $10
**Current Volume/Issue:** Issue 6
**Frequency per Year:** 2
**Backfile Available:** yes
**Unsolicited Ms. Received:** yes
**% of Unsolicited Ms. Published per Year:** 90%
**Format:** perfect
**Size:** H 8.5" W 5.5"
**Average Pages:** 100
**Ads:** no

## Water~Stone Review

**Type:** magazine
**CLMP member:** yes
**Primary Editor/Contact Person:** Mary F. Rockcastle
**Address:** GLS, Hamline University, MS-A1730
1536 Hewitt Ave.
St. Paul, MN 55104-1284
**Web Site Address:** http://www.waterstonereview.com
**Publishes:** essays, fiction, nonfiction, poetry, reviews, and translation
**Editorial Focus:** Water~Stone Review is published once a year by the Graduate School of Liberal Studies at Hamline University.
**Recent Awards Received:** Pushcart Prize, Best American Poetry, bronze prize for design excellence

from the MN. Magazine Publishers Association.

**Representative Authors:** Terry Tempest Williams, John Wideman, and Naomi Shihab Nye

**Submissions Policy:** Submissions accepted Sept.15-December 15. Submit, with SASE, up to 5 poems, 20 pages total, or up to 5,000 words of prose.

**Simultaneous Subs:** yes

**Reading Period:** 9/15 to 12/15

**Reporting Time:** 1 to 6 months

**Author Payment:** copies and subscription

**Contests:** Jane Kenyon Poetry Prize, Brenda Ueland Prose Prize alternate Years

See Web Site for Contest Guidelines.

**Founded:** 1998

**Non Profit:** yes

**Paid Staff:** 3

**Unpaid Staff:** 10

**Distributors:** DeBoer

**ISSN Number/ISBN Number:** ISSN 1520-457x

**Total Circulation:** 1,500

**Paid Circulation:** 700

**Average Print Run:** 1,500

**Subscription Rate:** Individual $14/Institution $15

**Single Copy Price:** $14

**Current Volume/Issue:** 8/1

**Frequency per Year:** 1

**Backfile Available:** yes

**Unsolicited Ms. Received:** yes

**% of Unsolicited Ms. Published per Year:** 60%

**Format:** perfect

**Size:** H 9" W 6"

**Average Pages:** 250

**Ads:** yes

**Ad Rates:** Full page, $250 Half-page, $150; 10% discount non-profits

See Web Site for Details.

## Waterways: Poetry in the Mainstream

**Type:** magazine

**CLMP member:** yes

**Primary Editor/Contact Person:** Richard Spiegel/Barbara Fisher

**Address:** 393 Saint Pauls Ave.

Staten Island, NY 10304-2127

**Web Site Address:** http://www.tenpennyplayers.org

**Publishes:** poetry

**Editorial Focus:** Contemporary poets and theme issues

**Representative Authors:** Albert Huffstickler, Joy Hewitt Mann, and John Grey

**Submissions Policy:** Themes are posted at our web site. Returns with SASE only. Rarely publish rhyme or haiku.

**Simultaneous Subs:** yes

**Reading Period:** Year-round

**Reporting Time:** 1 to 4 weeks

**Author Payment:** none and copies

**Founded:** 1977

**Non Profit:** yes

**Paid Staff:** 3

**Unpaid Staff:** 0

**ISSN Number/ISBN Number:** 0197-4777/0-934830

**Total Circulation:** 100

**Paid Circulation:** 50

**Average Print Run:** 100

**Subscription Rate:** Individual $25/Institution $25

**Single Copy Price:** $2.50

**Current Volume/Issue:** 24/9

**Frequency per Year:** 11

**Backfile Available:** yes

**Unsolicited Ms. Received:** yes

**% of Unsolicited Ms. Published per Year:** 60%

**Format:** stapled

**Size:** H 4 1/4" W 7"

**Average Pages:** 32

**Ads:** no

## Wave Books

**Type:** press

**CLMP member:** yes

**Primary Editor/Contact Person:** Joshua Beckman

**Address:** 1938 Fairview Ave. E

Seattle, WA 98102

**Web Site Address:** http://www.wavepoetry.com, http://www.versepress.org

**Publishes:** poetry and translation

**Submissions Policy:** Unsolicited manuscripts and proposals accepted only in February. See website for guidelines.

**Simultaneous Subs:** yes

**Reading Period:** 2/1 to 2/28

**Reporting Time:** 2 to 6 months

**Author Payment:** royalties

**Founded:** 2000

**Non Profit:** no

**Paid Staff:** 4

**Unpaid Staff:** 3

**Distributors:** SPD, Consortium

**Number of Books Published per Year:** 9-12

**Titles in Print:** 26

**Average Print Run:** Varies
**Average Percentage Printed:** Paperback 100%
**Average Price:** $12

## Weber Studies

**Type:** magazine
**CLMP member:** yes
**Primary Editor/Contact Person:** Brad L. Roghaar
**Address:** Weber State University
1214 University Circle
Ogden, UT 84408-1214
**Web site Address:** http://weberstudies.weber.edu/
**Publishes:** essays, fiction, nonfiction, poetry, and art
**Editorial Focus:** We seek quality work that provides insight into the environment and culture (both broadly defined) of the contemporary West.
**Representative Authors:** David James Duncan, Robert Dana, and Kate Wheeler
**Submissions Policy:** Submit cover letter and 2 copies of each manuscript÷3-6 poems, essays and fiction should not exceed 5,000 words, include SASE.
**Simultaneous Subs:** yes
**Reading Period:** Year-round
**Reporting Time:** 3 to 4 months
**Author Payment:** cash, copies, and subscription
**Contests:** O. Marvin Lewis Essay Award; Sherwin W. Howard Poetry Award; Neila C. Seshachari Fiction Award each ($500) awarded annually.
See Web Site for Contest Guidelines.
**Founded:** 1984
**Non Profit:** yes
**Paid Staff:** 2
**Unpaid Staff:** 3
**ISSN Number/ISBN Number:** ISSN 0891-8899
**Total Circulation:** 1,000
**Paid Circulation:** 800
**Average Print Run:** 1,100
**Subscription Rate:** Individual $20/Institution $30
**Single Copy Price:** $8
**Current Volume/Issue:** 22/2
**Frequency per Year:** 3
**Backfile Available:** yes
**Unsolicited Ms. Received:** yes
**% of Unsolicited Ms. Published per Year:** 10%
**Format:** perfect
**Size:** H 10" W 7 1/2"
**Average Pages:** 144
**Ads:** no

## Wesleyan University Press

**Type:** press
**CLMP member:** no
**Primary Editor/Contact Person:** Suzanna Tamminen, Editor-in-Chief
**Address:** 215 Long Ln.
Middletown, CT 06459
**Web Site Address:**
http://www.wesleyan.edu/wespress
**Publishes:** nonfiction, poetry, and translation
**Editorial Focus:** Scholarly books in the areas of music, dance, science fiction studies, film/TV/media, and poetry.
**Representative Authors:** Heather McHugh, Ann Cooper Albright, and Christopher Small
**Submissions Policy:** Poetry and all academic areas: submit proposal (see specific guidelines on website).
**Simultaneous Subs:** yes
**Reading Period:** Year-round
**Reporting Time:** 2 to 6 months
**Author Payment:** royalties
**Founded:** 1959
**Non Profit:** yes
**Paid Staff:** 5
**Unpaid Staff:** 0
**Distributors:** University Press of New England
**Wholesalers:** Ingram, Koen, Baker & Taylor
**ISSN Number/ISBN Number:** ISBN 0-8195-
**Number of Books Published per Year:** 25-30
**Titles in Print:** 412
**Average Percentage Printed:** Hardcover 10%, Paperback 90%

## West Branch

**Type:** magazine
**CLMP member:** yes
**Primary Editor/Contact Person:** Andrew Ciotola
**Address:** Bucknell Hall
Bucknell University
Lewisburg, PA 17837
**Web Site Address:** http://www.bucknell.edu/west-branch
**Publishes:** essays, fiction, nonfiction, poetry, reviews, and translation
**Editorial Focus:** Eclectic mix of traditional and innovative with preference for work displaying a strong attention to craft.
**Representative Authors:** John Haines, Nance Van Winckel, and Charles Harper Webb
**Submissions Policy:** Manuscripts must be accompa-

nied by a self-addressed envelope with sufficient return postage; we cannot respond by e-mail or post-card. All manuscripts should be typed and paginated, with the author's name on each page. Prose must be double-spaced.
**Simultaneous Subs:** yes
**Reading Period:** 9/2 to 4/15
**Reporting Time:** 4 to 6 weeks
**Author Payment:** cash and copies
**Founded:** 1977
**Non Profit:** yes
**Paid Staff:** 3
**Unpaid Staff:** 2
**ISSN Number/ISBN Number:** ISSN 0149-6441
**Total Circulation:** 1,100
**Paid Circulation:** 700
**Subscription Rate:** Individual $10/Institution $16
**Single Copy Price:** $6
**Current Volume/Issue:** Issue 53
**Frequency per Year:** 2
**Backfile Available:** yes
**Unsolicited Ms. Received:** yes
**% of Unsolicited Ms. Published per Year:** 2%
**Format:** perfect
**Size:** H 9" W 6"
**Average Pages:** 160
**Ads:** yes
**Ad Rates:** Please inquire

# West End Press

**Type:** press
**CLMP member:** yes
**Primary Editor/Contact Person:** John Crawford
**Address:** P.O. Box 27334
Albuquerque, NM 87125
**Publishes:** fiction, nonfiction, poetry, art, and transla-tion
**Editorial Focus:** Progressive literature emphasizing "the political is personal" and asserting art can help transform reality. Includes drama.
**Representative Authors:** Meridel Le Sueur, Cherrie Moraga, and Sharon Doubiago
**Submissions Policy:** Send brief letter, samples of work, SASE.
**Simultaneous Subs:** no
**Reading Period:** Year-round
**Reporting Time:** 1 to 3 months
**Author Payment:** royalties and copies
**Founded:** 1976
**Non Profit:** no

**Paid Staff:** two
**Unpaid Staff:** no
**Distributors:** University of New Mexico Press, Small Press Dist.
**Wholesalers:** Ingram, Baker & Taylor, etc.
**ISSN Number/ISBN Number:** ISBN 0-931122, 0-9705344,
**Number of Books Published per Year:** 4
**Titles in Print:** 36
**Average Print Run:** 1,000
**Average Percentage Printed:** Paperback 100%
**Average Price:** $14.95

# Western Humanities Review

**Type:** magazine
**CLMP member:** yes
**Primary Editor/Contact Person:** Managing Editor
**Address:** 255. S. Central Campus Dr., RM 3500
University of Utah
Salt Lake City, UT 84112-0494
**Web Site Address:** http://www.hum.utah.edu
**Publishes:** essays, fiction, nonfiction, poetry, and translation
**Editorial Focus:** Literary fiction, nonfiction, and poet-ry; critical articles of impressive humanistic scholar-ship.
**Recent Awards Received:** Best Spiritual Writing, 2005 Pushcart Prize, 2005 Best American Essays 2004
**Representative Authors:** Billy Collins, Alyson Hagy, and Richard Howard
**Submissions Policy:** See website
**Simultaneous Subs:** yes
**Reading Period:** 9/1 to 5/1
**Reporting Time:** 1 to 6 months
**Author Payment:** cash and copies
**Contests:** Annual Utah Writers' Contest, for Utah resi-dents.
See Web Site for Contest Guidelines.
**Founded:** 1947
**Non Profit:** yes
**Paid Staff:** 1
**Unpaid Staff:** 6
**ISSN Number/ISBN Number:** ISSN 0043-3845
**Total Circulation:** 1,000
**Paid Circulation:** 900
**Average Print Run:** 1,100
**Subscription Rate:** Individual $16/Institution $24
**Single Copy Price:** $10
**Current Volume/Issue:** 59/2

**Frequency per Year:** 2
**Backfile Available:** yes
**Unsolicited Ms. Received:** yes
**% of Unsolicited Ms. Published per Year:** 5%
**Format:** perfect
**Size:** H 9" W 6"
**Average Pages:** 170
**Ads:** yes
**Ad Rates:** Exchange . . . we run very few.

# Whereabouts Press
**Type:** press
**CLMP member:** yes
**Primary Editor/Contact Person:** David Peattie
**Address:** 1111 8th St.
Berkeley, CA 94710
**Web Site Address:**
http://www.whereaboutspress.com
**Publishes:** fiction
**Editorial Focus:** Literature in translation through our Traveler's Literary Companion Series
**Submissions Policy:** Not currently accepting submissions.
**Simultaneous Subs:** yes
**Reading Period:** Year-round
**Reporting Time:** 3 to 6 weeks
**Author Payment:** royalties, cash, and copies
**Founded:** 1993
**Non Profit:** no
**Paid Staff:** 0
**Unpaid Staff:** 1
**Distributors:** Consortium
**Wholesalers:** Ingram
**Number of Books Published per Year:** 2
**Titles in Print:** 12
**Average Percentage Printed:** Paperback 100%
**Backfile Available:** yes

# Whetstone
**Type:** magazine
**CLMP member:** no
**Primary Editor/Contact Person:** Dale Griffith, Editor-in-Chief
**Address:** P.O. Box 1266
207 Park Ave.
Barrington, IL 60011/10
**Web Site Address:** N/A
**Publishes:** essays, fiction, nonfiction, and poetry
**Editorial Focus:** The editors look for stories/poetry with engaging voices, fresh treatment of language, character situations, imagery, metaphor

**Representative Authors:** Eva Marie Ginsburg, John Kilgore, and Virgil Suarez
**Submissions Policy:** Six poems or 5,500 words of prose, original, unpublished, accompanied by SASE, with instructions to return or recycle ms.
**Simultaneous Subs:** yes
**Reading Period:** Year-round
**Reporting Time:** 4 to 6 months
**Author Payment:** copies
**Contests:** Whetstone Prize, John Patrick McGrath Memorial Award, Georgiana MacArthur Hansen Poetry Prize, Founding Editor's Award
**Founded:** 1982
**Non Profit:** yes
**Paid Staff:** 0
**Unpaid Staff:** 12
**ISSN Number/ISBN Number:** 1055-8659
**Total Circulation:** 500
**Paid Circulation:** 1%
**Subscription Rate:** Individual $8.50/Institution $8.50
**Single Copy Price:** $7
**Current Volume/Issue:** 19
**Frequency per Year:** 1
**Backfile Available:** yes
**Unsolicited Ms. Received:** yes
**% of Unsolicited Ms. Published per Year:** 90%
**Format:** perfect
**Size:** H 9" W 6"
**Average Pages:** 120
**Ads:** no

# Whit Press
**Type:** press
**CLMP member:** yes
**Primary Editor/Contact Person:** Claudia Mauro
**Address:** 1634 Eleventh Ave.
1634 Eleventh Ave.
Seattle, WA 98122
**Web Site Address:** http://www.whitpress.org
**Publishes:** fiction, nonfiction, poetry, translation, and audio
**Editorial Focus:** Women, Writers of Color, Emerging Writers, Literary projects focusing on environmental and social justice
**Submissions Policy:** Please read the Whit Press Mission. If your project fits our mission, send a brief outline and four to ten sample pages.
**Simultaneous Subs:** no
**Reading Period:** Year-round
**Reporting Time:** 1 to 2 months

**Author Payment:** royalties and copies
**Founded:** 2001
**Non Profit:** yes
**Paid Staff:** 1
**Unpaid Staff:** 1
**Wholesalers:** Partners West, SPD, Baker & Taylor
**ISSN Number/ISBN Number:** ISBN 0-9720205
**Number of Books Published per Year:** 4
**Titles in Print:** 8
**Average Print Run:** 5,000
**Average Percentage Printed:** Paperback 90%, Other 10%
**Average Price:** $17

## White Pine Press

**Type:** press
**CLMP member:** yes
**Primary Editor/Contact Person:** Dennis Maloney
**Address:** P.O. Box 236
Buffalo, NY 14201
**Web Site Address:** http://www.whitepine.org
**Publishes:** essays, fiction, nonfiction, poetry, and translation
**Editorial Focus:** We are a not-for-profit literary publisher.
**Representative Authors:** Pablo Neruda, Marjorie Agosin, and Rene Char
**Submissions Policy:** American poetry only as part of our annual competition. Others, send query letter.
**Simultaneous Subs:** yes
**Reading Period:** Year-round
**Reporting Time:** 1 to 3 months
**Author Payment:** copies
**Contests:** See Web Site for Contest Guidelines.
**Founded:** 1973
**Non Profit:** yes
**Paid Staff:** 3
**Unpaid Staff:** 1
**Distributors:** Consortium
**ISSN Number/ISBN Number:** ISBN 1-893996
**Number of Books Published per Year:** 12
**Titles in Print:** 150
**Average Print Run:** 1,200
**Average Percentage Printed:** Hardcover 1%, Paperback 99%
**Average Price:** $15

## Wild Berries Press

**Type:** press

**CLMP member:** yes
**Primary Editor/Contact Person:** Utahna Faith
**Address:** 1000 Bourbon St., #219
New Orleans, LA 70116
**Web Site Address:** http://www.wildstrawberries.org
**Publishes:** fiction, poetry, and art
**Editorial Focus:** Literary flash fiction and prose poetry
**Representative Authors:** Andrei Codrescu, Olympia Vernon, and Tom Bradley
**Submissions Policy:** Submissions considered for Wild Strawberries: a journal of flash fiction and prose poetry; see wildstrawberries.org
**Simultaneous Subs:** yes
**Reading Period:** Year-round
**Reporting Time:** 1 to 4 months
**Author Payment:** cash, copies, and subscription
**Founded:** 2003
**Non Profit:** no
**Paid Staff:** 0
**Unpaid Staff:** 1
**ISSN Number/ISBN Number:** ISSN 1552-4493
**Number of Books Published per Year:** 2
**Titles in Print:** 3
**Average Percentage Printed:** Chapbook 100%

## Wild Strawberries

**Type:** magazine
**CLMP member:** yes
**Primary Editor/Contact Person:** Utahna Faith
**Address:** 1000 Bourbon St., #219
New Orleans, LA 70116
**Web Site Address:** http://www.wildstrawberries.org
**Publishes:** fiction and poetry
**Reading Period:** Year-round
**Reporting Time:** 1 to 2 months
**Author Payment:** none
**Founded:** 2003
**Non Profit:** yes
**Backfile Available:** yes

## Will Hall Books

**Type:** press
**CLMP member:** yes
**Primary Editor/Contact Person:** Rebecca Newth
**Address:** 611 Oliver Ave.
Fayetteville, AR 72701
**Web Site Address:** http://www.willhallbooks.com
**Publishes:** fiction and poetry
**Editorial Focus:** We look for something unusual in the

area of literary fiction and fine poetry.
**Representative Authors:** Mary Morrissey and Paul H. Williams
**Submissions Policy:** year-round
**Simultaneous Subs:** yes
**Reading Period:** Year-round
**Reporting Time:** 4 to 6 weeks
**Author Payment:** copies
**Founded:** 1994
**Non Profit:** yes
**Paid Staff:** 2
**Unpaid Staff:** 1
**Distributors:** amazon.com and our website
**ISSN Number/ISBN Number:** ISBN 09630310
**Number of Books Published per Year:** 1-2
**Titles in Print:** 14
**Average Print Run:** 1,000
**Average Percentage Printed:** Hardcover 2%, Paperback 38%, Chapbook 60%
**Average Price:** $15

# Willow Springs

**Type:** magazine
**CLMP member:** yes
**Primary Editor/Contact Person:** Sam Ligon
**Address:** 705 W. First Ave.
Spokane, WA 99201
**Web Site Address:** http://willowsprings.ewu.edu/
**Publishes:** essays, fiction, nonfiction, poetry, reviews, art, and translation
**Editorial Focus:** We publish poetry, short fiction, and nonfiction of literary merit.
**Representative Authors:** Alison Stine, Robert Gregory, and Gary Fincke
**Submissions Policy:** See Web site for full submissions policy.
**Simultaneous Subs:** yes
**Reading Period:** 9/15 to 5/15
**Reporting Time:** 3 to 6 months
**Author Payment:** none
**Contests:** Fiction and poetry contests opens in February. Send $10 per submission, up to six poems per entry.
See Web Site for Contest Guidelines.
**Founded:** 1977
**Non Profit:** yes
**Paid Staff:** 5
**Unpaid Staff:** 30
**Distributors:** Ingram, DeBoer
**ISSN Number/ISBN Number:** 0739-

1277/7477086570
**Total Circulation:** 1,100
**Paid Circulation:** 70
**Subscription Rate:** Individual $11.50/Institution $11.50
**Single Copy Price:** $6
**Current Volume/Issue:** Issue 54
**Frequency per Year:** 2
**Backfile Available:** yes
**Unsolicited Ms. Received:** yes
**% of Unsolicited Ms. Published per Year:** 3%
**Format:** perfect
**Size:** H 8 3/4" W 6"
**Average Pages:** 144
**Ads:** yes
**Ad Rates:** Exchange only

# Wind: A Journal of Writing & Community

**Type:** magazine
**CLMP member:** no
**Primary Editor/Contact Person:** Rebecca Howell
**Address:** P.O. Box 24548
Lexington, KY 40524
**Publishes:** essays, fiction, nonfiction, poetry, reviews, and art
**Editorial Focus:** We operate on the metaphor of neighborly conversation between writers about the differing worlds in which they live.
**Representative Authors:** Wendell Berry, Yael Flusberg, and Ann Fisher-Wirth
**Submissions Policy:** Unsolicited and simultaneous submissions are accepted year-round. For guidelines, write or visit website: wind.wind.org
**Simultaneous Subs:** yes
**Reading Period:** Year-round
**Reporting Time:** 3 to 6 months
**Author Payment:** none, cash, and copies
**Contests:** The Joy Bale Boone Poetry Prize; The James Still Fiction Prize; The Quentin R. Howard Poetry Chapbook Prize
See Web Site for Contest Guidelines.
**Founded:** 1971
**Non Profit:** yes
**Paid Staff:** no
**Unpaid Staff:** yes
**ISSN Number/ISBN Number:** ISSN 0361-2481
**Total Circulation:** 1,000
**Paid Circulation:** 500
**Subscription Rate:** Individual $21/Institution $25

**Single Copy Price:** $9
**Current Volume/Issue:** Issue 91
**Frequency per Year:** 3
**Backfile Available:** yes
**Unsolicited Ms. Received:** yes
**% of Unsolicited Ms. Published per Year:** 1-2%
**Format:** perfect
**Size:** H 9" W 6"
**Average Pages:** 120
**Ads:** yes
**Ad Rates:** $100 for full page; $50 for half

## Windhover: A Journal of Christian Literature

**Type:** magazine
**CLMP member:** yes
**Primary Editor/Contact Person:** Audell Shelburne
**Address:** UMHB Box 8008
900 College St.
Belton, TX 76513
**Publishes:** essays, fiction, nonfiction, poetry, reviews, and art
**Editorial Focus:** Windhover is devoted to promoting good writers and quality literary efforts with a Christian perspective.
**Representative Authors:** Walt McDonald, Greg Garrett, and Marie (Giardano) Jordan
**Submissions Policy:** Subs regular mail only (not e-mail), max 3,500 words or 4 poems. May 15th deadline for next issue.
**Simultaneous Subs:** yes
**Reading Period:** Year-round
**Reporting Time:** 3 to 4 months
**Author Payment:** copies
**Founded:** 1996
**Non Profit:** yes
**Paid Staff:** 2
**Unpaid Staff:** 6
**Distributors:** University of Mary Hardin-Baylor
**Total Circulation:** 450
**Paid Circulation:** 350
**Average Print Run:** 500
**Subscription Rate:** Individual $15/Institution $15
**Single Copy Price:** $15
**Current Volume/Issue:** 10/1
**Frequency per Year:** 1
**Backfile Available:** yes
**Unsolicited Ms. Received:** yes
**% of Unsolicited Ms. Published per Year:** 10%
**Format:** perfect

**Size:** H 9" W 6"
**Average Pages:** 220
**Ads:** no

## Wings Press

**Type:** press
**CLMP member:** no
**Primary Editor/Contact Person:** Bryce Milligan
**Address:** 627 E. Guenther
San Antonio, TX 78210
**Web Site Address:** http://www.wingspress.com
**Publishes:** fiction, nonfiction, and poetry
**Editorial Focus:** Well crafted, intelligent, liberal-minded multicultural fiction and poetry.
**Representative Authors:** John Howard Griffin, Cecile Pineda, and Carmen Tafolla
**Submissions Policy:** We seldom accept open subs, and never from poets who do not read poetry. Send a bio and we will consider asking for a ms.
**Simultaneous Subs:** yes
**Reading Period:** Year-round
**Reporting Time:** 1 to 3 months
**Author Payment:** royalties
**Contests:** See Web Site for Contest Guidelines.
**Founded:** 1975
**Non Profit:** no
**Paid Staff:** 1
**Unpaid Staff:** 2
**Distributors:** Small Press Dist., Ingram, Baker & Taylor, Brodart
**ISSN Number/ISBN Number:** ISBN 0-930324- and 0-916727
**Number of Books Published per Year:** 10
**Titles in Print:** 56
**Average Percentage Printed:** Hardcover 20%, Paperback 70%, Chapbook 5%, Other 5%

# Witness

**Type:** magazine
**CLMP member:** no
**Primary Editor/Contact Person:** Peter Stine
**Address:** Oakland Community College
27055 Orchard Lake Road
Farmington Hills, MI 48334
**Web Site Address:** http://www.oaklandcc/witness
**Publishes:** essays, fiction, nonfiction, and poetry
**Editorial Focus:** Witness will now publish one special
issue per year on an announced theme.
**Representative Authors:** Joyce Carol Oates, Ron
Carlson, and Bob Hicok
**Submissions Policy:** send for guidelines
**Simultaneous Subs:** yes
**Reading Period:** Year-round
**Reporting Time:** 1 to 3 months
**Author Payment:** none, cash, and copies
**Founded:** 1987
**Non Profit:** yes
**Paid Staff:** 1
**Unpaid Staff:** 1
**Distributors:** Ingram, Ubiquity, DeBoer, Armadillo
**ISSN Number/ISBN Number:** 0891-1371/0891-1371
**Total Circulation:** 3,000
**Paid Circulation:** 800
**Subscription Rate:** Individual $10/Institution $18
**Single Copy Price:** $12
**Current Volume/Issue:** 19/11
**Frequency per Year:** 1
**Backfile Available:** yes
**Unsolicited Ms. Received:** yes
**% of Unsolicited Ms. Published per Year:** 5%
**Format:** perfect
**Size:** H 9" W 6"
**Average Pages:** 212
**Ads:** yes
**Ad Rates:** $100 pages

# Woman Poet

**Type:** magazine
**CLMP member:** yes
**Primary Editor/Contact Person:** Elaine Dallman
**Address:** 601 Van Ness Ave., Nr. 6
San Francisco, CA 94102
**Publishes:** poetry
**Editorial Focus:** Contemporary Poetry
**Simultaneous Subs:** yes
**Reading Period:** Year-round

**Reporting Time:** 1 to 2 months
**Author Payment:** none
**Founded:** 1978
**Non Profit:** yes
**Paid Staff:** 0
**Unpaid Staff:** 2
**Total Circulation:** 800
**Paid Circulation:** 60
**Average Print Run:** 500
**Subscription Rate:** Individual $16/Institution $16
**Single Copy Price:** $16
**Current Volume/Issue:** Issue 28
**Frequency per Year:** 1
**Backfile Available:** yes
**Unsolicited Ms. Received:** no
**Format:** perfect
**Average Pages:** 60
**Ad Rates:** none

# Women-in Literature

**Type:** press
**CLMP member:** yes
**Primary Editor/Contact Person:** Elaine Dallman,
Ph.D.
**Address:** 601 Vanness Ave. #6
San Francisco, CA 94102
**Publishes:** poetry
**Editorial Focus:** Poetry that is fine literature, from
established or new-to-the-field poets.
**Representative Authors:** Marilyn Hacker, Lisel
Mueller, and Marie Ponsot
**Submissions Policy:** Check with Poets and Writers.
When we are collecting we list there.
**Simultaneous Subs:** yes
**Reading Period:** Year-round
**Reporting Time:** 1 to 2 weeks
**Author Payment:** copies
**Founded:** 1970
**Non Profit:** yes
**Paid Staff:** 0
**Unpaid Staff:** 3
**ISSN Number/ISBN Number:** ISBN 0-910221
**Number of Books Published per Year:** 1
**Titles in Print:** 4
**Average Percentage Printed:** Hardcover 25%,
Paperback 75%

# The Worcester Review

**Type:** magazine

**CLMP member:** yes
**Primary Editor/Contact Person:** Rodger Martin
**Address:** 6 Chatham St.
Worcester, MA 01609
**Web Site Address:**
http://www.geocities.com/Paris/LeftBank/6433
**Publishes:** essays, fiction, poetry, art, and translation
**Editorial Focus:** Essays and features with a Central New England (particularly Worcester literary history) focus, poetry and fiction open
**Representative Authors:** Marge Piercy, Yusef Komunyakaa, and Jim Daniels
**Submissions Policy:** 3 poems, one short story or critical essay with a New England connection,
**Simultaneous Subs:** yes
**Reading Period:** Year-round
**Reporting Time:** 6 to 9 months
**Author Payment:** copies and subscription
**Contests:** Annual Worcester County Poetry Assoc. contest, see http://www.wcpa.homestead.org for guidelines
**Founded:** 1973
**Non Profit:** yes
**Paid Staff:** 0
**Unpaid Staff:** 12
**ISSN Number/ISBN Number:** ISSN 11607681
**Total Circulation:** 750-1m
**Paid Circulation:** 225
**Subscription Rate:** Individual $25/Institution $25
**Single Copy Price:** $12
**Current Volume/Issue:** XXII/2
**Frequency per Year:** 1
**Backfile Available:** yes
**Unsolicited Ms. Received:** yes
**% of Unsolicited Ms. Published per Year:** 3%
**Format:** perfect
**Size:** H 9" W 69"
**Average Pages:** 128
**Ads:** yes
**Ad Rates:** generally only inside front and back covers, $375
See Web Site for Details.

## Word Riot Press

**Type:** press
**CLMP member:** yes
**Primary Editor/Contact Person:** Jackie Corley
**Address:** P.O. Box 414
Middletown, NJ 07748
**Web Site Address:** http://www.wordriot.org/press

**Publishes:** fiction, nonfiction, and poetry
**Editorial Focus:** We are dedicated to the forceful voices of up-and-coming writers and poets.
**Representative Authors:** David Barringer, Stephen Oliver, and Ryan Robert Mullen
**Submissions Policy:** See our website:
http://www.wordriot.org/press
**Simultaneous Subs:** yes
**Reading Period:** Year-round
**Reporting Time:** 2 to 3 months
**Author Payment:** royalties and copies
**Founded:** 2003
**Non Profit:** yes
**Paid Staff:** 1
**Unpaid Staff:** 1
**Number of Books Published per Year:** 6
**Titles in Print:** 8
**Average Percentage Printed:** Paperback 50%, Chapbook 50%

## Word Riot

**Type:** online
**CLMP member:** yes
**Primary Editor/Contact Person:** Jackie Corley
**Address:** 114 Four Winds Dr.
Middletown, NJ 07748
**Web Site Address:** http://www.wordriot.org
**Publishes:** essays, fiction, nonfiction, poetry, and reviews
**Editorial Focus:** We encourage the forceful voices of up-and-coming writers and poets.
**Representative Authors:** Steve Almond, David Barringer, and Pia Z. Ehrhardt
**Submissions Policy:** See our submissions page:
http://www.wordriot.orgsubmissions/
**Simultaneous Subs:** yes
**Reading Period:** Year-round
**Reporting Time:** 4 to 6 weeks
**Author Payment:** none
**Contests:** See Web Site for Contest Guidelines.
**Founded:** 2002
**Non Profit:** yes
**Paid Staff:** 0
**Unpaid Staff:** 8
**Backfile Available:** yes
**Average Page Views per Month:** 2,700
**Average Unique Visitors per Month:** 1,800
**Frequency per Year:** 12
**Publish Print Anthology:** yes
**Price:** $10 (for anthology)

**Average Percentage of Pages per Category:** Fiction 60%, Nonfiction 15%, Poetry 20%, Reviews 5%
**Ad Rates:** See Web Site for Details.

## Word Smitten

**Type:** online
**CLMP member:** no
**Primary Editor/Contact Person:** Kate Sullivan
**Address:** 3115 Beach Blvd., Editorial Office
P.O. Box 5067
St. Petersburg, FL 33737-5067
**Web Site Address:** http://www.wordsmitten.com
**Publishes:** fiction, nonfiction, reviews, and art
**Editorial Focus:** Word Smitten's award-winning online and print publications seek to inform writers about the business of book publishing.
**Representative Authors:** Noy Holland, Louise Domaratius, and John Ravenscroft
**Submissions Policy:** E-mail first with one-page query. Accepting flash fiction (fewer than 500 words) and short fiction (fewer than 4,000 words).
**Simultaneous Subs:** no
**Reading Period:** Year-round
**Reporting Time:** 2 to 4 months
**Author Payment:** cash
**Contests:** Word Smitten sponsors two fiction contests (invited judges), Storycove Flash Fiction (May 1) and the Ten-Ten Award (July 1).
See Web Site for Contest Guidelines.
**Founded:** 1999
**Non Profit:** no
**Paid Staff:** 7
**Unpaid Staff:** 5
**Average Page Views per Month:** 38,000
**Average Unique Visitors per Month:** 30,000
**Frequency per Year:** 12
**Publish Print Anthology:** yes
Price: $11
**Average Percentage of Pages per Category:** Fiction 25%, Nonfiction 25%, Reviews 25%, Essays 10%, Art 15%
**Ad Rates:** See Web Site for Details.

## Word: Toronto's Literary Calendar

**Type:** magazine
**CLMP member:** no
**Primary Editor/Contact Person:** Beverley Daurio
**Address:** 22 Prince Rupert Ave.
Toronto, ON M6P 2A7

**Web Site Address:**
http://www.themercurypress.ca/word
**Publishes:** essays, fiction, nonfiction, poetry, reviews, and art
**Editorial Focus:** Word is a monthly literary newspaper that features reviews, columns, and Toronto event listings.
**Representative Authors:** Stuart Ross, Maggie Helwig, and Bill Kennedy
**Submissions Policy:** Reviews? Letters? Contact our editor about possible publication at wordeditor@themercurypress.ca.
**Simultaneous Subs:** yes
**Reading Period:** Year-round
**Reporting Time:** 4 to 6 weeks
**Author Payment:** copies
**Founded:** 1995
**Non Profit:** yes
**Paid Staff:** 1
**Unpaid Staff:** 3
**Distributors:** The Mercury Press
**Total Circulation:** 5,000
**Paid Circulation:** 200
**Subscription Rate:** Individual $18/Institution $18
**Single Copy Price:** free
**Current Volume/Issue:** 10/9
**Frequency per Year:** 9
**Backfile Available:** yes
**Unsolicited Ms. Received:** no
**Format:** Newspaper
**Size:** H 17" W 11"
**Average Pages:** 8
**Ads:** yes
**Ad Rates:** See Web Site for Details.

## Words Without Borders

**Type:** online
**CLMP member:** yes
**Primary Editor/Contact Person:** Blake Radcliffe
**Address:** c/o Center for Literary Translation
Columbia Univ., 415 Dodge Hall
New York, NY 10027
**Web Site Address:** http://www.wordswithoutborders.org
**Publishes:** essays, fiction, poetry, translation, and audio
**Editorial Focus:** A sampling of the world's best contemporary writing translated into English.
**Representative Authors:** MuXin, Najem Wali, and Witold Gombrowicz

**Submissions Policy:** Stories, excerpts of novels, poetry and literary nonfiction rooted in a sense of place; submission of translation preferred
**Simultaneous Subs:** yes
**Reading Period:** Year-round
**Reporting Time:** 5 to 6 months
**Author Payment:** none and cash
**Founded:** 2002
**Non Profit:** yes
**Paid Staff:** 3
**Unpaid Staff:** 4
**Average Page Views per Month:** 50,000
**Frequency per Year:** 12
**Publish Print Anthology:** yes
Price: $0
**Average Percentage of Pages per Category:**
Translation 100%
**Ad Rates:** upon request
See Web Site for Details.

# WordWrights Magazine

**Type:** magazine
**CLMP member:** no
**Primary Editor/Contact Person:** R.D. Baker
**Address:** 1620 Argonne Place NW
Washington, DC 20009
**Web Site Address:** http://www.wordwrights.com
**Publishes:** fiction and poetry
**Editorial Focus:** New and established poets and writers.
**Representative Authors:** David Franks, Rose Solari, and Grace Cavalieri
**Submissions Policy:** Open.
**Simultaneous Subs:** yes
**Reading Period:** Year-round
**Reporting Time:** 3 to 6 months
**Author Payment:** cash
**Founded:** 1995
**Non Profit:** no
**Paid Staff:** 0
**Unpaid Staff:** 25
**Distributors:** Argonne House Press
**Wholesalers:** Argonne House Press
**Total Circulation:** 1,000
**Paid Circulation:** 500
**Subscription Rate:** Individual $25/Institution $50
**Single Copy Price:** $5.95
**Current Volume/Issue:** Issue 30
**Frequency per Year:** 4
**Backfile Available:** yes

**Unsolicited Ms. Received:** yes
**% of Unsolicited Ms. Published per Year:** 10%
**Format:** stapled
**Size:** H 11" W 8.5"
**Average Pages:** 40
**Ads:** no

# Writecorner Press

**Type:** press
**CLMP member:** yes
**Primary Editor/Contact Person:** Mary Sue Koeppel
**Address:** P.O. Box 16369
Jacksonville, FL 32245
**Web Site Address:** http://www.writecorner.com
**Publishes:** fiction, nonfiction, and reviews
**Editorial Focus:** Writecorner Press is a companion to http://www.writecorner.com Publishes winning contest fiction and notable fiction and nonfiction
**Representative Authors:** Gregg Cusick, Sandra Bestland, and Martine Fournier
**Submissions Policy:** Interested in short fiction, memoirs, and essays under 3,000 words. Send fiction and nonfiction books to be reviewed.
**Simultaneous Subs:** yes
**Reading Period:** Year-round
**Reporting Time:** 1 to 2 months
**Author Payment:** copies
**Contests:** $1,100 E.M. Koeppel Short Fiction Annual Award. $100 Editors' Choice Award. $500 Scholarship. 3,000 words maximum.
See Web Site for Contest Guidelines.
**Founded:** 2002
**Non Profit:** yes
**Paid Staff:** 0
**Unpaid Staff:** 2
**Number of Books Published per Year:** 2
**Titles in Print:** 0
**Average Percentage Printed:** Paperback 95%, Chapbook 2%, Other 3%
**Backfile Available:** yes

# Writers Against War

**Type:** online
**CLMP member:** yes
**Primary Editor/Contact Person:** Jo-Ann Moss
**Address:** P. O. Box 28
West Linn, OR 97068
**Web Site Address:** http://writersagainstwar.com
**Publishes:** essays, fiction, nonfiction, poetry, and art

**Editorial Focus:** Creative and humanitarian expression against the use of war as conflict resolution, with anti-war and peace-themed work
**Representative Authors:** Robert Rabbin, Karen Ethelsdattar, and Rodrigue Tremblay
**Submissions Policy:** Please go to: http://writersagainstwar.com/submissions.html
**Simultaneous Subs:** yes
**Reading Period:** Year-round
**Reporting Time:** 1 to 2 months
**Author Payment:** none
**Founded:** 2004
**Non Profit:** yes
**Paid Staff:** 0
**Unpaid Staff:** 1
**Backfile Available:** yes
**Average Page Views per Month:** 1,000
**Average Unique Visitors per Month:** 1,000
**Frequency per Year:** 4
**Publish Print Anthology:** no
**Average Percentage of Pages per Category:** Fiction 10%, Nonfiction 25%, Poetry 30%, Essays 25%, Art 10%
**Ads:** no

## The Xavier Review

**Type:** magazine
**CLMP member:** no
**Primary Editor/Contact Person:** Dr. Richard Collins
**Address:** P. O. Box 110, Xavier University of LA
1 Drexel Dr.
New Orleans, LA 70125-1098
**Publishes:** essays, fiction, nonfiction, poetry, and reviews
**Editorial Focus:** Creative writing fm diverse cultures, including African-American, US South, Gulf/Caribbean basin
**Representative Authors:** Andre Codrescu, Catherine Savage Brosman, and Nachita Danilov
**Submissions Policy:** Print ms. using MLA style manual, accomp. diskette in ASCII, MS-DOS, or Mac, SASE. Fiction 8-12 pages, nonfiction 12-18 pages.
**Simultaneous Subs:** no
**Reading Period:** 9/5 to 1/31
**Reporting Time:** 4 to 8 weeks
**Author Payment:** copies
**Founded:** 1980
**Non Profit:** yes
**Paid Staff:** 0
**Unpaid Staff:** 5

**Distributors:** EBSCO
**ISSN Number/ISBN Number:** 0887-6681
**Total Circulation:** 100
**Paid Circulation:** 50
**Subscription Rate:** Individual $10/Institution $15
**Single Copy Price:** $5
**Current Volume/Issue:** 23/1
**Frequency per Year:** 2
**Backfile Available:** yes
**Unsolicited Ms. Received:** yes
**% of Unsolicited Ms. Published per Year:** 100%
**Format:** perfect
**Size:** H 9" W 6"
**Average Pages:** 95
**Ads:** yes
**Ad Rates:** $75/page, $35/half page

## XConnect Print Volumes & Web Issues

**Type:** magazine
**CLMP member:** no
**Primary Editor/Contact Person:** David E. Deifer
**Address:** P.O. Box 2317
Philadelphia, PA 19103
**Web Site Address:** http://xconnect.org
**Publishes:** essays, fiction, nonfiction, poetry, and art
**Editorial Focus:** Publishes a vast expanse of disciplines, from experimental to works well rooted in academia, tendency toward new writers . . .
**Representative Authors:** Gregory Djanikian, Tom Devaney, and Nicholas Montemarano
**Submissions Policy:** Send up to 10 poems or two stories including SASE and bio including address, phone number and e-mail if available.
**Simultaneous Subs:** no
**Reading Period:** Year-round
**Reporting Time:** 2 to 8 weeks
**Author Payment:** cash and copies
**Founded:** 1995
**Non Profit:** yes
**Paid Staff:** 2
**Unpaid Staff:** 6
**Distributors:** Ingram, DeBoer, SPD
**ISSN Number/ISBN Number:** 1087-0474/0-9651450-6-9
**Total Circulation:** 900
**Paid Circulation:** none
**Average Print Run:** 1,100
**Single Copy Price:** $12
**Current Volume/Issue:** V111/23

**Frequency per Year:** 2
**Backfile Available:** yes
**Unsolicited Ms. Received:** yes
**% of Unsolicited Ms. Published per Year:** 3%
**Format:** perfect
**Size:** H 8.5" W 5.5"
**Average Pages:** 200
**Ads:** no

## The Yalobusha Review

**Type:** magazine
**CLMP member:** yes
**Primary Editor/Contact Person:** Neal Walsh
**Address:** English Dept., University of Mississippi
P.O. Box 1848
University, MS 38677-1848
**Web Site Address:**
http://www.olemiss.edu/yalobusha
**Publishes:** essays, fiction, nonfiction, poetry, art, and translation
**Editorial Focus:** We seek quality work from any and all genres.
**Representative Authors:** Dan Chaon, George Singleton, and Charles Wright
**Submissions Policy:** Send disposable copy of manuscript w/cover letter and SASE for response to above address. See website for full guidelines.
**Simultaneous Subs:** no
**Reading Period:** 7/15 to 11/15
**Reporting Time:** 1 to 3 months
**Author Payment:** cash and copies
**Contests:** See Web Site for Contest Guidelines.
**Founded:** 1995
**Non Profit:** no
**Paid Staff:** 1
**Unpaid Staff:** 4
**Total Circulation:** 1,000
**Average Print Run:** 500
**Subscription Rate:** Individual $8/Institution $8
**Single Copy Price:** $10
**Current Volume/Issue:** X/2005
**Frequency per Year:** 1
**Backfile Available:** yes
**Unsolicited Ms. Received:** yes
**% of Unsolicited Ms. Published per Year:** 5%
**Format:** perfect
**Size:** H 10" W 7"
**Average Pages:** 125
**Ads:** yes
**Ad Rates:** Free Exchange

See Web Site for Details.

## Zephyr Press/Adventures in Poetry

**Type:** press
**CLMP member:** yes
**Primary Editor/Contact Person:** Christopher Mattison
**Address:** 50 Kenwood St.
Brookline, MA 02446
**Web Site Address:** http://www.zephyrpress.org
**Publishes:** essays, fiction, nonfiction, poetry, and translation
**Representative Authors:** Charles North, Hsia Yu, and Anatoly Naiman
**Simultaneous Subs:** yes
**Reading Period:** Year-round
**Reporting Time:** 1 to 3 months
**Author Payment:** royalties, cash, and copies
**Founded:** 1980
**Non Profit:** yes
**Paid Staff:** 2
**Unpaid Staff:** 2
**Distributors:** Consortium and SPD
**ISSN Number/ISBN Number:** ISBN 0939010
**Number of Books Published per Year:** 6
**Titles in Print:** 50
**Average Print Run:** 1,500
**Average Percentage Printed:** Paperback 100%
**Average Price:** $14

## zingmagazine

**Type:** magazine
**CLMP member:** yes
**Address:** 83 Grand St.
New York, NY 10013
**Web Site Address:** http://www.zingmagazine.com/
**Publishes:** essays, fiction, nonfiction, poetry, and audio
**Reading Period:** Year-round
**Reporting Time:** 1 to 2 months
**Author Payment:** none
**Founded:** 1995
**Non Profit:** no

## Zoetrope: All-Story

**Type:** magazine
**CLMP member:** no
**Primary Editor/Contact Person:** Tamara Straus, Editor in Chief

**Address:** 916 Kearny St.
San Francisco, CA 94133
**Web Site Address:** http://all-story.com/
**Publishes:** essays, fiction, art, and translation
**Editorial Focus:** Classic short fiction with purpose, compelling ideas, and intelligent prose.
**Representative Authors:** Susan Straight, A.M. Homes, and Adam Haslett
**Submissions Policy:** Stories and one-act plays under 7,000 words accompanied by SASE. First serial rights required.
**Simultaneous Subs:** yes
**Reading Period:** Year-round
**Reporting Time:** 1 to 5 months
**Author Payment:** cash, copies, and subscription
**Contests:** See Web Site for Contest Guidelines.
**Founded:** 1997
**Non Profit:** no
**Paid Staff:** 4
**Unpaid Staff:** 25
**Distributors:** Ingram, Small Changes, OneSource, IPD, Kent, Total
**ISSN Number/ISBN Number:** ISSN 1091-2495
**Total Circulation:** 20,000
**Paid Circulation:** 10,000
**Subscription Rate:** Individual $19.95/Institution $19.95
**Single Copy Price:** $6.95
**Current Volume/Issue:** 8/3
**Frequency per Year:** 4
**Backfile Available:** yes
**Unsolicited Ms. Received:** yes
**% of Unsolicited Ms. Published per Year:** 50%
**Format:** perfect
**Size:** H 10.75" W 8.25"
**Average Pages:** 128
**Ads:** yes
**Ad Rates:** See Web Site for Details.

# Zone 3

**Type:** magazine
**CLMP member:** yes
**Address:** P. O. Box 4265
APSU
Clarkesville, TN 37044
**Web Site Address:** http://www.apsu.edu/zone3
**Publishes:** fiction and poetry
**Reading Period:** Year-round
**Reporting Time:** 1 to 2 months
**Author Payment:** none

**Founded:** 1986
**Non Profit:** no
**Backfile Available:** yes

# Zoo Press

**Type:** press
**CLMP member:** no
**Primary Editor/Contact Person:** Caitlin Phelps
**Address:** P. O. Box 3528
Omaha, NE 68103
**Web Site Address:** http://www.zoopress.org
**Publishes:** poetry
**Editorial Focus:** Contemporary Literature/Popular Music
**Representative Authors:** Rachel Hadas, Eric Ormsby, and Jeff Tweedy
**Submissions Policy:** Please visit our website at zoo-press.org for our submission guidelines.
**Simultaneous Subs:** yes
**Reading Period:** 7/1 to 7/31
**Reporting Time:** 3 to 6 months
**Author Payment:** royalties
**Contests:** Paris Review Prize in Poetry, Kenyon Review Prize in Poetry
See Web Site for Contest Guidelines.
**Founded:** 2000
**Non Profit:** yes
**Paid Staff:** 5
**Unpaid Staff:** 5
**Distributors:** University of Nebraska Press
**ISSN Number/ISBN Number:** ISBN 1932023
**Number of Books Published per Year:** 15
**Titles in Print:** 20
**Average Percentage Printed:** Paperback 100%

# Zora Magazine

**Type:** magazine
**CLMP member:** yes
**Address:** P.O. Box 588
Raleigh, NC 27606
**Web Site Address:** http://www.zoramagazine.com
**Publishes:** essays, fiction, nonfiction, poetry, and art
**Reading Period:** Year-round
**Reporting Time:** 1 to 2 months
**Author Payment:** none
**Non Profit:** yes
**Backfile Available:** yes

# ZYZZYVA

**Type:** magazine
**CLMP member:** no
**Primary Editor/Contact Person:** Howard Junker
**Address:** P.O. Box 590069
San Francisco, CA 94159-0069
**Web Site Address:** http://www.zyzzyva.org
**Publishes:** essays, fiction, nonfiction, and poetry
**Editorial Focus:** West Coast writers
**Representative Authors:** Margaret Weatherfor, Susan Parker, and Katherine Karlin
**Submissions Policy:** We publish writers who are currently living on the West Coast (CA, OR, WA, AK, HI).
**Simultaneous Subs:** no
**Reading Period:** Year-round
**Reporting Time:** 2 to 6 weeks
**Author Payment:** cash and copies
**Founded:** 1985
**Non Profit:** yes
**Paid Staff:** 2
**Unpaid Staff:** 1
**Distributors:** Armadillo, Ingram, Small Changes, Ubiquity
**ISSN Number/ISBN Number:** ISSN 8756-5633
**Total Circulation:** 2,500
**Paid Circulation:** 1,600
**Average Print Run:** 3,500
**Subscription Rate:** Individual $24/Institution $44
**Single Copy Price:** $11
**Current Volume/Issue:** XXI/2
**Frequency per Year:** 3
**Backfile Available:** yes
**Unsolicited Ms. Received:** yes
**% of Unsolicited Ms. Published per Year:** 1%
**Format:** perfect
**Size:** H 9" W 6"
**Average Pages:** 192
**Ads:** yes
**Ad Rates:** See Web Site for Details.

# Indices

## Alabama

## Alaska

## Arkansas

## Arizona

## California

Another Chicago Magazine/Left Field Press 12
Blithe House Quarterly 36
Chicago Review 54
Common Review 61
CONTEXT 64
Contrary 64
Crab Orchard Review 67
Dalkey Archive Press 71
Electronic Book Review 80
Euphony 83
Hourglass Books 118
Journal of Ordinary Thought 129
Karamu 123
Light Quarterly 141
Mandorla: New Writing from the Americas 154
Midnight Mind Magazine 163
Newtopia Magazine 175
Ninth Letter 177
Other Voices 188
The Pikestaff Press 199
Poetry 206
Review of Contemporary Fiction 224
RHINO 225
The Spoon River Poetry Review 249
StoryQuarterly 251
TriQuarterly 268
Verbatim: The Language Quarterly 275
Whetstone 283

## Indiana
Bristol Banner Books 45
First Class 91
Indiana Review 123
insolent rudder 125
Jane's Stories Press Foundation 128
Nanny Fanny Poetry Magazine 169
The Notre Dame Review 182
Pathwise Press 194
Southern Indiana Review 245
Sycamore Review 256

## Kansas
Cottonwood Magazine and Press 66
First Intensity 91
Parakeet 191
Poetry Midwest 206

## Kentucky
Finishing Line Press 90
Georgetown Review 100
The Licking River Review 141

The Louisville Review/Fleur-de-Lis Press 148
Sarabande Books 232
Wind: A Journal of Writing & Community 285

## Louisiana
Bayou 25
Louisiana Literature 148
New Delta Review 171
Portals Press 209
Rive Gauche 225
The Southern Review 246
THEMA Literary Society 262
Wild Berries Press 284
Wild Strawberries 284
The Xavier Review 291

## Maine
Alice James Books 8
Beloit Poetry Journal 28
Century Press 52
Dan River Press 71
NorthWoods Journal 181
Northwoods Press 182
Tilbury House, Publishers 264

## Maryland
32 Poems 1
Baltimore Review 23
Etruscan Press 83
Feminist Studies 87
IBEX Publishers 120
Passager 193
Poet Lore 204
Potomac Review 210
Washington Writers' Publishing House 279

## Massachusetts
AGNI 7
ArtsEditor 17
Beacon Press 26
Boston Review 42
Coelacanth Magazine 58
Diner 74
Faux Press 86
Full Circle Journal 98
Harvard Review 111
jubilat 130
The Long Story 147
Massachusetts Review 158
Memorius: A Forum for New Verse and Poetics 161
Night Train Publications/Night Train 176

## North Carolina

& Journal for the Arts 1
2River 1
32 Poems 1
3rd bed 2
580 Split 2
6x6 3
88: A Journal of Contemporary American Poetry 3
A Gathering of Tribes 3
Absinthe Literary Review 4
Absinthe: New European Writing 4
Accent Miami 5
African American Review 6
African Heritage Press 6
African Voices Communications 6
AGNI 7
Ahsahta Press 7
Akashic Books 8
Alaska Quarterly Review 8
Alice James Books 8
All Info-About Poetry 9
Alligator Juniper 9
American Book Review 10
American Letters & Commentary 10
American Poetry Review 11
American Short Fiction 11
Anderbo.com 12
Anhinga Press 12
Antioch Review 12
Apalachee Review 13
Apogee Press 14
Archipelago 14
Archipelago Books 14
Arctoss Press 14
Argonne House Press 15
Arkansas Review: A Journal of Delta Studies 15
Arsenal Pulp Press 15
Arte Público Press 16
Artful Dodge 16
ArtsEditor 17
Ascent 17
Asian American Writers' Workshop 19
Atlanta Review 19
Atomic Quill Press 20
Aufgabe 20
Ausable Press 21
Backwards City Review 22
Backwaters Press 22
Ballyhoo Stories 22
Baltimore Review 23
Bamboo Ridge 23
Barrelhouse Journal 24

Barrow Street 24
Bayou 25
Bear Star Press 27
Belladonna* 27
Bellevue Literary Review 28
Bellingham Review 28
Beloit Poetry Journal 28
Berkeley Fiction Review 29
Best of Carve Magazine 30
Bilingual Review 31
Bilingual Review Press 31
Bitter Oleander 31
Bitter Oleander Press 34
BkMk Press 34
Black Clock 34
Black Issues Book Review 35
Black Lawrence Press 35
Black Square Editions/Hammer Books 35
Black Warrior Review 36
Blackbird: an online journal of literature and arts 36
Blithe House Quarterly 36
Blood & Thunder 37
Blood Moon Productions 37
Bloom: Queer Fiction, Art, Poetry & More 37
Blue Collar Review 38
Blue Mesa Review 38
Blueline 39
BOA Editions, Ltd. 39
Bogg 40
BOMB Magazine 40
Book/Mark Small Press Quarterly Review 40
Boston Review 42
Branches Quarterly 42
Briar Cliff Review 43
Bright Hill Press 44
Broken Pencil 45
Brook Street Press 45
Bullfight Media 45
Cabinet 46
Cafe Irreal 47
Callaloo 48
Calyx, a Journal of Art and Lit by Women 48
Canary 49
Caribbean Writer 50
Carolina Quarterly 50
Carousel 51
Carve Magazine 51
CavanKerry Press, Ltd. 52
Center for Literary Publishing 52
Chain Magazine/ 'A 'A Arts 52
Chatoyant 53

Chattahoochee Review 53

Chelsea 54

Chelsea Editions 54

Chicago Review 54

Chicory Blue Press 55

Cimarron Review 55

Cininnati Review 56

Circumference 56

Coach House Books 57

Codhill Press 58

Coffee House Press 58

Cold Mountain Review 59

College Literature 59

Colorado Review 59

Columbia: A Journal of Literature & Art 61

Common Review 61

Conduit 62

Confrontation 63

Conjunctions 63

Connecticut Review 63

Contemporary Poetry Review 64

CONTEXT 64

Cool Grove Publishing 65

Copper Canyon Press 65

Cortland Review 65

Coteau Books 65

Cottonwood Magazine and Press 66

Crab Creek Review 66

Crab Orchard Review 67

Cranky LIterary Journal 67

Crazyhorse 68

Creative Nonfiction 68

CROWD 69

Crying Sky: Poetry and Conversation 70

Curbstone Press 70

Cutbank 70

Dalkey Archive Press 71

Del Sol Review 72

Denver Quarterly 73

descant 73

Diagram 73

Dicey Brown 74

Diner 74

Dirt Press 74

Dirty Goat 75

divide 75

Doorjamb Press 76

Dos Passos Review 76

Drexel Online Journal 77

Drunken Boat 77

Ducky Magazine 78

Ducts Webzine 78

Eclipse 78

Edgar Literary Magazine 79

edifice WRECKED 79

Electronic Book Review 80

Emergency Press/Emergency Almanac 80

Emrys Foundation 80

The Emrys Journal 81

Epiphany 82

EPOCH 82

Etruscan Press 83

Euphony 83

eye-rhyme 85

failbetter 86

Faultline 86

FC2 (Fiction Collective Two) 86

Fence 88

Fence Books 88

Fiction 89

FIELD: Contemporary Poetry and Poetics 89

Fine Madness 90

Finishing Line Press 90

Fire by Nite 90

Five Fingers Review 92

Five Points 92

Florida Review 93

Flume Press 94

Folio 94

Foreword 95

Four Way Books 95

Frigate 96

FriGG: A Magazine of FIction and Poetry 97

Fugue 97

Full Circle Journal 98

FuseBox 98

Futurepoem Books 99

Gargoyle Magazine 99

Geist 100

Georgetown Review 100

Georgia Review 101

Gettysburg Review 101

Gingko Tree Review 102

Gival Press 102

Glimmer Train Stories 103

Good Foot 104

Grand Street 105

Graywolf Press 105

Great Marsh Press/The Reading Room 105

Great River Review 105

Green Hills Literary Lantern 106

Greensboro Review 107

## Magazine

## Press

## Essays

## Nonfiction

## Poetry

## Reviews

Water~Stone Review 279
West Branch 281
Willow Springs 285
Wind: A Journal of Writing & Community 285
Windhover: A Journal of Christian Literature 286
Word Riot 288
Word Smitten 289
Word: Toronto's Literary Calendar 289
Writecorner Press 290
The Xavier Review 291

## Art

13th Moon 1
2River 1
580 Split 2
A Gathering of Tribes 3
Abraxas Press 4
Absinthe: New European Writing 4
Accent Miami 5
Adirondack Review 5
African Voices Communications 6
AGNI 7
American Letters & Commentary 10
American Literary Review 11
Another Chicago Magazine/Left Field Press 12
Apalachee Review 13
Archipelago 14
Archipelago Books 14
Arkansas Review: A Journal of Delta Studies 15
Arsenal Pulp Press 15
Artful Dodge 16
Arts & Letters 17
ArtsEditor 17
Asian American Writers' Workshop 19
Asphodel Press 19
Aufgabe 20
Bamboo Ridge 23
Barrytown/Station Hill Press 24
Best of Branches 29
Big Bridge 30
Bilingual Review
Black Square Editions/Hammer Books 35
Black Warrior Review 36
Blackbird: an online journal of literature and arts 36
Bloom: Queer Fiction, Art, Poetry & More 37
Blueline 39
Bogg 40
BOMB Magazine 40
Border Crossings 41
Born Magazine 41
Branches Quarterly 42

Briar Cliff Review 43
Brick, A Literary Journal 43
BRIGHT HILL PRESS 44
Brilliant Corners 44
Callaloo 48
Calyx, a Journal of Art and Lit by Women 48
Caribbean Writer 50
Carolina Quarterly 50
Carousel 51
Chain Magazine/'A 'A Arts 52
Chattahoochee Review 53
Chelsea 54
Chicago Review 54
Cimarron Review 55
Cininnati Review 56
Coelacanth Magazine 58
Columbia: A Journal of Literature & Art 61
COMBAT 61
Common Review 61
Conduit 62
Confrontation 63
Conjunctions 63
Contrary 64
Cool Grove Publishing 65
Cortland Review 65
Crab Creek Review 66
Crazyhorse 68
CROWD 69
DIAGRAM 73
Dicey Brown 74
DINER 74
Dirt Press 74
Dirty Goat 75
divide 75
Doorjamb Press 76
Double Room 76
Drexel Online Journal 77
Drunken Boat 77
Ducts Webzine 78
edifice WRECKED 79
Ekstasis Editions 79
Electronic Book Review 80
Emergency Press/Emergency Almanac 80
Epicenter Magazine 81
EPOCH 82
Exhibition 83
eye-rhyme 85
Factorial Press 85
failbetter 86
Faultline 86
Feminist Studies 87

## Audio

32 Poems Magazine 1
3rd bed 2
580 Split 2
6x6 3
88: A Journal of Contemporary American Poetry 3
A Gathering of the Tribes 3
Absinthe: New European Writing 4
Accent Miami 5
African American Review 6
African Heritage Press 6
African Voices Communications 6
AGNI Magazine 7
Alaska Quarterly Review 8
Alligator Juniper 9
American Book Review 10
American Letters & Commentary 10
American Literary Review 11
American Poetry Review 11
Anderbo.com 12
Antioch Review 12
Apalachee Review 13
Apogee Press 14
Arkansas Review 15
Artful Dodge 16
Arts & Letters 17
Ascent 17
Atlanta Review 19
Aufgabe 20
Backwards City Review 22
Ballyhoo Stories 22
The Baltimore Review 23
Bamboo Ridge 23
Barrow Street 24
Bathtub Gin 25
Bayou 25
Bear Deluxe Magazine 26
Beginnings Publishing 27
Bellevue Literary Review 144 28
Bellingham Review 28
Beloit Poetry Journal 28
The Berkeley Fiction Review 29
Best of Branches 29
The Best of Carve Magazine 30
Bilingual Review
The Bitter Oleander 31
Black Warrior Review 36
Bloom: Queer Fiction, Art, Poetry & More 37
Blue Collar Review 38
Blue Mesa Review 38
Blueline 39
Bogg 40

BOMB Magazine 40
Book/Mark Small Press Quarterly Review 40
Border Crossings 41
Boston Review 42
The Briar Cliff Review 43
Brick, A Literary Journal 43
Brilliant Corners 44
Cabinet 46
Cairn 47
Callaloo 48
Calyx, a Journal of Art and Lit by Women 48
Canadian Literature 48
Canadian Poetry: Studies, Documents, Reviews 49
The Canary 49
The Caribbean Writer 50
The Carolina Quarterly 50
Carousel 51
Chapman Magazine 53
The Chattahoochee Review 53
Chelsea 54
Chicago Review 54
Cimarron Review 55
The Cininnati Review 56
COLLEGE LITERATURE 59
Colorado Review 59
Columbia: A Journal of Literature & Art 61
Conduit 62
Cottonwood Magazine and Press 66
Crab Creek Review 66
Crab Orchard Review 67
Cranky Literary Journal 67
Crazyhorse 68
Creosote: A Journal of Poetry and Prose 69
CROWD 69
Crying Sky: Poetry and Conversation 70
Cutbank 70
Denver Quarterly 73
descant 73
DINER 74
Dirt Press 74
The Dirty Goat 75
divide 75
Dos Passos Review 76
Eclipse 78
edifice WRECKED 79
Edgar Literary Magazine 79
The Emrys Journal 81
Epicenter Magazine 81
Epiphany 82
EPOCH 82
Essays on Canadian Writing 82

3rd bed 2
6x6 3
A Gathering of the Tribes 3
The Absinthe Literary Review 4
Absinthe: New European Writing 4
Accent Miami 5
The Adirondack Review 5
African Heritage Press 6
African Voices Communications 6
AGNI Magazine 7
Ahsahta Press 7
Akashic Books 8
Alaska Quarterly Review 8
Alice James Books 8
All Info-About Poetry 9
Alligator Juniper 9
American Book Review 10
American Letters & Commentary 10
American Literary Review 11
Anderbo.com 12
Anhinga Press 12
Anvil Press 13
Apalachee Review 13
Apogee Press 14
Arctoss Press 14
Argonne House Press 15
Arsenal Pulp Press 15
Artful Dodge 16
Arts & Letters 17
ArtsEditor 17
Ascent 17
The Asian American Writers' Workshop 19
Atlanta Review 19
Atomic Quill Press 20
Aufgabe 20
Ausable Press 21
Autumn House Press 21
Backwards City Review 22
The Backwaters Press 22
Ballyhoo Stories 22
The Baltimore Review 23
Barrow Street 24
Barrytown / Station Hill Press
Barrytown/Station Hill Press 24
Bathtub Gin 25
Bayou 25
Beach Holme Publishing 25
Beacon Press 26
The Beacon Street Review
Bear Deluxe Magazine 26
BEAR STAR PRESS 27

Beginnings Publishing 27
Belladonna* 27
Bellevue Literary Review 28
Bellingham Review 28
The Berkeley Fiction Review 29
Best of Branches 29
The Best of Carve Magazine 30
Big Bridge 30
The Bitter Oleander 31
The Bitter Oleander Press 34
BkMk Press 34
Black Lawrence Press 35
Black Square Editions/Hammer Books 35
Black Warrior Review 36
Blackbird / New Virginia Review 36
Blackbird 36
Blithe House Quarterly 36
The Blood Moon Productions 37
Bloom: Queer Fiction, Art, Poetry & More 37
Blue Mesa Review 38
Blueline 39
BOA Editions, Ltd. 39
BOMB Magazine 40
Book/Mark Small Press Quarterly Review 40
Border Crossings 41
Boston Review 42
Botton Dog Press 42
Branches Quarterly 42
The Briar Cliff Review 43
Brick, A Literary Journal 43
BRIGHT HILL PRESS 44
Brindle & Glass Publishing 44
Bristol Banner Books 45
Brook Street Press 45
Burning Bush Publications 46
Cabinet 46
Cairn 47
Calaca Press 47
CALYX Journal 48
The Canary 49
Canadian Poetry: Studies, Documents, Reviews 49
The Caribbean Writer 50
Carousel 51
Carve Magazine 51
CavanKerry Press, Ltd. 52
The Center for Literary Publishing 52
Century Press 52
Chapman Magazine 53
Chelsea Editions 54
Chicago Review 54
Chicory Blue Press 55

Cimarron Review 55
The Cininnati Review 56
Cinco Puntos Press 56
Cleveland State University Poetry Center 56
Coach House Books 57
Coelacanth Magazine 58
COLLEGE LITERATURE 59
Colorado Review 59
Columbia: A Journal of Literature & Art 61
COMBAT 61
The Common Review 61
Confrontation 63
Contrary 64
Crab Orchard Review 67
Cranky Literary Journal 67
Crazyhorse 68
Creative Nonfiction 68
Creosote: A Journal of Poetry and Prose 69
CROWD 69
Curbstone Press 70
Cutbank 70
Dalkey Archive Press 71
Dan River Press 71
DC Books 72
Del Sol Press 72
The Del Sol Review 72
Denver Quarterly 73
descant 73
DIAGRAM 73
DINER 74
Dirt Press 74
The Dirty Goat 75
divide 75
Doorjamb Press 76
Dos Passos Review 76
Double Room 76
Drexel Online Journal 77
Drunken Boat 77
Ducky Magazine 78
Ducts Webzine 78
Eclipse 78
Edgar Literary Magazine 79
edifice WRECKED 79
Ekstasis Editions 79
The Electronic Book Review 80
Emrys Foundation 80
The Emrys Journal 81
Epicenter Magazine 81
Epiphany 82
Etruscan Press 83
Euphony 83

Exhibition 83
eye-rhyme 85
failbetter 86
Faultline 86
FC2 (Fiction Collective Two) 86
Feather Books 87
Fence Books 88
Fence 88
Fiction 89
Finishing Line Press 90
Firewheel Editions 90
First Class 91
First Intensity 91
Five Fingers Review 92
Flash!Point Literary Journal 93
The Florida Review 93
Flume Press 94
Flyway: A Literary Review 94
Folio 94
Foreword 95
Four Way Books 95
Fourteen Hills 96
Frigate 96
FriGG: A Magazine of Fiction and Poetry 97
Fugue State Press 97
Fugue 97
Full Circle Journal 98
FuseBox 98
Future Tense Books 99
Futurepoem Books 99
Gargoyle Magazine 99
Geist 100
Georgetown Review 100
The Gettysburg Review 101
Gingko Tree Review 102
Gival Press 102
Golden Handcuffs Review 103
Good Foot 104
Grand Street 105
The Green Hills Literary Lantern 106
Greenboathouse Books 106
Guernica: A Magazine of Art and Politics 108
Gulf Coast: A Journal of Literature and Fine Arts 108
Gulf Stream 108
Haight Ashbury Literary Journal 109
Hanging Loose 109
Harbour Publishing 110
Harpur Palate 110
Harvard Review 111
Hawai'i Pacific Review 11
Hayden Ferry's Review 111